Nigeria

the Bradt Travel Guide

Lizzie Williams

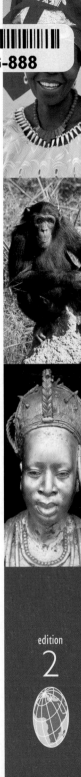

edition
2

www.bradtguides.com

Bradt Travel Guides Ltd, UK
The Globe Pequot Press Inc, USA

Nigeria
Don't
miss…

Lagos
Nigeria's bustling capital with
an estimated population of
13-17 million
page 109

Calabar Drill
Monkey Ranch
A refuge for chimpanzees
and monkeys
(DH) page 217

Obudu Plateau
(GG) page 226

Yankari National Park
Wikki Warm Springs
(KR) page 268

Oshogbo Sacred Forest
A World Heritage site where statues carved by Austrian artist, Suzanne Wenger, stand in honour of the Yoruba deities
(KR) page 176

top   *Kilish*, dried meat coated in groundnut and pepper paste (a northern delicacy) drying in the sunshine in Kano's old city (KR) page 78

above   Osun festival market stalls, King's palace, Oshogbo (KR) page 182

left   The weekly market in Akassa, Niger Delta (KR)

top   **Local school, Bida** (DH) page 260

above left   **In the Kano dye pits, cloth is traditionally dyed in indigo and ironed with mahogany pounds** (KR) page 309

above right   **Cocoa plant** (KR)

right   **Woman processing palm fruits** (Cercopan: Wright)

above Masquerade parade, Opobo Town. Each extended family has its own costume (KR)

below One of the groups of horsemen at the Kano durbar (KR) page 310

AUTHOR

Lizzie Williams is a travel writer based in Cape Town, South Africa. Originally from London, she has notched up over 12 years to date on the road in Africa and the Middle East. First as an expedition leader on overland trucks and now as a guidebook author, she has become something of an expert on border crossings and African beer. She has written numerous magazine articles, product brochures and websites on African travel, and is author of over a dozen guidebooks for various publishers on South Africa, Namibia, Kenya, Tanzania, Egypt and Turkey, among other destinations. These include the Bradt guide to Johannesburg. She has visited 20 African countries, none of which were quite as absorbing as Nigeria.

RESEARCHER

Kevin O'Rourke assisted with research for the northern cities for this edition. Hailing from the UK, he spent two and a half years with VSO as Information and Communication Technology coordinator for Nigeria's National Teachers' Institute and lived in Abuja and Kaduna. He's travelled widely in the north of the country and as a result has developed a liking for pounded yam, and no longer minds being squashed into bush taxis with goats and chickens. His favourite place in Nigeria is Sukur.

AUTHOR STORY

Bradt is the only publisher to devote an entire guide to this little understood country, and they are well known for giving their authors relative freedom to write as they see fit, especially in destinations that are difficult to travel in, such as Nigeria. When I wrote the first edition in 2005, Nigeria had only recently emerged from 16 years of military dictatorship and I was told by one Nigerian tourism official that during that period, the secretive military discouraged tourism so foreigners wouldn't see what was going on in the country.

What has surprised and delighted me while working on the second edition is to see what an impact the existence of a guidebook on Nigeria has had on encouraging people to visit the country. I've had an overwhelming response from readers, who have shared their experiences in Nigeria with me, and these haven't just been hardy expats and adventurous backpackers, who, admittedly, were the only people I had expected to buy the book. They have been people who spent their childhood in Nigeria when it was still under colonial rule, a group of ex-Peace Corps volunteers that served in Nigeria in the 1960s and wanted to revisit their old haunting grounds, a 19-year old Slovenian girl who wanted to visit her Nigerian boyfriend and whose father would only let her go after he read the book, parents of people who have married Nigerians visiting their grandchildren for the first time, and one poor chap who had succumbed to 419 fraud and went to Nigeria to try and recover his stolen money.

Totally unexpectedly many Nigerians bought the book too. After reading it, some have returned to Nigeria for a visit after living overseas for decades. One reader, who is half Nigerian and half British, and hasn't been to Nigeria since he was a small child in the 1980s, has made five visits in the last three years and has now moved to Lagos permanently. He has paid me the greatest compliment by saying, 'You showed me a side of Nigeria I had almost forgotten about. Thank you.'

PUBLISHER'S FOREWORD
Hilary Bradt

The first Bradt travel guide was written in 1974 by George and Hilary Bradt on a river barge floating down a tributary of the Amazon. In the 1980s and 1990s the focus shifted away from hiking to broader-based guides covering new destinations – usually the first to be published about these places. In the 21st century Bradt continues to publish such ground-breaking guides, as well as others to established holiday destinations, incorporating in-depth information on culture and natural history with the nuts and bolts of where to stay and what to see.

Bradt authors support responsible travel, and provide advice not only on minimum impact but also on how to give something back through local charities. In this way a true synergy is achieved between the traveller and local communities.

* * *

Bradt are thrilled to be publishing the second edition of this ground-breaking book. The many positive letters received from travellers inspired by the guide are proof of the fact that, whilst the scare stories about corruption and crime-rate are of concern, travellers getting off the beaten path will meet nothing but kindness and hospitality. An extra, unforeseen, bonus is the chord of resonance it struck with Nigerian residents past and present, many of whom wrote to Lizzie and thanked her for compelling them to look with new eyes at their continually evolving country.

Second edition published April 2008
First published in 2005

Bradt Travel Guides Ltd
23 High Street, Chalfont St Peter, Bucks SL9 9QE, England
www.bradtguides.com

Published in the USA by The Globe Pequot Press Inc, 246 Goose Lane,
PO Box 480, Guilford, Connecticut 06475-0480

Text copyright © 2008 Lizzie Williams

Maps copyright © 2008 Bradt Travel Guides Ltd

Illustrations © 2008 Individual photographers and artists

Editorial project manager: Emma Thomson

ISBN-10: 1 84162 239 7
ISBN-13: 978 1 84162 239 2

British Library Cataloguing in Publication Data
A catalogue record for this book is available from the British Library

Photographs Andrew Holt/Alamy (AH/Alamy), Anthony Casarotto (AC), CERCOPAN, Darren Humphrys (DH), Gatto Giallo (GG), Guiliano Colliva /TIPS (GC/TIPS), Kevin O'Rourke (KR), Mueller R/TIPS (MR/TIPS)
Front cover Boy drinking rainwater from banana leaf (Uwanaka/UNEP/Still Pictures)
Back cover People and horses on beach near Lagos (AH/Alamy)
Title page Christians dress up in their finest clothes for church on Sundays (DH), Chimpanzee (*Pan troglodytes*) (AVZ), Bronze cast, Benin City (DH)
Illustrations Carole Vincer
Maps Malcolm Barnes

Typeset from the author's disk by Dorchester Typesetting Group
Printed and bound in Italy by L.E.G.O. Spa-Lavis (TN)

Acknowledgements

This book wouldn't have been written without Darren Humphrys who shared 'the most obscure moment of the day' with me during research for the first edition. Thanks to all at Bradt for their continued support, especially former editor Tricia Hayne who spurred me on from the beginning. For this edition, thanks to Rupert Wheeler, Susannah Wight and Dominique Shead from Navigator Guides for the fine-tuning during the edit. Richard Pieterse provided books and maps, and first-hand reports on working in Nigeria, and Dan Isaacs, the former BBC correspondent in Lagos, gave encouragement. In Nigeria, I would like to sincerely thank Sharon and Paul Fay for their exceptional hospitality in Lagos, and all their friends who gave me an insight into expat life. A big Irish thank you goes to Alan Parke, a long-term expat, for his invaluable advice and useful comments after being the first person in Nigeria to read the book. Thanks to Anita Ibru and her team at the Federal Palace Hotel, to Peter Jenkins and Liza Gadsby from Pandrillus in Calabar for all their information, and to Sam who was such a special host at the Drill Ranch in Afi. The same goes to Zeena Tooze and Bob Baxter of Cercopan also in Calabar, and a special big thank you to Deputy Director of Cercopan, Claire Coulson, for helping me out with research in the final hour. Tunde Morakinyo of Environmental Resources Management gave me invaluable information on Nigeria's national parks, and thanks to Andie, Grant, Jeff and Steve from Oasis Overland for their route notes. Kevin would like to thank the staff of the Arts and Languages Department at Ahmadu Bello University in Zaria for their assistance, and Enoch O. Oyedele of the History Department for his information on Kaduna.

Thanks to readers of the first edition who wrote in with their stories and suggestions. These include Andrew Esiebo, Carol and Bob Walton, Gerard Adams, Nancy Ryer Bass and family, Ken from Northern Ireland, Eamonn Dunlea, Michael Fuenfzig, Cheryl Humphrys, Caroline Denham, Ursa from Slovenia, Michael Gbadebo, Idriys Abdulllah, Laurie Alper, Cate de Villiers and family, Fiona and Adrian Munn, Raphael Parker, Steve Tarry and family, Aagje Breetvelt and Papineau Salm and family, Caroline Todd-Earlam and Paul Delve. A special thank you to readers Mike Malaghan (sorry I couldn't make your kind invitation to dinner in Cape Town and best wishes for your 2008 ex-Peace Corps trip to Nigeria); to Michael Anderson for his wonderful email about going back to his roots in Nigeria; and to Jim Howard for saying it was the first guidebook that had made him laugh out loud (though I am not sure guidebooks are supposed to do that!). Lastly, I would like to express profound gratitude to Kevin O'Rourke for his help in northern Nigeria. The most sophisticated blogger on the internet, his warmth for Nigeria has been lucid and genuine.

Contents

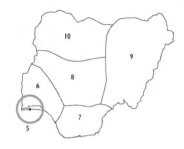

	Introduction	vii

PART ONE	**GENERAL INFORMATION**	**1**

Chapter 1   **Background information**   **3**
Geography and climate 3, History and government 5,
Economy 26, People 31, Language 32, Religion 33,
Culture and sport 39, Natural history and conservation 45

Chapter 2   **Practical information**   **51**
When to visit 51, Highlights 51, Tour operators 53, Red
tape 53, Nigerian embassies and high commissions 54,
Getting there and away 55, What to take 57

Chapter 3   **In Nigeria**   **61**
Information 61, Money and prices 62, Getting around 64,
Accommodation 72, Eating and drinking 73, Shopping
and bargaining 81, Women travellers 83, Gay travellers 83,
Cultural etiquette 83, Media and communications 85

Chapter 4   **Health and safety**   **89**
Health 89, Safety 101

PART TWO	**THE GUIDE**	**107**

Chapter 5   **Lagos**   **109**
History 110, Getting there and away 113, Getting around
117, Where to stay 121, Where to eat and drink 125,
Nightlife 131, Shopping 133, Practicalities 136, What to
see and do 142

Chapter 6   **Southwestern Nigeria**   **163**
Abeokuta 163, Ibadan 166, Ife 173, Oshogbo 175, Oyo
182, Old Oyo National Park 184, North from Oyo 185,
Benin City 186, Okomu National Park 191

Chapter 7   **Southeastern Nigeria**   **193**
Onitsha and Asaba 193, Enugu 195, Umuahia 197, Aba
199, Port Harcourt 200, The Niger Delta 207, Calabar
209, Cross River National Park 221, Rhoko Forest 223, Afi
Mountain Drill Ranch 223, Obudu Cattle Ranch 225,
Ikom 227

Chapter 8	**Central Nigeria**	**229**
	Abuja 229, Lokoja 246, Makurdi 252, Jos 253, West of	
	Abuja 260, Lake Kainji National Park 262	
Chapter 9	**East and Northeast Nigeria**	**265**
	Bauchi 265, Yankari National Park 268, Gashaka-Gumpti	
	National Park 272, Maiduguri 274, Around Maiduguri	
	278	
Chapter 10	**Northern Nigeria**	**285**
	Kaduna 286, Zaria 292, Kano 299, Katsina 314,	
	Gusau 317, Sokoto 318	
Appendix 1	**Language**	**324**
Appendix 2	**Glossary of Nigerian phrases**	**328**
Appendix 3	**Further information**	**330**
Index		**341**

FEEDBACK REQUEST

Given that there is little on-the-ground information available about Nigeria, this was an enormously difficult book to write, and a lot of it is based on first-hand experiences rather than on written information. The Nigerian people are hugely hospitable and charmingly humorous and I hope many more travellers go to Nigeria to meet them. I would like to hear about any experiences that could enhance the next edition of this book. Things change, though much more slowly in Nigeria than in other places in the world, so if a hotel or restaurant has closed down, a destination is no longer accessible, or you feel that an increasingly dilapidated sight is no longer worth the effort of getting there, I want to know. On a positive note, if the tourist office suddenly decides to print brochures and information for visitors, or if the National Parks office decides to count how many animals are left in Nigeria's parks, I want to know that as well. Write to me at info@bradtguides.com.

LIST OF MAPS

Abeokuta	165	Lagos: Victoria Island & Ikoyi	128–9
Abuja	234–5	Lokoja	248
Benin City	187	Maiduguri	275
Calabar	211	National parks	46
Central Nigeria	230	Nigeria colour section ii–iii	
Cross River National Park &	221	Northern Nigeria	284
Environs		Oshogbo	177
East & northeast Nigeria	266	Port Harcourt	202
Ibadan	168	Sharia States	36
Jos	255	Sokoto	319
Kaduna	289	Southeast Nigeria	194
Kano	302–3	Southwest Nigeria	162
Lagos, Greater	118	Zaria	295
Lagos: Lagos Island	144–5		

Introduction

Nigeria is Africa's most populous country and Lagos, with an estimated population that well exceeds ten million, is on the United Nations' list of mega-cities. As the sixth-biggest supplier of crude oil on earth, Nigeria by rights should be Africa's economic giant. It has also had the reputation for centuries of being one of the world's most chaotic and dangerous places; a warning to early sailors to the region was 'beware, take care of the Bight of Benin. Few come out though many go in.' To put it plainly, as travel destinations go, Nigeria is far from the most pleasant West African country to travel in – it's impoverished and the majority of the population lives on under US$4 a day. It's dirty and an environmental nightmare, with piles of rubbish literally everywhere, and its natural resources have been stripped bare. Nothing works and everything is seriously dilapidated, the infrastructure is totally inadequate, there are frequent shortages of fuel, electricity and water, and vehicle traffic and human congestion are tremendous.

The country has a history of despot military dictators, and corruption at all levels of society, and has witnessed overwhelming political upheavals. In the north, there's an ongoing religious and ethnic conflict that has killed between 10,000 and 15,000 people since 1999 – a conflict that is so primal that Nigerian people are killing each other in hand-to-hand fighting and mob violence. In the south, the creeks of the Niger Delta are controlled by militia warlords who are attacking Nigeria's oil industry, and over 200 foreign oil workers have been kidnapped since 2006. To the international community Nigeria is still sometimes regarded as a pariah nation, run by a government that is largely incapable of controlling the largest population in Africa.

Everywhere in Nigeria contrasts abound. Step outside Le Méridien Hotel in Port Harcourt, easily the most luxurious hotel in Nigeria, and you'll see people selling yams from wheelbarrows at the gate; outside the Virgin airline offices, you'll see goats in the car park. From 24-hour internet cafés to dead bodies in the street; from roadblocks where the policemen wear bandanas and mirrored sunglasses to the ladies going to church in the most beautiful dresses you've ever seen; from plane-loads of wealthy Nigerians going to Dubai on shopping trips to people so poor they resort to eating rats and maggots; from black-magic markets full of unexplainable fetishes and charms in a country where there are still rumours of human sacrifice going on, to more people carrying cell phones than perhaps anywhere else in the world. It's appalling and awful, fascinating and appealing, and funny and sad, all at the same time; Nigeria is that extreme.

In his Ghana guide, my colleague at Bradt, Philip Briggs, describes Ghana as 'Africa for beginners'. Well by the same token, I would describe Nigeria as 'Africa for the very experienced'. It is simply one of the world's most difficult places to travel in and the notion of travelling here conjures up a horrific reaction. It's far from a holiday destination, there's very little to see in the way of conventional sightseeing, and it's an environmental disaster. Nigerians themselves have little interest in conserving and preserving their natural or historical legacies, and there is no tourism industry to support the national parks or historic sites.

So why go to Nigeria? Well, it's impossible to deny its pride of place among the potential travel destinations of the world, and there are undeniably few of these left as the world gets increasingly smaller. For the adventurous traveller, Nigeria offers the opportunity to see the country in its raw and naked state. Travel is challenging and exciting and your experiences will be memorable and educational. Alternatively, you may have picked up this book because you intend to work there. Nigeria has wide market opportunities, and there are many foreign companies operating in industries such as pharmaceuticals, oil, roadbuilding and telecommunications. There is a large expat community, especially in Lagos, which has successfully made Nigeria its home. And if you are going to work there, you will find that there are effectively two Nigerias – one is the expat world of Lagos with its yacht clubs, societies, posh restaurants and supermarkets selling imported items, and the other is the rest of the country. I encourage you also to explore the latter.

Love it or hate it, Lagos has to be seen to be believed: nowhere on earth will you experience such mind-boggling, vibrant chaos as in this mass of humanity. In the waterlogged south of the country are deltas and lagoons where people's lives haven't changed for hundreds of years, and in the north are ancient kingdoms and walled cities, even today ruled by sultans and emirs. Nigeria has a fascinating and turbulent history, and the cultural assets of the nation are universally recognised, with more than 250 rich and diverse ethnic groups, several religions, and the warm-hearted hospitality of 140 million people. The highlight of travelling in Nigeria is meeting these culturally rich people; practically any person in any corner of Nigeria will offer a moment of their time to say 'welcome'. For the traveller with an open mind and friendly demeanour, meeting the people is an overwhelming experience – they are colourful, intelligent, curious, creative, imaginative and generous.

Travel in Nigeria can sometimes be stressful and is frequently stalled by inconvenience and inefficiency; not every experience will be pleasant. Away from the expat suburbs of Lagos, Westerners are a rare sight indeed, and without exception the Nigerians are absolutely dumbfounded to see *oyibos* (whites) walking along the streets, sitting in the local bush taxis, and eating in the local restaurants or food stalls. It just doesn't happen here. But if you're up to the challenge, it's one of the most exciting and engaging countries in the world and I have been treated with nothing but friendliness and helpfulness at all times. I have written for other guidebook publishers before, but the joy of writing for Bradt is that their authors are encouraged to write much more personally. Quite frankly there is no other way to write about Nigeria than personally. It's a destination that's not about Eiffel Towers or Serengeti Plains, but about a conversation or a unique moment. Every traveller to the country will experience a very personal and distinctive trip. I hope this book will greatly assist any travel to Nigeria and help to quell its awful reputation as a travel destination. It's a unique and compelling country with an enormous personality.

Part One

GENERAL INFORMATION

Location Between tropics of Cancer and Capricorn, on Gulf of Guinea

Neighbouring countries Benin, Niger, Chad, Cameroon

Area 923,768km^2

Altitude Rising to 2,419m at Chappal Waddi, on Cameroon border

Terrain Southern lowlands merge into hills and plateaux in centre; mountains in southeast; plains in north

Climate Tropical in south; arid in north

Status Federal republic

Government Bicameral presidential system

President Umaru Yar'adua (since 2008)

Capital Abuja (moved from Lagos in 1991); population 1.4 million approx

Other major cities Lagos (population 9 million officially; more likely to be 13–17 million), Port Harcourt (3.5 million approx), Kano (9.3 million approx)

Administrative regions 36 states and 1 Federal Capital Territory

Population 140,003,542 (2008)

Birth rate 40.02 births per 1,000 population (2008)

Life expectancy at birth 51.56 years (2008)

Age structure 0–14 years, 44%; 15–64 years, 53%; over 65, 3% (2008)

GDP per head US$1,500 per annum (2006)

Economy Oil provides 20% of GDP and 95% of foreign exchange earnings

Official language English

Major local languages Yoruba, Igbo, Hausa, Edo, Efik, Kanuri

Religion Muslim 50%, Christian 40%, indigenous 10%

Currency Nigerian naira (N)

Exchange rate £1=N250, US$1=N127, €1=N172 (2008; used to research this guide)

International airports Lagos, Abuja, Port Harcourt (currently closed for refurbishment), Kano

International telephone code +234

Time GMT +1

Electricity 220 volts at 50HZ; three-pin British-style plug

Weights and measures Metric

Flag Three equal vertical bands of green (representing agriculture), white (for unity and peace), green

National motto Unity and Faith, Peace and Progress

Public holidays 1 Jan, 1 May, 1 Oct; Christian and Muslim holy days

Background Information

GEOGRAPHY AND CLIMATE

LOCATION

The Federal Republic of Nigeria is located between the tropics of Cancer and Capricorn, on the Gulf of Guinea on the western coast of tropical Africa. It lies between latitudes 4° and 14° north of the Equator and longitudes 3° and 14° east of the Greenwich Meridian. It is part of West Africa, though borders Central Africa on its frontier with Cameroon to the southeast. Nigeria's total land area covers 923,768km^2 and it's one-and-a-half times the size of France, or one-third larger than the US state of Texas. It is five times larger than Ghana, 13 times as large as Sierra Leone and occupies one-seventh of West Africa. It is bordered by an 853km stretch of Atlantic Ocean coastline to the south, a 1,690km border with Cameroon to the east, a 773km border with Benin to the west, a 1,497km border with Niger to the north, and has a small 87km border region across Lake Chad, which it shares with Chad in the extreme northeastern corner of the country. Nigeria is roughly 1,600km from north to south and 1,100km wide.

GEOGRAPHY Nigeria has 800km of unbroken sandy beaches that are routinely pounded by the relentless Atlantic swells. Travelling inland from south to north, away from the coast, you first encounter the tropical coastal plain, an area that receives more rain annually than the rest of the country. The plain extends inland for about 75km before rising to an elevation of 40–50m at its northern boundary. The eastern and western sections are separated by the mangrove swamps of the Niger Delta that extends over an area of about 10,000km^2; it's characterised by soggy, mosquito-infested swamplands separated by numerous islands that hold Nigeria's most precious commodity, oil. Away from the coast, in the southeast, are forests full of oil palms, and away from the coast, on the western side, are tracts of ebony and mahogany forests.

The forest belt leads to higher savanna grasslands in the central regions where the Niger and Benue rivers converge, and further north the landscape is hot semi-arid bush that borders the Sahara Desert in neighbouring Niger. This is known as the Sahel region and consists purely of scrubby and sandy terrain. Some of the country's higher points are the Bauchi and Jos plateaux at 600–1,200m in the centre, and the Adamawa Massif (which continues into Cameroon) in the east, where Nigeria's highest mountain range, the Chapal Wadi, reaches heights of over 2,000m, with the Gangarwal Peak being Nigeria's tallest at 2,419m. In the far northwest, and in the northeast where the Chad Basin is located, elevation falls again to below 300m.

The Niger is West Africa's greatest river and the country's main geographical feature, together with its principal tributary the Benue. The Niger boasts an extraordinary course, rising little more than 300km from the sea in Sierra Leone, flowing northeastwards to brush the Sahara at Timbuktu, before completing its great bend across Nigeria's savanna and forest to the labyrinthine creeks and mangrove swamps of its long, mysterious delta. The Delta extends inland for more than 200km and along the coast for 100km, eventually reaching the sea at the Bight of Benin.

The Niger River traverses four countries – though the whole basin covers nine – that together represent a kaleidoscope of cultures and landscapes. The upper reaches of these rivers form narrow valleys with falls and rapids, though most of the lower parts are rapid-free, with extensive floodplains and numerous channels. The Benue rises in Cameroon, flows from the northeast, and joins the Niger at the confluence town of Lokoja. These two rivers form a great 'Y' in the southern part of the country and essentially divide Nigeria's three dominant ethnic groups: the Igbo in the southeast, the Hausa in the north, and the Yoruba in the southwest.

Although Nigeria has extraordinary biological diversity, it faces many environmental problems brought on by ever-increasing population numbers, poverty and industrial damage. These include frequent oil spills in the Delta region and rampant deforestation (in West Africa, only Ivory Coast cuts down more trees than Nigeria). A century ago there were five million hectares of trees and in 1897 two-thirds of Nigeria was covered by rich tropical rainforest. Today only 4% of this original rainforest remains, with most of the deforestation having happened since the 1980s – between 1981 and 1994 Nigeria lost 3.7 million hectares of rainforest through logging and bush burning. Causes include fuel wood gathering, conversion of natural forest to commercial tree plantations, oil exploration, mining

WHAT A WASTE . . .

Nigeria has got the most alarming rubbish problem I have ever seen and the main culprit is non-biodegradable plastic and the Nigerians' terrible attitude towards litter – they simply throw it on the ground, and there are few systems or services to dispose of it. Throughout the country there are unsightly heaps of rubbish everywhere – mountains of garbage are dumped on pavements, central reservations, under bridges and flyovers, in drains and canals, and on just about any available piece of land. The majority of it is plastic and the curse of the rubbish problem is the small half-litre water packets of what is known as 'pure water', which everyone relies on for drinking water and then simply drops on the ground as soon as they are finished. In markets, vendors believe in good presentation and almost all street food is presented in little plastic bags and even the cheapest market products are wrapped in plastic. If each of the 140 million people drops two pieces of plastic litter per day, you can imagine the immensity of the problem. Everywhere are ad hoc rubbish dumps, where pigs and cows forage, and where humans openly go to the toilet, which when set alight emit dangerous toxic fumes and terrible odours. They produce a number of health hazards and are breeding grounds for flies, cockroaches, rats and mosquitoes; when it rains the water mixes with the rubbish to create a toxic slush that contaminates water sources, causing typhoid and diarrhoea. In particular, vagrants and scavengers in the rubbish dumps are subjected to high health risks. There's one dump in the north of Lagos on the Ibadan road, which is overwhelmingly vast; it's the size of a small town and is in places 50m deep. Here an estimated thousand or so young boys known as 'pickers' comb through the rot, the stench and hazardous waste looking for wire, copper, wood or anything else they can re-sell. Home for them is a shantytown of dwellings made from plastic sheeting and scrap metal built on top of the mound of rubbish.

and urbanisation. And of what's left, over 3% is lost annually, and only a third is in protected areas, either under the protection of the forestry department or in national parks. Hundreds of plant species are threatened with extinction, as is some of the wildlife that is unique to Nigeria, such as the white-throated monkey, Sclater's guenon and the Niger Delta red colobus monkey.

CLIMATE Although Nigeria is wholly within the tropics, its climate varies from tropical at the coast, to sub-tropical further inland, to arid in the north. It experiences two distinct climates – dry and wet. The length of each season varies around the country depending on elevation and latitude but generally the dry season is November–March and the rainy season April–August, with shorter rains in September and October. However, on the coast the rainy season kicks in during February or March when a moist Atlantic air mass, known as the southwest monsoon, routinely batters the coast.

The coast, and predominantly the Niger Delta, receives more rain annually than the rest of the country – up to 4,000mm per year, approximately five times that of London. In contrast, the semi-arid Sahel in the northernmost part of the country receives the least rainfall – about 500mm annually. The peak of the rainy season here is in August, when air from the Atlantic covers the entire country. However, Nigeria has suffered from a number of droughts over recent years, particularly in the Sahel, and the 20th century is considered among the driest periods of the last several centuries, with well-publicised droughts during the 1970s and 1980s. These drought periods indicate the great variability of climate across tropical Africa.

Nigeria's temperature is high year round, and is frequently accompanied by high humidity in low-lying and coastal areas where temperatures average around 32°C. In the north, temperatures generally average 37°C, with extreme northern desert regions averaging 45°C during the day and 6°C at night. Temperatures are highest from February to April in the south and from March to June in the north and lowest from October to January over most of the country. The dry season brings cooler temperatures and chaotic dry northeast winds, referred to locally as the Harmattan, which carry fine sand from the Sahara across the country. The dust-filled air during this time can be irritating and uncomfortable and appears as a dense fog. The Harmattan is more common in the north but affects the entire country, except for a narrow strip along the southwest coast. However, an occasional strong Harmattan can sweep as far south as Lagos, pushing clouds of dust out to sea and providing relief from high humidity in the capital.

HISTORY AND GOVERNMENT

Before beginning any account on Nigeria's history, it should be stressed that modern Nigeria, like much of Africa, is a product of European colonial rule. Nigeria is a creation of the British Empire builder who, in search of new markets, raw materials and the need to exert political influence overseas, laid down borders at the end of the 19th century. Before this time Nigeria wasn't called Nigeria, and in the centuries leading up to colonialism all of West Africa was divided into smaller areas with different names, occupied by varying ethnic groups. Empires, kingdoms and states flourished, died, moved or changed identity in the geographical space that we know today as modern Nigeria. Even as recently as the 1850s, when Lagos became a British colony, few would have foreseen a political state with borders roughly matching modern Nigeria, and a whole lot of history had happened before then. It is usually presumed that Nigeria got its name from the River Niger, but it was actually Frederick Lugard's wife, Flora Louise Shaw, who in 1898 joined together the word niger, meaning 'black', with the word 'area', creating Nigeria. The following account of the historical development of the northern and southern regions in pre-colonial Nigeria, which follow distinctively different paths, is roughly based on modern Nigeria's Muslim–Christian divide (see map on page 36).

There are several dominant themes in Nigerian history that are essential in understanding contemporary Nigerian politics and society. First, the **spread of Islam** in the north a millennium ago and later the creation of the Sokoto Caliphate in the jihad (holy war) of 1804–08, which brought most of the northern region and adjacent parts of Niger and Cameroon under a single Islamic government (discussed under Religion, on page 35). This history helps account for the religious divide between north and south that has been so strong during the colonial and post-colonial eras. Second, the **slave trade** across the Sahara Desert and the Atlantic Ocean had a profound influence on virtually all parts of West Africa. Slavery was widespread, and many ethnic distinctions were reinforced because of slave raiding and trading, and the conversion to Islam and the **spread of Christianity** were intricately associated with issues relating to slavery. Third, the **oil boom** that since independence in 1960 has unleashed such rapid change and expansion in the economy has caused a severely distorted economic growth that subsequently collapsed in the 1980s. The social consequences of a declining economy and the internal movement of populations between regions and to the cities necessitated the reassessment of ethnic loyalties. This in turn was reflected in politics and religion, and led to a number of successful and failed military coups, a brutal civil war, and let corrupt governments siphon off billions of dollars of oil profits. As the most populous country in Africa, Nigeria has a history that bears scrutiny if for no other reason than to understand how and why this nation remains so divided today.

WEST AFRICA BEFORE AD1000 Very little is known about the history of West Africa before AD1000, though a 1960s archaeological dig at Akure in the forest area of today's western Nigeria unearthed stone artefacts dating back to 9000BC, indicating very early human habitation of the region. West Africa doesn't have archaeological sites as spectacular as those at Luxor in Egypt, Leptis in Libya, Great Zimbabwe in Zimbabwe, or the Olduvai Gorge in Tanzania to give us any clues. Only a little archaeological study has been undertaken in the region over the last 30 years or so, throwing but a few flashes of light into the dark centuries of West Africa's past. Generally, history can be pieced together by tracking the movement of West African people and defining its cultural groups.

The first inhabitants of pre-colonial Nigeria were thought to have been the Iron Age Nok people, skilled artisans who lived in the Jos region from 500BC to around AD200. It's a culture that takes its name from the village where the first archaeological discoveries were made during open-cast mining in the region in recent decades. Remarkable terracotta figures of men and animals of such technical detail were unearthed that they proved that the Nok must have achieved a level of material development not repeated in the region for another 1,000 years.

Information is lacking from the 'silent millennium' (1st millennium AD) that followed the Nok ascendancy, apart from evidence of iron smelting on Dala Hill in Kano from about AD600–700. It is assumed that trade linking the Niger region with North Africa played a key role in the continuing development of the area. Certainly by the beginning of the 2nd millennium AD there was an active trade along a north–south axis from North Africa through the Sahara to the forest, with the savanna people acting as intermediaries in exchanges that involved slaves, ivory, salt, glass beads, coral, cloth, weapons, brass and other goods. In the 8th and 9th centuries Arab geographers from as far away as Spain and Baghdad provided the earliest documentation of what are now the northern states of pre-colonial Nigeria, based on descriptions received from returning traders.

By 1000, it is assumed that the majority of West Africans were no longer living in the Stone Age and were using iron instruments and food-producing techniques. Important resources like the yam and the camel were influencing the lives of people in large areas and undoubtedly there must have been a substantial increase in population. West Africa's pattern of population must have already been one of considerable complexity with a great variety of groups differing in language, economy and culture. Nothing definite is known about the political organisation of these early communities, but it is assumed that they lived in small groups tied by kinship and presided over by a chief or spiritual leader.

WEST AFRICA BETWEEN 1000 AND THE 1470S

The northern states from 1000 Trade was the key to the emergence of organised communities in the northern savanna regions, and by the beginning of the second millennium the first trans-Saharan trade routes had been established from West Africa to the Mediterranean and Arabia. The routes established an avenue of communication and cultural influence that remained open until the end of the 19th century. The Hausa states developed into walled cities that engaged in trade and serviced caravans, as well as manufacturing cloth and leather goods, their wealth founded on the trade routes. By these same trade routes, Islam made its way south into West Africa. The Muslim traders arriving from north of the Sahara converted the early Hausa rulers to Islam. Acceptance of Islam was thought to have been gradual and was nominal outside the walled cities, where traditional religion continued. Nevertheless, the seven Hausa states – Hadejia, Daura, Katsina, Kano, Rano, Gobir and Zaria – with their famous mosques and Koran schools came to participate fully in the intellectual life of the Islamic world, and there was a blossoming of Islamic learning and culture. Over the next few centuries, they continued to have good relations with North African Muslim rulers.

A severe drought and famine struck the savanna region from Senegal to Ethiopia in the middle of the 18th century. There had been periodic droughts before, one of seven years' duration in the 17th century, but the great drought of the 1740s and 1750s probably caused the most severe famine that West Africa has known, including that of the 1970s during the Biafran War. The environmental and political instability provided the background for the momentous events of the first decade of the 19th century, when the jihad of Usman dan Fodio revolutionised the whole of northern Nigeria. The strongly Muslim Fulani people in the far north moved into Hausaland to escape areas where drought conditions were even worse, and conducted a violent Islamic revolution to create a single Islamic state, known as the Sokoto Caliphate (see Religion on page 35). Ever since then, the northern states have adopted a staunch Islamic regime and the two ethnic groups are linked, and are often referred to as one, the Hausa-Fulani.

The southern states from 1000 At the beginning of the second millennium, Nigeria's southwest region was occupied by many small communities lost in the forests, swamps and bush, the most significant being the Yoruba who possessed the longest traditions, possibly going back a further 800 years. A number of Yoruba empires flourished in the southern region from the 14th and 15th centuries, and the Yoruba cities of Ile-Ife and Oyo became major trading centres. These were ruled by traditional *alafins* (kings) with the *alafin* of Oyo being head of all Yorubaland, and Ile-Ife being their sacred city. The *alafins* ruled successfully until the early 19th century, when their powers began to crumble, partly through fighting with the Fulani over slaves and the spread of Islam, before the British stepped in and quelled the violence.

Meanwhile, further to the southwest, the Benin Empire, centred on the city of Benin, emerged as the region's most powerful state in the 15th century. The kingdom was to dominate the Yoruba, Igbo and Edo in the south of pre-colonial Nigeria, as far west as Lagos and as far east as the lower Niger, and went unchallenged for the next few hundred years. Ultimate rule lay with the *oba* (king) of Benin whose line dates from 1170 to the present day. The *obas* of Benin traditionally had good relations with the Europeans and in the 16th century no other kingdom in West Africa was on such cordial terms with the Portuguese. They even set up an embassy in Lisbon, allowed Portuguese missionaries to build a church in their capital, and requested Portuguese firearms for their army. As early as 1553 the *oba* of Benin could read, write and speak Portuguese. During this period Benin City itself was reputedly very magnificent, with walls, gates and wide streets, and may have housed 100,000 inhabitants at its height, spread over 25km^2. It was known for its grand palace and artisans who worked for the *obas*, producing many pieces of fine art, including the famous bronze-casting plaques and statues that adorned the palace walls and altars. Benin lost its authority over the region in 1897 when the British arrived, who, after finding evidence of human sacrifice, burnt the city down and looted the palace of its many treasured artefacts.

THE WEST AFRICAN SLAVE TRADE FROM 1471 A desire for global glory, profit from trade, and missionary zeal brought Portuguese navigators to the West African coast in the late 15th century. Locked in a seemingly interminable crusading war with Islamic Morocco, the Portuguese concluded that maritime expansion might bypass the Islamic world and open up new commercial markets. They hoped to tap into the fabled Saharan gold trade, establish a sea route around Africa to India, and link up with the mysterious Christian heartland. The Portuguese achieved all these goals. They accessed the gold trade on the Gold Coast (modern Ghana), explored the Indian Ocean securing a monopoly of the spice trade, and discovered the roots of Christianity in Ethiopia. Portugal's lasting legacy for present-day Nigeria, however, was its initiation of the transatlantic slave trade.

The outline history of the slave trade can be told simply enough. The first Portuguese sea captains captured unwary Africans whose sale for use as domestic servants elsewhere helped to defray the expenses of the voyage. But the trade soon began to assume a larger scale when labour was needed for the sugar plantations on the recently colonised Caribbean Islands and tropical American coast. After the pope gave permission for slaves to be taken from Africa in 1513, the number of Africans sent to the Americas steadily increased, and slaves were taken from an area that at its widest point stretched from Senegal to the Zambezi River in Angola. In the 16th century the annual export of slaves rose to about 13,000; in the 17th century it was 27,000; in the 18th century it was 70,000; and in the first decades of the 19th century, when slavery was finally abolished, numbers of slaves exported each year sometimes reached over 100,000. These figures indicate that at least 15 million slaves were transported across the Atlantic. But the loss of manpower to Africa was far greater, since many lost their lives in the wars that accompanied the trade, and many more died because of hardship, cruelty and hunger during transportation. A ship of slaves would take around five weeks to reach the Americas. Conditions were so cramped and unhygienic it wasn't unusual for half the human cargo to die *en route*. For every slave that landed in America, another one may have died because of the trade, putting the number of people lost to Africa nearer to 30 million. From pre-colonial Nigeria alone, some 3.5 million slaves were shipped across the Atlantic over the period of the whole slave trade.

White men were not the only criminals in the slave trade: the sale of Africans to other Africans had been practised for centuries in just about every ancient African society. Transportation of slaves had been going on since the earliest days of the trans-Sahara caravans when people captured in the sub-Saharan regions were taken to North Africa and sold into domestic bondage. In his 1826 book *Travel and Discoveries in Northern and Central Africa*, Captain Clapperton records: 'Slavery, of course, had existed since time immemorial, but the Fulani made a business of it on a scale hitherto unknown. Parts of the road to Tripoli were almost truly white with human bones. In 1822 Major Denham counted a hundred rotting skeletons round a well, and when he expressed horror the Arabs laughed, prodded the bones with their musket-butts and remarked that they were only blacks.'

The slave trade is singularly one of the most important events in human history, because it operated on such an unprecedented scale and its effects have been so shatteringly widespread. Leopold Senghor, a Senegalese poet and statesman, poignantly called the slave trade 'a bush fire, ravaging Black Africa, wiping out images and values in one vast carnage'. But it is worth noting that the trans-Saharan slave trade went on twice as long as the Atlantic slave trade. When the Europeans first arrived in West Africa and decided that they would transport slaves by ship to the New World, the slave trade in West Africa already existed, and the Europeans who conducted the trade had come from an environment where they were still burning witches and holding public hangings.

In 1471 Benin and the Niger Delta was the first region in tropical Africa to be reached by the Portuguese. Gwatto, the port of the Benin Kingdom, became a depot to handle peppers, ivory and increasing numbers of slaves offered by the Benin *oba* in exchange for coral beads, textiles from India, and tools and weapons from Europe. The Portuguese initially bought slaves for resale on the Gold Coast, where slaves were traded for gold. For this reason, the southwestern coast of pre-colonial Nigeria, neighbouring parts of the present-day Republic of Benin (not to be confused with the Kingdom of Benin), and present-day Ghana became known as the 'Slave Coast'. When the African coast began to supply slaves to the Americas in the last third of the 16th century, the Portuguese continued to look to the Bight of Benin as one of its main sources of supply.

Although the Portuguese were the first Europeans to take advantage of this human commodity, their monopoly on trade was broken at the end of the 16th century, when Portugal's influence was challenged by the rising naval power of other European states. The Slave Coast attracted an increasing swarm of foreign ships from Holland, Denmark, Sweden, France, Prussia and Britain. The British arrived in 1562, when John Hawkins took the first British boat of slaves to the West Indies. In exchange for slaves, they traded textiles, metalware, alcohol, tobacco and, later, firearms and also a variety of crops and vegetables imported from America that the Europeans had only just become familiar with themselves – tomatoes, pineapple, papaw, cassava and maize, food items that were to change the African diet forever.

Lagos and Badagry grew into important slave markets and ports, and inevitably the rich profits to be gained from the trade stimulated intense rivalry not only between the Europeans but among the local African ethnic groups. After the introduction of firearms in the mid-17th century, when Britain alone supplied some 100,000 guns to West Africa annually, the Europeans did not recognise cowries as currency and instead brought gin and guns. Even the most unwilling chief became embroiled in the trade because to be able to defend his people he needed firearms, and to procure firearms in the first place he needed to find slaves. (Even today, bright blue empty bottles of British-distilled gin are pulled up from the riverbeds around the Niger Delta.)

THE BREAKDOWN OF THE SLAVE TRADE FROM 1772 In the first decade of the 19th century, two unrelated developments that were to have a major influence on virtually all of the area that is now Nigeria ushered in a period of radical change. First, between 1804 and 1808 the Islamic jihad of Usman dan Fodio established the Sokoto Caliphate (see Islam, page 35), a great Islamic empire in the northern states that had a profound influence on much of Muslim Africa. Second, in 1807 Britain declared the transatlantic slave trade to be illegal, an action that occurred at a time when Britain was responsible for shipping more slaves to the Americas than any other country.

As the 18th century drew to a close, the anti-slave lobby became an increasingly powerful voice in Britain, brought on by strengthening liberal thinking that emerged after the Industrial Revolution, and by greater public awareness of the atrocities caused during the handling of slaves. In Britain, slavery was challenged by the humanitarian movement, which owed its origins to the Christian Church, and to the theories of equality and fraternity spread by the French Revolution. Already by 1772 British legislation decreed that no slave could be kept on British soil, and in 1807 the anti-slave lobby persuaded the British government to abolish slavery in West Africa altogether. Other countries hesitantly followed the British lead. The USA officially abolished slavery in 1808, as did Holland, Spain, Portugal and France between 1814 and 1817. (Denmark had been the first country to declare the trade illegal in 1792.) Also in 1817, many of the above countries signed the Reciprocal Search Treaty that permitted the British navy to search boats captained by other nationalities. For several decades, as much as one-sixth of all British warships were assigned to this mission, and a squadron was maintained at the Spanish colony of Fernando Po off the Nigerian coast from 1827 until 1844. British naval crews were permitted to divide cash derived from the sale of captured slave ships, and rescued slaves were usually taken to Sierra Leone where they were released. Apprehended slave runners were tried by naval courts and were liable to capital punishment if found guilty.

This considerably subdued the slave trade but by no means stopped it and, despite the British blockade, almost one million slaves were exported from pre-colonial Nigeria in the 19th century. A flood of captives taken in wars among the Yoruba in the 1830s were shipped from Lagos to meet the demand for slaves in Cuba and Brazil. The risk involved in running the British blockade obviously made profits all the greater on delivery. Britain soon recognised that it needed to do more and abolished slavery in all her colonies in 1833. Finally, Britain was determined to halt the traffic in slaves fed by the Yoruba wars, and responded to this frustration by annexing the port of Lagos in 1861, making it a British colony and ousting the last of the slave traders. The slave trade brought about its own demise when greater public awareness about its brutalities was provoked in Europe, which instigated the emergence of some dedicated European political and religious groups determined to compensate Africa for its sufferings. To do this they wanted to give to Africans the 'blessings of civilisation', therefore justifying increasing interference into African affairs. This was the main force behind European imperialism on the African continent.

EXPLORATION OF THE INTERIOR IN THE 1800S Although the Europeans occupied the coast during the slave trade, they had no incentive to travel inland and knew nothing about the interior of West Africa. But the campaign to eradicate the slave trade and substitute it for trade in other commodities increasingly resulted in the British needing to look inland. They knew that there was a great river, but did not know even the course of its flow, for the many openings of the Niger Delta were thought to be separate streams. Then in 1788 a group of learned Englishmen got together and formed the 'Association for Promoting the Discovery of the Interior Parts of Africa', more simply known as the 'African Association', financed by the British government.

In 1794 the African Association commissioned Mungo Park, an intrepid Scottish physician and naturalist, to search for the source of the Niger and follow the river downstream. Park reached the upper Niger in Sierra Leone by travelling inland from the Gambia River, and reported on the eastward flow of the Niger. He was forced to turn back when his equipment was lost to Muslim slave traders, but in 1805 he set out again to follow the Niger to the sea. He failed to complete the journey but covered more than 1,500km, passing through the western portions of the Sokoto Caliphate, before being drowned in rapids (near today's Kainji Dam). On a subsequent expedition to the Sokoto Caliphate, Captain Hugh Clapperton learned where the Niger River flowed to the sea. But he also died and it was his servants, brothers Richard and John Lander, who canoed down the Niger River in 1830 from its source in Bussa in Sierra Leone to its mouth in present-day Nigeria. The course of the Niger had been traced. Unfortunately for them, the Lander brothers couldn't enjoy their glory as they were seized by slave traders and sold down the river to a waiting European ship.

In 1841, at the behest of the slavery abolishment lobby, the British government sent a larger expedition up the river by steamship – the most technically advanced piece of equipment the West Africans had yet seen. From then on, the British became masters of the navigable stretches of both the Niger and Benue rivers, and by 1870 there were 14 British steamships operating on the rivers, and amicable contacts had been made with Nupe, one of the southern provinces of the Muslim north.

With the slave trade winding down, and using their newfound knowledge of the interior, the British began to look for other ways to exploit the region's resources. They took over the Jos tin mines, and discovered palm oil, which gradually took over from slaves as pre-colonial Nigeria's biggest export. It was used to lubricate machinery before petroleum products were developed for that purpose, and for making soap, and demand rose rapidly in Britain, which was caught up in the first grimy stages of the Industrial Revolution. The boom in palm oil preserved the prosperity of the Niger Delta where it was farmed, as much as it did of the British port of Liverpool to where it was sent and sold. Ultimately the transition from the slave trade to legitimate commerce was made without causing any economic disaster in the region, and palm oil exports were worth £1 million a year by 1840.

Expansion of the British 1849–1902
This new wave of commerce and British interest in the area led to the appointment of a full-time consul, John Beecroft, to 'the Bights of Biafra and Benin' in 1849, and the first British consulate opened in Calabar in 1851. Meanwhile, the slave trade was still being practised illegally along the coast, and the British were resorting to gunboat diplomacy to persuade local rulers to sign treaties renouncing the slave trade. This resulted in the complete annexation of Lagos by the British in August 1861, and Lagos became a British colony. Over the next few decades the city was administered under a British governor and a small legislative council of British officials, and the city's infrastructure developed rapidly. As the colony strengthened economically, trade links improved with the other regions in the interior. Over time, these other regions also came under the protection of the British, although all for different reasons.

During the 19th century the Yoruba to the north of Lagos had experienced a series of continual spats among themselves, and against the Fulani, mostly fighting over slaves or the encroachment of Islam from the Sokoto Caliphate to the north.

Missionaries in Yorubaland appealed to the British in Lagos to help restore order, and in 1881 the *alafin* (king) of Oyo requested the governor of Lagos to step in to stop the fighting. There was also a need to protect commerce disrupted by this fighting. The governor answered his appeal, and in 1883 concluded a round of treaties with the big Yoruba chiefs that inevitably led to further British annexations.

Along the coast, east of Lagos, the Kingdom of Benin was still independent despite the establishment of a British consulate in Calabar in 1851. The conquest of Benin in 1897 was sparked by the massacre of the British consul and his party, who were on their way to investigate reports of ritual human sacrifice in the city of Benin. In reprisal the British promptly stormed the city and destroyed the *oba*'s palace, sending the reigning *oba* into exile. A British Protectorate was established over what were referred to as the Niger districts – the area running along the coast from Lagos to the Cameroons, together with the banks of the Niger and Benue rivers as far inland as British traders were operating at Lokoja, the headquarters of the National African Company. It was first called the Oil Rivers Protectorate, after palm oil, the main commodity in the area, before being changed to the Niger Coast Protectorate. The essential purpose of the protectorate was to control trade coming down the Niger.

In 1886 the British government issued a royal charter to the National African Company, a major trading company in the Niger Delta formed by George Goldie, through an amalgamation of British firms in 1879. The charter gave the company the rights to govern the Niger districts north of Lokoja extending along the Niger and Benue rivers above their confluence, on behalf of the British, and it became known as the Royal Niger Company. The company negotiated trade treaties with Sokoto, Gwandu and Nupe. Meanwhile, the French were making progress in a southerly direction down the Niger from the French colonies in the northwest. The Royal Niger Company employed a Captain Frederick Lugard (who in later years became governor-general of Nigeria) to form a military force known as the West Africa Frontier Force to protect the northern states from possible invasion by the French. These military operations against a rival European colonial power soon proved too expensive for a private company and in 1897 the British government ended the charter, and by 1900 had taken control of the north, and Lugard became High Commissioner of the Protectorate of Northern Nigeria. His clear intent was to occupy the Sokoto Caliphate. Expansion continued towards Lake Chad, and after armed assault, Sokoto and Kano were occupied in 1902.

Lugard's success in northern Nigeria was attributed to his policy of indirect rule, which called for governing the protectorate through the rulers who had been defeated. If the emirs accepted British authority, abandoned the slave trade, and co-operated with British officials, then Lugard was willing to keep them in office. The emirs retained their caliphate titles but were answerable to British district officers, who had the final say over their administrations. One consequence of indirect rule was that Hausa-Fulani domination was confirmed, and in some instances imposed, on smaller ethnic groups, some of them non-Muslim, in the so-called middle belt.

Although Lagos retained its title as the British Colony of Lagos, these new areas inland were amalgamated and became known as the Northern and Southern British Protectorates of Nigeria. People living in the colony of Lagos passed for British subjects while those living in the protectorates were referred to as British protected persons.

THE 20TH CENTURY
Unification of Nigeria 1914
Lugard left Nigeria for six years to be governor of Hong Kong, but returned in 1912 as governor-general of Nigeria to set in motion the merger of the northern and southern protectorates with the colony of Lagos.

Finally, in January 1914, on the eve of World War I, the British officially joined the regions together as the Federation of Nigeria, with Lagos as its capital, though effectively they were administered separately until 1946. In 1916 Lugard formed the Nigerian Council to represent all of Nigeria, on which sat six traditional leaders, including the *oba* of Oyo, the sultan of Sokoto, and the emir of Kano. The principle of indirect rule administered by traditional rulers was applied throughout Nigeria, and colonial administrators were instructed to interfere as little as possible with the existing order. In practice, however, the system of indirect rule was modified to fit the needs of the distinctively different northern and southern regions. In the north, the colonial governor avoided any challenge with the local emirs over religion that might incite resistance to British rule, banned Christian missionaries from visiting the region, and permitted Islamic education to go on unhindered. In the south, meanwhile, the British promoted Christianity and Western education because the traditional beliefs of the Yoruba and the Igbo were not seen as contemporary enough. Hausa was recognised as the official language of the north but only English was taught in the south. The development of the infrastructure differed enormously too, with Christian missions contributing financially to schools and healthcare in the south, and the north quickly lagging behind in facilities, relying only on sparse government funds. In contrast, the north benefited from the railways and roads built to transport tin from the Jos mines, while people living in the Niger Delta in the south were still using ancient canoes as their only form of transport.

Lugard stepped down as governor-general in 1919, and was succeeded by Hugh Clifford, who had previously been governor of the Gold Coast. In contrast to Lugard, Clifford argued that Nigeria could only benefit from Western experience and was not an advocate for indirect rule. He was indifferent over what he thought was a backward north while in the south he saw great potential for building an elite through European-style schools and universities. He even argued for the division of Nigeria into two separate colonies. Although Britain did not permit this move, the 1922 constitution was modified to include Clifford's other recommendations, and a new legislative council taking in the southeast and southwest was established, replacing the Nigerian Council and the Lagos Legislative Council, while administration in the north was left untouched. By 1931 strong nationalist sentiments had begun to emerge against Britain's transparent neglect of the northern states. Despite increasing economic development in both regions, there was little political interchange and absolutely no pressure for further unification until after World War II. Interestingly, unlike other African colonies such as Kenya, the British granted access to very few white settlers, and those that did emigrate to Nigeria had to have proven skills essential for the country. By 1938 the whole of Nigeria was governed by only 380 British officials who administered indirectly through appointed local leaders.

Path to independence 1920–60 British colonialism created Nigeria, joining diverse peoples and regions in an artificial political entity, and inconsistencies in British policy reinforced regional animosities. The nationalism that rose during the inter-war period was derived not from any sense of country allegiance but from an older political allegiance to region, ethnicity and a broader feeling of pan-Africanism. In the north, nationalism, based on the foundation of Islam, was pointedly anti-Western, while the nationalists in the south, an elite influenced by European education, were opposed to indirect rule as it formed an unfair class system of government. For once, the country agreed on its sentiment: they wanted self-government, and all nationalists were critical of colonialism for its failure to appreciate the antiquity of indigenous cultures.

A new constitution in 1922 gave the opportunity to a handful of representatives to be elected on to a Legislative Council, giving politically conscious Nigerians something concrete to work on. One of these was Herbert Macaulay, the grandson of the legendary Bishop Samuel Crowther, Africa's first black bishop and a repatriated slave. Macaulay was often dubbed 'the father of Nigerian nationalism', and he aroused political awareness in Lagos through his newspaper, the *Lagos Daily News*.

The nationalist movement splintered into the National Council for Nigeria and the Cameroons (NCNC), led by Nnamdi Azikiwe, the political party that dominated the Igbo east; the Action Group (AG), led by Obafemi Awolowo in the Yoruba west; and the Nigerian People's Congress (NPC), led by Ahmadu Bello in the Hausa north. Meanwhile, after World War II weary Britain was beginning to regard Nigeria as a costly addition to the empire and expressed amenity in granting it more economic and political power. The first step towards de-colonisation was in 1946, when Britain devised a new constitution and a federal system with powers shared between a central authority and three regional legislatures, simply called the Eastern Region, Northern Region and Western Region. (A fourth region, the Mid-West Region, was added in 1962.) The three new regions were to choose representatives to sit on the Central Legislature in Lagos.

The 1951 constitution, in terms of population, gave over half the seats in the central parliament to the Muslim Northern Region. Despite holding the majority, however, the NPC were less advanced politically than the southerners and were still reluctant to have closer links with the other regions. By now, it was very clear that the introduction of democracy had promoted strong north–south regional loyalties that could potentially pull the country apart. If Nigeria was to achieve independence as a single nation, the regional governments were to be given more of the powers they wanted, and the responsibilities of the national government needed to be restricted to national affairs. In 1957 the Eastern and Western Regions were given internal self-government. The Northern Region continued to resist but finally faced the fact that if they wanted to retain access to the coast through the other two regions for trade, they needed to be part of the Federation of Nigeria. They were granted internal self-government in 1959, only after they agreed to direct elections.

Elections were held for a new and greatly enlarged House of Representatives in December 1959. Bello became premier of the Northern Region, Azikiwe premier of the Eastern Region, and Awolowo premier of the Western Region, and official leader of the opposition in the House of Representatives. The deputy leader of the NPC, which had the most seats in the federal parliament, Balewa, became prime minister, while Azikiwe, after aligning his party, the NCNC, with the NPC, assumed the role of governor-general. The government was answerable to a parliament composed of the popularly elected 312-member House of Representatives and the 44-member Senate, chosen by the regional legislatures.

When the federal government met for the first time in January 1960, in the presence of the British Prime Minister Harold Macmillan, they adopted a formal resolution for independence and admission to full membership of the Commonwealth. On 1 October 1960 Nigeria gained independence from Britain, and became a member of the Commonwealth of Nations and the United Nations. Queen Elizabeth II gained a new title – the Queen of Nigeria – and was represented at Nigeria's independence celebrations by Princess Alexandra, who formally handed over the Independence Constitution to Prime Minister Balewa. In his speech, he said that the Nigerians had known the British 'first as masters, then as leaders, and finally as partners, but always as friends'. A week after independence, Nigeria was admitted to the UN Security Council.

The first civilian government 1960–66 The British could never have dreamed of the political chaos that was going to grip Nigeria over the next few decades. The British colonial system had done little to unify Nigeria or prepare it for independence. It was a vast country that had absorbed a block of Africa with a bewildering variety of people, all forced to co-exist within artificial boundaries drawn up by the British. The new government faced an overwhelming task of unifying 250 ethnic and linguistic groups and a persistent historical religious conflict between north and south, a task, as it had transpired by 1966, that was unworkable, at least not without the influence of the military. The new government was short-lived; right from the start it was characterised by political antagonisms, increasing corruption and a fear of Nigeria breaking up into several minor countries based on regions and ethnic groups.

The first crisis occurred in 1962, with the Yoruba objecting strongly to the shape and location of both the Western Region and the newly formed Mid-West Region, because they split their people into different regional governments. Disagreements between Awolowo's Action Group and central government paralysed the Western Region and central authorities assumed control for ten months, when bloody rioting broke out and many members of the Action Group were put under house arrest. This loss of stability in one region gradually undermined the political structure of the whole country. Chief Samuel Ladoke Akintola, prime minister of the Western Region, managed to wrestle the position of Western premier from Awolowo, and immediately organised a new party, the United People's Party, which pursued a policy of collaboration with the NPC–NCNC government in the federal parliament. Then, in late 1962, investigations by the federal government found that Awolowo had funnelled several million pounds of public funds to the Action Group in the 1950s. In the course of the financial investigation, police uncovered evidence of a conspiracy to overthrow the government, and of 200 Action Group activists – who had received military training in Ghana – smuggling arms into Nigeria in preparation for a coup. Awolowo and other Action Group leaders were charged with treason and sentenced to 15 years in prison.

In 1963 Nigeria became a republic within the Commonwealth of Nations. The change in status meant that a president elected for a five-year term replaced the crown as head of state and Azikiwe, who had been governor-general, became Nigeria's first president.

The next crisis occurred during the 1964 general elections, which witnessed widespread electoral boycotts and violent and lawless protest against blatant vote-rigging. The elections were contested by two political alliances incorporating all the major parties: the Nigerian National Alliance (NNA), composed predominantly of the northern NPC and Akintola's western NNDP; and the United Progressive Grand Alliance (UPGA), which joined the eastern NCNC and the remnants of the western Action Group. The NPC-dominated NNA coalition won 108 seats in the House of Representatives and President Azikiwe asked Balewa to form a government with the NNA majority. The UPGA became the official opposition. But the new government wasn't sitting comfortably in the House of Representatives. After the elections accusations continued against vote-rigging and electoral abuse. In the six months after the election an estimated 2,000 people died in violent protests in the Western Region, events that set the stage for the end of civilian rule, but that were nothing compared with what was going to happen next.

Military coups 1966 In January 1966 more rioting broke out, and the military, mostly eastern Igbo army officers, staged a coup, taking Nigeria and the rest of the world by surprise and shattering the political foundations of the country. The coup, led by Major General Johnson T.U. Aguiyi-Ironsi, overthrew the federal government, wiping out many of the main players. His officers assassinated Prime Minister Balewa in Lagos, Akintola in Ibadan, and Bello in Kaduna, as well as senior officers of northern origin. Azikiwe escaped assassination as he was in London for medical treatment. Major General Ironsi was named president of a new military government, and placed military governors in each of the regions, suspended the constitution, dissolved all political parties, and proclaimed martial law as a solution to Nigeria's problems.

The new government announced itself as a source of national political cleansing to replace the corrupt, discredited civilian rule. It also announced plans to move away from the federal system that had forced politicians to play on tribal passions, and replace it with a unitary state. Surprisingly, despite the bloody character of the coup, these sentiments appealed directly to younger, educated Nigerians in all parts of the country. But the Hausa in the north did not see the coup as a bid for a 'clean' government, but as an Igbo plot to take over Nigeria and a Christian attempt to undermine the emirate states. Troops of northern origin became increasingly restless and fighting broke out between them and Igbo soldiers in garrisons in the south. In June, mobs in the northern cities massacred several hundred Igbo people living in the north and destroyed Igbo-owned property.

To try and prevent further chaos, in July, four months after the first coup, northern army officers staged a second military counter-coup. Ironsi and some of his senior officers were killed. The Muslim officers declared 31-year-old Lieutenant Colonel (later Major General) Yakubu 'Jack' Gowon, a Christian from a small ethnic group (the Anga) in the middle belt, as chairman of the federal military government. His first moves were restoring federalism and releasing Awolowo from prison.

Biafran War 1967–70 A return to a civilian government was negotiated between September and November 1966 but the regions failed to reach an agreement, in part because the representatives of the Eastern Region failed to appear after the first conference for fear of their safety. The tempo of violence increased, and chaos continued to reign in many of the northern cities, where some 20,000 Igbo living in the north were massacred by the Hausa, leading to a mass migration of over one million Igbo people to their native Eastern Region. The Igbo retaliated and began to kill Hausa living in Port Harcourt and other eastern cities, resulting in the military governor of the Eastern Region, Lieutenant Colonel Odemugwu Ojukwu, banishing all non-Igbo from his region.

More negotiations took place in 1967, when Gowon initiated a move to replace the four legislatures of Nigeria with 12 states (three of them in the east). This provision broke up the Northern Region, undermining the possibility of continued northern domination, but Ojukwu feared that Gowon desired to divide the Igbo into these new smaller states, and thus deprive the Igbo of its control over the oil fields and access to the sea. The situation quickly deteriorated, and in an attempt at secession, Ojukwu declared the Eastern Region as the Republic of Biafra on 30 May 1967, citing as the predominant cause for this action the Nigerian government's inability to safeguard the lives of the Igbo people. Gowon retaliated by declaring a state of emergency.

The most influential of the activists that protested during this time was the political dissident Wole Soyinka, one of Nigeria's foremost political campaigners and a prolific writer. Like Ojukwu, Soyinka spoke out against human rights violations and the right-wing policies of Gowon and his predecessor Ironsi. Troubled by the prospect of Nigeria's imminent war with Biafra, Soyinka went to Gowon's regime with the intention of making a personal appeal for peace, but Gowon reacted by jailing Soyinka without charge in solitary confinement for nearly two years.

The federal military government of Nigeria declared war against the new Republic of Biafra, a civil war that lasted three years and left behind between one and three million dead, and established 'Biafra' as a byword for mass destruction and famine. The Biafran army was an ill-equipped, understaffed and undertrained rebel force up against a Nigerian army 250,000 strong, but nonetheless had the benefit of superior leadership and superb morale. The bulk of Biafra's military supplies were homemade (see box page 198), but they also got unofficial assistance from France. Only four other African nations recognised Biafra as a republic: Tanzania, Ivory Coast, Gabon and Zambia. No doubt there was sympathy for the Biafran cause, but few African states dared to side with Biafra for fear of giving encouragement to secessionist movements within their own countries. The federal government of Nigeria gained official support from Britain and the Soviet Union (who supplied arms and warplanes to the Nigerian forces) and effectively accepted assistance from the east and the west during the Cold War. The USA remained neutral. It's worth remembering at this point that this was the first real era of television news broadcasting, when Biafra, like Vietnam, was flashed across TV screens worldwide, causing international uproar over disturbing images of widespread massacre and starvation. Some food and medical aid from international aid organisations got into Biafra by way of night-time drops from warplanes, but it wasn't nearly enough and the famine that ensued from the outbreak of war was deathly and determined.

At first the Biafran forces did well and advanced into the Mid-West Region. But by early October 1967, the Biafran side was weakening and the federal forces had already captured their capital Enugu. Despite attempts by the Organization of African Unity (OAU) to end the war, and an appeal by Ojukwu in October 1969 to the UN for mediation, the war raged on until 1970. The federal government insisted on Biafra's surrender, and Gowon observed at the time that 'rebel leaders had made it clear that this is a fight to the finish and that no concession will ever satisfy them.' On 12 January 1970, after 31 months of civil war, the Biafran forces surrendered at Owerri, the last major town in Biafran hands, and the Nigerian military government led by Gowon reasserted control and enforced the 1967 constitutional arrangement of dividing Nigeria into 12 states. Ojukwu had fled the country the day before and sought refuge in the Ivory Coast (he was pardoned a few years later and returned to Nigeria, and years later was a candidate in the 2003 and the 2007 elections). At the end of the war, Biafra was no more than 60km wide and just a few kilometres deep, crowded with some three million Igbo refugees. There were severe shortages of food, medicine, clothing and housing, and the region was shattered and in ruins. The cost in terms of human and material resources of the civil war – perhaps the worst civil strife experienced on the African continent at the time – was immense. The actual fighting was bitter enough but the worst sufferers were the civilian population. The federal forces had literally starved the Biafran population into submission.

After the war, Gowon assured the Igbo survivors that they would not be treated as defeated enemies, and a programme was launched to reintegrate them into a unified Nigeria. The federal government granted funds to the eastern states and much of the war damage was repaired. There were no war trials and few imprisonments, and it was Ojukwu, in exile, who was made the scapegoat. Relations were also mended with African states that had recognised Biafra during the war. One of the Igbo survivors was the writer Soyinka, who was released from prison and went on to write *A Shuttle in the Crypt*, a book of poetry that contemplates his time in jail and the critical period between 1966 and early 1971. Around this time he was also quoted as saying, 'as far as the regime is concerned, well, the play is sheer terror for them. Because they feel, how dare – how dare anybody lift his or her voice in criticism against us? We have the guns. Their level of paranoia and power-drunkenness is unbelievable.'

1970s oil boom and Gowon's six-year plan
In the post-war period, all significant political power remained with the federal military government and none of the three major, undoubtedly exhausted, ethnic groups had much of a political voice. In an environment where his role was unlikely to be challenged, Gowon announced in October 1970 that he intended to stay in power until 1976, which was set as the target year for the return to civilian rule. He headed the Supreme Military Council, a formidable bunch of military state governors, top-ranking policemen, and heads of the armed forces, that proposed a political plan for the country over the next six years until civil rule was reinstated. The plan was to include a national census, rebuilding of the war-torn east, a new constitution, an attack on corruption, the establishment of even more states, economic development, and organisation of political parties. Criticism of the six-year plan was widespread because the agenda was so broad, and many Nigerians feared that Gowon's programme was so ambitious that it would take much longer than six years to complete, keeping the military in power indefinitely.

Gowon conducted a national census in 1973, which produced some staggering results. Despite a loss of well over a million people during the Biafran War, the population was up 44% in ten years, a growth bigger than in any other developing country. On a more political issue, the north contained 64% of the total population, compared with 53.7% in 1963. The census, on which representation in a new elected parliament would be based, revived fears that one ethnic group would permanently dominate the others.

Gowon's government also made an effective attack on corruption. A damning anti-corruption police department dubbed, rather sinisterly, the 'X squad', made a number of investigations outing scams and extortion rackets in government and public departments and private industry. The list of offenders was endless: from state agencies and contractors who took bribes for sub-standard construction materials bought overseas, to hospitals that were buying expired medical drugs on the international black market for resale to the Nigerian people.

Gowon's economic plan charted Nigeria's transition from an essentially agricultural economy to a mixed economy based on both agriculture and industrial growth. In 1972 the government issued a decree that prevented foreign companies from investing in certain industries in order to stimulate home-based industry. At the time, some 70% of Nigerian industry was foreign-owned or managed, but by 1975 the federal government had bought 60% of the equity of the major oil companies operating in Nigeria. And the timing couldn't have been better for the economy. By the late 1960s, oil was the country's biggest foreign-currency earner, and in 1971 Nigeria was the world's seventh-largest oil producer, and joined the Organization of Petroleum Exporting Countries (OPEC). A heady rise in oil prices caused an instant economic boom in Nigeria, when between 1973 and 1974 the influx of oil revenue increased 350%. Later, in 1975, with Nigeria's full support, OPEC stepped in to regulate prices and Nigeria's exports were dominated by oil for the rest of the 1970s, until the bubble burst in 1981. Given that Nigeria had just emerged from a civil war and one of the worst famines the world had yet to encounter (at least in televised history), the country's excessive prosperity came as a huge surprise. Rocketing oil prices provided the Nigerian government with a chance to go on a spending spree of reckless proportions and industrialisation boomed throughout the rest of the 1970s.

Although the six-year plan had some successes, inevitably Gowon came up against obstacles that ultimately led to his downfall. The military had a grip on government, but it didn't have a grip over the urban populace who lived in increasing unemployment, poverty and lawlessness. Crime began to rear its ugly head as a threat to internal security and had a seriously negative impact on economic development. Armed gangs, often composed of former soldiers, roamed the countryside engaging in robbery, extortion and kidnapping, and pirates raided cargo ships awaiting entry to ports. Drug trafficking and smuggling were rife, and all crime was susceptible to the indifference of the police under the blanket of corruption at every level. The government used public executions by firing squads to curb crime but this had little impact on reducing the crime rate, instead promoting a callous public attitude toward violence.

With all these problems to contend with, Gowon, as expected, announced in January 1975 that he was backing off from the 1976 date scheduled for return to civilian rule. This announcement led to mass strikes throughout the country by an already agitated work force, and yet another bloodless coup ending Gowon's nine-year rule. The coup was led by Army Brigadier Murtala Mohammed, who became new chief of state. Gowon wasn't there at the time, but at an Organisation for African Unity (OAC) conference in Uganda, and soon after he swiftly exiled himself to the UK, where he remained on a Nigerian pension.

The regime of Mohammed and Obasanjo 1975–79 Murtala Mohammed was a 38-year-old Hausa-Muslim northerner, who had received military training at Sandhurst in the UK. In an attempt to restore public confidence in the federal government, he purged more than 100,000 employees in the civil service, police and armed forces, and the diplomatic corps and judiciary, citing malpractice and corruption as means for dismissal. Some were brought to trial, with one former military state governor executed for gross misconduct. His administration created a few more states, raising the number from 12 to 19, led by newly appointed military governors expected to administer federal policies handed down by the Supreme Military Council. The government took over the country's two largest newspapers and TV and radio stations, and took delivery of Soviet-built aircraft for the Nigerian air force.

But Mohammed didn't have the chance to do anything else, as his fellow army officers, disgruntled by his sweepingly harsh policies, assassinated him in 1976. He was replaced by army chief of staff General Olusegun Obasanjo. A Yoruba, Obasanjo had been Mohammed's deputy and retained the support of the military. He pledged to continue the programme towards a civilian government now set for 1979, and to continue the reform of the public service sector. He drafted a new constitution that was adopted in 1979, based on the Constitution of the USA, with provision for a president, a Senate and a House of Representatives. Nigeria was ready for local elections, to be followed by national elections, which would return the country to civilian rule. Plans were made to move the federal capital to Abuja, a location chosen for its central location and because it didn't identify with any ethnic group. Obasanjo set the 1979 elections in motion, after which he retired from the military to set up a farm in his home state, before emerging again years later to win the 1999 and 2003 elections and serving as president for two terms.

Return to civilian rule 1979 The 1979 elections were held on schedule in July and August, and attracted many of the key players from the parties that had existed prior to the 12-year-long ban on political activity. Just as the northern NPC had dominated the first civilian government of 1959, its successor, the National Party of Nigeria (NPN), dominated the second, and won the majority of the seats in the House of Representatives and the Senate, and its leader, Shehu Shagari, became president. The Yoruba United Party of Nigeria (UPN) came in second and formed the opposition, just as the Action Group had done the first time round.

The new civilian government was born amid great expectations. Oil prices were high and it appeared that unlimited development was possible. But it was all to be short lived. The world recession in the early 1980s sent oil prices plummeting and by 1981 the proverbial bubble had burst. Nigeria quickly sank into a cycle of massive debt, soaring inflation, large-scale unemployment and widespread corruption. The recession put severe strain on the new government, though government spending continued, mostly heavy investment in steel, and Nigeria increased its foreign debt almost five-fold between 1978 and 1982. In addition, the half-hearted attempts to license imports and to control inflation encouraged smuggling, which became a major crime that went virtually unchecked. There were many signs of tension throughout the country and the lack of confidence in their government by Nigerians was more than evident. In Sokoto in 1979, police killed or wounded hundreds of protesting farmers and burned their crops and villages, and in 1980 almost 4,200 people died in religious riots in Kano and Kaduna. The wealthy business community demonstrated their dissatisfaction by leaving, and an estimated US$14 billion of capital left the country between 1979 and 1983. The government responded by finding a scapegoat and expelled two million foreign workers, mostly from Ghana and Niger, who had come to Nigeria for jobs during the oil boom. As the 1983 elections drew near, the economy was in chaos, political despondency was at an all-time low, and the government was in sad shape. It was a perfect atmosphere for the military to step back in and exert control.

1980s wave of military coups Shagari was re-elected for a second term in 1983, but after only a few months army officers seized power on 31 December 1983, citing mismanagement and corruption on the part of the civilian government. Army chief Mohammed Buhari, a Hausa who had been Federal Commissioner for Petroleum and Mines during the height of the oil boom, led the coup. But he didn't last long and was largely ineffective during his two-year role as head of state. In August 1985 he was overthrown by General Ibrahim Babangida. The latter was assisted by one Sani Abacha, an army chief who remained valuable to Babangida throughout his presidency, and who Babangida appointed Minister of Defence in 1990. The Babangida regime had a rocky start. He survived several attempted counter-coups led by rival army officers, and serious opposition from unions and student bodies.

The economic crisis deepened further when, in 1986, there was heavy devaluation of the naira, causing a drop in real income, with per capita income falling below US$300, while unemployment was at 12%. Also by 1986, 44% of export earnings were being used to service the foreign debt. On 1 October 1986 the government declared a National Economic Emergency, which lasted for 15 months. Wages were cut in the army and public service sectors, import tax was increased to 30%, and petroleum subsidies were cut back. Despite these drastic moves, a drop in world oil prices further compounded Nigeria's situation and the government finally conceded that they could not alleviate their foreign debt without an International Monetary Fund (IMF) loan. In 1988 the World Bank stepped in and provided US$4.2 billion over three years.

Babangida announced that the country would be returned to civilian rule, though this promise was largely delivered to mollify the international community and the World Bank. Transition from military to civilian rule was originally planned for 1989, but scheduled elections were postponed. State elections finally happened in 1991. In preparation for democracy, the official capital of Nigeria was moved from Lagos to Abuja in December 1991 and the number of states increased to 30.

A presidential election was held on 12 June 1993, though the military did everything they could to ensure their favoured candidate was elected. However, much to their surprise the vote went in the opposite direction and the election was comprehensively won by Moshood Abiola, a former publisher promoted as a token opposition candidate. Enraged by the result, Babangida reneged on his promise, annulled the elections and returned the country to military rule, throwing Abiola in jail. However, Babangida did resign as self-proclaimed president in August 1993 and his senior aide and former defence minister General Sani Abacha became the new military strongman who, over the next five years, presided over an increasingly oppressive regime.

Abacha's iron-fisted rule Corruption, governmental inefficiency and harsh military rule dominated Abacha's term. He was notoriously authoritarian, and was never seen without his trademark sunglasses and a surrounding throng of soldiers from his 3,000-strong bodyguard unit. He immediately dissolved the national and state assemblies, putting generals and police officials in power, banned political parties, abandoned the not-yet-implemented 1989 constitution, and threw opponents of his regime into jail or out of the country. Abacha presented a budget that abandoned market reforms instituted in 1986, making it impossible to negotiate for aid from the IMF. Foreign debt deepened further and industrial output was at an all-time low. Meanwhile, Abacha's opponents maintain that he embezzled some US$1 billion of public funds into private bank accounts in Europe and the Persian Gulf. In the 1970s Nigeria was the 33rd-richest country in the world – by 1997, it had dropped to being the 13th poorest. (In 2002 it was ranked 26th-poorest country in the world.)

Abacha's government attracted much international condemnation, particularly through its treatment of the Ogoni people located in the oil-rich southeast of the country. Well-known political dissident and journalist Ken Saro-Wiwa was leader of the Movement for the Survival of the Ogoni People (MOSOP), which advocated for the rights of the Ogoni people. The Ogoni Bill of Rights, written by MOSOP, set out the movement's demands, including increased autonomy for the Ogoni people, a fair share of the proceeds of oil extraction, and remediation of environmental damage to Ogoni lands. This peaceful campaign of opposition was violently suppressed by the military and nine prominent Ogoni leaders, including Saro-Wiwa himself, were executed in 1995 on trumped-up charges. The incident sparked widespread rioting and civil unrest across Nigeria. International human rights groups claimed the charges against Saro-Wiwa were unfounded and that he had had an unfair trial without adequate defence. Many countries withdrew their ambassadors from Nigeria to protest the executions, the Commonwealth suspended Nigeria's membership until 1998, and the European Union (EU) imposed oil sanctions until 1998.

President Nelson Mandela of South Africa orchestrated much of the diplomatic isolation. This could have been in response to Mandela at the time calling for 'quiet diplomacy' over Saro-Wiwa's situation, a move he later deeply regretted, as he was as surprised as any by Saro-Wiwa's execution. Saro-Wiwa's son, Ken Wiwa, heard the news of the death of his father while he was imploring the world's leaders to do something about his release at the 1995 Commonwealth Heads of Government Meeting (CHOGM) in Auckland, New Zealand. A few years later, Wiwa wrote a brilliant book about what happened to his father called *In the Shadow of a Saint* (see Appendix 3, Further Reading).

In 1996 a UN fact-finding mission reported that Nigeria's 'problems of human rights are terrible and the political problems are terrifying'. The prominent Nigerian writer Chinua Achebe wrote an essay relating to this critical period entitled 'The Trouble with Nigeria': 'The trouble with Nigeria is simply and squarely a failure of leadership. There is nothing basically wrong with the Nigerian character. There is nothing wrong with the Nigerian land or climate or water or air, or anything else. The Nigerian problem is the unwillingness or inability of its leaders to rise to the responsibility, to the challenge of personal example, which is the hallmark of true leadership.'

Then on 8 June 1998 Abacha died very suddenly of a heart attack. He was in the company of two Indian prostitutes in the presidential villa in Abuja and it is alleged that the heart attack was caused by an overdose of Viagra or another virility drug. He was succeeded by another military ruler, General Abdulsalam Abubakar, who initially made positive moves to shed the country's pariah status and began to tackle Nigeria's neglected and now desperate economic situation. Like many of his military predecessors, he pledged to step aside for an elected leader, and provisionally predicted a general election for May 1999. Abubakar provided some early signs of hope of easing military rule when he released some political prisoners from jail – including Olusegun Obasanjo who Abacha had thrown in jail in 1995. However, the suspicious and unexplained death of Abiola, the man who had been imprisoned ever since he legally won the 1993 civil presidential election, was a crushing blow to democratic progress.

Despite this, there were concerted efforts towards a civil election and Abubakar drafted a new constitution in late 1998 proposing a US-style of political system. Under the provisions of this new constitution, executive power was to be vested in the president of the republic, and legislative responsibilities were to be entrusted to the National Assembly, comprising the 360-member House of Representatives and the 109-member Senate. The president and members of both houses were to serve a four-year term, and only two consecutive terms. Several political parties stepped forward claiming allegiance over the electorate from geographically based constituencies, though only three were permitted to contest the election – the People's Democratic Party (PDP), the Alliance for Democracy (AD) and the All People's Party (APP). The favourite in the presidential campaign was the former military ruler of the 1970s – Olusegun Obasanjo – who was only released from prison eight months before the February 1999 elections. Representing the People's Democratic Party (PDP), he won the elections with just less than two-thirds of the vote, and the PDP secured an absolute majority in both houses of the newly established parliament. Following nearly 16 years of military rule, the new constitution was adopted in 1999, and the transition from military rule to civilian government was finally completed.

Obasanjo's government After lurching from one military coup to another, Nigeria now had an elected leadership, and Nigerians were euphoric that they were finally free from military rule. Obasanjo's commitment to democracy and his pledges to fully restore Nigeria's international position after years of ostracism, and to tackle the country's endemic corruption that was crippling the economy, gained him high praise from the populace as well as the international community. He set up the Economic and Financial Crimes Commission (EFCC), which investigated and prosecuted highly-placed people in both the public and private sector on charges of corruption. It recovered tens of millions of dollars in stolen government money, including the majority of more than US$1 billion allegedly stolen from Nigeria by the family and cronies of Abacha. Abacha's eldest son, Mohammed Abacha, was arrested on charges of fraud, money laundering and embezzlement, and for the murder of the wife of Moshood Abiola, who was mysteriously assassinated in Lagos during Abacha's term. She had been at the forefront of the campaign for the release of her husband and was vocal in her support of efforts to restore democracy in Nigeria. Later, a deal was struck between the Nigerian government and the Abacha family, in which all criminal proceedings against Mohammed were dropped in return for 80% of the family's liquid assets. At least US$770 million of the stolen state cash has been recovered to date. Today, Nigeria is now 18 from the bottom of Transparency International's global corruption index, after occupying last place for many years.

In a country where a small group of soldiers held a tight grip on the reins of power for as long as most Nigerians can remember, Obasanjo was successful in steering the country to a point where few believed the military had any serious plans to take over again. He was also a champion for conflict resolution and was involved in international talks over Zimbabwe, Darfur and Liberia among others.

Despite these successes however, the inexperienced civilian government was criticised over its general handling of the economy – most famously symbolised by the building of the US$330 million National Stadium in Abuja for the 2003 All Africa Games, a cost that exceeded the combined budget for both health and education.

Nigeria approached fresh elections in April 2003 – the first transition from one elected government to another since independence more than 40 years ago. During the 1999 elections, only three parties were allowed to contest and they had to prove that they had support from across the country in order to prevent parties based on region or ethnicity from running. However, this wasn't the case in 2003, and 30 political parties registered to contest that year's poll. Nevertheless it was a tightly fought contest between Obasanjo and the People's Democratic Party, and Mohammed Buhari of the All Nigeria People's Party (both Buhari and Obasanjo led military governments in the 1970s and 1980s). Another presidential candidate was Emeka Odumegwu-Ojukwu of the newly registered All Progressive Grand Alliance (APGA) – none other than the former leader who tried to secede from Nigeria in the 1967 Biafran War.

The election was not without controversy. In September 2002, the electoral commission distributed 70 million registration cards, more than enough for every one of the country's eligible voters, but unaccountably, large numbers of these disappeared. Then in February 2003 the police in Lagos uncovered a scam to print as many as five million fake voters' cards – an unidentified man placed a US$800,000 order in a Lagos print shop for the cards – a retired general was the reported suspect. This was a vote-rigging scheme of huge proportions that could easily have swung the elections, representing 8.3% of the projected registration figure of about 60 million. In March that year a senior opposition politician, Harry Marshall, a senior figure of the All Nigeria People's Party who had been organising Buhari's first campaign rally, was shot dead at his home in Abuja.

Turnout on 12 April was around 50%, and Obasanjo's ruling party secured an outright majority in both the House of Representatives and the Senate. During his second term, Obasanjo's greatest success has been paying off Nigeria's foreign debt – the first African country to do so. In 2005 the Paris Club of rich lenders agreed to write off US$18 billion of Nigeria's US$30 billion foreign debt, and by April 2006, and thanks to money previously stolen from the government through corruption that was recovered by the EFCC, along with record-high oil prices, Nigeria paid off its remaining US$12 billion of foreign debt. This success was coupled with personal tragedy for Obasanjo, however, as his wife of nearly 40 years, Stella, died in 2005 from complications during a plastic surgery operation in Spain. In 2006 Obasanjo tried to change the constitution to allow him to stand for a third term, but failed, and in April 2007 Nigeria went to the polls again.

1957   Oil is discovered in the Niger Delta.

1960   Independence, with Prime Minister Sir Abubakar Tafawa Balewa leading a coalition government.

1962–63 A controversial census fuels regional and ethnic tensions.

1966   In January Balewa is killed in a military coup. Major General Johnson Aguiyi-Ironsi heads up a military administration. In July Ironsi is killed in a counter-coup, and is replaced by Lieutenant Colonel Yakubu Gowon.

1967   Three eastern states secede as the Republic of Biafra, sparking a bloody civil war that lasts for three years and leaves up to 3 million dead from fighting or famine.

1970   The Biafran leaders surrender and the former Biafran regions are reintegrated into the country.

1975   Gowon is overthrown and flees to Britain, and is replaced by Brigadier Murtala Mohammed, who begins the process of moving the federal capital from Lagos to Abuja.

1976   Mohammed is assassinated in a coup attempt, and is replaced by Lieutenant General Olusegun Obasanjo, who helps introduce a US-style presidential constitution.

1979   Elections bring Alhaji Shehu Shagari to power.

1983   Major General Mohammed Buhari seizes power in a bloodless coup.

1985   Ibrahim Babangida seizes power in a bloodless coup, and bans all political activity.

1993   Babangida allows elections, but when civilian Moshood Abiola wins, he reneges, annuls the elections and throws Abiola into jail.

1993   General Sani Abacha comes to power, and begins a dictatorship that suppresses all opposition.

1995   Ken Saro-Wiwa, a writer and campaigner against damage to his Ogoni

2007 Elections and Umaru Yar'Adua Obasanjo plucked a quiet northern state governor, Umaru Yar'Adua, as his successor. Never known as a 'mover or a shaker', he nonetheless won 70% of the votes and became president – the first time one civilian leader has taken over from another in Nigeria's history. The constitution does not allow for a president for more than two terms (eight years), but Obasanjo has at the time of writing kept his position as leader of the People's Democratic Party, so the question has arisen, just how much independent power Yar'Adua will have. Yar'Adua comes from Katsina State and is a former chemistry teacher and also the first leader since independence to be educated at university level. His brother was an army general when Obasanjo led a military government in the 1970s; Obasanjo served a prison term with him under Abacha. As governor of Katsina State, Yar'Adua was thought to be incorruptible and has a clean slate; in the first few weeks of office he publicly declared his assets for scrutiny. But he has been criticised as being meek and inexperienced for the role of president and a mere puppet of Obasanjo. He also suffers from ill-health and has a kidney disorder, which needs to be treated regularly by dialysis.

The 2007 elections, like the 2003 elections before, were also deeply flawed and were condemned by both local and international election observers as 'not credible'. The two primary opposition presidential candidates, Muhammadu Buhari and Atiku Abubakar, rejected the results, believing them to be rigged in Yar'Adua's favour. First, in the run up to the election, it was claimed that Obasanjo used a combination of inducements and threats of investigation by the EFCC to

	homeland by the oil companies, is executed following a hasty trial. In protest, the European Union imposes sanctions until 1998, while the Commonwealth suspends Nigeria's membership until 1998.
1998	Abacha dies suddenly and is succeeded by Major General Abdulsalam Abubakar. Chief Abiola is found dead in his prison cell a month later.
1999	Parliamentary and presidential elections for a civilian government are finally held, and Olusegun Obasanjo is sworn in as president.
2000	Sharia law is adopted by several northern states in the face of opposition from Christians. Tension over the issue results in 10,000–15,000 deaths to date in clashes between Christians and Muslims.
2003	The second civilian elections since the end of military rule in 1999 take place though polling is marked by delays, corruption and allegations of ballot-rigging. The People's Democratic Party wins for a second time and Obasanjo begins a second term of presidency. Violence in the Niger Delta kills about 100, injures 1,000, and displaces tens of thousands.
2004	Deadly clashes in Port Harcourt kill 500 and prompt strong crackdown by troops.
2005	The Paris Club of the world's rich lenders wipes off US$18 billion of Nigeria's US$30 billion foreign debt.
2006	Militants in the Niger Delta attack oil facilities and kidnap foreign oil workers – a situation that continues today. Helped by high oil prices, Nigeria becomes the first African nation to pay off its foreign debt to the world's rich lenders. The Senate rejects to change the constitution to allow Obasanjo to stand for a third term. Islamic spiritual leader, the Sultan of Sokoto, dies in a plane crash – Nigeria's third major air disaster in a year.
2007	Umaru Yar'Adua is proclaimed president in the 2007 elections.

persuade ten other state governors who were standing for president to withdraw and back Yar'Adua. These include Cross River State governor Donald Duke, who had been a popular favourite. Then over 200 people died in protests during election campaigns, and on election day itself on 21 April, many polling stations did not receive ballot papers in time for people to vote – just days before, 70% of the required ballot papers were still sitting in a warehouse at Johannesburg's airport. Bizarrely, in Abuja on the morning of the election, a petrol tanker loaded with additional gas cylinders was rolled down a hill towards the Electoral Commission's headquarters. It was plainly seen as an attack but thankfully came to a halt before hitting the building. Finally, when the results came in, the number of votes in some of the southern regions were neatly rounded to the nearest 1,000, which was suspiciously inept. Obasanjo acknowledged fraud and other electoral lapses but said the result reflected opinion polls. In a national television address he added that if Nigerians did not like the victory of his handpicked successor they would have an opportunity to vote again in four years' time.

Current issues Despite economic successes by Obasanjo's government, he failed to stop the spiralling violence between Muslims and Christians in an ongoing religious conflict (see page 38) that after 1999 was no longer threatened by army intervention. Since 1999 some 10,000–15,000 people have been killed in these clashes, many of which are set off by the most trivial of disputes. Obasanjo was a Christian from the south, while Yar'Adua is a northern Muslim and was involved in implementing Sharia law, which has been part of the problem; time will tell how he will diffuse this crisis.

There is also an ongoing violent dispute between communities in the Niger Delta and the oil companies. Some ethnic groups, namely the Ijaw, are demanding more political representation and compensation from oil companies operating in the area. More than 4,000 oil spills have polluted the delta over the past four decades, making it unfit for agriculture or fishing and creating health risks for the people of the delta, who are demanding a greater share of the oil wealth that comes from their traditional lands. Oil facilities are constantly being shut down and reopened because of sporadic violence; since 2003 Nigeria has periodically lost up to 30% of its oil output. These groups started out as gangs of youths with sticks, but have evolved in recent years into well-trained and organised militia groups with sophisticated weapons. Scores of people have been killed in fighting between different ethnic groups and the Nigerian navy, whose gunboats and troops have been blockading and firing on their villages from the rivers and creeks south of the town of Warri. Since 2006 almost 200 foreign oil workers have been kidnapped in this region to highlight the plight of the people living in the delta to an international audience, and oil platforms, installations and tankers have been blown up. In his inauguration speech, Yar'Adua said dealing with the crisis in the delta was one of his priorities, and the Vice President, Dr Goodluck Jonathan, has made the resolution of the Niger Delta crisis his major task. Soon after the 2007 election he relocated to Yenagoa, the Bayelsa State capital, in the delta itself. But to actually get the militants to surrender their new found power and come out of the creeks, having acquired huge arsenals of arms and money from ransom takings, will be difficult. Writer and activist Wole Soyinka, raised his voice again in 2007 and said Yar'Adua was an 'unknown quantity' being sworn into power at a 'perilous time'.

ECONOMY

Much of Nigeria's economic history has already been documented in the historical account above, simply because the health of the economy is directly linked to the character of those people that govern the country. Today, Nigeria's economy is one of the largest in Africa, with a variety of natural resources and a massive labour force. But despite great potential for high productivity and diversity, under Nigeria's military rule and thanks to political turmoil, years of economic mismanagement and corruption, as well as fluctuations in the world oil price, the economy was close to collapse. By 2002 it was rated the world's 26th-poorest country – in the 1970s, it was rated the 33rd-richest country in the world. However, although poverty and unemployment are still real problems today, since democracy arrived in 1999, the economy has been steadily strengthening. Businesses in the formal sector have doubled or tripled in size in recent years, there has been a substantial amount of inward investment, and some sectors such as telecommunications and banking are booming. Since 2003 GDP per head has almost doubled from US$800 to US$1,500. Most recently, and as the world's sixth-biggest oil producer, Nigeria has earned huge revenues from record oil prices – US$100 a barrel – and rather astonishingly in 2006 it paid off its foreign debt; the first African country to do so.

BEFORE OIL The British replaced indigenous food crops such as cassava with crops of palm oil, as well as groundnuts (peanuts) and cocoa, all intended for export. During the colonial period Nigeria basically survived on its agriculture for its economy, and for its food. At independence in 1960 agriculture accounted for well over half the GDP, and was the main source of export earnings and public revenue. But since the British left, agriculture has suffered from years of mismanagement, inconsistent and poorly conceived government policies, and the lack of basic infrastructure. Above all the sector has been dwarfed by oil, discovered in the Niger Delta in the 1950s. By the late 1960s oil had replaced cocoa, groundnuts and palm oil as the country's largest foreign-currency earner, and with an injection of oil money, Nigeria's manufacturing industry grew into its own from 1950 to the 1970s – before the discovery of oil there had been very few industries.

Nigeria started importing raw materials from other countries, and manufacturing became established. Industries included food processing and the manufacture of vehicles, textiles, pharmaceuticals, paper and cement. One of the effects of the oil and industry boom was that there was a significant rural-to-urban migration that took a lot of the labour force away from the rural areas. Not surprisingly, the largely subsistence agricultural sector declined, and failed to keep up with rapid population movement and growth. Nigeria, once a large net exporter of food, had to import food. Today, Nigeria still needs to import most of its food and only about 12% of the land is cultivated.

Other than oil, Nigeria is considerably rich in mineral resources. Nigeria was once the world's largest producer of tin, with huge deposits in the highland district around Jos. But production collapsed from an average of 10,000 tons per year in the 1970s to 300 tons in the late 1990s, with only an estimated 16,000 tons of tin reserves left. Although the reserves of tin have been exploited, other mineral resources have hardly been touched. Some estimates place iron ore reserves at over 800 million tons, but Nigeria's output is only around 50,000 tons per year. Deposits of uranium, lead, zinc, tungsten and gold have also not been exploited to their full potential. Gold has been located in some 65 sites around Nigeria though mining as yet hasn't begun.

THE DISCOVERY OF BLACK GOLD Since 1957, when Shell-BP discovered oil in Nigeria's Delta region, Nigeria's economy has overwhelmingly been dominated by oil. The majority of oil reserves are located in the Niger Delta but newer reserves have been discovered in deeper waters offshore. Today, production exceeds two million barrels per day, or 60.3 million per month, making Nigeria, a member of OPEC, the world's sixth-biggest oil provider. The majority of Nigeria's crude oil is exported to Europe, Asia and the USA. The low-sulphur content of much of Nigeria's oil makes it especially desirable in a pollution-conscious world. At present oil revenues constitute over 95% of Nigeria's export earnings, 90% of foreign-currency earnings, and 85% of total government revenue (over US$50 billion in 2006). Nigeria's largest joint venture oil company is Shell, which produces nearly 50% of Nigeria's crude oil, with the Nigerian National Petroleum Company (NNPC), the state-owned oil firm, having a 55% interest in Nigeria Shell. OPEC's 2003 estimate of Nigeria's proven oil reserves was put at another 35.2 billion barrels and with further exploration Nigeria wants this forecast to reach 40 billion barrels by 2010. Today, international oil prices have reached a record high and oil is a huge revenue earner for Nigeria.

However, oil production has not been without its disruptions. Thanks to a thriving black market for oil products, revenue has simply been lost through crime – from illegal siphoning from pipelines, to stolen oil being freighted out of Nigeria on ships. The government estimates that as much as 100,000 barrels per day of Nigerian crude oil is illegally 'bunkered' (freighted) out of the country and the Nigerian navy is under orders to capture any ship with oil aboard that is not accounted for. Pipeline theft has increased the number of explosions in recent years, with the most serious disasters being in 1998 at Jesse, when a fire killed over

1,000 people and on Boxing Day 2006 when fire killed over 250. Then there is the ongoing dispute with militants in the delta (see page 26) and today this crisis has reduced Nigeria's oil output by 30%.

Nevertheless, the oil revenue should indicate a wealthy country with a healthy economy, but this hasn't been the case at all. By rights the oil wealth should have filtered through the system from the oil wells in the Niger Delta to the man on the street, but roughly 57% of the population lives below the poverty line (compared with 43% in 1985). The problem has been that Nigeria neglected its agricultural and manufacturing bases in favour of an unhealthy dependence on crude oil. This didn't help Nigeria's millions who needed jobs, and it fuelled a massive migration to the cities, which in turn led to increasingly widespread poverty, especially in rural areas.

Nigeria faces a choice between privatisation and greater reliance on the private sector, or remaining dependent on the public sector, namely oil. Nigeria is also keen to attract foreign investment and needs foreign capital to reinvigorate the economy, but this is hindered by security concerns as well as by a shaky infrastructure. It also needs to build more oil refineries. Nigeria exports crude oil, but then imports the refined product at a far higher price. Exporting refined oil would earn far greater revenues and end the chronic fuel shortages that routinely plague Nigeria. The other priority is for the Nigerian government to lessen this unhealthy dependence on crude oil and perhaps develop the long-neglected agricultural sector.

One huge boost for the economy is the development of the natural gas industry – Nigeria is believed to have an estimated 3.5 trillion cubic metres of proven natural gas reserves, making it the world's ninth-largest source. But Nigeria currently flares 75% of the gas it produces – the World Bank estimates that Nigeria accounts for 12.5% of the world's total gas flare. (Gas, which is extracted at the same time as oil, is 'flared' or burnt off, which in turn causes major health and environmental problems such as respiratory disease and acid rain.) Shell has committed to end flaring completely by 2010, and in 1997 the US$569 million Escravos Gas Project became Nigeria's first gas exporter. In 1999 the US$4 billion Nigeria Liquefied Natural Gas Scheme, Africa's single-biggest engineering project, started producing liquefied natural gas from its plant at Bonny Island. The facility is capable of processing 77 billion cubic metres of natural gas annually. A proposed US$580 million pipeline will supply gas to central and northern Nigeria, as well as the Benin Republic, Togo and Ghana, and it is believed the World Bank will finance this.

INFRASTRUCTURE Nigeria's transportation infrastructure is a major constraint to economic development. Of the 200,000km of roads, only 60,000km are officially paved, but many are in very bad shape and have been decaying for years. Throughout the country are thousands of police and army roadblocks that hamper travel; most Nigerians have to pay a bribe, locally known as *dash* (whether personally or within the price of a bus ticket), to get through them. The principal ports at Lagos, Port Harcourt and Calabar charge docking fees for freighters that are among the highest in the world, and the inspection procedure for imported goods is riddled with corruption. Nigeria has four international airports at Lagos, Kano, Port Harcourt and Abuja, which are some of the busiest in the world, but there were two fatal air crashes in 2005 and another in 2006 and Port Harcourt's airport has been closed for urgent maintenance. The government-owned airline Nigerian Airways collapsed in 2003, due to mismanagement, high debt and an old and vastly shrunken fleet. Trains on the railways have all but stopped moving.

Basic resources are also plagued with problems. After years of neglect, the

Nigeria is divided into 36 states and one Federal Capital Territory (see map pages ii/iii in colour essay), all of which are referred to by their own rather unique titles that you will notice on car number plates throughout the country. Nigeria is governed by the Federal Capital Territory (FCT), of which Abuja is the capital, located in the middle of the country just north of where the Niger and Benue rivers converge.

State	Capital	State mottoes
Federal Capital Territory	Abuja	Centre of Power
Abia	Umuahia	God's Own State
Adamawa	Yola	The Highest Peak of the Nation
Akwa Igbom	Uyo	Promised Land
Anambra	Akwa	Home for All
Bauchi	Bauchi	Pearl of Tourism
Bayelsa	Yenagoa	Pride of the Nation
Benue	Makurdi	Food Basket of the Nation
Borno	Maiduguri	Home of Peace
Cross River	Calabar	The People's Paradise
Delta State	Asaba	The Big Heart
Ebonyi	Abakaliki	Salt of the Nation
Edo	Benin City	Heartbeat of Nigeria
Ekiti	Ado Ekiti	Fountain of Knowledge
Enugu	Enugu	Coal City State
Gombe	Gombe	Jewel of the Savanna
Imo	Owerri	Land of Hope
Jigawa	Dutse	The New World
Kaduna	Kaduna	Liberal State
Kano	Kano	Centre of Commerce
Katsina	Katsina	Home of Hospitality
Kebbi	Birnin Kebbi	Land of Equity
Kogi	Lokoja	Confluence State
Kwara	Ilorin	State of Harmony
Lagos	Ikeja	Centre of Excellence
Nassarawa	Lafia	Home of Solid Minerals
Niger	Minna	Power State
Ogun	Abeokuta	Gateway State
Ondo	Akure	Sunshine State
Osun	Oshogbo	State of the Living Spring
Oyo	Ibadan	Pace Setter
Plateau	Jos	Home of Peace and Tourism
Rivers	Port Harcourt	Treasure Base of the Nation
Sokoto	Sokoto	Seat of the Caliphate
Taraba	Jalingo	Nature's Gift to the Nation
Yobe	Damaturu	The Young Shall Grow

state-run National Electric Power Authority (NEPA) now produces below half its generating capacity of nearly 6,000 megawatts and power cuts are part of daily life. In Nigeria NEPA is commonly referred to as 'Never Expect Power Again', and for good reason. Faulty and ageing facilities are in desperate need of repair, and currently only 10% of rural households and approximately 40% of Nigeria's total

The Hausa inhabit northern Nigeria and southern Niger. In Nigeria, they live predominantly in the northern states, especially around Kano, Sokoto and Kaduna, a region referred to as Hausaland. There is no Hausa race as such, but a great many people speak the language, and are historically a fusion of nomadic people from North Africa, the Chad Basin and from present-day Sudan, who were absorbed, long ago, into Hausaland. According to legend, the Hausa trace their origins to Berber immigrants from Tripoli and Baghdad, and the Hausa rulers descended from a 'founding hero' named Bayinjida, supposedly the son of the king of Baghdad. In the 10th century he became *sarki* (king) of Daura, a dot on the map near Katsina, after killing a big snake at the Kusugu well that was terrorising people and only allowing them to fetch water once a week. He married the queen of Daura, and their children founded the other Hausa towns, which became known as the seven Hausa states (see box on page 316). The Hausa Empire controlled much of the northern region from the end of the 11th century, and converted to Islam in 1350. The seven Hausa states were centered on *birni*, or walled cities, where the Hausa developed techniques of efficient government, including a carefully organised feudal system and a highly learned judiciary that gave them a reputation for integrity, and the ability to administer Islamic law.

The Fulani people are scattered throughout West Africa from Senegal to Cameroon, including Nigeria. A number of African states, including ancient Ghana and Senegal, have had Fulani rulers. The Fulani also converted to Islam and were known to have arrived in Hausaland in the early 13th century, though their origin is more of a mystery. Once a pastoral nomadic people, theories and legends abound: descendants of gypsies or Roman soldiers who became lost in the desert, a lost 'tribe' of Israel, or relatives of the Tuareg who inhabit the southern edge of the Sahara. More realistically, it's believed the Fulani originated from Mauritanian shepherds who were looking for new pastures. Whatever their origin, the Fulani, with their olive skin and straight hair, settled in the cities and mingled freely with the Hausa, and mostly adopted the latter's customs and language. Historically, they have been a devoutly religious, educated elite who made themselves indispensable to the Hausa kings as government advisers, Islamic judges, and teachers. Between 1750 and 1900 they engaged in many holy wars in the

population have access to electricity – and then only sporadically so. In 2006 NEPA changed its name to the Power Holding Company of Nigeria (PHCN) – 'Problem Has Changed Name'! Access to water is another daily problem and only about 60% have access to safe drinking water in the cities, and only a third in rural areas. It rarely flows from any tap and households have resorted to buying plastic water tanks to store water, which are filled when it does miraculously appear from a tap, or from water sellers. All over Nigeria you will see men pushing handcarts with jerry cans of water for sale and crowds of people around public taps and wells.

Nigeria's government-provided public healthcare facilities are few and far between, of a very poor standard, and subject to shortages of doctors and nurses, drugs, equipment and electricity. Because of the lack of fundamental healthcare, many Nigerians resort to traditional doctors and medicine that could further endanger their health. Over 40% of the colossal population of nearly 140 million is under the age of 14, and although education is mandatory for all, finding school fees and places in schools and universities is difficult for the average Nigerian family. Many children are taught in rudimentary, privately run schools, often in the back street of a city or outdoors in a village. For a Third World country where the majority of people are living on a few naira a day, food prices are high, because of the lack of agriculture and the reliance on imported goods. Finally, with so many name of Islam, and during the first part of the 19th century, the Fulani carved out two important empires. One, based on Massina, for a time controlled Timbuktu; the other, centred at Sokoto, included the seven Hausa states and parts of western Cameroon. The sultan of Sokoto continued to rule over northern Nigeria until the British conquest in 1903. Other Fulani retained their traditional lifestyle and remained aloof from the Hausa and in some measure from Islam as well, herding cattle outside the cities and seeking pastures for their herds.

The Yoruba in the southwest of Nigeria and parts of the Benin Republic are made up of numerous smaller collections of people, united by a common belief that the spiritual city of Ile-Ife (today in Osun State) was their place of origin and 'Garden of Eden' and that the *alafin* (king) of Ile-Ife was their spiritual leader. The Yoruba are unusual in Africa in their tendency to form urban communities. It is assumed that their primary antecedents, the Odudua, came from Egypt, based on the resemblance of sculptures found in Ile-Ife to those in Egypt. Yoruba society was organised into kingdoms, the greatest of which was called Oyo from the 14th century, which extended as far as Ghana in the west and the banks of the Niger in the east. At one time of considerable power and importance, the Oyo Empire collapsed in the 1800s through a series of wars for which the slave trade was largely responsible. Today many of the large cities in Nigeria (including Lagos, Ibadan and Abeokuta) are in Yorubaland. Christianity has been the dominant Yoruba religion since the mid-19th century; some have converted to Islam and others retain their traditional spiritual religion. Vestiges of Yoruba culture are also found in Brazil and Cuba, where Yoruba people were imported as slaves.

The Igbo, also referred to as the Ibo, in the southeast, are again a synthesis of smaller ethnic groups. Their origins are completely unknown, as they claim to be from about 20 different places. Traditionally the Igbo have inhabited inaccessible areas and live in the Niger Delta and forested southeast of the country, where they were forced to retreat into the forest to escape the Fulani's slave raids. Their largest societal unit was the village, where each extended family managed its own affairs without being dictated to by any higher authority. Like the Yoruba, the Igbo were greatly influenced by Christian missionaries in the mid-19th century.

people and so few jobs, only a small section of the population works in formal employment. Most people eke out a living as traders on the streets and markets, as transport drivers and conductors, or as local service providers. The rising population will inevitably doom Nigerians to become even poorer.

PEOPLE

POPULATION The size of its population is one of Nigeria's most significant and distinctive features. When Nigeria became independent in 1960, the population was 35 million. At the time of writing, the population was put at a staggering 140,003,542 (2006 census) – a figure that represents almost 5% of the world's entire population. It's the largest population in Africa and, at the country's current 2.38% rate of growth, one that could reach 200 million by 2020. One in six Africans is Nigerian, and the country is home to a quarter of all sub-Saharan Africans and half of all West Africans. It has two of the largest cities in Africa: Lagos, with an official population of just over nine million, but with a more realistic estimated population of 13–17 million, and Kano, with an estimated population of 9.3 million. Several of Nigeria's 36 states have populations greater than those of entire African countries and there are several million Nigerians living overseas (for example three million in the USA and one million in South Africa).

Some of the reasons why the population is so high are that Nigeria has one of the lowest levels of modern family planning use in the world, coupled with a very high fertility rate – the average woman has over five pregnancies. Quality health services are hard to find throughout the country, and cultural and social pressures also limit access to family planning. In Muslim-dominated regions, where having many children is highly valued, some women need their husband's permission to seek medical care. And one man may have several wives, all producing children, so any man who is even an averagely successful trader supports perhaps up to 20 children. Some 45% of this colossal population is under 14 years of age. Population growth not only has an adverse effect on the health of Nigerian families, but stretches the availability of food, services and infrastructure. Merely to remain at current per capita levels, agricultural production, industrial and other economic output, and provision of health, education and other social services would all need to double within 25 years. This situation will be a challenge of historic proportions for Nigeria.

ETHNICITY Nigeria has a rich and diverse cultural history that extends back to at least 500BC, when the Nok people first inhabited the area. The ethnicity of Nigeria is so varied that there is no definition of a Nigerian beyond that of someone who lives within the borders of the country. The ethnic variety is both dazzling and confusing, and there are more than 250 ethnic groups with their own language and distinct cultural heritage, each with their own very strong sense of ethnic allegiance.

The following groups are the country's largest and most politically influential: the Hausa in the north (21% of the population), the Yoruba in the southwest (21%), the Igbo, also referred to as the Ibo, in the southeast (20%), the Ijaw in the east (6%), and the Fulani in the north (9%). The larger of the minor groups that make up the remaining population are the Tiv, Kanuri, Igala, Idoma, Igbirra and Nupe in the north; the Ibibio, Efik and Ekoi in the east; and the Edo, Urhobo and Itsekiri in the west.

In an area one-and-a-half times the size of France, with nigh on 140 million people all trying to retain their identity in 250 cultural groups, and speaking a different language, it's not hard to imagine the difficulties and ensuing chaos of governing such a vast variety of people. The boundaries of the former British colony were drawn up to serve commercial interests, largely without regard for the territorial claims of the indigenous ethnic groups, and the country's unity has been consistently under siege from alternating dominant groups that have wanted to take control of the whole country. Between 1914 and 1977 there were eight attempts at secession, the Biafran War being the last of the secessionist movements within this period. Even today, underlying tension continues between the Yoruba and Hausa, though it is predominantly religion, and not ethnicity, that divides the nation.

LANGUAGE

The country's official language is English, and is taught in schools and spoken with varying degrees of fluency by nearly 50% of the population, making Nigeria the largest English-speaking country in Africa. Those Nigerians that don't speak it consider English a foreign language, but Pidgin or 'broken' English, a mixture of English and indigenous Nigerian words, is often used in casual conversation and has been spoken and understood by almost all Nigerians for more than a century. It's a complete Nigerian fabrication (although local versions of Pidgin are found throughout the world) and a language in its own right, spoken with a lot of spirit and gesticulation. Hausa, Igbo, Yoruba, Fulfulde and Kanuri are spoken by millions of first- and second-language speakers. Three languages other than English are accepted in government: Yoruba, Hausa and Igbo, and nine are broadcast on television and radio. Each of the 250 ethnic groups has their own distinct language, with scores of dialects within each group, and the Index of Nigerian Languages published in 1992 records over 500 languages spoken in modern Nigeria. Some have developed written traditions but most are pre-literate, with only a small number of speakers, and some of the minority languages are endangered, simply through lack of use. Educated Nigerians are often fluent in several tongues, and the more widespread languages are taught in schools and universities in Nigeria and abroad. Indeed, the BBC news website gives the option of presenting the world news in Hausa, proving that many millions worldwide speak it. (See also Appendix 1 on page 324.)

RELIGION

In order to appreciate fully how Nigeria's complex religious character shapes and affects all walks of life in Nigerian society, the religion practised in the country needs to be looked at in a little more depth than in the average guidebook. I have never visited a country where almost all of its inhabitants are so fervently religious. A rough line divides Nigeria in an east–west direction between the predominantly Muslim north and the Christian south (see map on page 36).

Around 50% of the population are Muslim, and 40% are Christian (the remaining 10% follow indigenous beliefs), and churches and mosques are prolific around the country. Islam was introduced to West Africa from the 11th century onwards via the trans-Saharan trade routes, and European missionaries spread Christianity when they arrived on the coast in the 18th century. Many Christians and Muslims also incorporate some traditional worship into their daily lives that pays homage to gods and spirits. These practices play an important part in Nigerian culture and pre-date the introductions of both Islam and Christianity.

Although most traditional religions coexist, there has been a historical and recently increasingly violent conflict between the imported religions, Islam and Christianity, which continues to separate the country religiously, politically and socially between the north and the south. Over the last few years, violent religious clashes have intensified since Sharia law was introduced in the northern states. Nigerian politics is plagued by escalating religious rivalries and public unrest over the issue of Islam versus Christianity and under whose rules people in different areas should live. Despite most of the north being Muslim, there are pockets of communities that are Christian, just as there are Muslims living in the south. This is the root of the problem.

ETHNIC NIGERIAN RELIGIONS Nigeria's people worship a variety of complicated traditional religious beliefs, and terms such as fetish or *juju* have produced much confusion. While ancestral spirits and membership of cults still exist, the main object of worship remains a common belief in a supreme being; Olorun or Olodumare (names given to God in Yoruba belief), Chineke or Chukwu (God among the Igbo) and Obangiji (God in the Hausa language). Of the three major groups of people, the traditional religion of the Yoruba is God-worship; the Igbo ancestral spirit-worship; while the Hausa-Fulani have been Muslim for almost a thousand years. The other traditional religions are too numerous to mention.

There are some 400 Yoruba gods each with a specific role. As might be expected in a culture with only oral records of the past, the same god may be male in one village and female in the next, and have a variety of names, differences that probably arose as myths were passed by word of mouth over the centuries. They serve under one all-powerful god who is variously known, among other names, as Olorun ('the owner of the sky') or Olodumare (roughly translated as 'the almighty'). He or she was creator of the world and had the ability to shape human bodies. The Yoruba explained to early missionaries that the 400 or so minor gods descended from this single god, and all are thought to have been once human, if not mythical, characters in ancient Yoruba history. Traditionally, the Yoruba pay homage to their gods at shrines, some of which still exist, and at certain festivals make animal sacrifices and pray to the gods to look over them. During the 19th century the traditional religion of the Yoruba altered significantly because of missionary-inspired Christianity, and again in the early 20th century under the dominance of colonial rule, when the British put restrictions on their religious practices, many of which, such as human sacrifice, they thought were barbaric. The British also insisted on burying the dead in communal graveyards rather than allowing the traditional Yoruba practice of burying them in the house.

The Igbo people traditionally believe in worshipping karma and spirits, and that they have two souls; their eternal soul or Maw, and one that belongs to an ancestor that is always watching over them, the Nkpuruk-Obi. Both souls leave the body when it dies but it is the Maw that goes on to form a shadow or ghost and becomes an Nkpuruk-Obi for somebody else. For this reason, the Igbo consider it bad luck to step on a shadow as they could be trampling on somebody's soul. As in the God-worship of the Yoruba, there is a hierarchy in the Igbo spirit world. This is headed by the ghost king or Eze Ala Maw and the ghost messenger or Onwu, who appear as skeletons and bring death to a person by striking him at the base of the skull with a large staff. A ferryman or Asasaba brings good souls across the river of death to be reincarnated into a Nkpuruk-Obi or other spirit representing humans or living things such as trees or animals. The living pray to the deceased to look after them and provide a secure future. Death and the afterlife play a large role with elaborate funeral ceremonies and continued pilgrimage to the dead person's grave, though several types of deaths such as suicide are considered shameful.

CHRISTIANITY The arrival of missionaries in the 18th and 19th centuries on the coast made their impact on the southern regions, though they failed to penetrate the Muslim north. Roman Catholic priests accompanied the first Portuguese slave traders to the West African coast and introduced Catholicism to the Kingdom of Benin in the 15th century. Several churches were built to serve the Portuguese traders and a small number of African converts, but the influence of Catholicism dwindled when the Portuguese withdrew, and had all but disappeared by the 18th century. Although churchmen in Britain had been influential in the drive to abolish the slave trade, missionaries only arrived again on Nigeria's coast in the 1840s. Mostly British Protestants, they set up the first mission stations in Calabar, and in Abeokuta, just north of Lagos, and by 1850 had made a considerable impact on the people they were working with. The Roman Catholics arrived again in the 1880s, by which time Christianity was a force to be reckoned with in the southern states.

Other European and American missionaries subsequently arrived, as well as a considerable number of African Christians – returning slaves who had been exposed to Christianity elsewhere. There were some 3,000 returned slaves from Sierra Leone and from Brazil in Lagos by 1870. Among them was Samuel Crowther, a Yoruba by birth, who had been rescued as a boy from a slave ship by a British warship and taken and educated in Sierra Leone. He came to Yorubaland to concentrate on the mission stations along the Niger, and at the beginning of the

19th century was the first West African to be ordained an Anglican bishop. (He was the grandfather of Herbert Macaulay, one of Nigeria's leading nationalists in the 20th century.) With the arrival of colonialism at the end of the 19th century, which the missionaries supported, some African Christian communities formed their own independent churches because many European missionaries were racist, and because European Christianity refused to incorporate their local practices and traditions. The number of Nigeria's independent Christian churches grew steadily; today Christians make up over 96% of the population in the east and southeastern states, which is where Nigeria's largest concentration of churches are found, ranging from Orthodox to Pentecostal.

In these regions, *everybody* goes to church. Southern Nigeria is a place where millions and millions of people, every Sunday, dress up, pick up their Bibles, and go to church, and on weekday nights there are additional services and Bible study groups. On Sundays Nigerian women wear their best and biggest shiny headdresses, men wear their full traditional robes, and children are dressed in their smartest clothes. Many churches have their own sort of uniforms and you'll see several women dressed in the same fabric. There is much hymn-singing and praising the lord, and preachers (male and female) are mostly self-styled evangelists; traditional clergymen are found only in the traditional Roman Catholic churches. Any makeshift building can become a church, stuffed to the gills with plastic seats or wooden benches, sometimes with a microphone system or electric organ or guitar. Whole streets are closed off on Sundays for open-air church services, and outside the big cities you will see what are termed as 'campgrounds'. These are not for camping at all, but are vast areas used for evangelistic gatherings that often go on until dawn. There is one outside Lagos that can reputedly hold three million people! All over the south you will see billboards advertising well-known preachers and events. Some are even black evangelists from the US, who come to Nigeria to tap into this monumental thirst for religion that Nigerian Christians seem to have.

Society in the south is shaped by God. It is a region where people frequently break out into impromptu hymn-singing; where conversations are peppered with plenty of amens and praise-the-lords; where women in minibuses sing religious songs under their breath for their entire journey; where lay preachers wander motor parks with a microphone and The Word; where cassette stalls in markets belt out never-ending religious tunes; where hundreds of thousands of how-to pamphlets are published on how to live life through the eyes of God; and where businesses are named in the name of God – God's Will Motors and Vote for Jesus Motors (both bus companies); Thank the Lord Bakery; Let God be my Witness Tyre Menders; Pray Harder Hairdressers; Praise the Lord Optical Services; or Jesus Loves You Nursery School. It is remarkable – nowhere else in the world have I seen such a deep and revered attitude to Christianity.

ISLAM Northern Nigeria was the southernmost outpost for the sweep of Islam that was carried from North Africa across the Sahara between the 10th and 19th centuries, but the penetration stopped before it reached southern Nigeria. It was practised unchallenged for some 500 years, though before the 19th century it was the religion of the elite few. Then, from the beginning of the 19th century, while the British were embroiled in the slave trade on the coast, other significant events were occurring in the north that had nothing to do with European intervention.

There were a series of spats between the flexible and easygoing Hausa and the more religiously devout Fulani, both living in the northern states. In 1802 one of the Fulani chiefs, Usman Dan Fodio, raised the standard of revolt against the Hausaland rulers, calling for a jihad or holy war. Although the Hausa were

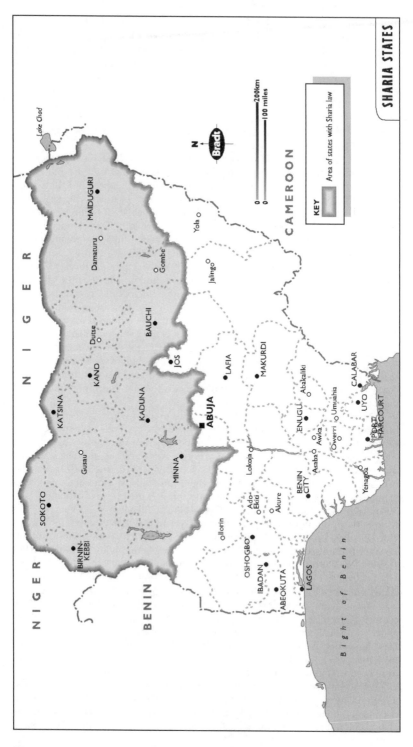

predominantly Muslim, many were not so strict and some still practised traditional religions. Dan Fodio campaigned for the purity of the Islamic faith and against the evil ways into which many of its followers had fallen. He intended the jihad to protect and expand the faith, to denote that the authority of local rulers was shaped in religious terms, and to stress that the imam was the local leader for religious prayer and study.

Dan Fodio became known as *sarkin musulmi* or 'Lord of the Muslims', and was leader of what became known as the Sokoto Caliphate, the religious heartland of his movement in the extreme northwest, with the city of Sokoto as its capital. The Caliphate was a loose confederation of emirates that recognised the regime of the commander of the faithful, the sultan. His supporters rallied around him in such numbers that he found himself head of a formidable army of warriors all burning with religious fervour and intent on jihad, which eventually resulted in a series of wars between the Fulani and the Hausa. By 1808 the jihad had invaded the Hausa states of Kano, Zaria and Katsina, and the jihad war-bands went about conquering neighbouring pagan communities and built up a string of new states – Bauchi, Gombe, Adamawa and others – which all became tributaries to the Sokoto Caliphate, an empire founded by Muslim-reforming zeal. They moved further south, deep into non-Muslim Yorubaland as far as the city of Oyo, shattering the relatively peaceful relationship that had existed in the past between the various Yoruba states. Thousands of Yoruba refugees retreated south and built new cities, where they carried on their resistance to the Caliphate and fought among themselves as well. One of these cities was Ibadan, founded as a war camp in 1829 by a group of soldiers from Oyo, which became the largest city in Black Africa during the 19th century.

The movement retained its momentum well into the second half of the 19th century, when the Sokoto Caliphate stretched 1,500km from Dori in modern Burkina Faso, across what is now Nigeria, and into southern Cameroon. In addition, Dan Fodio's jihad provided the inspiration for a series of related holy wars far beyond Nigeria's borders that led to the foundation of Islamic states in Senegal, Mali, Ivory Coast, Chad, Central African Republic and Sudan. An analogy has been drawn between Dan Fodio's jihad and the French Revolution in terms of its widespread impact. Just as the French Revolution affected the course of European history in the 19th century, the Sokoto jihad affected the course of history in Africa from Senegal to the Red Sea. It introduced new forms of political and religious organisation and succeeded in planting deep-rooted Islam, irrevocably affecting the way of life of the region's inhabitants. Today, of the 50% of Nigerians who practise Islam, almost all live in the northern states.

Again, like Christianity in the south, Islam is practised with devoutness and fervour, particularly as many northern states have now adopted Sharia law (see below). Northern Nigerians are strict Muslims and live their lives to the Islamic letter. The north is scattered with mosques and open prayer compounds, and most males pray every few hours. Nigerian Muslim women live their lives as most Muslim women do around the world, though they are not expected to completely cover up. Most wear headscarves and flowing robes but their faces are not covered. Unlike other Islamic areas such as Turkey and the Middle East, but like more staunch regions such as Iran, the female children from walking age (and not puberty) wear headscarves and long clothes.

SHARIA LAW Sharia law was first introduced in Nigeria's Zamfara State in January 2000, and is now practised, to a greater or lesser extent, in 12 other northern states. But what exactly is it? To Muslims, Sharia is a God-given code for how life ought to be lived. Calling it 'law' can be misleading, as Sharia extends beyond law, and governs all aspects of religious, political, social, domestic and private life. It's often dubbed Islamic law, but this is arguably incorrect as only part of it is based on the text in the Koran. The Sharia law system is thought to be the work of Muslim scholars during the early centuries of Islam, who fused the messages in the Koran with older Arabic, and other, law systems. There are similarities with ancient Bedouin law, commercial law from Mecca in the 7th and 8th centuries, and laws from conquered or conquering countries over the millennia, such as Roman and Jewish law. Despite this, most Muslims believe it to be based on the Koran and hence think of it as the 'will of God'.

Used in varying degrees, for most Muslims it governs their religious way of life. Beyond that, many Islamic countries have adopted Sharia as their civil law. Some countries use Sharia as their criminal law, applying its judgements and penalties to offences such as adultery or theft, known in Sharia as Hadd offences. These are Saudi Arabia, Sudan, Iran, perhaps most famously Afghanistan under Taliban rule, regions of Pakistan, and since 2000 practically one half of Nigeria, where an estimated 70 million Muslims found themselves faced with criminal sentences that differed greatly from those handed out to non-Muslims.

These include floggings for gambling and consumption of alcohol, amputations for theft, and even death for crimes such as adultery. But then there was the infamous story of 30-year-old Amina Lawal, who was sentenced to death by stoning for committing adultery. The man identified as her lover was released, because the court said there was insufficient evidence against him and he swore on the Koran that he had never had sex with Lawal. But a baby was enough evidence for them to convict Lawal. The story brought worldwide condemnation, and the sentence was later reversed in the wake of international pressure. Human rights' groups complained that these religious laws are archaic and unjust, and they also represent a constitutional threat because they undermine the national, secular legal system. Since then and to date, none of the harsher penalties have been carried out. The reaction of the government has been to do nothing, and the issue has largely gone away.

RELIGIOUS CLASHES Islam and Christianity both gained momentum throughout Nigeria in the 20th century at the expense of the smaller, increasingly unfashionable indigenous religions. Since 1980 there have been several outbreaks of religious or ethnic-driven violence, resulting in thousands of deaths, injuries or arrests. The first dramatic religious disturbance was in 1980, incited by a Muslim sect known as the Maitatsine Movement. They demanded absolute obedience to Islam, and violent riots broke out in Kano, killing more than 4,000. After 11 days, the army and air force eventually suppressed the riots after the surprised police had failed to restore any order. Muslim extremists sparked further riots in 1981, and destroyed several of Kano's state government buildings. Then in Kaduna, in 1982, fighting broke out between the Maitatsine Movement and the police, during which an estimated 500 were killed. The government banned the sect and many of its leaders were arrested. Nevertheless, the Maitatsine sect continued to demonstrate violently, and in 1984 struck again, this time in northeast Nigeria at Yola, the capital of Adamawa State. The army used artillery to quell the disturbances, but was ill-equipped for riot control and another 700 people died and some 30,000 were left homeless. In 1985 Maitatsine riots claimed more than 100 lives in Gombe and dozens of suspected sect members were arrested.

Until this point in what is a very recent history, the lives lost were either of rioting sect members or of those in the police or army. But the violence took on a new dimension in 1987 when unprecedented violence broke out in several high schools and universities. Muslim and Christian students attacked each other, and

12 died in rioting at one college in Kaduna. Within a few days the violence had spread to Zaria, Katsina and Kano, where some 50 Kano churches were torched and many students were injured. All universities and schools were closed in Kano and a curfew was imposed in Kaduna State.

In February 2000 more than 2,000 people were killed in religious unrest in Kaduna. In 2001 at least 500 were reported to have died in Jos, and in 2002 another 200 died, 1,000 were injured and some 11,000 were left homeless in Kaduna over the Miss World controversy. These riots were triggered by an article in the Lagos-based newspaper, *This Day*, which suggested that Mohammed, Islam's prophet, would have approved of the Miss World competition, which was to be hosted in Nigeria. Isioma Daniel, a 21-year-old fashion journalist, wrote, 'The Muslims thought it was immoral to bring 92 women to Nigeria to ask them to revel in vanity. What would Mohammed think? In all honesty, he would probably have chosen a wife from one of them.' After the incident, the government of Zamfara State issued a fatwa against her – a religious injunction calling for her death. The Miss World competition was moved to London. There were further sporadic deaths during the 2003 elections. On 11 May 2004 there were riots in Kano that subsequently left 30 people dead; they had begun in response to another massacre a few weeks earlier in a village near Jos, which killed a reported 200. There were demonstrations all over the north because of the Danish cartoon controversy in 2006, and churches were burned and over 100 Christians were killed.

Since the return to democracy it has been suggested that there's often been a strong link in the north between these 'ethnic' or 'religious' incidents and the activities of local politicians. It's no coincidence that Sharia law was first introduced in Zamfara State, where former governor Ahmed Sani Yerima didn't even bother to launder the money he was stealing from the state treasury through shell companies. In the 2007 election he was rewarded for his loyalty to the ruling party with a seat in the House of Representatives, ensuring his immunity from the law for at least another four years. In Kano State whenever the populace start to become unhappy about the lack of public services Governor Shekarau usually responds with a crackdown on some form of 'immorality' such as the sale of alcohol in the Sabon Gari. And another great way to improve politicians' popularity with Muslims (the majority) in the north is to encourage local youths (often hired thugs) to attack a church or burn down some Christian businesses.

This slice of violent history is so recent for Nigeria it's difficult to envisage how it will be resolved. Various explanations, some bordering on applied sociology, have been offered to explain this crisis, though many of the underlying causes are probably as old as the nation itself, even if they only simmered beneath the surface before. There are suggestions that it is a passing phase in a nation that has found its freedom after many years of dictatorship, a freedom that Nigeria's people are unequipped to deal with, leading to a heady demonstration of that very same freedom, which unfortunately has chosen the path of violence.

CULTURE AND SPORT

FAMILY LIFE Family structures in Nigeria are shaped by religion and vary from one ethnic group to another, but almost all are male dominated. The practice of polygamy is not uncommon as it is allowed under Islamic law and in traditional culture; a Muslim male can have up to four wives with the consent of the others and the law requires him to provide for each wife equally. The status of Muslim women in Nigeria is similar to that of Muslim women in other Islamic countries. Most non-Muslim women enjoy more freedom, influence family decisions, and work outside the family home – generally non-Muslim women have made more

NAME CALLING

In many Nigerian homes a traditional child-naming ceremony is even more important than a baptism. A few days after a child is born, the Igbos gather friends and family for a feast and ceremony, when after food, and perhaps kola nuts and palm wine are served the baby is produced. First the grandmothers give the child a name, followed by the father, and then the baby's mother. Guests can also then suggest names. When the guests have departed, the household gathers to review the suggested names and selects one. Igbo names include *Adachi* (the daughter of God), *Akachukwu* (God's hand), *Nwanyioma* (beautiful lady) and *Ndidikanma* (patience is the best).

The Yoruba child-naming ceremony takes place on the ninth day after birth for boys and on the seventh day for girls. Twins are named on the eighth day. Again friends and family gather for a feast and an elder performs the ceremony using kola nuts, a bowl of water, pepper, oil, salt, honey and liquor. Each of these items stands for a special life symbol: kola nuts are for good fortune; water for purity; oil for power and health; salt for intelligence and wisdom; honey for happiness; and liquor stands for wealth and prosperity. The baby tastes each of the above, as do the rest of the group. The name of the child is chosen before the ceremony and the elder touches the forehead of the baby and whispers the name into the baby's ears, before shouting it aloud for all around to hear. Some Yoruba names are *Jumoke* (loved by all), *Amonke* (to know her is to pet her), *Modupe* (thanks), *Foluke* (in the hands of God) and *Ajayi* (born face downwards).

Hausa children are generally given names of Islamic origin. The Muslim name is often followed by the father's name. Hausa names include *Tanko* (a boy born after successive girls), *Labaran* (a boy born in the month of Ramadan), *Gagare* (unconquerable) and *Afere* (a girl born tiny).

gains in Nigeria than in other African countries.

Marriage customs vary, but the payment of a bridal dowry is common throughout the country and the groom is expected to give money or property to the bride's family. Western-style dating is not common in rural areas, where arranged marriages are still sometimes practised, but is increasingly common among young people in the cities. Women usually marry by the time they are 20, men in their mid-20s, though living together before marriage is common, as many couples simply find a wedding to be too expensive. Names given to children at birth are usually based on events surrounding their birth – for example, Sunday. Although over the last few decades there has been a great migration from rural areas to the cities, most Nigerians keep kinship alive and frequently visit their 'village', which is either their place of birth or where they might still have relatives living. This explains the massive amount of travelling people do all over Nigeria. Once upon a time, when Nigeria was largely rural, they were probably mostly visiting villages. This is not always the case today – I met one lady and her husband who lived in Kaduna and were on their way home from visiting their 'village'. It turned out that their village was Bauchi – a village of a couple of million people.

ART In the north, because Islam frowns on the representation of people and animals, art forms such as ceremonial carvings are virtually absent, while in the south indigenous people had produced their own art long before the Europeans arrived. Nigerian crafts are grouped into textiles, pottery and ceramics; bronze, brass and iron works; woodworks, calabash decorations and leather works; and jewellery. Nigeria has over 2,000 years of art history, going back to the Iron Age

Nok culture that existed between 500BC and AD200. This era is represented by sophisticated terracotta sculptures found in present-day Kaduna State that depict the early life and spirituality of the Nok people. Here clay figures of 10–120cm in size, with detailed patterns of elaborate hairstyles, jewellery and clothing, were unearthed in the first few decades of the 20th century.

Some of the sculptures can be seen in Nigeria's museums, but many were lost during the colonial period when they were taken overseas. Besides the Nok terracotta figures, Benin City is famous for its wax bronze casting, which decorated the palace of Benin for centuries before the British burnt and looted it at the end of the 19th century, though today there has been some revival of the art, and bronze casters again practise their unique tradition in Benin. The Yoruba are famous for their art and craftwork, and everything in this society was traditionally carved, from doors and drums to ritual masks. Doors were often covered with carved panels of scenes of everyday life, history or mythology. Even the hinge posts were carved with figures. Their masks are simple facial carvings that represent different types of Yoruba religious people like the trader, the servant and the seducer, as well as the many Yoruba gods.

Cloth plays an important role in Nigerian society for use in traditional dress, and has been used as an item of trade for centuries. Although these days much of it is manufactured, traditional home-made weaving and dyeing techniques are still used by some women. These include Yoruba batik, which uses wax and natural dyes (such as the distinctive indigo) to depict traditional themes and motifs. *Adire* is the traditional Yoruba hand-painted cloth on which patterns are made by tying and stitching with raffia or cotton thread, or by using chicken feathers to paint cassava paste on the cloth which then acts as a resist dye, much like the wax method used on the batiks. *Asa-oke* is hand woven on horizontal looms and is sold in strips which are then sewed together to make material for men's gowns and women's scarves.

For centuries beads have been used as trade goods in Nigeria and indeed throughout West Africa. The earliest beads found so far date back to about the 9th century, and would have been traded via the long-established Sahara route. Even today they are worn by many Nigerians – men and women, young and old, and even babies. You'll see the most impressive beads around the necks of the chiefs and other dignitaries. Bead types and styles can symbolise wealth and status or they can be used to ward off evil. Apart from the old stuff, Nigeria has many good contemporary artists. Oshogbo is the country's art capital, see page 175.

FESTIVALS Nigeria's cultural heritage is woven from threads of history, legend and conquest, and is rich in oral traditions, philosophy, rites and rituals, which are traditionally expressed through festivals. Nigeria has many local festivals, which cover an enormous range of events, from harvest festivals, betrothal festivals and festivals marking events in traditional religions, to the investing of a new chief and funerals. It seems odd to Western ways of thinking to see a funeral as something to be celebrated, but for many of Nigeria's ethnic groups, death means joining the ancestors, and the deceased must get a good send-off. Many festivals feature dance, acrobatics, music and masquerades, though in modern Nigeria they have in recent years started to fall out of fashion and young Nigerians seem less intent to carry these traditions on (as is the case with traditional art).

A festival that still occurs every year in the south is the Osun Festival at the Oshogbo Sacred Forest, generally held at the end of the rainy season (August to September), which pays homage to Osun, the Yoruba goddess of fertility and the river (see box on page 182). The Iriji-Mmanwu (masquerade) Festival is sometimes staged in Enugu around August, with a colourful parade of masquerades from different parts of Igboland, considered in Igbo tradition to be a reincarnation of the dead with supernatural powers. The Benin Festival takes place at the end of the rainy season in Benin State, after the harvest has been gathered. Partly a kind of harvest festival, it's also an opportunity for eligible young men and women to take part in the matchmaking ceremony. The festival only occurs once every four years, and only the very wealthy can afford to have their children put on display, although everyone joins in the festival atmosphere.

The people living in the Niger Delta hold the Ikwerre, Kalabari and Okrika festivals, to celebrate the water spirits of their region. The masqueraders wear carved headdresses that imitate the heads of fish or water birds. Many communities, including those in the north, have a version of the harvest festival. In the south, this is often a new yam festival, celebrated when the first of the season's yams are ready to eat, between August and October. This is also when the Maidens Coming of Age Festival is, when traditionally girls go into rooms to learn how to be good wives and mothers, and during this time they are allowed to eat the best of foods to emerge robust and radiant – the rooms are dubbed fattening rooms.

In the predominantly Muslim north, festivals are associated with Islam rather than the older traditional beliefs, and the Muslim year revolves around the three major festivals, Eid-el-Fitir, Eid-el-Kabir and Id Al Maulud. The main event in the Islamic calendar is Ramadan, a month-long observation of fasting. During the hours of sunlight no one must eat or drink; some very religious people will not even swallow. Each evening at dusk there is a celebration of sorts, as the family prepares to break the fast. In towns people do so by going out to one of the markets, where stallholders will be prepared for the hungry people. At the end of Ramadan there is a celebration, which varies in style among the different Muslim groups.

Also featured in northern communities are *durbars* (see box, page 310), long lines of horsemen led by a band, the horses in quilted armour with the riders wearing quilted coats and wielding ceremonial swords. Usually celebrated to mark the annual Eid-el-Fitir and Eid-el-Kabir festivals in major cities of northern Nigeria, the *durbar* is a colourful parade of gaily dressed riders on horses and camels displaying their riding skills, battle readiness, and loyalty to the traditional institutions. Drumming, dancing and singing accompany the parade. Also in the north, the Argungu Fishing Festival (see box, page 322) occasionally takes place in Argungu, in Sokoto State, during February or March. The festival involves traditional methods of fishing and dates back to the 16th century. During the festival, hundreds of local men and boys enter the water armed with large fishnet scoops, and the competition is to catch the biggest fish.

DRESS One of the distinctive features of Nigeria, as in other countries in West Africa, is the brightly coloured and elaborate dress. Nigerian fabrics are known for their vivid colours and unique patterns, and there's a wide range of traditional dress distinctive to each ethnic group. Outside the cities traditional dress is worn every day. Traditional Nigerian dress for men is loose and comfortable and they usually wear caps when in their full regalia. *Buba* and *sokoto* is top and trousers, while *agbada*, mostly by worn by men in the north, is similar to *buba* and *sokoto* but has extra widths of material in the top, which is then folded back across the shoulders in layers. A long man's dress without trousers is a *kaftan*. Some men in the north, particularly those with some rank in the community, wear elaborate and heavy turbans; the emirs, palace guards, chiefs and local dignitaries are always the best dressed, with grand flowing gowns and elaborate head gear.

An *akede* is a woman's scarf, which most women use to make intricately folded and glamorous headdresses. On Sundays and special occasions they become bigger and shinier, and married women wear the largest and most complicated ones. An *oshoke* is a matching two-piece scarf set, one for the head and one draped around shoulders or tied around the waist. In the north Muslim women wear traditional headscarves, though not veils like in other strict Islamic countries, and their flowing dresses are even more colourful than in the south, with lots of bright patterns worn together. Most women in the south wear the traditional *iro* and *buba*, a long, wraparound skirt and short-sleeved top. Men and women select fabric in the market and discuss with their tailors (who are all men) what sort of design they want for their outfits. On Sundays in the south you will see a glittering display of traditional clothing when everyone dresses up for church.

For women, despite frequently covering up their hair in headdresses, their hair is also an important aspect of their appearance and there are some wonderful plaited and weaved styles, some with extensions or with wire woven into it. There are hairdressers everywhere or, more informally, women 'do' each other's hair while they tend to their stalls in the markets. For many ethnic groups facial scarring is also a method of decoration. If you can picture the singer Seal (who is Nigerian) you'll know what I mean. Faces are cut in slices around the corner of the mouth or nose or sliced in lines across the cheeks and sometimes neck.

MUSIC Traditional Nigerian music is played on a number of instruments from an *obo* (a stringed zither), used during masquerade festivals in the villages of the Niger Delta, to trumpets heralding the arrival of an emir in the north, to the Yoruba 'talking' drum used to accompany a story teller of oral traditions – though you won't hear much traditional music in Nigeria these days, except at festivals or important ceremonies, and the average Nigerian listens to tapes or CDs of either church or pop music.

From independence to the late 1980s (when the last international record company packed up and left the country) Nigeria was a hotbed for African popular music and there was something of a renaissance in African music during this period thanks to some notable musicians that acquired worldwide fame and success. These include the world-renowned King Sunny Ade and Fela Kuti, and a number of types of music emerged from this era including juju, Afro-beat, highlife and makossa. These days the Nigerian live music scene is somewhat overrated. In recent years many of the more popular musicians have moved overseas – you're just as likely to hear a Nigerian band in London as in Lagos. At one concert we went to see at the Jazz Hole Bookshop, most of the musicians had airline tags on their instrument cases, and had flown in from overseas especially for the occasion, though the good people of Jazz Hole are attempting to revive Lagos's music scene, and now organise a series of concerts over an annual calendar at a variety of venues.

One of the most phenomenal success stories in African music as a whole was the release of Prince Nico Mbarga's 1976 mega-hit 'Sweet Mother'. This heartfelt tribute of a son's affection and gratitude sold an amazing 13 million copies, and its mix of Nigerian highlife, Cameroonian ashiko, and Zairean rumba managed to please just about everyone on the entire continent of Africa. Prince Nico, the son of a Cameroonian father and a Nigerian mother, sang in Pidgin English.

Highlife is considered the first of Nigeria's contemporary music styles, with its origins in the 1930s in Ghana, and in Nigeria in the 1950s. It's like an early African jazz using wind and brass instruments, and is very easy to dance to. The first major Nigerian highlife star was Bobby Benson, who formed his first band in Lagos in 1947 and created such classic songs as 'Taxi Driver'. He was elected the first president of the Nigerian Musicians Union, formed in the independence year of 1960, and continued to be active in music until his death in 1983. Victor Olaiya and Rex Lawson are the other highlife greats.

Juju music is hugely popular all over West Africa and beyond. It was originally traditional Yoruba music before the guitar and other western instruments were introduced. It's essentially infectious dance music with upbeat tempo and rhythms, and the word is thought to be a corruption of the Yoruba word *jo jo*, meaning dance. In the early 1960s, Chief Commander Ebenezer Obey cut his first record in 1963, and was followed shortly by his main rival, King Sunny Ade, who released his first album in 1967. For decades these two battled it out over the juju throne, and Ade gained ascendancy when he was signed to Island Records in 1982. Following the success of reggae singer Bob Marley, Island was open to incorporating other world artists and in the early 1980s Nigerian music, and especially King Sunny Ade, enjoyed unprecedented international limelight. However, this was short-lived, and Island dropped the King after three albums. In Nigeria, he occasionally still performs at the MUSON Centre as well as internationally.

Fuji music is traditional Yoruba Muslim music blended with the more contemporary *juju* sound. Ayinde Barnster and Wasiu Ayinde Marshall are famous Nigerian fuji artistes. Makossa is pop music imported from Cameroon, a mixture of highlife and soul; its rhythms are purely dance music. Afro-beat is a fusion of African music with jazz and soul played on non-African instruments such as guitars and saxophones. Its creator was the Nigerian Fela Kuti, who studied music in London and who went on to discover James Brown and black politics in the USA in the 1960s. When he returned to Nigeria, he created the lively Afro-beat music, sung in Pidgin English and mostly with a strong protest element. Songs such as 'Expensive Shit', 'Zombie', 'Sorrow, Tears and Blood' and 'ITT' (International Thief Thief), which attacked such targets as corrupt politicians, hypocritical businessmen, and societal suffering, earned him the enmity of the authorities. Fela's complete rejection of governmental authority through the establishment of his 'Kalakuta Republic' in the Surulere suburb of Lagos and his flagrant marijuana use were other challenges to the establishment, and the government unleashed a series of attacks on Fela, his family and property. Fela died of AIDS in 1997, but his son Femi Kuti continues the musical tradition and regularly plays in Lagos and overseas.

Another Nigerian Afro-beat and jazz musician popular today is Funsho Ogundipe, a pianist and a barrister living in the UK where he has a band which also returns to Lagos on occasion for concerts. Lagbaja! occasionally plays in Lagos at his own venue on the mainland, Motherlan'. He is a skilful saxophone player but also sings and tells stories about life in Lagos and is usually accompanied by a female vocalist. He wears elaborate costumes made from West African cloth such as batik and *aso-oke* and his fans haven't seen his face for many years as he always performs wearing a traditional Yoruba masquerade mask. His real name is Bisade Ologunde, but in Yoruba, Lagbaja! can mean: somebody, anybody, everybody or nobody. It refers to those without identity, and Lagbaja! sings on behalf of the faceless masses.

Younger Nigerians tend to listen to the same chart-topping music as their contemporaries all over the world, and FM music radio stations are popular in the south. Especially popular are US rap bands, and the likes of Sean Paul, Snoop Dog and Jay-Z have previously performed in stadiums in Lagos. Up-and-coming Nigerian bands are following suit and aggressive rap is perhaps giving the more soulful and jazzy melodies of the music coined in the 1960s and 1970s a run for its money among Nigerian record labels.

SPORT Nigerian sport only appeared on the international scene in the 1950s, with Nigeria's first appearance in the 1952 Olympic Games at Helsinki. Nigeria was awarded its first international medal in 1954, when Emmanuel Ifeanjuna won the gold in the high jump at the Commonwealth Games in Cardiff. Nigeria emerged on the international football scene in 1960 when it first entered the World Cup, but failed to qualify for the finals. It eventually qualified for the 1970 World Cup in Mexico, and the Nigerian National Football League was established in 1972. Since then Nigeria has consistently fared well internationally in the fields of football and athletics. Nigeria hosted the 2003 All Africa Games in Abuja, for which a new 60,000-seat National Stadium was built. Abuja is currently bidding to become the first African city to host the Commonwealth Games in 2014 (www.abuja2014.org), which in terms of numbers of athletes and spectators involved is actually smaller than the All Africa Games, so Abuja clearly has the capacity to host them. The only other city it is competing against is Glasgow in Scotland. Nigeria also made a bid for the first FIFA Football World Cup to be held on African soil in 2010, but lost out to South Africa.

Football is hugely popular among millions of Nigerian men, and is played and watched throughout the country. *Everywhere*, whether it is a cleared spot in a city rubbish dump, a dusty pitch in the middle of a village, or even a pitch on an unfinished road, people play and watch football. If people don't have their own TVs showing local and European league games, they can watch football even in the smallest village or side street where a satellite TV will be set up for an important match. There is a small fee of, say, N10 to watch, and even in the remotest possible places are blackboards and scribbled posters proclaiming 'UK Premier Division; Liverpool v Blackburn; tonite; 19.30' or 'Real Madrid qualifying match; here 18.00; with suya' (barbecued meat). Football shirts are also hugely popular, and I saw perhaps thousands of David Beckhams! The Nigeria Football Association introduced the Professional League in 1990. Now the Nigerian Premier League, it has 20 teams from throughout the country. Other football clubs feature in division two or three or in the amateur leagues.

Nigeria has produced seasoned soccer players, and the national Super Eagles team, who usually make it to the football World Cup, was at one time regarded as the best in Africa and one of the world's top football teams. The Super Eagles won the gold medal for football at the 1996 Olympics in Atlanta (when Nigeria also won long jump gold) and routinely do well in African competitions such as the FIFA Africa Cup of Nations. Nigeria last won this in 1994, but lost out to Cameroon on penalties in the final in 2000 when it was played in Nigeria. Since then they have come third in the 2002, 2004 and 2006 competitions, and the under-17 squad, known as the Golden Eaglets, won the 2007 Africa Under-17 Championship. Unfortunately the Super Eagles didn't qualify for the 2006 World Cup, but today there are more than 360 Nigerian players playing for European and South American teams. These include Nwankwo Kanu, who used to play for Arsenal until 2004, and currently plays for Portsmouth, Yakubu Aiyegbeni of Middlesbrough, and Obafemi Martins and Celestine Babayaro, who both play for Newcastle United.

In other sports, Nigerian athletes do well in the Olympics and have won a number of medals in track and field events. In professional boxing, Nigeria has produced three world champions – Hogan 'Kid' Bassey (featherweight, 1957–59), Dick Tiger (middleweight, 1962–63) and US resident Bash Ali (cruiserweight, 1987). At the end of the 1990s, a Nigerian based in the USA, Hakeem Olajuwon, was considered to be the best basketball player in the world.

NATURAL HISTORY AND CONSERVATION

NATIONAL PARKS Despite rapid deforestation in Nigeria, there are still a number of reserves dotted around the country, and Nigeria currently has eight national parks. In 1979 the first Obasanjo administration established Lake Kainji National

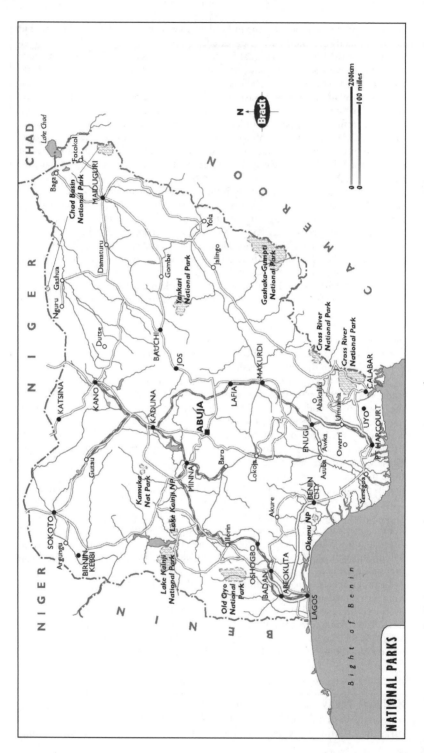

NATIONAL PARKS

Park as Nigeria's first national park and since then seven others have been created, mostly carved out of former forest or game reserves. They cover about 3% or 24,000km² of the country, though only two of these are well known, or even visited regularly – these are Lake Kainji National Park and Yankari National Park. The others are Cross River, Gashaka-Gumpti, Okomu, Kamuka, Old Oyo and Chad Basin national parks.

All except Yankari National Park, now managed by Bauchi State, are run by the Federal National Parks Service (FNPS), which receives funding direct from the federal government. For many years they suffered from serious underfunding, poor protection and weak management, and poaching was a serious problem in all the parks. Added to this is the complete lack of knowledge of what and how many animals are left in each park. Even the park rangers have no idea! And again, despite what the Federal National Parks Service says, their figures are likely to be seriously over-inflated, given that there hasn't been a game census in Yankari since 1991, and that in some of the other parks there hasn't been a game count ever.

On a more promising note, however, Nigeria has 904 documented species of birds thanks to a survey by Birdlife International in 2002, so figures for birds, unlike animals, should be fairly accurate. Of these, 436 species are breeding residents, and the rest are migrants, many of them from Europe, which come to northern Nigeria during the winter months – the wetlands of the Chad Basin National Park have been declared a Ramsar site, so called after the 1971 Convention of Wetlands, held in Ramsar, Iran. In recent years gorillas (once thought to have left the area long ago) were discovered in the forests of Cross River National Park and reclassified from a lowland gorilla to a Cross River gorilla (thought to be a new sub-species of gorilla – see box on page 222).

Today there has been some progress in the management of the parks, and the National Park Decree of 1999 gives the park staff special powers and regulations to fine and capture anyone found poaching. Poachers caught in the environs of the park can be tried and punished under national park laws and not in the local courts, because the national parks are federal land, which has had some success at Lake Kainji National Park.

Other developments include a complete refurbishment of the accommodation at Yankari now that Bauchi State has recently taken over the management, and 250 animals (various antelope, wildebeest, zebra and giraffe) were given to Nigeria in 2006 by Namibia to help kick-start its tourist industry. These animals all now reside in Yankari. A private lodge has been built in Okomu National Park and Gashaka-Gumpti is now accessible through the Gashaka Primate Project, which has a base in the park and is doing much towards its protection. Also, several non-governmental organisations (NGOs) devoted to environmental protection in Nigeria have been formed, some of which are very active. This has been accompanied by a gradual increase in environmental awareness throughout Nigeria, including in the government, which is starting to adopt conservation strategies. It is to be hoped that Nigerians will become more conscious of their natural heritage.

WILDLIFE The first animal you will see in Nigeria is the comical and colourful agama lizard; they are everywhere, so you'll have to get used to lizards scurrying around your feet and up walls. The much brighter males have bright orange heads and brilliant blue bodies and can reach lengths of 20cm, while the plainer and smaller females are brown. As a result of the problems experienced by national parks (see above), you are very unlikely to spot much wildlife in Nigeria so there's little point in producing an extensive list of what might or might not be there. Sadly, you are more likely to see wildlife dead than alive, for sale as bushmeat at the side of the road, fashioned into so-called curios in the markets, or as black magic ingredients on a *juju* doctor's stall. The animals listed below are all very seriously endangered in Nigeria and it is imperative that they are protected immediately before they completely disappear from Nigeria's forests. For that reason alone they are grouped here in this way to highlight this fact, although you are unlikely to see them.

There used to be several species of big game in Nigeria, as attested to by the skins and pelts hanging up in museums and curio and *juju* markets, cheetah and leopard being prime examples, but it's very unlikely that they still exist in the wild, though there are still lions in Yankari. Of all the parks Gashaka-Gumpti holds the most hope of still having relatively large populations of animals, and researchers have discovered a healthy-sized community of chimpanzees there. It's very remote and inaccessible, so the problem of poaching hasn't been so intense here.

Endangered species
Birds There are some 30 sites around Nigeria that meet the criteria of Birdlife International for important bird areas, and birds endemic to Nigeria are the **Anambra waxbill**, the **Jos Plateau indigobird**, the **rock fire-finch** and the **Ibadan malimbe**. Nigeria is home to one of the most endangered birds in Africa, the **grey-neck picathartes**, of which there may be as few as 2,500 individuals in the forests of Cross River State. **Secretary birds**, *Sagittarius serpentarius*, are occasionally seen in Yankari and Lake Kainji national parks. This tall bird with a raptor's beak, long legs and a stalking gait has black and grey plumage and is largely terrestrial. They feed on snakes, which they pound to death with their strong feet. The **African grey parrot**, *Psittacus erithacus*, is an unmistakable grey parrot with a scarlet tail. It draws attention to itself by flying directly between roosting and feeding grounds screeching loudly, and it grips the branches of trees while climbing. It is seriously threatened by trapping, deforestation and the international pet trade. In Nigeria you are most likely to see them in inadequately sized cages hanging outside people's houses. **Ostriches**, *Struthio camelus*, can only be found in small groups in northeastern Nigeria around the Chad Basin, and are seriously threatened by egg collection. They are distinguished by their great size; males have black plumage and a long pink neck, while the plainer females have grey feathers and are smaller.

The giant forest hog The **giant forest hog**, *Hylochoerus meinertzhageni*, is a huge pig, heavily built with a rump higher than its shoulders and relatively long legs and a long head with tusks. Its coat is coarse and entirely jet black, and it could possibly still exist in Gashaka-Gumpti.

Antelopes Antelopes are seriously endangered in Nigeria, as antelope meat is considered a delicacy, and, in the poorer rural areas, a source of free food. The **sitatunga**, *Tragelaphus spekei*, is a large antelope with hindquarters higher than its forequarters, giving the animal a peculiar hunched appearance. The coat is fairly long and shabby, and the males have long and twisted horns. It is a very shy and timid animal that spends its time hidden among thick vegetation along river banks, and it only ventures from its watery refuge at night to feed on drier ground. As soon as it senses danger it slips into the water and swims away, and can remain submerged with only its muzzle above the surface of the water. It was once common around the swamps of Lake Chad, but is now very rare.

The **roan antelope**, *Hippotragus equinus*, is one of the largest of the antelopes and resembles a horse in terms of its proportions. It has contrasting black and white face markings, very long pointed ears with tufts on their tips, and moderately long horns that curve backwards. It is particularly susceptible to drought and is only present in Lake Kainji, Yankari and Gashaka-Gumpti national parks. The **bohor reed buck**, *Redunca redunca*, is a medium-sized graceful antelope with a thick coat and short tail, with a fawn colour on its back and a bright white underbelly seen clearly when the tail is held erect. Only males have horns, which are curved backwards and then sharply forward forming hooks on their tips. They are very seriously threatened in Nigeria, but may possibly still exist in the remote northern savanna regions.

Hippopotamus The **hippopotamus**, *Hippopotamus amphibius*, is a semi-amphibious mammal that spends the greater part of the day submerged in a lake or river, and comes out at night to feed on the swampy borders of forest streams. These animals have to be near water; they cannot spend too much time on dry land during the day as their thick skins are sensitive to the sun. They are known to attack if their path back to water is blocked. In Nigeria there are small populations in Yankari and Kainji national parks. Pygmy hippopotamuses used to occur in the Niger Delta, but these haven't been spotted for decades.

Lions The **lion**, *Panthera leo*, is a large powerful cat that used to stalk most of West Africa. In Nigeria there are small populations of lion in Yankari, Lake Kainji and Gashaka-Gumpti national parks. They are very sociable and are rarely seen alone and the female is more lightly built than the male, and doesn't have a mane. It's the females that hunt in a combined operation by stalking or ambushing their prey, such as antelope and buffalo, before killing them by strangulation.

Elephants The **African elephant** is the largest terrestrial animal and adults weigh up to 6,000kg. It uses its trunk for feeding, drinking, grooming and fighting, while its third upper incisors grow tusks which grow throughout its life. There is a marked difference between the African savanna elephant, *Loxodonta Africana*, and the forest elephant, *Loxodonta Africana cyclotis*. The latter has straighter tusks and more rounded ears and is considerably smaller. Despite their size elephants can run very quickly over a short distance and can live to be up to 70 years old. There may perhaps still be forest elephants in Okumu, Omo and Cross River national parks and there's a fairly big herd of savanna elephant in Yankari National Park. They used to be found in Lake Kainji but this population has all migrated to Benin due to hunting pressures. There is also a sad pair of elephants in a ridiculously inadequate enclosure at Jos Zoo. The World Wildlife Fund believes there maybe fewer than 500 elephants left in Nigeria and unfortunately ivory is still openly sold.

Primates All primates are seriously endangered in Nigeria, not because they are necessarily eaten (though that does sometimes happen), but because of deforestation and the popularity of using monkeys for *juju*. **Sclater's guenon**, *Cercopithecus sclateri*, is Africa's rarest and least-known monkey. Rather frighteningly it is only found in Nigeria, in a few isolated patches of forest between the Niger and Cross rivers in the southeast. The characteristic features of the species are its white ears, white nose, and red and grey tail. The monkey is a sacred animal in two Igbo villages, but it is still seriously threatened with extinction due to hunting, habitat loss and the erosion of traditions. The **white-throated monkey**, *Cercopithecus erythrogaster*, is another seriously threatened species of monkey endemic to Nigeria, though it has recently been spotted in the Benin Republic. This unique primate has a beautiful gold crown and striking white throat. In Nigeria its last hope for survival is in the Okomu National Park, although there are a few in some zoos. **Preuss's guenon**, *Cercopithecus preussi*, is only found in forests higher than 1,000m and is restricted to southeast Nigeria, around the Obudu Plateau, and southwest Cameroon. It has dark smoky fur with a ruff of white under its chin. The **red colobus monkey**, *Procolobus badius waldroni*, was only discovered in Nigeria in recent years and is a red, long-furred and limbed forest monkey. It lives in forest pockets of the Niger Delta and could be endemic to Nigeria in West Africa, after becoming extinct in other countries such as Ghana.

The **chimpanzee**, *Pan troglodytes*, can easily be distinguished from the gorilla by its large characteristic turned-out ears, big eyes and long arms. It is regarded as the most man-like of all the apes, not only because of its anatomy, but because of certain behaviours, such as community defence and the use of tools. One of their daily rituals is to build a nest five metres or so above the ground in the canopy of the forest for the group to sleep in at night. They were once found in all of Nigeria's southern forests, but have been poached and hunted for bushmeat or for the illegal trade in pets or zoo animals. There is, however, a fairly healthy population in the remote and unexplored forests of Gashaka-Gumpti National Park, and visitors can visit rescued chimps at the Afi Drill Ranch.

The **gorilla**, *Gorilla gorilla*, is the strongest and largest of all the primates. It has a big head, protruding brow, large nostrils and arms longer than its legs. Dominant adult males have a band of silver hairs on their back, hence the term silverback. As with the chimpanzee, the group builds nests to sleep in at night some five metres up in the canopy of the forest and they seldom spend two successive nights in the same place. Thought to be extinct in Nigeria for many years, a few individuals have been discovered in small pockets of forest in Cross River State and across the border in Cameroon. They have recently been re-classified as the Cross Border gorilla and it's believed there are fewer than 300 gorillas in the Nigeria– Cameroon (Cross River) area, making them the most critically endangered gorillas on earth (see also box on page 222).

Finally, another primate that is critically endangered is the **drill monkey**, *Mandrillus leucophaeus,* which is a short-tailed rainforest monkey restricted to the forested parts of the southeast of Nigeria, parts of Cameroon, and on Bioko Island, Equatorial Guinea. The males are much like a baboon in shape, with a big head, a bright pink scrotum, and a black face surrounded by a ring of brilliant white fur. They are seriously threatened by habitat loss and hunting, especially by dogs. When confronted by a dog, a drill will instinctively stand and fight rather than flee in confusion. This usually gives the hunter ample opportunity to shoot and slaughter a whole troop in a matter of seconds. It's not known for sure how many drills remain in the wild, but the population is generally believed to be fewer than 10,000, and possibly as low as only 3,000 (see also box on page 217).

2

Practical Information

WHEN TO VISIT

Nigeria is consistently hot all year round with very little change in temperature, and in the south there is a constant uncomfortable humidity. Temperatures are highest from February to April in the south and from March to June in the north, and lowest from October to January over most of the country. This is the dry season, when there are cooler temperatures but chaotic dry northeast winds, referred to locally as the Harmattan, which carry fine sand across the country from the Sahara. The dust-filled air during this time can be irritating and uncomfortable and appears as a dense fog. The Harmattan is more common in the north but affects the entire country except for a narrow strip along the southwest coast. However, the dry season is still the best time to go, as heavy rains during the rainy season (April–August) severely hamper travel when roads are flooded, motor parks become quagmires, and streets in Lagos turn into rivers of rubbish. On the coast, the rainy season kicks in earlier than in the rest of the country and starts in February or March, continuing until August. It's best to avoid travel in the south during this time – the sky is continually overcast, it's hot, humid and wet, and if travelling by public transport, you'll need gum boots to wade through the mud in the motor parks.

HIGHLIGHTS

If the truth be known, there is very little in the way of conventional sightseeing in Nigeria and the real joy of travelling here is meeting its culturally diverse peoples. The historic sights that do exist are very dilapidated, badly maintained or ignored, and Nigerians generally have little interest in their historical heritage. (The **Kano Wall** is a fine example – a thousand-year-old wall is today a sorry mound of earth that is covered in rubbish. People routinely dig out chunks of it and cart it home in wheelbarrows to be used as house bricks.) Nigeria also has an awful attitude to its natural heritage, as the several pitiful zoos and eight largely empty national parks attest to (as do all the bi-products made from dead animals found in the curio and *juju* markets). And there obviously has never been a tourism industry to support such things as old architecture or Nigerian animals.

There are places in more remote spots of the extreme east of Nigeria along the border with Cameroon that few people have ever seen, and although these are not impossible to reach by public transport, they are best visited in your own self-sufficient 4WD vehicle. These include the **UNESCO World Heritage Site** at **Sukur**, and some of the national parks such as the **Gashaka-Gumpti National Park**. Other 'sights' are perfectly accessible by public transport but are really not worth the effort of getting there – **Zuma Rock** near Abuja being our favourite 'why did we bother?'. The real reason for going to Nigeria is to immerse yourself in the cultures of millions of people, and to see how they live in a place where hardly anything works; to talk to people who have so much personality and rhythm in their souls; and to enjoy and embrace the unexpected, the bizarre, the enchanting, the appalling, the funny, and the downright obscure aspects of everyday life in Nigeria.

The Nigerian character can be enjoyed in all the main cities, and **Lagos** is without doubt West Africa's wildest and most vibrant metropolis; despite the chaos it is the place where you can experience a few Western comforts. If Lagos becomes too overwhelming then leave the city and visit the other Yoruba towns in the cluttered southwest of the country. **Abeokuta** is famous for its sacred **Olumo Rock**, while **Ife**, as the centre of the Yoruba culture, has palaces and a museum, and **Oshogbo** has its eerie collection of weirdly shaped shrines in the **sacred forest**. If you are interested in the Yoruba culture then the better museums in this region are the **National Museum** in Lagos and the **Ibadan Museum**. Further to the east is **Benin City**, once the capital of a powerful and wealthy kingdom, where you can see examples of the traditional art of **bronze wax casting** in the museum and in the workshops along Igun Street.

To the southeast of Nigeria, where the River Niger spills into the creeks and watery channels of the **Niger Delta**, there are some nondescript towns that support the massive oil industry in the Delta. Because of ongoing disputes between the communities that live around the oil fields, not all of these are especially safe to visit. **Port Harcourt** to the extreme south is an industrial giant heaving with people, and far more interesting is the colonial town of **Calabar**, easily one of Nigeria's most relaxed and even relatively clean cities, with an excellent museum and a couple of conservation projects for Nigeria's endangered wildlife that are well worth a visit. To the north of Calabar are the dense tropical rainforests of Cross River State, some of which have been cordoned off into the **Cross River National Park**. There are no facilities as yet for visitors, but it is possible to appreciate the forests at the **Afi Drill Ranch**, a sanctuary for the endangered drill monkeys and chimpanzees, or the **Rhoko Forest**, another sanctuary for monkeys. In recent years, the former Cross River State governor, Donald Duke, has been a great instigator of tourism investment in this region of the country and there are now the new attractions of **Tinapa**, a giant shopping centre in Calabar, and incredibly a new cable car at the recently upgraded resort on the **Obudu Plateau**.

Central Nigeria has a higher terrain of grassy plains dotted with outcrops of giant rocks. In the new capital of **Abuja** there is little to see, though people crossing Nigeria overland may need to stop here to obtain onward visas. As a relatively new city, it is already of considerable size and has some Western trappings associated with governments and embassies such as large hotels and conference centres. To the east of Abuja is the pleasantly located city of **Jos** on a high plateau with nice countryside, which has an interesting line of museums. To the east of Jos is Nigeria's best-known national park, **Yankari National Park**, which still contains some wildlife, including a fairly healthy population of elephant. Here are the **Wikki Warm Springs**, a stunning swathe of mildly warm crystal-clear water in a forested valley.

The north of the country is dominated by the Hausa-Fulani walled cities, which for over a thousand years have been powerful centres founded on trade and Islam. In these you will meet the more interesting of Nigeria's peoples, for whom traditional dress, language and deeply devout religion are an important part of everyday life. Some of the mosques here fill with thousands of worshippers for Friday prayers, and the **durbar festivals** at the end of Ramadan are among the most colourful and spectacular events in West Africa. In **Kano** are the famous **dye pits**, which produce some of the traditional cloths of Nigeria, and the ancient and claustrophobic **Kurmi Market**, where for centuries trans-Sahara camel caravans exchanged a wealth of goods with the Hausa traders. In **Zaria** is a fine example of an emir's palace. To the extreme northeast are the shrinking watery channels of **Lake Chad**, once one of Africa's superlakes that has now largely disappeared, but if you make it this far you will be rewarded with the sight of the ancient Kanuri people, who still trade with people in Chad by canoe, and who could plausibly be one of the least-visited peoples of the world.

TOUR OPERATORS

The only operators to go through Nigeria are the overland operators. The ones listed below are reputable companies with decades of experience in the overland game, running trans-Africa overland tours through West Africa at least once or twice a year. Generally the trucks spend two to three weeks in Nigeria crossing from the Benin border through Abuja, and then out of Nigeria to Cameroon in the southeast. No trucks go through Lagos, as visas for onward countries are now obtainable in Abuja, but there's no reason why you can't jump truck for a few days if you want to visit Lagos or elsewhere.

African Trails ☏ 020 8422 5545; www.africantrails.co.uk. African Trails operates two departures a year from Malaga is Spain in Mar & Nov, which come down through West Africa to Cape Town & then back up on the east side & continue through the Middle East & finish in Istanbul 43 weeks later. You can travel short sections of this trip.

Dragoman ☏ 01728 861133; www.dragoman.com. Dragoman has two departures per year between the UK & Cape Town in each direction that take 30 weeks; they leave from Cape Town in Aug & the UK in Sept, but these long trips are broken into much shorter sections – the one that covers Nigeria is the 4½-week Accra–Douala tour.
Oasis Overland ☏ 01963 363400; www.oasis overland.co.uk. Oasis runs 2 yearly trips departing from the UK & finishing in Nairobi via Cape Town.

RED TAPE

A **passport** (valid for at least six months and preferably with several blank pages) and a Nigerian **visa** are required for entry into the country. Visa exemptions are granted only to citizens of some of Nigeria's neighbouring West African countries. Nigerian embassies or consulates are located in the capitals of most European, North American and African countries together with Hong Kong, Tokyo and Canberra. Some countries may have several visa offices (for example Washington, New York and San Francisco in the USA). British consulates often represent Nigerian overseas missions if there is no Nigerian embassy in the country. The two visas readers of this book are likely to apply for are the short-term tourist visa, valid for a stay of not more than one month (though they are generally extendible to a maximum of three months in-country), or, for those going to work, a business visa, issued to expatriate 'experts' to work on specific projects, which is initially valid for three months but can be extended for up to a maximum of six months (if the expat stays long term it can be changed into a long-term residency visa).

When applying for a tourist visa, you need to produce (along with your passport) your return airline ticket, evidence of funds that you will spend in Nigeria (bank or credit card statements), one passport picture, evidence of a hotel booking or a letter from friends or family in Nigeria, a return or onward air ticket if flying on, and the non-refundable fee; at the time of writing (autumn 2007) this was US$60 but it varies among the issuing authorities. In most countries you are required to attend the embassy in person to apply for a tourist visa, though not in the case of a business visa. For these, you will also need to produce a supporting letter from your employer stating the nature of your business and guaranteeing sufficient financial support for the visit, or alternatively have an invitation letter from the business you are dealing with in Nigeria. For both visas, some embassies may also require to see your return airline ticket. Generally, visa turnaround is three to seven days. For more information visit www.nigeria.embassyhomepage.com.

Once you have a visa, ensure that you make a photocopy of it and the passport page with your photograph on it. Some travellers choose to scan them in and store them at their email address so you can always access your documentation and print it out. For security reasons it is advisable to detail all your important information on one document, photocopy it, leave a copy with family or friends at home and distribute copies through your luggage. Details might include things like passport and visa number, travel insurance policy details, a 24-hour emergency contact number, and details of relatives or friends to be contacted in case of an emergency. Other guidebooks recommend that you also put credit card details and travellers' cheque numbers on this document, but this is *not* the case for Nigeria – not because you aren't going to be able use either travellers' cheques or credit cards anyway, but because of the prevalence of fraud.

If you are going to Nigeria to work or are staying a considerable time, it might be an idea to register with your embassy or high commission on arrival. Staff can advise you of travel warnings, keep records of next of kin, provide passport services, absentee voting arrangements and so on. They will also put you on what is referred to as the Warden System, which enables them to contact you in case of an emergency in Nigeria.

Should there be any possibility that you will want to drive in Nigeria, obtain an **international driving licence** (available at post offices in the UK, and from www.nationalautoclub.com in the USA, for a nominal fee). Although most expats have drivers, there are occasions at night and the weekends when they drive themselves. Overlanders will need additional paperwork for their vehicle such as a **carnet de passage**, registration document and third-party insurance.

NIGERIAN EMBASSIES AND HIGH COMMISSIONS

The following countries have embassies unless otherwise stated. A complete list of Nigerian embassies and high commissions worldwide can be found at www.nigerianembassy.org.

Australia (High Commission), 7 Terrigal Crescent, O'Malley ACT 26, Canberra; ☎ +61 6 286 5332
Canada (High Commission), 295 Metcalfe St, Ottawa, Ontario K2P 1R9; ☎ +1 613 236 0521–3 or 236 0527; www.nigeriahighcommottawa.com
France 173 Av Victor Hugo, 75116 Paris; ☎ +33 1 47 04 68 65–6
Germany (Consulate-General), Neue Jakobstrasse 4, 10179 Berlin; ☎ +49 30 21 23 00, www.nigeriaembassygermany.org/
Ireland 56 Leeson Park, Dublin; ☎ +353 1 660 4366

Italy Via Orazio 14/18, 00193 Rome; ☎ +39 6 689 6231; www.nigerian.it
Netherlands Wagenaarweg 5, 2597 LL, The Hague; ☎ +31 70 355 1110
UK (High Commission) 9 Northumberland Av, London WC2N 5BX; ☎ 020 7839 1244; www.nigeriahc.org.uk
USA 3519 International Court, Washington DC 20008; ☎ +1 020 986 8400; www.nigeriaembassyusa.org

If you are travelling overland from Europe, you will probably need to get a Nigerian visa *en route*. Below are some of the embassies in countries north of Nigeria. By all accounts, and speaking to experienced overlanders, the Nigerian High Commission in Accra is the best bet.

Côte D'Ivoire 35 Bd de la République, 0I-BP 1906, Abidjan; ☏ +225 1 211982

Benin Av de France, Marina, Cotonou; ☏ +229 301142

Burkina Faso 36 Rue de L'Hopital, Ouagadougou; ☏ +226 315202

Ghana (High Commission) Josif Broz Tito Av, Accra; ☏ +233 21 776158–9 or 777280

Morocco 70 Av Umar Ibn El Khattab Agdat, Rabat; ☏ +212 778325 or 770367

Senegal Rue IXFA, Point E, Dakar; ☏ +221 825 8136

Togo 311 Bd Du 13 Janvier, Lome: ☏ +225 215976

GETTING THERE AND AWAY

✈ **BY AIR** Nigeria's international airports are Murtala Mohammed International Airport, Lagos; Aminu Kano International Airport, Kano; and Nnamdi Azikiwe International Airport, Abuja. Port Harcourt Airport is currently closed. Many international airlines operate to and from Nigeria and there are a huge number of flights – not, unfortunately, because lots of tourists are visiting the country, but because many millions of Nigerians want to live anywhere else in the world but Nigeria. Established airlines serving Nigeria include Air France, British Airways, Egypt Air, Emirates, Ethiopian Airlines, Ghana Airways, Kenya Airways, KLM, Lufthansa, South African Airways, Swiss (formerly Swissair) and Virgin, variously offering good connections with London, Paris and Dubai, and a number of Dutch and German cities, as well as with Addis Ababa, Nairobi and Johannesburg in east and southern Africa. From Lagos to London, it's a six-hour flight. Most airlines fly to Lagos, but KLM and Air France fly between Amsterdam and Abuja and Kano. Travellers from North America have the option of going via Europe or North American Airways offers a service between New York and Lagos.

In September 2004, the Nigerian government signed an agreement with Virgin for the establishment of a new airline, Virgin Nigeria (www.virginnigeria.com), to be based at Murtala Mohammed International Airport in Lagos. The airline now operates both on domestic and regional routes and has services to London and Johannesburg.

With all these airlines serving Nigeria you should be able to get a competitively priced ticket from Europe, but be warned the flights are very popular and fill up quickly. The Emirates and Kenya Airways (via Nairobi) flights from Lagos to Dubai are extremely popular with wealthy Nigerians on shopping trips. London especially has dozens of travel agents specialising in cheap flights to Africa, many of which can be combined for onward travel. Remember, it is essential that you have a return or onward ticket to get a visa for Nigeria. For a starter you can try these, most of which have several branches around the UK and some of which have outlets in Australia, New Zealand and the US: **Flight Centre**, www.flightcentre.com; **STA Travel**, www.sta-travel.com; and **Trailfinders**, www.trailfinders.com.

🚢 **BY SEA** You can get to Nigeria by boat from Cameroon, but this trip is not for the faint-hearted and I have heard stories about motor boats packed full of people simply disappearing. Boats arrive and depart from Orun in Cross River State – see the Calabar section.

OVERLAND The major overland route from Europe through West Africa roughly runs through Morocco, Mauritania, Senegal, Mali, Burkina Faso, Ghana, Togo, Benin, Nigeria and Cameroon. From Cameroon it's sometimes possible to cross into East Africa via Chad and Sudan but this route is routinely closed because of the unrest in these countries. You can do all or part of this epic journey with an

2

overland company (see above) or in your own vehicle, though of course you will have to be fully kitted out and self-sufficient, with a 4x4 and all the gear. For inspiration to start your own overland, visit www.africa-overland.net, the website for the Africa Overland Network, which has lots of useful information and links to over 200 websites of people's individual trips by land, bicycle and motorbike. Also pick up a copy of Bradt's *Africa Overland* for lots of practical advice.

You can enter Nigeria by road from Benin, Cameroon and Niger. The easiest and quickest route is from Zinder in Niger through to Kano, then west to Maiduguri, and into Cameroon at Mora. But it's much more interesting to continue south to Jos and then on down to Calabar via perhaps Yankari National Park. The alternative overland route is from Benin along Nigeria's coastal highway, the fastest route between Lagos and Cameroon. When crossing into Nigeria get rid of all money from the previous country as it's hard to change once across the border. Also fill up with diesel, as diesel is not always available everywhere in Nigeria. Once in Nigeria fill jerry cans or water tanks whenever you can, as water is also hard to get (for a small fee you can fill up from public taps). Finally, if you're not in your own vehicle, public transport links the closest cities in the neighbouring countries with the closest cities in Nigeria, so feasibly backpackers can move about from country to country.

Via Benin The principal link and the busiest border crossing is at Kraké on the Benin side of the Badagry–Lagos Expressway. Roads on both sides are tar-sealed and in reasonably good condition, but the traffic's heavy and the border is notoriously slow. You can get public transport from Cotonou direct to Lagos. Be aware, however, that there have been violent robberies on vehicles on this road in recent years. Alternatively get yourself to Porto Novo on the Benin side and cross into Nigeria at the Idi-oroko border post some 30km to the north of Kraké. From here the road goes to Ikeja in northern mainland Lagos, and public transport from Porto Novo arrives at the Oshodi Motor Park, from where you could feasibly get transport for onward travel without going into Lagos proper if you didn't want to. Recommended to me by one of the overland companies is the crossing at Kétou, on the Benin side, which is approximately 120km north of Porto Novo via Pobé. Andi from Oasis Overland says: 'Customs is in Kétou town; 17km further on is Benin immigration, and then you need to go to the Nigerian immigration which is very easy to miss as it's not on the road at all. Ask lots of people for directions. Meko is the first town on the Nigerian side 10km further on. You can change money with the border guys. This is a good border and really quiet. After Meko for 5–10km the road is dirt and is really bad, with huge potholes, then it's tar-seal to Abeokuta.'

Via Cameroon and Chad There are two principal borders between Nigeria and Cameroon, one in the south near Ikom north of Calabar and one in the north near Maiduguri. Mfun border is 30km to the east of Ikom where the road is tar-seal to the border. Here there is a rather grand suspension bridge over the Cross River, which forms part of the border. From Ekok, the first town on the Cameroon side, you simply walk down the hill to the Cameroon customs and immigration sheds before crossing the bridge to complete the Nigerian formalities on the other side. There are hotels and money changers in Ekok if you get stuck here.

In Cameroon there are bush taxis from Mamfé to the border on a horrendous road, and there are regular vehicles on the Nigerian side to Ikom. There is another road directly from Calabar to this border but it's not tar-sealed and I hear it's in very bad shape. It may be better to go the long way round via Ikom if coming from Calabar. Andi from Oasis Overland says of this border: 'The Nigerian side was very easy and only took an hour; we just had to fill out a few forms. The dirt road on the other side was terrible, with huge, deep ruts. It took us five hours to go 20km once we were in Cameroon and we had to keep stopping to build the ditches up as the bottom lockers of the truck were scraping the ground and we had to remove the exhaust. Avoid this road if it's wet.'

The main crossing in the north is from Mora in Cameroon to Maiduguri. This is an infrequently used border and relatively simple to negotiate; again the road on the Cameroon side is nothing more than a rough track, though the Nigerian side is tar-sealed. From Mora it is possible to get a vehicle to the border and change there on to one to Maiduguri; vehicles are fairly frequent, and money changers hang out on both sides of the border. If you are in your own vehicle this is the most sensible crossing if you want to go to Waze National Park in Cameroon.

To get to Chad (despite sharing a border with Chad, Nigeria and Chad do not have a road crossing), the best border to cross is the Ngala border, in the extreme northeast of the country about 140km east of Maiduguri, that crosses to Fotokol on the Cameroon side, where the road leads directly across a 100km bottleneck of Cameroon to Kousséri. Here a bridge over the confluence of the Chari and Logone rivers links Kousséri with the capital of Chad, Ndjamena, on the other side. From Maiduguri, get a vehicle to Ngala, and another to cover the short distance to the border, and then a bush taxi on the Cameroon side to take you to Kousséri. The total journey is roughly 250km and can be managed in a day. You'll need a visa for Chad but if you are only crossing this small section of Cameroon and not going elsewhere in the country, free transit visas are issued at the border at each end.

Via Niger There are several tar-sealed roads between Niger and Nigeria that many Hausa traders use frequently. The most common crossing and the closest to the Niger capital of Niamey is from Birnin-Nkonni in Niger to Ilela in Nigeria, 85km north of Sokoto. The other main crossings are Maradi in Niger to Katsina, 45km from the border; and Zinder in Niger to Kano, which is roughly 140km from the border. All crossings are reasonably straightforward and roads are tar-sealed, though they do have a few potholes. In Niger, there are buses from Niamey to the borders at Birnin-Nkonni and Maradi, and another service to Zinder, from all of which you can get public transport to the borders themselves, though the best bet is Birnin-Nkonni, which is right on the border itself. Here you can find a bush taxi going directly to Sokoto. In Maradi you can get a bush taxi to the border town of Dan-Issa and change vehicles there for onward travel to Katsina in Nigeria, and in Zinder you can again get a bush taxi to the border, where you can change on to another one heading towards Kano.

WHAT TO TAKE

It is necessary to put some thought into what to take to Nigeria because you need to dress for the constant heat and humidity and, at certain times of the year, for the rain; because it is necessary to adhere to a certain dress code in the Muslim north; and because medical supplies and other basic necessities are inadequate or simply not available. The initial choice is to take everything that you may possibly need, but at the same time it's important not to carry too much. You need to strike a balance, something that probably depends on personal experience more than anything else.

CARRYING LUGGAGE Unless you are only ever going to see Nigeria from the compound of the Sheraton Hotel, Nigeria is not a place where you want to lug several suitcases around, or even leave them free-standing for any length of time.

Keep luggage small and light enough to keep on you at all times while you travel until you can safely deposit it in a hotel room. If you are travelling by public transport, space for luggage in vehicles is extremely limited, and you will often have to put your luggage on your knees. You need to take strong luggage that will survive bouncy potholed roads, sudden breaking by manic drivers, and the brute force of vehicle conductors, who fill every conceivable space in a vehicle with luggage and people.

Rather uniquely to Nigeria, because of the traffic (and human) congestion, you cannot always rely on taxis in the form of cars to take you from A to B – for example, often a motor park will be on the edge of town, and the only way to get into town and to a hotel is to cover the distance by *okada* (motorbike taxi), as inner-city public transport has even less room for luggage than inter-city transport. You can get away with carrying a 50-litre backpack on the back of an *okada*, as long as it's not too heavy, and this keeps hands free to hold on. It may be worth having two different-sized backpacks – for example 50-litre and 20-litre – as drivers and conductors of minibuses then only have to find space for the bigger one, while the smaller one can be kept on your knees if necessary. You could consider carrying just a daypack during excursions.

Avoid taking a backpack with several pockets on the outside and if possible lock the zips with padlocks. There is the danger of wandering hands making their way inside unlocked pockets not just in hotels or on public transport but also by baggage handlers at the airports (and not just in Nigeria). If you can, get one with one of those extra flaps that cover the straps on a backpack as this helps to avoid damage when the pack is shoved into small spaces in vehicles. The only other problem we encountered with packs and public transport was the dirt and sometimes oil on the floor of the vehicles, which leaves nasty stains on your clothes once you put your pack on your back – insist that your luggage goes in the back of the vehicle at all times if possible.

CLOTHES Nigerians are generally snappy dressers and the various dresses, robes and head gear they wear are spectacular and colourful. It always amazed me how neat and unruffled Nigerians looked in their elaborate clothing, while we managed to attract all the dirt and melted in the heat. Women travellers to Nigeria should **dress modestly**, and respect local customs regarding dress, especially in the Muslim north, where it is inadvisable for women even to wear trousers. But a word of advice for women – if wearing a long skirt, ensure that it is quite full; I had a few problems sitting astride an *okada* in a too-tight long skirt that showed too much leg.

As hard as it is not to wear typical summer clothes in such heat it is important to cover up. Men and women should avoid revealing shoulders and legs, and women should avoid tight-fitting clothing, bare midriffs, cleavage and so on. A staunch Muslim emir in northern Nigeria will not want to see your belly ring. Also avoid military or combat style clothing, especially camouflage print. If you are on business in Nigeria, a lightweight suit and tie may be necessary for men for formal meetings, and a jacket in some upmarket restaurants. If it's the rainy season, you'll need a light raincoat, and you may want to throw in swimwear and shorts (only to be worn at the beach). You are very unlikely to need anything warm to wear anywhere except at the top of Obudu Plateau.

Take **light cotton clothes**, not heavy material like denim or even T-shirt material (heavy, hot, and takes forever to dry), but thin (not transparent) cotton trousers, skirts and loose-fitting shirts. Ideally, you want fabrics that you can rinse out each night when there is water available; hang them up over the back of a chair, and with the help of a little air conditioning, they will be dry by morning. Remember that Nigeria is hot and humid all year round – you will sweat a lot walking around the streets in the humidity and crowded public transport, so expect to have to wash your clothes at the end of each day when possible. Small packets of washing powder are available to buy for next to nothing, so if you have clothes that can be easily washed and dried, you will have to take very little with you. Once in Nigeria, manufactured clothes are available in all the markets but they are not especially cheap. Fabric is also available everywhere and most Nigerians who wear traditional clothing choose a fabric and then get a tailor to make up a dress or robe.

Shoes are a personal choice, given that you'll be trudging around a fair number of rubbish-filled streets: boots or trainers are unbearably hot but offer greater protection from the filth, while thongs or sandals are cooler but less protective. Careful choice of open shoes is needed to give better protection. We found that the only time closed shoes were essential was in the national parks and forests in the east of Nigeria where the insects and ants were a constant problem.

My personal recommendation for men and women, and an item I never go travelling without, is a **sarong**, or a more masculine East African version, a *kikoi*. They have a multitude of uses and take up very little room. The obvious use is as a wrap-around long skirt for women and men (this is very acceptable all over Africa), or if you suddenly have to cover up, say when leaving the beach. They can be used for shade, as a towel (as they are quick drying and much lighter than a fluffy version), or as a woman's headscarf. If it's unbearably hot at night or you have a temperature, you can lie underneath a sarong soaked in cold water. And finally, you can even use your sarong to tie up your laundry.

OTHER USEFUL ITEMS Most budget travellers carry the obligatory **sleeping bag**. This is not necessary in Nigeria, where it never cools down enough for you to want to climb into it. Unless you are in an overland vehicle you won't be camping anywhere and most hotels provide adequate bedding. All you really need is a **sheet sleeping bag**, something you can easily make yourself, to use in places where the sheets look somewhat dubious. Very few hotels provide a **towel** so take a small hand towel, a travel towel or a sarong.

Other **basics** include medical kit (discussed in Chapter 4), sunglasses, torch and spare batteries, alarm clock, sun protection cream, and a Swiss army knife or Leatherman. Also essential is a **money belt** that is not too big and has an elastic waistband, as this will make it far more comfortable when you're scrunched up in a minibus.

Toiletries should be kept to a minimum and basics like soap, toilet paper and toothbrushes and toothpaste are readily available in Nigerian markets (in motor parks just look out for the toothbrush man with everything you need for oral hygiene perched on his head), though items that Nigerians are less likely to use, such as razors, shampoo and conditioner, and deodorant, are only available in the few upmarket supermarkets dealing in imported goods, and are very expensive. Also, beware of buying toiletries such as moisturisers and face cream in Nigeria – their shelf life is dubious and counterfeit products abound. Items that are not easily found in Nigeria include contact lens solution, sanitary products, mosquito repellent and medical supplies, so bring enough with you to cover the length of your stay. You may want to consider leaving **contact lenses** at home and reverting to glasses. The tremendous dust, pollution, air conditioning and the fact that your hands may never be entirely clean when putting them in and taking them out, leads to all sorts of irritations and possible infection.

Other items you may want to consider taking are a **cell phone** and charger (plus adaptor if your charger doesn't have a three-pin British-style plug). If your phone is on international roaming, you can get cell phone reception just about all over Nigeria, and although you may not have much luck getting through to any

Nigerian telephone numbers, it's good to carry one in the event of an emergency. A **calculator** is useful to work out exchange rates, and I never go anywhere without one of those **electrical elements** and a Thermos cup to make tea first thing in the morning. There will be the opportunity to read **books** on long journeys and perhaps by torchlight when the power and the TV go off. Rather than lugging expensive novels around, buy cheap, locally produced books in Nigeria at the various bookshops – Nigeria is well known for its writers and this is a good opportunity to delve into some Nigerian literature. Finally, all washbasins and baths in Nigerian hotels are plugless, so to wash with a limited amount of water or to wash your clothes, you may want to consider bringing a universal plastic **plug**, usually found in travel-gear shops.

3

In Nigeria

INFORMATION

Nigeria has a network of tourism offices, but you'll be hard pushed to actually get any tourist information out of them. Most come under the wing of the **Nigerian Tourism Development Council** (NTDC), which has its central offices in Abuja. The NTDC has a few regional offices and they are well staffed, but if you were to go into any of these offices and present yourself as a tourist and ask for some information, the above-mentioned staff are likely to fall off their chairs. Other than a few dusty leaflets that were printed circa 1975, they usually haven't got anything to give out or any information to tell you. It's not that they are unfriendly or unhelpful, just that they have *no* tourist information. In addition to branches of the NTDC there are some **state tourist offices**, which are just as ineffectual, and where you will be required to make an appointment. All of these offices are nothing more than government or state civil service departments employing people to sit at empty desks. Many staff do not understand our need for tourist information. I had to go through a whole rigmarole of making appointments with the local director, who invariably had nothing to offer and who politely wanted to know what I was doing wasting his time. I even found this at the head office of the Nigerian Tourism Development Council in Abuja, where we struggled to talk to anyone. In short, *there is no tourist information*, so don't bother trying to find these offices. If you are in Nigeria long term, it might be worth contacting the **Nigerian Field Society**, which is run by expats, as they occasionally organise field trips out of Lagos, particularly to the durbar festivals in the northern cities. You'll find up-to-date telephone numbers if you ask around expat circles or visit www.nigerianfield.org.

MAPS There are two country-specific maps of Nigeria available: The *Spectrum Road Map, Nigeria* (1:1,500 000) was last published in 2002 by Spectrum Books in Nigeria, and is available there at many of the bookshops, and *Nigeria* (1:1,900,000) from International Travel Maps, Vancouver, Canada (ISBN 1553413512), www.itmb.com. Both are perfectly functional, though they're a little outdated and do not show some of the new roads and new names for the national parks that were created out of old game reserves. Of the two, the one from International Travel Maps, on which the regional maps in this book are based, is the most detailed and the most lightweight. The *West Africa* Michelin map is very detailed for Nigeria, with fairly accurate kilometre markings, and is essential if travelling through West Africa overland.

HOLIDAYS In Nigeria, public holidays fall on: 1 January (New Year's Day), 1 May (Labour Day), 1 October (National Day).

In addition, Christian and Muslim holy days are celebrated throughout the entire country. Muslim holidays vary according to the lunar calendar and include Maulid an-Nabi, which is Mohammed's birthday, usually celebrated in September or October; Idul Fitr, a three-day feast that ends the month-long fast of Ramadan; and Idul Adha, a feast that commemorates the faith and obedience of the prophet Ibrahim (Abraham) in his preparedness to sacrifice his own son, usually held in June or July. Christian holidays include Easter (Friday to Monday), Christmas Day (25 December) and Boxing Day (26 December). Additionally, in the urban areas Sanitation Day is the last Saturday morning of the month when people are supposed to stay home and clean up around them.

$ MONEY AND PRICES

Nigeria's unit of currency is the naira (pronounced *nieera*), which is written as an 'N' preceding numbers. 1 naira (N) = 100 kobo (k). Notes are in denominations of N1,000, 500, 200, 100, 50, 20, 10 and 5. Unfathomably, a N2 coin was introduced in 2006, which is virtually worthless. In 2007, new N50, 20, 10 and 5 notes were introduced, which have a thin plastic coating to make them far more durable than the old ones and evidently they are harder to forge. Each has the number written in the three major languages: Yoruba, Igbo and Hausa. The higher notes remain the same. Exchange rate figures are included as a guide to the movements of the Nigerian naira against the pound sterling and the US dollar in recent years.

EXCHANGE RATES 2003–2007

	2003	2004	2005	2006	2007*
US$1	N127	N138	N133	N128	N127
GB£1	N200	N243	N256	N252	N250

*used in researching this guide

FOREIGN EXCHANGE It is not easy to change foreign currency into naira, despite there being banks everywhere. In Lagos alone there are over 90 bank companies (with many branches) but most are very reluctant to change money. Very oddly, the banks give out US$ cash but don't take it in. Many are affiliated to Western Union, and offer a service of supplying US$ cash. This may be because of the large number of Nigerians who travel abroad. The best currency to take to Nigeria is the good old greenback (US$) – you'll have a great deal of difficulty changing anything else.

There is an active and tolerated black market in Nigeria referred to as the 'parallel market', which offers slightly higher exchange rates than the official bank rate published in the newspapers alongside the black market rate. You are very likely to have to resort to changing money with black marketeers on the street. However, although in the past the only way to change money on arrival at the international airports in Lagos, Kano and Abuja was to negotiate with black market money changers outside the terminals in the car parks (which you can still do), there are now 24-hour Travelex bureaux de change at the airports. These are hassle free and offer commutative exchange rates. Elsewhere most hotels in the large cities offer foreign exchange services to their guests, and if you get stuck it is still worthwhile asking at one of them, even if you're not staying at the hotel. At the very least your hotel should be able to point you in the right direction to local money changers.

When changing money on the street (which is deemed acceptable in Nigeria) try and go to the money changer's office or shop if possible, and count out the naira carefully before handing over your US$. If you feel hurried or distracted, abort the transaction immediately. You'll find that you'll get a lower exchange rate for small denomination US$ notes than for bigger ones, so in Nigeria small notes are not much use. Most Nigerian money changers are sharp businessmen with whom you may have to haggle over the exchange rate, but most are also pretty straightforward and honest, and you'll experience few problems.

In this guide I have listed the very few places where you can change money, and as there are only a handful around the country, read ahead and make sure that there is somewhere to change money to avoid being caught short. In general it is sensible to change money when you can. One piece of advice is to approach other foreigners – expats or Lebanese businessmen. Many expats get some of their salary paid in naira and may be happy to change it over into hard currency. Then there are a few Lebanese shops and restaurants where the Lebanese owners may also be happy to change money given that they import much of their produce.

ATMs have started to appear on the scene and over 6,000 had been installed at principal banks across the country. Diamond Bank for example has ATMs at all their branches and at some petrol stations and branches of Mr Biggs fast food restaurants. These are used with local cards, and Nigerians themselves now have the option of pre-loading a credit card, which they can use in these machines, and use ATMs and pay for things overseas. Some of the ATMs are now Visa linked, but it's ill-advised to use them as there is a very real risk of credit card fraud. The only places that change travellers' cheques in Nigeria are the Travelex offices in the international arrivals and departures halls at the airports and the first branch of American Express (AMEX) in Nigeria at 109 Awolowo Rd, Ikoyi, Lagos; ↘ 01 271 5797/8.

If you are travelling overland and arrive in Nigeria on a land border, it's usually possible to exchange US$ cash and eastern and western CFAs (Communauté Financière de l'Afrique francs) used in the West Africa Francophile countries, with money changers at the border, though you will get a poorer rate than elsewhere. When I spoke to people who came through on overland trucks from the Republic of Benin, their advice was to fill up the truck with diesel in Benin (diesel is only found sporadically in Nigeria, though petrol is not such a problem) and to change enough money at the border to cover the journey to Abuja (where money changers near the Sheraton offer a much better exchange rate – see page 240). All overlanders will inevitably end up in Abuja as this is where they obtain onward visas.

The western CFA is used in certain countries to the west of Nigeria: Benin, Burkina Faso, Guinea-Bissau, Ivory Coast, Mali, Senegal and Togo, and Niger to the north of Nigeria. The eastern CFA is used in countries to the east of Nigeria: Cameroon, Central African Republic, Chad, Equatorial Guinea, Gabon and the Republic of Congo. The two types of CFA are not interchangeable, so if you are crossing Nigeria overland you need to get rid of either excess western or eastern CFAs (depending in which direction you are travelling in) at the border.

Finally, it's important to remember that the climate in Nigeria will make you sweat. On more than a couple of occasions I fished out some rather damp US$100 notes from my money belt to exchange with a Lebanese shop owner who was not impressed! Keep your money in a plastic bag.

SMALL CHANGE You'll need to keep a lot of your naira in small change – preferably N20 notes, which are the most useful. Nigeria seems to print more of these than any other note, as this is seemingly the cost for any vehicle to get through a road block, and inexplicably there are many more N20 notes than any other notes. N10 and N5 notes are not of much use, except perhaps for buying packets of *pure water* or a small snack such as peanuts. N20s are very useful for short bus fares, *okada* trips and soft drinks, and if the vendor or driver can't give you change from a N20 then it's not going to really matter. Most notes are pretty dirty and have changed hands thousands of times. People hold money all the time – just look out for the conductors in the motor parks or market traders and you will see them constantly counting the wedge of cash in their hands. If you can, refuse any particularly ragged notes and ask for cleaner or newer ones.

PRICES Nigeria is not the cheapest of African countries, even for Nigerians. Budget travellers can get around on roughly US$80 a day for two people, including accommodation, local food, extensive long-distance travel by public transport, frequent short-distance transport around the cities, and the odd entry fee and *dash* (see *Dashing*, page 84) for a guide. Prices for food and accommodation are fixed, though the cost of inter-city or intra-city transport varies depending on distance, type of vehicle and the haggling power of the individual, and you may spend an average of about US$10–15 a day if you move around by bush taxis, minibuses and *okadas*. You pay about US$30–40 for a very basic double room and perhaps about US$15 each on food and the odd beer.

Expect to spend more in Lagos where the cost of accommodation and restaurant meals, and even *okada* rides, is much more than elsewhere in the country (see *Chapter 5* for some idea of prices). A business traveller who stays and eats in the best hotel in any city and pays for what is generally known as car hire (comes with a driver) may spend US$300–500 a day. Lagos expats who have some experience of costs and facilities in Nigeria can feasibly move around Nigeria with their own vehicles and stay at mid-range hotels for around US$80–130 for two, and eat at the few upmarket restaurants for roughly US$50–60 for a meal for two with drinks.

Although I have quoted in US$ for the most part, you will have to pay for everything in naira, which has been pretty steady against the US dollar in recent years. I have used N127 = US$1 and N250 = £1 as the exchange rates. To help you digest the prices, work in N1,000s – US$8 or £4 is about N1,000.

GETTING AROUND

BY AIR There are 22 paved runways around the country and most of Nigeria's state capitals have their own airports; as there are several domestic airlines, in theory it is feasible to travel around by air. Until recently there used to be many more airlines, 30 or so, but following two fatal air crashes in Nigeria in 2005, the government got tougher with airline operators and new standards were set. The airlines were required to meet stricter standards of safety and the international airport at Port Harcourt (where one of the disasters occurred) was closed down. Many of the airlines failed to meet the new standards and their licences were revoked by the Ministry of Aviation. Unfortunately, despite this move, another fatal crash occurred in 2006, which killed the Sultan of Sokoto among many others (see page 319). Nevertheless, despite this appalling aviation record, conditions in safety have improved overall lately and, to put it in perspective, it's worth remembering that between seven and eight million Nigerians take domestic flights annually. In addition, Richard Branson made the ground-breaking move in 2004 of introducing Virgin Nigeria, which offers both domestic and international flights. He thinks that Lagos is an ideal transport hub for West Africa.

At the bigger airports such as Lagos and Abuja, you just pitch up for a ticket at the airport, though in the smaller cities some of the airlines have desks in local hotels where you can purchase a ticket. Domestic airfares are reasonably cheap, though they vary slightly between the various airlines. Expect to pay roughly the following prices: Lagos–Abuja, US$100; Lagos–Warri, US$160; Lagos–Benin City, US$90; Lagos–Calabar, US$70; Lagos–Kano, US$140; Lagos–Sokoto, US$140; and Lagos–Enugu, US$90. There are scores of additional fares from Abuja to these destinations and between the other cities, but you can get an idea of price versus distance from the above. Compared with some of the others, the Lagos–Calabar route is especially good value at the moment, probably because many flights have been rerouted there since the airport at Port Harcourt was closed. All domestic airlines now have websites listing full schedules, though use these as a guide only as they can change frequently. See also the 'Getting there and away' sections of destination chapters for details of flights to and from the major cities.

Airlines

✈ **Aero Contractors** ☎ 01 497 9122; www.acn.aero

✈ **Arik Air** ☎ 01 279 9999/496 6606; www.arikair.com

✈ **Bellview Airlines** ☎ 01 270 2700/262 1373; www.flybellviewair.com. Bellview is a domestic airline but also has services to Abidjan, Accra, Banjul, Conakry, Dakar, Doula, Freetown, Libreville & Monrovia. It has flights to & from London four times a week & to & from Johannesburg twice a week.

✈ **Chanchangi Airlines** ☎ 01 493 9744/55; www.chanchangi.com

✈ **IRS Airlines** ☎ 01 773 8014/5; www.irs-airlines.com

✈ **Overland Airways** ☎ 0803 535 5003; www.overland.aero

✈ **Sosoliso Airlines** ☎ 01 496 1962; www.sosolisoairline.com. Domestic flights plus services to Accra, Freetown & Monrovia.

✈ **Virgin Nigeria** ☎ 01 460 0505/271 1111; www.virginnigeria.com. As well as domestic flights, Virgin flies to Accra, Dakar & Doula in West Africa as well as London & Johannesburg.

CAR RENTAL AND DRIVING The national road system links all the main centres, and traffic drives on the right. Roads in Nigeria are generally very poor, causing damage to vehicles and contributing to hazardous driving conditions. Of Nigeria's 200,000km of roads, only about 60,000km are paved, but many of these are in very bad shape and have been decaying for years. Some have lost their asphalt surface or have reverted to being gravel roads; many are barely usable, especially in high rainfall areas of the south. Excessive speed, unpredictable driving habits, and the lack of basic maintenance on many vehicles are additional hazards (as burnt-out wrecks and mangled vehicles along the road will attest). The rainy season from May to October is especially dangerous because of flooded roads. The worst roads are in the southeast of the country. There are few traffic lights or stop signs, and drivers seldom yield the right of way or give consideration to pedestrians and cyclists.

Gridlock is common in urban areas, especially in Lagos, which is known for its 'go-slow', and outside the cities traffic is made worse by trucks and buses having to make up for the inadequate rail system. Chronic fuel shortages lead to long queues at service stations, which can disrupt or even block traffic. Night driving should be avoided as the streets are very poorly lit and many vehicles are missing one or both headlights. (See also 'Road accidents' in *Chapter 4*, page 101.)

Road travel in Africa is generally erratic, but in Nigeria you will also have to get used to the whole ethos of 'me first' – each motorist has absolute power and authority over the road, regardless of whether a pedestrian is walking in front of his vehicle, whether he is on the wrong side of the road and a truck is heading down a hill towards him, or whether he wants to get from point A to point B via an

DISTANCES BETWEEN MAJOR CITIES (KM)

	Abeokuta	Abuja	Bauchi	Benin City	Calabar	Enugu	Ibadan	Ilorin	Jos	Kaduna	Kano	Katsina	Lagos	Lokoja	Maiduguri	Makurdi	Port Harcourt	Sokoto
Abeokuta	—																	
Abuja	740	—																
Bauchi	1,072	445	—															
Benin City	329	450	893	—														
Calabar	765	857	998	436	—													
Enugu	577	400	741	248	283	—												
Ibadan	77	659	1,069	291	530	539	—											
Ilorin	236	500	913	362	826	649	159	—										
Jos	995	313	132	761	866	609	863	781	—									
Kaduna	836	180	412	791	1,015	765	759	600	280	—								
Kano	1,086	410	321	1,057	1,283	1,074	1,009	850	421	242	—							
Katsina	1,169	563	494	1,230	1,425	1,095	1,052	893	575	398	173	—						
Lagos	81	800	1,199	328	766	526	147	306	986	906	1,156	1,199	—					
Lokoja	489	173	603	290	610	382	580	310	471	505	767	899	539	—				
Maiduguri	1,536	908	464	1,357	1,462	1,179	1,520	1,377	596	876	614	776	1,660	1,067	—			
Makurdi	950	323	471	492	529	270	871	824	339	502	760	851	820	319	935	—		
Port Harcourt	693	700	996	364	184	255	625	799	864	987	1,230	1,370	662	557	1,460	525	—	
Sokoto	969	793	778	1,095	1,498	1,249	892	732	646	487	583	428	1,050	938	1,183	985	1,214	—

embankment, a pavement or a central reservation. There is a good reason why hire cars only come with a driver in Nigeria, and why the more comfortable front seats of a go-when-full minibus are often the last to fill – the views through the eyes of the driver can be very unnerving! Finally, driving without honking the horn is considered discourteous and dangerous.

When you are on the road, signposts are sporadic, but do look out for the white marker stones next to the road featuring the first three letters of the next and previous towns and the distances to each in kilometres.

As from 2003 it has been a law for Nigerian drivers and front-seat passengers to wear seat belts. This law is taken quite seriously, particularly in Lagos, where most taxi drivers buckle up and ask you to do the same.

Petrol and diesel Petrol and diesel costs N70–80 a litre, though the price routinely changes depending on fluctuations in Nigeria's oil-based economy, which is also reflected in fares for public transport. Price hikes often cause strikes and riots. Of the two, diesel is harder to find, and overland vehicles need to fill up whenever they can. All the petrol stations have rather comical signs outside saying 'Yes petrol, Yes diesel, Yes paraffin'. If they don't have one of these products they simply scrub out the 'Yes' bit! Cheating at petrol stations is quite common (pumps are either tampered with or the displays on them don't work at all). Another scam is to fit extra-long nozzles on pumps that trap an accurate measure of fuel going into a tank whereby the tank reader gives a misreading of how full the tank is, or to fail to zero the pump before starting to fill a tank.

Car hire Very few foreigners actually drive in Nigeria because of high accident rates, hectic traffic, and confusing or non-existent traffic rules – expats usually have their own chauffeur-driven cars and car hire always includes a driver. There is effectively no such thing as traditional car hire, and the division between taking a taxi and hiring a car is somewhat blurred. You cannot hire a car without a driver and it's the driver who pays for the petrol, so in essence you're just taking a taxi. It's not difficult to hire a car in the bigger cities, but it is best to go through one of the major hotels who can recommend a driver. Expect to haggle over rates, and remember that deals can be done for periods of more than a day. In the Sheraton, for example, reasonable cars with a driver cost upwards of US$120 a day, with cheaper rates for three days or more, while elsewhere a beat-up old Peugeot with a driver costs about US$70 a day. There really is no such thing as taking a car and driver from city to city – to do this you will have to negotiate with a driver, which basically is the same as taking a bush taxi (see below) as a drop, meaning you have got the vehicle for your exclusive use and that you will therefore have to pay the same as if it was full of passengers.

RAIL Nigeria has over 3,500km of railways and the two main railways are from Lagos to Kano (via Ibadan–Oyo–Ogbombosho–Kaduna); and from Port Harcourt to Maiduguri (via Aba–Enugu–Makurdi–Jos). The railways are run by the Nigeria Railway Corporation (www.nrc-ng.org), which has been in and out of bankruptcy for the last 20 years, and years of neglect of both the rolling stock and tracks have seriously reduced the capacity and utility of the railways; passenger services have been largely suspended because of sabotage and a lack of maintenance. There is now one weekly (erratic) service between Lagos and Kano, but there are often significant delays and derailments. At the time of writing, the government were negotiating with the Chinese to rehabilitate this Lagos–Kano line – no doubt in an exchange for oil. There has also been talk of building 'light' railways linking the airports in Lagos and Abuja to the city centres.

3

Motor parks are chaotic, crowded and usually filthy, stuffed to the gills with vehicles and market stalls, and are frequented by hawkers, food-is-ready stands, and conductors and touts shouting out destinations and arguing over passengers. They are full of life and great places to observe daily Nigerian street life. Once everyone has got over the shock of the arrival of an *oyibo* (white person) and you have located and decided what vehicle you are going to take, you'll receive no hassles and it's a fabulous opportunity to see everyone at work and chat to the people around you.

Motor parks are frantic places where everyone wants to sell you something. The hawkers do their rounds with loaves of bread, peanuts, sticks of *suya*, soft drinks, *pure water*, various other street food, boxes of imitation watches, underwear and handkerchiefs (a very useful item in a sweaty bus). Other hawkers offer services such as the shoe doctor or mobile tailor (amazingly these men walk around with old black Singer sewing machines on their heads), and – my absolute favourite – International Finger Cutter men. These are manicurists who wander around the motor parks clacking their scissors and administering what look like rather harsh manicures and pedicures to any man who desires to have his nails buffed (presumably women conduct this grooming procedure at home). Then there are beggars – the blind, crippled and maimed – who throw their hands through minibus windows and rattle their enamel plates.

There are also lay preachers, who come to each vehicle and pray to God for all the passengers to have a safe journey. This often turns into a bit of impromptu hymn-singing, after which the passengers are expected to pay the preacher some *dash*. We were often 'sprinkled with the blood of Jesus' for safe travelling. Quite often a passenger in the vehicle will say another prayer before departing. Finally there are traditional doctors, who roam the motor parks proclaiming through loudspeakers that they have the medicine, the book and the power to cure all the ailments of the world, which on one occasion included 'unfriendly body odour' and a 'weeping penis'! This same gentleman advised putting undiluted petrol on a tooth three times a week to cure toothache, washing your hair in urine to cure dandruff, and using an onion to cure premature ejaculation. The man I was sitting next to on the bus, who was a real doctor, told me irritably that the traditional doctor was 'confusing the common man'. It was a priceless moment.

MINIBUSES AND BUSH TAXIS Except for the smallest of villages, every settlement in Nigeria has a motor park, and some of the larger cities have several. All public transport goes from these and you will inevitably spend a great deal of time hanging around them waiting for vehicles to go-when-full. Sometimes you may be lucky and arrive at a motor park and find a vehicle with only a couple of seats left and depart almost immediately; at other times you may be the first to arrive and have to hang around for another 16 or so people who want to go in the same direction as you.

It's best to go to a motor park early as the first vehicles of the day fill quickly. The exception of this is Sunday in the Christian cities, where nothing moves until church finishes about 13.00. Although they seem completely chaotic at first, motor parks are fairly organised and someone will point you in the right direction of the vehicle you want. Always look out for the men in the green and white uniform of the National Union of Road Transport Workers (NURTW), who patrol the motor parks and take the fee paid by the drivers for the use of the motor park. He will take you straight to the right bus. There are queues of vehicles and the one that is filling up first will have a wooden pyramid sign on top with the first three letters of the town or city it's going to. When the vehicle departs, this is simply plonked on to the top of the next one. In nearly all of the motor parks you can hire a wheelbarrow and driver to carry your luggage.

No vehicle moves until the required amount of people are in place. In a minibus this means when two people are in the front plus the driver, five are on the back seat, four are across the middle seats (with another couple of additional people squashed on to the engine cover at the back of the front seat), and the conductor is sitting in the doorway. In a bush taxi (any kind of car), it's when two people are on the front seat plus the driver and four are on the back seat. In the case of Peugeot 504s, another three are on the second back seat fixed into the boot.

Expect to be completely squashed and uncomfortable. There is not enough space for everyone to sit back on their seats so you will have to get used to frequently 'shifting' as the Nigerians like to call it – as in 'shift up', 'shift back' and so on. This means everyone in the vehicle takes random turns at sitting to the front of the seats while other passengers sit back, and arms and legs are routinely shifted to accommodate everyone else's limbs.

In a minibus, if you are sitting opposite someone sitting on the engine cover behind the driver you'll also have to weave your knees with theirs, and on the middle seat at the front and in the passenger seat of a car (which takes two people) expect to sit astride the gear stick (with the driver negotiating gear changes from between your legs!). I've even seen an impossibly small Toyota Startlet (three door hatch-back) with four in the back, two on the front passenger seat and another passenger sharing the seat with the driver! If you are doing a lot of travelling in these vehicles it might be a good idea to try out all the positions in the vehicle to find the most comfortable so that you know which to bag first at a motor park. Also, always eye up the other passengers; you most certainly don't want to be pinned up against a six-foot hulking man on the front seat of an impossibly small car like a Golf.

You'll pay a few hundred naira more for a bush taxi than a minibus. The reason for this is that bush taxis fill up and go quicker. If it looks as if you may be waiting around for a long time for a minibus to fill up, hold off paying your fare to give you the option of switching to a bush taxi if you get fed up with waiting. Occasionally you'll hear that a minibus is 'taking three across'. This means that one less person is put on each seat and that the vehicle is actually comfortably full, with more or less the amount of people it was designed to carry. For this, though, you'll pay considerably more. Quite bizarrely, on some of the longer routes you will be required to fill out a form with your contact details for insurance purposes in case of an accident, and N50 or so of your fare will go towards an insurance policy.

All fares are set and everyone pays the same. Occasionally, if a vehicle is taking a long time to fill up the passengers will club together and pay for the extra seat so the vehicle can get going. In a minibus expect to pay roughly US$5 for a journey of about 100km or two hours, rising to US$15–20 for a journey of 500km and several hours, and add on approximately 30% to this for a bush taxi. If there's a fuel shortage, which happens several times a year, then fares go up and the drivers and conductors try and squash more people in.

As a foreigner, you will inevitably be asked at every motor park if you want a drop – meaning that you can take the vehicle for your exclusive use but will have to pay the same as if the vehicle was full of the correct amount of people. This is easy enough to work out: if a small car takes six at, say, N500 per person, it will cost N3,000 for you to have the car to yourself. The longest journey you can take on a minibus or bush taxi is around six or seven hours (more than long enough to be stuck in a squashed and sweaty vehicle). I think our longest ride was from Maiduguri to Kano, which was roughly seven hours. For longer distances you will have to break your journey and swap vehicles in a motor park.

Finally, the vehicle is ready to depart, luggage is strapped on the roof, squashed under seats, goes in the boot, and sometimes has to sit on your knees, and the conductors use brute force to fit everything in. When all that's done and the door is shut someone goes off to find the driver. When he eventually turns up and gets in, what follows is an obligatory argument with the National Union of Road Transport Workers man about how much the driver should pay to use the motor park.

'LUXURY' BUSES Inter-city, or 'luxury' buses as they are known (basically big coaches), are more comfortable than minibuses or bush taxis as you will have more leg room and your own seat all to yourself. Some newer ones also have air conditioning, toilets and play Nollywood movies. These buses cover longer distances than the smaller vehicles but are also not in great condition, and they nearly always travel at night so are not generally recommended, even by Nigerians, because of the danger of armed robbery. The 'luxury' buses connect all the main cities, and there are dozens of companies, many with delightful names: Young Shall Grow Motors, Fruit of Labour Motors, God's Will Transport, Vote for Jesus Motors or Glory is My Shepard Motors.

Each bus company has its own bus stand which is often close to the motor parks. The buses are too big to fit inside the motor parks proper and collect on a vacant side of the road that's big enough to accommodate them nearby. Unlike the minibuses and shared taxis, you have to pre-book a seat on a 'luxury' bus earlier in the day that you want to travel. This means you have to find the bus, book and pay for a ticket, and then return again at the departure time later in the day. Finally, and rather awkwardly, if they fill up they leave earlier than the scheduled time of departure. Fares vary between the companies, but expect to pay US$25 for the almost 1,000km overnight trip from Lagos to Jos, for example. The best of the bunch is ABC Transport (✆ *01 791 1365; www.abctransport.com*), which connects all the Nigerian cities, runs some services during the day and has the newest buses. A meal (usually of chicken and rice) is often included in the fare. A daytime journey between Lagos and Abuja is roughly US$30 and they also operate long-distance buses between Lagos and Togo, Benin and Ghana.

OKADAS AND CITY TRANSPORT There must be hundreds of thousands, if not millions, of motorcycle taxis in Nigeria. In the south they are generally called *okadas* (after a defunct airline); in the north they are known as *achabas*. If you get stuck, just simply say machine. You'll see the odd meaty Suzuki, but the majority of Nigerian *okadas* are Jinchengs imported from China. Millions of young men make a living as *okada* drivers, and if they are successful, as they get older and when they can afford to buy a car, they become taxi drivers. They usually carry one person on the back but it's not uncommon to see two or more people plus an assortment of luggage. In the cities they are faster than regular taxis but are not for the faint-hearted, though you can always tell your driver to slow down.

You will always have to negotiate a ride, which will be as little as N30 for a short hop outside of Lagos, and N50 in Lagos, while a journey of a kilometre or two will cost upwards of N150. Given that you won't have a crash helmet, it's not a good idea to take *okadas* on busy expressways where the traffic is moving fast. Accidents are common and in the large cities in particular *okadas* are driven very aggressively. Finally, Kevin says, 'If you ask an *okada* driver to take you somewhere and they

Police roadblocks are frequent (I counted 22 roadblocks on a 100km stretch of road between Lagos and Abeokuta). These are manned variously by men in black police uniforms, men wearing army fatigues or armoured vests, and men in nothing more than baseball caps, T-shirts with the sleeves ripped off, and mirrored sunglasses. Whatever the attire, no-one argues with the AK47s or pistols that these men invariably carry. These roadblocks can also be extra intimidating at night.

If you are on public transport you have nothing to worry about, as it is the driver who has to deal with the situation and not the passengers. Only very occasionally will the passengers be asked to get out so that the vehicle can be searched. When setting off in a bush taxi or minibus, you will notice the driver roll up a pile of N20 notes and stick them in a row above the driver's door. These are for what I like to call the '20km/h handshake'. The driver slows down at a roadblock, takes a couple of the rolled-up N20 notes, and neatly deposits them in the policeman's hand as he drives past.

Nigerians seem to have two differing opinions about roadblocks. In some of the vehicles we were travelling in, everybody groaned and tutted in disapproval when the driver handed over a *dash* or if we got delayed. In one, someone even complained to the driver that he shouldn't have dashed the policeman as he was only carrying a stick and not a gun. Then, by contrast, there were many other people who wholly approved of the roadblocks: it was explained to us that they caught armed robbers, and were doing a good job in keeping the roads safe, and that it was only right that they should be dashed as a thank you. One passenger commented that the police had a very hard job standing on the road in the hot sun all day, and that it was only fair to give them money for a Coke.

Foreigners in their own vehicle are usually just waved through. If you are stopped it's likely that the police are just curious and want to have a chat; as long as you are not breaking the law (by not having your licence with you, or not wearing a seatbelt, for example), there is nothing to be nervous about. If you have your own driver, they are in the best position to answer police questions, or try and be diplomatic when asked what you've got for them – 'just a smile for you today' often works. The police may attempt to try and 'fine' you if the steering wheel is on the wrong side, for a number plate that is not big enough for their liking, or for advertising (displaying an overland-company logo on the side of the vehicle).

There are also incidents of so-called 'tax collectors', often wearing yellow work vests and setting themselves up on roads leading into and out of towns. They have been known to throw down a piece of wood spiked with nails in front of your car and to demand a 'tax' that entitles you to free access to the town or city. This is nothing short of extortion; if you are stopped in this manner try to deal with it with a sense of humour and patience, and try and talk your way out of it. Try to avoid stopping for anyone who is not in a uniform. If you are stopped, ask for ID and say that you want to go to the police.

Reports suggest that things have improved greatly over recent years, which is good news if you are travelling overland through Nigeria. Many of my overland truck-driver friends tell me that a decade ago it cost several hundred dollars in bribes to police and army checkpoints simply to drive from one side of Nigeria to the other. However, they now tell me how refreshing it is not to be asked for *dash*, and that when they are stopped, it is often only so the police can have a look at their trucks or talk to their passengers. One proudly told me that when he crossed recently, all he paid in *dash* was one can of peaches!

hesitate *at all* it means that they don't know the place. Rather than admitting this, they will drive around randomly until you catch on.'

Taxis are available everywhere (though less so at night); although some are painted in specific colours, nearly all cars serve as taxis for the right price. Agree on the fare before getting in and remember that a drop is when you specifically want the vehicle to yourself. Expect to pay about three times more for a drop in a car than you would pay for an *okada*, but remember if there are a few of you then a drop will work out cheaper than you all taking individual *okadas*. Minibuses and shared taxis operate along specific routes that you simply hail down on the side of the street in the general direction you want to go. The price for both is usually set at about N20–40 depending on the distance you travel in them. Pay the correct fare, and pay it only once, no matter how many times the conductor or driver goes around collecting.

BOATS AND FERRIES There are some local ferry services, which are dealt with in the relative chapters.

 ## ACCOMMODATION

Apart from Lagos, Abuja and Port Harcourt, which each have several international-standard hotels (there is no star grading system in Nigeria), Nigerian hotels are generally run down, dilapidated, poorly maintained, have limited services, are often not wholly clean, and have not seen a lick of paint for perhaps 20 or 30 years. That said, as long as you know what to expect, then you will find adequate and comfortable accommodation just about everywhere.

In 2001 there was a decree that all foreigners must pay for hotels in foreign currency. This never happened and you'll struggle to find anywhere to accept your US$ except at the very top end of the market – unless otherwise stated all rooms must be paid for in naira. Also, hotels are supposed to use a two-tiered price system for residents and non-residents – this never happens either, except at a handful of hotels, so expect to pay the same as everyone else. You'll always be asked to pay up front and to pay a sizeable deposit, and in the more expensive hotels a 5% VAT levy and a 10% service charge will be added to the bill (see below).

If you are prepared to pay over US$200 for a room, you'll get one of a good standard, but at the very bottom end of the scale, where hotel rooms go for as little as US$20, you'll get ancient and scuffed furnishings, dirty carpets, frequent power and water cuts, rattling or defunct air-conditioning units, leaking fridges, and bad smells. Budget travellers will really want to be checking if there are clean sheets and that there is water available, even if it's in a bucket. Even for a little more, roughly US$60–100, you'll get the same in the so-called state hotels. These were obviously built during the 1970s–80s oil boom, and although they are huge, with vast public areas, cavernous empty restaurants and often defunct shops, no maintenance work or improvements have been done on them since they were built, and everything is very faded and old-fashioned. For what you do or do not get, accommodation in Nigeria is not especially good value (and Lagos hotels are particularly expensive), though on the upside even the cheapest establishments have en-suite rooms with air conditioning and TV.

It's almost impossible to pre-book a hotel in Nigeria, not only because of the inefficient phone and email services, but because the only way to reserve a room is by paying the deposit upfront, and as you are strongly urged not to use a credit card, this is almost impossible to do unless you are already there. The only exception to this is at the very top-end, international-chain level such as the Sheraton or Hilton, which you can book through the websites. The South

African chain Protea manages a number of hotels across the country and is opening more in 2008 and 2009. Again, they have an efficient website for reservations. Elsewhere, you will rarely find that a hotel is full, unless there is a large conference on.

CAMPING Camping is not really an option in Nigeria and there are no formal campsites with ablution blocks. Though self-sufficient overlanders manage to cross Nigeria and bush camp in quarries, timber yards and down dirt tracks on the side of the road without any problems, there are no facilities. Be wary of camping near towns and cities or any congested areas as you are bound to attract unwanted attention and news of your impromptu bush camp will spread like wildfire. Many of the hotels have large compounds and car parks (essential if you are driving) and at these places there's no reason why you can't ask if you can put a tent up, though you'll have to negotiate a price for camping. This is really only suitable for large groups as they will be expected to take at least one room for use of the shower and toilet. In the southeast of the country ignore the signs that say 'camp ground' – these are not campsites at all but venues for large religious gatherings that frequently take place on Sundays and go on all night.

LONG-TERM ACCOMMODATION If you have gone to Nigeria to work then it makes sense to live in rented accommodation. Most companies provide accommodation for their employees, and in Lagos there are many large expat communities on Victoria Island and Ikoyi living in apartment blocks, company compounds or private houses. There may sometimes be waiting lists for accommodation and it's not uncommon for new expats to spend the first few months of their stay in a hotel. Bear in mind rents can be upwards of a whopping US$50,000 a year for a two-bedroomed apartment in a compound, plus an annual service charge of US$10,000 or more, though it's the companies that usually meet these expenses.

Most apartment blocks have their own boreholes and generators for uninterrupted water and power supplies, and extras such as a swimming pool and tennis court, and service charges cover all maintenance. In houses, however, which tend to rely on the public water supply, the tenant is responsible for services and maintenance, and it's essential that you get a generator rigged up and consider some sort of security.

There is the added hassle of organising things to be fixed in your house. Many expats employ a steward or maid who lives in separate staff quarters. If you need to employ your own staff, it's essential that you talk to other expats for recommendations; reference letters are easily forged and previous employers may be hard to contact once they have left Nigeria.

Potential expats and their wives are usually invited to Nigeria for a few days by their sponsoring company on what is termed in expat language as a 'look-see', before they decide to commit to a contract. They are usually put up in a very nice hotel, making the prospect of living in Lagos seem slightly brighter, and are often shown around by another expat or his wife. Work contracts tend to be long (at least two or three years), and it's essential that you go on a 'look-see', and talk to lots of other expats, before committing to a lengthy stay in Nigeria.

EATING AND DRINKING

EATING Although typical of what is found throughout West Africa, traditional Nigerian food is more diverse because of the number of ethnic groups in the country. It differs between the south and north depending on what food products are available.

THE 15% In addition to the quoted fee, hotels and many restaurants are supposed to charge an additional 5% VAT and a 10% service charge. In the bigger cities such as Lagos and Abuja they do this, making a room or a meal significantly more expensive here than elsewhere, and you have to remember to include this in your budget. In the cheaper establishments, the 15% is either included in the rate or they don't bother with it at all.

AC AC is a universal acronym for air conditioning, though if you said air conditioning and not AC to the average Nigerian hotel receptionist, he or she would have no idea what you were talking about. Surprisingly, even the cheapest of hotels almost always has AC, but whether it works or not (no NEPA – power from the Nigeria Electric Power Authority) is another thing. In many hotels the AC units are as old as the ark; be wary of touching the control knobs or power points if they look especially hazardous. All rooms listed in this book have AC unless otherwise stated.

BED SIZE There is no such thing as a single bed in a Nigerian hotel. A standard room advertised on the tariff is often presumed by the hotel staff to be for one person, but it has generally got a normal-sized (for Europeans) double bed in it. Hotel receptionists in Nigeria will find it difficult to comprehend that two people might want to spend the night in a bed that size. A double is usually a room with a queen- or king-sized bed, while a so-called suite or executive room contains a bed so vast that it is wider than it is long. Room rates on the tariff often vary because of the size of the bed, so it's up to you how much you pay for sleeping space. Room rates are per room and not per person. Most hotels supply a top and bottom sheet, though where there is no top sheet and where the sheets do not look especially clean, I would advise you to use your own sleeping sheet (see page 59).

BREAKFAST ITEMS Some of the more expensive hotels have a menu of breakfast items. These usually cost around N200–300 each and you make up your own breakfast from tea, coffee, bread, toast, eggs, baked beans, chips, yam chips, sometimes Vienna sausage, and very occasionally bacon.

BUCKET SHOWERS Almost all hotel rooms are en suite with either a bath or shower or both. Although these facilities in themselves may be perfectly functional, running water through the shower head or taps is not. Even in the more expensive Nigerian hotels buckets and scoops are provided. You'll need to keep the bucket constantly filled from the tap when there is water, as you'll need it to flush the loo as well as for washing when there isn't any water. If there is never any water in the taps then ask for someone to fill the bucket for you from the hotel's main water tank.

CATERING SERVICES If a hotel offers a catering service, it means it provides food. Not all hotels have restaurants, but those that don't may offer the option of cooking you a plate of food and bringing it to your room; sometimes they have beers and soft drinks as well. When checking in ask what sort of food they have that day as all the items shown on a menu will not necessarily be available.

CHECK-OUT TIME In just about all of Nigeria's hotels check-out time is 12.00 midday and check-in time is 14.00. These are much later and earlier than in, say, European hotels, when check-out time is usually 10.00. The advantage of this is that you can leave your luggage in the room undisturbed until 12.00, giving you time in the morning to explore somewhere without lugging everything around. Most hotels will happily store your gear safely at the reception desk after this time·and you do not have to worry about theft. On just about all the tariffs it says that check-out after 12.00 will incur an additional charge of 50% of the room rate, and full room rate is charged after 18.00.

CONFERENCE FACILITY If a hotel advertises a conference facility, this usually means that the hotel has anything from a shed at the back of the cheapest hotels, to a vast range of halls in the plusher hotels, which can be hired out. This may be for conferences, but they are usually hired for weddings, funerals, memorials, church services and similar events that draw hundreds of people, especially at the weekend. These can get noisy and you have the additional concern that there are hundreds of non-hotel guests wandering around, so give the hotel a miss if there's a large 'conference' on.

DEPOSIT A deposit is required for even the cheapest hotel room. Deposits vary between 25% and 50% of the room rate. When you are checking into a hotel you pay the deposit price, which is considerably higher than the room rate, but when checking out you get the balance back, minus any additional expenses such as minibar, meals, telephone calls and so on. A room at a mid-range hotel in Abuja, for example, costs N16,000 (US$125) but the deposit is N22,000 (US$173). When you check in you must pay the N22,000 deposit and get the difference of N8,000 back in the morning when you check out after staff have deducted any additional expenses. This system is the same at just about all hotels in Nigeria whether it costs N1,000 or US$1,000 a night. Always take the deposit into consideration when budgeting because this is the amount of ready cash you'll need to stay anywhere for the night, though invariably you'll get a portion of this back. Also, always keep all your receipts for any piddly amount of deposit money you expect back; as Nigerians are rather officious about their paperwork, you may not get the remainder of your deposit back without it.

FRIDGE Many hotels have (usually empty and ancient) fridges in the rooms. This could be a throwback to a few decades ago when perhaps someone entertained the idea of offering a minibar service. They are NEPA (power) dependent, but we found them useful to keep water cool.

GEN Gen is short for generator (electricity provider run on diesel). In any hotel always make sure there is a generator – I found even the cheapest fleapit had one. The generator kicks in (assuming that there is diesel available) as soon as NEPA (the power) goes off. There is generally a few moments' overlap as NEPA dies, and someone runs to crank up the gen, and the noise of the gen roaring into action becomes quite familiar. The generator systems in some hotels are very elaborate and resemble small electricity sub-stations, particularly if they have to power hundreds of rooms, while at the smaller and cheaper places it's often just a single unit. In these cases the gen is often switched off between 23.00 and 07.00 to conserve diesel – an important consideration if it's stinking hot and you are relying on AC to ward off mosquitoes, or if you happen to be midway through a good movie on TV. Candles and a torch are essential. Remember the terms 'on' and 'off' as verbs when enquiring about hotel accommodation, as in 'What time do you off the generator?'

continued overleaf

LUXURY This word is frequently used on hotel tariffs describing the most expensive rooms. It doesn't mean luxury in the normal sense at all, and the 'luxury' rooms are usually the biggest suites with the biggest beds. An 'executive' room usually means that it has got a desk. *Always* look at a room before deciding.

NEPA The Nigeria Electric Power Authority (NEPA) in theory supplies Nigeria with electricity. Locally it's dubbed Never Expect Power Again – and for good reason. The power routinely goes off several times a day; often it's not even on during daylight hours, and when it comes on at dusk there is such a power surge, it fails within minutes. 'No NEPA' is a familiar term throughout the country. Despite fuelling lights, air-conditioning units and fans, NEPA also powers pumps to get water from water tanks to the taps in hotel rooms. In 2005 NEPA was privatised and changed its name to the Power Holding Company of Nigeria (PHCN). However everyone still refers to it as NEPA, although a new nickname has been quickly dubbed to the new title – 'Problem Has Changed Name...'.

SUITE A suite (sometimes spelt *suit* on the tariff) is quite simply a hotel room with more than a bedroom and bathroom. The extra room(s) will perhaps have a sofa, a table and chairs (often plastic), an additional TV, or an old desk (in which case it's confusingly very similar to an 'executive' room). In every sense it's a suite of rooms, but very far from the expectations of a suite in the real world of hotels.

TARIFF The tariff is a list of room rates, which is almost always available at the hotel reception. There is often a mind-boggling array of rates and types of room, from 'standard' or 'classic' rooms to all different types of suites, family rooms and specific rooms for diplomats, presidents and even monarchs. Except in the most expensive hotels such as the Sheraton and the Hilton, the difference is usually that the more expensive rooms are bigger and/or have bigger beds (Nigerian beds reach mammoth proportions). Always ask the difference between each room rate, and always look at one or more rooms before you decide. Note that the 15% and the deposit (see above) are also outlined on the tariff, so it's imperative that you study it before filling out the registration form and paying for a hotel room.

Starch As a general rule of thumb, Nigerians are fond of some kind of starchy staple accompanied by an (often spicy) soup – this is actually more like a sauce or relish and is not runny like a soup. They use a lot of palm oil, a reddish coloured oil made from ground palm kernels, and a lot of chillies ground into a red powder (known in Nigeria simply as pepper). The starches include pounded yam, which is boiled yams literally pounded in a giant pestle and mortar until the consistency is light and fluffy; it looks a bit like mashed potato. Others are *eba* or *garri*, porridges made from pounded cassava; *amala*, ground yam peels, which are boiled into a stiff paste and have a darker brown colour; and *semovita*, made from maize flour, another mashed-potato-looking concoction and similar to *mealie meal* or *pap* eaten all over eastern and southern Africa. Most of these starch-based staples have little taste and are very bland, and some have a fairly slimy texture, but they are cheap and filling and soak up the flavour of the sauce that comes with them. Alternatively you can opt for rice, which is served plain or cooked with peppers and palm oil; the latter is called *jollof rice*, which is bright orange, fairly hot and very tasty.

Soup Most of the soups are made with lots of palm oil and some meat-based stock, and a few pieces of your chosen meat are plonked on top. Nigeria is renowned for

TEA-BREAD-AND-EGGS Inexplicably, breakfast is sometimes included in the price of a hotel room for *one* person. This is always tea-bread-and-eggs, the standard Nigerian breakfast – Lipton tea with powdered milk and sugar, a hunk of bread and a pale-looking fried and greasy omelette. Rather confusingly, if you ask for just tea (as in a cup of tea) it will also come with bread, so you must always stipulate if you only want the tea (something that is not always got across very easily). If breakfast is not included in the room rate, tea-bread-and-eggs is generally available for around N200–300.

TOILET ROLL AND SOAP Rather amusingly, when checking into a hotel you will be presented with a toilet roll and a small bar of soap stuffed down the middle of the cardboard tube at reception – if you run out they will not be replaced automatically but if you ask, you'll get more. Towels are only provided in the upmarket hotels.

TV Even the cheapest of hotel rooms normally has a working TV (when of course there is power). LOCAL TV is the national station, which is run by the state television corporation, and all you'll usually get is the local news broadcast between 18.00 and 20.00, read by women in enormous shiny headdresses in bare television studios. DSTV (Digital Satellite Television) is South African satellite TV, with a handful of channels. These include Supersport, a sports channel with a South African slant popular because of its coverage of football; CNN and BBC World news channels; MNET movie channel, reasonably current Hollywood movies; MNET Open Time, South African soaps between 17.00 and 19.00; and Africa Magic, a clever business move by DSTV as this channel shows only Nigerian 'Nollywood' movies and is specifically broadcast in Nigeria 24 hours a day. 'Nollywood' movies are hugely popular low-budget dramas usually filmed on hand-held video cameras, and it is estimated some 70 a week of these movies are released on to the video market in Nigeria. You have to watch one – they are hilariously badly made with the most bizarre story lines. In the top hotels you'll also get BBC Prime, the History Channel, Discovery and the like. Except at the top range hotels, whoever is sitting at the reception desk of the hotel gets to choose what to watch. For example, you could be midway through watching a movie and the man at reception gets tired of watching it himself and flicks channels to watch the football and suddenly you are watching David Beckham instead of Brad Pitt and there is nothing you can do about it!

its fiery *obe ata* (pepper soup), which effectively is the country's national dish; it's a thick sauce made by boiling tomatoes, ground pepper, meat or fish broth, onions, palm oil and other spices. A Nigerian must-do is to try dried fish, beef or chicken pepper soup with your choice of starch and be prepared for your eyeballs to melt and your nose to explode, though you may choose to pass on the hugely popular *isiewu* (goat's head pepper soup) – every part of the goat's head is swimming around in it.

Other soups include the tasty *egusi soup*, made from ground melon seeds and bitter leaf (a sort of spinach); *okra soup*, made from okra, also known as ladies' fingers; *draw soup*, made from palm nuts, which is horribly slimy and viciously hot and is so called because the spices are 'drawn' out; *groundnut soup*, which is made from peanuts and lends a slight satay flavour to the sauce; and *efo*, a vegetable soup (but vegetarians need to remember that even the vegetable soups have a meat-based gravy).

You can add additional meat to these meals, which usually consists of a few pieces of very tough beef or goat, cooked dried fish with its head still intact, or a piece of chicken; the latter ranges from delicious KFC-styled fried chicken to a piece of bone with hardly any flesh on that has been boiled dry. It's worth

Nigerians in the south are great beer and Guinness drinkers, but in the Muslim north Sharia law prevents the consumption of alcohol. This doesn't mean alcohol cannot be found at all though. Although the northern cities are predominantly Muslim there are also considerable populations of Christians living there. Sabon Gari is Hausa for 'foreigners' town' (often meaning the Yoruba or Igbo, and sometimes Christian quarter) and in some (not all) of the northern cities bars can be found in these areas. Beer is also sold in a few hotels, as they are cater for visitors from other parts of the country and not local Muslims.

Government-owned or federal land doesn't come under the local state's law. These areas include military land, where soldiers are permitted to drink alcohol, and regions of interest to the visitor, such as the national parks. Yankari and Lake Kainji national parks lie within Sharia states, but as they are federal property they have bars selling beer. At the time of writing the driest cities were Katsina, Sokoto and Maiduguri.

Still on the wet–dry subject, swimming pools at the hotels in the Sharia states are generally empty. Sharia law does not permit public swimming. At one pool that had water I asked if we (male and female) could swim at the same time, and the confused receptionist answered that it was 'a very difficult question to answer'. I presume that because so few foreigners visit she was not sure how Sharia deals with this predicament. If there is water in your hotel pool, my advice is to speak to the manager about actually swimming in it.

remembering that you'll get very good or very bad versions of these meals; there is often no way of telling which it's going to be. Nevertheless, if you're lucky you'll get a big plate of steaming starch, tasty soup and tender meat. If there's also *dodo* on the menu add this – it's a delicious dish of fried plantains.

Fish, meat and vegetables Because of the prevalence of tsetse fly, cattle are scarce in the coastal regions, so consequently more fish is eaten in the south, while meat is more popular in the north. Look out for *suya*, which is delicious barbecued beef on sticks, though you can also get offal and goat *suya*, and *kilishi*, spiced dried meat that is very thinly sliced and dried outside in the sun. You'll often see bushmeat on the menu, which is considered a delicacy. Sometimes it's antelope that's unfortunately been poached out of the countryside, but more often than not it's *grasscutters* (cane rats) or giant rubbery snails called *igbin*. In the southeastern regions where meat is rare, beans are used to supplement protein in soups, and *moin-moin*, or bean cakes with a slightly gelatinous texture about them, are served as snacks wrapped up in banana leaves.

Vegetables such as onions, tomatoes, bitter leaf and yam are plentiful throughout Nigeria, though more exotic vegetables can be found in Lagos and the markets of the bigger cities. Outside Lagos we only really saw potatoes (and chips) on the menu in the north. Strangely given the dry climate, we also found more salads in the north, and they were surprisingly delicious, with lettuce, onions and tomatoes, a spattering of tinned baked beans, hard-boiled eggs, and a big dollop of mayonnaise. Fruit is plentiful and bananas, mangos and slices of fresh pineapple, or even coconut, are often seen on the side of the road, as are imported apples and sometimes pears from South Africa. Dairy products are scarce and you are unlikely to see cheese apart from in the posh restaurants on Victoria Island, though tinned condensed milk, milk powder and canned margarine are available. One brand of margarine that's popular is Blue Band, about which one reader said, 'I didn't entirely trust a food product that doesn't go off when kept in a warm cupboard for a year. My suspicion is that Blue Band is actually a form of spreadable plastic.'

RESTAURANTS Lagos has by far the best restaurants in the country for international fare – elsewhere you will struggle to find a non-Nigerian meal, though you'll sometimes find basic items such as omelette or chicken and chips and a rare stab at something continental, even if it's not always terribly authentic – on one menu I saw 'marshed potatoes' and 'spaghetti boneless'. But the imported ingredients and accompanying wine and other imported alcoholic drinks on Lagos menus and at the few outlying continental restaurants in the rest of the country come at a price. In a Nigerian restaurant outside Lagos you can expect to pay around US$5–7 for a Nigerian dish and perhaps US$1.20 at the most for a local beer. In a Lagos restaurant serving 'Western' food, a main dish alone averages US$15–20, without extras such as drinks and the 15% VAT and service charge, which nearly all Lagos eateries add on (unlike restaurants in the rest of the country). Even a not very special meal for two with drinks in Lagos can cost more than US$70 and much more in the better restaurants.

Away from Lagos, those with a bit more cash can splurge at the various Lebanese, Indian or Chinese restaurants found in the larger cities. Also worth a mention are the fast-food chains Tantalizers, Tastee Fried Chicken (also known as *De Tastee Fried Chicken*) and Mr Biggs – these are relatively new chains that are found in practically all of the big cities serving eat-in or take-away Nigerian fast food in a clean AC environment not too dissimilar from any other Westernised fast-food chain. Food here has been standardised throughout the branches – box of

3

chicken *jollof* rice, beefburger, *moin-moin*, Scotch egg, meat pies, doughnuts and so on. Mr Biggs now has branches in most cities and is one of the few places in Nigeria where you can buy a ready-made birthday cake. Their slogan is 'what a delicious experience', while Tastee Fried Chicken claims 'we do chicken right' and Tantalizers maintains that 'every bite a promise kept'. You'll either love it (easy food in AC), or hate it (everything is deep fried), so make up your own mind. Additionally in the northern cities a new chain of bakeries has opened up. The Chinese-owned Oasis Bakery sells cold drinks, tubs of ice cream, fresh bread and cakes and very good meat pies. Very inexplicably and very Nigerian, some of the branches are called Ostrich Bakery.

DRINKING Starting with the obvious, international branded soft drinks such as Coca-Cola, Fanta, Sprite and Schweppes lemon are available everywhere, from roadside stalls to buckets on top of people's heads, and in all the country's restaurants and bars. They're not always cold so check first before handing over the N50 or so it costs for a 350ml bottle – you give the bottle back as soon as you have finished. Occasionally you'll see disposable cans but these are quadruple the price of a bottle.

There are several brands of locally produced and hugely popular malt drinks in brown bottles; one such drink is brewed by Guinness, and is served very cold. It tastes like a thick, non-alcoholic Guinness. They're advertised as being very good for you and it's common to see a couple in a bar with the man drinking a beer and a woman drinking a malt drink. A drink called Chapmans is hard to find except in the more upmarket restaurants, and is expensive at about N250 for a glass, but is very refreshing; it's a deep red berry colour and tastes a bit like a non-alcoholic Pimms and is made with a good dose of angostura bitters and either tonic or lemonade with ice and a slice – like lemon or lime bitters. At most motor parks you'll see men trundling around on bicycles selling chilled flavoured yoghurt drinks. These taste nice, but I'd give them a wide berth as despite being served out of cooler boxes, you have no idea how many times they've warmed up in the sun. You're better off buying these from a supermarket.

Lipton tea bags are readily available, as are small tins of condensed milk, small packets of milk powder, and small tins of Nescafé. When ordering tea and coffee in a restaurant, this is what you get, and it invariably comes with bread. If you are unable to speak to anyone in the morning before a caffeine fix, I suggest you bring one of those electric elements you heat water with and a plastic or Thermos mug, as all the ingredients are available in Nigeria. In a hotel, you may wait for an hour before a simple cup of tea emerges from the hotel kitchen. All over Nigeria in the mornings, on the side of the road and in the motor parks, you'll see tea-and-bread sellers who serve huge plastic mugs of tea and a hunk of bread, but as they boil the sugar in the water, the tea is exceptionally sweet.

Bottled water is available, though sporadically so, so try and buy it when you see it. Expect to pay around N100 for a half-litre bottle. Much more common and sold literally everywhere are half-litre plastic packets of what is known as *pure water*. Not everyone trusts the purity of *pure water* and it's generally believed to be tap water, neatly packaged by *pure water* packaging machines that are freely advertised in the newspapers for anyone to buy and set up their own *pure water* business. (One Lebanese businessman I spoke to told me that this is exactly what happens.) Always presume that you are drinking ordinary tap water and not any kind of special mineral water. For this reason I would probably avoid them in Lagos and the bigger cities, where tap water is more likely to be contaminated. One *pure water* brand I saw in Sokoto was called 'Acceptable Water', which says it all.

The two main terms for food are *chop* and *food-is-ready*. Chop simply means food or a meal, and informal budget restaurants are generally referred to as a chop house, while a snack is a small chop. Food-is-ready needs little explanation; it simply means that there is food ready to eat instantly which doesn't have to be cooked after it has been ordered. In a restaurant, despite the fact that there are often extensive menus, you'll get used to asking 'what food-is-ready?' Alternatively, if you choose something from a menu that isn't already prepared, you'll be told that the 'food-isn't-ready' and that you will have to wait. Here is Kevin's account of ordering food in a chop house:

> One of the things that makes life in Nigeria more interesting is the process of ordering food at one of the many chop houses. You usually end up playing a guessing game that's oddly reminiscent of the Monty Python Cheese Shop sketch. The main rule of the game seems to be that the waiter/waitress must never reveal what food they actually have except in answer to a specific question. For example, asking 'what food do you have?' won't work. Instead you have to ask about each individual item that may or may not be available – pounded yam, rice, stew, egussi soup, white soup, garri, semovita, draw soup, etc. The staff won't tell you what's not available or list what is, instead you have to keep guessing until you find something they actually have.

Except in the northern cities, you won't have a problem finding alcohol, and there are many excellent brands of locally brewed beer, which are sold in big half-litre re-usable bottles for about N150. The most popular are Star and Gulder; of the two, Star has the lighter taste. Big bottles of dark Guinness are hugely popular, but it's not served in quite the same way as it is in the emerald isle; you'll get it very cold and, quite bizarrely, it usually comes with a straw. It's brewed to a recipe that keeps the tropical heat from spoiling it, so it's more strong and bitter than the Irish original. You'll need to ask for a glass. As Nigerian Breweries is under licence to the Heineken label, you'll sometimes see cans of Heineken, but, as it comes in cans and not re-usable bottles, they are more expensive at around N400–500.

Local drinks include *emu*, or palm wine, the favourite drink in southern Nigeria, which is a natural sweet, frothy juice with a foul smell. It has to be drunk fresh and is potently alcoholic, and gets more so as the day wears on; administer with care. The distilled version of palm wine is *ogogoro*, a strong local gin, but it's very discreetly sold. You'll sometimes see Gordon's Spark, which is a Nigerian version of an alcopop made with gin. Imported spirits and wines are expensive and can only be found in upmarket restaurants and hotels, and the few supermarkets dealing in imported goods, and are very rarely seen outside Lagos, Abuja or Port Harcourt.

SHOPPING AND BARGAINING

Nigeria is one big market and the country's economic and social character is founded on trade. Everyone is a buyer or seller and there are markets simply everywhere. As in many other African countries, shopping from a vehicle from streetside vendors is common, especially in Lagos where traffic is almost at a standstill anyway. You'll see hundreds of people hawking their wares on any city street, and you can buy the most unbelievable items, from cold drinks, *pure water*, towels, belts and net curtains, to blow-up Santa Clauses and god-awful oil paintings of God.

There are a few upmarket supermarkets in Nigeria dealing in imported goods, which tend to sell everything from food to household goods and clothes. More recently, modern glitzy malls are beginning to appear in Lagos and Abuja such as the Palms on the Lekki Peninsula (see page 136). These are home to local shops and imported South African chain stores as well as new cinemas showing Hollywood, not Nollywood, movies and to date are proving to be very popular. Then there is the mega shopping mall development of Tinapa in Calabar (see page 216), which hopes to attract shoppers from all over West Africa. These top-end shops are generally frequented by the expat community or the Nigerian elite, who can afford to buy at over-inflated prices, while the man and woman on the street shops right there on the street.

Prices in shops are fixed, but in the markets everything is negotiable. The Yoruba and the Hausa have their own accepted ways of bargaining. A Hausa trader uses the standard African method. It is expected that you offer about one-third of the asking price and go from there until a mutually agreed price is reached. However, a Yoruba trader bargains completely differently. They will give you a price and you immediately reduce it by N100, and if he or she agrees you reduce it again by N100; this goes on until the trader stops agreeing and that is the price you will pay. For both methods, if you still think the price is too high, walk away, and if you are not called back to continue the negotiations again, it means that the price is probably about right.

Visitors will find a number of curios and souvenirs to pick up and specific markets and shops are listed in the relevant chapters. Of these, cloth is the most prolific and is for sale in all the markets – Nigeria is renowned for the rich variety of designs, colours, materials and production techniques of its textile craftsmen (see under *Art*, page 40). There is also a fair amount of pottery, leatherwork, wood carvings, beads, jewellery, basketry, drums and masks on offer. Designs vary greatly, with many cities having their own distinctive style.

Crocodile products, cowrie shells and ivory can be bought in Nigeria, but it may be illegal to import them into your own country. Much of the ivory seen in the curio markets is plastic. However, the skins of leopard, cheetah, caracal, civet cat, and black and white colobus monkey; the elephant feet; the handbags from lion fur; and the various dried monkey heads, snakes and amphibians in the *juju* markets are very real and explain why these animals are now so rare in Nigeria's national parks. If you are buying antiquities (remember a trader can make something look old even if it isn't) then you are required to get a permit from the National Commission for Museum and Monuments to export it from Nigeria. In theory export permits can be obtained at any of the national museums in the country, but your best bet is to go to the museum in Lagos.

BUSINESS HOURS Most shops and offices are generally open from 08.00 to 17.00, Monday to Friday, and sometimes for a few hours on Saturday morning. Local markets are open Monday to Saturday 08.00–19.00, though some districts have night markets which stay open until midnight, and food stalls are usually the last to close. Government offices usually close by 15.00 each day. In the south the day of rest is usually Sunday; in the north it is Friday, reflecting the Christian–Muslim divide, though in the north you'll find that all Christian-run businesses will stay open on Friday and vice versa on a Sunday in the south. Note that Sanitation Day is the last Saturday in the month, when between 07.00 and 10.30 traffic is not allowed on the streets, and in theory people are supposed to clean up around them. This does actually happen, although a little half-heartedly, in Lagos.

WOMEN TRAVELLERS

Nigerian women all over the country travel on their own, be it on long journeys by bus or for a short hop on the back of an *okada*. Every time I jumped on the back of an *okada*, however, everyone stopped and stared incredulously. But the attention you get stops there, and you will soon get used to having a million pairs of eyes on you. The most prevalent attitude you are going to meet is complete bemusement. Nigerian society is conducted on the street and Nigerians are by character great socialisers and talkers, and they'll often approach you for a chat. Almost all of the time it is just out of inquisitiveness and simply just to say 'welcome'. Not once did I receive any rude or suggestive comments, and (only!) once was I approached in a bar environment to ask if I wanted company – as happens anywhere in the world. The guy in question left when I declined. But remember to turn down unwanted attention very politely – pride is important for Nigerian men.

One word of advice for women travellers (at least for anyone over the age of 21!) is to say that you are married even if you're not. This is not for any practical reason; you certainly won't be asked if you are married to get a hotel room, even in the Muslim north. But if you are over 21 and not married, Nigerians, male and female, will not get it, and you'll be embroiled in a lengthy and analytical conversation about why you're not married. Believe me, it's just easier to say you are.

Although there have been occasions in Nigerian history where rape and sexual assault have been prevalent, they have only really occurred during war times when the army has used rape as a weapon against women. Other than that, sexual crime is not common in Nigerian society. Hopefully this is because it doesn't happen rather than because it's not being reported.

The most important thing for a woman to consider is to dress modestly, especially in the Muslim north, though despite the strict Sharia code, Western women are not expected to cover their hair. This is because many Christians live in the northern cities and wear what they like, though as a visitor it's always sensible to respect the local customs. There are other Islamic considerations to take into account: women are generally not welcome at mosques, particularly at prayer times, and as prayers often happen outside mosques or in open prayer compounds at the side of the road or in markets, it is a good idea not to get too close, and under no circumstances should you stop and stare. In the northern cities, my male fellow traveller went to the main Friday prayers to see several thousand men praying in and around the main mosque. It wasn't appropriate for me to go and he says that all the women in the area simply melted away during prayer time.

GAY TRAVELLERS

In early 2007, the National Assembly deemed homosexual activity as illegal in Nigeria. It's now punishable by up to five years in prison in the south and, under Sharia law in the north, possibly by death.

CULTURAL ETIQUETTE

GREETINGS Greetings are highly valued in Nigeria and neglecting to greet another person is a sign of disrespect. Shaking hands with everyone is customary on meeting and departing. Because of the diversity of cultures, customs and dialects in Nigeria, English is widely used throughout the country for exchanging greetings even if the conversation continues in another language. Before any conversation, even if it's a quick request to ask directions or if you are buying something in a shop or at a stall, you will be expected to go through a whole range of greetings, first starting with 'Hello' and 'How are you?' and responding politely to the answers. Everywhere you'll go you'll hear 'You are welcome', a phrase which is used simply to say 'Hello', shouted at you from the street. And more formally, 'Good afternoon madam' – in fact, rather wonderfully you'll get 'Good morning', 'Good afternoon' and 'Good evening' from the same person if you see them at various occasions during the day. We also got *oyibo* or *batauri* (both meaning white person in the south and north respectively) yelled out to us in the street, but unlike in East Africa where people yell out *mzungu* (white person) repeatedly and aggressively when they are usually asking for things, in Nigeria *oyibo* and *batauri* fall out of people's mouths as yelps of surprise. Rather amusingly, we also got Mr and Mrs White!

It is respectable to address Nigerians by their surnames until you know them very well, and titles are important. There are many chiefs, high chiefs, doctors, professors, madams, princes, emirs and honorable so-and-sos, and Nigerians love to have lengthy names. Children generally address their elders with a title – Mr or Miss before someone's name, even if they are using the first name. Seniority matters. Treat anyone older than yourself with civility and respect, whether it's a chauffeur, a gate man or a corporate director. Nigerians often wink at their children if they want them to leave the room.

Gestures differ from one ethnic group to another. In Yorubaland it is a sign of respect for women to curtsey when meeting someone (we got 'bobbed' at a lot), and to enquire after relations. You'll have to adapt slightly to avoid further questions: 'Yes my grandmother is very well' (dead for 20 years) or 'My husband's business is going very well' (not married). Visiting family and friends is an important part in maintaining ties, and unexpected guests are welcome, simply because planning ahead is not always possible in areas where there are no phones. Finally, no matter how run down it may appear in Western eyes, Nigerians are generally proud of their country. Complaints from visitors about the traffic, rubbish, power cuts, people urinating in the streets and so on will not go down well.

DASHING *Dash* = bribe, tip, donation, give (verb and noun). Despite Nigeria's huge reputation as one of the most corrupt countries in the world (which it is at business and government level), as a simple tourist you are unlikely to experience many instances of being asked for a bribe. The notable exception is at the roadblocks (see box page 75), and even then you'll only be asked if you are driving your own vehicle. The only time we paid *dash* was when we extended our visas at the government immigration department.

However, it is a different story if you are working in Nigeria, when bribery is very much part of getting things done on a business level. One story I heard was from an expat who was working for a telecommunications company installing reception towers for a cell phone company. The *dash* needed to pay landowners for the proposed sites was included in his official company budget. In the event that someone performs a 'kind' act for you, such as carrying your luggage to your room, then of course you should offer them a small tip.

There are also odd occasions when (quite rightly) you need to pay *dash* for a museum guide or to people who very kindly agree to be photographed. Generally Nigerians do not tip, and in the more upmarket restaurants and hotels, 10% service charge is added on to your bill. And even in the cheapest of hotels, if someone brings food or drink to your room, a small fee for 'room service' is added to your bill. It's up to you if you want to leave any extra tip: it will be greatly appreciated, but certainly not expected.

The only other times you'll be asked for a *dash* is from beggars. They are prevalent all over Nigeria and unfortunately some are seriously handicapped. One lady in the south asked me why we wanted to travel to the north: 'There, people only have one leg or arm,' she declared. Whatever southerners think, this is obviously not true, but there are certainly more beggars in the poorer regions. There will be countless occasions on the streets and in the motor parks where someone will shove a plate in front of you, but not once did we find beggars irritating or intrusive – I live in South Africa and the beggars there are far more aggressive. And very refreshingly, nowhere in Nigeria did we hear '(Please) give me...', a phrase uttered all over Africa in any country that is used to seeing tourists. In Nigeria there simply are no tourists and the people there have no idea about the concept of asking and being readily handed something by a Westerner who doesn't know any better. Nigerians themselves tend to respond to beggars, especially better-off Muslims who frequently *dash* poor people who collect around mosques. In vehicles in motor parks, after people have paid for their seat, they'll often hand over the small change to a beggar through the window, and if at the end of the day a chop or food-is-ready stall has left-over food, the women running the stalls will often feed the street children and beggars.

PUBLIC TOILETS What public toilets? The only communal toilets you will find are in a few hotels and restaurants; none of them are that flash and remember that the more basic chop houses or food-is-ready stalls are not going to have any facilities. As an *oyibo* you will get away with asking if you can use them, regardless of whether or not you are eating or staying in that establishment. Everyone, especially men, goes to the toilet in public. Oddly, the Muslim men in the north squat and urinate beneath their long cloths, whereas men in the south just get their tackle out. Although you will see women crouching down in their skirts at the side of the road and behind walls, it's not as common a sight as it is for men.

If you get caught short the problem is deciding where to go – there are people everywhere and there's very little privacy. If travelling by public transport sometimes someone will stop the driver if there is some urgency to go to the toilet. If this happens go then, as once at your urban destination there may not be anywhere to go until you get inside your hotel room. If you are absolutely desperate, ask a local of the same gender and perhaps she or he can recommend somewhere. Most Nigerians are not going to know the terms bathroom, restroom, take a leak or a piss, or even the words dump or shit; in one restaurant I asked a waiter where the toilet was and he replied by asking if I wanted 'to easy myself'? Even if you have found a toilet, the chances are there will be no water, the toilets themselves won't flush, and you won't be able to wash your hands. You may want to consider carrying wet-wipes with you, and you'll most certainly need to have a roll of toilet paper handy.

All over Nigeria you will see the rudimentary signs painted on walls that say 'Do not urinate here'. On a wall in Ibadan I saw the words 'Do not urinate here (again)' and in Calabar 'Do not urinate here by order of a native doctor' accompanied by the skull and crossbones sign! In one motor park in Lagos we actually saw a few modern 'port-a-loos' with signs saying 'Pay as you shit' and an advertisement for the company saying 'Our business is shit business'. Fabulous!

MEDIA AND COMMUNICATIONS

Nigeria has all the modern communication systems any country in the developing world could wish for – landline telephones, cellular networks, internet service providers and satellite television. But with a massive demand for communication tools and an infrastructure that is perilously overloaded, and with unreliable power sources and high maintenance demands, communication is far from reliable and interruptions in services are the norm. Go there expecting nothing to work, and when it does be gratefully delighted.

TELEPHONE The national phone company is called **NITEL** (Nigerian Telecommunications). Nigeria's landline telephone system is totally inadequate and poorly maintained, and phone lines are more than not often out of order. It's rapidly approaching total collapse, with whole cities being without landline services for weeks. You will notice from our listings that we often give more than one telephone number for businesses and organisations, because many companies have installed multiple phone lines as one or more of their lines may be down. This is attested to by the thousands of tangled telephone wires hanging between all the telephone poles. Many hotels have given up on landline numbers altogether and are increasingly giving out cell phone numbers. However, these are usually the personal numbers of the reception staff, so can change frequently.

There are public NITEL offices in the main cities, from where in theory you can make local and international calls. You need to buy a **phonecard** from the attendant, who usually has a list of call charges so you can work out what price to pay for a card depending on how long you think you may want to talk. A N300 card will give you around two minutes to Europe. There are only usually one or two phones that you can phone internationally from and you'll need a specific international card. A scam here is that touts buy up all the international cards from the NITEL office and then sell them outside for more than they are worth.

For some unfathomable reason it is sometimes easier to get an international line out of Nigeria than to make a local phone call around the corner, and if you do get through anywhere expect to be cut off at any time. To get a line out of Nigeria first dial 009 followed by the country code. Dialling into Nigeria, the international code is 234. To make a reverse-charge (collect) call, phone the international operator on 191. Note that the fax machine has become almost obsolete in Nigeria and fax numbers rarely work. International calls can be made directly from a few of the more upmarket hotels, with the usual premium rate attached, and some internet cafés double up as call centres.

The use of **cell phones** (commonly referred to as GSM in Nigeria: Global System for Mobile Communications) has soared in Nigeria and 2007 estimates put the amount of cell phones in the country at almost 40 million, and for the large part cell phones have replaced the landline system. If your own cell phone has international roaming, you should be able to pick up coverage, and you can buy Sim cards and top-up cards everywhere. The local providers include MTN, V Mobile, Globacom and MTEL. The latter has the largest rural coverage in the country. Again, like the landlines, services can be hopelessly erratic and unreliable. Here is an anecdote from Kevin:

> On my travels I've ended up watching a lot of TV in hotel rooms. Tonight the
> Nigerian version of *Who Wants to be a Millionaire* was on. The contestant was a bit
> stuck, so phoned a friend. The friend's side of the conversation went something like
> this: 'Hello? I can't hear you. Who is speaking? Hello?...' It continued like that until
> his 30 seconds ran out. The joke is that the show is sponsored by MTN.

Phone stalls Other than personal cell phones, the most common way that Nigerians make local phone calls is from the phone stalls on the street, which offer both landline phones (brought out from the nearest building on a very long extension cord) and GSM or cell phones. Many thousands of people have their own business of a phone stall that usually consists of one plastic table, two plastic chairs (one for the attendant with a working wrist watch, and one for the caller), one yellow umbrella usually sponsored by the cellular company such as MTN, and one phone. You give the attendant the telephone number, he or she dials it (sometimes repeatedly) until someone answers and then hands the phone to you. It's marvellously simple. Throughout the country costs are around N30–40 per minute nationally, and slightly less for a local call. Very occasionally you'll see phones that can call internationally and they cost around N100 per minute.

MAJOR CITY CODES

City	Code	City	Code	City	Code
Abeokuta	039	Ibadan	020	Maiduguri	076
Abuja	090	Jos	073	Makurdi	044
Bauchi	077	Kaduna	062	Oshogbo	035
Benin City	052	Kano	064	Port Harcourt	084
Calabar	087	Katsina	065	Zaria	069
Enugu	042	Lagos	010		

POST The Nigerian postal service is run by Nipost (www.nipost.gov.ng) and the website lists addresses of all post offices. Post used to be painfully slow, but these days it's fairly reliable, though never send anything valuable by post – use a courier company. Stamps are in denominations of N20, N30, N40 and N50, and it costs about N120–150 to send a letter to Europe, which should take 2–3 weeks. Post offices are generally open Monday to Friday 08.00–17.00 and Saturday 09.00–13.00. Some offer services for EMS Speedpost and some, like nearly all of the banks, are agents for Western Union.

ELECTRIC DEVICES Electricity is 220 volts at 50Hz. If an appliance does not fall within this specification then you need an adapter or voltage converter. Three-pin British-style 13 amp plugs and sockets are the norm in Nigeria but don't assume all sockets have been earthed. In most buildings the electricity supply is precariously overloaded and in parts broken – there are wires hanging all over the place and a Nigerian fuse box would take pride of place in an electricity museum if such a place existed. Be very wary of touching any electrical socket or appliance that looks especially dodgy.

Power cuts are common all day every day, particularly during the dry season when there is not enough hydro-electric power to feed the national grid. A torch and spare batteries are essential, though almost all hotels have backup generators. In the event that you are travelling with a laptop, remember that power surges can be especially damaging (and if you're visiting from the USA, you may need to bring a voltage regulator).

RADIO AND TELEVISION The Nigeria Television Authority has some 40 stations across the country, which are generally all local state stations. Programmes are broadcast in English as well as Yoruba, Hausa and Igbo. You are not going to watch much on these except the local news between 18.00 and 20.00, although they occasionally show CNN during the day. The South African media corporation, MTN, has set up multi-channel subscription television under its offshoot company called DSTV (Digital Satellite Television). An increasing number of hotels, even some of the cheaper ones, as well as bars and restaurants, subscribe to DSTV and, although the packages vary, the service generally includes M-Net (South Africa's best-quality channel with up-to-date movies, documentaries and serials), Movie Magic (mostly one- to two-year-old movies), BBC World, CNN and Supersport (South Africa's 24-hour sports channel).

3

More and more individual Nigerians are subscribing to the service if nothing more to watch the football (including the Manchester United FC TV satellite channel, whose existence I didn't even know about before going to Nigeria) and Africa Magic (a channel that only shows Nigerian 'Nollywood' movies). Even in the cheapest chop house you may find all the occupants glued to an especially gripping 'Nollywood' movie on the TV in the corner. (See under TV in *Glossary of accommodation terms* on page 81 for more details.)

Nigeria has well over 200 radio stations, so the best way to find out what is available is to use the search button on your radio. Consequently, radio is hugely competitive and a number of FM stations have emerged, with Ray Power (100.5 FM), Cool FM (96.9 FM) and Rhythm (93.7 FM) being the most popular. Travellers with short-wave radios can pick up Voice of America, the World Service and Radio France Internationale. However, these do not broadcast 24 hours a day and their frequencies and times change throughout the year. It is worth checking their websites for schedules and programming.

INTERNET AND EMAIL Internet cafés are open everywhere for easy and affordable internet access, though speed and availability of the web varies depending on whether the café uses an international service provider via satellite or the inferior and unreliable NITEL. Remember never to use internet banking in a Nigerian internet café. Servers are painfully slow compared with those in Europe or the USA, though on occasion you'll find one that is super-quick. Increasingly, Nigerians are accessing the internet by using their phones as modems and in the cities the internet service providers have established radio connectivity. Often, as you do for photocopying, you pay slightly more for an hour's internet time 'during gen' than 'during NEPA' (see pages 79 and 80 for an explanation of these terms). Expect to pay in the region of N150 per hour. Finally, be aware that locals may well use the term 'cyber café' rather than 'internet café'.

NEWSPAPERS AND MAGAZINES In Lagos, thanks to the frequency of arrivals of international airlines, you can buy up-to-date international newspapers and magazines at vastly inflated prices from the bookshops of the major hotels. These include one- or two-day-old newspapers including the *Telegraph*, *The Times*, the *European*, *Le Monde*, *USA Today* and the *International Herald Tribune*, and magazines as far ranging as *PC World* and *Hello!* The Nigerian press is mostly privately owned, though the *New Nigerian* is state-owned, and thus is fairly open and opinionated (and sometimes downright funny). Local English-language newspapers include the *Guardian*, the *Comet*, *This Day* (the paper whose articles caused controversy during the 2002 Miss World competition), *Daily Times*, *Daily News*, *Vanguard* and several others, though few feature much international news. There are also scores of weekly news magazines that in presentation at least have copied the style of the US *Times* and *Newsweek* (also available).

4

Health and Safety

Nigeria's poor infrastructure, colossal population, poverty, terrible roads and high crime rate combine to create what can only be described as not a very healthy or safe place to visit. Travelling in tropical Africa exposes us to diseases caused by parasites, bacteria and viruses, some so bizarre we may never have heard of them before. Illnesses are passed around in food and water, or by insects and bugs, and can even be contracted from passing an infected person on the street. Added to this is the high crime rate and manic, highly publicised congestion on the roads. If you are still in some doubt about going to Nigeria then this is the chapter that is likely to scare you off for good. However, remember that with the right precautions and a sensible attitude, the following events or illnesses are unlikely to trouble you. Getting fully acquainted with them in the first place, and knowing what to do if something goes wrong when you get there, can minimise all Nigeria's health and safety risks. Prevention is the best way to stay healthy and safe. For this reason it's important to digest the information in this chapter right through to the end, which will help you to prepare for your trip effectively. To put things in perspective, after malaria, which can be prevented by taking the right precautions, the biggest danger for a traveller in Nigeria is being involved in a road accident.

✚ HEALTH   *with Dr Felicity Nicholson*

It's important to mention right from the start that Nigeria's healthcare system is seriously inadequate. Do not even consider going if you have an existing medical condition that needs regular attention or if you think you might be pregnant. On the other hand, if you are a traveller with adequate medical insurance or an expat with healthcare sponsored by your company, then the chances are that top-class facilities will be made available to you in the case of an emergency, and people who contract serious injury or illness will be evacuated to their country of origin. Obviously there are under-developed areas, urban as well as rural; Lagos is one of the unhealthiest places on earth, with poor sanitation, dire healthcare facilities, and waste and rubbish problems. These are places where infectious diseases thrive, but they won't pose too much of a threat to tourists or business travellers who pay attention to hygiene and to what they are eating and drinking, and who stay in an adequate hotel.

BEFORE YOU GO
Preparation Ideally you should visit your GP or travel clinic at least eight weeks before your departure to discuss your health generally and to organise the relevant immunisations and malaria medication. If you don't already know it, this is the time to find out what blood group you are. Visit your dentist if you are going to be away for some time, and if you have a serious allergy or long-term condition such as diabetes or epilepsy make sure someone knows about it, or get a Medic Alert

bracelet. Nigeria has a serious problem with fake drugs (see box on page 95) – some of which can be lethal – and imported medical products, if they are genuine in the first place, are very expensive. Ensure that you bring any necessary prescription or over-the-counter medication with you, and if you have to buy drugs in Nigeria only go to a reputable recommended pharmacist.

Travel insurance Don't leave home without it. Comprehensive medical insurance is essential and the cover must include repatriation to your home country by air in case of an emergency. Remember to carry the details and phone number of the insurance company with you.

Immunisations Immunisation against **yellow fever** is essential and proof may be required on entry, and always if you are coming from another yellow fever infected area. There is a real risk of contracting yellow fever, particularly in the bigger cities. **Cholera** is a serious risk in high-density urban areas, so if you have time then consider having the oral cholera vaccine (Dukoral) now available in the UK. This palatable berry-flavoured drink is said to offer about 75% protection against the more common strains of cholera. For adults and children six years and over, two doses are needed, taken at least one week but no more than six weeks apart. Ideally the second dose should be taken at least one week before entering an infected area. Two doses of vaccine will provide cover for two years. For children aged two to five, three doses are needed for the same efficacy, but protection lasts only for six months. Despite World Health Organisation guidelines issued in 1973, stating that a cholera vaccination certificate is not a condition of entry to Nigeria, there have been instances of certain nationals being asked to produce proof of vaccination on entry. If you don't have time to take the vaccine or are going for just a short visit (less than three–four weeks) the easiest way round this is to get your doctor to stamp your vaccination card with a 'cholera exempt' stamp.

Typhoid and **hepatitis A** and **B** are present in Nigeria and immunisations are highly recommended. **Meningitis** and **rabies** immunisations should also be seriously considered. Routine immunisations, such as for **tetanus**, **diphtheria** and **polio**, should be reviewed and updated. If you do decide to have an armful of jabs, start organising them at least six weeks before departure, and remember that a yellow fever certificate becomes valid only ten days after you've had the vaccination.

Children If you are travelling with children, especially if you are an expat who intends to take your family with you to Nigeria, they should in addition be properly protected against whooping cough, haemophilus influenzae, mumps, measles and rubella (German measles). An invaluable book is *Your Child Abroad: A Travel Health Guide* by Dr Jane Wilson-Howarth and Dr Matthew Ellis (Bradt Tavel Guides, 2005).

Malaria Malaria exists *all* year round *all* over Nigeria, including in urban areas, and is the biggest health threat to Nigerians. It's essential to take sensible malaria preventative steps. The obvious advice is to avoid getting bitten in the first place. Wear long trousers and sleeves in the evening and use insect repellents, and choose a hotel room that is as mossie proof as possible. (See *Insects and bugs*, page 97, for further advice on how to avoid mosquito bites.)

Malaria kills an estimated one million Africans annually, and is the biggest health threat to travellers in tropical Africa. There are four types of malaria, but only one, the falciparum strain, can lead to death if not treated promptly. In Nigeria 90–95% of all malaria is caused by the potentially deadly falciparum strain. As someone who has had malaria more times than she would care to remember, I cannot stress here strongly enough how important it is to prepare yourself against catching malaria *before* going to Nigeria. All malaria is dangerous but the falciparum strain of malaria has been known to kill in less than 24 hours.

Malaria is caused by a parasite carried in the saliva of the female *Anopheles* mosquito, which flies between dusk and dawn, generally near to the ground. The parasite is transmitted into the bloodstream through a mosquito bite, where it will multiply and infect the blood, liver and eventually the brain. It starts out as something resembling severe flu, with symptoms such as headaches, fever, lethargy and aching limbs, and sometimes vomiting and diarrhoea. Soon after the sufferer experiences extreme fevers that come in waves, inducing excessive sweating and shivering, a rapid rise in body temperature, and fluid loss. If the disease is allowed to develop further, what follows are fits, delirium, coma, organ failure and eventually death.

It's important to remember that malarial symptoms can subside for up to 48 hours before returning, so just because you may start to feel better it doesn't mean you don't have malaria – still get treated. The disease has an incubation period of between a few days and several weeks so you can fall ill some time after an infected mosquito has bitten you. If you are pregnant or have very small children, it would be wise to consider *not* travelling to such a high-risk malarial area; such travellers are likely to succumb rapidly to the disease.

Prophylactic drugs Despite valiant efforts there is still no vaccine against malaria, so the only sensible option is to take prophylactic drugs and use insect repellents. Prophylactic drugs greatly reduce the chances of getting the disease and if you still contract malaria while taking the drugs, you are likely to get a milder bout. Travellers to Africa are unable to build up any resistance to malaria and those who don't take prophylactic drugs will be risking their lives. The falciparum strain has been reported to be resistant to chloroquine. So, the combination prophylactic of chloroquine and Proguanil/Paludrine is only used as a last resort when there is no other tablet suitable. At the time of writing, the prophylactics advised are mefloquine (Lariam), doxycycline or atovaquone (Malarone). Because no malaria drug is 100% effective, seek immediate medical attention for any fever or flu-like symptoms occurring within three months of your return home, and be sure to tell your doctor your travel history.

Lariam or mefloquine (250mg tablet once a week) is effective but doesn't suit everyone; 20–30% of users suffer from significant side-effects and have to discontinue use and change to an alternative prophylactic. Psychological effects such as paranoia and psychosis have been reported in some cases and it is not advised for anyone with a history of psychiatric problems or epilepsy. It should only be taken on a doctor's recommendation and if you have never used it before then you should start at least two and a half weeks before departure to check that it suits you. If you have used Lariam before then you can start one week before, and either way the drug should be continued for four weeks after leaving the last malarial area.

Doxycycline (100mg daily), a broad-based antibiotic, is a good alternative prophylactic if you can't take Lariam, and you only need to start taking it one day before arriving and again four weeks after being in a malarial area. Doxy is not advised for pregnant women or children under 12. There are few side-effects, but women on the pill should use alternative forms of contraception for the first four weeks, and between 1% and 3% of people taking it suffer from sun sensitivity on their skin. If this happens then you must stop taking the doxycycline as it is an allergic reaction which may get worse. Malarone is a newer and very effective drug that is started one to two days before arriving and that needs to be taken for only seven days after visiting a malarial area. Reports so far record that it is as effective as Lariam and both are probably slightly more effective than doxycycline. It is expensive but it has the advantage of having fewer side-effects.

If you are going to Nigeria to work on a long contract, it's perhaps not advisable to continually take anti-malarial drugs for what feasibly could be a number of years. Discuss this with your doctor. Some expats I spoke to took nothing and never got malaria, though they often rarely left their air-conditioned homes, offices and cars, while another I spoke to had been taking Lariam for six years and when he stopped he got malaria! However, this practice is not to be recommended as Lariam should not be continued for more than two years.

Diagnosis and treatment Self-test kits for malaria are now available from some pharmacists and you may want to consider carrying one with you. However, they are far from 100% accurate, and if you've never had malaria before I would strongly advise against using them. For anyone who has had malaria before and instantly recognises the symptoms that are unique to their body, they are useful to carry. But for those who have contracted the disease for the first time, don't know what is happening to their body, and are probably too ill to carry out the test correctly enough to make the right diagnosis, it is dangerous to rely on self-test kits.

If you think you may have symptoms, and have a very high suspicion of all symptoms however vague they may be, get a full malarial blood test taken by a doctor as soon as possible. Local doctors in Nigeria are more than familiar with the disease and any clinic or hospital will be able to give you a malaria test. The most common form of treatment is quinine and Fansidar, because it is cheap. However, it is no longer considered to be the most effective treatment. Consult a specialist before you go to get the most appropriate medication. Newer and more effective treatments include Malarone and Riamet. Halfan – a previously popular treatment – is no longer recommended for anyone. Note that the Royal Homeopathic Hospital in the UK does not advocate any homeopathic options for malaria prevention or treatment.

✚ **TRAVEL CLINICS AND HEALTH INFORMATION** A full list of current travel clinic websites worldwide is available from the International Society of Travel Medicine on www.istm.org. For other journey preparation information, consult www.tripprep.com. Information about various medications may be found on www.emedicine.com. For information on malaria prevention, see www.preventingmalaria.info.

UK

Berkeley Travel Clinic 32 Berkeley St, London W1J 8EL (near Green Park tube station); ☎ 020 7629 6233.
Cambridge Travel Clinic 48a Mill Rd, Cambridge CB1 2AS; ☎ 01223 367362;
e enquiries@travelcliniccambridge.co.uk; www.travelcliniccambridge.co.uk. Open Tue–Fri 12.00–19.00, Sat 10.00–16.00.
Edinburgh Travel Clinic Regional Infectious Diseases Unit, Ward 41 OPD, Western General Hospital, Crewe Rd South, Edinburgh EH4 2UX; ☎ 0131 537 2822; www.mvm.ed.ac.uk. Travel helpline (☎ 0906 589 0380) open weekdays 09.00–12.00. Provides inoculations & antimalarial prophylaxis, & advises

on travel-related health risks.
Fleet Street Travel Clinic 29 Fleet St, London EC4Y 1AA; ☎ 020 7353 5678; www.fleetstreetclinic.com. Vaccinations, travel products & latest advice.
Hospital for Tropical Diseases Travel Clinic, Mortimer Market Bldg, Capper St (off Tottenham Ct Rd), London WC1E 6AU; ☎ 020 7388 9600; www.thehtd.org. Offers consultations & advice, & is able to provide all necessary drugs & vaccines for travellers. Runs a healthline (☎ 0906 133 7733) for country-specific information & health hazards. Also stocks nets, water purification equipment & personal protection measures.

Interhealth Worldwide Partnership House, 157 Waterloo Rd, London SE1 8US; ☎ 020 7902 9000; www.interhealth.org.uk. Competitively priced, one-stop travel health service. All profits go to their affiliated company, InterHealth, which provides health care for overseas workers on Christian projects.

Liverpool School of Medicine Pembroke Pl, Liverpool L3 5QA; ☎ 0151 708 9393; f 0151 705 3370; www.liv.ac.uk/lstm.

MASTA (Medical Advisory Service for Travellers Abroad) Moorfield Rd, Yeadon, Leeds, West Yorkshire LS19 7BN; ☎ 0113 238 7500; www.masta-travel-health.com. Provides travel health advice, anti-malarials & vaccinations. There are over 25 MASTA pre-travel clinics in Britain; call or check online for the nearest. Clinics also sell mosquito nets, medical kits, insect protection & travel hygiene products.

NHS travel website www.fitfortravel.scot.nhs.uk. Provides country-by-country advice on immunisation & malaria, plus details of recent developments, & a list of relevant health organisations.

Nomad Travel Store Clinic 3–4 Wellington Terrace, Turnpike Lane, London N8 0PX; ☎ 020 8889 7014; travel-health line during office hours ☎ 0906 863 3414; e sales@nomadtravel.co.uk; www.nomadtravel.co.uk. Also at 40 Bernard St, London WC1N 1LJ; ☎ 020 7833 4114; 52 Grosvenor Gardens, London SW1W 0AG; ☎ 020 7823 5823; & 43 Queens Rd, Bristol BS8 1QH; ☎ 0117 922 6567. For health advice, equipment such as mosquito nets & other anti-bug devices, & an excellent range of adventure travel gear. Clinics also in Bristol & Southhampton.

Trailfinders Travel Clinic 194 Kensington High St, London W8 7RG; ☎ 020 7938 3999; www.trailfinders.com/travelessentials/travelclinic.htm.

Travelpharm The Travelpharm website, www.travelpharm.com, offers up-to-date guidance on travel-related health & has a range of medications available through their online mini-pharmacy.

Irish Republic

Tropical Medical Bureau Grafton Street Medical Centre, Grafton Bldgs, 34 Grafton St, Dublin 2; ☎ 1 671 9200; www.tmb.ie. A useful website specific to tropical destinations. Also check website for other bureaux locations throughout Ireland.

USA

Centers for Disease Control 1600 Clifton Rd, Atlanta, GA 30333; ☎ 800 311 3435; travellers' health hotline f 888 232 3299; www.cdc.gov/travel. The central source of travel information in the USA. The invaluable *Health Information for International Travel*, published annually, is available from the Division of Quarantine at this address.

Connaught Laboratories Pasteur Merieux Connaught, Route 611, PO Box 187, Swiftwater, PA 18370; ☎ 800 822 2463. They will send a free list of specialist tropical-medicine physicians in your state.

IAMAT (International Association for Medical Assistance to Travelers) 1623 Military Rd #279, Niagara Falls, NY14304-1745; ☎ 716 754 4883; e info@iamat.org; www.iamat.org. A non-profit organisation that provides lists of English-speaking doctors abroad.

International Medicine Center 915 Gessner Road, Suite 525, Houston, TX 77024; ☎ 713 550 2000; www.traveldoc.com.

Canada

IAMAT Suite 1, 1287 St Clair Av W, Toronto, Ontario M6E 1B8; ☎ 416 652 0137; www.iamat.org.

TMVC Suite 314, 1030 W Georgia St, Vancouver BC V6E 2Y3; ☎ 1 888 288 8682; www.tmvc.com. Private clinic with several outlets in Canada.

Australia, New Zealand, Singapore

IAMAT PO Box 5049, Christchurch 5, New Zealand; www.iamat.org.

TMVC ☎ 1300 65 88 44; www.tmvc.com.au. Clinics in Australia, New Zealand & Singapore, including Auckland, Canterbury Arcade, 170 Queen St, Auckland; ☎ 9 373 3531; Brisbane, 75a Astor Terrace, Spring Hill, QLD 4000; ☎ 7 3815 6900; Melbourne, 393 Little Bourke St, 2nd floor, Melbourne, VIC 3000; ☎ 3 9602 5788; Sydney, Dymocks Bldg, 7th floor, 428 George St, Sydney, NSW 2000; ☎ 2 9221 7133.

South Africa and Namibia

SAA-Netcare Travel Clinics Sanlam Building, 19 Fredman Drive, Sandton, P Bag X34, Benmore, JHB, Gauteng, 2010; www.travelclinic.co.za. Clinics throughout South Africa.

TMVC NHC Health Centre, Cnr Beyers Naude & Waugh Northcliff; PO Box 48499, Roosevelt Park, 2129 (postal address); ☎ 011 888 7488; www.tmvc.com.au. Consult website for details of other clinics in South Africa & Namibia.

Switzerland

IAMAT 57 Chemin des Voirets, 1212 Grand Lancy, Geneva; www.iamat.org.

Further reading
Wilson-Howarth, Dr Jane, and Ellis, Dr Matthew *Your Child Abroad: A Travel Health Guide*, Bradt Travel Guides, 2005
Wilson-Howarth, Dr Jane, *Bugs, Bites & Bowels*, Cadogan, 2006

MEDICAL KIT A comprehensive medical kit is an important part of your luggage when going to Nigeria, especially if you are staying long term. Although nobody wants to lumber themselves up with too heavy a medical kit when travelling, it is important to remember that Nigeria has an appalling reputation for supplying fake and out-of-date drugs, so it is best to go well prepared. None of the items listed here are readily available in Nigeria so take sufficient amounts with you.

Your medical kit should contain:
- malaria prophylactics
- malaria treatment (only to be used if prescribed for you by a doctor)
- soluble aspirin or paracetamol (good for gargling for mouth and throat infections and to reduce fever and aches and pains)
- iodine (for sterilising water and cleaning wounds)
- antiseptic cream or powder
- antihistamine cream or tablets (for irritated mossie bites)
- Imodium (a standby for when diarrhoea occurs at an awkward time)
- oral rehydration sachets (to replace lost salts during diarrhoea)
- a broad-based antibiotic such as doxycycline or Ciproxin (Ciprofloxacin) or Flagyl or tinidazole (for problem diarrhoea)
- bandages, plasters and tweezers
- sunblock
- mosquito repellent
- condoms
- contact-lens cleaning solution
- sanitary wear (all rarely found in Nigeria).

HEALTHCARE IN NIGERIA
Medical facilities Nigeria's government-provided public healthcare facilities are of a poor standard and are subject to shortages of doctors and nurses, drugs, equipment and even electricity. Indeed, at one point in 1995, at the height of the 'brain drain' during Abacha's term, there were more Nigerian doctors operating in the USA than in the whole of Nigeria. You would be ill advised to seek treatment in a public hospital and it is essential that you take a sufficient supply of drugs or medication to meet personal needs. There are some adequate private facilities in Lagos and Abuja where the standards approach those of Europe, but facilities are expensive and doctors and hospitals often expect immediate cash payment up front for health services. Medical insurance is essential. In this book we list medical facilities recommended to us by Nigeria's expat community, but if you are in any doubt consult your embassy in Nigeria for their recommendation of a clinic or hospital used by diplomats.

Health hazards
Bilharzia Bilharzia or *schistosomiasis* is a tiny parasite carried by freshwater snails and is prevalent in Nigeria's rivers and dams. The parasite burrows into human skin and multiplies in the bloodstream, eventually working its way up to the bladder and intestine, where it lay its eggs. Symptoms vary but can include blood in the urine or faeces, fever and flu-like symptoms, lethargy and swelling of the liver or spleen. The disease is much harder to treat when advanced, though it doesn't cause too much discomfort if caught early enough and it's just a matter of taking a one-

The National Food and Drugs Administrative Control (NAFDAC) is the Nigerian government agency in charge of the regulation and control of processed food and drugs. In Nigeria all locally produced items are supposed to go through checks with NAFDAC that ensure that it is fit for consumption. You'll see the NAFDAC logo on packets of *pure water* for example. It's a powerful organisation and since 2001 the head of NAFDAC, Dora Akunyili, has been embarking on a campaign to root out fake, sub-standard and adulterated drugs, and to ensure that items imported into Nigeria and made in Nigeria meet the required standards. When she started the job, the World Health Organisation had estimated that 50% of drugs on the market in Nigeria were fake.

The illegal production of fake drugs has been big business in Nigeria over the last 20 years and sugar or aspirin, for example, are often substituted for the real ingredient of any given drug, though sometimes more sinister ingredients such as arsenic have been used. In some cases, diseases such as malaria and tuberculosis were being treated by nothing more than sugar syrup or chalk tablets.

Akunyili has had much success in recent years and has regulated imports and closed down medicine markets and pharmacies. Interestingly, she chose mostly women to be members of her team of pharmacists and inspectors as she believes women are less likely to take bribes than men. There are enthusiastic campaigns on Nigerian TV showing mounds of 'unwholesome' products being burned, that appeal to the public to report 'perpetrators' of counterfeit food and drugs manufacture to their local NAFDAC office – on the TV ad, one such perpetrator is shown (dramatic music and all) being led away in handcuffs for ultimate effect.

NAFDAC has offices at the old Federal Secretariat buildings on Ikoyi in Lagos. The buildings are about a dozen storeys high and one section of one of the blocks was completely burnt out in 2004. It was started deliberately by a group of criminals dealing in counterfeit drugs, and supposedly Akunyili kept much of her paperwork there, which the arsonists managed to destroy. A similar inferno razed its Kaduna office a few hours later, which destroyed state-of-the-art laboratory equipment used for testing drugs, and within two weeks of this incident there were two attempts on Akunyili's life. Despite these dangers and set backs, she continues her fight against fake drugs and has won numerous human rights awards. Akunyili's sister, a diabetic, died in 1988 after taking a shot of fake insulin.

off treatment of the drug praziquantel. Avoid swimming and paddling in fresh water and if there is any chance you may have contracted bilharzia have a blood test as soon as you get home. Swimming pools that are well maintained and chlorinated are safe.

Cholera Cholera is caused by bacteria carried in polluted water or contaminated vegetables, and infects the lining of the intestine. Symptoms include abdominal cramps, diarrhoea, vomiting and rapid dehydration. Diarrhoea can be so severe that several litres of fluids can be lost from the body in a single day, and it is especially dangerous in small children who dehydrate very quickly. Treatment consists of fluid replacement and antibiotics, but as it tends to break out only in overcrowded areas with poor sanitation, it poses little threat to the well-nourished traveller. For those at higher risk, for example if you have a chronic and potentially debilitating disease such as diabetes, or if you are living and working in areas of poor sanitation, then consider taking the newer oral cholera vaccine Dukoral.

Health and Safety **HEALTH**

4

Food and drink Quite a few diseases, including hepatitis A and typhoid, are transmitted by unsanitary food handling and contaminated water. *All* tap water in Nigeria should be regarded as being potentially contaminated – especially city water such as that in Lagos, which is most definitely not suitable for drinking, or anything else for that matter save flushing the toilet. Water used for drinking, brushing teeth or making ice throughout the country should have first been boiled or sterilised; otherwise stick to bottled water. Beware of salads washed in water and ice in restaurants and hotels – as painful as it may seem, order drinks without ice (not that you'll see it very often) or order hot drinks such as tea and coffee.

Be careful when buying bottled water, especially on the side of the road where bottles may have been filled up from the tap – check the seal is intact. Bottled water is not always easy to find so buy it when you see it. Most water in Nigeria is sold in half-litre plastic bags generally called *pure water*, which are sold everywhere and are usually cold – the plastic bags are the scourge of Nigeria's rubbish problem. They are, however, far from pure, and are presumably filled from a tap. My advice is to avoid them like the plague in Lagos and perhaps the other bigger cities, but in the outlying regions they should be OK. We certainly didn't get sick from drinking *pure water*, but the problem is you can never be sure where the water has come from. Like other African countries, water in Nigeria does not contain fluoride supplements so those who are staying long term may want to consider fluoride treatments from their dentists before and after leaving home.

Milk is not pasteurised and should be boiled. Powdered or tinned milk is available and is the better bet, but make sure it is reconstituted with clean water. Avoid dairy products that are likely to have been made from unboiled milk, and only buy dairy products from one of the supermarkets specialising in imported goods. Many expats first freeze dairy products before using them just to be on the safe side and rinse their fruit and vegetables with a sterilising solution such as Milton before use.

Heat and humidity Nigeria is hot and humid pretty much all year round and sensible sun protection is essential. Tanning causes wrinkles and over-exposure to the sun is directly related to skin cancer. Use sunscreen with a 15+ SPF (sun protection factor) and wear a broad-brimmed hat. Bring sunscreen with you, as it's not readily available in Nigeria. If you are coming from a cooler climate get used to the sun gradually or you will get burnt. On your first day start by only exposing your skin for a 20-minute period and increase this slowly to a maximum of two hours per day, avoiding the sun altogether in the middle of the day. Don't be lulled into complacency on cloudy days, as this is when UV levels can be especially high. Short-term over-exposure leads to burning, headaches and nausea, and in the extreme can lead to heatstroke and dehydration. If on your return home you notice any changes to moles on your body get them checked out. Melanomas can be removed if caught early enough, but malignant melanomas cause skin cancer if ignored.

In humid weather, we sweat more than normal, which can lead to dehydration, and Nigeria is a very sweaty place. As soon as you leave the confines of an air-conditioned room you will begin to sweat. It is important to remember to replace lost fluids and salt by drinking plenty of liquids and adding more salt to your food. There isn't much salt in Nigerian food, and outside Lagos you are very unlikely to see a salt shaker on a restaurant table, so I strongly suggest that salt is something you should think about travelling around with.

Prickly heat, a fine pimply rash caused by sweat trapped under the skin, is common and harmless, but can be uncomfortable and itchy. Dab with cold water or soothe with a cooling lotion such as aloe vera. Humidity can also promote fungal infections, particularly on the scalp, feet and groin, so wear loose-fitting, preferably cotton clothing and pay attention to personal hygiene. If you notice an itchy and flaky rash between your toes or in the groin area this is likely to be a fungal infection and will need treating with Canesten (clotrimazole) cream.

Hepatitis Hepatitis is an infection of the liver which can be caused by one of several viruses spread by contact with blood, saliva and nasal mucus. It can also spread through contaminated food or foodstuff that has come from polluted water such as raw shellfish and, in the case of hepatitis B, through unprotected sexual intercourse. Symptoms include jaundice (yellowing of the skin and eyes), weakness, loss of appetite, abdominal pain, pale-coloured stools, and dark yellow urine.

The severity of the illness varies considerably, and depending on which virus is involved some people may experience liver problems in later life. Some people may also show no symptoms but will still act as unwitting carriers. There is a growing list of types labelled from A through to E, with A and B being the most common. Both diseases are prevalent in Nigeria so immunisation against both of these is highly recommended. However, if you have not received these vaccines and suspect that you have been in contact with either disease, seek medical help at once. Immunisation, if given quickly after exposure, can be highly effective in preventing the disease.

HIV/AIDS and sexually transmitted diseases The estimated 3.5 million Nigerians living with HIV/AIDS is a figure larger than entire populations of other African nations and it has the world's third largest number of HIV/AIDS victims after India and South Africa. As with most African countries, the transmission of HIV/AIDS in Nigeria is through heterosexual activity, and the danger of catching the virus through unprotected sex is very real. Any exposure to contaminated blood or body fluids may put an individual at risk. There is widespread prostitution, and a high proportion of this population is likely to be HIV positive. Gonorrhoea and syphilis are also rampant in Nigeria and many strains are resistant to antibiotics. Abstinence from sex is the only 100% effective prevention, but using condoms or femidoms reduces the risk considerably.

Catching the AIDS virus does not necessarily produce an illness in itself, though if you notice any genital warts or discharge seek prompt medical attention. The only way to feel sure if you have been put at risk is to have a blood test for HIV antibodies when you get home. Unfortunately, Nigeria has one of Africa's most inadequate HIV/AIDS educational programmes, and one of the highest rates of unsafe blood transfusions in the world. For peace of mind, pack a few needles and hypodermic syringes in your medical kit in the unlikely event that you have to have a blood transfusion in a public or remote hospital.

Insects and bugs Apart from malaria (see page 94), Nigeria's mosquitoes, flies, fleas, bugs and worms transmit a variety of diseases, or can simply just use your body as a temporary home. Personal protective measures are extremely important since insects are almost impossible to avoid. Most insects, including mosquitoes, are attracted to light. In hotel rooms, be aware that the longer you leave a light on, the more bugs you are likely to attract as bedmates. Even the cheapest Nigerian hotels have air conditioning or fans, which help combat the bug problem, but remember that the AC goes off when there's no NEPA or when the generator is switched off for a few hours in the middle of the night. Electric mosquito-zappers that you fit with a pad each night are reasonably effective, but again require electricity. It's also worthwhile blasting your room with a fly spray a couple of hours before going to bed. When choosing a hotel room check that the mosquito netting on the windows is intact; often it can be full of holes.

Wear long trousers, long sleeves, and socks from dusk onwards, and cover exposed parts of your body with an insect repellent, preferably a DEET (Diethyltoluamide) based product. Apply every few hours, and more often if you sweat heavily. If you prefer not to use a DEET product in case of allergy or reaction, then use a validated non-DEET product; non-DEET, Mosiguard and non-DEET Autan have all been tested by the London School of Tropical Medicine and Hygiene. When walking through bush and forest areas through the day, it's also a good idea to use a repellent and to cover yourself to protect against irritating midges.

Dengue fever is contracted from the *Aedes* mosquito, which has a particular passion for shallow pools of water and freshly watered flowerpots and gardens where they like to breed. Also, these mosquitoes fly during daylight hours so make sure you apply repellents at all times. It's another severe flu-like illness; symptoms include fever, lethargy, a rash and aching muscles. The disease follows a rather rollercoaster type of cycle, usually lasting around a week, though it can last much longer. It kicks in suddenly for about two to three days, and then appears to get better for a couple of days, before attacking again for another two to three days. There is no specific treatment save for rest, rehydration and recuperation.

Hookworms are parasitic worms that live in the soil in areas of poor sanitation or in the sand on beaches contaminated by dog faeces. They enter the bloodstream through the soles of your feet so avoid walking barefoot. They move around under the skin causing an unpleasant skin reaction of slowly moving itchy red lines, but can be effectively treated with antibiotics.

Jiggers or **sandfleas** latch on to your feet if you walk barefoot in contaminated places, such as damp soil and sand, or wet grass. They burrow under the skin of the foot, especially in the soft places between the toes where they cause a painful, hard, boil-like swelling. To get them out you need to break the surface carefully and draw out the worm by winding it around something like a pencil. It is repulsive, and as your feet are not easy to reach, it's best to let a local expert do it. If the jigger bursts on eviction, douse the hole with spirit alcohol to prevent further infestation.

River blindness or *onchocerciasis* is rare but present in many West African countries and is spread by small black flies that breed near fast-flowing rivers and rapids. An egg is laid beneath the skin that in turn hatches into a worm, which will live in, and feed off, your bloodstream. Symptoms vary and as the worm can live inside your body for a considerable time (up to 18 years), it's difficult to diagnose. The most common symptom is irritable skin rashes caused by the worms moving around under the skin. In extreme cases, the worm will pass through the eyes causing damage, hence the term river blindness. The only prevention is to wear long sleeves and trousers to help keep them at bay. Citronella repellents don't work against them. Treatment is by an 150mg oral dosage of Ivermectin every 6–12 months. This doesn't kill the parasites, but prevents the disease progressing under the skin.

Tick bites can cause several unpleasant illnesses in Africa, the most common being tick-bite fever, which produces swollen glands, severe aching of the bones, backache and fever. There is no specific treatment; you just have to let it run its course for three to four days. The good news is that ticks you may find on yourself will not inevitably give you some disease, and you are unlikely to catch anything if you get the tick off quickly and completely. Grasp the tick as close to your body as possible and pull out cleanly at a right angle. Make sure you pull out the head as well as the body – it's not painful. Douse the wound with iodine or alcohol and if redness appears indicating an infection, you may need antibiotics.

Tsetse flies administer a sharp painful bite, which while irritating is on the whole harmless. Bigger than houseflies, they are prevalent in much of Nigeria and are much more of a threat to cattle, which explains the lack of dairy and beef products throughout the country. Tsetse flies are found in outlying rural areas, bite in daylight and are attracted to the colours blue and green. They can carry sleeping sickness but the disease is very limited to the tsetse fly's range and is of minimal threat to travellers.

Tumbu or **putsi** flies lay their eggs in wet clothing, bedding, or in damp soil. Expats living in Nigeria complain about them in the cushions of their garden furniture and most do not dry their washing outside. The eggs hatch in the fabric and can penetrate your skin to lay yet more eggs. After a day or two, the larvae develop into worms and an inflamed boil-like infection will appear on the skin that can sometimes be quite severe. After about eight days, they will emerge from the skin by themselves, but applying Vaseline to the lesion can speed up the process. This starves the worm of oxygen and brings it to the surface quicker, where it can be extracted with tweezers. Always dry clothes on an airy clothesline in direct sunlight until they are crisp, or iron with a hot iron afterwards – the heat kills the eggs.

Meningitis Meningitis is an inflammation of the meninges, the membranous coverings of the brain and spinal cord, and can be caused by one of several bacteria or viruses. The seriousness of the disease depends on the causative organism, which can spread through the air through coughing and sneezing. Infection can spread from something as simple as an ear or sinus infection to other parts of the body via the bloodstream. Symptoms include respiratory illness, fever, headaches, skin rashes and sometimes vomiting. If you show symptoms, go to a doctor immediately, as prompt treatment with antibiotics is required. Immunisation against the most severe form of bacterial meningitis is available (meningitis ACWY vaccine) and is recommended for Nigeria.

Rabies Rabies, also known as hydrophobia, is a potentially fatal disease spread through blood or saliva. The most common way to get it is to be bitten by an infected animal but it can also be transmitted by a scratch, or a lick of an open wound. It's prevalent in African dogs and monkeys but can be carried by all mammals. The virus travels from the wound to the spinal cord and brain, and the incubation period can be as long as twelve months. Symptoms include fever, restlessness and depression, proceeding to more dramatic symptoms such as salivation, muscle spasms and a fear of drinking water (hence it being called hydrophobia).

If you are bitten you must always assume that the animal is rabid and seek medical help as soon as possible. In the meantime, wash the wound with clean water and soap and then apply an iodine or alcohol solution, which will help stop the rabies virus entering the bloodstream and prevent other infections such as tetanus. Effective treatment is in the form of a vaccine, and remember to tell the doctor if you have already had a pre-exposure vaccine. If you haven't you will also need an injection of something called immunoglobulin, which is expensive and in short supply.

For those who are specifically working with animals or will be away from medical help for prolonged periods, pre-exposure vaccination is advised. Ideally, three vaccines should be taken over a minimum period of 21 days for maximum protection.

Tetanus Tetanus, or lockjaw, is caused by bacteria living in soil or animal faeces and is transmitted through deep dirty wounds, such as those caused by a rusty nail or an animal bite. Ensure wounds are kept thoroughly cleaned and be sensible about first aid. The bacterium produces a poison that attacks the spinal cord nerves controlling muscle spasm. This leads to stiffness, especially in the jaw, difficulty in swallowing, restlessness and fever. A tetanus vaccination gives good cover for a ten-year period so make sure your immunisation is up to date or get a tetanus booster before you leave home. If you are involved in a serious accident or get bitten badly by, say, a dog, it's also wise to seek treatment.

Travellers' diarrhoea Most travellers to tropical Africa will suffer from a bout of diarrhoea, and the newer you are to tropical travel the more likely you are to get it. Indeed, one study showed that up to 70% of *all* travellers anywhere may suffer during their trip, so be fully prepared for a stomach bug in Nigeria. Nigerians refer to it quite aptly as a 'running stomach'; it needs no more description than that!

Diarrhoea is caused by bacteria spread through unhygienic food handling, and to a lesser extent, contaminated water. (See *Food and drink*, page 96 for precautions you can take when eating and drinking.)

Dehydration or excess fluid loss is the reason diarrhoea makes you feel so awful, so the best cure is to rest and drink lots of clean water to flush the bacteria out of your system. The loss of salts cause stomach cramps and oral rehydration sachets such as Electrolade are a good idea. If these are not available, then make your own by adding a spoonful of salt and sugar to a glass of water topped with a tot of lemon or orange juice to improve the taste. If no safe drinking water is available than you can do the same with a glass of, preferably flat, Coke or similar carbonated drinks. Stick to plain starchy food such as dry biscuits, boiled rice and potatoes, and drink as much fluid as you can, especially if you have lost your appetite.

Avoid jumping for drugs immediately. Instead, let the diarrhoea run its course for at least the first 36–48 hours, which in most cases is long enough for it to clear up on its own. Blockers such as Imodium or Lomotil not only block the diarrhoea but the bacteria that caused it in the first place and don't cure anything, though you may need to resort to these temporarily if you are in an awkward location, such as when travelling on a bus, and do not have easy access to a toilet. If the diarrhoea persists for over 36 hours without improvement or is accompanied by other, unusual symptoms then see a doctor. Ciproxin (ciprofloxacin) is the antibiotic usually administered for severe diarrhoea with blood and/or slime in the stools and/or a fever. A single 500mg dose repeated 6–12 hours later usually does the trick if it is going to work at all. Ideally no medication should be taken until you have seen a doctor, but this may not always be possible.

Giardiasis is also a common form of gut illness which produces greasy, bulky stools, stomach cramps and characteristic 'eggy' burps. If you are suffering from these symptoms seek medical help as soon as possible. More experienced travellers may wish to carry tinidazole – an effective treatment for giardia. At the first sign of infection take four 500mg tablets in one go and if symptoms persist repeat the dose three to seven days later. Again it is always best to seek a doctor's advice before doing this.

Tuberculosis Tuberculosis (TB) is common in all developing countries, but Nigeria has a prevalence of over 100 cases per 100,000, putting it in the highest World Health Organisation risk category. TB is a highly contagious bacterial infection spread via respiratory secretions such as coughing and sneezing. Eating or drinking unpasteurised dairy products can also lead to pelvic TB that can cause infertility and intestinal blockage. Respiratory symptoms include coughing blood, night sweats, weight loss and shortness of breath, and developed TB can spread to other organs causing a variety of serious symptoms. Treatment is a long course of antibiotics over at least six months. There have been cases of Nigerian expats contracting the disease from long-term exposure to infected household help. Although it's almost impossible to do, particularly in downtown Lagos, the only practical advice is to avoid people coughing in your face in crowded public places. Travellers planning to stay more than three months who have not received a BCG (Bacillus of Calmette and Guerin) vaccination before should consult with a doctor at least six weeks before travelling, in case vaccination is recommended. If you have an unexplained illness on your return home, ask your doctor to consider TB.

Typhoid Typhoid is a bacteria spread through contaminated food and water or through direct contact with an infected person's faeces. Flies carrying the bacteria from faeces to food may also spread the disease. Symptoms include loss of appetite, aching muscles, vomiting, fever, abdominal pain and headaches. Some people get the infection without any symptoms, but can still pass it on to others and act as carriers for the disease. Symptoms are similar to malaria so in the event of testing negative for malaria ask your doctor to test for typhoid. It is treated with antibiotics. A typhoid vaccine is extremely effective and recommended for Nigeria. Also, pay particular attention to sanitary food handling and drinking clean water.

SAFETY

ROAD ACCIDENTS Bugs, bowel movements and tropical diseases aside, your safety during any trip to Nigeria is most likely to be endangered by getting around by road. Traffic everywhere, and most famously in Lagos, is one big aggressive snarl-up. The city roads are choked and congested beyond belief, while the highways and expressways between the cities are poorly maintained, and they are used by manic drivers who have no respect for oncoming traffic. Road accidents are common, as attested to by the millions of battered vehicles in the country, and the thousands of mangled buses and cars on the sides of the road. If you are travelling around in a chauffeur-driven car, by overland vehicle or by overcrowded public transport, always exercise caution on the roads.

Always be aware of your driver's road sense as soon as you get in a vehicle – which you should be able to judge pretty quickly. If you are very uncomfortable with his method of driving then stop him, get out of the vehicle and find an alternative one.

Always avoid driving, or being driven, after dark. There are very few street lights, many vehicles do not have headlights, and there's the added problem of pedestrians and domestic animals on the road. Additionally, though there are countless police roadblocks during the day, there are far fewer at night on the roads and this is when armed robberies of vehicles tend to take place. If you are taking public transport over quite some distance, set off early in the day as you will inevitably have to wait for some time in the motor park for a vehicle that goes-when-full, and you will want to ensure that you reach your destination before dark. I would also not advise you to travel on the so-called 'luxury' buses (dealt with in the *Getting around* section, page 70) simply because they nearly always travel at night.

MARINE DANGERS Nigeria's coastline has extremely strong undercurrents, whirlpools and frequent riptides, particularly in windy or rainy weather. Steep drop-offs and heavy surf mean the water can be deceptively deep. A few steps further out from being in knee-deep water can result in finding yourself totally out of your depth. Moreover, the surf is very powerful and can quickly drain one's energy. When the volume of water backed up against a steep beach becomes greater than the incoming surf, it will find the point of least resistance and funnel out to sea in a riptide. They look like a small river on the water's surface flowing away from the beach, and are sometimes brownish and foamy and can flatten incoming waves, making the sea look calm. These currents can reach a speed of eight to ten knots, much faster than any swimmer, and it's not unheard of for a riptide to sweep a swimmer out to sea for a kilometre or so.

Be very wary when swimming off the beaches and never swim alone or without someone knowing that you have gone into the water. If you are a weak swimmer, it's probably best to stick to paddling. If you do get caught in a riptide don't panic or try to fight it; it's a dangerous waste of valuable energy. Instead, swim or float on your back parallel to the shore until you reach the end of the rip, and only then try to get back to land.

On the beach itself, always wear shoes, as there are man-of-war jellyfish in Nigerian waters that can inflict a nasty sting both in and out of the water. It goes without saying that you should never turn your back on a child playing in the surf – some expat parents insist on their children wearing life jackets when on the beach in Nigeria.

FRAUD Financial fraud is very common in Nigeria. Keep all personal financial documents safe and don't let anyone know your home bank account details. The fraudsters are so sophisticated they can trace financial information to your home country. Avoid sending bank account details by post, phone, fax or email to and from Nigeria or checking internet bank accounts. Above all **do not** use a credit card in Nigeria – the number on your card can easily be used again and again once it's in the system. We spoke to one expat in Lagos who had specifically instructed her UK bank not to send her bank statement through the post to her address in Lagos. The bank ignored her request, the statement never arrived and her UK bank account was cleaned out.

Advance Fee Fraud (AFF) is known internationally as '419' fraud after the section of the Nigerian penal code which addresses fraud schemes. Indeed the term '419' is used so often in Nigeria, it's now used to describe all fraud, including the 'This house is not for sale' scam (see box). AFF simply means the demand for and payment of an advance fee in the form of a tax or loan under the pretence to close a business deal or transaction. It's particularly prevalent on the internet and

---

THIS HOUSE IS NOT FOR SALE

All over Nigeria you will see 'This house is not for sale' painted on walls and gateways of houses. Sometimes the signs are more specific with 'This shop is not for sale', 'This block of flats is not for sale' or even 'This estate is not for sale'. I even saw 'This petrol station is not for sale' and 'This land is not for sale by order of Jesus'. Often scribbled next to this is 'Beware 419' – '419' being the common term used for all fraud. There's a scam going on that a so-called owner of a house will find a willing buyer of his or her property and take them to show them the house. If the buyer wants it, he pays the seller a considerable deposit or even all of the money for the house or property. The seller is of course not the owner of the property at all, and breaks into a property that is either standing empty or where the real owner is away, and sells it. In Nigeria I also saw in a cheap magazine an article entitled: 'What to do if your wife sells your house while you are at work'!

your email account may have been targeted by these fraudsters before – an email about how you could receive millions of US dollars for simply offering the use of your foreign bank account.

Many of the emails originate from internet cafés in Festac Town, Lagos, although some originate from other parts of West Africa or are sent by overseas Nigerians in cities ranging from Amsterdam to Bangkok. Some of these emails look extremely official, supported by a Nigerian government agency or law firm, or impersonating persons of social distinction, giving themselves bogus prefixes such as Doctor, Prince, Engineer, Chief, His Royal Highness and so on. The usual story is that the sender is the owner of spectacular wealth in or out of Nigeria and for some reason or other needs to move the cash so he can gain access to it. To enable him to do this he needs to use a foreigner's bank account. In exchange, the holder of the bank account will receive a huge cash payment for providing this service, often running into millions of dollars. It is of course a blatant way of getting hold of your bank account details, and there have been countless incidents of people's accounts being cleaned out. Indeed it happened to one of the readers of the first edition of this book, who bought the book to go to Nigeria to chase up his money!

These emails and letters will appear ridiculous to most, but unfortunately a large number of victims are enticed into believing they have been singled out from the masses to share in a multi-million dollar windfall for doing absolutely nothing, and Nigerian '419' fraud is believed to gross hundreds of millions of dollars a year. Do not respond to these emails.

On the next page is an example of an email, spelling mistakes and all, which wormed its way into my yahoo account from (supposedly) Mrs Abacha.

CRIME AND CORRUPTION Nigeria has a reputation for crime and corruption and has more than its fair share of challenges to safety and security – it is advisable always to be security conscious. Things do happen – armed robberies and carjackings are prevalent in Lagos and there is a threat of mugging. More disturbing are the huge numbers of guns in private possession and in the police and armed forces; both are susceptible to bribery and corruption, and thus could provide arms to civilians at the right price. There have also been incidents when the police themselves have been the perpetrators of crime.

Some of the more outlandish crime that occurs in Nigeria is piracy, or armed robbery on ships anchored in Nigerian waters, or the illegal 'bunkering' of oil on to ships belonging to other nationalities. It's also not uncommon for gangs to hijack oilrigs off the coast to extort money from the oil companies. Also be aware that there have been many recent incidents of hostage-taking for ransom, particularly in the Niger Delta, because of local community problems with the oil companies (see page 26). People working in Nigeria for these companies should be especially vigilant and follow their employer's security guidelines.

Although it doesn't produce any drugs of its own, Nigeria is known as a major drug-trafficking country for Asian heroin smuggled to Europe and the USA, and for South American cocaine trafficked to Europe. Nigerian drug organisations are also heavily involved in other criminal activities such as document fabrication, illegal immigration and financial fraud. But Nigerians in Nigeria are generally not drug users. I live in Cape Town and at the end of my road is a large Nigerian community (a reported one million Nigerians live in South Africa, and three million in the USA, with other large communities in Europe and elsewhere in the world). Some of Cape Town's Nigerian community, as well as many Capetonians, sell drugs on the street for a living. We never once got offered drugs on the street by a Nigerian in Nigeria.

I am Mrs Marriam Abacha, the wife to the late Head of State, of the federal Republic of Nigeria from 1993–1998 – General Sani Abacha.

My late husband made a lot of money as the Head of state of Nigeria for 5years. He has different accounts in many banks of the world. He has not left any stone unturned in accruing riches for his family.

The present democratic government of Nigeria led by President (Gen.) (Rtd) Olusegun Obasanjo has not find favour with myfamily since their inception. This may be as a result of his hatred for my late husband who kept him in jail for over two years for a coup attempt, before the death of my father. He was released immediately my husband died and he was later made the present President.

He has confiscated and frozen all my family account in Nigeria and some other American, Europe and Asian continents, It has been in both the local and international news.Presently my son mohammed Abacha has been languishing in different prison centers in Nigeria for a case against his father which he knows nothing about.

Now, my purpose of all these introduction and proposal is just seeking for your candid assistance in saving this sum of $30.8.000,000.00 [USD THIRTY.EIGHT MILLION.DOLLARS] which my late husband had hidden from the Nigerian govt. during his regime. and which is presently somewhere in a financial and security company outside the entire Nigeria and West African region.

This is a huge sum of money, I cannot trust much on most saboteur friends of my family in Nigeria who could not be trusted. I got your contact through our trade mission. I deemed it necessary to contact you for this trustworthy transaction.

All whom I needed is a sincere, honest, trustworthy and God-fearing individuals whom my mind will absolve to help me in this deal.If you have feelings about my situation, don't hesitate to stand for me. If my proposal is sudden to you, all I need now is for you to stand as the Beneficiary of this money to claim it and save for me.

There is no difficulty, I will send your name as the recipient as well as the beneficiary of the money.On your identification and confirmation from me, the fund will be handle to you.

all i need is your confirmention of willingness and i will give you the full details. You will be compensated with 25% of the total fund for all your

efforts in this transaction,provided this fund is save for me for your account in your country.

Please this is a very serious matter, it is a save my soul request from you and I will be delighted too much to receive a positive response from you in order to move into action. I will give you details on request from you.

THANKS

YOURS FAITHFULLY

MRS M ABACHA

Many Nigerians complain that the illegal activities of the offending minority have damaged the whole nation's image. It was also explained to me that most of Nigeria's criminals were not in Nigeria at all, and made up the huge populations of Nigerians living overseas. These were the people who were capable of forging, stealing or bribing to get passports and visas, and, as illegal immigrants in other countries, resorting to criminal activity to make a living. Despite all this, Nigeria's awful reputation for crime is largely exaggerated, especially outside Lagos where you will rarely feel threatened or be a victim of crime. Even in Lagos, long-term visitors may never see an Area Boy or someone out of uniform carrying a gun. But always remember that there is a criminal element in Nigeria and keep up your guard.

Finally, on a lighter note we once saw a man in Lagos selling those boxes of airplane food, complete with the little plastic bags of plastic cutlery and salt and pepper from the back of his car – 'fell off the back of a plane' perhaps? And in one Lagos market, we found six-packs of Fosters lager – 'fell off the back of an Australian diplomatic bag' perhaps?

Petty theft The culture of cheating is alive and kicking in Nigeria and you are more likely to be cheated out of something than having it simply stolen off you. This was one of the biggest surprises I had in Nigeria. As a seasoned traveller in eastern and southern Africa, where you guard your bags and possessions fiercely, I didn't feel the need to do this so attentively in Nigeria. Not once did we have anything stolen out of a hotel room, and after the first few outings on public transport when we crouched over our bags jealously, we would quite willingly throw them into the open back of a vehicle surrounded by hundreds of people and go for a wander around a motor park while waiting for the vehicle to go-when-full.

We could just have been lucky, but there was definitely a general feeling that people don't openly steal from one another. They might scam, swindle, demand bribes or dupe you, but I really don't think they literally pick up something that does not belong to them and keep it. This could be because of the strong religious sentiment, both Christian and Muslim, that thou shall not steal, preached in churches and mosques daily throughout the country.

I spoke to an expat in Jos, who one night went out, got horribly drunk, and left his wallet on the back seat of a taxi on the way home – the following morning the taxi driver found out where the expat was working and dropped off his wallet untouched at his place of work. If anyone has any less positive experiences I would be happy to hear their stories. Nevertheless, there will always be opportunist thieves wherever you travel, so don't put temptation in their path. Keep your valuables hidden, never flash your wealth, and leave anything of financial or sentimental value at home.

Political risks There is no doubt that political and religious tensions in Nigeria are high, and there has been a category of riots and violent incidents since Nigeria gained independence in 1960. There is no real science of assessing political risk, though it's a good idea to check your nationality's foreign office advice before you leave home and keep a close eye on Nigerian news. Outbreaks of localised civil unrest and violence can occur all over Nigeria without warning. If something does occur while you are in Nigeria, it is unlikely that a traveller will be targeted or involved, and most violent eruptions are based on local ethnic or religious spats. Potential trouble spots are in the northern cities, and in the Niger Delta where the local communities resent the presence of the multinational oil companies. Here is the one place where foreigners could be specifically targeted if they are identified (mistakenly or not) as oil employees and at the time of writing the region was completely off-limits to foreigners because of a continual spate of kidnappings.

It's worth being prepared for a threat to personal safety, so look out for the following: traffic suddenly becomes very light and the streets mysteriously clear of pedestrians (extremely unlikely in Lagos); armoured vehicles or truckloads of armed police or soldiers; the noise of shooting or explosions, however distant; the disruption of TV and radio broadcasts; or streets thronged with chanting or stone-throwing groups. If unrest does occur, it is wise for a foreigner to be discreet and not join in on the action. Stay in your hotel and listen to the advice of the hotel manager who knows the area and situation much better than you do. Because the cities are so populated and everyone talks to each other, news of events going on elsewhere quickly does the rounds. If events get really bad, phone your embassy so that they are aware of your whereabouts, and listen carefully to the advice of embassy officials.

NOTES FOR DISABLED TRAVELLERS

Nigeria, like the majority of African countries, does not have the needs of disabled travellers – or even those of its own disabled population – high on its agenda of 'things to improve'. Unless you stay in the confines of the Sheraton, wheelchair access is zero.

PLANNING AND BOOKING I know of no operators specialised in disability who run trips in Nigeria, and there are no local operators.

ACCOMMODATION Few establishments, except perhaps the international hotels in larger cities (about three or four at most), have made any considerations for wheelchair users. Many places have ground floor rooms and if you can cope with a standard bathroom then accommodation should not be impossible to find.

TRANSPORT

Air travel Aisle chairs are not guaranteed at airports and assistance may not be as experienced or highly trained as you are used to. However, if you explain fully how you like to be helped, you should have few problems.

Buses and trains There is no effective legislation in Nigeria to facilitate disabled travellers' journeys by public transport; therefore, if you cannot walk at all then both of these options are going to be difficult. Even an able-bodied person would have difficulty finding any space at all on public transport, never mind an actual seat.

Health and Insurance Doctors will know about 'everyday' illnesses, but you must understand and be able to explain your own particular medical requirements. Except for a handful in the cities, all Nigerian hospitals and pharmacies are very basic, so it is wise to take as much essential medication and equipment as possible with you, and it is advisable to pack this in your hand luggage during flights in case your main luggage gets lost. Nigeria can be hot; if this is a problem for you then try to book accommodation and vehicles with fans or air conditioning, and a useful cooling aid is a plant-spray bottle.

Most insurance companies will offer insurance, but the following companies specialise in people with pre-existing medical conditions and older travellers:

UK Age Concern; ☎ 0800 169 2700; www.ageconcern.org.uk
Free Spirit; ☎ 0845 230 5000; e freespirit@pjhayman.com; www.free-spirit.com
USA Travelex Insurance Services; ☎ 0800 228 9792; e customerservice@travelex-insurance.com; www.travelex-insurance.com

Australia Travel Insurance Direct; ☎ 1300 843 843; e infoAUS@travelinsurancedirect.com.au; www.travelinsurancedirect.com.au
New Zealand Mike Henry Travel Insurance Ltd; ☎ 09 377 5958 or 0800-657 744; f 09 309 5473; e info@mikehenry.co.nz; www.mikehenry.co.nz

SECURITY Although the vast majority of people will only want to help you, it is worth remembering that, as a disabled person, you are more vulnerable. Stay aware of who is around you and where your bags are, especially during car transfers and similar.

Part Two

THE GUIDE

5

Lagos

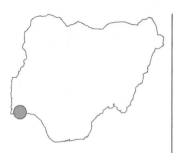

Although Nigeria's capital city is Abuja, with a population of just under 1.5 million, it took over from Lagos as the country's official capital only in 1991, and Lagos remains Nigeria's largest and most overwhelmingly principal city. The city is the capital of Lagos State, lying in the southwestern corner of the country. It's the smallest state in the federation, and occupies an area of just 3,577km^2, 22% (or 787km^2) of which consists of lagoons and creeks. This is not much bigger than a British county, but with a vastly higher population density. It shares its boundaries with Ogun State in the north and east, the Republic of Benin to the west, and has 180km of Atlantic coastline to the south. The Nigerian name for Lagos is Eko. It wasn't until the 17th century that the Portuguese renamed it Lagos, meaning 'lagoons'.

Lagos is situated in one of the few gaps in the 200km-long sandbar that stretches from Benin to the eastern side of Lagos State. It lies in a swampy mangrove zone and is entirely flat, with no natural point being any higher than a metre or so above sea level. The metropolitan area covers three main islands and an ever-increasing section of the mainland spreading out in all directions. The waters of Lagos's lagoons stretch from a few hundred metres to 15km across, and in recent years landfills in the lagoons have been used for urbanisation. The city is basically a collection of islands that are connected together and to the mainland by long bridges – similar to Manhattan in New York City, though the comparison stops there.

Before the 2006 census Lagos was believed to be the the largest city in Africa, with an estimated population of at least 13 million. Completely unexpectedly, and still under serious debate, the 2006 census's results for Lagos State came in at 9,013,354, while Kano State was put at 9,383,682, a difference of some 370,000. Officially Kano is bigger, although the census has been largely disputed. It has been suggested that as the days of the census were declared as public holidays, many Lagos residents, who come from all over Nigeria, used the opportunity to 'visit their village' (go back to their place of birth or where they may have family) and that the census results were distorted because of this. The United Nations estimates that Lagos has a population of between 13 and 17 million, which is likely to be more accurate than the 2006 census figure. This enormous population represents every socio-economic level – evident from the sprawling, overcrowded shanty towns that are home to a mass of humanity, to the spacious leafy mansions on Victoria Island housing the wealthy and privileged.

The mere mention of its name evokes strong reactions from visitors and Nigerians alike. Most people either passionately love or virulently hate Lagos, but no visit to Nigeria is complete without experiencing this overpowering and mind-boggling city. It is stimulating and vibrant, and dirty and dangerous, all at the same time. Those who love Lagos do so because of its diversity, and the majority of Lagosians proudly confess that they can't see themselves living anywhere else in

Nigeria. Those who hate it find it a volatile place, with perhaps one of the world's worst reputations for congestion, crime, poverty and chaos. Whether you love it or hate it, you will undoubtedly find Lagos mind-blowing! That's the only word that even vaguely captures the essence of Lagos, where the super-rich meet the mega-destitute, cacophony meets peace and quiet, searing heat and humidity meet icy air conditioning, life meets death, hi-tech meets ancient, filth and squalor meet hygiene, and natural beauty jars head on with pollution.

HISTORY

Early settlements of hunters and fishermen, protected by the lagoon swamps and mangrove forest, marked the beginning of Lagos. It is believed that the first settlers on Lagos Island were the Olofin people in the 14th century. Their chief first settled on the Iddo Peninsula and divided the land on Lagos Island between his ten sons. One son, Aromire, used his land to grow vegetables, including peppers, and built his farm on the site that is today the location of the King's (Oba's) Palace, otherwise known as the Iga Idunganran or Pepper Palace. The town of Lagos then steadily grew as the fertile grounds attracted a number of farmers, and the sea attracted fishermen. In the early 1400s, a quarrel broke out between the Olofin people and a wealthy woman named Aina, who they had falsely accused of being a witch. Aina sent for help from the king of Benin, who sent an army that defeated the Olofins, and Lagos became the southern outpost of the Benin Empire. They called it Eko, which was the Benin name for war camp. A Benin warrior called Ashipa was made king of the town and was given a royal drum, or *gbedu*, by the king of Benin.

Since then, all of Lagos's kings have been descendants of that first king, Ashipa. His son, King Ado, built the Oba's Palace on Lagos Island, and Ado's successor, King Gabaro, went on to move the seat of government from Iddo to the Oba's Palace in the late 15th century. Although still under the jurisdiction of the Benin Empire, Gabaro was more lenient towards the Olofins than his predecessors and gave them land and chiefdoms. The descendants of these Olofin chiefs are today Lagos's chiefs or *idejos*, which means 'landowners'.

THE SLAVE TRADE The first Europeans to arrive in Lagos were the Portuguese, who landed on the coast in 1472, and for the next four centuries traded with the kings and people of Lagos. They named the settlement Lago de Curamo, and finally Lagos, after the port in Portugal of the same name. In 1730 Gabaro's brother Akinshemoyin became king and invited Portuguese slave traders to Lagos. The Portuguese had already established trade links with the Kingdom of Benin and by the mid-18th century the empires on the coast were flourishing with wealth generated by the slave trade. Most of the slaves passed through the Lagos slave market en route to Europe and America, and Lagos continued to grow over the next hundred years.

Although the British government outlawed slavery in all her territories in 1833, in Lagos the slave trade continued to operate well into the middle of the 19th century. In 1845 Kosoko wrenched the throne from his uncle Akitoye, who was not the rightful heir to the kingdom. Akitoye went to the British Consul John Beecroft and appealed to the British to help him get the throne back, in return for which he promised to stop the prohibited slave trade once and for all, and to strengthen trade links with Britain. Queen Victoria sent a message to Kosoko requesting that he end the slave trade and insisting that Lagos must sign an official treaty with Britain. Kosoko refused and the British retaliated in 1851 by attacking Lagos Island with five battleships and defeating Kosoko's army. On 1 January 1852, Beecroft reinstated Akitoye as king of Lagos and the treaty with the British was signed, stating that the slave trade was to be abolished.

In 1852 Akitoye died suddenly and was succeeded by his son Dosunmu, who over the next five years also failed to close down Lagos's slave markets. His failure resulted in the complete annexation of Lagos by the British and finally, in August 1861, Dosunmu signed the declaration of cessation and Lagos became a British colony. Dosunmu retained his role as *oba* and received an annual salary from the British – 1,200 bags of cowries that was worth about £1,000 – but overall his authority over Lagos was reduced to a minimum. Allegedly, the British took occupancy of Lagos 'not without some reluctance', but they had succeeded in finally stamping out the slave trade for good.

LAGOS UNDER THE BRITISH Over the next few decades, Lagos was administered under a British governor and a small legislative council of British officials, and it became the main base for British imperial activities and penetration into the hinterland. As the colony strengthened economically, the British influence spread into Yorubaland and beyond, and trade links were established between other regions of the interior. Although Lagos retained its title as the British Colony of Lagos, these new areas inland were amalgamated and became known as the British Protectorate of Nigeria. People living in the colony of Lagos passed for British subjects, while those living in the protectorate were referred to as British protected persons. Finally, in January 1914 the British officially joined the two regions together as the Federation of Nigeria with Lagos as its capital, though effectively they were administered separately until 1946.

After Nigeria gained independence from Britain in 1960, Lagos became the capital of the Federal Republic of Nigeria. This position was ceded to Abuja in 1991, since the latter occupies a more central location in the country, a move that is hoped will take the pressure off the already exhausted infrastructure of Lagos as the centre of commerce and industry, and the seat of government. Today Lagos remains the capital city of Lagos State, with its administrative centre in Ikeja on the mainland.

GROWTH OF THE CITY Although the city's growth and structure were influenced by its status as a colonial capital, there were never a large number of British settlers, and the social life and the culture remained largely Nigerian. As a formal capital city, Lagos grew phenomenally quickly from the end of the 19th century. In 1885 schools were built, by 1886 the railway had arrived and telephone links with Britain were established, and by 1898 the streets were lit with electric lights.

People streamed in from all over Nigeria and other parts of West Africa, including repatriated slaves and their descendants. Returnee slaves, known as Creoles, returned to Lagos from Brazil, the West Indies and Freetown in Sierra Leone, swelling the population of the city. They had been introduced to Christianity and had the privilege of a Western education, and made remarkable contributions to education and the rapid modernisation of Lagos. They returned with knowledge of the wider world and the European way of life, and many of them had received training as doctors, architects or lawyers. Others were skilled workers: carpenters, bakers, mariners or tailors. Brazilian returnees brought with them the skills they had acquired in Brazil. Most were master-builders and masons, and gave the distinct characteristics of Brazilian architecture to their residential buildings (some dilapidated examples can still be seen today on Lagos Island). For all practical purposes their arrival marked an era of modernisation in Lagos and Nigeria as a whole. With their educational, professional and technical qualifications, many got employment in the colonial civil service and from Lagos were transferred to other parts of the country that were under British control. The Creole families of Lagos formed the nucleus of African colonial staff in the early decades of British administration.

From the 1920s these people pioneered modern political activity in the country and agitated African participation in government – one of the leading nationalist movement's players, Herbert Macaulay, was a member of one of the Lagos Creole families, and the grandson of the legendary Bishop Samuel Crowther. Lagos became the centre of the anti-colonial struggle and was the headquarters of Macaulay's Nigerian Democratic Party, the Nigerian Youth Movement, and the National Council for Nigeria and the Cameroon, as well as home to the anti-colonial press that helped get the message across to the common man to cast off the yoke of imperialism and alien rule.

The city was also the centre of the trade union movement, which began to challenge British rule and fight for the rights of the working classes through a series of protest marches and strikes – a 45-day general strike in 1945 seriously disabled the whole country. From 1967, the two-and-a-half year Biafran War caused a further massive migration to the city. This, coupled with a huge wave of refugees and migrants from other African countries fleeing famine and drought, produced a population boom, with hundreds of thousands of people pouring into the city looking for jobs as an alternative to rural poverty. The growth of light industry in post-independence Lagos and the petroleum-related industry that boomed in the 1970s also directly affected the rapid growth of Lagos.

During the oil boom of the 1970s a masterplan was drawn up with the help of the United Nations Development Program. This was meant to guide the development of the city over the following two decades. There were to be 35 self-sufficient district centres, each with their own commercial, industrial and residential zones, to ease the congestion on the commercial centre of Lagos Island. A fourth mainland bridge was intended to connect Victoria Island with the Lekki Peninsula (today, land fill does this), and there was to be a light rail and ferry system. But in 1982, 16 years of military rule began, the masterplan was abandoned, and so began a series of governments that had no interest in investing in an infrastucture to cope with the millions who had moved into Lagos.

LAGOS TODAY Lagos has grown too big too fast. On the eve of independence in 1960, the population was put at a little less than half a million. In the disputed 2006 census, it was put at 9.2 million, but it's generally believed to be 13–17 million. Population growth today is put at 3–5% annually and the United Nations has classed Lagos as a megacity, which is defined as a metropolitain area with an excess of 10 million inhabitants with a population density of at least 2,000 people per square kilometre. Based on an estimated figure of 15 million and with a 3,577 km^2 land mass of Lagos State, the population is nearer 4,200 people per square kilometre. This phenomenal growth comes at the expense of decent social services and infrastructure, which are stretched to breaking point, and have failed to keep up with the population growth. Energy and water access, sewage, transportation and housing have all been adversely affected by the haphazard development of a geographically disjointed city. Lagos consumes 45% of the energy of the whole country, but suffers frequent power cuts and fuel shortages. There is a worsening water supply that has resulted in people sinking bore holes in contaminated soil; because of inadequate sewage, much of the city's human waste is carried through rainwater drains and ditches to end up on the city's tidal flats.

Nigeria's failure to dispose of its rubbish is at its most acute here, and everywhere there are piles of garbage. Everything seemingly appears broken, disused or seriously dilapidated, and waste and discard are the order of the chaotic

Lagos day. The streets are littered with abandoned yellow vehicles driven until they die, there are half-finished, derelict or burnt-out buildings, dysfunctional telephone and electricity wires are wrapped around broken poles, and sometimes even dead bodies can be seen decomposing in the gutters. I've even seen a photograph of someone walking down a Lagos street with two muzzled and chained hyenas!

There is the push-and-shove traffic and the thousands of yellow buses, minibuses and taxis, covered in scratches and dinks, with doors hanging off and rusting undercarriages, battered beyond recognition. And many more thousands of motorbikes, their handlebars shortened so they can squeeze through the traffic better, their toot-toot horns replaced with truck horns, which can be driven so recklessly I hear stories of the rider's legs being taken off. Snarl-ups and go-slows are a constant daily problem – it takes an average of two to three hours to travel 10–20km. And finally, despite there being pockets of adequate housing, for the majority of Lagos's many millions, home is in appalling slums that stretch as far as the eye can see, where people's aspirations for a decent lifestyle seem doomed to flounder in the filth and decay.

Despite all this, on a visit to Lagos you'll discover a city far more welcoming than the ferocious Lagos of modern myth. And although there are limited so-called sights, these various elements are what Lagos is all about and its major attraction. It's a Third World megalopolis all right – no-one would ever use words like 'pleasant' or 'relaxing' to describe the commercial capital of West Africa, but Lagos is a lively, noisy, chaotic and fast-moving city. It has its own dynamic, if perhaps sometimes unappealing, personality, but go with confidence and get into its vibrant rhythm and don't be surprised if you leave Nigeria with a certain fondness and respect for Lagos. It will not fail to surprise.

GETTING THERE AND AWAY

BY AIR
Lagos Murtala Mohammed International Airport Lagos Murtala Mohammed International Airport (LOS) is 22km, or roughly one hour's drive (depending on the traffic), north of the islands that are the centre of Lagos proper. This airport used to have a notorious reputation for corrupt officials, con artists, bogus taxi drivers and pickpockets, and travellers were harassed inside and outside the airport. In addition, planes were routinely attacked by criminals on the actual apron who robbed their cargo holds. But following the democratic election in 1999, the security situation at LOS began to improve. Airport police instituted a shoot-on-sight policy for anyone found in the secure areas around runways and taxiways, malfunctioning and non-operational infrastructure such as air conditioning and luggage belts have been repaired, the entire airport has been cleaned, and many new restaurants and duty-free stores have opened.

Today LOS by and large resembles any other busy international airport with ongoing improvements; procedures for immigration, customs and baggage collection are all straightforward and you will experience few problems. Indeed, my experience was a very friendly encounter with all the various officials. However, as in any airport it is still necessary to keep on your guard at all times, and to keep valuables close to you and your passport hidden. Do not hand over your passport to anyone other than the immigration authorities, and under no circumstances offer to pay *dash*.

If you are arriving on a 30-day visa, providing you can show that you have an airline ticket with a date of departure on it, it is worth asking here on arrival if you can get a 90-day entry stamp. The officials may or may not oblige, but if they do this saves the hassle of extending your visa once in Lagos. You can hire a porter and a trolley for about US$1 (and can use US$ cash so bring some small notes with you). When you leave the baggage hall an official will inspect your airline ticket against the tag on your luggage to make sure you've got your bag and no-one else's.

To change money there are two bureaux de change at arrivals. The first is an unnamed counter within the baggage collection hall (⊕ 08.00–20.00 daily); look to the left of the Virgin baggage carousel. The second is beyond customs next to the exit and is a brand new Travelex counter (⊕ 24hr), which is very efficient and can change most major currencies. At both, exchange rates are competitive and only a small amount of commission is charged. Alternatively, there are hordes of money changers in the car park and it's pretty straightforward to change money with them if you are confident enough. But have the cash ready, as you don't want to be dipping into your money belt in such a public place.

Only a certain number of taxis are allowed to trade at the airport and prices are generally fixed at about US$45/N6,000 from the airport to the islands, though going from the islands to the airport you'll be able to negotiate a cheaper ride for about US$32–40/N3–4,000 with any taxi, but as usual for Lagos the price depends on the traffic and weather, and the price and availability of fuel. The big hotels and some of the travel agents can arrange a meet-and-greet service at the airport, and all expats will be picked up by drivers from their respective companies. It's not really necessary, and a bit of a nightmare, to pre-arrange this, as catching a taxi is straightforward enough – just ensure that the driver knows the way to your destination. Outside the building there is a throng of people behind a makeshift fence and gate across from the main concourse – only people with valid airline tickets are allowed beyond the fence so any drivers meeting you will be on the other side of this fence, and this is where you'll find taxis.

On departure your luggage will inevitably be searched on a big table at the check-in desk, and as a foreigner you will be asked if you are carrying any antiquities. If you have bought souvenirs declare them, but unless they are really old pieces of Nigerian art for which a licence is required, you shouldn't have any problems (see page 82). Also on departure you may be asked by immigration how much naira you have. This is not a request for a bribe; it is illegal to take more than a small amount of Nigerian currency out of the country.

The domestic terminal If you are departing from Lagos on a domestic flight note that the domestic terminal is in a separate building off Agege Motor Road about one kilometre from the international terminal. Look out for the old Nigeria Airways jumbo jets parked rather forlornly in a hangar next to the car park – like abandoned vehicles dumped all over Nigeria, since the demise of the national airline in 2003 the planes have just been left to grow rusty and be covered in the city's grime. Rather confusingly, however, Virgin Nigeria and Arik Airlines operate their domestic flights to Abuja, Enugu, Port Harcourt and Calabar not from the domestic terminal but back at the international terminal. In early 2007 a new domestic terminal at the same site of the international terminal had been commissioned, so some of the other airlines may follow suit: check with the airline which terminal your aeroplane is departing from before heading out to the airport.

Taxis to and from the domestic terminal cost roughly the same as to and from the international terminal. It is almost impossible to pre-book a ticket for a domestic flight, and to fly from Lagos to anywhere else in Nigeria you just have to pitch up at the domestic terminal. One reason for this is that the flights are relatively cheap and popular, and the domestic airlines do not pay commission to local travel agents, so it's simply not worth their while to sell and ticket domestic flights.

The domestic departure hall is a tad chaotic, but once you get your bearings you'll find it is organised, in a manic sort of way. There are some 15 check-in desks for the different airlines, and above each desk are signs showing when the next plane is going where. Here is where you buy your ticket (which is hand-written) and then point out your luggage to the luggage attendant who will take it (in theory) to the right plane. You won't get a boarding pass and the seat number is written on the front of the ticket. Once through into the frantically busy and noisy domestic departure hall, you'll find some small snack bars, a bookshop, and public phones next to a kiosk where you can buy a phonecard.

There are a dozen or so flights per day to Abuja, so it's just a case of turning up at the airport and getting on the next one. There are also several direct flights a day to the other major cities but they run less frequently and you may find yourself sitting at the airport for a few hours. Check out the websites for schedules, though these invaribly change, and see the 'Getting there and away' sections of the relevant destination chapters and the main 'Getting around' section for details of fares and timetables.

Airlines

✈ **Aero Contractors** Airport desk; ✆ 01 497 9122; Federal Palace Hotel; ✆ 01 261 7934; www.acn.aero.

✈ **Air France** ICON House, Plot 98 Adeola Odeku St, Victoria Island; ✆ 01 461 0777; www.airfrance.com.ng.

✈ **Arik Air** Airport desk; ✆ 01 279 9999, 496 6606; www.arikair.com.

✈ **Bellview Airlines** Airport desk; ✆ 01 270 2700; www.flybellviewair.com. Bellview is a domestic airline but also has flights to Abidjan, Accra, Banjul, Conakry, Dakar, Doula, Freetown, Libreville & Monrovia. It now flies to London 4 times a week & Johannesburg twice a week.

✈ **British Airways** Plot 5, Oninkan Abayomi Drive, Ikoyi; ✆ 01 461 1002–6. There is also a desk at the Sheraton Hotel in Ikeja; www.britishairways.com.

✈ **Chanchangi Airlines** Airport desk; ✆ 01 493 9744/55; also has desks at the Federal Palace, Airport & Eko hotels; www.chanchangi.com.

✈ **Egypt Air** 22b Idowu Taylor St, Victoria Island; ✆ 01 497 0339; www.egyptair.com.eg.

✈ **Emirates** Churchgate Tower, 30 Afribank St, Victoria Island; ✆ 01 271 7600; www.emirates.com/ng.

✈ **Ethiopian Air** 3 Idowu Taylor St, Victoria Island; ✆ 01 774 4711, 461 1869; www.ethiopianairlines.com.

✈ **Ghana Airways** 128 Awolowo Rd, Ikoyi; ✆ 01 269 2363, 269 1397; www.ghanainternationalairlines.com.

✈ **IRS Airlines** Airport desk, ✆ 01 773 8014/5; www.irs-airlines.com.

✈ **KLM and Kenya Airways** Churchgate Tower, 30 Afribank St, Victoria Island; ✆ 01 461 2555, 461 2538; www.klm.com; www.kenya-airways.com.

✈ **Lufthansa** 150 Broad St, Lagos Island; ✆ 01 266 0222, 266 0088; www.lufthansa.com.

✈ **North American Airlines** Silverbird Galleria, 133 Ahmadu Bello Way, Victoria Island; ✆ 01 716 3801–4; www.flynaa.com. Now has direct flights between New York & Lagos.

✈ **Overland Airways** 17 Simbiat Abiola Road, Off Mobolaji Bank Anthony Way, Ikeja; ✆ 0803 535 5003; www.overland.aero.

✈ **Sosoliso Airlines** Airport desk; ✆ 01 496 1962; www.sosolisoairline.com. Domestic flights plus services to Monrovia, Freetown & Accra.

✈ **South African Airlines** 28c Adetokunbo Ademola St, Victoria Island; ✆ 01 262 0607/9, 262 5783; www.flysaa.com.

✈ **Virgin Nigeria** 19 Adeyemo Alakija Street, Victoria Island; ✆ 01 460 0505, 271 1111; www.virginnigeria.com. There's also a desk at the Sheraton in Ikeja. As well as domestic flights, Virgin also flies to Accra, Dakar, Doula, Johannesburg & London.

BY ROAD

Motor parks There are several motor parks on mainland Lagos that serve other destinations in Nigeria. The most useful are Mile Two for vehicles to the east of Lagos and to the border of the Benin Republic; and the Ojota old and new motor parks serving just about everywhere else. There are direct minibuses from these to the Obalende motor park between Lagos Island and Ikoyi. Except for those vehicles coming into Mile Two from the east, if you are arriving in Lagos on public transport from any other direction, vehicles could end their journey in motor parks at Oju Elegba, Iddo, Yaba, Ebute Eru or Oshodi (the latter being well known for its Area Boys (see box on page 120), where you'll be knee-deep in mud if it's raining). But nearly all first stop at Ojota, so if you are catching a vehicle from an outlying city ask if it is going to Ojota and get the driver or conductor to tell you when to get off.

The Ojota Motor Park is roughly spread around Ikorodu Road, that joins the Lagos–Ibadan Expressway, with the New Ojota Motor Park being about 300m or an N50 hop on an *okada*, to the south – it's a filthy and chaotic area where every last space is filled with rubbish and thousands of vehicles. You'll have to ask around for a vehicle going in your direction and expect to get hopelessly lost, but most people will helpfully assist you. Sometimes there are the wooden pyramid signs that sit on top of the vehicle with the destination written on, which are simply plonked on the next vehicle when the first one is full and ready to depart. Look out for a National Union Road Transport Workers (NURTW) man (they patrol the motor parks and take the fee off the drivers for the use of the motor park), who usually wears a green and white shirt and cap, and he will show you which vehicle to get on. We experienced no problems walking around Lagos's motor parks even with our luggage, but nevertheless always exercise caution.

Bus companies There are scores of 'luxury' bus companies that operate out of Lagos, though as mentioned in the general 'Getting around' section, my advice is not to use these as they nearly always travel at night. Most 'luxury' bus stands are located near the main motor parks. It might be the case that you get to a motor park, find out where the buses go from and then make another journey to the 'luxury' bus stand. Major bus stands for buses heading north and east are on Western Avenue in Surulere near the National Stadium, and near Ojota and Oshodi motor parks, and for buses also heading north as well as west to the Benin Republic, on the Badagry Expressway near the Mile Two Motor Park. One of the most established 'luxury' bus companies is Ekene Dili Chukwu Transport Company (℄ 01 774 1596; www.ekenedilichukwu.com), which runs services from its stand near Oshodi to Abuja, Port Harcourt, Aba, Kaduna, Kano and Maiduguri. Also near Oshodi, ABC Transport (℄ 01 791 1365; www.abctransport.com) is another long-distance bus company that runs to all the major cities plus Cotonou in Benin and Acrra in Ghana. ABC also has a booking office at the Airport Hotel in Ikeja.

BY RAIL The Lagos train station is just north of Lagos Island across the Carter Bridge, on Murtala Muhammed Way, not far from the Iddo Motor Park. Services have been erratic for years and the track has largely fallen into disrepair but in theory there is a service between Lagos and Kano once a week. It's supposed to depart from Lagos on Friday night and reaches Kano on Monday or Tuesday, before leaving again for Lagos the following day. A seat in second class is N1,025 and a first-class sleeper berth is N2,670. Check at the station to see if it's running.

ORIENTATION The Lagos metropolitan area covers a whopping 3,500km^2 and spreads over much of Lagos State on four principal islands and adjacent parts of the Nigerian mainland. Most visitors will spend the majority of their time on the islands, which are the real heart of the city, while the mainland is made up of a myriad of mostly poverty-stricken neighbourhoods and suburbs stretching as far as the eye can see.

The principal islands are **Lagos Island**, which is the site of the original settlement and today the predominant commercial district of the city; and **Ikoyi**, which is now merged with Lagos Island by landfill and is an area of leafy suburbs and big houses that was once the Government Reserved Area (GRA) during colonial days, and was the location of some federal buildings during the time when Lagos was capital before it moved to Abuja. Between the two is the working-class district of **Obalende**, where the Obalende Motor Park serves as the link for public transport between the islands and the rest of Lagos; **Victoria Island,** to the south of Ikoyi, is the business district where banks, embassies, hotels and most of the restaurants can be found. The **Lekki Peninsula**, to the east, is now joined to Victoria Island by another landfill that is today being hurriedly covered up by new development and middle-class housing estates. Ikoyi and Victoria Island are separated by the **Five Cowrie Creek**, so called because it used to cost five cowries to cross it by ferry long before any bridges were built.

Lagos Island is joined to the northwestern tip of Victoria Island by **Independence Bridge**, while Ikoyi connects with Victoria Island by what must be one of the busiest roads in the city, the **Falomo Bridge**. Three bridges connect Lagos Island with the mainland: the oldest is **Carter Bridge**, built in 1900 and repeatedly bolstered by new concrete; the **Eko Bridge**; and the **Third Mainland Bridge**, which stretches over ten kilometres across the Lagos Lagoon to join the Lagos–Ibadan Highway (look out for the hectic shanty town built on stilts between the bridge and the mainland). This is the longest bridge in Africa.

Whether you come to Lagos by road or air, your point of entry will be on the mainland. The airport is near the district of **Ikeja**, the mainland's most upmarket suburb, where there are a few hotels serving the airport. The main **motor parks** for long-distance road transport are scattered around the mainland in various working-class suburbs, from which you can feasibly get to the islands by public transport.

Initially it is a bit confusing finding your way around the islands as landfills have merged existing islands and street names have changed several times over the years, to appease certain government characters, and are often referred to by more than one name. Kingsway in Ikoyi that leads to the Falomo Bridge is a prime example: it is now called Alfred Rewane Road, though everyone still refers to it by its old name. If you can get hold of a street map (see *Maps and publications* in *Listings*, page 138) it helps a lot. I found that two completely defunct buildings made good landmarks and were helpful to get my bearings. The first, and about as central to the islands as you're going to get, is the **1004 apartments** to the left of Falomo Bridge on Victoria Island. This is a massive sprawl of run-down concrete blocks that used to house government ministers and officials when Lagos was the capital city before it moved to Abuja. It now stands forlornly empty and the buildings have been completely gutted, though there are rumours of redevelopment. The second is the former **Federal Secretariat** that lies roughly on the border with Ikoyi and Lagos Island. The cluster of tall blocks used to be where the government had offices before moving to Abuja, and again they're completely gutted.

GETTING AROUND

PUBLIC TRANSPORT

Public transport in Lagos is absolutely chaotic, but it is perhaps the rusting and overcrowded *molues* (big yellow buses), the swarm of yellow Peugeot 504 taxis, the thousands of battered *danfos* (minibuses), and the hundreds of thousands of customised *okadas* (motorbikes) that give Lagos some of its frantic charm. The city suffers from chronic traffic congestion, which makes it impossible for buses and taxis to operate efficiently, especially during the rush hours. All of Lagos's vehicles are scratched, dented and smashed up beyond belief – the sides have thousands of scratches on them where they have jostled with each other in the chaotic motor

AGEGE

Airport

OBAFEMI
AWOLOWA
WAY

LAGOS-IBADAN ROAD EXPRESSWAY

Ibadan

ALLEN AV

MOBOLAJI

BANK ANTHONY WAY

Afrika
Shrine

Sheraton

New China Restaurant
Motherlan'

IKEJA

Bank
House

AKINOBI ST

Domestic
terminal

Murtala
Mohammed
International
Airport

Tamarin

IKORODU ROAD

Ojota Motor Park

Ojota New
Motor Park

Oshodi
Motor Park

AGEGE MOTOR ROAD

ILUUPEJU

OSHODI

APAKI

IKORODU RD

IKORODU EXPRESSWAY

SHOMOLU

MUSHIN

ISOLO RD

MARKET ST
ST

MUSHIN RD

LAFYA

UNIVERSITY RD

Lagos University

N

Bradt

OWORONSOKI EXPRESSWAY

MASHA RD

WESTERN

Yaba Market

MURTALA MOHAMMED WAY

National
Stadium

0   2km
0   2 miles

APAPA

SURULERE

AVENUE

EBUTA
METTA

3rd Mainland
Bridge

Lagos Lagoon

LAGOS BADAGRY EXPRESSWAY

CEMETERY RD

National Theatre,
National Gallery

Railway station

see pages 000-0

Cotonou,
Badagry

OLD OJO RD

Eko
Bridge

Carter
Bridge

RING RD

Mile Two Motor Park

MALU RD

BADIA

Lagos
Island

BROAD ST

OBALENDE

A REVANE RD

KIRIRKIRI RD

APAPA

LIVERPOOL
RD

Excelsior

WAREHOUSE RD

Obalende
Motor Park

IKOYI

AWOLOWO RD

Thistle Bar

St Elmo's, Chicken Licken,
Frenchies

Apapa docks

Five
Cowrie
Creek

Falamo
Bridge

Tin Can Island

Porto Novo Creek

Victoria Island

AHMADU BELLO WAY

Bar Beach

Kuramo Lagoon

Lekki
Peninsula

see pages 000-0

Lighthouse
Beach

Tarkwa Bay

ATLANTIC
OCEAN

GREATER LAGOS

parks, and the vehicles are so ancient there are rust holes in the bodywork, doors have fallen off, and tail lights hang off rusted bumpers. They are simply driven until they die, and all over Lagos you will see abandoned, wrecked yellow vehicles on the side of the road, sometimes with chickens living inside, where they were just left when they finally stopped working.

Buses and minibuses Most of the minibuses, buses and taxis in Lagos are yellow, and they are an ubiquitous part of the city. The exceptions are those on Victoria Island and the adjoining Lekki Peninsula, which are green and white. The story goes that the one-time Minister of Transport did some deal with a paint company (from which he got a huge *dash*) to lay down a decree that all the vehicles on Victoria Island must be painted with a particular colour of green that was only available from this particular paint company. On the streets, vehicles do not run to any timetables – you just hail one down in the general direction that you want to go and they'll stop if they have a space. Around Victoria Island are bus stops denoted by either a square green sign or a round blue sign with a picture of a bus on them, where all public transport is supposed to stop (though they stop anywhere if they are not already in a 'go-slow'). Although vehicles run along all the main arteries, there is no way of telling what destination they are going to. But it's simple enough to jump on one in the direction you want to go, and if it turns off towards somewhere else, get off and jump on another that is going towards your destination.

Motor parks If you are beginning a journey at a motor park, vehicles go-when-full – nothing moves until the required amount of people are in place. In a motor park you'll have to ask around for a vehicle going in the direction you want to go, and some of them have the name of their destination (usually another motor park in a different part of the city) painted in small letters on the side of the vehicle towards the back. Also look out for a National Union Road Transport Workers man, and he will show you which vehicle to get on. There are several motor parks in mainland Lagos where vehicles depart to other destinations outside Lagos (dealt with under 'Getting there and away'). To get to any of these from the islands, you need to go to Obalende Motor Park between Ikoyi and Lagos Island. This massive motor park with its queues of yellow vehicles snaking their way down all the access roads is under a tangle of flyovers that eventually lead to the mainland via the Carter or Third Mainland bridges. Here you will find vehicles that go-when-full going directly to Ojota, Mile Two and Oshodi, the main motor parks for long-distance vehicles, and the journey from the islands across the city in a minibus should cost around N70.

Lagbuses Introduced in 2007 are the government red buses known as *Lagbus* and to date 280 have been been put on the roads. These are normal full-size public buses that bring commuters in to the city and run along set routes along the main roads from six mainland depots to points on the islands. Fares are a standard N80 whatever the distance. Routes can be seen on the website (*www.lagbusonline.com*). In theory they are supposed to run in a dedicated bus lane marked with a yellow line every 5–10 minutes. They do use this lane – and so does everyone else in Lagos. Painting a yellow line the length of the Third Mainland Bridge was perhaps in hindsight rather a waste of time, and how they actually managed to paint it given the traffic is a mystery.

Okadas Note that *okadas* are infinitely quicker than taxis – it's not uncommon for an expat with a car and driver to jump out of the car if it's stuck in traffic and to hop on an *okada* to get to a meeting. But they are also infinitely more dangerous – indeed far more so in Lagos than Nigeria's other cities and *okada* accidents and injuries are a

'Area Boys' are local hoodlums and thieves, who have been prevalent in Lagos since the 1960s. They use physical intimidation to get what they want and simply stop people and demand money or property while threatening them with belts, whips, sticks or guns. It's basically mugging – and in broad daylight and in front of thousands of other people. They also get aggressive towards drivers of vehicles who they will not let pass until they've received their *dash*, often snatching the keys out of a vehicle, and they think nothing of throwing a punch at an *okada* or minibus driver. If a brave victim objects, there is also the further threat of calling in more Area Boys to deal with him. They typically hang around the bus stops and motor parks, and under flyover bridges or major road junctions, mostly in mainland Lagos. Notable spots on the islands are Bar Beach on Victoria Island, and under the flyovers and bridges on Lagos Island.

Someone told us to go to Oshodi, a particularly notorious motor park on the mainland, 'early, as the Area Boys don't wake up until late morning'. He also added that this spot was known locally as the 'Area Boys' University'. That said, you are very unlikely to be a victim of an Area Boy; an attack on someone who is an obvious visitor to Nigeria and a white person would draw too much attention. Only very rarely will foreigners be stopped in their cars and the driver asked for a *dash*. Nevertheless keep your wits about you at all times. Area Boys are relatively unique to Lagos and are not found much in other Nigerian cities.

common daily sight. Consider the traffic, state of the roads, weather conditions, look of the bike and the colour of the whites of the driver's eyes before jumping on one.

Tuk-tuks New to Lagos Island are the three-wheeled *tuk-tuks*, which are imported from China and are beginning to feature in many African cities. Basically a motorised buggy with a covered seat behind the driver that is designed to carry three people across, but may well carry more. They cost a little more than an *okada* and to date I only saw them around the Obelende Motor Park, but as in Kano further north where they have been introduced so Muslim women don't have to get on the back of a motorbike driven by a strange man, they are likely to catch on soon. Nairobi in Kenya and Dar es Salaam in Tanzania also now have them.

Fares Minibuses and buses are not negotiable; taxis and *okadas* are always negotiable, and you'll have to bargain harder in Lagos than in any other part of the country. Minibuses within the islands cost N50 for a short hop; taxis or 'drops', meaning you have a car to yourself, cost in the region of N500 for a short journey, and N800–1,000 for a longer journey across the islands; *okadas* cost N50 for a short journey (roughly under a kilometre), while to go from one island to another, for example for a ride across the Falomo Bridge (never walk across here), expect to pay N150–200. Expect to pay about three times more for a drop in a car than you would pay for an *okada*, but remember if there are a few of you than a drop will work out cheaper than you all taking individual *okadas*.

Ferry In the residential area of southeast Ikoyi, on Oyinkan Abayomi Drive, is a ferry service across Five Cowrie Creek to a point midway between Victoria Island and Lekki. It is very useful and avoids a drive through the traffic on Falomo Bridge. On the Ikoyi side there's a small makeshift jetty where passenger motorboats generally go-when-full. Life jackets are available. Most Ikoyi *okada* drivers seem to know where it is and many hang out there waiting for passengers coming off the boat. The ride across takes less than a minute and costs N40. There's also now a slower car ferry; a sort of flat motorised punt that can hold four cars and is accessed down a short concrete ramp. The cost per car and occupants is N1,000. Both go to the Tarzan jetty and double-storey Tarzan bar on the opposite side of the creek, which is in walking distance of the Palms Mall and is where boats also go to the beach at Tarkwa Bay (see page 156 for details).

CAR HIRE As explained in Chapter 3, there is effectively no such thing as car hire and the division between taking a taxi and hiring a car is somewhat blurred. You cannot hire a car without a driver and it's the driver who pays for the petrol, so in essence you are taking a taxi, although the phrase 'car hire' is often used. You can find cars and drivers outside all the major hotels – ask the hotel reception staff to recommend a particular driver. Alternatively, if you come across a taxi driver you like and trust, who happens to have a cell phone, make him an offer and expect to bargain hard. Budget around N1,000/US$8 per hour.

WHERE TO STAY

In a city the size of Lagos, there are many hotels catering for the large expat community and for local business people – very, very few can say that they've actually received a tourist as a guest. Most are scattered over Victoria Island and Ikoyi, or in the upmarket suburb of Ikeja near the airport. Despite there being a competitive range of hotels, given that their customers are nearly always business-orientated, none of them are cheap and there aren't many budget options. There are cheap local hotels in more dubious parts of mainland Lagos, but you'd be ill-advised to spend the night in these areas. For the most part you are looking at spending not less than US$70 a night for two people in a double room, rising to US$300–400, which is considerably more than in the rest of Nigeria. As outlined in Chapter 3 under 'Accommodation', don't expect the same sort of quality that you would get for these prices as you would back home. Re-read the 'Glossary of Accommodation Terms' on page 74 and modify your expectations accordingly.

In any hotel always ask to see a room first, and remember that just because a hotel advertises facilities and services such as a business centre or even a tennis court, it does not necessarily mean that they are functioning. Nevertheless, Lagos does have some of the nicest hotels in Nigeria, and there are a couple of establishments that could qualify for international-class standards (in particular the Protea chain). Many of these are used by visiting Nigerian government officials from Abuja, or to house new expats while they wait for long-term accommodation to become available, and upper-crust hotels are used by companies to host potential expats on their look-sees. For the international chains, it's quite feasible to book through the websites.

The hotels listed here are grouped by area and price, based on the price of the cheapest double room. This is because many have 'suites' – a hotel could have a whole selection of rooms of different sizes and with bigger beds resulting in some instances of room rates ranging from US$70 to US$800 in one establishment. Unless otherwise stated all rooms have en-suite bathrooms and AC, and all hotels have their own generators, so power is pretty consistent.

IKOYI

⌂ **Sofitel Moorhouse** | Bankole Oki Rd; ☏ 01 461 540922; www.sofitel.com. This intimate & professional guesthouse has excellent service & friendly staff & is part of the international Sofitel chain. It's Lagos's finest boutique hotel, located in a quiet corner of Ikoyi & well signposted off Alfred Rewane Road (formerly Kingsway). It's also consistently full as this is the place expats stay when they come to Lagos for a 'look-see' & the companies want to impress them. The 44 rooms &

8 suites with DSTV & minibar are modern & immaculate, & some have an additional balcony & lounge area. There is fine dining to be had in the L'Aquarelle restaurant (guests only), & there's a separate bar, reliable business centre, swimming pool & gym. You can book through the website, which attracts a discount. $$$$$

⌂ **The Elion House** 7–8 Agbeken Rotinwa St, off Hannat Balogun St, Dolphin Estate; \ 01 461 4190–4; www.elionhousehotel.com. This is a newish 2-storey boutique hotel tucked away in a quiet suburb of Ikoyi. There's stringent security to get through the gate & even into the housing estate where it's located. To find it you need to be on the expressway that goes from the Third Mainland Bridge across the top of Ikoyi & then take the turn-off (past a huge pile of rubbish & a resident family of pigs) signposted to the Federal Secretariat – the 3 abandoned high-rise buildings to the northwest of Ikoyi. This road comes to what is effectively a dead end just before the Federal Secretariat, but the Elion House is on the last road to the right (there is a signpost). You can't get here by road from Alfred Rewane Rd in the middle of Ikoyi – you have to go via the expressway. Once at the hotel, look out for the clocks above the reception desk that show times in Lagos, London & Beirut – the Lebanese management imports paint from Lebanon each month to maintain the place! There are sweeping staircases, marble floors, fine art on the walls & antiques everywhere, & the 24 enormous rooms are individually decorated, with DSTV, minibar, safe & sometimes a corner bath. There's 24-hour room service, a secure car park, a water-treatment plant, gym, & an immaculate swimming pool. Fine wines & Italian & Lebanese food are served in the Olive Garden restaurant (guests only), & the Classico bar & lounge serves cocktails while someone plays the piano. Rates are not bad for this quality & include

breakfast but not the 15% that goes on everything. At the time of writing they also didn't require a deposit, but again that may change. $$$$

⌂ **Bogobiri House** 9 Maitama St; \ 01 474 7421, 270 7436; www.bogobirilagos.com. This is a new treat to Lagos & conveniently located right across the road from the Nimbus Art Centre (see *Nightlife*) & close to Awolowo Road's restaurants. With just ten rooms, the décor is stunning with rattan cane furniture, four-poster beds, African prints on the wall, shelves of African pots & giant flat-screen TVs. Some of the bathrooms have lovely mosaic tiling & the front door with its statues & lanterns is a piece of artwork in itself. There's internet access; you can arrange car hire & airport pick ups; there's a beauty therapist on site for massages, manicures & facials; & you can even rent a cell phone. $$$

⌂ **YMCA** 77 Awolowo Rd; \ 01 773 3599; www.ymcaoflagos.org. This is strictly men only, so for blokes on a budget this is the cheapest place to stay in Lagos, though it's pretty grim & I cannot be sure how secure it is. A block back from Awolowo Road, though well signposted behind the BG Mart shop (look up for the sign), the 'Y' has several rooms around a cool courtyard in a concrete block. The bare dorms (US$3) have 2 double bunks in each with a separate bathroom with little more than a loo, tap & bucket, while the rooms (US$20) have an additional shower, a fan & a chair. It's very basic & not wholly clean, there's no AC or reliable gen, & you'll need your own bedding. On the plus side the doors lock & there is intact mossie screening on the windows. The maximum stay is 7 days & you'll need to be a member (about US$2.50 to join) – many of the guests are from other West African countries & may be staunchly religious. There is a YMCA in Lagos on Lagos Island but it is inadvisable to stay there. $

VICTORIA ISLAND

⌂ **Victoria Crown Plaza** 292b Ajose Adeogun St, Victoria Island; \ 01 621 3133; www.vcphotel.com. New to Lagos & probably its finest boutique hotel, which is topped by a lavish presidential suite that takes up the entire floor. There are 39 standard rooms & a number of suites with a pool, bar, antique furniture & gold & gilt in the bathrooms. The suites have additional double jacuzzis & goose down pillows & you can arrange a personal butler. The Alo Alo restaurant is very plush with thick carpet & silverware & white linen on the tables &

specialises in Italian, plus there's fine dining to be had on the terrace or in the piano bar. The grilled prawns & calamari here are excellent. $$$$$

⌂ **Blue Sea Hotel** 24 Amodu Tijani St; \ 01 270 8820/1; www.blueseahotels.com. In the same quiet cul-de-sac as the Camelot (see below), this is a smart personal option in a bright blue building with secure parking & imported made-for-hotel Italian furniture. Rooms have safes, DSTV, wireless internet & minibars. There's a neat swimming pool at the back with umbrellas & sun loungers, plus a restaurant bar, gym & business centre. The staff here are exceptionally friendly. $$$$

🏠 **Federal Palace Hotel** Ahmadu Bello Way; ☎ 01 262 3116–25. The Federal Palace is a landmark on VI — a tall concrete tower with a big circular orange symbol on the side standing to the east of Victoria Island overlooking Lagos Harbour. The standards here are not on the same level as Lagos's other big hotels in the same price range although a new, more modern wing has been built (but at the time of writing wasn't open yet). The Executive Floor on the 14th floor of the existing block has however been refurbished, & these 18 rooms have much nicer furniture than elsewhere in the hotel & wooden floors, with a private check-in desk, international newspapers & magazines, business centre & a lounge with complementary tea & coffee, where you can also take breakfast or eat meals sent up from the restaurant. The other 600-odd rooms & 80 suites are spacious, with one or two enormous double beds, but they smell terribly musty & have old-fashioned furniture. All rooms, however, have a balcony, DSTV & minibar, & face the harbour. Facilities include the completely overhauled swimming pool & terrace with wooden sun loungers, which have a great view of the harbour, a curio market out in the car park, a conference venue built out on a concrete island in the water, useful desks in the lobby for courier services and car hire, an Aero Contractors desk upstairs and a Chanchangi desk in the car park, & restaurants (covered under *Where to eat & drink*). $$$$

🏠 **Protea Hotel** Victoria Island Violet Yough Close; ☎ 01 320 4717/27/37; www.proteahotels.com. This is a fairly new & quality hotel on a prime site on Victoria Island managed by the South African Protea chain with a rim-flow swimming pool, modern restaurants & hi-tech bar, conference & business facilities, & a gym with equipment air-freighted in from South Africa. The 42 rooms have all working mod cons, imported hotel furniture & good views of the city. Airport transfers can be arranged. $$$$

🏠 **Protea Hotel Kuramo Waters** off Ogunlewe St; ☎ 01 271 2962–4; www.proteahotels.com. This is Protea's latest offering in Lagos, which is very nicely located with views of the Kuramo Lagoon. The 60 rooms & suites are arranged in a row of red-tiled blocks & are equipped with internet access, DSTV, cool tiled floors & dark wood furnishings. There's a lovely 12m pool surrounded by a terrace right on the water's edge, plus an excellent restaurant (guests only) & piano bar. $$$$

🏠 **Eko Hotel** Adetokunbo Ademola St; ☎ 01 262 4600-19; www.ekohotels.com. This is a largely business travellers' hotel set in a central spot on Victoria Island on a huge wedge of land with nice gardens backing on to the Kuramo Lagoon. The open & airy reception area is contemporarily decorated with plants, African prints & *objets d'art*, & with wooden walkways leading through to the swimming pool, where there are sun loungers & a great outside bar overlooking the lagoon. The 492 rooms have phone, internet access, minibar & DSTV, while the new Eko suites that opened in 2004 have additional kitchenette, fax & photocopier. Slightly cheaper accommodation is available in the adjacent & newly refurbished Eco Gardens. Facilities include a gym, sauna, tennis & volleyball courts, & several top-class restaurants & bars listed individually in *Where to eat & drink*. The 15% is added to all rates. The Eko is one of Lagos's nicest hotels, but the open lobby is not especially secure, & there have been security problems here in the past. Rooms $$$; suites $$$$$

🏠 **B-Jay's Hotel** 24 Samuel Manuwa St; ☎ 01 270 4861/2; www.bjayshotel.com. A reasonably small hotel with friendly staff on the outer rim of Victoria Island overlooking Five Cowrie Creek & just two blocks from the new Palms Mall. The 34 very attractive rooms have just had a refit & now have polished wooden floors, are decorated with modern African art, & have DSTV, small fridge & phone. Ask about weekend specials — sometimes three nights for the price of two. The L-shaped Cowrie bar & restaurant has recently had a refit & is stunning; it's definitely worthwhile coming to eat or drink here even if you're not staying (see *Where to eat & drink*). You can hire cars from a stand across the street. Rates are inclusive of the 15% & include tea or coffee & toast in the morning. Rooms $$$; suites $$$$

🏠 **The Camelot Rest House** Plot 1425b Amodu Tijani Close; ☎ 01 261 2103/262 5797; www.camelotresthouse.com. Another good new hotel with enthusiastic staff (the chef will greet you personally) in a central location on Victoria Island at the end of a quiet cul-de-sac. It features all-new furniture & appliances, including a state-of-the-art reservations system & hairdryers in the rooms, & a huge car park with security guards. The medieval theme continues in the Dragon's Den Bush Bar on the roof, which is open 24 hours, with good views of the city; the downstairs Merlin's Bar & Coffee

Shoppe, which serves snacks & sandwiches; & the King Arthur restaurant, which serves a range of Oriental, Lebanese & continental dishes & Italian wines. The 32 rooms have enormous beds, minibar, DSTV & phones; the bigger suites have balconies & fat sofas. Rooms $$$; suites $$$$

🏠 **Hotel Victoria Palace** 1623 Saka Jojo St; ℡ 01 262 5901/8. This has 30 rooms on three floors in a surprisingly quiet street & with exceptionally friendly staff. The rooms are basic but adequate, with fridge, DSTV & big old beds, & the bathrooms have seen a lick of paint in recent years; shame they couldn't have replaced the ancient bathroom

fittings at the same time. The back rooms look out on to the noisy launderette, so ask to see a few rooms before you decide. The Bombay Palace restaurant serves Indian, Nigerian & continental dishes, but this is rather dependent on what ingredients they've got, & there's a pool table & dart board in the guest lounge. The best thing about this hotel is the row of clocks in reception – you know, time in London, time in New York etc. They have one for the time in Timisora (in Romania). Room rates are inclusive of the 15% & b/fast. $$

LEKKI PENINSULA

🏠 **Protea Hotel** Oakwood Park Lekki Expressway, opposite Chevron; ℡ 01 270 2900; www.proteahotels.com. Another new Protea with very high standards, though it's primarily aimed at the conference market. There are 65 very comfortable rooms with all the trimmings, a large pool with terrace & pool bar, fine dining in the formal restaurant (guests only), gym & sauna, a cocktail bar & extensive conference facilities with modern equipment that caters for up to 600 people. $$$$

🏠 **La Campagne Tropicana** to the eastern end of Lekki Beach, approx 20km along the Lekki Expressway from Victoria Island, turn right at the

Total petrol station; ℡ 0805 222 7226; www.lacampagne.org. This is an attractive beachside resort spread around 60 acres of woodlands surrounding a lagoon that offers safe swimming & excellent bird watching. The neat & tidy 2-storey bamboo huts & chalets have an upstairs bedroom & downstairs lounge with DSTV, & either a shower or bath. The more expensive ones have an additional jacuzzi. Each unit has a fridge with complimentary soft drinks, & rates are inclusive of three meals a day. The beach is wide & very clean here & you can walk through the woodlands & sample palm wine at a rustic bar. Huts & permanent tents $$$; chalets $$$$

THE MAINLAND
Apapa

🏠 **Excelsior Hotel** 3–15 Ede St; ℡ 01 587 6095; ℮ excelsior@infoweb.abs.net. This is in the suburb of Apapa near the port area on the mainland, but be aware this is a rough area. Built in the 1960s & not renovated since 1989, it's a popular but very rundown hotel, with dusty nicotine-coloured walls throughout, but nevertheless it is one of the cheapest places to stay. Facilities include a bright red Chinese restaurant called the Double O, a very

faded hotel dining room for basic Nigerian meals, & a dodgy bar for hard-core drinking. The 111 rooms on 3 floors have local TV, fridge, scratched furniture & dusty armchairs, & dilapidated bathrooms with buckets, though they are clean enough to use. Rates include the 15%. Outside the hotel are a few curio sellers & some Hausa money changers, & a few blocks south of here, on Warehouse Road, are a couple of fast-food joints. $

Ikeja

🏠 **Sheraton Lagos Hotel and Towers** 30 Mobolaji Bank Anthony Way; ℡ 01 280 0100–300; www.starwood.com/sheraton. Conveniently located near the airport, the hotel runs a shuttle service (airline crews stay here). There are 332 spacious rooms with DSTV, iron & ironing board, & minibar; the more expensive rooms & suites in the Towers section are on the sixth floor with a separate check-in desk, lounge & café, & other extras, such as someone to turn down your bed. Facilities

include a business centre, ballroom, tennis courts, mosque, swimming pool, various conference halls & several top-notch restaurants dealt with under *Where to eat & drink*. The expensive hotel shop sells books & curios & international magazines & newspapers. In the lobby are desks for Virgin Nigeria & British Airways, & a desk for Planet Car Hire. Although all the rooms have been newly refurbished, the lobby is a bit dated – this is what one reader says of it: 'The lobby looks like the set of a 1970s porn movie, & combined with the awful music from the band that plays the same songs every night, it could well have been once.' Another complaint here is that prices for food & drink are exceptionally high. Given that most airline crews are instructed not to leave the grounds, the hotel can more or less charge what they want. There is a supermarket in the block next to the hotel for cheaper items such as bottles of water. Rooms $$$$; suites $$$$$

🏠 **House J** 1 Sir Michael Otedola St, off Joel Ogunnaike St, GRA; 📞 01 497 2288/0423; www.housej.com. A friendly mid-range option with just 14 rooms only 1km from the airport's domestic terminal & 3km from the international terminal in a quiet Ikeja suburb. Although with dated furnishings, the rooms are clean & compact with DSTV & start from an affordable US$130. There's a nice pool, secure parking in the compound, which is surrounded by manicured trees, & a gym. The neat restaurant & bar serves Nigerian staples & some simple continental dishes & they can organise car hire & airport shuttles. $$$

🏠 **Airport Hotel** 111 Obafemi Awolowo Way; 📞 01 493 7573; www.lagosairporthotelltd.com. This is a huge complex close to the roundabout that joins Obafemi Awolowo Way & Allen Avenue in Ikeja, a few kilometres north of the Sheraton in the Ikeja GRA, among the heaving mass of markets & vehicles that is the centre of Ikeja proper. It's a terribly tired-looking old hotel, the bulk of it having been built in 1961, & with seemingly not much being done to it since. However, it provides an alternative if the Sheraton is out of your league. It started life as the Grand Hotel, Lagos in 1942 with just 5 rooms. The present 1960s monstrosity has 277 rooms spread over 3 L-shaped blocks. All the rooms have fridge & local TV, but the décor is hideous, with beaten-up & old-fashioned dressing tables & garish flowery curtains & sheets. There are 3 car parks, 4 bars, 1 Nigerian & 1 Chinese restaurant, an Olympic-sized swimming pool, & 6 vast conference halls, which are often overrun with conference delegates or noisy weddings, funerals, church services & the like. Facilities include car hire, an airport shuttle bus, & in the shopping arcade outside are some bureaux de change & travel agents. With 4 giant generators & 3 boreholes, the power & water supply is fairly consistent, & the staff are generally good, as many of them have worked there for years. Their brochure was clearly printed many years ago, but it amused me greatly – 'Tired or bored? Spooky or dingy? Make a way to any of our bars & wash off a little.' $$

🏠 **Tamarin Hotel** 158 Adekunle Fajuyi Way; 📞 01 497 9160–9; www.tamarinhotels.com. This is an affordable & well-run hotel in the relatively peaceful Ikeja GRA not too far from the airport (the domestic terminal is only about a 10min drive). To get here, either make use of the hotel's shuttle service (though you will struggle to pre-arrange this before arriving), or get a taxi straight from the airport as most drivers will know the way. Adekunle Fajiuyi runs parallel to Agege Motor Rd with the railway line separating the two streets so you can see the hotel from Agege Motor Rd as well. There's a restaurant & bar serving mainly Nigerian food, a swimming pool, a gym, & you can arrange car hire. The range of comfortable rooms & suites are spread over several wings, & are spacious with DSTV, fridge, enormous beds & old furniture. The best value rooms are the Olive Chalets, but out of a total of 103 rooms there are only nine of these. Rates are inclusive of the 15% & breakfast. Chalets $$; rooms $$$

AROUND LAGOS STATE: BADAGRY

🏠 **Soketta Hotel** Hospital Rd, a short walk around the corner & north from the Heritage Museum near the cemetery; 📞 01 723 4318 (the telephone code in Badagry is the same as in Lagos). Rather astonishingly, part of the ground floor is taken up by an internet café powered by a 24-hour gen. The 14 double rooms & 2 suites are dark & grim but have giant beds, local TV & fridge. There are a few chairs outside in the pleasant garden area under a thatched hut, but it's very noisy here if the gen is on. Nigerian meals are available, plus occasional continental dishes, such as not-so-fiery chicken curry & rice. $

✗ WHERE TO EAT AND DRINK

Lagos has by far the best restaurants in the country for international fare – elsewhere you will struggle to find a non-Nigerian meal – but the imported ingredients and accompanying wine and other imported alcoholic drinks on the menus come at a price. In a Lagos restaurant serving international or 'Western' food, a main dish alone averages N2,000/US$15, without extras such as drinks and the 15% VAT and service charge, which nearly all Lagos eateries add on, so even a not very special meal for two with drinks can cost around N6,500–7,500/US$50–60 and much more in the better restaurants. Nevertheless, Lagos has an excellent variety of international restaurants and plenty of people prepared to pay from the expat community and upper elite of Lagos society. European, Lebanese and Oriental food are readily available, and most menus feature international dishes and Nigerian food, of which the latter is always cheaper. However, one of the biggest problems in Lagos restaurants is the inconsistency of the food and service, and not all the dishes are terribly authentic. You might have a great meal there one day, and a truly awful one the next – it all depends on which chef or waiter is on duty.

For very cheap Nigerian food, as is the case everywhere in Nigeria, there are the street food hawkers and the food-is-ready stalls. Although they are plentiful in the market areas of Lagos Island and the mainland, they are not found readily in the more upmarket Ikoyi and Victoria Islands, though cheap chop can be found around the Obalende Motor Park on Ikoyi and along Bar Beach on Victoria Island. These islands have a smattering of fairly modern fast-food joints for those on a budget. In Ikoyi, most moderately priced restaurants are clustered along or around Awolowo Road, while the more expensive options are dotted around Victoria Island or in the upmarket hotels and increasingly in the new shopping malls.

LAGOS ISLAND

✕ **La Scala** MUSON Centre, 8–9 Marina (entrance opposite the National Museum on Awolowo Road); ☎ 01 264 6885, 264 6391; ⏰ lunch 12.00–15.00 Mon–Fri; dinner 19.00–22.30 Mon–Sat, though it's sometimes closed for private upscale functions. Consistently known as the best restaurant in Lagos with quality continental cuisine, silver service, luxurious décor with wooden floors & ceilings, crisp tablecloths, fine china & silverware, & an intimate bar. Don't miss the sole in lemon butter or the jumbo grilled prawns in garlic sauce. There's an extensive albeit expensive selection of fine wines from France, Italy & South Africa, & don't forget the 15% which adds considerably to the bill here. There is secure parking in the MUSON Centre's car park. Unbeatable atmosphere & very elegant; reservations are essential & you need to dress up. $$$$$

✕ **Al Dente** City Mall, Awolowo Rd, Lagos Island; ⏰ 12.00–22.30 Mon–Sat. Italian restaurant on the top floor of the mall with veiws out over the Muson Centre across the street. It has warm a décor of muted greens & browns & pictures of statues of Adonis & Eros. Standard Italian food such as pizza & pasta, but short on specials like veal. $$$

IKOYI

Flowerstalk 114 Awolowo Road; ☎ 01 270 1629; ⏰ 10.00–18.00 daily. This is a fairly new upmarket florist above a bank with an attached tearoom serving gourmet salads, fresh juice & good coffee, & occasional treats such as foie gras. The shop sells trendy plants, vases & some stunning flowers, & it's a lovely place to sit surrounded by all the greenery, but the food is very overpriced. $$$$

✕ **Golden Gate** Alfred Rewane Rd; ☎ 01 269 5337/9; ⏰ 12.00–16.00, 19.00–22.00 daily. A very formal & upmarket Oriental restaurant serving good but pricey Chinese, Japanese & Thai food in different restaurant areas; you can request that no MSG be put in your food. The terrace on the roof has great views of the city & is a popular venue for company/embassy receptions. $$$$

✕ **Tanjia** 54 Raymond Njoku St, Ikoyi; ☎ 01 897 2117; www.tanjialagos.com; ⏰ 13.00–late Tue–Sun. Moroccan cuisine & DJs on Friday night in a lovely set of lounges decorated with Asian & Moroccan motifs, brass platters, giant vases, velvet cushions & low wooden tables. Happy hour is Tue–Thu 18.00–20.00 & there are regular events from film shows to corporate parties. Food includes authentic tajines & keftas or you can get cheaper soups & sandwiches. $$$–$$$$

✕ **Coconut Grove** 108 Awolowo Rd; ☎ 01 269 6111/2; ⏰ 12.00–15.00 daily; on Sun last orders for lunch 17.00; dinner 19.00–23.30 Mon–Sat. There's an odd mixture of things here. The décor is

Carribean style with murals of palm trees & toucans on the walls, although most of the food is standard steak or fish with rice meals. $$$

✗ **Double Four** 44 Awolowo Rd; ☏ 01 269 3012, 269 3524; ⊕ 11.00–23.00 daily. Predominantly a Lebanese restaurant but which also has burgers, pizzas & ice cream, with some 150 dishes on the menu — more Western ones include beef stroganoff, chicken Kiev & prawn curry. The atmosphere is noisy with blaring television, but it's popular with business people at lunchtime for the good food, & there's a bar area with a real espresso machine. The general manager, Awni, is quite a character & we managed to have quite an animated conversation with him about the state of Middle East politics (on which he has a lot of opinions). A bunch of Lebanese men at the table next to the door appear to do the same all day over coffee & cigarettes. At the time of writing a new branch was in the process of opening in the City Mall (see page 135) on Lagos Island. It should have a

similar menu, & the smart new décor features Italian prints on the wall, linen table cloths & a curved cocktail bar. $$$

♀ **British High Commission Club** (also known as the Kingfisher Club), 4 Reeve Rd; ☏ 01 461 5661/2. Wed nights are open nights for guests outside the High Commission (though if you go regularly you will be expected to pay a fee to join), when you can get very cheap British beer & traditional fish & chips. You must first apply at the gate of the club for an ID card for which you'll need two passport photos. There's also a range of sporting facilities here such as netball, tennis & squash courts, & the expat gatherings are very social. $$

✗ **Home Cooking** 38 Awolowo Rd; ☏ 01 267 1043; ⊕ 10.00–22.00 Mon–Sat. This is a good Nigerian restaurant specialising in cheap & tasty food from the Effik/Calabar region, including goat's head, cow's leg, bushmeat or oxtail pepper soup, plus dried fish, snails & a variety of starches & soups. Friendly atmosphere but slow service. $$

VICTORIA ISLAND

✗ **Churrasco** on the same property as The Lagoon (below), 1c Ozumba Mbadiwe Av; in a circular building in the car park; ☏ 01 262 9961; ⊕ 12.00–16.00, 19.00–midnight. The first Brazilian restaurant in Lagos that serves all-you-can-eat meat dishes for US$40, in which waiters carve off strips of meat from skewers on to your plate, or all-you-can-eat salads for US$20 from the salad bar. There's also a broad selection of snacks such as hummus, couscous & rice & beans. The name churrasco is Portuguese for a cut of steak or grilled meat & it's cooked in an open pit of coals referred to as a *churrasqueira*. $$$$$

✗ **Foods of the Sun Eko Hotel** Adetokunbo Ademola Street; ☏ 01 262 4600/19; www.ekohotels.com; ⊕ 19.00–22.30 Mon–Sat. The best French restaurant in Lagos with a small but exquisite menu, with daily chef's specials & the finest of French wines. Although the décor is very ordinary, in a plain-looking hotel dining room, & there's not much atmosphere, the food is to be relished; try a starter of goose liver pate with caramelised apples, followed by a main course of veal, lamb or crocodile. Don't forget the 15% which adds considerably to a bill here. $$$$$

✗ **Kuramo Sports Café Eko Hotel** Adetokunbo Ademola Street; ☏ 01 262 4600–19; www.ekohotels.com; ⊕ 06.00–10.30, 12.00–16.00 & 20.00–01.00 daily. A cavern of a place decorated, as the name suggests, with all things sporty, including giant TV screens

showing the South African sports channel Supersport. There are continental & Nigerian all-you-can-eat buffets, & the Nigerian dishes include bushmeat stew & chicken pepper soup. The bar serves local & imported beers, spirits & wines. A good place to be if you want to stuff yourself silly in front of a big match. The hotel's Poolside Terrace at the front of the restaurant has a snack menu & it's a perfect venue for an afternoon drink overlooking Kuramo Lagoon. $$$$$

✗ **Villa Medici** 1 Alhaji Babatunde Jose Rd (formerly Festival Rd); ☏ 01 262 1717, 261 0484; ⊕ 12.00–14.30 & 19.00–22.30 Mon–Fri, 19.00–22.30 Sat. Pricey but serves excellent French & Italian food & wine in a lovely atmosphere with elegant dressed-up tables with black tablecloths, sparkling silverware & crystal glasses, arranged around an indoor pond with its own footbridge. Expect the likes of beef fillet medallions & lobster — don't forget to add on the 15%. The service is superb & you'll need to dress up. Recommended for a special night out. Security guards outside watch your car. It's a bit hard to spot but look for a green fence & lots of trees. $$$$$

✗ **Lagoon** 1c Ozumba Mbadiwe Av; ☏ 01 261 1616, 261 6888; ⊕ 12.00–23.00 daily. A formal dining room overlooking Five Cowrie Creek serving continental, Chinese, some Indian & West African dishes washed down with French wine. Upmarket & good quality but with extremely slow service. There's

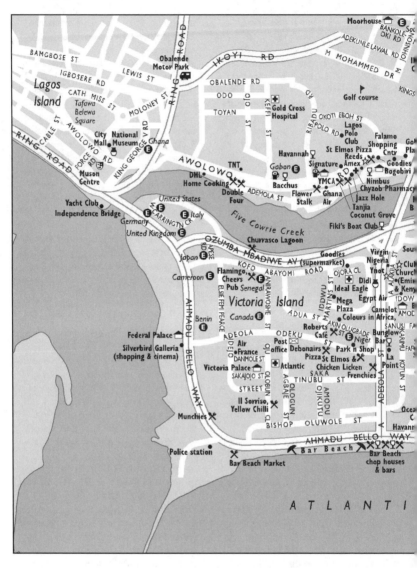

a huge & secure car park here, & cheaper takeaways such as burgers & pizzas are available from a kiosk outside on the terrace. The whole complex is a large venue popular for functions & the annual draw for Nigeria's FA Cup is held here. $$$$

✕ **Bangkok Restaurant** 244a Muri Okunola Street; ☎ 01 461 0666; ⏰ 11.00–23.00 daily. Excellent Thai & other Asian dishes flavoured with traditional lemon grass & coconut, great authentic green & red curries & pad Thai noodles, in an informal setting with efficient service & friendly owners. There is parking & security guards outside to

watch your car & takeaways are available. The menu here is delightfully misspelt – try the spaer ribs or the sring rools! There's another branch of the Bangkok in Cape Town, South Africa, that also has an excellent reputation. $$$

✕ **Casa Chianti Eko Hotel** Adetokunbo Ademola St; ☎ 01 261 4570; ⏰ 12.00–23.00 daily. Pleasant & homely hotel Italian restaurant with friendly staff, red & white checked table cloths, booth seating & separate bar & lounge area outside surrounded by tropical gardens. Classic dishes are on offer such as spaghetti carbonara, seafood

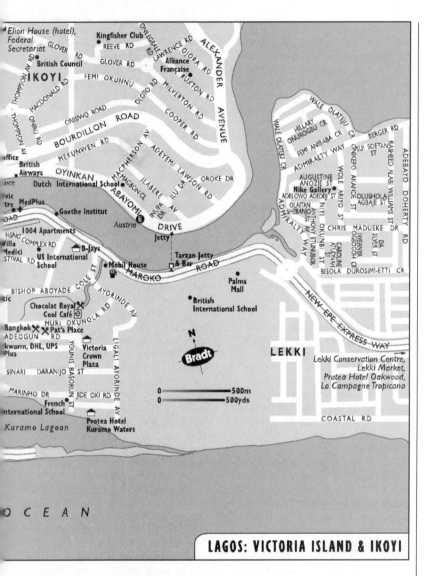

LAGOS: VICTORIA ISLAND & IKOYI

tagliatelle & tiramisu for dessert & the food's authentic & comes in large portions with plenty of crusty bread & olive oil. $$$

✕ **Cowrie Restaurant and Bar in B-Jay's Hotel** 24 Samuel Manuwa Street; ☏ 01 774 6900/1, 270 4861; www.bjayshotel.com; ⊕ 10.00–22.30 daily. This is in an L-shaped room with one arm as the bar & the other as the restaurant. It's a very stylish place with good service, relaxing music, sociable atmosphere & recently refurbished earthy décor – lose yourself in the enormous leather sofas. There's also an outside terrace, but unfortunately it's right

next to the traffic. The cuisine is continental & Nigerian; there's a full buffet on Wed & Sun with live music, low-calorie specials on Thu, & a happy hour 19.00–20.00 on Fri. The bar has a broad selection of wine & imported spirits. Bizarrely, the menu not only lists the dishes & the prices, but also the time it takes to make the food. So Cordon Bleu steak (40min) takes the same time as an egg sandwich! There are occasional jazz nights here which are worth asking about. $$$

✕ **Il Sorriso** 27a Oju Olobun Close; ☏ 01 261 0153, 461 1719; ⊕ 11.00–23.00 daily. The best traditional Italian restaurant & pizzeria in Lagos with a trattoria atmosphere, run by an authentic & friendly Italian family — even the menu is in Italian & all the wines come from Italy. Popular with the expat community & deservedly so, & as it's small & intimate, reservations are essential. There's a full range of pasta & risotto dishes plus truffles, prawns & salmon, & tiramisu, profiteroles & Italian ice cream for dessert. Just in front of the entrance is another restaurant with a smart bar upstairs, the Yellow Chilli, that serves good & cheap Nigerian food-is-ready. $$$

✖ **Lighthouse Restaurant Federal Palace Hotel** Ahmadu Bello Way; ✆ 01 262 3116–25; ⏰ 06.00–22.00 daily. A relaxing restaurant with buffets for breakfast, lunch & dinner, with a variety of continental, Chinese & Nigerian food on offer. There are also à la carte items like fish & chips & spaghetti. Enjoy a drink or a cocktail in the hotel bar first for a fine view of the shipwrecks in Lagos Harbour. You can also get snacks at the hotel's Poolside Café during the day. $$$

✖ **Ocean Pearl Oceanview Complex** Adetokunbo Ademola St, Victoria Island; ✆ 01 261 3555; ⏰ 11.00–23.00 daily. A very ordinary looking but established Chinese restaurant with a big menu that's popular for business lunches. There's good dim sum, the prawn dumplings are delicious & service is speedy. There's a long fully stocked bar & next door is the Coral Snack Bar where you can get a cheaper wrap or burger & a glass of freshly made Chapmans. $$$

🍽 **Chocolat Royal** AIM Plaza, next to the Cool FM radio building, 267 Etim Inyang Crescent; ✆ 01 262 3055/6; ⏰ 07.00–22.00 daily. A glitzy French-style patisserie serving the best pastries & fresh cream cakes in Lagos, & the place to be seen for besuited executives with cell phones attached to their ears at lunchtime — from the outside tables note the line of BMWs & Land Cruisers with waiting drivers. Serves sweet & savoury snacks, huge salads with all the trimmings, ice cream, muffins, divine handmade chocolates, cappuccino & freshly ground coffee. It's packed to the gills, the waiters glide around in crisp white uniforms, there's wireless internet & a very buzzy atmosphere. It's pricey but fabulous & great for a treat. Across the street & a few metres up, opposite Cool FM, is the hi-tec Cool Café, which offers just about the fastest & most reliable internet access in Lagos. Snacks $$; meals $$$

✖ **Flamingo Restaurant and Cheers Pub** 10 Kofo Abayomi Street; ✆ 01 262 2225, 261 0387; ⏰ 12.00–23.30 daily. This has a huge range of Chinese, Indian & continental dishes, of which the Indian food is the best: good nan bread, vindaloo, tikka & sizzling tandoori dishes. It's great for vegetarians, with several dishes just for them, including veggie curries & cutlets, & Chinese soups they will cook without the meat. Home delivery available. $$

🍽 **Frenchies** 29 Akin Adesola Street; ✆ 01 261 0096, 261 0186; ⏰ 08.00–22.00 Mon–Sat; 14.00–21.00 Sun. A ground-floor café with a bakery selling pies, cakes & pizza, & a first-floor licensed restaurant serving grills & kebabs with an outside terrace overlooking the traffic. Excellent affordable sandwiches thanks to the great freshly baked white bread. There's another branch in Lekki Market. $$

🍽 **Robert's Café** Akin Olugbade Street; ✆ 01 270 2606; ⏰ 09.00–18.00 Mon–Fri, 10.00–19.00 Sat. Opposite the Colours in Africa shop (see *Shopping*), just around the corner from both the Mega Plaza & Park 'n' Shop, so it's the perfect venue for expat ladies to take tea while they are out shopping. This is one of Lagos's most elegant & expensive coffee-and-cake cafés, with bright white tablecloths, stylish furniture, intimate music & personalised service. Drink freshly brewed coffee or tea from china cups & indulge in rich chocolate cake, Black Forest gateaux, or cheesecake for around N600 a slice. There's also a menu of authentic cocktails such as margaritas & bloody Marys. Very nice! $$

🍽 **Mega Plaza Food Court** next to the main entrance of the Mega Plaza, 14 Idowu Martins St, Victoria Island; ⏰ until 21.00 daily. There are a number of cheap stalls here serving fancy wraps, subs, hot dogs, spring rolls, burgers, chips & salads as well as Nigerian snacks, though you may choose to stay clear of the liver, gizzards & snails. Unusual (for Nigeria) items on the menu include bacon & mushrooms, but prices reflect the imported ingredients (presumably bought from the supermarket upstairs in the food court). Personally, I would be wary of the milkshakes. There are outside tables in the centre in the baking sun, & as most of the food at the stalls is fried, this is stinking hot during the day — it's better to come in the early evening when you can fill up with good, cheap food & a cold beer. $–$$

✖ **Chicken Lickin and St Elmo's Pizza** 80 Adeola Odeku St; ⏰ 09.00–22.00 daily. Both part of South African chains that are popping up all over Africa. Chicken Licken is a bit like KFC, serving fried chicken, fries & coleslaw, while St Elmo's serves excellent pizzas & some pasta dishes. A few doors down is a branch of Debonairs Pizza, which is similar to St Elmo's. $

THE MAINLAND
Apapa

✗ At 20 Warehouse Rd in Apapa is another branch of **Chicken Licken** and **St Elmo's** (both ⊕ 09.00–22.00 daily), & there's also another branch of **Frenchies** a few doors along at 14b Warehouse Rd (⊕ 08.00–20.00 Mon–Sat).

♀ **Thistle Bar** 36 New Marine Rd; ☎ 01 545 5226; ⊕ 09.00–midnight Sun–Thu; 09.00–03.00 Fri–Sat. There's an odd mixture of things here but it's a fun & lively venue, the food is excellent & is almost worth a special trip out to Apapa in itself. Be warned that it's a haunt for 'nightriders' in the evenings. There's an outside thatched bar with fans, happy hour is on Mon & Wed 17.30–19.30, & on Wed, Fri & Sat there's live music. The menu is called the Investment Schedule; starters are called Opening Accounts; & Nigerian dishes, African Development Banks. There's a wide range of good & affordable food from pizzas & pastas, prawns & fish, & authentic Western dishes such as chilli con carne & beef stroganoff, plus daily specials. In the main building at the back is a much smaller bar frequented by a mostly German expat clientele & at the entrance is a stall selling a surprisingly large variety of international magazines & newspapers from the UK's *Marie Claire* to Germany's *Stern* & just about every German newspaper there is. Finally, upstairs to the back of the outside bar there is a gym which has a few weight machines, bikes & treadmills. $$$

Ikeja

✗ **New China Restaurant** Opic Plaza, next to the Sheraton, Mobolaji Bank Anthony Way, Ikeja; ⊕ 11.00–23.00 daily. When they're allowed out of the hotel, airline crews eat here as an alternative to the expensive Sheraton. Set menus are from N3,300, which is not bad value considering they include soup, spring rolls, beef & chicken dishes & plenty of rice or noodles. Plates are piled high, specials include lobster & shrimp in oyster sauce & décor is typical Chinese red lantern style. $$$

✗ **Sheraton Hotel & Towers** (see *Where to stay*). The best place to eat in Ikeja is in the restaurants in the Sheraton but they are very expensive. The hotel's best gourmet restaurant is the **Pili Pili** (⊕ 18.30–22.30 Mon–Sat; $$$$$), which offers chef's specials such as scallops, tiger prawns or crusted fillet of beef followed by fine cognacs & cigars. The **Crockpot** (⊕ 24 hours; $$$$) has b/fast, lunch & dinner buffets with speciality themes on some evenings. The **Pool Bar** (⊕ 10.00–22.00 daily; $$$$) does the same, with an American night on Wed, an Arabian night on Sat & the like, while **La Giara** (⊕ 12.30–15.00, 17.30–22.00 daily; $$$$$) is an Italian restaurant that serves pizzas & pastas using authentic ingredients. All the restaurants have good wine lists & plenty of options for vegetarians. Finally, the informal British-style pub Goodies provides live music on most nights & satellite TV, & stays open until 03.00.

NIGHTLIFE

For the adventurous, Lagos has a vibrant and pumping nightlife scene that often doesn't even begin to get going until well after 23.00 – if you show up before then you'll be helping the bartender polish the glasses – with bars, discos and live-music clubs carrying on until dawn. Some daytime restaurants mentioned above have dance floors and crank it up after 21.00 when they attract cover charges, particularly at the weekends. Expect to pay in the region of N1–2,000/US$8–15 to get into a club and up to N5,000/US$40 for a venue with live music. Safety on the streets after dark in Lagos is a major concern, so exercise caution and preferably go clubbing accompanied by a local – essential if you are going to the clubs on the mainland. As with any major city, Lagos has its fair share of prostitutes, locally known as 'nightriders', and they tend to target venues popular with foreigners.

♀ **'A' (Atlantic) Bar** 14 B Adeola Hopewell St, Victoria Island; ⊕ 12.00 until the early hours daily. Here you'll find a younger, well-heeled Nigerian crowd in a sophisticated setting of polished wooden floors & bright sofas, with very good music from enormous speakers with makossa on Wed nights & DJs & live music from 23.00 at the w/ends. Bar snacks & light meals are available & there's now also wireless internet access.

♀ **Bacchus** 57 Awolowo Road, Ikoyi; ⏰ from 18.00 until the last person leaves daily. A Lebanese restaurant serving shwarmas, burgers & pizzas in the early evening, & then a late-night disco with thumping Western music & 'nightriders'. The new 6 Degrees Lounge has red upholstered walls, plasma TVs & 1960s-style booths. It's hugely popular with Lagos's younger Lebanese community & there's live music on Thurs. If you are out & about on Awolowo Rd at night, Bacchus is a good central location to find a taxi home as there are bouncers at the door & loads of cars & people outside. Be wary of the beggars in wheelchairs & on skate boards who target the wealthy Lebanese as they go in & out.

♀ **Bungalow Bar** Plot 1296, Akin Adesola St, Victoria Island; ⏰ 10.30–midnight, later at the weekends, daily. A new spot on Victoria Island serving pub grub such as potato wedges with dips, chilli con carne, chicken wings & club sandwiches, & on Sun there's a good Lebanese mezze menu on offer from 12.00 to 16.00. Décor is modern & bright with African art adorning the walls, there's a fully stocked bar & happy hour is Mon–Fri 16.00–18.00; a jazz band plays on Thurs night & there's a DJ from 23.00 on Fri & Sat nights. Expat run but a lively mixed crowd.

♀ **Caffé Vergnano** upstairs in the City Mall, Awolowo Rd, Lagos Island, & another branch in the Palms Mall, Lekki; ⏰ 11.00–late daily. All still very smart modern bars as they are located in the new malls with full bars, coffees & some cakes. There are polished wooden floors, tall director's chairs, large windows, mirrors & subtle lighting. Live music on Fri evenings.

♀ **Club Towers** 18 Idowu Taylor St, Victoria Island; ⏰ 21.00 to the early hours Wed–Sun. On two storeys with a bar & dance floor downstairs & quieter lounge upstairs. There's a full range of dance music from reggae to RnB from the sophisticated sound system, a mixed clientele including expats, complementary bar snacks & very good security with bouncers in full tuxedos. Wed is jazz night & there's a karaoke bar next door. Drinks are very expensive here though.

♀ **Fiki Palace** Fiki Boat Club, Ozumba Mbadiwe Rd, almost under the Falomo Bridge, Victoria Island; ⏰ 24hr. A basic bar, with a terrace & plastic chairs next to Five Cowrie Creek. Fish, chicken, chips

& rice are on offer & the Star & Heineken beer is always cold. There is a live makossa & highlife band on Wed, Fri & Sun nights.

♀ **Havanna Bar** Ribadu Rd, Ikoyi, & Plot 1411, Adetokunbo Ademola St, Victoria Island; ⏰ 10.00–late daily. The Ikoyi branch is a good late-night drinking option after eating in one of the restaurants on Awolowo Rd, & both have a huge menu of imported alcoholic drinks, shooters & cocktails, & good pub-like atmospheres, & the giant bouncers at the door will help you find a taxi to get home. Bar snacks such as chicken wings & onion rings are available, there's a very mixed crowd, including expats, & regular live music at the weekends.

♀ **New Afrika Shrine** Pepple St, Agidingbi, Ikeja. The original Shrine was where famous Afrobeat star Fela Kuti played for two decades before the military destroyed the club along with other of his properties. Kuti died of AIDS in 1997 & one million people paraded through the streets of Lagos on the day of his funeral. In 2000 his son, renowned saxophonist & Grammy-award nominee Femi Kuti, re-established the club on the same spot & now regularly plays here when he is in Lagos. He's famous for his own personalised form of Afro-beat, his showmanship is said to be as good as his father's was & he's accompanied by over 20 musicians & dancers. & it seems the Afro-beat rhythm is staying in the family too. Femi's 12-year-old son, Made Kuti, started playing the trumpet when he was 4 years old & now plays 5 different instruments. He's only allowed to join his father on stage during the school holidays! There's a haze of dope in the air here & you can sample palm wine & suya. Bar open most of the day, performances Thu–Sun 20.00–dawn, Femi Kuti plays on Sun night when he's in Lagos.

♀ **Nimbus Art Centre** 10–12 Maitama Sule St, Ikoyi; ⏰ 10.00–late daily. A comfortable, relaxed bar & restaurant at a stylish art gallery for drinking & conversation & the place to meet Lagos's expat press corps (the Associated Press building is near here). Standard but filling chicken & chips & other Westernised basics are on offer, as is the popular Nigerian drink Chapman's. There's a stage in the garden that features anything from a lone guitarist during the week to a full jazz or highlife band at the weekend.

♀ **Pat's Place**, Plot 292C Ajose Adeogun St, Victoria Island; ☎ 01 320 0424/5; ⏰ from 10.00 & closes when the last person leaves. A Lagos expat institution run by the larger-than-life Pat Roberts, the congenial host & ex-rugby player (he played for Zambia & England) who has lived in Lagos for over 25 years. There are 4 bars & several rooms decorated with dart boards & framed rugby shirts and, oddly, a US combat jacket. Very attentive waitresses serve up huge portions of English-style pub grub such as steak & kidney pie & chicken & chips. Major sports are shown on a big DSTV screen, & Pat boasts that he has the largest selection of single malt whiskies in West Africa. It's a fun atmosphere, especially when there's a crucial rugby match on. On Thu from 20.00 there's live music from two female singers who belt out jazz & blues, & there's a disco on Sat night when the place is heaving. Parking is on the street, but there are security guards.

♀ **Reeds** 190 Awolowo Rd, above St Elmos Pizza; ☏ 01 763 7475; ⏱ 13.00–02.00 Tue–Sun. Stylish & smartly decorated with a backdrop of wine bottles & glasses illuminated with green lights, this has an extensive selection of cocktails, wine & champagne & some delicate Thai snacks are on offer.

♀ **Tarzan Jetty Bar** Maroko Rd between Victoria Island & Lekki; ⏱ 24hr. This is a 24hr bar on two storeys overlooking Five Cowrie Creek with lots of cold beer & Guinness, comfortable cane furniture, pool table & a stage where a makossa band plays from 17.00 to 23.00 on Sun, which attracts a huge crowd, in front of which is a gravel space for dancing. This is where you can catch a boat to Tarkwa Bay (see page 156).

♀ **Sure** upstairs in the City Mall, Awolowo Rd, Lagos Island; ⏱ daily 12.00–02.00. Completely enclosed so you won't know you're in a shopping mall, with West African cloth covering the windows, low sponged seating in pastel colours, giant flat screen TVs for music & sport, & a stylish if not smokey long cocktail bar with a full range of drinks.

♀ **The Motherlan',** 64 Opebi Rd, Ikeja; ⏱ midnight–dawn. An enormous outdoor amphitheatre on the edge of a canal in Ikeja, which has been designed to look like a typical West African market square with a hi-tech sound system, & it has live performances by Lagbaja (another saxophonist) & The Colours Band, usually on the last Fri of every month. At other times it's a venue for other bands &, increasingly, comedians. Lagbaja is the guy who plays a fusion of Yoruba music & jazz & always performs in elaborate costumes & a mask (see page 44). Performances from 23.00.

♀ **YNot** Adayemo Alakija St, Victoria Island; www.ynotclub.com. A large, popular venue that's open 24/7 with various bars, a mirrored dance area, pool tables, a video game arcade, an army of besuited bouncers & waitresses, & the main entrance is flanked by two illuminated statues of horses rearing up. It heaves with people on weekend nights when a DJ spins house & trance music & prostitutes probably number 10–1 to every male customer. Not for the faint-hearted.

SHOPPING

BOOKS AND MUSIC

Bookworm Unit 6, Eko Hotel Shopping Complex, Ajose Adeogun St, Victoria Island; ☏ 01 461 3180, 320 0606; www.bookwormlimited.com; ⏱ 09.00–19.00 Mon–Fri, 10.00–17.00 Sat. Not to be confused with the bookshop in the Eko Hotel – this shopping centre is outside & to the north of the hotel complex where there are also a couple of courier companies & a branch of MedPlus pharmacy. By far the best bookshop in Nigeria, with a range of imported books from the UK; hardbacks, new novels, some CD ROMs, children's books, board games such as Monopoly & Scrabble, & some classical music CDs. The staff here are knowledgeable & friendly, & can order just about anything you want from their UK suppliers. Not that you cannot do this directly from Amazon & the like over the internet, but if you are wary about sending credit card details through the web from Nigeria then this is a good alternative option.

CMS Book Shop 50–52 Broad St, Lagos Island; ⏱ 08.30–17.30 Mon–Fri, 09.00–15.00 Sat. This sells a huge range of text & school books & a big selection of Bibles & religious books, but most are curled & covered in dust. There are only a few dated novels for sale here.

Glendora Shop 4, Falomo Shopping Centre, Awolowo Rd, Ikoyi; ☏ 01 895 3498; www.glendorabooks.com; ⏱ 08.00–18.30 Mon–Sat. Other branches at the Jazz Hole & Eko Hotel (see below) & two well-stocked kiosks in the departure halls of the airport's international & domestic terminals (⏱ 06.30–22.00 daily). It's an old-fashioned & somewhat dusty shop with floor-to-ceiling shelves of new & secondhand novels, text & school books, literature & classics, children's books, & some of Nigeria's (limited) selection of maps. They publish the quarterly *Glendora Review*, which is a fat magazine on West African art & music available at all their outlets.

Glendora Eko Hotel Book Shop in the far corner past the main reception area; ⊕ 08.00–21.00 Mon–Fri, 08.00–19.00 Sat. An excellent range of foreign publications including up-to-date French & English newspapers & magazines, & the likes of *Time* & *Newsweek*. This is also one of the best places to pick up a street guide to Lagos & Abuja & it has a similar, though much smaller, range of books to the other Glendora branches above.

Jazz Hole 168 Awolowo Rd, Ikoyi; ☎ 01 895 3498; glendora@glendorabooks.net; ⊕ 10.00–19.30 Mon–Sat. A wonderful, cavernous shop stuffed with interesting things; you could spend hours browsing in here & the music is great. Sells art & photography books, magazines & newspapers, intelligent novels, all the famous Nigerian writers, social, political & philosophy journals, coffee-table books, plays, sheet music, & an excellent variety of African & world music CDs, from West African chant reggae to Latino American blues. The helpful staff will let you listen before you buy. If you email them you can get a regular listing of what's on at the shop, which includes jamming sessions, intellectual discussions & book readings. They have their own record label, which is keen to promote Nigerian new talent & resurrect forgotten names. They also produce great compilations in unique 'Jazz Hole' covers, & host regular concerts (often free) to plug their CDs. Owner Olakunle Tejuoso heads up the Jazzhole All Stars Band. Finally, they have just added a coffee shop serving fresh fruit juices, cappuccino & organic sandwiches & it's a wireless hotspot.

Media Store Silverbird Galleria, Ahmado Bello Way; ☎ 01 773 7116; & in the Palms Mall; ⊕ 10.00–21.00 daily. New excellent book, DVD & CD stores that rank with a modern international bookshop chain. Items are imported from South Africa & the UK & there's a full range of world music & novels, & if you can't find what you're looking for, again they can order in. The only downsides are that most of the books are sealed in plastic so it's difficult to browse & they have limited stocks of Nigerian literature so the other bookshops are a better bet for that. The cafés do excellent cappuccino.

CRAFTS AND CURIOS There are several craft markets in Lagos, though the cheapest and the best is in Lekki Market (see *What to see and do*, page 155). Nigerian crafts include wood carvings, masks, drums, decorated calabashes, leather goods, gold, bronzeware, silver, bead jewellery, pottery, batiks and other colourful fabrics. Outside the **Eko Hotel** is a market in a cabana to the left of the main entrance of the hotel as you enter the driveway. It's stuffed to the gills with arts and crafts – I hope that the large quantity of ivory on offer is not real even though the traders insist it is. Very unfortunately the leopard and cheetah skins hanging on the walls are very real. Do not purchase these items – you will be encouraging an illegal trade and the chances of you getting them into your home country are zero.

When bargaining, which you'll have to do very hard, make out that you live in Lagos even if you don't. This usually gives you a bit of an edge as the trader will think you have had daily experience of bargaining. The target is usually about a third of the asking price. There's another similar market outside the **Federal Palace Hotel** to the right of the car park just before the entrance of the circular elevated driveway. *Both are* ⊕ *daily 08.00–20.00*. Finally, there's a whole range of craft and curio shops in the international departure lounge of the **Murtala Mohammed Airport**, but prices here are obviously more expensive, though still negotiable.

Colours in Africa 5a Akin Olugbade St, Victoria Island; ☎ 01 270 1346; ⊕ 09.00–18.00 Mon–Fri, 10.00–19.00 Sat. This is a very stylish shop on two floors with the trendy Robert's Café opposite (see *Where to eat & drink*). It's stuffed with high-quality curios from all over Africa, including baskets from Swaziland, pots from Kenya, wood carvings from Zimbabwe, & wire sculptures from South Africa. I especially liked the brightly painted Nigerian trucks & buses on the wall, made from shiny metal in the character of the beat-up vehicles decorated with stickers & slogans. There's also furniture, screens, jewellery, crockery, some batik clothing & handmade leather shoes. Well worth a browse followed by tea & cake in the café.

Quintessence Falomo Shopping Centre, Awolowo Rd, Ikoyi; ✆ 0803 327 5401; www.quintessenceltd.com; ⏰ 09.00–18.00 Mon–Sat. One of the best & most upmarket book & craft shops in Lagos, with hefty price tags to match. Here you'll find trendy clothes, coffee-table books on Africa, batiks & Nigerian fabrics, stylish jewellery, international magazines, & high-calibre souvenirs. Look out for some unique clay sculptures by artist Reuben Ugbine (sold here, at Signature, & in Colours in Africa). They are of Nigerian people in a variety of poses, from old bent men, young muscled boys or women pounding yam, to people chatting or individuals pondering with heads in hands. They are quite remarkable, unique to Lagos, & there's a lot of warmth & life in the figures. The gallery to the side of the shop shows about 10 exhibitions a year of usually very talented artists. It's also a good place to pick up leaflets & flyers on what's on around the city, & they sell tickets for concerts, plays & events at the MUSON Centre on Lagos Island.

Signature 107 Awolowo Rd, Ikoyi; ✆ 01 776 0900, www.signatureafrica.com; ⏰ 10.00–17.30 Mon–Fri, 10.00–16.00 Sat, longer hours in the smaller Palms Mall branch. If you are at all interested in Nigerian art, check out this website. Here is a wonderful collection of *objets d'art* from all over West Africa, & a few pieces from eastern & southern Africa; oil, watercolour & charcoal paintings, sculpture, exquisite furniture, antiques, fabric, mirrors, vases & wood carvings. Downstairs is the main shop; upstairs is a gallery with changing exhibits of local artists. All the pieces are of very high quality with prices to match. Paintings go from US$400 while a small drum is US$150. They can arrange to air-freight items worldwide. They also sell imported art materials such as oil, watercolour & acrylic paints, paint brushes, canvasses & paper, & have a picture-framing service.

FOOD AND GENERAL GOODS If you are living in Lagos than you will no doubt depend on the few shops specialising in imported food. Modern shopping malls are starting to appear on Lagos's skyline.

City Mall next door to the National Museum, Awolowo Rd, Lagos Island; ✆ 01 271 4300; www.lagos-citymall.com; ⏰ from 09.00 daily; the shops close at 18.00, cinema & bars close later; Goodies 10.00–21.00 Mon–Sat, 10.00–18.00 Sun. This is a new complex with 50 shops & restaurants on 3 levels including a large branch of Goodies Supermarket, & two modern cinema screens showing Hollywood releases. Useful outlets include a modern internet café, the Tonark Pharmacy, & the rather strangely named 3 Fold Cord bookshop that sells some novels among the mostly religious & self-help books. The smart coffee shop & bakery at Goodies is a good place to take a break if exploring Lagos Island or you can get cheap chop such as *shawarmas* & soft drinks in the kiosk in the car park, which incidentally is guarded by armed guards.

Goodies 192 Awolowo Rd, Ikoyi; ⏰ 10.00–21.00 Mon–Sat, 11.00–18.00 Sun. A supermarket selling expensive goods that are hard to find elsewhere. There's a good selection of toiletries, & wine & spirits, a deli counter, & a fruit & veg stall in the car park outside. Next door you can grab a snack at St Elmos Pizza. There's another branch on Ojora Close on Victoria Island & in the new City Mall on Lagos Island.

La Point Akin Adesola St, opposite the Bungalow Bar, Victoria Island; ✆ 01 261 1971; ⏰ 09.00–18.00 Mon–Sat. This is a quality delicatessen for imported goods such as Belgian chocolates, fine wines & champagnes, with a deli counter selling cured hams, a broad selection of cheese, & excellent cuts of fresh meat including pork & lamb, which are usually hard to find – according to some expats this is the best meat in town.

Mega Plaza 14 Idowu Martins St, Victoria Island; ✆ 01 774 4477; www.megaplazamall.com; Mega Plaza ⏰ 10.00–22.00 daily; supermarket & food court ⏰ 09.00–23.00 daily. This is a shiny glass building very centrally located on VI where you'll find probably the best selection of imported goods in the country, but it's expensive – I saw a flat-screen TV here for N1.9 million. There was a damaging fire here a couple of years ago & the Mega Plaza is in the throes of refurbishment. Four floors are completed & are up & running, while the top floor will eventually feature more retail space, a Chinese restaurant & a bar with picture windows overlooking the skyline of VI. In the basement is office equipment, generators & white goods; on the ground floor stereos, & thousands of TVs, around sound systems & DVD players; on the 1st floor is an extensive collection of phones & cameras; while the 2nd floor features household goods from pots & pans to linen & furniture. Adjacent to the main complex is a large & well-stocked Lebanese-run supermarket & a food court (dealt with under

Where to eat). For those visitors who don't necessarily need to buy a washing machine, the Mega Plaza is handy for hard-to-find items such as batteries, toiletries & razors. At the time of writing they were building a multi-storey car park across the road. If you speak to the Lebanese management they can organise car hire.

Park 'n' Shop 47 Adeola Odeku St, Victoria Island; ⏱ 10.00–21.00 Mon–Sat, 11.00–18.00 Sun. This is another similar set up to Goodies (above) that also sells household items such as white goods, crockery & linen as well as imported food.

The Palms I Bis Way, Lekki; ✆ 01 271 4491–3; www.thepalmsshopping.com; shops ⏱ 10.00–20.00 Mon–Fri, 10.00–18.00 Sun; cinema & bars open until at least 23.00. Opened in 2006, this is another new shopping & entertainment mall & is a first of its kind in Nigeria, on a par with similar shopping centres elsewhere in the world. It covers a 44,000m^2 site with parking for over 700 vehicles. The anchor stores are South African brands; Game is a hypermarket that sells just about everything imaginable from household goods & electronics to jewellery & beauty products; Shoprite is a supermarket chain; while Nu Metro is a 6-screen cinema. There are some 60 or so additional shops & restaurants including a branch of Signature (see above), Newscafé; a South African coffee shop chain, Nando's; South African grilled chicken chain; & numerous boutiques & household shops. The Media Store has a large range of books, CDs & DVDs imported from South Africa & the UK. The food court has a good range of places to snack at & at the time of writing a bowling alley was being built.

Silverbird Galleria 133 Ahmadu Bello Way, Victoria Island; ✆ 01 270 1412; www.silverbirdcinemas.com. This is another new modern mall with a variety of shops on 4 levels & the 5-screen Silverbird Cinema. There's another branch of the Media Store, fast-food restaurants, an office for North American Airlines, banks & ATMs, & a selection of boutiques & specialist shops.

THE WORLDWIDE WEB

There are hundreds of internet cafés all over Lagos, but although within the last couple of years there has been an internet boom, many of these establishments are today non-functioning, not just because of the inconsistent NEPA, but because the service providers, like cell phone networks, come and go rapidly or fail miserably to maintain their connections. You will find internet access, but you may have to do some leg work to find a place that is actually working. There's no shortage of places to try and just about every street on Victoria Island has a few spots.

PRACTICALITIES

CHANGING MONEY As explained in Chapter 3, there are thousands of banks all over Lagos where you will *not* be able to change money. There are hundreds on Victoria Island alone, many of which are agents for Western Union, where you can take out US$ cash but not exchange US$ cash or other currencies for naira. Best bet is to change money on arrival at the airport at the Travelex offices in both the international departures and arrivals terminals, or the money changers in the airport car park, or alternatively try the reception of your hotel, which mainly provide a foreign exchange service to their guests.

After that, and particularly for budget travellers, you're likely to resort to the black market money changers who hang out at various locations. These are Broad Street on Lagos Island, outside the Excelsior Hotel in Apapa, and outside the Eko and Federal Palace hotels on Victoria Island (at the Federal Palace you can make transactions in the car park without even getting out of your car). Changing money on the black market is illegal but tolerated – they print the black market rate along with the bank rate in the newspapers, so you shouldn't have too many problems. Just ensure that you count all the naira first before handing over US$ cash. If you feel uncomfortable with this than try the Mega Plaza on Victoria Island – the Lebanese management here gave us good US$ and GBP rates. You'll find them in the cash desk behind all the TVs.

Finally, if you know of an expat who may want to change money, this is the best bet. Many get a certain part of their wage in naira and are more than willing to swap it over for hard currency. If you are travelling to other parts of Nigeria read those chapters carefully, as there are few other options to change money outside Lagos and you may need to do the bulk of money changing here. Visa machines can be found at Standard Chartered Bank, while MasterCard and Maestro machines are found in Ecobank and some Zenith Bank branches, but you'd be ill-advised to use credit cards to get cash in Nigeria because of the possibility of fraud.

CINEMAS Although Nigeria has a vibrant home-grown video industry dubbed Nollywood, regular cinemas that were once popular in the 1960s and 1970s all closed down during military rule. However, in the last couple of years, new multi-screen complexes have appeared on the Lagos scene; they are part of the shopping complexes listed on page 135 and they generally open *11.00–23.00 daily*. They show Hollywood blockbusters and other mainstream movies, not Nollywood, and so far are proving hugely popular, so the trend may well have a ripple effect across the country. Abuja has one already. Despite these new cinemas having counters for popcorn and cold drinks, a Nigerian phenomenon seems to be sneaking chicken and chips in to a movie. Additionally, expat organisations and the foreign cultural centres occasionally show films.

COURIER SERVICES DHL (*www.dhl.com.ng*) has various offices around Lagos. The better located are the offices at the Eko Hotel Shopping Complex at the roundabout just north of the hotel itself on Ademola Street, Victoria Island, at 32 Awolowo Road in Ikoyi, and another at the top end of Isaac John Street near the Sheraton in Ikeja. Other courier companies include United Parcel Service (*www.ups.com*) at 12 Idowu Taylor Street, and, like DHL, there's a branch in the Eko Shopping Complex, Victoria Island.

CULTURAL CENTRES

Alliance Française (French Cultural Centre) 4 Ruxton Road, Ikoyi; ✎ 01 269 2035; ☼ 10.00–19.00 Mon–Sat. French films are shown once a week, usually on Monday nights, and there is a café plus French newspapers and magazines and a library with over 800 mostly French books. There are occasional live music performances. For a small fee and deposit members can borrow books, DVDs, videos and CDs. If you are living in Lagos, you can learn to speak French here with four- to six-week courses starting each month. These courses come highly recommended. The centre produces a useful leaflet listing what's on in Lagos each month.

British Council 20 Thompson Av, Ikoyi; ✎ 01 269 2188/2192; www.britishcouncil.org/nigeria; ☼ 10.30–16.00 Mon and Sat, 09.30–18.00 Tue–Thu. There is a lounge area with English newspapers and magazines, an internet café with over 20 reliable terminals, a library with a good selection of books and videos, and a good café. Anyone is allowed inside to browse, but to borrow items from the library there is an annual membership of about US$35, which includes unlimited use of the internet.

Goethe-Institut (German Cultural Centre) 10 Ozumba Mbadiwe Av, on Five Cowrie Creek, not far from B-Jay's Hotel and opposite the 1004 apartment complex, Victoria Island; ✎ 01 461 3416; www.goethe.de/ins/ng/lag; ☼ 10.00–13.00 and 15.00–17.00 daily, and until 19.00 on Tue and Thu. In the library, with an extensive range of German books and newspapers, you can browse for free but to borrow there's a very small annual fee of N500. The centre is set in big grounds and the gardens and an inside gallery (sponsored by Lufthansa) hold regular exhibitions of contemporary art. It's well worth checking out what's showing, and the centre also has information on other cultural events in Lagos.

Terra Culture Plot 1376 Tiamiyu Savage, off Ahmadu Bello Way, Victoria Island; ⟍ 01 270 0588; www.terrakulture.com; ⊕ 09.30–22.30 Mon–Thu, 09.30–24.00 Fri–Sat, 12.00–22.00 Sun. A multifaceted cultural centre that offers language lessons in Yoruba, Hausa and Igbo, a vast choice of arts and crafts lessons for adults and children from tie-dying to basket weaving, a library and bookshop, internet access and an art gallery of changing exhibitions upstairs. You can also sample Nigerian specialities such as palm wine or a plate of snails in the trendy café, which is decorated in some lovely rustic hand-crafted wooden furniture, or you can buy crafts from the shop.

EMBASSIES AND HIGH COMMISSIONS

❸ **Austria** 65 Oyinkan Abayomi Dr, Ikoyi; ⟍ 01 461 3586/7 or 269 0423; www.austriantrade.org/nigeria.

❸ **Benin** 4 Abudu Smith St, Victoria Island; ⟍ 01 261 4411.

❸ **Cameroon** 5 Elsie Femi Pearce St, Victoria Island; ⟍ 01 261 2226.

❸ **Canada** 4 Anifowoshe St, Victoria Island; ⟍ 01 271 5650; www.dfait-maeci.gc.ca/Nigeria.

❸ **France** 1 Oyinkan Abayomi Dr, Ikoyi; ⟍ 01 269 3427–30; www.consulfrance-lagos.org.

❸ **Gabon** 8 Norman Williams St, Ikoyi; ⟍ 01 268 4566, 268 4673.

❸ **Germany** 15 Walter Carrington Crescent, Victoria Island; ⟍ 01 261 1011/1082; www.abuja.diplo.de.

❸ **Ghana** 21/23 Island Club Rd, Onikan, Lagos Island; ⟍ 01 263 0015/0934.

❸ **Italy** 12 Walter Carrington Crescent, Victoria Island; ⟍ 01 261 9881/4066.

❸ **Japan** 24/25 Apese St, off Kofo Abayomi St, Victoria Island; ⟍ 01 261 4929/3797.

❸ **Niger** 15 Adeola Odeku St, Victoria Island; ⟍ 01 261 2300/2330.

❸ **Senegal** 12/14 Kofo Abayomi St, Victoria Island; ⟍ 01 261 1722.

❸ **South Africa** 10 Club Rd, Ikoyi; ⟍ 01 461 2067, 461 2981; www.dfa.gov.za.

❸ **Togo** Plot 976, Oju-Olobun Close, Victoria Island; ⟍ 01 261 7449.

❸ **UK** 11 Walter Carrington Crescent, Victoria Island; ⟍ 01 261 9531/9537; www.britishhighcommission.gov.uk.

❸ **USA** 2 Walter Carrington Crescent, Victoria Island; ⟍ 01 261 0150/0139; www.nigeria.usembassy.gov.

HOSPITALS The following hospitals have been recommended to me and all have 24-hour emergency units, but in the event that you do have to go to hospital, if you possibly can, contact your embassy, high commission or company first and ask them which hospital they currently recommend in Lagos.

✚ **Atlantic Medical Centre** 7 Oju Olobun Close, Victoria Island; ⟍ 01 262 0316. This is one of the best private hospitals in Lagos & is on a retainer with many US companies.

✚ **Gold Cross Hospital** top of Keffi St, Obalende, Ikoyi; ⟍ 01 269 5670.

✚ **Ideal Eagle Hospital** Plot 247, Ojora Close, Victoria Island; ⟍ 01 262 0953; www.chagourygroup.com/idealeagle.

✚ **Radmed Diagnostics** 3b Ligali Ayorinde St, Victoria Island; ⟍ 01 444 8108, 270 0354; www.radmeddiagnostic.com.

✚ **St Nicholas Hospital** 57 Campbell St, Lagos Island; ⟍ 01 260 0070; www.saintnicholashospital.com. This is currently the preferred hospital for many of the foreign companies operating in Lagos for emergency treatments, including malaria cases.

MAPS AND PUBLICATIONS The indispensable **Lagos Street Map** (West African Book Publishers Ltd) can be found at most of the bookshops for around N1,500/US$12; I found the branch of Glendora Books at the Eko Hotel was the best place for maps, and if you are also going to Abuja, pick up a map here as well as they are not readily available in Abuja itself. The Lagos Street Map is clear and concise and as close to an A to Z as you are going to find for Lagos. It's published as both a book and a fold-out version. A small booklet, **What's New: The Lagos City Guide**, is published bi-monthly and can be found at the Jazz Hole and the other bookshops on Awolowo Road in Ikoyi for N600/US$5. It lists galleries, restaurants, nightclubs and cultural events and has a couple of basic maps at the back.

The weighty **Lagos Easy Access** is the expat bible and deservedly so. It's in its second edition now and quite rare. It is published by the American Women's Club (the first edition came out in 1998) and it tries to fill the vast gap between what an expat has heard about Lagos from his or her home country and what it is actually like – as I hope to do in this book. There is a wealth of information in the book about coming to Lagos, domestic staff, shops and markets, social clubs, housing, buying furniture, shipping things to and from Nigeria, and a full directory of shops and services in Lagos. At the time of writing it was being updated for a third time so it may be out again by the time you read this.

NEWSPAPERS AND MAGAZINES One- or two-day-old international newspapers including the the *Daily Telegraph, The Times*, the *European, Le Monde, USA Today* and the *International Herald Tribune* are available at the bookshops in major hotels such as the Eko Hotel on Victoria Island and the Sheraton Hotel in Ikeja. Also at the Eko, in the grounds at the back of the curio market, is a useful shop selling a broad range of international newspapers and magazines, where you'll be able to pick up new and old copies of anything from *Time* and *Newsweek* to *Cosmo*.

PHARMACIES There are pharmacies all over Lagos but, because of the prevalence of fake drugs, it's a good idea to check out locally what places are being recommended if you're staying in Lagos for some time. These two have been recommended.

✚ **Chyzob Pharmacy** 168 Awolowo Rd, Ikoyi (next to the Jazz Hole bookshop); ✆ 01 269 4545; ⊕ 08.00–20.00 Mon–Sat, 13.00–18.00 Sun. They import drugs from the UK & US.
✚ **MedPlus** Mega Plaza, 14 Idowu Martins St, Victoria Island; ✆ 01 262 1223; Eko Shopping Centre, Ajose Adeogun Street, Victoria Island;

✆ 0803 304 2789; & there are another two branches at the Civic Centre opposite the 1004 Apartments on Moroko Rd on Victoria Island & another branch at the Palms Mall in Lekki; www.medicinesplusltd.com; ⊕ 10.00–21.00 Mon–Sat, 13.00–21.00 Sun. Again, they import drugs & you can order specific items from abroad.

POST The main post offices are located at Adeola Odeku Street, Victoria Island (which is also an agent for Western Union and EMS Speed Post); about 200m east of where Alfred Rewane Road (formerly Kingsway) joins Awolowo Road on Bourdillon Road near the Falomo Bridge in Ikoyi; 33 Marina, Lagos Island; and the corner of Mobolaji Bank Anthony and Medical Road, Ikeja, close to the domestic airport. All are generally open 08.00–17.00 Monday–Friday; and 10.00–15.00 Saturday. There are also post offices in both the domestic and international terminals at the airport.

SAFETY Lagos is often dubbed the most dangerous city in the world, and, as with any impoverished city in the Third World, it has problems of crime brought on by the millions of people trying to eke out a living in a confined space. But remember crime statistics are high because of the colossal population, and the islands are considered lower risk than the mainland. As a foreigner it will be assumed that you have relative wealth, and muggings, carjackings and armed robberies occur. If you talk to Lagos's expats, stories abound, and most of this excessively paranoid community live in highly secure compounds and travel around with drivers, some of them armed.

On one of my visits to Lagos, there was in incident at the Eko Hotel on Victoria Island when a party of Chinese businessmen arranged a transfer to another part of the city by coach. The coach pulled up in front of the hotel where they all piled in, and they were then driven off to a remote spot and robbed at gunpoint. A few moments after they had departed, the 'real' coach pulled up outside the hotel. The Eko Hotel now advises guests not to believe early-morning phone calls telling guests that their pick-up time has changed. Other incidents that happened while I was in Nigeria included an airline flight crew being robbed at gunpoint while eating in a restaurant close to the Sheraton Hotel in Ikeja, and an armed robbery at a bar on Victoria Island popular with expats. Fairly frequent armed robberies on vehicles occur, which have the disadvantage of being trapped in the traffic, and the airport road after dark is a particular black spot for this.

However, it seems likely that high-powered business people are generally the target for robbers and fraudsters, and our personal experience as budget travellers was that we had no problems whatsoever, and even negotiated the motor parks on the mainland unscathed, which are notoriously known as stomping grounds for Area Boys (see box on page 120). Nevertheless, it's obviously essential that you take note of your surroundings at all times and develop a sense of street savvy. Most people get through their stay in Lagos safely, and are surprised to find the city a friendly rather than dangerous place.

Finally, when you are on the streets beware of the traffic, which is possibly the biggest threat to your safety in Lagos. Pedestrians most definitely do not have the right of way; it's survival of the biggest and the heaviest, and Lagos drivers are renowned for their aggressive tactics. Often walking on pavements is impossible as these are used to park cars. Be very wary of walking along the edge of the road as this is the part of the congested road that the *okadas* use too – on my last visit to Lagos, I was hit by an *okada* from behind outside the Virgin Nigeria office on Victoria Island. I came off alright, just bruises and burns on the back of my legs; the *okada* driver flipped, skidded, took half the skin off his face and broke both his legs. In retrospect, it could have been so much worse; take heed.

SPORTS

British High Commission Club (also known as the Kingfisher Club) 4 Reeve Rd, Ikoyi; ↘ 01 461 5661/2. You must first apply at the gate of the club for an ID card, for which you'll need two passport photos. There's a range of sporting facilities here such as netball, tennis & squash courts, & the expat gatherings are very social.

Hash House Harriers Contact Pat Roberts at his bar, Pat's Place, Plot 292C, Ajose Adeogun St, Victoria Island; ↘ 01 320 0424/5; www.lagosh3.com. Pat has all the details about the local Hash club, which runs around three times a week, but be warned the drinking games involved are rather disgusting & the pictures on the website are just about X-rated.

Ikoyi Club Ikoyi Club Rd, Ikoyi; ↘ 01 269 5075, 269 5133; www.ikoyiclub-1938.org. Here is the only 18-hole golf course in Lagos & there's a full range of other sports on offer such as badminton, squash, gym, fitness classes & tennis. Again the atmosphere is very sociable, with a club bar suitable for long-term visitors, & there is an annual membership fee.

Lagos Yacht Club ↘ 01 496 3511, 496 6742; www.lagosyachtclub.org.uk. Just south of the museum & Tafawa Balewa Square on Lagos Island; the entrance is down an alley off the ring road just a few metres before it goes across the bridge to Victoria Island. Established in 1932, the yacht club is a hugely popular members-only expat haunt, & if you are new in Lagos it's a great place to meet people. There's a club house with bar & restaurant & a nice outdoor terrace right on the very tip of Lagos Island almost under the bridge itself. If you are living in Lagos for a while you may want to consider joining (about US$1,200 per annum) & even buying a boat or hobie-cat. The yacht club can help with this — boats tend to change ownership among expats as they come & go.

Despite being highly sociable the members of the yacht club take their sailing seriously & it's not just a venue for a few beers, so you do obviously have to know how to sail as membership is dependent on a certain amount of sailing experience — you will be expected to sail about eight times a year. If you don't have your own boat, it's possible to hook up as a crew member with another member who does. There are races in the harbour every Sat afternoon, & on Sun there are often sails out to one of the private beach resorts up the creek or out to sea, & every year there's a race to Badagry. They also organise various functions, parties & balls. The barman here has been serving expat sailors for over 20 years.

Swimming Unless you are staying in one of the very few hotels with a pool, choices for swimming are limited to the Eko and the Federal Palace hotels, both of which have very nice pools. But these are not much good for short-term visitors as the Eko charges an annual fee to use the pool, gym, tennis courts and sauna, while the Federal Palace charges an annual, quarterly or monthly fee to use the pool. Swimming off Bar Beach on Victoria Island is not encouraged; this is not the sort of beach to sit and sunbathe on or where you would want to frolic in the waves: the water is filthy and covered in a sheen of oil. The best place to go in Lagos is Tarkwa Beach (see page 156), where the sea is cleaner and the environment safer.

TELEPHONE For international phone calls, try the big hotels, though the cost of calls will be at a premium. There are **NITEL** offices on Cable Street on Lagos Island and just to the east of the roundabout at the northern end of Falomo Bridge in Ikoyi, at 3 Alfred Rewane Road (formerly Kingsway Road); the entrance is through the Mammy's market (⏰ *24 hours*), where you can buy a phonecard for an international call and try your luck at actually getting through. For local calls, there are **MTN cell phone stands** all over the place, especially on Victoria Island – just look for the distinctive yellow umbrellas – and some **landline stands**. Expect to pay around N40–50 per minute. You may come across the odd public phone box, but there are no phones inside.

THEATRE Lagos is not renowned for its theatre and the only venues of note are the Eko Hotel, which has an auditorium popular for beauty pageants and fashion shows, and the **MUSON (Musical Society of Nigeria) Centre** (☎ *01 264 6670, 264 6663; www.musonigeria.org*) opposite the museum on Awolowo Road on Lagos Island. Here is a relatively modern theatre that holds regular concerts, recitals, operas and plays (a local version of the *The Lion King* was showing when we visited). To find out what's on, ask at the box office, or visit the **Goethe-Institut** (German Cultural Centre) on Victoria Island (page 137) or **Quintessence**, the book and craft shop in the Falomo Shopping Centre on Awolowo Road in Ikoyi (page 135). Both have full programmes of events at the centre and Quintessence also sells tickets.

TRAVEL AGENTS There are hundreds of travel agents all over Lagos, mostly dealing with flights out of Nigeria, and very few are used to dealing with inbound travellers. I found the following travel agents particularly helpful.

First Dolphin Travels and Tours on the 1st floor of the Federal Palace Hotel, Ahmadu Bello Way, Victoria Island; ☎ 01 261 4927, 262 6112; www.firstdolphintravels.com. Flights & IATA ticketing, & can organise meet-and-greet services at the airport.

Five Star Travel Falamo Shopping Centre, Awolowo Rd, Ikoyi; ☎ 01 269 0184–92; www.5star.com. Represents most airlines.

Soltan Travel and Tours Glitter House, 214c Eti-Osa Way, Dolphin Estate, Ikoyi; ☎ 01 269 3358; www.soltantravel.com. Ask for the charming Victoria Soluade, who is in charge & extremely friendly & helpful.

VISAS If you need to extend your visa once you have arrived in Nigeria you need to go to the **immigration office** on Alagbon Close in Ikoyi (this street is not marked on any map I can find). To get there, take a taxi or *okada* to the Federal Secretariat in Ikoyi – the three big high-rise blocks, all of which are gutted and derelict. Alagbon Close is a small road with a busy little market running down the west side of the compound of buildings (if you are facing the Federal Secretariat it is on the left). Walk down and on the right-hand side is a jumble of low-rise tatty buildings that are the immigration offices. There is a sign for the Alien's Immigration Office. You need to have a huge amount of patience and you may be asked for certain paperwork such as your invitation letter. Above all be very friendly as the immigration officers have a somewhat boring job, so if you can brighten their day, you may get somewhere.

You are also very likely to be asked for a *dash*. Our experience was that we paid N3,500 (US$28) each to extend our visas and there was no way of knowing if this was the fee or an outright bribe. I am assuming the latter as the starting price was much higher, and I was involved in a bit of negotiation about the price without either of us admitting that the official was offering to extend our visas for a bribe. This was the only time I paid *dash* during our whole time in Nigeria.

If you don't feel comfortable with this, you can alternatively, for a fee, go through **Quartum Resources Limited** (*22 Child Avenue, Apapa;* ✆ *0803 328 6596;* ✆ *0803 717 6616;* f *+ 1 928 222 1639* (this is a US e-fax number); e *quartum@nigol.net.ng*). Hugh is an expat who runs a service in Lagos for advice and anything to do with Nigerian visas, quotas, work permits, etc. If you give him your passport, he will extend your visa at Alagbon Close on your behalf. This is a reliable company that many of the foreign organisations use to sort out paperwork for expats. You'll also catch Hugh at the Yacht Club on Saturday afternoons.

WHAT TO SEE AND DO

Like the rest of Nigeria, Lagos doesn't have a great deal in the way of architecture or old buildings, or museums and galleries, and what there is in the city is generally so dilapidated it's in danger of collapse. But Lagos has atmosphere, and it's definitely well worth exploring some of it by foot. Given that the expat community is ferried around in chauffeur-driven cars, an *oyibo* walking or riding an *okada* around any part of Lagos attracts some attention. Very few white people do this and you can spend a whole week on the streets of Lagos without encountering another white face. But although people will be surprised to see you, you'll be most welcome wherever you go and receive very little hassle.

Don't be afraid to walk around the islands of Lagos during the day – sometimes it's much quicker to walk than to travel by car because of the hectic traffic. Just try and avoid carrying anything valuable. It's another story on the mainland and anywhere at night, however. As there is very little to do or see on the mainland there's little reason to venture there. Taxis are easy to catch after dark on the islands, so this shouldn't present any problems.

THE ISLANDS
Lagos Island NB Although it is reasonably safe to walk around the central lanes and streets of Lagos Island during the day, stay well clear of walking under the flyovers and major road intersections on the outer rim of the island, as these are territories of the notorious Area Boys (see box on page 120). And I stress, *never* go on to the island after dark.

Lagos Island is home to the row of high-rise concrete blocks that dominate the skyline of Lagos, and it's the site of the first settlement and the oldest part of the city. Today it's no longer an island marooned in the lagoon, but has instead been joined by a landfill with the more upmarket district of Ikoyi, the working-class district of Obalende serving as a buffer zone between the two very different suburbs. Despite being a somewhat daunting experience, a wander through the people-packed narrow lanes and heaving markets of Lagos Island will reward you with a real insight into what is the heart of the city – one of the most frantic and densely packed areas of Africa, if not the world. The 2006 census put the population of Lagos Island at 209,437 in an area of just 8.7km^2.

It is a fascinating area to explore. At first glance the streets appear to be one massive market, but a surprisingly organised one at that, with each section selling one kind of product. The limited sights in the area include the Oba's Palace, the National Museum and a few examples of Brazilian architecture, built by freed slaves repatriated from Brazil to Nigeria when slavery was finally abolished that today struggle to survive against the onslaught of time and indifferent attitudes towards both modern practical maintenance and historical pride. The highlight here is to immerse yourself into the street life – to drink in the chaos, breathe in the electric atmosphere, and inhale the sights, smells and sounds of millions of African people going about their daily lives.

Driving is all but impossible in downtown Lagos Island; the streets are too crowded and narrow, there are many dead ends and one-way systems, and the traffic is choked to a virtual standstill. Here, I have put together a walking tour starting at the National Museum at Onikan. This is a good start and finish point simply because as a landmark it's reasonably straightforward to get to by public transport, and because there's safe parking available if you have your own car. There is an *okada* park opposite the museum, so you shouldn't have any problems picking up a drop taxi here, and there is secure parking in the museum grounds, at the MUSON Centre on the opposite side of Awolowo Road or at the new City Mall which is next door to the museum (see page 135), where there is also a wide choice of modern restaurants to stop at for a snack or drink.

Give yourself a few hours to complete the tour, which includes a couple of hours in the museum itself, and enough time before dark to get back to your car, or by public transport, to get back to where you are staying off Lagos Island. Although there are a couple of accommodation options on Lagos Island itself, they are nothing short of flea-pit hotels, and because of the prevalence of Area Boys and crime in general, you are strongly advised not to be here at night.

Once in the throng of streets, if you get completely overwhelmed or claustrophobic, or if you simply get lost, grab an *okada* back to the museum or an outer road such as the Marina, where you should be able to find a taxi. You are unlikely to encounter any safety problems, but make sure that you are not carrying or wearing anything valuable. Don't bring a camera as it's unlikely that you will be able to take pictures freely – there are just too many people who will object.

It's also worth considering dressing reasonably conservatively; as a traditional area for commerce and markets, many of the market traders are Hausa-Fulani Muslims who have settled here over the centuries. And if you are a non-Muslim, it's a good idea not to be too intrusive at the local mosques or the open-air designated prayer compounds found throughout the markets – the people here can be a little hostile to non-worshippers.

The National Museum The National Museum is on Awolowo Road, about 150m east of Tafawa Balewa Square (⊕ *08.00–16.00 daily; admission N200 – photography is not permitted and if you do have a camera, you will be asked to leave it at the entrance, another reason not to bring your camera on to Lagos Island*). The museum is set back in large grounds and houses numerous exhibits of Nigeria's ancient civilisations, including some famous bronze and terracotta sculptures. Guides are available for the museum itself for a small *dash*, but everything is labelled reasonably clearly so it's

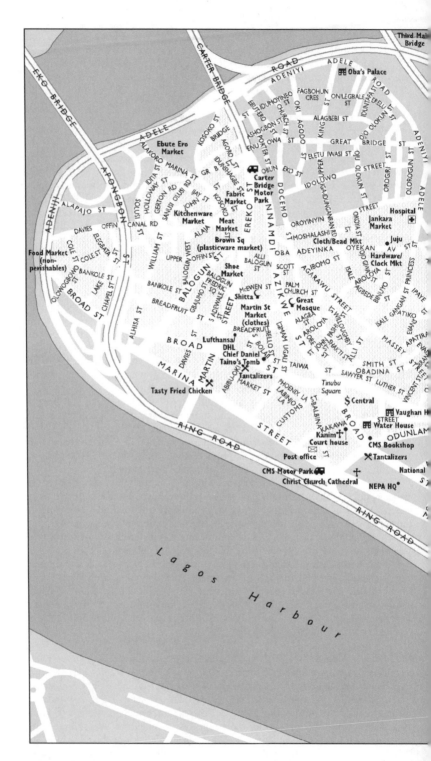

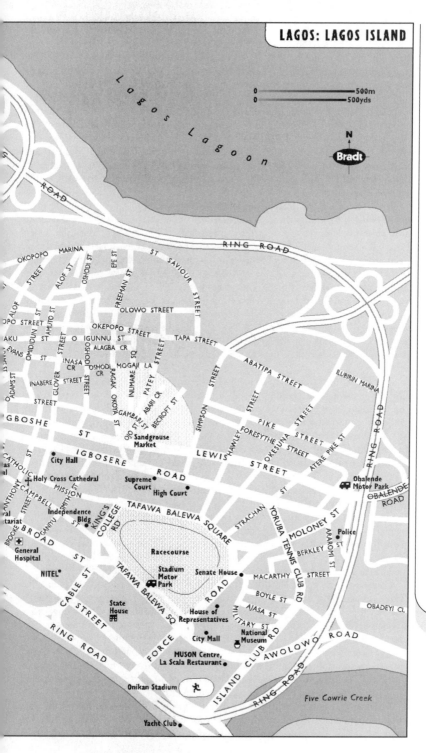

0   500m
0   500yds

N

Bradt

Lagos Lagoon

ROAD

RING ROAD

OKOPOPO   MARINA
STREET   ALOF ST   OSHODI ST   EPE ST   ST SAVIOUR STREET
ALOF ST   AMUTO ST   FREEMAN ST
PO STREET   OMIDIDUN   OLOWO STREET
AKU   ST   O IGUNNU ST   OKEPOPO STREET
EVANS   ST   OSHODI   ALAGBA CR   TAPA STREET
INASA   MOGAJI LA   ABATIPA STREET
ADAMS ST   CR   OSHODI   INUMARE SQ
INABERE   GLOVER   STREET   CR   RAGAK   PATEY   ST   ILUBIRIN MARINA
STREET   OGAMBARI ST   OKOYA   ABARI CR   SIMPSON
GBOSHE   ST   BECROFT ST   STREET   STREET
IGBOSERE   Sandgrouse   PIKE   STREET
CATHOLIC   City Hall   Market   LEWIS   HAWLEY   FORESYTHE STREET
las   ROAD   STREET   OKESUNA STREET
al   Holy Cross Cathedral   Supreme   STREET   ATERE PIKE ST
ANTHONY   MISSION   Court
CAMPBELL   High Court   Obalende
al   STREET   Independence   Motor Park
tariat   ONGANTU   Bldg   KING'S   TAFAWA BALEWA SQUARE   OBALENDE
BROOKE   BROAD   COLLEGE   RD   STRACHAN   YORUBA TENNIS CLUB RD   ROAD
General   ST   Racecourse   MOLONEY ST   Police
Hospital   ST   BERKLEY   ST
NITEL   CABLE ST   Stadium   Senate House   MACARTHY   STREET
TAFAWA BALEWA   Motor   Park   ROAD   BOYLE ST
State   SQ   House of   AJASA ST   OBADEYI CL
CABLE   House   Representatives   MILITARY ST
STREET   City Mall   National   AWOLOWO   ROAD
RING ROAD   FORCE   MUSON Centre,   Museum
La Scala Restaurant   ISLAND CLUB RD
Onikan Stadium   RING ROAD
Five Cowrie Creek
Yacht Club

easy enough to wander around by yourself, though rather infuriatingly there are no dates marked on anything, so there is no way of telling how old things are, and even the guides, who do little more than read off the labels anyway, are a little vague on the age of the exhibits. There are a few dusty old books and magazines for sale in the reception area but nothing of great interest.

The museum's exhibits cover Nigeria's traditional religions such as the Yoruba gods and deities and masquerade festivals, which many ethnic groups use to connect with their ancestors and to express their cultural traditions. Many of the masquerade costumes and masks on display are elaborately decorated with raffia, cowrie shells, beads and horns. There is an extensive selection of old musical instruments on display including drums, flutes and horns, the most elaborate being the trumpets still used in the north to signal the arrival and departure of the emir at Friday prayers or special events.

In the **Symbols of Power and Authority Gallery** is a selection of royal paraphernalia, including thrones and footstools that once graced the royal palaces, and clothing and crowns worn by traditional rulers (rather comically worn by papier maché heads and arms), Yoruba beaded crowns, Igbo felt crowns decorated with plumes, and Hausa-Fulani turban crowns. Old jewellery on display includes giant brass, iron and ivory bracelets, and manacles and anklets that were also used as currency during the slave trade. There are some scary-looking war dresses and shields, presumably used in the Yoruba wars of the 19th century. Some are made from chain mail – reminiscent of *orc* costumes from *Lord of the Rings* – and all are designed to instil fear into the enemy, and are prepared by witchdoctors who laid spells on the outfits and attached fetishes and charms. Other exhibits include decorated household calabashes and pottery used to store water and grain.

One of the most important displays is of the Benin bronze plaques in the **Benin Gallery**, which once adorned the royal palace at Benin City. Benin brass casters only worked for the Benin royal household and the unique and delicate figurines and plaques showing traditional ceremonies or royal scenes were used to decorate altars and walls within the palace. When the British conquered the Benin Empire in 1897, they looted the Oba's Palace of many thousands of these artworks, many of which are now on display in the British Museum and other European museums. There is also a rumour that the few on display in the Lagos museum are fake – stolen during the various military regimes and replaced with wax castings. When looking at them it's hard to tell if they are the real thing or not, as it is looking at the hoard of carved ivory tusks that also used to adorn the Oba's Palace at Benin.

In the museum's courtyard, there are some interesting photographs on body painting, women's hairstyles and scarring – many of Nigeria's ethnic groups still use facial scarring as a form of decoration. (The UK singer Seal is Nigerian by birth and has deep facial scars from the side of his nose to the corners of his mouth.)

Outside the main museum block, a separate building houses a display entitled **The Government of Yesterday and Today**. Here there are some early drawings and faded photographs of some pre-colonial traditional rulers, colonial governors, and some photographs of Queen Elizabeth II's visits to Nigeria – of her watching the durbar in Kaduna in 1956, and her overseeing independence proceedings in 1960. There's also a chronological line of photographs of Nigeria's presidents, governors and military generals from independence through to 1993 and General Abacha. (The exhibit hasn't been updated since then, and quite frankly it doesn't look like the room has been cleaned since then either.)

The most interesting exhibit is the car of Murtala Mohammed, one of Nigeria's more popular leaders, a black Mercedes limousine in which he was assassinated in February 1976. There are three bullet holes through the windscreen directly over the front passenger seat leaving spidery cracks through the windscreen, more bullet holes in the side, and several in the back seat of the car where presumably he was sitting. When he was shot dead (by disgruntled members of the military), his car was stuck in a traffic jam between a mosque where he had just been to Friday prayers and Lagos Airport where he was heading – the airport was subsequently named the Murtala Mohammed Airport in his memory. Finally, at the side of the museum is the office where you get export permits if you are exporting any antiquities from Nigeria.

The MUSON Centre and around Opposite the museum on Awolowo Road is the **MUSON (Musical Society of Nigeria) Centre** (see page 141), a tall modern office block in well-kept gardens that contains the relatively modern theatre, the Glover Memorial Hall, and other smaller venues. One of the finest restaurants in Lagos, La Scala, is also at the MUSON Centre (see *Where to eat*, page 126).

From the MUSON Centre it's a few metres' walk to **Tafawa Balewa Square** – though it's actually not a square at all, but a huge oval stadium and race course (though no horse races have been held here since the colonial years). When the British arrived in the early 1900s, they built barracks and partly prefabricated houses on the site. The story goes that accompanying each set of structures that were shipped from England was a team of British craftsmen: two bricklayers, two joiners, one plasterer and three coffins – early expats clearly suffered serious health problems in Lagos. In later years, the British built a race course, and at independence in 1960 the shift of power was officially handed over to the new Nigerian government at the race course when temporary grandstands were built for the occasion. The present grandstand and shopping complex was built in 1975 and named after the first president of the federation. The venue is still used for major political events and inaugural ceremonies for new ministers, governors and so on. The main entrance to the south is flanked by four larger-than-life statues of men dressed in Yoruba masquerade costumes with pointed hats and masks, and four concrete horses rearing up, behind a chaotic motor park full of battered yellow buses and taxis.

A few metres southwest of the square on Cable Street is the **NITEL building** (☉ *24 hours daily*) for local and international telephone calls. It's an ugly concrete tower, but is reputedly the tallest building in Nigeria. It was renovated in the 1980s after a large fire. Look out for sculptures of traditional musicians and praise singers around the main entrance door.

From Cable Street, two of Lagos Island's main thoroughfares run roughly northwest and parallel with each other: **Broad Street** and **Marina Street**. The latter is simply referred to as Marina, and, as its name suggests, it was once next to the water and was the location of the docks, before the area was filled in to build the ring road that circles Lagos Island in the 1970s. Apparently it was once lined with tall almond and palm trees, with benches where people could sit and admire the views of Lagos Harbour. There also used to be buildings here for the customs and port authorities, and booking offices and waiting rooms for passengers awaiting a berth on a steam ship to Europe. Little remains of this era today, and the area is now dominated by concrete high rises – mostly bank or oil buildings – and Marina lies 200m or so back from the water beyond the ground level and elevated sections of the ring road.

The only building of note in this area of Marina is **State House**, which was the residence of the governor during colonial times. At independence in 1960, it became the residence of the president, including that of the first military ruler, Major General Ironsi, after the first coup of 1966. But when General Gowon became head of state after the second coup of 1966, he chose to live in the perhaps

The Eyo (pronounced Err-your) Masquerade is a Yoruba festival unique to Lagos Island, and it is widely believed to be the forerunner of the modern-day Rio Carnival, thanks to slaves from Nigeria ending up in Brazil. On Eyo Day, the main highway in the heart of Lagos Island, Nnamdi Azikiwe Street, is closed to traffic from the end of Carter Bridge to Tinubu Square to allow for a procession. The participants pay homage to the *oba* of Lagos and it takes place whenever occasion and tradition demand, but is usually held as the final burial rites at the death of a Lagos *oba*. The first performance in Lagos was in 1854 in memory of Oba Akintoye, and since then it has been performed over 70 times, the last being at the funeral of Oba Adeyinka Oyekan, who died in 2003. The procession is led by Eyo dressed in masquerade costume, an elegant white-clad and veiled figure with a European-looking hat who carries a tall staff and various charms and fetishes under his cloak. There is much dancing and chanting to oversee the *oba*'s spirit joining his ancestors. You can see statues of Eyo at the entrance of Tafawa Balewa Square.

more secure Dodon Barracks in Ikoyi. You can still make out some of the colonial-style architecture on the State House, such as the vertical columns on the outside and its imposing entrance, but you'll have to look really hard as the building was modified almost beyond recognition in the 1970s.

Lagos Harbour and around Lagos Harbour is the biggest and busiest in Africa, and hundreds of ships and tankers line up out to sea waiting to unload their cargos or be pumped full of oil at the Apapa Docks to the south of Lagos Island. Apapa has a vast container terminal, which is capable of processing over 300 containers a day and 65% of Nigeria's exports and imports pass through the port. Until recently it was owned by the government but was sold off to Danish company AP Moller in 2005 for a reputed US$1 billion. Young boys dive 40m to the bottom of the harbour to collect buckets of sand from the ocean bed, which must be very heavy to pull back up. It is subsequently dried and sold off as building material.

Back at Tafawa Balewa Square and Cable Street, the walk continues along Broad Street, which increasingly gets busier and busier as you head north. Broad Street was once widened by the British colonial government to create a fire break through Lagos at a time when most buildings had thatched roofs. On your left between Broad Street and Marina is the very dilapidated and non-functioning **General Hospital** that dates from the 1930s, on the site of the original hospital built in 1895, when it was called the African Hospital. Apparently, at one time coffin sellers strategically set up their wares at the entrance of the hospital's morgue around the corner on Brooke Street.

From Broad Street, at the junction with Bank Anthony Way turn right and continue across the intersection with Campbell Street to the next intersection where the **Holy Cross Roman Catholic Cathedral** is on the right. The history of this cathedral begins with a priest who came from Dahomey in 1863 but who left again two years later after failing to convert anyone in early Lagos to Christianity. A second group of missionaries arrived in 1869 and built the first church on the spot from bamboo, after a group of Brazilian slave repatriates known as *Agudas,* who had been Roman Catholic in Brazil, were brought into the church and successfully converted local people to Christianity by combining Catholicism with the worship of Yoruba gods. The present cathedral was built in 1934 under the supervision of Father Aime Simon, a French priest who based it on 18th-century European church architecture, with Gothic columns, vaulted arches, side altars and buttresses. Some of the materials were imported from France. If the door is open you can go inside, and it's a welcome relief from the frenetic streets – look out for the French *fleur-de-lis* motifs in the mouldings in the side chapels.

Back along Broad Street are the decaying buildings of what used to be the **Old Secretariat** during colonial times. Built in 1906 in the shape of the letter E, there is little evidence of colonial architecture today, as over the decades the exteriors have been added to and plastered with concrete, and today they are simply falling down. Until the New Federal Secretariat complex opened on Ikoyi in the 1970s, these offices were home to the government ministries – there is still a sign on the corner of one proclaiming it as the home of the Federal Ministry of Transport and Aviation.

Continuing along Broad Street and just after Joseph Street is the **Shell headquarters** tower block on the left. A few metres up and also on the left is the **NEPA building,** with a bronze statue outside of Shango, the Yoruba god of thunder holding up his staff of power. Beyond here, at 50–52 Broad Street on the northeastern corner of the junction with Odunlami Street, is Bookshop House, with the modern **CMS Bookshop**, which sells a huge range of text and school books and some paperbacks. If you take Odunlami Street right, past Bookshop House, there are street vendors around King Street selling more textbooks. Diagonally across the junction from Bookshop House is the old and now defunct CMS Bookshop – you can still see the sign on the front of the two-storey building, which during colonial times also had its own printing press. On this corner is also **Tantalisers** fast-food restaurant, with its filthy plastic tables and dodgy fried chicken, which is a good stop for a whoosh of air conditioning and a cold drink and to use the OK toilets. (Don't be fooled by the pretty pictures of the food – it's pretty grim – and stay well clear of the ice cream.)

The markets and around It's in this area that the markets of Lagos Island start proper, and a range of meat is for sale at this junction, including pungent dried fish and goats' heads. And more of the distinctive yellow buses and taxis converge at what is known as the CMS Motor Park. You'll find black marketeers on the corner outside Bookshop House and you're likely to be asked by several if you want to change money. (More money changers hang out to the west of Lagos Island on Breadfruit Street.) It's probably reasonably safe to do so and they offer competitive exchange rates, but you certainly do not want to be carrying wads of cash on a walk around Lagos Island.

Just to the south of the Broad and Odunlami street junction, and back on Marina, is the **Christ Church Anglican Cathedral**. There has been a church on the site since 1867, but construction of the present cathedral began in 1925 and was finally finished in 1947. It's easily one of the largest churches in the city, and it's a fine white (though traffic-stained) building with a commanding square steeple and a cavernous interior. The design is classic neo-Gothic, with arched stained-glass windows and a wooden pulpit, but with additional Brazilian decorative single-flower motifs in the plasterwork. Again, if you can get inside, it offers a relatively peaceful moment away from the busy streets. Just up Marina, on the northwestern side of Odunlami Street, is Lagos's main **post office.**

Continue from Odunlami Street along Broad Street for a couple of hundred metres to Kakawa Street. On the left-hand corner is the old colonial magistrates' **Court House**, built in 1925 – note the inscription to King George V on the façade. Next door is the **Trinity Methodist Church** built in 1966, on the site where Methodist missionaries built their first church out of bamboo in 1861.

Turn right into Kakawa Street, which was once a fashionable street of Brazilian architecture, but which today is little more than a run-down alley, and look for the **Water House** on the right at No 12, and the **Vaughan House** on the left at No 29 – though you will have to look very hard, as they are seriously falling down and masked by busy shops. The Water House was built in 1885 by the Da Rocha family, some of the first people to lead repatriated slaves from Brazil, and the house was named after the water the family used to sell from the well in their back yard. At the time, Lagos's drinking water was brought by canoe down the Oyan River from Abeokuta, so the family's well was in great demand. A new wing was added in 1967, which by and large hasn't disturbed the original style of the building. The Vaughan House was built in 1900 by the Vaughan family, who were freed American slaves. Both today are used as shops and residences.

From here, Broad Street opens up into **Tinubu Square**, but what with the rapid increase of market activity you will hardly be aware that you are in a square at all. It's named after Efunroye Tinubu, a successful female trader and an anti-slave trade activist. The Central Bank of Nigeria building dominates the southern corner, where there is another busy motor park. In the middle of the square, among the stalls, is the now-defunct Independence Fountain – a gift to the city made in 1960 by the Lebanese community during independence celebrations. Whichever direction you follow from Tinubu Square into the heart of Lagos's commercial area, you will inevitably get lost, but these streets are well worth a wander to soak up the atmosphere. You'll lose sight of any street names, but if you can, roughly follow Nnamdi Azikiwe Street.

Along this street is the **Central Mosque**, which was rebuilt in the 1980s to replace an older one, with its large central dome and ornate minarets, serving Muslims in an area that has traditionally been occupied by Hausa-Fulani immigrants to the city for centuries. The stalls outside the mosque sell items of an Islamic nature, such as copies of the Koran or scripture boards. Another notable mosque in the area is the **Shitta Mosque**, a few blocks south of the Central Mosque on Martin Street, built by Shitta Bey, a repatriated slave from Sierra Leone who returned to Lagos as a wealthy merchant and a Muslim, and who built his own mosque in 1892. It was officially opened by the then British governor of Lagos, Governor Carter, in 1894. The architecture is typically Brazilian with traceries on its canopy and floral motifs on its pinnacles. Just to the south of here on Broad Street is another branch of **Tantalisers** and a similar set-up can be found around the corner at **Tasty Fried Chicken** on Martin Street. A few metres across from Tantalisers is **Chief Daniel Taiwo's tomb**, an ornate white statue in a fenced-off square, and a memorial to the chief who died in 1901, reputedly at the grand old age of 120. He had come to Lagos as a simple basket maker's apprentice to become an eminent person in the political circles of the city.

If at this point you have not felt you were in the commercial centre of Lagos, then you will now. From here on the markets are heaving, and every inch of space on these streets teems with stalls, where you will wade through crowds of thousands of people and crawling traffic. From Tinubu Square, to the north and east the buildings and streets of Lagos Island disappear under one massive blanket of a market.

Unlike the skyscrapers around Marina and the southern end of Broad Street, most of the buildings in this district of Lagos Island are only a couple of storeys high and were built as part of a central renovation project in the 1950s. Over the years, each family has developed their commercial activity, and now each house and structure burgeons with trade at the front while many trading families still reside above or behind their overflowing shops.

You can find almost anything for sale in these streets. Stalls are frequently grouped together depending on what they sell. For example, all the stalls in one

Here are a few lines from a poem called 'The Search', written by Nigerian Helon Habila (see page 332). He has won numerous prizes for his poetry. His first novel, *Waiting for an Angel*, was voted one of the five best debut novels of 2002 by the *Observer* newspaper, and he's presently teaching creative writing at a university in Washington DC.

Bus stops
The hawkers are a blur in motion
Needle weaving through metal fabric
Yellow buses that come and go, their anaemic limbs
Joined each to each by rust, 69 seated, 99 standing.
Prehensile bus conductors monkey on and off running boards
Calling bus stops, places...

Broad Street
On Broad Street there are no people
Only streams of intentions; sellers, buyers, opportunity addicts
Sidling to you, flashing wristwatches, jewellery, and drugs
The money-changer waits by the kerb
Catching your eye, beckoning in pounds and dollars
Floating from Tinubu Square to Marina...
You soon discover
Here are all predators, and you the only prey...

alley may only sell clocks, another hardware, or manufactured clothes, shoes, batteries, car parts, plastic piping, beds, meat, etc; even the smallest items such as padlocks or pens are all sold from a hundred stalls next to each other. Rather amusingly, and so very traditionally, you may find that in the areas that sell cloth, meat or vegetables, females are approached by the vendors as the 'madam', while in the hardware, car parts or trouser districts, it's the males or 'master' who receives all the attention. Among all the permanent stalls are the informal traders who wander around all the districts selling their wares – sour milk sold in little plastic packets out of buckets, dead cane rats hanging off a string, packets of dried fish bones and plastic water bags balanced on heads, shiny imitation gold watches and jewellery in a presentation glass box, fresh chicken thighs on an enamel platter, or giant yams stacked up in a wheel barrow.

If you can stomach it, one worthwhile detour is to the **Jankara Market**, which sells locally dyed cotton and hand-woven cloth, leather goods, musical instruments, beads, and one sight that you have to see – *juju* (black magic) items. To get there head west from Nnamdi Azikiwe Street along Oba Adeyinka Oyekan Avenue (also known by its old name Idumagbo Avenue) for about 200m. After the junction with Okoya Street, Jankara is a low-rise section of stalls on your left. Keep walking past the market until you reach the end at Princess Street and then enter; the *juju* section is in this southeastern corner of the market. In the middle of mud, corrugated rusted roofs, dark alleyways, open drains, and where thousands of people live on the premises, you'll find piles of dried monkeys' heads and hands, snake vertebras, animal skins and fur, bizarre collections of twigs and sticks, dried frogs, chameleons and insects, bottles and jars of ointments and potent poisons, and a whole host of other weird and wacky things used by the 'doctors' that run the stalls as charms, fetishes and for traditional medicine. (Here I was asked by one giggling lady if I wanted something to 'make my man grow bigger'!) It's fascinating, absorbing and appalling all at the same time, and a few years ago there were reports of human body parts turning up at Jankara.

For fabrics and beads, head up Okoya Street to the northwestern corner of the market before heading in. Once inside the market, a word of warning – watch where you're stepping; there are myriad open drains, rough ground and the inevitable rubbish. Like the stalls outside on the streets, Jankara and other similar designated markets sell just about anything. The only difference is that these were originally built as markets with narrow walkways between the stalls rather than stalls lining the traffic-choked streets.

The Oba's Palace The other (not very good) distraction in the northern part of Lagos Island is the **Oba's Palace**, the site of the official residence of Lagos's kings. It was originally built by the Portuguese in 1705 during the reign of Oba Akinsemoyin and most of the construction materials came from Portugal, but it was renovated beyond recognition in 1960. Follow Adeniji Adele Road from Jankara around the top of the island and beneath the shadow of the Third Mainland Bridge. The unremarkable Oba's Palace is a few metres down Upper King Street, but there's nothing really to see. The squat building has a couple of old cannons outside, a few fat goats wandering up and down the steps and, judging by the amount of Mercedes parked outside, probably a few fat-cat councillors inside. The present king is Oba Akiolu, who ascended the throne in 2003 and is the 19th Oba of Lagos.

From either the Oba's Palace or Jankara Market you can head back to Nnamdi Azikiwe Street and to the junction with Martin Street, just to the south of Carter Bridge that crosses to the mainland. At this junction is another chaotic motor park where every inch of available space is taken up by the ubiquitous decrepit yellow vehicles hemmed in by yet more market stalls. From here it's possible to catch a vehicle back in the direction you've come from to the southwest of Lagos Island, somewhere near the museum. Try asking for a vehicle going to the motor park at the front of Tafawa Balewa Square and you'll more or less be back where you started. But given that the traffic hardly moves on Lagos Island, you'd be better off walking or catching an *okada*. Notice that towards the end of the day another layer of markets on the already-congested narrow lanes appears – of traders selling dried fish, chicken pieces, chillies and tomatoes for shoppers heading home to make dinner.

Ikoyi When the first European settlers arrived on Lagos Island in 1852, they were badly affected by bad sanitation and malaria from the mosquito-infested swamps, and sought refuge on neighbouring Ikoyi Island. Palatial European-style houses were built on the island in the late 1800s and early 1900s, and a sprawling leafy suburb was created as a Government Reserved Area (GRA); reserved, that is, for Europeans. Very little of this architecture survives today and the space is slowly being given over to high-rise apartment blocks, though it is still the location of some of the biggest houses in Lagos, and there are many expat compounds here.

Ikoyi was once separated from Lagos Island by the MacGregor Canal, but this has been long since filled in, and there is no discernible border between the two islands except for a tangle of flyovers. There is little to see as such, and Ikoyi lacks the frantic atmosphere and teeming streets of Lagos Island, though there are some worthwhile shops and restaurants in the area, and there's a very convenient motor park at **Obalende**, the district where Ikoyi ends and Lagos Island begins, where you can get minibuses out to all the outlying motor parks on the mainland, from where public transport goes out of Lagos to other areas of the country.

Ikoyi is bisected neatly by Alfred Rewane Road, formerly and still known as Kingsway Road. The main shopping district of Ikoyi is on **Awolowo Road** in southwest Ikoyi off Alfred Rewane Road, where some of the most expensive and exclusive shops are located, as well as the Polo Club. It's worthwhile going for a stroll along Awolowo Road, though it is always filled with choking traffic, but there is an excellent selection of restaurants here as well as some good bookshops. It's also recently been upgraded with smooth tar and level concrete pavements (and even pedestrian underpasses – though on the last look these were gated shut and full of rubbish).

Starting from Alfred Rewane Road, Awolowo Road heads east to Lagos Island via Obalende. It's the first few hundred metres or so at the Ikoyi end that has the most interesting of distractions. At this junction, the **Falomo Bridge** rises over Five Cowrie Creek as it takes a constant stream of traffic over to Victoria Island. The bridge is littered with hawkers selling anything and everything, and beggars making the most of the go-slow. One reader writes, 'On one trip across the bridge from Ikoyi to Victoria Island (half a mile long tops) during a go-slow, I saw cold drinks, ties, tools, machetes, calculators, shoes, mops, watches, sunglasses, toilet seats, oil, floor mats, hats, CDs, DVDs, lamps, and clocks with the picture of the Last Supper on them.' A Lagos joke is that you can leave home naked, and get to work fully dressed, shaved and with clean teeth, from what you can buy in the traffic! To ride an *okada* over the bridge is far from being the most sensible thing to do in Lagos, but it's certainly an exhilarating experience.

At the Awolowo Road end of the bridge is a giant roundabout with a surprising patch of garden on top of it. Just to the east of the roundabout is a **NITEL** office for international phone calls, and there's a **post office** on Bourdillion Road. To the southwest of the roundabout and behind a petrol station is the **Golden Plaza,** with nine floors of mainly fairly upmarket Chinese and Indian shops selling imported items such as clothes and shoes, furniture, electronics and household goods. On the ground floor is a small café called the Cafeteria where you can get a cappuccino or espresso in icy air conditioning with a spring roll or samosa and watch (though not necessarily understand) Chinese CNN on the TV in the corner.

Once on Awolowo Road, the **Falomo Shopping Centre** is on the left behind a fence, where there is the good **Glendora** bookshop, and the upmarket souvenir shop **Quintessence** (see *Listings*) that are well worth a browse. At the back of Falomo Shopping Centre, down Raymond Njoku Street, is the small **Falomo Market**, with a few stalls selling clothes made from traditional Nigerian fabrics and some batiks. Back on Awolowo Road on the other side of the street, you can peek through the gates of the **Polo Club**, where the elegant polo horses graze on the field. Remarkably these horses are often taken through the hectic traffic of Lagos and even over Falomo Bridge to be exercised along Bar Beach on the south side of Victoria Island.

Victoria Island Locally dubbed VI, Victoria Island is reached by crossing the Falomo Bridge from Ikoyi, though the island is no longer an island as landfill has now joined it with the Lekki Peninsula. It started out as a residential area divided up into thousands of plots, but today it is the location of many hotels, banks, offices, embassies and very few sights per se, though there are some useful shops, and the best of Lagos's restaurants are on VI. Unlike Lagos Island or Awolowo Road, there's little sense in walking around here as everything is spread out.

The **Didi Museum** (*175 Akin Adesola Street, the main road that runs south from Falomo Bridge;* ☎ *01 262 9281, 433 0408;* ⊕ *09.00–17.00 Mon–Fri; free entry*) is a privately owned gallery of truly uninspiring Nigerian art next to the owner's house. There are only about half a dozen paintings here of different styles, none of which especially stand out, but if you are trawling around the hot and noisy streets of Victoria Island you can take a breather and sit down in the peaceful garden outside the gallery. The occasional temporary art exhibitions are of more interest, when you can aso buy paintings.

Bar Beach, also known as Victoria Beach, is very popular though not especially attractive or clean, and is the main beach that runs along the south of Victoria Island parallel to Ahmadu Bello Way. It's not safe for swimming and the water is truly filthy and covered with a sheen of oil. In places the sand used to routinely get washed away by the sea but that problem seems to have been fixed thanks to a new sea wall with pathway on top that has been built at the western end. There's a small market at the western end selling a few shells and batiks, but mostly fruit and veg. You can walk along Bar Beach reasonably safely during the day, though there are a few Area Boys asking for a 'fee' to get on to the beach.

At night it's a different story – then it's frequented by drug pushers, prostitutes and people smoking dope on the sand, and – by contrast – makeshift churches, though if you take sensible precautions you can visit the line of bars and chop houses at the eastern end, which sell a good range of cheap food and plenty of beer. It's certainly a lively enough place and the area attracts up to about 3,000 people a night, and there's often live music. Just don't go too far away from the bright lights and don't go on to any isolated stretch of sand in the dark. Note that some expats visit here with armed guards.

LEKKI PENINSULA
Getting there and away The Lekki Peninsula is to the east of Victoria Island. To get there take a minibus along Maroko Road for about 2km. After B-Jay's Hotel you'll pass the Mobil House Building and then the British International School and the Palms Mall (see page 136) on the right-hand side, then you'll get to a series of roundabouts on the Lekki–Epe Expressway, which is Lekki proper.

Nike Okundaye's house There is currently a huge building project going on here and a large housing estate of big homes is going up, one of which is the house and gallery of the famous batik artist, **Nike Okundaye** (*4 Augustine Anozie Street, off Admiralty Way, off the Lekki–Epe Expressway;* ✆ *01 270 5964–5; www.nikeart.com;* ⊕ *10.00–20.00 daily*). To get there take a minibus to the first roundabout in Lekki. From here take an *okada* or walk about 700m along the road to the left, which is Admiralty Way, and follow it around a big bend and turn right on to Wole Ariyo Road. Nike's house is down the third road to your right. Some of the minibuses that go along Makola Road have 'Lekki estate' marked on the side – these turn left at the roundabout on to Admiralty Way into Lekki housing estate, and will take you much closer to Nike's house. Pick up one of these from outside B-Jay's Hotel.

Nike Okundaye's house on three floors is full to the brim of exquisite Nigerian art of excellent quality and this is easily the best display of art in the country. The gallery exhibits her own work as well as that of other Nigerian artists, and there are several rooms of paintings, batiks, sculptures, and the unique indigo dresses that she favours herself. There are also samples of all of the most popular Nigerian cloths, so you can order whatever you want to be made up. The gallery has recently been extended and Nike now offers air-conditioned guest rooms for US$100 per night if you want to stay with her and she can organise transport from the airport. She's also opened a small workshop nearby at 'Roundabout 2' on the Epe Expressway a couple of kilometres to the east of the house, which offers short courses in batik and indigo dyeing, weaving, embroidery and quilting to interested groups. Nike is charming and a clever businesswoman. Along with her husband,

Born to a family of craftsmen, Nike was brought up by her great grandmother, who was a cloth weaver, adire maker, indigo dyer and head of the village women. She had an extremely tough early life, with her problems beginning at age six when her mother died and she was sent out to make a living selling banana leaves. At the age of 16 she ran away from her father and an arranged marriage to join a travelling theatre group, and later wed a well-known contemporary artist who was a graduate of the Oshogbo art workshops during the 1960s. As one of 15 wives, she spent 16 years in a violent, abusive and deprived polygamist marriage.

Throughout her life Nike has been determined to inspire other women to expand their horizons, and her principles have been to empower other Nigerian women through art. She opened the Oshogbo Nike Centre for Art and Culture (see page 178) in 1983 and took on around 150 students, some from overseas. Art mediums included adire, batik, wood carving, painting, beadwork, mosaics, drum making and dancing. One of her own most famous pieces is a batik called Breastless Blind Woman, which tells the story of a woman born blind and without breasts, and of her will and determination to overcome her handicaps in a society where the handicapped are normally kept behind closed doors.

Nike has done much to keep the traditional Yoruba art forms alive, and, aside from her Lagos and Oshogbo galleries, she has a representative and gallery in New York run by Stanley Ledermann (Apartment 3D, 200 East End Avenue, NY 10128; ✆ 01 212 427 1253). There's a book about her life, The Woman of the Artistic Brush (A Lifestyle of a Yoruba Batik Artist – Nike Davies) by Kim Marie Vaz, and she has produced her own video, Adire Among the Yoruba, on the traditional Nigerian method of adire and indigo dyeing.

who is quite a character, and her very smiley sister, she makes you feel very welcome in their home even if you don't buy anything.

Lekki Market Further along the Lekki–Epe Expressway and about nine kilometres from the centre of Victoria Island is the Ilasan Market, confusingly also known as the Ola Elegushi Market, or simply just as **Lekki Market**. Get off the minibus at the roundabout near Heroes furniture shop (the bus drivers and conductors should know where the market is if you ask). If you see the Chevron building from the bus it means you have gone too far. Once off the minibus, follow the road south from the roundabout, by foot or *okada*, for about 50m and then turn left for another 200m or so, and you'll find the sprawling market on your right. It is full of fruit and vegetables and all sorts of mundane household items, but if you walk through to the back, you'll find the excellent curio section, which sells arts and crafts from all over West Africa. The market traders are known for their aggressive tactics, but if you bargain hard, this can be the cheapest place to buy such items in Lagos. It's best to go on a weekday, as prices are higher at the weekends. If you're feeling peckish, look out for the branch of Frenchies (also on Victoria Island and Apapa) at shop number G1 in the market. There is no point trying to describe where this is, but someone will point you in the right direction once in the market.

Lekki Beach Another kilometre or so along the expressway is a dirt road that leads down roughly two kilometres to **Lekki Beach**. This is an attractive beach with shelters made of palm fronds and umbrellas available for rent and some local chop stalls, though the surf can be dangerous for swimming and it's far from rubbish free. Occasionally live bands play here, and Lekki Beach hosts Nigeria's answer to Jamaica's famous musical Sunsplash Festival each year on Boxing Day. Be very cautious here, as we had a run-in with some Area Boys who guard the entrance of the beach with a selection of sticks, belts and whips and no-one could get past them without paying a *dash*. At the far end of the beach is the La Campagne Tropicana (see *Where to stay*) where the beach is far nicer and kept clean.

Lekki Conservation Centre The **Lekki Conservation Centre** is at Km19 on the Lekki–Epe Expressway, which is also the location of the office for the Nigerian Conservation Foundation (NCF) (✆ *01 264 2498; www.africanconservation.org; entry N200 and there's a whole range of ridiculous fees for cameras – N700 for a fixed lens camera, N1,000 for a zoom lens and so on;* ⊕ *08.00–19.00 Mon–Fri, 12.00–18.00 Sat–Sun*). To get here you can catch a minibus along the Lekki–Epe Expressway, and the entrance to the conservation centre is opposite the Chevron Complex, so ask to get off there.

This is a small 78ha nature reserve enclosed by a concrete wall. It's a rectangular-shaped piece of swampy marshland between the Lagos Lagoon and the Atlantic Ocean. The vegetation consists of grassland and flooded mangrove forest that can have a water depth of around a metre during the rainy season. There is a figure-of-eight path through the reserve, which follows an elevated wooden walkway, that's around a kilometre long; it's a fairly pleasant walk through a patch of forest and for a moment you will forget you are in Lagos. A newly built treehouse which you can climb up to see the monkeys in the canopy of trees. A member of staff is on hand to help you up and down the ladder.

Inhabitants include mona monkeys, monitor lizards, cane rats (grass cutters), small crocodiles, giant forest squirrels, giant rats, pangolins, bush buck and Maxwell's duikers. It also attracts a number of birds, such as kingfishers, herons, hornbills, kites, wagtails, egrets and cuckoos, and some 118 bird species have been recorded in the reserve. As you can imagine, there are plenty of lizards and amphibians.

The centre was established in 1990 to preserve a piece of the Lekki Peninsula not earmarked for development, and as an education centre for awareness of natural resources, particularly for Lagos schoolchildren. At the entrance there's a rondavel with an excellent exhibition of photographs of some of the animals in Nigeria's national parks that was put up for the benefit of Prince Philip who visited here in 2003. There's also a small library of wildlife publications (⊕ *09.00–16.00 daily*), and the staff canteen here doubles up as a café for visitors offering big plates of cheap Nigerian fare such as fiery *jollof* rice and meat, soft drinks and tea. At the picnic area near the entrance reside three large tortoises, which have recently been donated to the centre. The centre is practically deserted during the week but it's popular at weekends. Unfortunately, despite being surrounded by a wall, the reserve is not free from the scourge of poaching, and Tunde, a tame sitatunga that was donated to the reserve by the people that run the Drill Ranch in Calabar, was killed by poachers for bushmeat in 2002.

TARKWA BAY There are a number of beaches in the Lagos area, but the sea can be unpredictable (see *Marine dangers* in Chapter 4, page 101). The major problem is the amount of rubbish on the beaches and the oil in the water – oil tankers flush out their tanks before filling up with oil again at Lagos Harbour and the sea is covered with slimy film. Up the Porto Novo Creek, or up-the-creek as it's generally known, on the sand bar between the ocean and the creek that goes all the way to the border with Benin, are a number of private beaches and beach houses lined with mangroves and palms, but you have to have your own boat (or know someone that does) to get there, as there are no roads. The water is much cleaner up here and once past the environs of Lagos there's much less rubbish.

The best public beach closest to the city is Tarkwa Bay, which is a reasonably sheltered beach located on the sand bar between the city and the ocean, and next to the main entrance of Lagos Harbour – you'll get one hell of a shock when an oil tanker passes by seemingly only metres away! The bay is manmade and was created during the construction of the harbour when it was covered with sand dredged from the bottom of the channel. As a result the water is a lot calmer than the exposed coastline elsewhere areound Lagos, and is safe for swimming, even for small children, as there's no surf.

This is a popular spot as a day trip and only accessible by boat, from Maroko Road or from under the Falomo Bridge on Victoria Island (see below). The beach is about 800m long and is mostly kept clean and there's a long line of deck chairs for which you will have to negotiate a price with one of the beach touts. Behind the deck chairs and sun shades are a few makeshift stalls selling *suya* and food-is-ready, as well as cold beers and soft drinks. Beach vendors casually walk up and down selling beads, baskets, carved calabashes and pieces of sarong-sized cloth, as well as watches and belts. You'll have to be firm with them so they leave you alone.

If you walk to the south end of the beach, sandy paths lead up to an old jetty built out of a line of boulders and then on, 500m or so, to the adjacent **Lighthouse Beach** on the other side. Lighthouse Beach is on the Atlantic Coast proper, while Tarkwa Bay is in the lip of the harbour and Lagos Lagoon. Unlike Tarkwa, Lighthouse Beach is pounded by the Atlantic waves and has a very strong undercurrent and is not safe for swimming, although previously, adventurous and experienced surfers have actually surfed here. Also unlike Tarkwa, there has been no effort to keep it clean and what would normally be a majestic swathe of white sand is full to the brim with countless discarded items of plastic rubbish that have been swept here by the ocean from Lagos. In the far distance, you can see a shipwreck of an oil tanker leaning into the waves as they break over the beach and this is a great, if isolated walk (walk on the shoreline where the waves break as there's less rubbish). Lighthouse Beach also has the best view of the hundreds (literally) of oil tankers and other ships queuing up in the sea to get into Lagos Harbour. It's a staggering sight, and there are ships moored way out into the ocean as far as the eye can see.

If you are here on a Sunday, you may see a church service on the beach, with the worshippers dressed in flowing white robes and fervently throwing themselves down in the sand in prayer. Between the two beaches are some ad hoc stables where you can negotiate a horse ride along either beach. Try not to ride in the middle of the day when the heat is at its most intense – although you may be able to manage this, it's not good for the poorly looked-after horses.

Getting there and away You can catch a boat to Tarkwa daily from the **Tarzan** jetty on Victoria Island on Maroko Road as it heads towards the Lekki Peninsula. From the Falomo Bridge, you'll need to catch a minibus or *okada* along Maroko Road, past Mobil House, and get off roughly when you see the British International School. Tarzan is to the north of here through a jumbled boat yard. From here there are also speed boats that go directly to Ikoyi on the opposite side of Five Cowrie Creek every few minutes for N30. This is a very useful service and saves a long journey from Ikoyi to Victoria Island through the traffic. Throughout the morning and early afternoon, the small speed boats to Tarkwa go-when-full and carry about half a dozen people. They take about 20min and as no life jackets are provided you'll need to hang on tight! The cost is N1,000 return, and you pay the full price up front and get a ticket that covers the return journey.

A boat returns from Tarkwa at 14.00, 15.00, 16.00, 17.00, and 18.00, and you must stipulate which boat you want to come back on when you buy your ticket so the boatman has some idea of how many people he is picking up. On the way out to Tarkwa, look out for the two massive oil pipelines in the harbour that stretch out to sea where the oil tankers dock to fill up with oil. One of them is abandoned and full of holes, while the other is the newer one in use today. Once at the beach, the boats dock on the south side where you will have to jump out and wade in. Hang around in the same area to catch the boat back and someone will point you to the Tarzan boat.

The Tarzan jetty is not a bad place to wait, despite being surrounded by abandoned boats and a rubbish-strewn beach. There's a 24-hour bar here (see *Where to eat and drink*, page 125) where a band plays on a Sunday evening. Plan to come back from Tarkwa on a later boat and enjoy a few sundowners at Tarzan. At the weekends other boats for the same sort of price and arrangement go to Tarkwa from the **Fiki Boat Club** on Ozumba Mbadiwe Road, almost under the Falomo Bridge, on the Victoria Island side. Like Tarzan there's also a 24-hour bar here.

THE MAINLAND
National Theatre and Gallery The **National Theatre and Gallery** rises out of a cluster of ring roads and flyovers just north of Lagos Island across the Eko Bridge in the Ebute-Metta suburb of the mainland. Its distinctive white concave roof is a notable landmark on the skyline of the mainland. Because of the confusing road system, the only way to get here is to take a drop taxi from the islands. The 32,000m² building was built in the 1970s for the 1977 Festival of African Arts and Culture (FESTAC), which featured a number of international performers, including Stevie Wonder and South African songbird Miriam Makeba, but today it's very run-down and poorly maintained.

The entrance to the National Gallery, with its exhibition of contemporary art including sculpture and pottery, is at Entrance B of the theatre (⊕ *09.00–17.00 daily; entry N200, plus a dash for the guide; no photography is permitted and you have to leave any bags at the entrance*). In the **Portrait Gallery** are huge oil paintings and some sculptures of Nigeria's leading statesmen, such as past premiers Abello and Azikiwe. There is an interesting range of portraits of famous characters from Nigeria's history painted in 1976 by a certain Mr Emokpae, including prominent *obas*, war lords, chiefs, emirs and missionaries – there's also one of Samuel Crowther, the first African bishop and a repatriated slave, and Herbert Macaulay, founder of the Nigerian Nationalism Movement. There are also portraits of modern writers and academics such as Wole Soyinka and Chinua Achebe.

In the **Contemporary Hall** are abstract works and modern art, and some pottery and batiks. Look out for the excellent pieces by celebrated Nigerian artist Bruce Onabrakpeya, who worked in the 1970s; they are unusual and lively plaster-cast paintings of busy market scenes and abstract people.

After visiting the gallery, you can get a drink or snack at the small bar at the main theatre entrance. The theatre itself is huge, but since the FESTAC event it has only really been used for seminars or conferences and is not much more than a big, run-down white elephant of a place. There are rumours that it is going to be sold off by the government and privatised or even turned into a casino if investors can be found. More recently the theatre has been used to show Nigerian 'Nollywood' movies on a Sunday afternoon (known as **The Theatre on a Sunday**), which has proved a popular move – so much so that often stars and producers of the movies pitch up to meet their fans! Shows start at '12-to', and '3-to' – 12.00 and 15.00. To the northwest of the theatre complex is a line of drinks and snack stalls, which literally heave at the weekends, when people come to socialise and picnic on the lawns.

AROUND LAGOS STATE

Badagry Badagry is 45km from Lagos and provides a reasonably interesting day out; it is a popular day trip for Lagos schoolchildren and Lagos people at the weekends. It's a small town pleasantly located on the Porto Novo Creek, called here the Badagry Lagoon, which extends from Lagos to the border with the Republic of Benin, cutting off the long sand bar that lies between the mainland proper and the Atlantic Ocean. It has an interesting if sombre history, as Badagry was a major slave port and a key entry point for many of Nigeria's missionaries. A slave market was established here in 1502, and on the sand bar across the lagoon often referred to as Coconut Island is the 'point of no return'. Slaves left the mainland of Africa by rowing boat to this strip of land between the creek and the ocean, where they were herded along a sand path for a few metres to the waiting ships in the sea on the other side. 'The point of no return' was probably the last they saw of their African homeland.

Slavery was finally abolished in Badagry in 1886. Badagry is also the site of the first two-storey building in Nigeria, built in 1845 and still standing on its original site. The townspeople are exceptionally friendly and will often offer to act as your guide. In 2001 and 2002 a Black Heritage Festival was held here, but this hasn't happened in recent years. Also, the town has been visited in the past by black Americans keen to discover their slave 'roots'. About 20–30km beyond Badagry, towards the border with Benin, are some stretches of attractive beaches lined with coconut palms, but you'll need a car to get to them.

Getting there and away Badagry is about an hour and a quarter's drive or 57km west of Lagos on the Badagry Expressway, towards the Republic of Benin. Minibuses and bush taxis go from the Mile Two Motor Park in Apapa for around N180. If you are coming from the Lagos islands, catch a vehicle from Obalende to Mile Two first. Badagry can also be reached by boat along the Porto Novo Creek, though there are no commercial boats. At Badagry, the motor park is on the Expressway, and from here you will need to catch an *okada* into the town proper, which lies a kilometre or so to the south on the creek. Tell the driver you want to go to Chief Mobee's house, as this is on the waterfront and as good a place as any to start exploring.

What to see and do The best place to start exploring Badagry's slave relics is to begin at the **chief's house** on the Marina, which is the road running along the creek to the south of town. Here you can pick up a guide (for a small *dash*) who will take you to all the places of interest along the Marina and in the back streets a short walk from here. The present chief is Chief Menu-Toyon II, also referred to as the Mobee of Badagry, and his house is at 127 Marina, on the corner of Mobee Street, just around the corner from the Mobee Museum. He also now has his own website (*www.mobeetoursinternational.4t.com*).

The chief is a charming man and part of a long line of chiefs whose family line has been in Badagry since the 15th century. The story goes that Mobee means 'take koala nuts', presumably an offering from the local chief when the Europeans first pitched up, who thought that was his name and it stuck. The present chief spends his days in the front room of his house, attending to chiefdom matters, such as consulting on his neighbours' disputes and problems. Here is his throne, and the room is adorned with photos of his coronation, and he will happily show you his scrapbooks and photo albums or let you take photos. In front of the throne is a pot where you will be expected to make some sort of offering or *dash*. Next to the chief's house is another house where the family sell cold Cokes and Fantas or, if you're really lucky, the chief's wife might offer you a Nescafé.

5

Like most southern regions of Nigeria, Badagry is split into a number of quarters, each under the jurisdiction of a different chief, who then reports to the *oba* (king) of the town or region. Their powers are limited as far as governing the town is concerned, and their roles are largely ceremonial these days, but they are consulted on local matters and are held in high regard as upright and wise members of the community. To be chosen as a chief, an application (usually from the same family line as the existing or previous chief) is sent to first the local government and *oba*'s office, and then on to the state government for consideration. If there is no objection, the proposed chief goes through a three-month period of isolation and contemplation in his quarters to prepare himself for his coronation. Coronation festivities go on for nine days, before he is finally crowned by the *oba* on his new throne.

The **Slave Relic Museum**, on Mobee Street (⊕ *daily; entry N100*), is in Chief Mobee's compound and is maintained by the Mobee family. The museum consists of a single room at the back of his house with a row of slave chains on the wall, some supposedly from the 1600s, and one of the giant water pots that slaves were made to drink out of crouched down like dogs. There's also a horrific iron 'lip-lock' which was used to stop the slaves eating sugarcane when they were on the plantations of the New World, and a leg shackle with a spike through it that went through the slave's foot to immobilise him. Also in the room is the headstone and grave of a previous Chief Mobee who died in 1893, and who was involved in selling slaves to the European slave traders at the Badagry slave market (black Africans were also part of the slave trade).

A few metres along the Marina to the east is Nigeria's **first two-storey building**, built in 1845 by a Reverend C A Gollmer of the Church Missionary Society as the first parsonage in Nigeria. This is also where Bishop Samuel Crowther, a freed slave and Nigeria's first black bishop, translated the Bible from English to Yoruba in 1846. The house has shuttered windows, a rusty tin roof and an outside staircase leading up to the second floor. The house next door has much grander architecture – though it's on the verge of falling down – with arches and a balcony, and a sweeping staircase up to the second level. Built in 1919 this is where Lord Lugard once stayed.

The **Black Heritage Museum** around the next corner (⊕ *09.00–17.00 daily; entry N100*) is an excellent museum, and here we had a superbly informative guide who was very easy to understand – though it's a little gloomy inside if there's no NEPA. The two-storey, pale blue building has been restored in recent years, although it was first built in 1853 as the district officer's office. Allow at least an hour or two here as there's an excellent display of exhibits all about the slave trade, from old photographs, slave chains and a mock-up plywood model of a slave ship demonstrating how many thousands of slaves were crammed inside, to pictures and drawings of slaves working on plantations in the New World.

Visitors learn about over 300 years of trading when the people of Africa were simply seen as 'goods'. One of the exhibits is an advertisement published in the USA in 1794: 'Negroes For Sale: A cargo of very fine stout men and women, in good order and fit for immediate service, just imported from the windward coast of Africa. . .'. Another advertisement in New Orleans in 1835, says, 'Chloe, aged 36 years. She is without exception, one of the most competent servants in the country; a first rate washer and ironer, does up lace, a good cook, and for a bachelor who wishes a housekeeper she would be invaluable.' There are also a few local masquerade costumes, and the guide will explain how masquerades were used to warn off unwelcome European slave traders on the coast centuries before any police force was established.

A few streets back from the Heritage Museum on Old Post Office Road is the

missionary cemetery, which has over 200 tombs of the first missionaries that arrived on the coast, and the tomb of George Fremingo, also known as Huntokomu, the first Portuguese slave merchant to arrive in Badagry, who was killed when he got there in 1620.

A few streets back from the Marina (you will need a guide to find all these things) is the site of the first Christian church and the **Agla Tree Monument** on Market Street. It was supposedly under this tree that Christianity was first preached in Nigeria by Thomas Birch Freeman, a Methodist missionary, and Henry Townsend, an Anglican missionary, who both arrived in Badagry in 1842, though there are other spots in Nigeria that have staked this auspicious claim. The tree survived another century or so before being blown down in a storm in 1959. Today there is a simple cross and a concrete monument and a little lizard-filled garden enclosed by a fence marking the spot, but there's not much to see.

Not far from here is the Badagry **Slave Market**, which was established in 1502. This is where the Europeans met the African middle men to barter for slaves, of which 900 would be sold on an average week. They were auctioned for commodities like iron bars, cotton, gin and arms. It has been recorded that a single cannon was worth 100 slaves, while a bottle of gin was worth two, and estimated that some 18 million slaves were sold from this market over a 400-year period. Inside the simple compound is a yard of deep sand surrounded by concrete walls, and to the left of the gate is a small shrine that, judging by the chicken feathers scattered around, is still in use today. The well here is also still used by the townsfolk and the water is supposed to have magical properties. This is presumably the last place the slaves got to drink, from the big communal pots seen in the museums, before being carted off to the slave ships.

Back on the Marina and opposite the chief's house is the **Slave Port** (*entry N100*) that was in use between the 15th and 18th centuries. The slaves were taken here from the slave market and then transported across the lagoon to 'the point of no return', and then on to the slave ships waiting in the sea at the other side of the sand bar. There's a garden here and a stone wall and gate leading on to a short jetty, and a couple of rusty cannons that were used against the slave traders during the abolition of slavery in 1886. Across the street and next to the chief's house is the **Brazilian Baracoon**, built in the 1840s; it's a low, squat and crumbling brown building with a tin roof that used to hold up to 40 slaves at a time as they were being ferried from the slave market to the jetty.

You can arrange a **boat ride** across to the 'point of no return' with the man that takes the entry fee for the Slave Port for about N600 per person, though less if there are more than two people in the boat. You can get out on the sand bar and walk though the 'point of no return' and imagine what it was like for the slaves in their last moment on African soil. There's an arched monument right on the beach to mark the spot where the waiting ships would take on their cargo. You can stroll along the beach for a bit while the boat waits for you to take you back to Badagry. It's very moving to imagine that it was on this breezy palm-fringed shoreline that millions of human beings were traded like farmyard animals for the benefit of capitalists thousands of miles away.

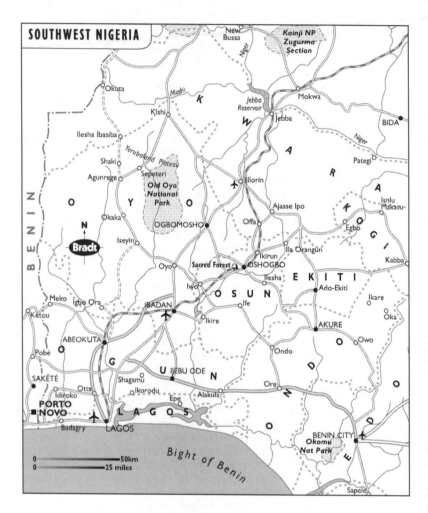

SOUTHWEST NIGERIA

6

Southwestern Nigeria

Aside from Lagos, the southwest of Nigeria is easily the most densely populated part of the country. This is Yorubaland, and there are many cities here steeped in history and the mythical origins of the key players in the traditional Yoruba religion. These towns are still governed to some extent by *obas* (ostensibly kings, though they come under an array of other names too), who sit regally in old palaces and wield a certain degree of political clout. While their positions in the communities are largely ceremonial these days, their stature and spiritual role are still important and all can trace their origins back to the founders of the powerful Yoruba empires, many of whom were (supposedly) the Yoruba gods themselves. Throughout the region are testaments to the Yoruba religion, such as shrines where sacrifices are still made, which at times may seem strange and complicated, but are without doubt a compelling sight. In recent years much of traditional religion has been lost under the cloak of Christianity that chokes much of the southwest, but it's worth exploring the Sacred Forest at Oshogbo, the Olumo Rock at Abeokuta, and the mythical city of Ife, the spiritual home of all Yorubas, for an insight into the Yoruba religion, and to hear the stories and oral traditions that have been passed down through the centuries. Finally, there is Benin City, which has its own unique history, and which is near enough to Lagos to be lumped in with this chapter. Between the heavily populated urban areas the countryside is a rich and tropical expanse of dense green palms dotted with busy villages, and travelling between the major centres is not difficult. It's easy enough to hop from one motor park to the next, and all of the places mentioned in this chapter can feasibly be visited on a day trip from Lagos. The southwest of Nigeria is also renowned for its art, especially in Oshogbo, which underwent an art renaissance in the 1960s, and where there are still some good galleries to purchase some unique pieces of art. It's also a region that is highly educated and industrialised, and is home to a number of educational institutions such as Nigeria's premier university, the University of Ibadan, established in 1948 during colonial times, and the Obafemi Awolowo University at Ife.

ABEOKUTA

Abeokuta is the capital of Ogun State and is around 100km north of Lagos on the old Ibadan road. It's a historical town for the Yoruba people and its most famous landmark, the Olumo Rock, is considered sacred. Abeokuta was founded in the 1830s by the Egba clan of the Yoruba, who were seeking refuge from the Yoruba civil wars. They had traditionally lived in scattered villages, but with the threat of war with more powerful neighbours, they sought strength and protection in unity, and giving themselves a king they gathered together on the defensive western side of Olumo Rock. Abeokuta means literally 'under the rock'. The Egba were essentially middlemen in the slave trade, providing slaves from the interior to the slave markets on the coast, and with European guns obtained in exchange for slaves, they managed to protect their newly formed kingdom during the Yoruba wars.

By the 1840s, and towards the end of the slave trade, some 500 returnee slaves, or Creoles as they were known, settled in Abeokuta and were the early nucleus of the Christian community. Among them was Samuel Crowther, a Yoruba by birth, who had been rescued as a boy from a slave ship by a British warship and taken and educated in Sierra Leone. He returned to Yorubaland and was the first West African to be ordained an Anglican bishop. He ran a prestigious Christian mission in the town, and word of his good works got sent back to Queen Victoria in England who sent two Bibles – in English and Arabic – to the Alake (king) of Abeokuta. When Crowther later went to England he was granted an audience with the queen, when he recited the Lord's Prayer in Yoruba. She reputedly described it as 'soft and melodious'. The town is not only famous for its easily climbable rock; there's a good selection of traditional adire and batik cloth on offer in the market, and it's also the birth place of the famous Nigerian writer Wole Soyinka, the late musician Fela Kuti and now ex-President Obasanjo.

GETTING THERE AND AWAY Abeokuta is roughly two hours' drive northeast of Lagos; pick up a vehicle in **Ojota Motor Park** in Lagos for around N200 and it will drop you at Kuto Motor Park in Abeokuta, which is just to the south of the main roundabout at the top end of town near the Gateway Hotel. Vehicles from Ibadan, roughly the same distance away as Lagos, but to the north, also drop off at **Kuto Motor Park**, where you can pick up taxis and *okadas* to get around town. The road to Ibadan has a few pot-holes.

WHERE TO STAY AND EAT

Gateway Hotel, just off Ibrahim Babangida (IBB) Bd & clearly signposted from the roundabout; ☎ 039 241904/244652. This is the town's principal state hotel & is a vast property on extensive grounds. The place is cavernous with tall corridors, a vast lobby & enormous conference halls making you feel a bit like a shrunken Alice in Wonderland. The Wonderland comparison stops there though, as it was obviously built during the 1970s oil boom by the government, when no expense was spared, but it now looks very tired & frumpy. The restaurant serves basic dishes of Nigerian food & occasionally there are evening buffets of continental dishes. The 200 rooms are old-fashioned but adequate, & there's a 24-hour gen, swimming pool & tennis court. Rooms $$; suites $$$

Dusmar Presidential Hotel | IBB Bd, just around the corner from the Kuto Motor Park; ☎ 039 245179/245218; e dusmarhotels@hyperia.com. By far the nicest hotel in town & good value too, this has 41 rooms in a tidy 3-storey block with secure car park next to the MKO Abiola Stadium, with a very neat restaurant with crisp white tablecloths, silver cutlery & glasses, muted music & a well-stocked bar. It's relatively new & the rooms have good furnishings

with DSTV, a fridge & a desk. Rooms $; suites $$

Ajol Castle at 4 Aduke Ayorinda Av, around Oba Alake Rd, which is in the quiet GRA part of town called the Ibara Housing Estate; ☎ 039 242220/241712. This has clean & neat rooms with fridge & DSTV, & the bigger rooms have 2 king-sized beds next to each other, which equates to about 3m of bed space. There are cold beers in the fridge in reception, the small restaurant serves Nigerian food & the odd continental dish like chicken & chips, & there's a car park. It's friendly & seems quite popular & deservedly so, so try & phone the owner, Mr Johnson, first. $

Ayo Inn at 6 Aduke Ayorinda Av, next door to the Ajol Castle; ☎ 039 241735. This is very rough & ready, with 7 dark & gloomy rooms with stained walls & battered AC units. Tea-eggs-and-bread breakfast is N300 & they can rustle up a plain rice dish for dinner on request, & there's beer for sale at reception. The cheaper rooms at the back have a shared bathroom & go for as little as US$20 & there's no deposit. $

Mokland Inn around the corner at 7 Oba Alake Rd; ☎ 039 240060, 242054. A big range of rooms spread through a row of 4 houses behind big gates where there is plenty of parking. You can get cold

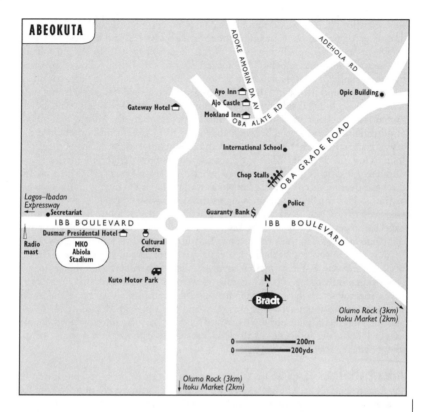

ABEOKUTA

ADOKE AMORIN DA AV

ADEHOLA RD

Ayo Inn
Ajo Castle
Mokland Inn

Opic Building ●

Gateway Hotel 🏠

OBA ALATE RD

International School ●

OBA GRADE ROAD

Chop Stalls

Lagos–Ibadan
Expressway
←   ● Secretariat

Guaranty Bank $

● Police

IBB BOULEVARD

IBB   BOULEVARD

Radio
mast

Dusmar Presidential Hotel 🏠

MKO
Abiola
Stadium

Cultural
Centre

Kuto Motor Park 🚐

N

Bradt

Olumo Rock (3km)
Itoku Market (2km)

0 ▬▬▬▬ 200m
0 ▬▬▬▬ 200yds

Olumo Rock (3km)
↓ Itoku Market (2km)

beers & soft drinks at reception & there's a fairly wide choice of food on the menu, such as spaghetti & some sort of meat & chips, which they can bring to your room. The rooms are spacious, with local TV & new fans, & water actually comes out of the big shower heads. There's a row of slightly cheaper but smaller rooms at the back of one of the buildings. $

WHAT TO SEE AND DO
Olumo Rock You can climb the **Olumo Rock** for an impressive view of the city (*entry N200; parking N25; camera N150; video camera N250; plus dash for the guide*). The rock is 3km through town beyond the markets, and a taxi from the Koto Motor Park will cost about N100 (less for an *okada*). Taxis in Abeokuta are green with a horizontal yellow stripe. Olumo is an impressive outcrop of large granite boulders and the founding site of Abeokuta; the highest point of the main rock is 137m. It's quite a steep walk from the car park up 52 steps with a railing to the base of the main boulder, or for those feeling lazy there's a new lift! In 2006 Ogun State revamped the car park, laid out a park with benches at the bottom of the rock, and built a visitors' centre and an elevator to the top of the rock – an ugly concrete structure and a lift shaft tower, which completely ruin the naturalness of the rock, but nevertheless saves a steep climb.

The first thing you'll see here in a cave under a lip of the rock is the main Olumo Shrine with bits of fur and feathers stuck to the door and stoop – if a recent sacrifice has been made then you may also see decomposed pigeons, cow parts, kola nuts and snails. People still come regularly to pop money in the door to appease the Yoruba gods and to ask for wealth, and barren women pray to become pregnant. At one time, and reputedly within the last hundred years, human beings

6

were sacrificed here. The Olumo Festival takes place on 5 August each year, when thousands of people come at midnight to make sacrifices, and a priest will pray over each one. Traditionally a new *oba* of Abeokuta will spend four days in solitary confinement in the cave behind the locked door of the shrine, followed by three months of solitary contemplation in a room in his palace before his coronation.

Further around the base of the rock is a bigger cave several metres wide, but only a metre or so high. Inside the cave are remains of some low walls, with bowls carved into the floor and light niches into the walls where the Yoruba leaders hid out during the Yoruba wars between 1820 and 1830. Around the corner from the cave are a few huts where some women and children live as guardians of the Orisa Igun (God of thunder) Shrine decorated with sticks that represent iron and thunder. Next to the shrine is a tree where the *oba* takes a leaf to put on his forehead during his coronation, known as the Akoko leaf. There is another shrine to the god of smallpox, and another to the devil, where people pray and make sacrifices to ask the devil to stop doing whatever he is doing wrong. You are expected to pay a small *dash* to the keepers of the shrines. The guide will also point out some faces etched out in the stone of Yoruba warriors decorated in cowries.

To get to the very top of the rock there's a steep set of iron steps up a cleft in the boulder, and the last few metres involve a bit of daredevil scrambling on the smooth granite surface. There are great views over the brown rusted tin roofs of town, from where you can hear the drifting music from the cassette sellers in the markets. Ex-President Obasanjo was born and went to high school in Abeokuta, and the guide will point out the big white school next to a radio tower on the top of a neighbouring hill. Olumo Rock also serves as a police post, because of the views over the town.

Itoku Market Abeokuta is also famous as a centre for cloth, especially adire, the tie-dyed indigo cloth. The **Itoku Market** is located in the centre of town near the white pyramid obelisk that sits on a roundabout, from where the market spreads out in all directions; you can catch any vehicle from Kuto Motor Park and ask for the market. There are huge amounts of cloth here stacked up in bales at hundreds of stalls, and all the women are beautifully dressed in colourful fabrics. The market also has a large *juju* section where you'll see live chameleons in tiny cages, dried frogs and insects, more of the appalling dried monkey's heads, crocodile and snake skins, bits of twigs and dried leaves used to make magical potions, and tails, paws and heads, or beaks of various small animals and birds used as fetishes and charms. The market is fine to walk around and have a look at the weird and wonderful bits and pieces, but if you are female expect to get a bit of friendly hassle from the women who sell the cloth.

IBADAN

About 125km north of Lagos and a prominent transit point between the coast and the north, Ibadan is spread over acres of hills and valleys and is the capital of Oyo State. During the first half of the 20th century and before Nigerian independence, Ibadan was reputedly the largest city in sub-Saharan Africa. It started life as a military camp in the 1830s, and the phenomenal growth in size is derived largely from the Yoruba wars, when hundreds of thousands of retreating and displaced refugees gathered in one place. In 1840 Ibadan forces defeated Fulani invaders from the north at the battle of Oshogbo, thus protecting south Yorubaland from further attack and stopping the advance of the jihad through Yorubaland towards the sea. Easy access to fertile land encouraged people to settle there, and even today the region is the most important agricultural area in Nigeria – it essentially feeds Lagos.

The city came under British protection in 1893, and was later the capital of Nigeria's former Western Region. The introduction of the cash crop cocoa by the British brought increasing prosperity and Ibadan became the centre of Nigeria's cocoa belt, which for decades assured the prosperity of the Yoruba. Little cocoa is grown today in the region, but the 25-storey Cocoa House is one of the only high-rise buildings on Ibadan's skyline and serves as a good landmark. Its population was put at 2.5 million in the 2006 census.

There's not a great deal to see or do here; Ibadan is most famous for its university and its market (one of the biggest in Nigeria) and very unfortunately a god-awful zoo, though it is a convenient base for trips to the other, more traditional, old towns of Oyo State. It's a sprawling metropolis that goes on seemingly to all points on the horizon, over several hills dotted with granite boulders affording good views of the rusty corrugated iron rooftops of yellow stucco-walled houses. The University of Ibadan (founded as a college of the University of London in 1948, and as an autonomous university in 1962) was Nigeria's first university, and several libraries and research institutes are located in the city.

The city is very religious for both Muslims and Christians, and there are scores of churches and mosques; on Sundays whole streets close to traffic for open-air church services. In the evening look out for the thousands of kites that fly over Ibadan at sunset – it's a remarkable sight. Finally, the popular songstress, Sade, was born in Ibadan and lived here until the family moved to the UK when she was four years old. Her Nigerian father was an economics lecturer and her English mother was a nurse.

GETTING THERE AND AWAY Ibadan is two hours' drive north of Lagos and one hour 45 minutes from Abeokuta, and there are regular vehicles throughout the day. However, be aware that the 147km-long Lagos–Ibadan Highway is the worst road in the country; it's plagued with pot-holes, most of it is in near collapse and the traffic is very heavy. There are countless fatal accidents on this road. In Ibadan, you are likely to be dropped off at the Dugbe Market around Oyo Road (confusingly here also called Dugbe Road), which is a pretty central destination, and where there are plenty of *okada*s and taxis to take you to a hotel.

If you are coming from elsewhere or if you are leaving Ibadan you need to get to one of the bigger **motor parks** listed below, which are several kilometres away on the edge of the city. To get to any of these go to the Mokola roundabout 1km to the north of Dugbe, and here you will find lines of shared taxis and minibuses that go to all the motor parks. It's a very spread-out city and the traffic is bad, so give yourself at least an hour to get out to an outlying motor park.

For destinations to the southeast such as Benin City, Warri and Onitsha, and for Lagos, you'll need to go to New Garage to the southeast of the city, though there are some vehicles going directly to Lagos from near the Dugbe Market on Oyo Road. To get to New Garage you first have to get a vehicle from the Mokola roundabout to somewhere called Challenge (it's very vaguely beyond Cocoa House and the GRA, and around the ring road of Ibadan). Once at Challenge (a suburban motor park surrounding a petrol station) you need to swap on to another vehicle going to New Garage.

For buses to the north and northeast (with the exception of Oyo – see below), vehicles go from Agodi Gate Motor Park in the east, simply referred to as just 'Gate'. To get here take a vehicle directly from the Mokola roundabout. Everyone will help you find the right bus and it shouldn't cost much more than N30 to get from the centre of Ibadan to the motor parks.

To get to and from Oyo, only 52km directly north of Ibadan, buses go from a

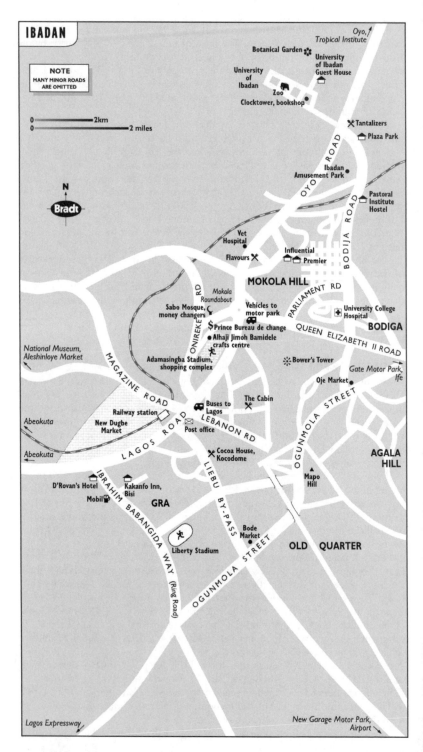

IBADAN

NOTE
MANY MINOR ROADS
ARE OMITTED

0 ————— 2km
0 ————— 2 miles

N
Bradt

Oyo,
Tropical Institute

Botanical Garden ❀

University
of Ibadan
Guest House

University
of
Ibadan

Zoo
Clocktower, bookshop

✕ Tantalizers

🏠 Plaza Park

Ibadan
Amusement Park ●

Pastoral
Institute
Hostel

OYO ROAD

BODIJA ROAD

Vet
Hospital ●

Flavours ✕

Influential ●
🏠🏠 Premier

MOKOLA HILL

PARLIAMENT RD

✚ University College
Hospital

BODIGA

Mokola
Roundabout

Sabo Mosque,
money changers 🌙

Vehicles to
motor park

ONIREKE RD

💲 Prince Bureau de change
● Alhaji Jimoh Bamidele
crafts centre

QUEEN ELIZABETH II ROAD

Adamasingba Stadium,
shopping complex

☀ Bower's Tower

Gate Motor Park,
Ife

Oje Market ●

National Museum,
Aleshinloye Market

OGUNMOLA STREET

MAGAZINE ROAD

🚌 Buses to
Lagos

The Cabin
✕

Railway station 🏠

New Dugbe
Market

LEBANON RD

LAGOS ROAD

✉ Post office

✕ Cocoa House,
Kocodome

Mapo ▲
Hill

**AGALA
HILL**

Abeokuta

Abeokuta

D'Rovan's Hotel

Mobil ⛽

Kakanfo Inn,
Bisi 🏠

IBRAHIM BABANGIDA WAY

GRA

🏃
Liberty Stadium

LIEBU BY-PASS

Bode
Market

OGUNMOLA STREET

OLD QUARTER

(Ring Road)

Lagos Expressway

New Garage Motor Park,
Airport

motor park in a sprawling market roughly three kilometres north of the university on Oyo Road. To get there take any city bus or shared taxi heading north up Oyo Road. Ibadan is a central transit point for vehicles going further north, so you may find yourself changing vehicles here between Lagos and other points north, which may involve a trip from one motor park to another by city transport.

The train station is on Dugbe Road, which is an extension of Oyo Road. Ibadan's airport is 12km southeast of town, but given its proximity to Lagos there are very few flights. Overland Airways (↘ *0803 535 1158, desk at the airport; www.overland.aero*) flies between Ibadan and Abuja (one hour) Monday to Friday at 07.00, and 15.00; and from Abuja to Ibadan Monday to Friday at 12.45 and 17.30.

PRACTICALITIES The commercial centre of the city is effectively the area around the train station, Dugbe Market and Cocoa House, where you'll find most of the market activity. Oyo Road bisects the city neatly, though it confusingly changes name; it is referred to as Dugbe Road near the Dugbe Market, and to the very south it's Lagos Road. There is a stream of minibuses and shared taxis going up and down this main road and a short hop will cost N30. Ibadan's cloth market, supposedly every 16 days, is at the corner of Ogunmola Street and Bodija Road, and you will have to ask in the area when it's next on. There are bread sellers here all the time. Opposite the entrance to the university are book and stationery stalls. On Oyo road are a number of internet cafés, some open 24 hours if there is NEPA; there's a particularly dense crop of them about 100m north of the Mokola roundabout, along with some pharmacies.

The chaotic **post office** is on Dugbe/Oyo Road, more or less opposite the train station (⊕ *08.00–17.00 Mon–Fri, 09.00–13.00 Sat*). To **change money**, ignore all the banks and head for the area around the Sabo Mosque, where you will find plenty of Hausa money changers, some with their own offices. From the Mokola roundabout take the road left or to the east (I could not find the name of this street) for about 100m and just before the Sabo mosque, which is on the right-hand side, you'll find money changers on either side of the road. Look out for Prince Bureau de Change, a small office with mirrored glass doors, on the left.

WHERE TO STAY

⌂ **International Institute of Tropical Agriculture** Oyo Rd, 5km north of the university; ↘ 02 241 2626 & ask for the International House; www.iita.org. The best place to stay in Ibadan, but you have to make a reservation. The International Institute of Tropical Agriculture (IITA) is a research institute founded in 1967 & its mission is to improve food security through agriculture for the poor in Africa. This is a private guest house set in a 600-acre tropical estate, with pool, tennis, badminton & squash, a 9-hole golf course & fishing in a large lake. It's also a great place for hiking & birdwatching. There is a poolside café, a bar & there's excellent food in the main buffet restaurant. Accommodation is in singles & doubles & 1- to 2-bedroomed flats with fully equipped kitchens. $$$

⌂ **Kakanfo Inn** 1 Nihinlola St, off Ibrahim Babangida Way, which is also referred to as Mobil Petrol Station Ring Rd; ↘ 02 231 1471–3/751 8000; www.kakanfoinn.com. This is very

professionally run & is one of the nicest hotels in Ibadan, opened in 1989 & tucked away in a quiet area of the GRA. The 68 rooms & 14 suites all have balconies, with slightly dated but comfortable furnishings with fridge & DSTV, 24hr power & running hot & cold water. There's a good restaurant serving Indian & Nigerian food, an L-shaped swimming pool & relaxing poolside terrace, a curio shop in the lobby, & a small gym with some weight machines. Unusually you are quite likely to be charged the non-resident rate on the tariff here, though pay the actual bill in naira. Try & negotiate with the receptionist to pay the lower resident's rate & don't forget the 15%. Discounts are available at the w/end. Rooms $$; suites $$$

⌂ **Premier Hotel** Mokola Hill; ↘ 02 241 1234/ 4122/4245; www.premierhotelibadan.com. This is the state hotel perched on top of Mokola Hill, & it is easily seen from any approach to the city. Built in

1966 & 6 storeys high, it's recently be spruced up by repainting; it has new baths & AC. The comfortable 80 double rooms & 6 suites have DSTV, & the best views in the city. In the huge car park you can arrange car hire, & there are a few batiks & wood carvings for sale. The hotel has its own boreholes & giant gens, tennis court, gym, another vast lobby, bakery, mosque, bureau de change (guests only), bookshop, comfy bar with TV showing CNN, & an Olympic-size pool. You can swim here for a small fee even if you're not staying. Finally there is a Chinese restaurant (see *Where to eat*). Rates are discounted by 25% at the w/end. $$

🏠 **Hotel Influential** Mokola Hill, a few metres to the south of the main entrance to the car park of the Hotel Presidential on M. Fadahunsi Onilegogoro St; 🕿 02 241 4894, 415039. This is a nice & neat, reasonably new, business hotel with just 15 rooms, also at the top of Mokola Hill, with a smart lounge & dining room, modern cool tiles, fat sofas, a cosy bar area, plants, friendly staff & welcoming Spanish flamenco music. The spotless rooms have giant beds & there are a few spaces for cars in the compound & a 24hr gen. Breakfast items go from N100–200, & they offer dinners of beans & dodo, meat & a variety of soups plus continental dishes of chicken & fried rice. $$

🏠 **D'Rovans Hotel** Chief Francis Aiyegbeni Close, Ring Rd; 🕿 02 231 2907/8364; www.drovanshotel.com. Rooms here are tiny but not too tired-looking, with reasonably modern furniture, & there's a consistent power supply, too. There's a great bar next to the swimming pool with comfy seats & fans & sometimes live *juju* or highlife bands. Other facilities include a small gym, a restaurant serving unremarkable meals, conference facilities & plenty of parking. Rooms $; suites $$

🏠 **Pastoral Institution Hostel** Bodija Rd; 🕿 02 810 3928. This is a well-looked-after pale blue building set in very peaceful grounds not far from the university. It's nice & it's cheap, but it is very much a God-fearing place, with a strict curfew from 22.30, & you have to be well behaved. The sister in charge usually lets guests stay for a week at a time, but if you are very polite & it's not already full, she may let you stay for one night for US$15 per person. There's a whole list of house rules here about being courteous & not deceiving God & there is a church service in the main hall downstairs each morning at 06.15, more on Sun, plus a Christian bookshop. Basic meals can be arranged in advance at the canteen & there is no booze. Rooms are sparse but spotlessly clean, the showers work & there's mossie netting at the windows. A basic b/fast is included but pay extra for AC. $

🏠 **Plaza Park Hotel** Bodija Rd; 🕿 02 810 2221/3569/3370. Also near the university; there's a clean bar & restaurant in a brick shed serving Nigerian staples & a new wall around the compound provides secure parking. It's all very concretey though, & the rooms with local TV are very plain, though they have been scrubbed up & painted in recent years. Rates include the 15% & rooms start from US$20. $

🏠 **University of Ibadan Guest House** 🕿 02 273 9864, 810 2143, 810 2297. This is located on the campus of the university – to get here follow the road from the entrance of the campus for 300m or so to the main buildings, & specifically the large bookshop, & turn right; the guesthouse is a few metres along this road on the right-hand side. There are just over 100 rooms here in 3 two-storey wings of faded brown paint. The corridors & stairwells are grimy & musty & the staff surly, but the rooms themselves are actually quite clean & spacious, with local TV & fridge. There is a huge car park, reasonable gardens, a hotel dining-room serving food-is-ready, & at the back a small internet place for students & a tatty bar with old sofas, crates of beer stacked everywhere & a blaring TV. $

✖ WHERE TO EAT AND DRINK

✖ **Bisi Kakanfo Inn** (see above); ⏰ 11.00–21.30 daily. A great albeit expensive Indian restaurant serving authentic biriyani, masala & jalfresi dishes in nice surroundings, & it has several vegetarian choices. The hotel also has a barbecue at the weekends next to the pool with live music. $$$

✖ **Golden Dragon** Premier Hotel (see above); ⏰ 12.00–15.00 & 19.00–22.30; closed Mon lunch. Serves fairly authentic Chinese food in red lantern type décor, though it's not especially cheap, but Chinese people eat here & the food is quite delicious. If you are not staying at the Premier, this is within walking distance of the Influential Hotel but beware of bumping into goats on the way home in the dark! $$$

✖ **Kocodome** in the car park at Cocoa House; ⏰ 09.00–23.00 daily. This serves Lebanese & continental food & is hugely popular. It boasts all sorts of treats, including a swimming pool open until 19.00, & frequent live music. Downstairs is a bar serving Chapmans, tea & coffee, & plenty of beer & Guinness; upstairs is a more formal restaurant. In both there is the same extensive & excellent-value menu of Nigerian dishes, plus toasted sandwiches & Lebanese *shawarmas*, grills & kebabs, & a good mezze selection. Next door is a thumping nightclub which is open from 23.00–dawn on Fri & Sat; if you eat at the restaurant first there is no charge at the door. $$$

♀ **The Cabin,** Onireke St, off Lebanon St. This is in a smart new double-storey brick building with a car park, & is a well-stocked bar with tall bar stools, pool tables, loud music & some Western food such as chicken & chips & Lebanese snacks like *shawarmas*. $$

⌴ **Flavours,** just off Oyo Rd at 3 Okommade St, opposite the vet hospital & just north of the

Makola roundabout; ⊕ 08.00–22.00 Mon–Sat; 12.00–22.00 Sun. A fairly new café serving good Nigerian food, with an internet café next door. Both are in a small compound with a garden & there is a big signpost off Oyo Road. Eat at the outside tables or inside in the cool AC at bright white plastic tables & chairs. It's spotlessly clean & modern & there's a good variety of Nigerian food & beers on offer. Dishes start from as little as US$3 for goat's head pepper soup, & there's snails & bushmeat on the menu. For the timid I recommend the fried chicken. $

⌴ **Tantalizers** opposite the entrance to the university on Oyo Rd. Cheap Nigerian fast food such as sausage rolls, *jollof* rice & sugary cakes. Obviously popular with students. $

WHAT TO SEE AND DO

The University of Ibadan The **University of Ibadan** (*www.ui.edu.ng*) is Nigeria's premier university; it was established in 1948 as a college of the University of London, and as an autonomous university in 1962. It's on an enormous campus with lots of mosques and churches, and the main buildings are 300m from the entrance on Oyo Road; there are plenty of minibuses and *okada*s if you don't want to walk. The University **bookshop** is worth a look and has a wide selection of Nigerian-published books. From the main entrance of the university go straight down towards the clocktower and the bookshop is on the right (⊕ 08.00–16.30 Mon–Fri). You may be able to pick up some Nigerian maps here (though none of Ibadan), and we found some old copies of *National Geographic*. There's a vast selection of text books and a comprehensive section on Nigerian writers, plus Christian books and dog-eared romantic novels.

At the back of the University Guest House, a few metres north of the bookshop, are a few stalls selling batiks and clothes, but the traders are often aggressive. To the north of the guest house is the university's botanical garden (⊕ 08.00–dusk daily), which is situated on a pretty, green 70-acre plot on the banks of the sluggish perennial River Ona. There's an impressive collection of palms and conifers and a collection of plants and shrubs found in Yankari National Park in Bauchi State. For a *dash*, guides are often available in the mornings and you can buy plants from the nursery.

The university also has a **zoo** (⊕ 08.00–18.00 daily), with a large collection of monkeys and large primates. It's along the road to the left of the bookshop and clocktower; just follow it around and someone will direct you or get an *okada* – having said that, however, I implore you not to go there, pay the piddly N100 gate fee, and encourage the existence of this zoo anyway! It is thoroughly depressing and archaic, and has been neglected for decades. Just through the entrance is a juvenile chimp in an inadequately small cage where people were throwing peanuts at it through the chicken wire. The ducks and the 'selection of water birds' had a bigger cage than the chimp. Next up were several porcupines in a bird cage – the cage was very tall but the animals had no space whatsoever on the floor.

The saddest inhabitant was an old, lonely female gorilla in a patch of grass about 7m by 10m surrounded by a moat, with only about half a metre of shade. When we visited she was sitting forlornly against the bars, wanting to get inside her night cage, with absolute despair on her face and sighing heavily. A keeper was trying to get her to stand up for a bunch of disinterested school children by throwing mangos at her. Many of the monkeys are housed next to the kids' playground, where many of the same uninterested school kids were yelling and screaming, which completely unnerved all the primates, most of which were totally mad – this is, after all, the country that dries monkey heads for *juju*. The lions, including some new-born cubs, were kept in dark concrete cages all day. In the grounds is the Department of Psychology Experimental Animal Laboratory Unit, with mice in cages and ominous-looking concrete slabs. I could go on, I won't; don't go there, it's terribly sad.

Transwonderland Amusement Park On a lighter note **Transwonderland Amusement Park**, just south of the university, is a very bizarre place (*entry N70*). It's a bleak spot of open ground, but it seems popular with families for its ancient and rusty amusement rides, most of them now defunct, though the Ferris wheel and dodgems are still working. Consider carefully the state of all machinery in Nigeria, and the fact that the power goes off and on all the time, before hopping on a ride. You can get a soft drink and a snack at the shops.

The National Museum The most worthwhile of Ibadan's limited sights is the **National Museum** (\ *02 241 2797;* ⊕ *09.00–17.00 daily; entry N200, plus dash for the excellent guides; no photography is permitted and you may be asked to leave your camera at the entrance*). It's off Dick Road near Aleshinloye Market, and although *okada* drivers probably won't know where the museum is, they will know where the market is, and it's easy enough to find the museum from there. It's located in a little park where there is a museum kitchen popular for weddings and functions and where you might sometimes be able to get a cold drink.

This is a fairly new museum (it only opened in 2001), and is one of the best I saw in Nigeria. It's not too dusty and the exhibits are presented in three bright halls with everything clearly labelled. One hall is packed to the gills with drums, including a pair of very tall Badagry drums that you have to jump up and down to play. Ayan is the Yoruba goddess of drums, so Ayan is added to all the individual names of the drums in the museum. There is a selection of masquerade masks and costumes; the one from Cross River is covered in raffia and bells and looks particularly scary.

Look out for the beautiful *oba*'s coat, which is covered with hundreds of thousands of brightly coloured beads. Another hall is full of over 300 pots; some were used as incense burners, some for storage, and some as stoves, and there are ritual pots that were once presented to widows and new brides, or used for sacrifices or to bury the placenta of a new-born baby. There are also displays on the traditional art of ironmongery, tie-dyeing indigo cloth, weaving Aso Oke cloth, and wood carving.

The Alhaji Jimoh Bamidele Crafts Centre For more art that you can buy, Ibadan has a good shop. The **Alhaji Jimoh Bamidele Crafts Centre** is at 75 Lekan Salami Shopping Complex, at the back of the stadium. Here are two shops next to each other stuffed full of traditional carvings from all over the country, though it's mostly Yoruba artwork, plus antiques and furniture.

Mapo Hill For views of Ibadan, you can climb up **Mapo Hill** in the oldest quarter of the city, where Mapo Hall was built in a commanding position on the summit by the British in the 1920s. On a neighbouring hill to the north of here is the **Bower's Tower**, a white 20m-high cenotaph-like looking structure that was erected in 1936 to honour Ibadan's first colonial commissioner, Captain R. L.

Bower. The hill it's on is called Oke Aare (*aare* in Yoruba means commander-in-chief). These are both good spots for taking photos of Ibadan's densely packed houses with their rusting brown roofs; go later in the day when the light enhances them better.

IFE

Ife is a southwestern city with perhaps around 500,000 inhabitants The Obafemi Awolowo University sprawls over expansive land, and a wide spectrum of disciplines and the presence of many thousands of students in Ife brings some life to an otherwise unremarkable town. Like Ibadan it used to be another important centre on Nigeria's cocoa belt. Look out for the single-storey 1940s colonial houses scattered around that were built during the height of the cocoa trade. Some are still standing in a reasonably good, if rather faded, state of repair, showing perhaps that things were built to a higher standard back then.

Ife has special significance for all Yorubas, as they regard it as their first city, and Ile-Ife, the ancient name meaning 'old Ife', is the cradle of Yoruba culture and religion. All Yoruba chiefs and *obas* trace their descent from Oduduwa, the first mythical ruler of Ife and the founder of the Yorubas, and they regard the reigning *oba* (here called Oni) of Ife as their ritual superior. Archaeological excavations have put Ife's origins in the 9th century, and from the 12th to the 17th centuries it was the most powerful Yoruba kingdom.

There are two theories of where Oduduwa came from. According to Yoruba mythology, earth was originally a marshy, watery wasteland and in the sky lived the gods, including the supreme god Olodumare, the owner of the sky. He threw down an iron ladder from the heavens to the world, and ordered his son Oduduwa and his lieutenants down it to create earth and the human race. He gave him a ball of sand, a palm nut and a chicken. The ladder landed in Ife, where he accomplished his task. He threw sand on the water and created land, on which he let the chicken loose to scratch around to spread the land and planted the palm oil tree.

The other theory is that Oduduwa and his people migrated to Ife from Egypt after a political crisis over the rise of Islam. Terracotta sculptures made in the area as early as the 12th century, some of which are displayed in the Ife Museum, vaguely resemble artefacts found in Nubia in Egypt, a fact which lends itself to the migration theory. Once he established his own kingdom at Ile-Ife, Oduduwa gave his children crowns and sent them off to establish the other Yoruba towns. The newer town of Ife was built on the spot of Ile-Ife in 1882.

GETTING THERE AND AWAY Ife is 86km from Ibadan, where you'll have to change vehicles if coming from Lagos. Vehicles to and from Ibadan drop off outside the university gate first, and then in town itself, around the Lagare roundabout. From here you can also get vehicles to some of the other southern towns including Oshogbo and Benin City. There's a masquerade statue in the middle of the roundabout. Within Ife, plenty of shared taxis and minibuses ply the main routes for about N20–40.

WHERE TO STAY AND EAT

Hilton Hotel NITEL Rd, just down the hill from the main Ife/Ilesa road; 036 232819. A good budget option, the 20 rooms have AC & a fan, one or two giant beds, brand new fridges & satellite TVs, nice tiled floors & they have seen a lick of paint in recent years. There's hot water in the bathrooms, & new shower curtains, an item rarely seen in Nigeria. There's a bar with outside tables & a few umbrellas in a courtyard, parking within the compound, & the restaurant serves up cheap Nigerian food. Rooms start from an affordable US$20 & there's only a small deposit. The Hilton is opposite the **Mayfair Hotel**, which is truly awful, so avoid it. $

🏠 **Hotel Diganga** | Ife-Ibadan Rd, near the entrance to the university; ☏ 0803 442 5970. Here, presumably because of its location near the university & visiting students, you have to sign a 'lodging regulations' slip stating that 'This hotel does not under any circumstances allow lodgers to turn their hotel room into a disco night meeting or any form of gathering. This has been done by some people under the disguise of ordinary being a lodger. . .' Despite the no disco rules, this is the best option in town & not badly priced at around US$25. The rooms are perfectly presentable, with clean bathrooms, DSTV & phones that work, & you can order room service. The only downside is there is no gen, & you will be woken up by chickens in the morning, as there is a chicken coop right against the back wall of the hotel. There's secure parking behind a security-manned boom gate. The comfy bar has fat velour sofas & fish tanks, there's a good restaurant serving individually priced breakfast items & the likes of chicken & rice, & the staff are very friendly. $

WHAT TO SEE AND DO

The town Most of the few sights in town are clustered around Enuwa Square, a kilometre or so from the Lagere roundabout along Aderemi Road; jump on an *okada* and ask for the Oba's Palace. Once in the square and with your back to the palace, look down the street and you'll see two imposing towers, both about six storeys high, opposite each other. The one on the left is a modern red building with windows all the way up and is part of a mosque; the older one on the right is white and square with a cone on top and slit windows. The latter is a memorial to Oduduwa and is surrounded by gardens that are well looked after, with lawns and flower beds, but unfortunately it's locked.

This is the **Oduduwa Afewonro Park**, where there is also a statue of Oduduwa draped in robes and jewellery holding up a staff and chicken, with another chicken at his feet.

Oba's Palace At the **Oba's Palace** one of the palace guards at the gate will show you around the grounds for a small *dash*. There's a big hall used for ceremonial occasions, with a carved door and elephant tusk above it, a statue of Oduduwa in Egyptian dress (giving the theory that he came from Egypt some credence), and in the middle of the compound a large statue of Moremi wrapped in beads and holding a staff. This was the woman who was supposedly the earliest leader of Ife, with whom Oduduwa had to battle for power when he arrived in Ife.

Also in the compound is the local criminal court, with two basic steps for the criminals to stand or sit on and a line of chairs where the *oba* and chiefs decide their fate. To one side is the shrine of Ogun (the god of war and iron) – it's a rectangular piece of earth surrounded by a low concrete wall decorated with shells, where people come regularly to pray and make sacrifices, and there are several mounds of earth covered in feathers, dollops of pounded yam and snail shells.

Ife Museum Next door to the palace is the **Ife Museum** (⊕ *08.00–18.00 daily*; *entry N50 plus dash for the guide; though it's often closed and you may need to ask around for someone to open up*), which has many fine bronze and terracotta sculptures dating back to the 13th century, a collection of brass heads that were unearthed in the town in 1938, and that are thought to be from the 11th–12th centuries, a rock thought to be a piece of 11th-century Ife pavement, and a terracotta royal footstool that is one of the largest pieces of terracotta found in Africa. Also on display are some *juju* (black magic) items – *juju* was described to us by the museum guide as 'modern-day Africa's remote control', and I am struggling to put a meaning to this! There's quite a good display of fading drawings of *obas*, farmers, chiefs and prominent community members in their traditional dress, much of which is still worn today. Everything is displayed around a lovely and serene courtyard with a garden of shrubs and aged farming implements, and the building itself is an old circular colonial building built in 1948 – look out for the original wooden louvered windows and parquet floor.

The Opa Oranmiyan The **Opa Oranmiyan** is an engraved monolith 5.18m high, which is popularly believed to be the walking stick (*opa* means staff) of the giant Oranmiyan, who was the warrior son of either Oduduwa or the god Ogun. According to legend Oranmiyan was the powerful first *oba* of Oyo, and after his death the obelisk was erected supposedly on the spot where he was buried, though there's no grave. There is, however, a more mythical story. Oranmiyan, a giant warrior, left Ife and marched south conquering all that got in his way, but he promised his people back home that if he was ever needed by them he would return. Ife was under threat and all the people got together and shouted out his name in a plea for Oranmiyan to help them in their hour of need. Oranmiyan heard and came striding back to Ife, still slaying anyone that got in his way. When he looked down at one warrior he had killed, he recognised him as a friend and realised he was again among his own people. He was so distressed that he'd killed someone from Ife, he plunged his staff into the ground, where it petrified and became the monolith, and strode off into the forest never to be seen again. On one side of the staff are some faded carvings, and inexplicably there are some nails driven into it. The meaning of these is unknown.

The staff is just to the south of the palace off Ikyekere Street and to get to it you'll need to jump on an *okada*, but it's just a very straight, rather phallic-looking piece of granite in a small unkempt garden which is locked. If you ask around someone should go and get the caretaker for you, but it really isn't worth the trek when you can see pictures and learn the story at the museum.

The university Ife's Obafemi Awolowo University (*www.oauife.edu.ng*), on the Ibadan road, a few kilometres to the west of town, is Nigeria's biggest university with a capacity for 55,000 students, 7,000 staff and 13 faculties. The University of Ife was established in 1962, and was renamed after one of its leading founders, and the first premier of the Western Region, Obafemi Awolowo after his death in 1987. The main buildings of the university are a bunch of 1960s hideous concrete blocks, and some evidently were never finished, as a few are derelict. Nevertheless, there are some attractive squares and gardens, the campus is relatively rubbish free, and it's teeming with students, lecturers and staff.

In recent years the university has been plagued by intermittent strikes by the students in protest at rising fees, and in 2005 one strike lasted 11 months. Then in February 2007 police were called in to order students to sit their exams; they had been refusing to do this because they hadn't been granted a pre-exam lecture-free week. This incident turned into a bloody riot, many students were beaten by police, part of the campus was burnt down and the university was closed. It reopened again in February 2008.

OSHOGBO

Oshogbo (also known as Osogbo) is 88km to the northeast of Ibadan and 100km south of Ilorin and is the capital of Osun State, which is dubbed the 'State of the Living Spring' (on car number plates) because of the Osun River that runs through Oshogbo. The Yoruba city was thought to have been founded in the 17th century, and in 1839 it was the site of a decisive battle between the Yoruba from Ibadan and the Fulani from **Ilorin**, but the Fulani did not succeed in taking Oshogbo and it remained an important town in the Yoruba culture. An influx of refugees after the battle swelled Oshogbo's population, which is currently at about 850,000 (a small town by Nigerian standards).

It's primarily a farming and commercial city, with cotton gins, a steel-rolling mill and a cigarette factory, but it's best known as being the centre of Nigerian art. Oshogbo is the founding centre of the internationally renowned School of Oshogbo, which in the 1960s produced a collection of artists who went on to become successful and wealthy on an international scale. Historically the town has always been an art centre for the Yoruba, but it underwent a renaissance in the late 1950s when three European artists – the Austrian sculptress Susanne Wenger, the writer Ulli Beier (who used to be married to Susanne Wenger) and the artist Georgina Beier – started a series of art schools that rejuvenated Nigeria's art world and produced some excellent local contemporary artists. These include Jimoh Buraimoh, Twins Seven Seven ('the Art Man'), Nike Davies-Okundaye (who now lives in Lagos but has a gallery in Oshogbo and used to be married to Twins Seven Seven) and many others. Oshogbo remains the centre of Nigerian art and there are some good galleries to visit. It's also home to the shrines and grove of Osun, the Yoruba goddess of fertility, in the Oshogbo Sacred Forest, where the Osun Festival takes place in August each year.

Despite being the state capital, Oshogbo is a particularly scruffy town and there are some pretty awful accommodation options in the town centre, which are so bad I'm not going to bother to list them. Nevertheless it's well worth coming here to visit the galleries and the Sacred Forest, and there are a couple of good mid-range places to stay in.

GETTING THERE AND AWAY Oshogbo's **motor park** is spread haphazardly around Okefia Road and the two roundabouts near Dugbe Market. From here you can find vehicles to Lagos, Ilorin, Oyo, Ife, Benin City and Ibadan. Just walk around and someone will show you which area you need to be in for a vehicle going in your direction. The train station is on Alhaji Sonmonu Hassan Road in the event a train ever pulls into Oshogbo again.

PRACTICALITIES All Oshogbo **taxis** are painted the same colour – blue with a yellow stripe over the top and middle. Most city transport is by way of *okadas*, or shared taxis that go up and down the major streets, and a short ride will cost N30 on either. The **post office** is at the north end of Station Road; **NITEL** is to the south, towards King's Market (just look for the tower).

 WHERE TO STAY If you ask around town for a hotel you will be directed to the **Osun Presidential Hotel** on Old Ikirun Road, as it's the state hotel, but it's terribly run down. There are better options.

⌂ **MicCom Golf Hotel and Resort**, Ibokun Rd, Ada; ☏ 035 241386; www.miccomgolfhotels.com. Just under a 15km drive out of town to the northeast in Ada; follow the road Susanne Wenger's house is on out of town. Arranged in pink blocks with bright blue windows & red tiled roofs, this a very neat new option that opened in 2004 & is set on an 18-hole golf course, which rather astonishingly has golf carts. The 90 rooms range from small studios to lavish royal suites & all are very comfortably furnished with DSTV & fridge. There's a very attractive pool, two golf pros in the golf shop, a smart bar & restaurant that serves Nigerian & continental food, tennis courts & 24hr electricity.

Rooms $$; suites $$$
⌂ **Nike Ambassador Guest House** roughly 6km to the west of the gallery, almost in the countryside, at Ido Osun Junction on the Ede Rd (go the Nike Gallery; ☏ 035 242254, first, to tell them of your arrival & the staff will direct you). By far the nicest place to stay in Oshogbo, & a very peaceful retreat, this is one of Nike Davies-Okundaye's houses & you must pre-arrange a visit here at her gallery in Lagos (see page 154). If you are in a group, Nike will use a 12-seater minibus & driver to bring people from Lagos to Oshogbo for US$200 per day. It's a big house in lovely gardens in a quiet suburb & ambassadors

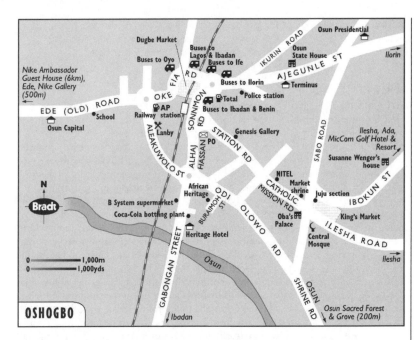

OSHOGBO

have stayed here, hence the name. There are over a dozen rooms in 2 bright white blocks, with several living & dining rooms all decorated with art from Nike's shops, & extras include slippers & dressing gowns in the rooms. Only two of the rooms are en suite, but there are several palatial bathrooms. Meals are served on a balcony or on the grassy lawns where ducks, peacocks, antelope & turkeys wander around. Nike can also organise a cultural troupe to entertain at the guesthouse with singing & dancing. It's US$10 for b/fast, US$15 for lunch, & US$25 for dinner; coffee, tea & beer are available. $$

🏠 **Hotel Heritage International** Gbongan/Ife Rd (behind the Coca-Cola bottling plant, & well signposted off the main road); 📞 035 241881/ 240228; www.buraimoh.com/hotel. One of the better choices for budget travellers, the 46 rooms are in 3 big blocks painted brightly outside, but they are very dark inside, with old furniture. Nevertheless accommodation is clean & good value & there are 24hr gens. The better & newer rooms are in the blocks in the car park, but they fill up quickly — arrive early to get one of them. It's a great spot if you are in a party mood, as

there's a big & lively bar with comfy old red velvet booths, loads of cold beer & a brand new, large-screen satellite TV showing football. There is a disco at the weekends that goes on until 08.00! You can get food here, but you'll wait at least an hour. When I asked what they had I got 'rice & plantain, rice, fried rice, egg & rice, & bread & rice' — you'll get to love those carbohydrates! There's also a chop house in the car park for *suya*. The rooms start with basic doubles with fan & bucket, through to suites with AC & a shower, plus the 15%. All have local TV & a fridge. This hotel is owned by the artist Jimoh Buraimoh (see below), who sometimes pops in for a beer in the evening. $

🏠 **Osun Capital Hotel** Ede Rd; 📞 035 240396. Newly painted outside, but pretty seedy inside, with dusty halls & peeling paint, there are 20 basic rooms with buckets, the water supply is very hit & miss, & there's no parking, but it's cheap with rooms for under US$20 & the sheets & tiles in the bathroom are clean. The restaurant serves Nigerian starch & there's a busy bar that keeps going well into the night. $

✕ WHERE TO EAT

✕ **Lanby Restaurant** 3 Alekuwolo St; 🕐 10.00–17.30 daily. A clean, single-storey detached

building with a big sign where you can get cheap & filling food-is-ready & soft drinks. $

B System Supermarket Gbongan Rd. This has a very exciting variety of things for sale, & it's open fairly late, should you get stuck for something to eat in the evening. You'll find things like Mars bars, Twix & other chocolate bars, Pringles, peanut butter & loads of booze. Other useful items include batteries & razor blades.

WHAT TO SEE AND DO

Art galleries Oshogbo is renowned for its art and, other than the galleries, you may be approached in the street by hopeful artists who offer their cards and invite you to their studios or homes to look at their work. To the east of Oshogbo on Old Ede Road is the **Nike Gallery** (✆ *035 242254; www.osunarts.org.uk/nikeart*), a studio and shop of one of Nigeria's most celebrated artists, Nike Davies-Okundaye (see *Chapter 5* for more information on Nike, page 154). It's open practically all the time as there is always someone around, and all the staff are artists and very friendly.

The gallery is on two storeys and the items on sale are similar to what's available in the Lagos gallery: unusual furniture, batiks, paintings, wood carvings, metal sculptures and baskets. Upstairs (the staircase is completely carved) is the cloth: ready-made clothes, quilting, embroidery, antique Hausa cloth over 80 years old, *aso-eke* strip cloth and adire indigo cloth. Along with the Nike Gallery in Lagos, this is one of the best collections of cloth and art there is in the country.

Some 500m west of the shop on the other side of the road is a group of huts that are home to the studio where some 70 students work. Ask at the shop and someone will take you there on weekdays to watch the many young artists at work for a small *dash*. It's recently attracted students from Europe and North America too. There's another good gallery on Station Road called **Genesis Art**; look out for the tall statue outside of a woman carrying a flame and a calabash. There are paintings, wood carvings and metal sculptures.

At the **Africa Heritage Gallery**, in a big house just off Odi Olowo Road (*1 Buraimoh Street;* ✆ *035 241864; www.buraimoh.com*), is a wonderful display of vividly coloured abstract paintings made from tiny beads and oil paint by artist Jimoh Buraimoh (so famous they named the street after him). If he is at home (he frequently exhibits in the USA) you will meet him, and he's a charming man. Some of his work is sold through galleries in London and New York, and he has four paintings on display in the National Gallery in Lagos. He's the first painter to be known to use tiny glittering beads in his art; the same method is used to decorate Yoruba traditional royal cloaks and crowns, and each painting takes two to three weeks to make. Buraimoh's work is expensive but stunning; if you want to buy he can ship paintings abroad and accepts payment into his US bank account. You can visit his house and gallery any day before 17.00. He's also the main organiser of the Osun Festival (see below).

The town There's a cluster of sights around the crossroads of Catholic Mission Street and Osun Shrine Road. The **central mosque** is on the southeastern corner and is a large domed building with an 'Islamic' market outside selling worry beads, Korans and stickers of Allah and, oddly, of Jesus. There are few mosques in the southern regions and Muslims often have to resort to open prayer compounds – indeed, many of the southern states forbid the building of mosques as some of the northern states forbid the building of churches. Opposite the mosque is the **King's Market** where you might want to gawp at the teeming *juju* section, where we saw python skins and domestic cat's heads. It's in the north of the market on the Sabo Road side.

Susanne Wenger's house Behind the market, follow Ibokun Street for a couple of hundred metres and you'll get to **Susanne Wenger's house** with its large

One of Nigeria's most successful artists is Twins Seven Seven, so named because he is reputedly the only surviving child of seven sets of twins born to his mother. He was born in 1944 and was one of the students of the Oshogbo art movement in the 1960s. At one time he was married to Nike Davies-Okundaye (see above). His house in Oshogbo is down an alley off Ede Road near the Boras petrol station, but as he now lives in Philadelphia it's currently closed up.

Twins Seven Seven's career began in the 1960s as a student in workshops run by European artists, Susanne Wenger, Ulli Beier and Georgina Beier, and by the end of the 1960s, and thanks to exhibitions in Prague and Munich, he had made it on to the international art circuit. His paintings are vividly colourful and concentrate on the mythology of the Yoruba culture; his canvases are crowded with people, gods, motifs, animals and plants. He traditionally paints with palm leaves but uses other techniques such as sculpture, metalwork, engraving and fabric-painting.

Today, Twins Seven Seven's work is exhibited in private collections and museums around the world including Washington's Smithsonian Institution, the Museum of Modern Art in New York, the Philadelphia Museum of Art, Tropenmuseum in Amsterdam, the Georges Pompidou Centre in Paris, as well as the National Gallery in Lagos. In 2005, Twins Seven Seven was named UNESCO's Artist for Peace for that year 'in recognition of his contribution to the promotion of dialogue and understanding among peoples, particularly in Africa'. Nigeria's then president, Obasanjo, attended the ceremony in Paris with Twins Seven Seven when he received his award. The ceremony took place on Africa Day.

keyhole-shaped door and elaborate sculptured fence studded with gargoyles. It's a weird-looking house on four storeys behind a huge flowering bougainvillea, and is quite broken down, with lots of kids and chickens running around outside. There is a line of chairs where we met her doctor (who was having his nails done by International Finger Cutter Man at the time!), who allowed us to look at the first floor of the house, where there are some of her sculptures and statues similar to those found in the Sacred Forest (see below).

Wenger's art is very surreal and she uses a lot of symbolism, and the room is quite spooky and eerie. She still lives here on the second floor and it's possible to visit her, but she's frail and over 90 now. When Wenger got to Oshogbo in the 1960s she became a born-again Yoruba and later a high priestess (Adunni is her Yoruba name), and all her art in the house and at the Sacred Grove is intricately woven around the storeys of the Yoruba gods. You can see photographs at www.susanne-wenger.org.

The Market Shrine and Oba's Palace Opposite the market is the **Market Shrine**, a low building made from brown earth with a rusted roof that is so dilapidated it leans to one side and has a tree growing in part of it. This was the original Oba's Palace, and could feasibly be quite old. If you look through the door edged with carved wooden door posts, you'll see a line of broken thrones. Also at this crossroads is the dilapidated **Oba's Palace** – the entrance is opposite the Market Shrine, but there's nothing really to see except another line of old thrones under a balcony. Once through the various buildings you'll find (with difficulty) the **Oba's Shrine** in a squat building painted red and black, where you might be invited inside – but don't bother. There's nothing to see inside. Along Catholic Mission

Street to the northwest are a number of two-storey buildings characterised by **Brazilian architecture**.

The sacred forest Now a UNESCO World Heritage Site for its cultural significance, the **Osun Sacred Groves and Forest** (☉ *10.00–18.00 daily; entry N200, plus dash for the guide, N500 for a camera, N2,500 for a video camera, and a staggering N20,000 if you want to take commercial photos*) are Oshogbo's main attraction, if not one of the biggest attractions in Nigeria (all the signs for them say 'Sacred Grooves'). In the traditional Yoruba religion groves are sacred places reserved for rituals or shrines and Osun is today believed to be the last remaining one in the Yoruba culture – hence its inclusion as a World Heritage Site.

When the artist Susanne Wenger came to Oshogbo from Austria in 1960, she was dismayed to find a culture in ruin. She set about studying the Yoruba, took part in the rites and religion of the culture, and in time was initiated as a priestess of Osun and Obatala, two of the principal gods. She soon became known as Adunni (adored one) by local people and Mama by those who knew her well. She has done much to revive the Yoruba religion, and together with Yoruba artists restored the site from the 1960s and created many strange and interesting sculptures and shrines representing various gods and goddesses. Wenger calls it a refuge for homeless gods who have been abandoned by modern society, and each one is essentially a reflection of the activities, life and preoccupations of the gods while they established Oshogbo. Some of these are the first market, the first palace and courtyard, shrine and temple.

YORUBA GODS

Olodumare is the divine spirit who sent his son Oduduwa to Ife to create the Yoruba. Of the other important Yoruba gods, Shango, who had four wives each personified by a major Nigerian river, is the god that creates the weather. He does this by casting down to earth 'thunderstones' that create thunder and lightning. Ogun is the god of war, of the hunt, and rather curiously, of ironmongery, and is patron god to blacksmiths, warriors, and all who use metal in their occupations. He also presides over deals and contracts, and, in traditional Yoruba courts, witnesses swear to tell the truth in the name of Ogun.

The Yoruba consider Ogun fearsome and terrible in his revenge, and if someone breaks a pact made in his name, swift retribution will follow. He added yet another feather to his formidable cap when, according to legend, he built Africa's first road, as he was the only god who had the right implements to carve through the dense jungle. Eshu is the god of Ifa, a form of writing using a complex system of nuts, signs and squares that the Yoruba use to predict the future. Today many Yoruba do not make a major life decision without consulting it. He is also the divine trickster and is responsible for many of the world's ill doings, and needs regular attention to maintain harmony in the community. Shokpona is the god of smallpox – he became a high-ranking god because of the smallpox plagues spread by various inter-ethnic wars over the centuries.

Priests of Shokpona wielded immense power and it was believed that they could give smallpox to their enemies. They reputedly made potions from the skin of those who died from smallpox, which they would pour in an enemy's house or village to spread the disease. Osun is the goddess of the river that flows through Oshogbo, and is the bringer of fertility in women. Lyamapo is the goddess of all women's crafts, including childbirth, and is held responsible for Aje, the destructive or malevolent aspects of womanhood.

The forest is a 75-hectare patch of delightful, butterfly-filled greenery that was once inhabited by the early settlers and founders of Oshogbo some 400 years ago (see box). Despite being completely surrounded by Oshogbo, the forest supports a remarkable diversity of monkeys, birds, snakes, forest antelopes and other fauna. The sacred nature of the forest means that it is protected, and none of the animals are hunted because they are regarded as physical manifestations of the goddess Osun. This is a rare example of protected rainforest in Nigeria, and an example of conservation as a local initiative, where indigenous people have endeavoured to protect their culture and their environment. Many of the animals in the groves, particularly the monkeys, are fairly tame and easy to see as they jump around overhead in the trees.

You can wander around with a guide on a trail that winds throughout the forest. To get there it's little more than a N50 hop on an *okada* or N100 for a drop taxi from town, but you can easily walk the 700–800m from the King's Market down Osun Shrine Road, and the chances are you will have to walk back as there is no transport around the groves. On the road leading up to the entrance are clay walls with abstract figures on them, and on the main gate are elaborate abstract metal sculptures of elephants, mermaids, soldiers and farmers. There's a thatched reception area with a few curios for sale; as there are no refreshments, bring water, as it's a hot walk around the forest.

The sculptures are scattered through the forest on either side of the approach road, but from the main entrance you are led first to Oya Grove, which reaches a tranquil spot on the Osun River, where there is the statue of Osun built beneath giant sycamore trees. The river is full of tangled vines and surrounded by ferns and you have to look carefully among the rocks and tree roots to see some of the smaller statues and figurines, as they are overgrown and covered in moss. Other shrines and statues depict the various gods, and one very tall structure is called Aiye Dakun Yipada, literally meaning 'the world, I beg you to reconsider your ways'.

Obatala, the white god, who is responsible for giving people human form, is represented in a statue where he sits with hands stretched towards heaven on the top of an elephant, and surrounding the base of the elephant are lions, his messengers. Another statue of three elderly men holding hands represents compromise. Over the river is an old suspension bridge that has nothing to do with the shrines – it was built in 1936 by a Welsh colonial officer. It's just about falling down now, but there are nice views from it of the meandering river.

Away from the river and further into the forest are other statues, some several metres high, including two alien-looking creatures with giant teeth, a massive chameleon, and one of Lyamaro, the messenger of Osun, which has a big eye, tentacle-like legs and several pointing arms, over 12m tall. Another is of Obaluaye, another messenger of Osun, which has a fly-like head and a mix of spidery legs and arms beneath which people are begging. Ela, another messenger, is a very straight sculpture over 20m high with hands outstretched to the sky.

Another imposing statue is that of Lyamapo, the god of all women's craft, including childbirth. She is represented on her back with her children at her feet and with three pairs of arms which gesture advice, blessing, and regrets. The meaning of this is that if you take positive advice you will be blessed and if you don't you will regret it. She also has wings to represent her supernatural power of flight. They all must have looked very surreal when they were first made in the 1960s. The first-ever market in Oshogbo is said to be the Oja Ontotoo – a market for supernatural and subterranean beings represented by a fantastic market scene of heavenly and earthly characters riding to market on flying tortoises, pigs, elephants, and giant snakes.

At the end of the tour you will be expected to give a small *dash* to the Osun priest

The Osun (sometimes spelt Oshun) Festival usually takes place on the second Friday in August, and is popular enough to be shown live on state TV, and in 2005 even CNN got in on the action. It attracts thousands of people and if you are in Nigeria at that time foreigners are allowed to attend, but you must get permission from the Osun priests first. Osun is the Yoruba word meaning 'water of life' and is given to the river goddess who is the spiritual mother of Oshogbo and an important deity in the Yoruba religion.

Legend has it that Osun was the youngest of the three wives of Shango, the god of thunder, who was at one time also *alafin* (king) of Oyo. Oba and Oya were his other wives but Osun was his favourite. This resulted in Oya and Osun having a fight and Osun left Oyo and went on to marry Larooye, who created Oshogbo (loosely translated as the place of wizards) some half a millennium ago. Larooye and his migrant people were cutting down a tree to build huts for a new settlement when the tree fell into the river and the forest, in a loud and furious voice, shouted '*pele o, Osogbo ikoko aro mi le ti fo tan*' – meaning 'in the forest, all my dye pots have been broken by you'.

In appeasement Larooye and his people offered a sacrifice to the gods of the forest and the river. In response the gods instructed Larooye to move his settlement to higher ground away from the river's floodplains and pledged abundant blessing and protection of the people. The banks of the river became Osun's centre of activities and the sacred waters were renamed the Osun River. She became learned in medicine and the water of the river was said to have the healing power to cure infertility. When the river burst its bank, Osun was said to have made offerings to it to appease its anger, as people still do today during the Osun Festival. Osun became a Yoruba goddess and was also credited for playing a part in protecting Oshogbo during the Fulani jihad in the early 19th century, when she disguised herself as a food seller and sold poisoned bean soup to the Fulani enemies, causing a fatal epidemic in their war camp.

The Osun Festival is regarded as a celebration of the founding of Oshogbo, commemorating the pact or marriage of Larooye and Osun. The week-long Osun festival still asks the gods for protection, and during rituals the priests lay down their offerings and sacrifices to the statue of Osun standing next to the river with her arms open, indicating she is the goddess of fertility, care, protection, cure and mother to all. On the last day a virgin maid of Osun carries a symbolic calabash at the head of a procession of worshippers, chiefs and priests, through the Oshogbo Sacred Forest, to present to Osun, and to ask for blessing and protection for all the people of Oshogbo. While the men beat drums and chant to ward off evil spirits, the women pray to Osun to give them more children.

who sits at reception, as well as to the guide. This is a weird and wonderful place and the sculptures are completely unique and mysterious, but after 50 years they are somewhat weather-beaten; all the more reason why they should be preserved. Susanne Wenger made these structures to invite the misplaced Yoruba gods to live in them, and as complicated as the Yoruba spirit world is to understand, the peacefulness and serenity here in what is a beautiful tract of forest is indisputable.

OYO

Oyo, 52km north of Ibadan, is a bustling town of perhaps 250,000 people, but there isn't really anything to see or do there, though you are quite likely to pass through it on the way to somewhere else. If that is the case, then it's worth jumping off a bus or pulling over to visit the drum shops (see below). It has some old Portuguese-style houses with rusting brown roofs similar to those in Ibadan, and is best known as the capital of the old Oyo Empire, established by the Yoruba, who controlled a wide area between the Niger and the Volta rivers in present-day Ghana in the mid-17th century, and which was the biggest of the Yoruba kingdoms.

According to legend, Ile (old) Oyo was established by Oduduwa's son, Oranmiyan (of the Ife staff fame – above), some time around the 12th century on a site north of modern Oyo in what is today Old Oyo National Park. Because of frequent spats with neighbouring communities in the 16th century, the Kingdom of Oyo established an army of 1,000 foot soldiers and 1,000 horses; the area was relatively free of tsetse fly so horses could be used for war and transport in the region. From then until the early 18th century the Oyo army was highly developed and went about conquering neighbouring lands. It was the largest political unit in Yorubaland, if not West Africa, during the mid-17th century, and remained so until the Yoruba wars in the 1820s–30s, when the Oyo Empire all but collapsed when they lost against the invading jihadists from the north. Ile-Oyo was abandoned and many Oyo refugees either fled to Ibadan or further south, where they founded the city of Oyo in its present location. Oyo is still referred to as 'the city of warriors'. The British bombarded the capital in 1895 with shells, and burnt down the *alafin*'s palace, though the *alafin* was permitted to stay in Oyo under the British system of indirect rule.

GETTING THERE AND AWAY Minibuses and bush taxis pick up and drop off at the **motor park** opposite the Mobil petrol station, a few metres south of the Agip petrol station on the Ilorin–Ibadan road as it goes through the district of Owode in the centre of town. There are frequent vehicles between here and Ibadan and to Ilorin to the north, 109km away via Ogbomoso. In Ilorin you'll need to change vehicles to get anywhere north; in Ibadan you'll need to change to get to Lagos and the south, or any point east. All the roads in any direction from Oyo are full of pot-holes.

WHERE TO STAY AND EAT

 La Bamba roughly 1km south of Owode on the Ibadan road; ☎ 038 230443, 240444. The only hotel in town with 50 well-kept chalets (pronounced by the staff as it is spelt – take the French accent off the word to make *shalett*) in unusually expansive grounds full of flame & neem trees. The complex is set a few hundred metres back from the road, though the first thing you'll see is the open-air chop stall & bar just within the gate, which according to my *okada* driver sells the best *suya* in town. You order meals from reception & beers & soft drinks from the fridge behind the reception desk, & everything will be delivered to your room. Choice depends on what is available in the kitchen, so expect a plate of *jollof* rice & chicken & the like. Built in 1979 the décor in the rooms hasn't changed much, but there's running water & DSTV. From outside the hotel gate you can flag down a minibus to Ibadan. Overlanders can negotiate camping here as there's loads of grass & space for vehicles & it's reasonably secure. §

WHAT TO SEE AND DO

Drum shops Yoruba drums and calabashes are for sale on Oyo Road in Owede. There are two shops next to each other that are well worth a visit – the first selling predominantly drums, and the second selling carved calabashes – about 100m north of the Agip roundabout on the left-hand side. If you are in your own car there is reasonable space to pull up and park directly outside.

The drum shop is the Owode Co-operative. A big drum is called an *iya ilu*, a small drum a *kanango,* and there are also the famous Yoruba talking drums called *dundun.* Also for sale is a selection of leather bags, poufs and fans, plus some wood carvings, and the traders are happy to let you 'look for free' without too much hassle. Most of the items have prices on, but you could try a spot of bargaining with the good-natured traders and prices are cheaper here than in Lagos's markets. Perhaps unique to this shop (I certainly didn't see them anywhere else) are the hand drums called *sakara,* which are made by stretching a piece of skin over a clay ring and which are beaten with a bamboo stick decorated with scraps of material called a *congo.* All of the drums have stickers on them with the name of the person who made them.

In the shop next door are carved and painted calabashes. There's another drum and craft shop just a few minutes' walk away to the south of the Mobil petrol station, more or less opposite the motor park, and more calabashes can be found in the main market where you might see them being worked on. The main market is called Akesan Market, and Akesan Market Road goes west from the main Agip roundabout. Catch a minibus for about a kilometre and ask to be dropped off at the post office; the myriad streets to the market are opposite the post office. Just ask around and someone will point out the calabash stall, which is only a few metres in among the piles of yams and buckets of bright red palm oil used to make the fiery *jollof* rice.

Old Oyo National Park

Old Oyo National Park covers an area of 2,512km^2 and was established in 1991, when it was carved out of the Upper Ogun Game Reserve that was first established in 1936. It's located in the northern part of Oyo State, roughly two hours' drive from Oyo on rough roads, and you'll only get there in your own vehicle. Very few people visit the park and it's only open in the dry season between December and April, so you'll need to be completely self-sufficient. There are four very basic chalets at Ibuya within the park, but don't expect them to be functional or open.

The park entrance is at the village of Sepeteri (on arrival ask around for the gateman, who will perhaps have a vague idea of how much it is to get in). From Oyo it's approximately 160km to Sepeteri, on a back road through Kwara State via Iseyin, a large Yoruba agricultural town.

There is very little reliable information on what species exist in the park, and for years it has suffered from mismanagement and neglect. Park rangers know little about the interior of the park, and hunting, cattle grazing, logging and bush-burning have gone on undeterred. Villages surround the park boundaries, and the species that do still exist are restricted to small, remote areas of the park. The terrain is savanna scrub with patches of tropical rainforest along the rivers, and while it was once home to lion and elephant, the chances of these still being present in the park are virtually zero, though it may still be home to a few species of antelope, baboons, black and white colobus monkeys, and possibly a few hardy buffalo.

The national park also contains the ruins of the ancient Yoruba city of Ile-Oyo, the historical capital of the Oyo Empire (see above), which are located in the north-eastern part of the park, but nothing has been done to protect them and very few people even know where they are.

The Old Oyo National Park office is on the outskirts of Oyo on Iseyin Road (✆ *038 240125/240690*). There is a signpost at the Agip petrol station at the roundabout in the centre of town from where you follow Akesan Market Road, but with the headquarters being located so far away from the park itself, the management effectively do not run the park, and quite frankly this is just another fine example of civil servants in a government institution being employed to do and know nothing.

Palace guard, Zaria; one of hundreds who would accompany the Emir at all times (DH) page 296

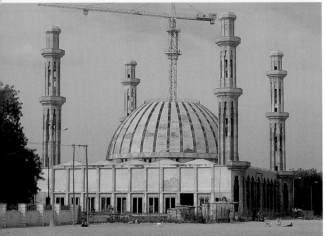

top   **Emir's palace, Zaria**
(KR) page 296

above   **Interior of Emir's palace, Kano**
(GC/TIPS) page 309

left   **Mosque beside the Shehu's palace, Maiduguri**
(KR) page 278

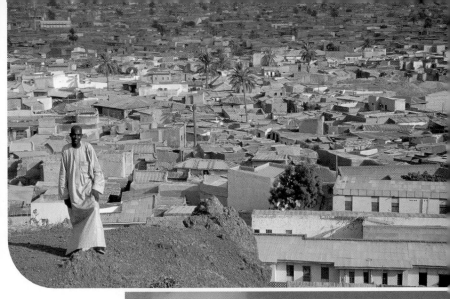

above Looking across old
Kano from Dala Hill
(DH) page 312

right Gobarau minaret in
Katsina city. The
tallest remaining
mud-built structure
in Nigeria
(KR) page 317

above **Hiking to Sukur: one of Nigeria's two World Heritage sites** (KR) page 282

below **Lokoja and the confluence of the Niger and Benue rivers from Mount Pati** (KR) page 246

above Zuma Rock, Suleja, considered to be the geographical centre of Nigeria (DH) page 246

below Gurara Falls near Abuja, during rainy season (KR) page 246

top **Pygmy hippopotami**
(Choeropsis liberiensis)
**are now rarely seen
in Nigeria**
(AC) page 49

centre **African elepant**
(Loxodonta Africana)
(AVZ) page 49

left **Lion** *(Panthera leo)*
(AVZ) page 49

above left **Sclater's guenon**
(*Cercopithecus sclateri*)
Africa's rarest
monkey, indigenous
to Nigeria
(Cercopan / Paule) page 49

above right **Red-headed
agama lizard**
(*Agama agama*)
(MR/TIPS) page 47

centre **Warthog**
(*Phacochoerus africanus*)
(KR)

below left **Red-capped
mangabey**
(*Cercocebus torquatus*)
(Cercopan / Sherrard)

below right **Putty-nose monkey**
(*Cercopithecus nictitans*)
(Cercopan / Hogan)

above All aboard! The local transport, known as 'mammy wagons' (KR) page 64

below Ferry to Brass Island through the khaki waters of the Niger Delta (DH) page 208

North from Oyo Heading north from Oyo along the A1, the main road that neatly bisects the west of Nigeria all the way to Sokoto in the far north, you'll pass through some of the other Yoruba towns, but there's little reason to stop. There are frequent vehicles going up and down the A1 from centre to centre, and you're most likely to be travelling along this road if you're heading towards Lake Kainji National Park (see page 262). It's worth noting that this road is a blackspot for accidents, as attested to by the mangled wrecks on the side of the road, and it's horrendously busy.

From Ibadan through to Ilorin it's pot-holed and fairly hilly, and drivers of big trucks think nothing of overtaking when going up hills. Between Ilorin and Mokwa, where it crosses the River Niger, there's a new and broad highway that hasn't been opened yet, and traffic still uses the old road alongside. Work on this road started and then stopped goodness knows when (I heard a rumour that the government was in huge debt to the foreign-owned road-building companies) – when this will be finished and opened is anyone's guess. For now people graze their cows on the grass that has grown on the new embankments and kids play football on the unfinished gravel surface.

You are likely to pass through unremarkable **Ogbomosho**, 53km north of Oyo, which was thought to have been established by the Yoruba in the 17th century. It resisted Fulani invasions in the early 19th century and grew rapidly by absorbing refugees from other towns destroyed by the Fulani. Today it is a sprawling industrial centre with a population of 1.2 million and there's nothing to see. There is however a very good place to stay at the town of Offa, 47km north of Ogbomosho on the road to Ilorin. The **Avalon Hotel** (*Salandeen Adetoyi Avenue;* ☏ *031 800103–7;* $$) is a neat and tidy block with secure parking behind a boom gate, with spotless rooms with modern furnishings and some two- and three-bed chalets with kitchenettes. There's Western food in the restaurant, which also serves a good Sunday lunch, a well-stocked bar with wine and international spirits, and a swimming pool and tennis court.

Ilorin Ilorin is the capital of Kwara State, roughly 100km north of Ogbomosho along the A1, where you are likely to swap vehicles in Ilorin's sprawling motor park if heading further north or east. It's a large market town for livestock and vegetables and is surprisingly clean, with a population of around 850,000. As part of the Fulani Empire in the 19th century it has a strong Muslim influence and, at just over 300km northeast of Lagos, is considered to be the gateway of the south–north, Christian–Muslim religious divide.

Ilorin was the capital of a Yoruba kingdom that, with the assistance of the Fulani, successfully rebelled against the Oyo Empire in 1817. In the 1820s it became a Muslim emirate associated with the Fulani caliphate of Sokoto, and increased its territory through wars against Oyo and Ibadan in the late 19th century. In 1897 it was conquered by troops of the British-chartered Royal Niger Company, led by Sir George Goldie.

There are flights on weekdays with Overland Airways (☏ *0803 5351190, airport desk; www.overland.areo*) from Lagos to Ilorin which depart at 07.15 (45 minutes), and return to Lagos at 17.45, and from Abuja to Ilorin at 16.30 and Ilorin to Abuja at 08.15. The airport is 2km from the city centre and rather remarkably has its own website (*www.ilorinairport.com*) as it's currently undergoing a revamp and a new 5,000m^2 cargo terminal is being built. *Okadas* are called *express* in this region of the country. If you get stuck here, try the **Kwara Hotel** (*Ahmadu Bello Avenue, in the GRA;* ☏ *031 221490;* $$). It's another white elephant of a state hotel, but has recently been given a refurbishment and has a functioning swimming pool and tennis courts; the Chinese restaurant here is about the only place to eat non-Nigerian food.

Jebba Just over 100km north of Ilorin, Jebba is an unremarkable town set on the south banks of the Niger. It was taken under the control of the British in 1897 and temporarily served as the capital of the Protectorate of Northern Nigeria from 1900 to 1902. The railway reached here in 1909 and a bridge was built over the Niger in 1916. Its principle attraction is a huge sandstone obelisk overlooking the river that is the memorial to Mungo Park and Richard Lander, who were the first explorers to trace the course of the Niger. It's about 15m tall but despite its impressive size is a plain honey-coloured block with a plaque on one face bearing the inscription 'To Mungo Park, 1795, and Richard Lander, 1830, who traced the course of the Niger from near its source to the sea. Both died in Africa for Africa'. I couldn't find out when it was erected, but its location in Jebba doesn't really make sense. Mungo Park made it as far along the Niger as New Bussa, 150km to the north of Jebba, where he drowned in rapids and from where Richard Lander subsequently picked up the trail, so there's no real reason why the monument should be where it is.

From Jebba, you can head west to the Kainji National Park (page 262), swing east to Abuja or continue north to Kaduna and the other northern cities.

BENIN CITY

The capital of Edo State is Benin City, which is about 320km east of Lagos and is famous for its unique bronze, brass and ivory works of art. Modern Benin City is a rapidly developing metropolis with a population of 1.2 million and is the centre of Nigeria's rubber industry, but there are a few reminders of its long and turbulent history. The old city's moat and wall survive in places, and the National Museum houses an interesting collection of Benin royal art. Benin is to the west of Igboland, and it's mainly populated by the Edo and Bini people, hence its name.

An early traveller, a Mr Cyril Punch, wrote of Benin before it was destroyed in 1897:

Benin has an extraordinary fascination for me which I cannot explain. All the rest of West Africa that I know is squalid. Benin in the old days was more than squalid, it was gruesome. . . No-one who went there came away without being impressed.

Benin served as the capital of the Benin Kingdom, which ruled much of the Yoruba, Igbo, Ijo and Itsekiri peoples, and was probably founded in the 13th century. According to legend the warrior Oranmiyan stalked south from Ife and married a local woman. Their son Eweka became the first *oba* of Benin and the palace was thought to have been built during his reign. The kingdom flourished in the 14th–17th centuries, when it was ruled under the dynamic leadership of a chain of warrior kings and traditional *obas*.

Benin City was the first inland settlement to be visited by the Europeans, despite not being near the sea or having a river port, but the reputation of the Benin civilisation motivated the Portuguese in the 15th century to seek it out. By the early 16th century, Benin Kingdom had sent an ambassador to Lisbon, and in return the king of Portugal had sent missionaries to Benin. Portuguese was to remain the foreign language for the Benin aristocracy for centuries, and elements of the language have continued to survive in palace circles even today. Early trade items included cowries, ivory, pepper and palm products. Although some slaves were exchanged for goods, Benin was not a slave-dealing nation, preferring to use its manpower and prisoners of war as construction workers to build and maintain the royal palace, the expansive residencies of the aristocracy, and the city walls, moats, and ditches that surrounded the city.

At the height of the Benin Kingdom, great walls were built between 1450 and 1550, and the city was split up into the Oba's Palace and 40 wards. The network of walls stretched from the city and enclosed the surrounding villages in a radius of

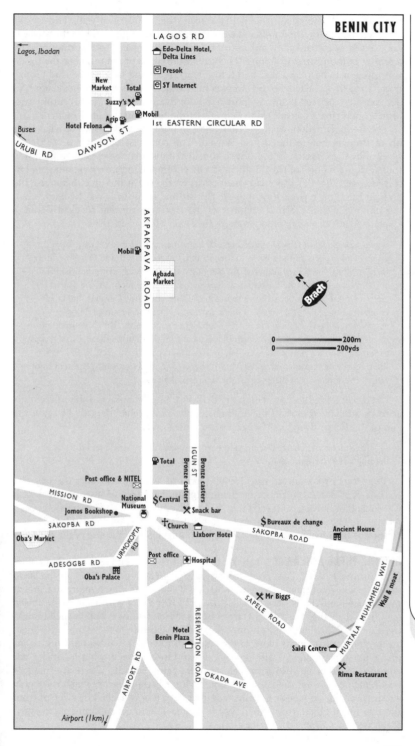

BENIN CITY

LAGOS RD

Lagos, Ibadan

Edo-Delta Hotel,
Delta Lines

Presok

SY Internet

New
Market

Total

Suzzy's

Mobil

Agip

Hotel Felona

Buses

URUBI RD

DAWSON ST

1st EASTERN CIRCULAR RD

AKPAKPAVA ROAD

Mobil

Agbada
Market

N
Bradt

0   200m
0   200yds

Total

IGUN ST
Bronze casters

Bronze
casters

Post office & NITEL

MISSION RD

National
Museum

Central

Jomos Bookshop

SAKOPBA RD

Snack bar

Church

Bureaux de change

Ancient House

Oba's Market

URHOKOPTA RD

Lixborr Hotel

SAKOPBA ROAD

ADESOGBE RD

Post office

Hospital

Oba's Palace

Mr Biggs

SAPELE ROAD

RESERVATION ROAD

Motel
Benin Plaza

AIRPORT RD

OKADA AVE

Saidi Centre

MURTALA MUHAMMED WAY

Wall & moat

Rima Restaurant

Airport (1km)

Southwestern Nigeria BENIN CITY

6

187

over 100km. There could have perhaps been over 5,000km of wall. These walls enclosed over 500 compounds and were 9m tall at their highest. Then the palace is said to have been flanked by an enormous gate of two towers, each surmounted by a bronze python some 15m long. The walls were made of red mud but the inside was thought to be very ornate and full of ivory, brass and iron figures and bronze busts. In each of the city's wards were communities of artisans who made items to decorate the palace. Benin is known predominantly for its 15th-century wax bronzes, which are considered to be some of the finest African ancient art.

The Benin Kingdom declined after 1700, and not much is known of what went on in the city before the British arrived. The conquest of Benin in 1897 was sparked by the massacre of the British consul and his party, who were on their way to investigate reports of ritual human sacrifice. Human sacrifice *was* going on, but it is assumed that this was a last-ditch effort by the *oba* at the time to appease the gods and stop the encroachment of the British, and in the only way he knew. Here is a chilling account from a member of the British party that attacked Benin, a Captain Alan Boisragon, who wrote in *The Benin Massacre* in 1898:

> As we neared Benin City we passed several human sacrifices, live woman slaves gagged and pegged on their backs to the ground, the abdominal wall being cut in the form of a cross, and the uninjured gut hanging out. Men slaves, with their hands tied at the back and feet lashed together, also gagged, were lying about. As we neared the city, sacrificed human beings were laying in the path and bush – even in the king's compound the sight and stench of them was awful. Dead and mutilated bodies were everywhere – by God! May I never see such sights again! In the King's compound, on a raised platform or altar, beautiful idols were found. All of them were caked over in human blood. Lying about were big bronze heads, dozens in a row, with holes in the top, in which immense carved ivory tusks were fixed. The whole place reeked of blood. Fresh blood was dripping off the figures and altars.

On discovering these atrocities, the British promptly ransacked the palace of its artwork, massacred most of the heathen people, and torched the city. That was the end of the Benin Kingdom. Boisragon went on to say:

> . . . fire, smoke and charcoal seemed to have removed all the smell, and the city became sweet and pure again.

The British took an estimated 5,000 pieces of artwork, and only the few that escaped their notice remain in the Benin Museum and Lagos Museum. Much of it was sold off in Europe (some of it is in the British Museum), but most has never been recovered. The reigning *oba* was exiled to Calabar where he died in 1913, and a new palace was built by his son; it was said to be about a tenth of the size of the old one.

GETTING THERE AND AWAY There are daily **flights** between Lagos and Benin City (50 minutes) with Associated Aviation (\ *01802 317 8971 airport desk; www.associatedaviationlimited.com*) at 08.30, 13.00 and 16.00, which return to Lagos at 09.30, 14.30 and 17.30. Arik Air (\ *01 279 9900 central reservations; www.arikair. com*) has a daily flight (except Sat) from Lagos to Benin City at 11.00 which returns to Lagos at 12.20. The airport is only 2km from the centre to the southwest. There are several **motor parks** close to the centre of town, and you should find a bus going in any direction from up and down Urubi Street, where vehicles are clumped together in little groups close to the petrol stations. There are frequent buses, including three-across, to the Ojota Motor Park in Lagos, which is roughly a four-hour ride, as well as the other southwestern towns. Delta Lines depart from the Edo Delta Hotel, from where you'll also be able to get to Onitsha and Warri (dealt with in *Chapter 7*; see page 193).

PRACTICALITIES City transport is mostly in the shape of red and yellow and shared taxis, and minibuses go up and down the main roads. Expect to pay around N30 per ride. *Okadas* are reasonably cheap and you can get just about anywhere for N50, but here unusually they are not allowed to drive at night and have to be off the roads between 18.00 and 07.00 – a rule that seems to be either respected or enforced.

Benin City is fairly easy to navigate around, with most things of interest being centred around King's Square, which is not a square at all but an enormous roundabout with the **museum** in the middle of it. There is a string of **internet** places opposite the Total and Mobil petrol stations on Akpakpava Road. Try Presok Cyber Café at No 128, or the Sy Cyber Café at No 90; both are open 24 hours. If you need to **change money** there is a line of bureaux de change between about 40 and 50 Sakpoba Road or try your hotel.

WHERE TO STAY

🏠 **Hotel Felona** 6 Dawson Rd; ☏ 052 251194. A good option & fairly new, so consequently everything is quite fresh, & this is a good-value, mid-range hotel with reliable power & water. Comfortable rooms are spread over 4 floors, the large restaurant & comfortable bar is wood-panelled, with a good atmosphere & proper tablecloths & napkins, & there's lots of chicken on the menu & some attempt at Western dishes. There's good security with parking behind a manned boom gate. $$

🏠 **Saidi Centre** 271 Murtala Muhammed Way, between Sapele & Sakpoba roads; ☏ 052 240460/242125. This is a totally kitsch place, with all sorts of different décor, & it looks a bit like a castle complete with turrets & all. There are psychedelic murals, curved staircases & gilt mirrors, & the restaurant has very Arabic décor, with lots of gold & padded booths, & is in an old disco equipped with a glittering DJ's podium. The chef will have a stab at continental food, such as chicken chasseur but you might be better off sticking to the oriental dishes, given that the chef is Chinese. The fabulous pool has deep blue tiles & crystal clear water, & the pool bar is a big meeting place for expats working in Warri, & it serves up *suya* & *shawarmas*. Rooms have balconies or patios. $$

🏠 **Motel Benin Plaza** 1 Reservation Rd, GRA; ☏ 052 254779; www.motelbeninplaza.com. In a good location just a 10min walk from Kings Square, the

135 comfortable chalets & rooms here have internet access, fridge, DSTV & motel-style parking & there's a pool & gym. In the excellent restaurant you can build your own breakfast from a long list of items including – wait for it – sausage & bacon. They'll take guests to the airport for free after their stay & rates are inclusive of the 15%. Rooms $; suites $$

🏠 **Edo-Delta Hotel** 128–134 Akpakpava St; ☏ 052 252722. There is a rabbit warren of rooms here in chalets & in a 2-storey building, behind which is a makeshift church that is hugely noisy on a Sun morning thanks to the very loud PA system & a very enthusiastic preacher. There's a good bar with cheap food & very friendly staff & there's a kiosk for snacks (and bottles of gin) in the car park. The rooms are basic but there's water in the showers & satellite TVs (in cages) showing BBC World. $

🏠 **Lixborr Hotel** 4 Sakpoba Rd; ☏ 052 256699. This is in a big compound with a snack bar in the car park selling meat pies & drinks, & there are larger-than-life statues of a drummer & mother & child at the front door. It's the best-value hotel in town, with 40 rooms on 3 storeys, & it's in a great location, right opposite the bronze casters on Igun St. There's a very comfortable modern bar & restaurant, with reasonable Nigerian & some continental dishes, & it's deservedly popular, so you may need to try & get through by phone to make a reservation. The rooms have working showers in tiled bathrooms, new AC units & fans, & DSTV. $

WHERE TO EAT

✗ **Motel Benin Plaza** 1 Reservation Rd, GRA; ⏰ 24hr daily. The best place to eat in town & the highlight here is the great bar around a small swimming pool under fans with big sofas, a big range of spirits & a live band most nights. There's

also a *suya* spot here, & it's a fun place when there's football on the strategically placed TVs. The lovely restaurant has white tablecloths, good service, some wine, & well-priced continental dishes including pizza & unusual specials like chicken &

spinach pancakes or grilled lamb chops. Alternatively, try mud fish or cow intestine pepper soup in the bar! $$$

✗ **Rima Restaurant** 226 Murtala Muhammed Way in the Imaro House; ⏲ 09.00–22.00 daily. There's a snack bar & bakery to the left selling meat pies & sandwiches, & a more formal dining area behind a curtain to the right serving steak & chips with pepper sauce, & some spaghetti dishes, & a cheaper full Nigerian menu. $$

✗ **Suzzy restaurant** 2 Hudson Lane off Akpakpava Rd; ⏲ 08.00–20.00 daily. A cheap canteen serving hot & tasty food-is-ready, & a variety of soups & starch, but no booze. It's a yellow building up the lane behind the Mobil petrol station. $–$$

✗ **Mr Biggs** 43 Sapele Rd. The usual & convenient fast food: boxes of *jollof* rice, bean cakes & scotch eggs; also whole roast chickens & fresh salads. $

WHAT TO SEE AND DO

The National Museum The **National Museum** (⏲ *09.00–18.00 Mon–Fri, 10.00–16.00 Sat–Sun; entry N200*) is in the middle of the central roundabout at King's Square, but one must navigate several lanes of traffic to reach it. Just before the museum is a statue on a tall pillar of the Tomb of the Unknown Soldier, commemorating both world wars. The museum is in a circular building and there are three floors of exhibits, including some of Benin's famous bronze plaques, but unfortunately some of the glass cases are empty, and rather infuriatingly nothing is dated. Most of the plaques are of the *obas* in traditional or supernatural forms, and they are very detailed, with the tiny *obas* carrying swords and shields. Some plaques show Portuguese traders holding manilas (used as currency), and one plaque is of the messenger of Ogiuwu, the chief of all executioners – if past inhabitants of the Kingdom of Benin got presented with this, it reputedly sentenced them to death. Also on display is an executioner's sword.

Upstairs are masquerade costumes, a replica of a pair of wooden stools sent from Benin to the king of Portugal, with a coiled snake around the stand and monkey heads and snakes at the base, and a big map of what Benin City used to look like, with its wards and walls. On the third floor is an ad hoc display of some Yoruba art and carvings, drums, masks, weapons, musical instruments and old fishing tackle from the Niger Delta.

Oba's Market and around To the northwest of the roundabout on Oba Market Street is the **Oba's Market**, a big grey concrete block on two levels, which is easy to navigate. Downstairs is fresh food while upstairs are manufactured clothes and shoes, with lots of impromptu hairdressers on the stairs in between. Nearby, on Mission Road, is a bunch of bookshops; look out for **Jomos Bookshop** at No 3, which has a lot of secondhand novels, and which sells the Spectrum map of Nigeria. The **Central Market** further up Akpakpava Road sells fresh produce, materials and everything plastic. It's sort of covered but has big holes in the corrugated roof.

Back at the roundabout and to the southwest is the **Oba's Palace**, in a huge compound with unassuming low wooden buildings, a vast car park and a basketball court! The present *oba*, Omo Akpolokpolo, has been on the throne since 1979. At the gate on Monday–Friday between 08.00 and 16.00 you can ask if there is someone to show you around the grounds for a small *dash*, and tell you a bit about the present *oba* and his role in the city.

Bronze casting If you follow Sakpoba Road to the east of the roundabout for a few metres, you'll find Igun Street opposite the Lixborr Hotel. This is the home of Benin's **bronze casters**, on a bricked street with an arched entrance that was done up a few years ago from money donated by UNESCO. To the left as you walk up the street is a small café for beer, soft drinks, meat pies and pepper soup. Since old Benin was destroyed the art of bronze casting had been extinct for many decades, until the UNESCO project turned Igun Street into a series of shops and workshops where many young artists turned their attention to bronze casting. There are about 20 stalls here, with the craftsmen working outside each on the street, and hundreds of pieces on display, and despite the fact the traders get very few visitors they don't hassle you too much.

The casting technique is as follows: first, the bronze caster makes a rudimentary mould out of clay, which he covers in wax and moulds into shape using thin strips of wax to make the relief details. He then covers the statue with more clay and the wax is melted out by holding it over hot charcoal. Then the hot bronze is poured into the space left by the wax and when it has cooled the clay is removed from the outside and chiselled out from the inside, and he is left with a rough casting which he then grinds and polishes. The ancient Greeks made similar castings, but they were solid, without any clay core.

You can see the bright yellow figures and heads of elaborately dressed *obas*, sword-wielding maidens, decorated (bronze) elephant tusks, replicas of items that once decorated the old *oba*'s palace, and more modern busts of local chiefs. You'll also see British soldiers and the whole of Benin's history reflected in these figures. The bigger pieces are very heavy and you are unlikely to be able to shift them without a vehicle, but there are plenty of small statues of fishermen, farmers and drummers, all of which are unique. It's wonderful that this ancient craft has been revived again and the craftsmen will happily let you watch; they are imaginative in their designs and proud of their artwork.

The Ancient House The **Ancient House**, at 97 Sakpoba Road, was the house of Chief Ogiamen, and is thought to be one of the few buildings that survived the 1897 fire that gutted the old city. As such it is probably the only example of old Benin City architecture still in existence. It's a long, one-storey building built of red mud with a rusted tin roof, and there are mysterious cowrie shells above the door, and bits of snail shells, bird wings and jaw bones of unidentified small animals in the two small shrines inside. You can wander through the door into the courtyard and have a look around, but people still live in the corridor of rooms at the back. Unfortunately it's right next to an outside welding stall, whose equipment covers up part of the front.

The city walls Further down Sakpoba Road and along Murtala Muhammed Way are some pathetic remains of old Benin's **city walls** and moats. At their highest point, the walls were 9m high and the moat 9m deep. Unfortunately in the past few years, the walls and moats have been the victim of extensive soil excavation and used as a source of building materials, and are so overgrown it's hard to even make out what you're looking at. The wall is now just a mound of brown earth covered in rubbish, and the moat is a green slimy area full to the brim with plastic garbage.

OKOMU NATIONAL PARK

Okomu National Park (*entry N300 pp*), about 40km to the west of Benin City, is one of the largest remaining rainforest reserves in Nigeria, and Nigeria has less than 5% of its original rainforest left.

GETTING THERE AND AWAY To get here, you'll have to be in a car. Take the road that runs more or less parallel to the Benin–Lagos Expressway to the south, where there is a sign to the park near the village of Orah. Follow this road south for 2km to Udo and Okomu National Park is 20km or an hour's drive beyond this village.

WHERE TO STAY AND EAT Accommodation can be found at the newly opened ⌂ **Okumu Resort** (☎ *080 468 0294; www.okomuecoresort.com*), which offers 12 reasonably comfortable chalets on stilts with balconies in a beautiful lush forested spot just inside the park entrance. Each has twin beds and en suite bathroom with hot water, there's a large dining room and both the onsite chef and indeed the manager like to cook, so you'll get a variety of food and they'll discuss what you want to eat with you; there's also beer, wine, whisky and gin on offer. Their speciality for dessert is lime mousse made with limes from the forest. Guides will take visitors on forest walks, there's a swimming pool, and the camp is surrounded by fig trees, a favourite food of mona monkeys which are frequently seen. The tracks into the forest are suitable for 4x4s only, but if you're in a normal car, it can be parked up at the village of Udo and the camp's management will pick you up. They also offer free transfers from the airport in Benin City ($$).

WHAT TO SEE AND DO Okomu was carved out of the old Ologbo Game Reserve and expanded to 19,712ha and declared a national park in 1999. But today it's under serious threat from logging, and less than a third of the forest of the original reserve remains. It's shrinking fast, with villages encroaching on all sides. The terrain is typical rainforest, swamp forest and some patches of open scrub, and again nobody really knows what's in there, though it is regarded as one of the last habitats for the white-throated monkey. There are a few forest elephant and buffalo left, and possibly red-capped mangabey, the Sclater's and putty-nosed guenon. More common are mona monkey, bush pig, Maxwell's duiker, civet cat and pangolin.

Nevertheless, it's a beautiful spot, with a mist-shrouded forest of tall trees including giant mahogany, ironwood, and silk-cotton trees. Some 200 species of birds have been recorded here, including five species of hornbill, and over 700 species of butterflies. There is a nature trail that goes through the forest, and a ladder up to a viewing platform 50m high in a lofty silk-cotton tree, which provides a fantastic panoramic view of the forest. You'll also see many butterflies and birds. If the Arakbuan Stream is full it's possible to swim, and as this stream is also worshipped by the local community you might see bits of snails and chickens left as sacrifices.

7

Southeastern Nigeria

The southeast of Nigeria is crowded with industrial and commercial towns, but away from the urban centres the region is perhaps the most scenic corner of the country, thanks to the forests of Cross River State and the watery channels of the Niger Delta. This is Igboland, though there are numerous other ethnic groups, and some of those living in the delta still retain traditions that are centuries old. This was the region that proclaimed itself as a Republic in 1967, a move that started the Biafran War, when many of the cities were ravaged by heavy military bombardment, and the Igbo people shifted around the region as the Nigerian army beat and starved them into submission.

This was one of the first regions to be visited by Europeans, first during the slave trade and then by early missionaries and colonial officers, whose legacies can still be seen in Old Calabar's 19th-century architecture. Calabar is the location of the country's best museum, two excellent primate sanctuaries, and the brand new Tinapa, which is an incredibly ambitious shopping and entertainment complex. It's also a convenient base from which to explore the area around the Cross River National Park, an ancient but fragile patch of beautiful rainforest of enormous trees and craggy peaks, and serves as a springboard to the Obudu Cattle Ranch, perhaps one of Nigeria's most appealing tourist attractions. There is not a great deal to see or do in the towns and cities except for Calabar, but you will inevitably find yourself moving from one to the next even if you don't venture out of the motor parks.

In the extreme south in Bayelsa, Rivers, Anambra and Delta states, the River Niger fans out in endless meandering lagoons and creeks to form the Niger Delta. Here there are beautifully forested islands of mangroves and ancient fishing communities, but unfortunately the additional presence of oil has damaged the environment and the peaceful existence of the delta people. Today, the region is witnessing a volatile crisis over the unfair distribution of oil wealth – there are violent spats between government gunboats and creek warlords and frequent kidnappings of foreign oil workers – so it's not a safe place to venture to. As we went to press (in early 2008) even Port Harcourt, the capital of Nigeria's oil industry, was considered well and truly off the map.

ONITSHA AND ASABA

Onitsha and Asaba are twin cities that sit opposite each other on either side of the Niger River, about 160km north of Nigeria's coast. They are joined by an impressive road bridge, built in 1965, which serves as a vital link between eastern and western Nigeria. The river is well over a kilometre wide here. As one of the few road crossings over the Niger, the bridge is usually gridlocked and it can takes hours to cross. It's also in danger of falling down as bolts and girders are missing, and in 2007 the government announced plans to build a second bridge between the two cities.

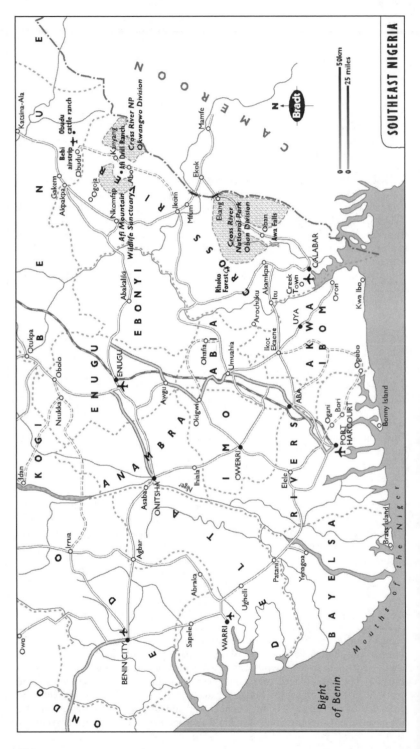

SOUTHEAST NIGERIA

Asaba lies on a hill on the west bank of the river about 140km to the east of Benin City and is the capital of Delta State. As it's not an oil city, it's not part of the crisis going on further south in the delta itself. It was once the colonial capital of the Southern Protectorate of Nigeria and was where the Royal Niger Company administered trade on the river. Onitsha is a port on the eastern bank just over 100km to the west of Enugu. The growth of Onitsha over the centuries probably derives from its strategic location on the river, and it's believed immigrants from Benin probably established the city in the 16th century. Long before the British arrived it was a centre for trade and a meeting place for a variety of the region's tribes.

Despite being in Igboland Asaba has historically been inhabited by people from other parts of the country, and even today there is a large Hausa-Fulani community. Onitsha was hit harder than most during the Biafran War, and was almost completely destroyed by shelling. Today's concrete monstrosities are from the 1970s rebuilding era, and it's a rather ugly, commercial town, with nothing to see except for the river.

WHERE TO STAY AND EAT

The Grand Hotel 112 Nnebisi Rd; 056 282030. Lying adjacent to a park in Asaba on the riverbank with wonderful views of life on the river, this is the best place to stay in the region. There's a large kidney-shaped swimming pool with sun loungers, a pleasant outside terrace, a giant chess set in the garden & a new gym. Very nicely furnished rooms are arranged in garden suites, the bigger rooms have steam baths & complimentary dressing gowns, & there's secure parking. Rather hefty non-resident rates of US$223 (US$300 deposit) are charged but you'll have to pay in naira; b/fast for one person inc. $$$$

ENUGU

The capital of Enugu State is sprawled at the foot of the Udi Hills and is the gateway city to the southeast of Nigeria; it is effectively the capital of Igboland. Less formally, Enugu State is also known as 'Wawa State' because the people in this area use the word '*wa*' for 'no' rather than '*mba*' used in other parts of Igboland. It's a fairly prosperous city with many manufacturing plants around its outskirts, including a vast 7 UP bottling plant, a Nigerian Breweries brewery, and a Mercedes assembly plant. It doesn't have a long history, as the Igbo people generally never gathered in cities as the Yoruba did, preferring their village life among the watery channels of the Niger Delta.

In 1909, a British expedition set out to the Udi Hills to explore for silver but instead located a seam of coal below the village of Enugu Ngwo (*enu ugwu* means top of the hill in Igbo). This was the beginning of Enugu on its present site, referred to as the coal city, and a colliery was opened in 1914 by Lord Lugard, who initially called it Enugu Coal Camp to distinguish it from Enugu Ngwo. The railroad to Port Harcourt was completed in 1912, from where the coal was shipped to Lagos. Coal workers here took part in the general strike of 1945, and again went on strike in 1949 when 21 miners were shot by the British, an incident that fuelled the nationalist movement. Today the coal mines are still here, but the need for coal has fallen away since the railways switched to diesel, though the local cement factory still uses Enugu coal for fuel. Enugu was also the capital of the secessionist state of Biafra (1967–70) and managed to survive the Biafran War pretty much intact.

If you are travelling by public transport there's a good chance that you will change vehicles at Enugu's motor park to get to any point to the southeast from anywhere else in the country. There are a couple of decent accommodation options at each end of the budget scale. The only place to visit is the **National Museum**, which opened in 2001, but as it is difficult to find, three kilometres north of the city on Abakaliki Road, it receives so few visitors that it is locked most of the time. You'll see the usual display of masquerade costumes, musical instruments and pots if you find it open.

GETTING THERE AND AWAY Enugu's **Akanu Ibiam Airport** is roughly 10km north of the city. Aero Contractors (↘ *042 559688; www.acn.aero*) and Sosoliso Airlines (↘ *042 553500, airport desk;* ↘ *042 557000, desk at Nike Holiday Resort; www.sosolisoairline.com*) have daily flights to Lagos, and Sosoliso has a daily service to and from Abuja. The **railway station** is on Ogui Street next to the unmissable National Stadium, and the crazy **Ogbete Motor Park** is clustered around Market Road where it joins Okpapra Avenue in the heart of the city.

There are so many vehicles here that the roads are hugely congested and the frantic market along Market Road means that even walking is difficult among the throngs of people, animals and cars. However, despite the chaos, the motor park is surprisingly well organised, though you'll have to ask around to find the area for vehicles going to your destination (don't forget the National Union of Road Transport Workers men in the green and white uniforms). There are vehicles to all destinations in the southeast, as well as to Makurdi, Onitsha and Benin City, and overnight 'luxury' buses to Abuja and Lagos. Some of these go to Abuja during the day.

WHERE TO STAY AND EAT

Nike Holiday Resort Nike Lake Rd, Abekpa-Nike Village; ↘ 042 557000/557679/550001; managed by the South African Protea group; www.proteahotels.com. You can also make a reservation through the website or South African office, which you may want to consider doing if you want to use a credit card over the phone; ↘/f +21 (21) 430 5330. This relaxing resort is 7–8km from Enugu. To get there follow the airport road out of town & turn off on to the Onitsha/Abakpa road & follow the signs. The resort is set on the Nike Lake that has rowing boats & short walking trails through the bird-filled

surrounding forest. It's an old structure & briefly served as the HQ for the Biafran army during the civil war; Nike means 'with power' in Igbo. Now completely refurbished by Protea, the hotel has 216 luxury rooms & suites with DSTV, minibar & balconies. There is a mini-golf course, tennis courts, a brand new gym & a large pool. There are also several houses that are rented out to expats working on local projects. There's a hi-tech business centre, a few shops in the lobby, & a big modern restaurant serving buffet meals for about US$20. If you want to come here for the weekend from Lagos, for around US$10 you can make use of the shuttle service between the resort & the airport. Rates include breakfast but not the 15%. Rooms $$$; suites $$$$

🏠 **Placia Guest House** 25 Edinburgh Rd; ☏ 042 251565/255851. This is a good budget option not far from the motor park, though far enough to get an *okada*. Follow Market Rd south across the railway line & turn right into Zik Av. Edinburgh Rd is opposite the post office. This is a good-value spot with refreshing tiled floors, good bathrooms, high ceilings & DSTV. There is no restaurant or bar, but (very good) Nigerian food & beers are brought to your room & the staff are friendly. Rates include tea-bread-and-eggs that is brought to your room in the morning at an allocated time. Across the street from the main gate are a couple of palm wine-drinking joints, & the street vendors sell *suya*, & prepared slices of pineapple & paw paw, & finally there's an internet café on the 2nd floor of the building opposite. $

UMUAHIA

Umuahia straddles the main Enugu–Port Harcourt Expressway roughly 120km south of Enugu. Today, it is an unremarkable town, but it's best known as being the central military headquarters during the Biafran War, though things are very peaceful now. Writers Ken Saro Wiwa and Chinhua Achebe both went to Umuahia's Government College. The only reason to stop here is to visit the **National War Museum**, which is a worthwhile detour off the expressway. If you are coming from the Enugu direction, get off the vehicle at the roundabout that has a big unmissable sign and statue that says 'Welcome to Abia; God's Own State'. Vehicles stop on the top right-hand corner of this roundabout if you have Enugu behind you, where there is a mini motor park with plenty of bush taxis and minibuses to and from Enugu, Aba and Port Harcourt.

WHAT TO SEE AND DO

The National War Museum To get to the National War Museum take the left-hand road from the roundabout called Mission Hill, which goes east through town proper; the museum is roughly three kilometres on the other side. Expect to pay around N100 on an *okada* or N400 in a drop taxi for the journey out there. A couple of hundred metres down this road from the roundabout is the **Novotel International Hotel** (*62 Mission Hill;* ☏ *088 220440/1;* $), a neat and tidy two-storey hotel with a restaurant and bar and adequate rooms if you get stuck in Umuahia and need to stay the night. But you should be able to visit the museum on the way to somewhere else.

The National War Museum (🕐 *open 10.00–18.00 daily; entry N400*) opened in 1985 and is largely a collection of military supplies used by both sides in the Biafran War (see box). The differences between the home-made Biafran items and those made in proper international arms factories are more than evident, and many of the exhibits are usefully displayed next to each other to highlight the differences. The main collection is outdoors – armoured vehicles, artillery and planes, spread about in a field among some mango trees. The first thing you'll see on approaching the museum is the 1966 NS *Bonny*; it comes as quite a shock to see a warship in the middle of a field miles away from the sea.

An informative guide will show you around for a small *dash*, starting at a shed housing the Biafrans' rudimentary 'red devil' armoured cars. These are displayed in chronological order from the first ones built, which are nothing more than simple box-like metal cars, through to the ones built later in the war, whose shape had been modified, rocket launchers added, the wheels removed and replaced by tank tracks. They are still not a patch on the meaty Nigerian Russian-built tanks standing next to them, however. Also on display is a home-made, box-like assault boat with an anti-submarine gun and some torpedoes that were used in the sea off Port Harcourt before the Nigerians recaptured the city, and then in the Niger Delta.

Not all the military hardware was hand-made; the Biafrans also resorted to using ancient World War II items, including Russian-built heavy artillery guns and anti-tank guns that they had to fix up and make useable again. The ones on display date from 1943 but were used again in 1969–70.

There are several Nigerian fighter planes, including one MiG, all imported from Russia, including the Ilyushin, nicknamed 'Genocide', a four-crew bomber capable of carrying 1,000kg of explosives, which was brought into Nigeria by an Egyptian pilot for the Biafrans but was actually used on both sides of the war as it was subsequently captured by the Nigerians. This plane completely dwarfs the 'Biafran Baby', an impossibly small two-seater sports plane that was donated to the Biafran side by one Count Von Rosen, who flew it from Sweden. It could carry 12 rockets and, as it could fly low, went undetected by radar and in 1969 managed to bomb and destroy many much more superior Nigerian planes and MiGs when they were sitting on the tarmac in Port Harcourt, after Nigeria had taken the city.

The NS *Bonny* was built by the British in 1966 and used by the Nigerian side to

THE BIAFRAN WAR

Lieutenant Colonel Odemugwu Ojukwu declared the Eastern Region as the Republic of Biafra on 30 May 1967, citing the predominant cause for his action as the Nigerian government's inability to safeguard the lives of the Igbo people. The federal military government of Nigeria declared war against the new republic and a brutal and disastrous civil war raged over the next three years and left an estimated one to three million people dead through fighting and starvation. The Biafran army was an ill-equipped, undermanned and under-trained rebel force up against a Nigerian army 250,000 strong. Some of Biafra's military supplies came with unofficial assistance from France and its former West African colonies, but it wasn't enough.

Meanwhile, the federal government of Nigeria got its artillery, fighter planes and gunboats from the international arms market, with official support from Britain and the Soviet Union. The United States remained neutral. Without international help, the Biafrans resorted to making their own artillery and vehicles, and at the beginning of the war set up a group of engineers, railway workers from Enugu and university professors to design and assemble fabricated weapons. These people had no experience of making guns or armoured cars and had to invent them from scratch – the resulting artillery was a lot less sophisticated than that on the Nigerian side. Nevertheless they worked, and Biafra had some successes during the war; they even made their own landmines and called them *ogbinigwe* meaning 'muscular'. But Biafra's homemade anti-aircraft guns, tanks, and rocket launchers were constantly beaten down by Nigeria's superior firepower.

Throughout the war the fighting was confusing and vicious, and many of the major cities such as Port Harcourt, Enugu, Aba, Calabar and Umuahia kept changing hands and were routinely attacked by air and at the coast by gunboats. The Nigerians eventually retook the coast and when the Nigerians captured Port Harcourt they found that the Biafrans were distilling their own petrol from crude oil in makeshift refineries to fuel their war vehicles. The Biafran army was eventually reduced to an enclave in the Niger Delta around Owerri. On 12 January 1970, after 31 months of civil war, the Biafran forces surrendered and by the end of the war Biafra was no more than 60km wide and just a few kilometres deep, crowded with some three million Igbo refugees.

bomb and capture Calabar and Bonny. It came to the museum in parts and was reassembled. You can clamber over the boat and wind the anti-aircraft gun up and down. It's now rather charmingly a restaurant, though it's stinking hot below deck, but there are plastic chairs and tables on the outside deck; you can get a cold drink and food-is-ready. The site of the museum was chosen as it was here that the Voice of Biafra was transmitted on the radio from the former Eastern Nigeria Television Station. This was the method the leaders of the ill-fated republic communicated with their people throughout the war. At one stage the radio station was moved to a bunker, which is still there today. Ask to go inside, and notice as you go down the stairs the rows of photographs of the key political and military leaders of the war; to the left are portraits of Biafran leaders and, on the right, those of their Federal counterparts. There's also an indoor display of old uniforms, weapons and photographs, some of which are harrowing, a mother and child for example, emancipated beyond imagination.

ABA

Further south on the Enugu–Port Harcourt Expressway, approximately 60km south of Umuahia, and one hour's drive from Port Harcourt, is Aba, a large town in Imo State on the Aba River. Inexplicably, it's also known as Enyimba City (Enyi is Igbo for elephant). Its biggest claim to fame is that it is home to Enyimba International Football Club, popularly called 'the people's elephant', one of Nigeria's most successful teams. Aba is an important regional market town, attracting people from all around because of its strategic position in the fertile belt of the Niger Delta, and is a manufacturing centre for cement, textiles, pharmaceuticals, tyres, plastics, soap, and the proverbial two opposites, beer and mineral water.

Originally a village, Aba was developed by the British as an administrative centre in the early 20th century. It is famous for the 1929 Aba Women's Riots involving Igbo, Ibibio and Opobo women who rioted against Britain's arbitrary use of indigenous persons as rulers, and also in protest at the local chiefs of the time including women in their head count and making them pay taxes. There was a series of mass protests, and women burnt buildings and attacked the local chiefs. Colonial troops were sent in and opened fire, and some 50 women were killed at Aba and another 50 or so in the surrounding region. After the incident the British set up an inquiry and the event was a leading milestone in the history of Nigerian nationalism.

Even by Nigerians, Aba is known to be the filthiest city in Nigeria. Its massive Ariara Market spills out on the Port Harcourt Expressway. The edges of all the roads are stacked high with plastic rubbish, broken-down and abandoned oil tankers and tractor units, and the central reservations are full of derelict cars. Allegedly, this is a result of an overwhelming influx of people migrating to Aba from the northern cities in the last three years. The local authorities are no longer able to cope with the mountains of garbage accumulated by the increasing population.

WHERE TO EAT AND DRINK You can grab a cold drink from the stalls in the garden of the museum (see below), where there are a few wooden carvings and pieces of cloth for sale. If you have to stay in Aba, the best option is the 75-room **Crystal Park Hotel and Flamingo Restaurant** (*Crystal Park Avenue off Port Harcourt Road;* ℡ *082 221588, 221742;* **$$**), which has adequate rooms and Indian and Chinese food in the restaurant. Everything else is pretty rough, so budget travellers may as well move on.

WHAT TO SEE AND DO
The Museum of Colonial History Aba's only sight per se is the **Museum of Colonial History** (⊕ *09.00–17.00 daily; entry N200*), which is within walking distance of the main motor park on Ikot Ekpene Road as it heads out to the east of town. (Vehicles running between Port Harcourt and Calabar drive straight past it so you could feasibly break your journey here.) The museum is housed in a freshly painted, bright yellow colonial consulate building and was opened in 1995. Exhibits include old photographs of colonial times recalling the early growth of Aba, and portraits of Nigeria's movers and shakers during the build-up to and after independence, but you'll struggle to see anything if there's no NEPA.

PORT HARCOURT

The approach to Port Harcourt, the capital of Rivers State, is from the Aba Expressway, which gets busier and busier, until you eventually join the go-slow on the Aba Road in the city proper. The pollution is palpable here and you'll immediately see the oil flares to the south of town emitting big black clouds of smoke. This is the centre of Nigeria's oil industry. Port Harcourt, the capital of Rivers State, has long been an important merchant port, and is an industrial giant in a region producing steel and aluminium products, pressed concrete, tyres and motor vehicles. But predominantly Port Harcourt is the collection point for all the oil pumped out of the wells of the Niger Delta. Pipelines carry oil from the delta directly to Port Harcourt's wharfs and on to Bonny Island to be pumped into the tankers for export.

Port Harcourt is a relatively young city and was founded by the British in 1912 as southeastern Nigeria's railhead and sea port for the shipment of coal mined from the new Enugu coal fields. The spot was chosen because of a natural deep-water harbour on the Bonny River and was named after Viscount Lewis Harcourt, secretary of state for the colonies (1910–15). In addition to its physical advantages, the area had the advantage of being sparsely inhabited by fishing folk and was not under the jurisdiction of any meddlesome traditional leaders.

Like Jos, Kaduna and Enugu, Port Harcourt became one of the colonial new towns. Its port grew quickly, and after Lagos it's now the second-busiest and biggest in the country, taking away business from the pre-colonial ports of Calabar, Brass and Bonny islands. As a new town it attracted people from other regions and other countries, including Lagosians and Creoles (returned slaves), and a fair number of British traders. Asian entrepreneurs from Lebanon, India, and Syria formed the bulk of the middlemen between the big European firms and the African traders. (There are still Lebanese supermarkets on Azikiwe Road.) Pidgin English has its roots in Port Harcourt as a general language for people of varying tongues to use during the city's formative years. The original one square mile town was designed by orderly British town planners, with plenty of open spaces, parks, and playing fields – few of these serve their purpose today, but nevertheless it earned the city the title of Nigeria's 'Garden City'.

Since the discovery of oil in the delta, Port Harcourt has been primarily an oil city and the first shipment of Nigerian crude oil left here in 1958. The Nigerian National Petroleum Corporation, the federal government's agency for oil, has its headquarters here, and there are two oil refineries and a petrochemical complex near Okirika, about 20km southeast of Port Harcourt. Today the city is huge and choked with traffic on almost the same scale as Lagos, and its population is estimated at between three and four million.

Warning! At the time of this update (January 2008) Port Harcourt and the Niger Delta were completely off-limits to foreigners. There is an ongoing dispute between local communities and the oil companies about the unfair distribution of the oil money; most of it goes straight to Abuja and not to the people who live next to the oil wells, often in abject poverty. Routinely oil pipes are blown up, oil tankers bombed and oil platforms sabotaged, and the crisis has resulted in a 25–30% cut in Nigeria's oil output in the last few years. Indirectly, it has also contributed to a spike in global oil prices.

From the beginning of 2006, the number of attacks in the region involving foreigners has risen dramatically – remember it will always be assumed foreigners are oil workers. At first, attacks were carried out by politically motivated gangs of youths, yielding sticks or pistols, protesting for the rights of their respective ethnic group against the oil companies operating in the delta. Since early 2006 it's been a different story. Militia groups are now well organised and led, have an arsenal of sophisticated weapons including rocket launchers, assault rifles and machine guns, and are heavily financed from the rich pickings earned from ransom taking. The political or ideological agenda is perhaps now leaning towards a more criminal element.

To date more than 200 foreign oil workers, including many Britons and Americans, have been kidnapped from Port Harcourt or from oil rigs and installations in the delta. Five were abducted from a Port Harcourt nightclub, another seven from a Port Harcourt compound for expats, and three were taken from a Port Harcourt public minibus. In December 2006, car bombs exploded at Port Harcourt's Agip compound and at Shell's residential compound, and again in January 2007 another bomb went off at the Shell compound. There were no casualties but Shell was forced to evacuate the majority of their foreign employees from Port Harcourt, Bonny Island and Warri. Also in January 2007, 24 Filipinos were kidnapped off a ship making its way into Warri.

To date at the time of writing, three foreign abductees have been women, and during my visit in July 2007 three children were taken including a British three-month-old baby. Most hostages have been released unharmed, although in a poor physical state, after a ransom has been paid by the oil companies (or as suggested, by the government, which they always deny), though there have been some fatalities.

Militants in the Niger Delta have explicitly and repeatedly told foreigners to leave the region, and have recently warned of expanding activities well outside the Niger Delta states. Their demands have included the creation of additional states for Ijaws (the delta's dominant ethnic group), amenities and jobs for rural communities, contracts and oil concessions for faction leaders and even calls for independence. Most attacks are thought to have been launched by the Movement for the Emancipation of the Niger Delta (MEND); the group has admitted responsibility for some of the incidents, is threatening further attacks on oil companies, and has publicly warned China (which is tapping into oil resources all over Africa) to stay away from the Niger Delta. Interestingly, MEND denied involvement in the case of the kidnapping of the three-month-old British baby in July 2007, and even offered assistance in looking for the child (she was released after five days). This re-enforces the theory that although MEND perhaps operates under a shadow of political motivation, there are other criminal groups using the same kidnapping tactics simply to extort ransoms.

There were further outbreaks of violence on the streets of Port Harcourt in August 2007, and soldiers implemented an 11-hour nightly curfew on the city. At the time, weeks of fighting between the military and militia members on motorbikes carrying automatic weapons resulted in an unconfirmed death toll, blazing buildings across the city and government helicopters firing on to the streets. Anyone who is considering visiting Port Harcourt or the delta should get up-to-the-minute advice.

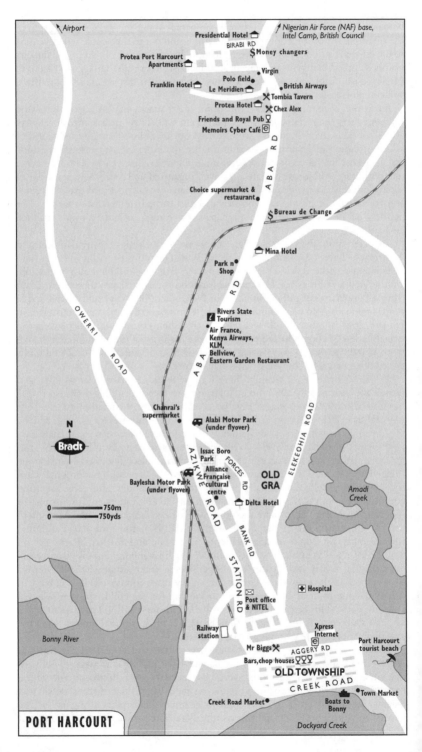

Airport

Nigerian Air Force (NAF) base,
Intel Camp, British Council

Presidential Hotel
BIRABI RD
Money changers

Protea Port Harcourt
Apartments

Virgin

Franklin Hotel
Polo field
British Airways
Le Meridien
Tombia Tavern
Protea Hotel
Chez Alex

Friends and Royal Pub
Memoirs Cyber Café

ABA RD

Choice supermarket &
restaurant

Bureau de Change

Mina Hotel

Park n'
Shop

ABA RD

Rivers State
Tourism

Air France,
Kenya Airways,
KLM,
Bellview,
Eastern Garden Restaurant

OWERRI ROAD

ELEKEOHIA ROAD

Chanrai's
supermarket
Alabi Motor Park
(under flyover)

N

Bradt

Issac Boro
Park

OLD
GRA

Amadi
Creek

AZIKWE ROAD

FORCES RD

Alliance
Française
cultural
centre

Baylesha Motor Park
(under flyover)

Delta Hotel

BANK RD

0   750m
0   750yds

STATION RD

Hospital

Bonny River

Post office
& NITEL

Railway
station

Xpress
Internet

Port Harcourt
tourist beach

Mr Biggs
AGGERY RD

Bars, chop houses
OLD TOWNSHIP

CREEK ROAD

Town Market

Creek Road Market
Boats to
Bonny

PORT HARCOURT

Dockyard Creek

GETTING THERE AND AWAY

By air Port Harcourt International Airport is 40km or about 45 minutes' drive (depending on the traffic) from Port Harcourt, north on Owerri Road. However, the airport closed in August 2006 for essential repairs. An electrical fire had gutted its power plant, the runway was in need of an upgrade and the perimeter of the airport needed fencing. This was where a Solsoliso plane crashed in December 2005, killing 106 people, and where a few months earlier an Air France jet narrowly missed having a serious accident; it was taxiing to arrivals when it ran over and killed several cows that had wandered on to the runway. There is no indication as to when the airport will reopen, and work was abandoned in June 2007 because of safety concerns for foreign engineers.

Meanwhile, some **domestic airlines** such as Virgin Nigeria and Aero Contractors are using the runway at the Nigerian Air Force (NAF) base off the Aba Expressway; other airlines are re-routing to Owerri or Warri, which are both some distance away, and there's the added security risk of travelling by road through the delta towns. For now Virgin Nigeria and Aero Contractors have daily flights between Port Harcourt (NAF) and Lagos, and Aero Contractors also has flights between Port Harcourt (NAF) and Calabar (35 minutes) and Warri (30 minutes). Other airlines may follow suit and use the NAF airstrip, so check the websites.

Airlines

Air France upstairs in the shopping plaza at 47 Aba Rd, above the Eastern Garden Chinese Restaurant; ☎ 084 486901/2; www.airfrance.com.ng
Aero Contractors NAF airport desk, ☎ 084 230110; www.acn.aero
Bellview upstairs in the shopping plaza at 47 Aba Rd, above the Eastern Garden Chinese Restaurant; ☎ 084 230518/9; www.flybellviewair.com
British Airways in the Corporation Building, 180 Aba Rd; ☎ 084 238350/1; www.britishairways.com
Chanchangi Airlines Airport desk, ☎ 084 231920; desk at the Presidential Hotel, ☎ 084 234937; www.chanchangi.com

KLM and Kenya Airways share an office; ☎ 084 231645, 235468; www.kenya-airways.com, www.klm.com
Lufthansa has an office at the Hotel Presidential; ☎ 084 232014/230634; www.lufthansa.com.ng
Sosoliso Airlines has a desk at the Presidential Hotel; ☎ 084 571946; www.sosolisoairline.com
Virgin Nigeria 175 Aba Rd (above the Zenith Bank); ☎ 084 467000/6; www.virginnigeria.com

By road The sprawling Alabi Motor Park is on Aba Road and you can look down at the chaotic compound stuffed to the gills with vehicles from the flyover that takes Aba Road into the city proper, where it turns into Azikiwe Road. Just to the south of here and under the flyover is the Baylesha Motor Park, opposite the gate to the Issac Boro Park, which is far less frantic and where the slightly more expensive private companies such as Crosslines or Delta Transport go from, offering a 'three-across' service (fewer people). Vehicles in each of the motor parks go to all the cities in the southeast and as far as Benin City, where you'll need to change for Lagos, Enugu and points north. There are overnight 'luxury' buses to Lagos, Kano and Abuja. Non-trainspotters should head for the train station at the end of Azikiwe Road.

GETTING AROUND Port Harcourt is bisected neatly by the Aba Road that goes over a series of flyovers and starts life as the Aba Expressway 64km north in Aba, turns into **Aba Road** as it enters the city, and then **Azikiwe Road** as it heads towards the Old Township and the wharfs to the south of the city. This is literally the end of the road in southeastern Nigeria, and any point south of here in the Niger Delta is reached by boat (or by the oil companies' helicopter). This road is routinely choked with traffic to the point that a pedestrian will be unable to cross the road, thanks partly to a big concrete buffer in the middle of it. There is the odd pedestrian bridge but they are some distance apart. Street vendors hound vehicles in their droves. *Okadas* are useful here but, as in Lagos, can be dangerous given the heavy traffic and they are not allowed on the roads after 18.00.

The city is roughly divided into five suburbs – **Old GRA**, **GRA 1**, **GRA 2**, **GRA 3** and **Old Township**. The latter is a bustling (though not necessarily safe) area of frantic commerce and congested streets. The further south you get towards the wharfs on Creek Road and Bonny Street, the less likely you are going to be able to navigate this area by car. **Shared taxis** and **minibuses** in Port Harcourt can be any colour, but the majority are blue with a white stripe on the side, and they run up and down the major arteries.

WHERE TO STAY Accommodation in Port Harcourt is reasonably good and there are a couple of upmarket spots that clearly cater for international oil company executives. The better hotels are located in the GRA areas off the Aba Road to the north of the city. There are budget hotels in the Old Township, some of which are passable, but this is an especially dangerous part of the city and not recommended after dark. There are a number of compounds around Port Harcourt for employees of the big oil corporations – Shell, Elf, Schlumberger, Bristows and others have their own residential areas with security and generators – so if you are working, you may find yourself staying at one of these.

Le Méridien Ogeyi Place 45 Tombia St, GRA 2; ✆ 084 461770; www.starwoodhotels.com. Reservations can be made directly through the website or from the UK, through Le Méridien's toll-free number; ✆ 08000 282840. This is without doubt the best hotel in Nigeria & is the only one that hits the 5-star mark by international standards – it is stunning. It's a new luxury hotel overlooking the Port Harcourt Polo Club, with 84 modern rooms, 6 penthouses, a health club, business centre & swimming pool. The Ororo Restaurant & bar faces the polo field & overlooks the pool terrace. Rooms have all the trimmings you would expect of an international 5-star hotel & are super luxurious, & the suites have extras such as flat screen TV, kidney-shaped bath tubs & walk-in showers. There are certainly no power or water problems here & it's probably the best you're going to get in the whole of West Africa. Deposits are 25% more than the room rates. $$$$$

Protea Hotel Port Harcourt Apartments 3 Isaiah Odulu St, GRA 1; ✆ 084 231557; www.proteahotels.com. These are luxurious apartments, but each of the several rooms in the 8 apartments can be let out separately from about US$200 per room inclusive of full English breakfast & the 15%. This is an odd, almost Gothic-looking slate-coloured building, but it's very modern & all the uncluttered bedrooms & communal areas are decorated with polished wood, sumptuous brown leather sofas & gleaming white tiles & mirrors. Each apartment is spread over 7 floors of living rooms, bedrooms, studies & bathrooms. The apartments can also be taken for long stays & are fully serviced with DSTV, AC & balconies. There's a small restaurant & bar serving continental food exclusively for the guests, & a small pool & tiled barbecue area. Of interest to long-term guests, Nigerian Breweries is next door, where you can buy slabs of Heineken from the side of the road. $$$$$

Presidential Hotel at the northern end of Aba Rd before it turns into Aba Expressway, GRA 1; ✆ 084 461500–12, 575802–4; www.hotel-presidential.com. This has been the city's principal hotel for decades, & there are lots of useful services here; it has recently been nicely refurbished. There are several bars & restaurants, a swimming pool with terrace where you can play table tennis, a welcome desk for Shell (as many expat oil workers arrive & start their term of service here), & a coffee shop in the lobby. In the row of shops are domestic airline desks, & a bookshop where you can pick up a map of Port Harcourt that quite frankly makes no sense whatsoever. There are no fewer than 12 types of accommodation in 307 rooms, all with myriad names. The cheapest are the Garden Rooms, which come in at just over US$200. Rooms $$$$; suites $$$$$

🏠 **Protea Hotel Garden City** 1c Evo Crescent, GRA 2; ☎ 084 463401–3; www.proteahotels.com. You can also make a reservation for both Port Harcourt's Proteas through the website or the South African office, which you may want to consider if using a credit card (☎ +27 (0) 21 430 5000). This is another excellent brand new option close to the Méridien, which has 103 rooms & suites in a newly built block with imported hotel furnishings, DSTV, a fully functioning business centre, a gym, nice spacious pool & each floor has its own lounge area. The two presidential suites have additional flat-screen TVs & computers. There's good international food in the restaurant & a choice of cocktails in the bar. Wi-fi is available in the public areas. $$$$

🏠 **Franklin Hotel** 10 Obagi St, GRA 2; ☎ 084 240183/4; www.thefranklinhotelsandsuites.com. Obagi St is an extension of Tombia St so to get here, go straight on after the Méridien (above). Another new option so everything is still very fresh, the Franklin is in a peaceful suburb & the ordinary looking white block has 52 rooms popular with oil workers. Indeed they offer a service for cleaning uniforms. There's a marble lobby, a smart bar with a stage for live music, restaurant serving both Nigerian & continental dishes, & a spacious lounge

with pillars & fat sofas. Discounts at the weekends. Rooms $$$; suites $$$$

🏠 **Mina Hotel** 23 Igbodo St, Old GRA; ☎ 084 236356–7. In a good location just off Aba Rd, the décor is still in very good condition & things work reasonably well. The 41 rooms have DSTV & fridge, & are newly painted & modern with new carpets & tiles in the bathrooms. The restaurant & bar serve Nigerian & continental food, there's a Sosoliso Airlines desk & you can arrange car hire. Two giant gens provide 24hr power & this place even has its own water-treatment plant to treat the tap water. Rates include the 15% & there are discounts at the w/end & for long-staying guests. Rooms $$; suites $$$

🏠 **Delta Hotel** 1–3 Harley St, Old GRA; ☎ 084 236650. A great budget option in a quiet area set in nice tree-filled grounds where there is plenty of parking & friendly & attentive service (they will spray your room with fly spray to attack the mossies before you retire). There's an old-fashioned but comfy bar, & the good restaurant serves some continental dishes such as chicken, coleslaw & chips. The only drawback is that the gen goes off at 22.30. Rooms have new AC units & fridges, lots of furniture & satellite TV. $

🍴 **WHERE TO EAT AND DRINK** Restaurants in Port Harcourt are of a good standard thanks to the expat presence, though prices are high to reflect the international cuisine. For cheap eats, in the Old Township on Victoria Road are lots of bars (and brothels) serving plates of hot pepper soup, and there are good *suya* stands on the corner. Exercise extreme caution in this area and stay within the confines of the brightly lit bars, but if you do go for a drink down here you'll certainly see some sights. There is a branch of **Mr Biggs** on Aggery Road.

🍴 **Amadi Creek Restaurant** in the Intel Camp, to the north of the city off the Aba Expressway near the Eastern Bypass roundabout; ⏰ 18.00–22.30 Tue–Sun. If you are an expat, you may find yourself living at the Intel Camp. Non-residents can visit the coffee shop for good cappuccino & pizza, the food shop that sells imported Italian items & the Amadi Creek Restaurant. Fully geared to expats & professionally run with a maître d', this has a cocktail lounge with grand piano & outside tables next to the camp's swimming pool, & serves up superb continental food accompanied by varied imported wines. $$$$$

🍴 **Ororo Restaurant** in the lobby of the Le Méridien Hotel (see *Where to stay*); ☎ 084 571488; ⏰ daily. A superb spot, although pricey, but it is one of the few places in Nigeria where you can get

a glass of Moet, a tot of Remy Martin or a bottle of French wine. The themed buffets & Sun lunch cost US$18 but include a soft drink & children go for half price, & there's frequently changing dishes on the à la carte menu. Even if you just pop in for coffee you need to be dressed very smartly. Watch the well-groomed polo horses trotting around the polo field, & if there is a match on you'll get a bird's-eye view from the pool terrace. Ororo means oil in Yoruba. $$$$$

🍴 **Presidential Hotel** There are several restaurants & bars here including the **Why Not** Lebanese restaurant & **4-5-6** Chinese restaurant, that both serve authentic food. The **Rivers restaurant** on the second floor is a plain hotel dining-room serving over-priced buffets of Nigerian & continental food for around US$20, though the Sun buffet brunches

✕ **Chez Alex** 143 Aba Rd; ☎ 084 232358, 235200; ⏱ 12.00–15.00, 19.00–22.30 daily. A charming restaurant run by a very extended Lebanese family, with nice décor, a long bar & candlelit tables. There's an enormous menu (though you may want to skip the brains, tongue & gizzards), with mezze items, main dishes of seafood paella, lobster or fried prawns, & cheaper oriental dishes & pizza. Wines are Italian & French. $$$

✕ **Eastern Garden** in the Air France building, 47 Aba Rd, to the side of a flyover; ⏱ 11.30–23.00 daily. This is a very stylish Chinese restaurant on two floors with big tall pillars, large windows & a packed car park. There's an enormous 16-page menu of every imaginable Chinese dish there is with lots of meat, seafood & vegetarian options. Be warned about the vicious pepper sauce on the tables. $$$

✕ **Tombia Tavern** 8 Tombia St, GRA 2; ⏱ 12.00–22.00 daily. This is an odd little place with only 4 tables & a couple of bar stools; look for a red gate as there's no sign. Nevertheless it serves up excellent & affordable Indian food, cooked from scratch so you may have to wait a while. It's best known for its delicious chicken tikka & prawn vindaloo. Takeaways are available & there's a full range of beers & spirits. $$–$$$

✕ **Mrs Jolly Singh** ☎ 084 486193, 235129. For those that do not want to venture out from their expat compound, Mrs Singh offers a delivery service of every kind of Indian meal imaginable & it's priced by weight; US$12 for a kg of chicken korma for example. $$

✕ **Choice** 107 Aba Rd; ☎ 084 572860. Another Lebanese supermarket with a restaurant next door & you may be able to change money here. There's a full deli with cheese & hams & smoked salmon, & a full range of imported food, & the plain restaurant next door has a menu of Lebanese food of mixed grills & all things meaty. The portions are huge & they also offer excellent takeaway rotisserie chicken & *shawarma* sandwiches. $–$$

✕ **Friends** and **Royal Pub** 131 Aba Rd. Cheap & seedy, with prostitutes ('nightriders') galore, but it's an atmospheric bar & disco serving Nigerian snacks & is open from 17.00 to dawn with an enormous dance floor. There's a small cover charge later in the evening. $

✕ **Park n Shop** 97 Aba Rd to the west of a flyover. A huge supermarket dealing in imported goods & similar to the branch in Lagos. There's a good bakery here for meat & cheese pies & the **Curry in a Hurry** kiosk sells Indian snacks. Further south is a similar set up at **Chanrai's** supermarket. $

PRACTICALITIES If you need to **change money**, try and approach the management of one of the supermarkets (see above) or the Hausa money changers who hang out on the street to the south of the Presidential Hotel just off Aba Road. There's also an official bureau de change at 90 Aba Road and most of the hotels change money. For **internet access** there are several spots in town, including Memoirs Cyber Café at 169 Aba Road next to the defunct Nigerian Airways office, or Xpress Internet on Aggery Road in the Old Township. The **post office** is on Station Road and the **NITEL** office is directly behind it. The office for **Rivers State Tourism** is at 37 Aba Road, a couple of blocks to the north of the Air France building. There is a sign, but if you go down the filthy corridor and actually find the office, you will first have to wake up the receptionist at his desk and ask to see the director, who will be most surprised to see you and somewhat embarrassed that he hasn't got anything to give out (as was my experience). The **British Council** is at Plot 127, Olu Obasanjo Road, GRA 2 (☎ 084 237173; 231776; *www.britishcouncil.org/nigeria*); while the **Alliance Française** is at 13 Azikiwe Rd, Old GRA (☎ 084 231408). Both offer similar services as they do in Lagos, such as libraries and language tuition.

WHAT TO SEE AND DO Again there's not much to see, but if you happen to be walking up and down Aba Road the **Isaac Boro Park**, opposite a flyover and near the Abali Motor Park, may distract you. The 5.7ha patch of green grass was named after an army officer, and it's also the location of the cenotaph of the Unknown Soldier, where there are concrete models of a tank, warplane and warship. It's a very ordinary park, but it's litter-free where people actually sit on the grass, though it's hardly peaceful being next to the flyover and the packed motor park.

The **Port Harcourt Tourist Beach** (*N100 entry*) is to the extreme east of the Old Township and overlooks an area of harbour and creek, the rubbish-infested city shorelines and a pile of shipwrecked boats. It's not a beach right next to the water, but a swath of clean sand in a park where there are plenty of tables and a couple of bars to have a beer or soft drink, and it is a popular spot for families and couples at the weekend. There is a small arts centre with the odd statue and animal skin, and obligatory portraits of local chiefs, governors and the president, plus a couple of horses that children can take short rides on, and a dreadful zoo. We saw some terrible zoos in Nigeria but this was the worst. It was overgrown, full of rubbish, all the enclosures were falling down and it contained only two dead-looking crocodiles, one insane baboon and one ostrich that constantly ran up and down in a concrete pen about one metre wide. Shocking. Despite the zoo, which you can easily avoid as it's behind a wall, the tourist beach is not a bad place for a drink in the afternoon. Back on Aggery Road, look out for the Saros building, an imposing white block, which was Ken Saro-Wiwa's publishing house and where he spent much of his time.

THE NIGER DELTA

To the south and east of Port Harcourt are the numerous islands separated by the ever-expansive creeks and waterways of the Niger Delta. It covers some 70,000 km^2 and makes up around 7.5% of Nigeria's land mass. The forested creeks and khaki waters are full of mangroves that are the habitat of storks and kingfishers, while the delta people travel to and fro in canoes with tiny sails, fishing or moving around between the small settlements. Larger, more colourful slower boats packed with people and cargo and crates of Coke and beer wend their way from village to village. In contrast, tugs and launches pull the big pieces of equipment needed at the oil installations and oil rigs, such as cranes and the oil pipelines that carve tracks through the forests.

The most accessible points in the delta are Bonny and Brass islands and the city of Warri. In the 18th and 19th centuries Bonny and Brass were powerful sites for slave exportation from West Africa, and later important bases for the British colonists, and on both there are still some old colonial buildings and cemeteries featuring headstones of past missionaries and colonial officers. Further west on the road to Benin City is Warri, another port and collection point for oil with a large refinery. Today, the region is witnessing the worst of the delta violence, and many of the delta waterways and remote island settlements are controlled by ethnic militia groups. Get up-to-the-minute advice before heading into the delta.

BONNY From 1885 to 1894 Bonny was the administrative centre of the British Oil Rivers Protectorate. It declined in the 20th century but was revived after 1961, when its port was modernised as the export point for oil, and today it is the principal port for the Niger Delta. It is home to massive oil installations for international oil companies such as Shell, Mobil, Chevron, Agip and Elf, as well as the US$4 billion liquefied natural gas project, which was built in 1999 and at the time was Africa's single biggest engineering project. Like Port Harcourt, there are large residential areas for oil and gas workers. Once there, sights include fishing villages, oil installations, shipwrecks on the shores, and the hundreds of brooding oil tankers waiting out to sea to dock at the pipelines to get their bellies filled with oil.

Getting there and away If it's considered safe to go, then direct ferries to Bonny go from Creek Road in the Old Township of Port Harcourt and take just over an hour.

Open boats with outboard engines depart when full from 05.30 to 19.00 and cost around N700 each way. Port Harcourt's Old Township is not renowned for its safety and there are always a few unsavoury characters hanging around. It's a heaving area of trade in large goods such as timber, steel and aluminium sheets. It's also the region of the city where it's rumoured that the militants are based, and at the time of writing the government was threatening to bulldoze parts of the Old Township.

BRASS Brass is located at the very tip of the delta to the southwest of Port Harcourt. The village is on the northern creek side of an island and the sea is on the other side. It's populated by the Nembe people and was named Brass because when the British arrived a colonial officer grabbed a woman by the arm and asked a little too eagerly, 'Where are we?' The woman replied 'Barasi' ('leave me alone' in the Nembe language) and the name stuck. Around the jetty there are a couple of old colonial buildings, in the same architectural style as the Lugard houses found in Lokoja and elsewhere, built on stilts because of the reptiles and flooding. But today they are hopelessly falling down. To the east of the jetty a track leads to the older fishing village, which is much more primitive than the main section of Brass that has seen some modern building in recent years. You may see the odd Italian expat here, as Brass is home to a big Agip oil installation that is Italian-owned.

Everyone is very friendly here and you can wander around the village alongside very large cows with enormous horns, and chat to the people. Brass's enormous church is a very smart affair built in 2003 with a shiny aluminium roof, which is full to the brim with shiny headdresses on a Sunday. Opposite is the village's football pitch, where you can watch future Nwankwo Kanus battle it out on a Saturday afternoon, in full football strip but with no shoes.

Accommodation on the island is in ad hoc rooms in people's houses and *okada* drivers will take you from where the boat lands to places, but they don't serve food. Near the football pitch is a bar with a pool table and there are others in the back streets, some of which do very basic food-is-ready. In the boat house is a small café serving tea-eggs-and-bread in the mornings and food-is-ready in the afternoons. Opposite the boat jetty is a line of chop and drink stalls for snacks – look out for the skewers of deep-fried palm tree maggots.

Getting there and away Again if it's considered safe to go, boats go to Brass from Yenagoa, the capital of Baylesa State, approximately 120km to the west of Port Harcourt and halfway to Warri. You can get a minibus from Port Harcourt for around N300. Once at Yenagoa, a sprawling commercial town, things start to get confusing. Yenagoa is on the Orashi River, a tributary of the Niger, which begins to spread its arms here and turn into a number of creeks that get wider and wider until they reach the sea.

From the motor park in the centre of town you need to head to the boat office at the new market at Nembe. *Okadas* are the only vehicles that will get into the densely packed market and the boat office is right in the middle of it. It's so hectic you'll have to walk the last few metres and get the *okada* drivers to park their bikes and go with you because you'll never find it by yourself. In the shed is a desk for the Brass boat that goes-when-full and costs around N1,500 each way. Other boats go to Abk and Silga, other villages in the Niger Delta. The man at the desk will ring a hand bell when the boat is ready to depart, and there is a line of benches to sit on and wait, or you can wander around the market (listening out for the bell).

The motor-boat ride to Brass takes about 1½ hours. It goes very fast, and once out in the wider creeks closer to the sea it's a very bumpy and painful ride, so you'll need to hang on as there are no life jackets, and it's also very squashed. If it rains the boat driver pulls a tarpaulin over the passengers. It is not a comfortable journey.

WARRI Warri is 205km northwest of Port Harcourt in Delta State. According to legend, a Benin prince called Ginuwa founded Warri in the 15th century, and by the 17th century it was independent of Benin, and its natural harbour was visited by Portuguese Roman Catholic missionaries and subsequently served as the base for Portuguese slave traders. Home to the Itshekiri, Urhobo, Ijaw and Isoko-speaking peoples of the Niger Delta, it became a major trading centre and relations were good with the Portuguese. Many of Warri's residents converted to Catholicism, others assumed Portuguese names, some visited or sent their children to schools in Portugal, and one of the Itshekiri kings married a Portuguese woman.

After the slave trade was abolished, the British replaced the Portuguese as trade partners, and by the 19th century it had become wealthy in the palm oil trade. Britain was determined to keep her claim on the Niger Delta and, after a peaceful treaty with local leaders failed, Britain resorted to using force when in 1894 they attacked the most powerful of the Itshekiri rulers, Chief Nana. This particular battle featured one of the earliest uses by the British of the newly invented automatic, self-firing guns, which were later to become known as machine guns, against which the people of Warri didn't stand a chance. Chief Nana was captured and exiled, and Itshekiriland came under British administration with Warri as the regional capital.

The subsequent British conquest of the city of Benin three years later opened up the western Niger Delta for British commerce in palm oil, timber and rubber, and Warri port was developed to transport goods back to Europe. On return voyages, ships would bring back consumer and household goods from Europe. The people of Warri acted as middlemen and distributed these goods by canoe through the creeks and waterways before the British built roads between Warri and Sapele and Benin City.

Today Warri is still a major sea port and an oil and steel city. Oil and natural gas fields are prolific in the area, there's a refinery here, and Warri is also home to the headquarters of the Nigerian Petroleum Institute. Refined oil is transported via pipeline from here to northern Nigeria. There's also an enormous steel plant that sprawls across the Aladja district of Warri, and a major petrochemical complex producing plastics, pharmaceuticals and paints.

Getting there and away Aero Contractors (✆ *053 250713, 256279; www.acn.aero*) has daily flights in each direction between Warri and Lagos (50 minutes) and Port Harcourt (35 minutes).

CALABAR

The capital of Cross Rivers State in the extreme southeastern corner of Nigeria, Calabar is a pleasant town in a beautiful setting high on a hill above a curve in the Calabar River. It was originally called Old Calabar to distinguish it from another town called Kalabari. It has a long history of being Nigeria's eastern port on an estuary of the Gulf of Guinea, and an estimated third of the slaves that left Nigeria were transported through Calabar. The town is also the cultural centre for the Efik people who dabbled in the slave trade as middlemen. It's made up of the old Efik settlements of Creek Town (Obio Oko), Duke Town (Atakpa), Old Town (Obutong) and Henshaw Town (Nsidung).

Calabar is well known as the home of the Scottish missionary Mary Slessor, who arrived in 1878 from the United Free Church of Scotland. It grew as an important Niger Delta trading state in the 19th century, thanks to the lucrative palm oil trade, and today rubber and timber pass through Calabar's port; tyre manufacturer Dunlop has rubber plantations around Calabar. It's surrounded by saltwater swamps and dense tropical forest, and the markets are full of fish, pineapples, bananas, plantains, cassava and palm oil. For a short time (1893–1906) it was the capital of the British Protectorate of Southern Nigeria, before the capital was moved to Lagos, and was the region's principal port during the early colonial days before it was eclipsed by Port Harcourt.

The older part of town along the Calabar River has some beautiful colonial buildings but they are in various stages of decay. These were shipped from Liverpool frame by frame, with the carpenters, and were not only used by the colonial offices; many of the local chiefs liked the British architecture so much that they ordered their own houses and period furniture from England and this architecture became the hallmark of Old Calabar. These chiefs even took British names: there were the Dukes, the Jameses, and the Henshaws. The best place to explore Calabar's history is in the excellent museum (see page 214). By contrast, Calabar today is also home to two interesting conservation organisations that are doing something worthwhile to help Nigeria's primates in the nearby Cross River forests.

More recently, and rather incredulously, Calabar is in the throes of constructing the largest duty free zone in West Africa: an enormous project called Tinapa, which when completed hopes to attract shoppers and traders from the whole region. This is the brain child of former Cross River State Governor Donald Duke, who has done much to support tourism and investment in the state in recent years. Along with Tinapa, he's upgraded the Obudu Cattle Ranch (see page 225), which includes the building of a state-of-the-art cable car, instigated the construction of two forest canopy walkways in the state, and has organised the annual Calabar Carnival on Boxing Day, which is a wonderful experience with over 10,000 colourfully dressed participants.

At a local level Duke was a well liked governor who still has tremendous support, and in 2006 the BBC reported that he was the only state governor in Nigeria not to be investigated by the Economic and Financial Crimes Commission on issues of corruption. Under his eight-year governance of Cross River State, schools were overhauled and text books were made available, health facilities improved, over 90% of the state was electrified, and in Calabar and other towns, roads were fixed and trees planted. The campaign against HIV/AIDS in Cross River State is the most intensive in Nigeria.

Calabar born and bred, Duke held two terms of office as governor but had to step down in May 2007 as the constitution allows only for two consecutive terms. He stood as a presidential candidate in the 2007 elections and his presidential campaign was anchored on the platform of visible and credible achievements of his administration of Cross River State. However, he stepped down from the race in line with the People's Democratic Party's policy of promoting a candidate from the north (previous president, Obasanjo, was from the south). He's so highly regarded in the southeast, it would have been interesting to know if he would have won Nigeria's presidency. Although he's not governor any more, he is unlikely to go away quietly.

Finally, on an environmental note and thanks to another Donald Duke initiative, while not being totally rubbish free, Calabar has been named the cleanest city in Nigeria, and the state government is doing something to address the rubbish problem. Here I saw a rare creature to Nigeria indeed – a rubbish truck!

GETTING THERE AND AWAY

By air Calabar's Margaret Ekpo Airport is accessed from IBB Way and is very centrally located. Margaret Ekpo was a leading Nigerian women's activist in the 1950s who was born in Calabar, and the airport was named after her in 1991. Not surprisingly, there has been a recent spurt of airlines extending their schedules to Calabar in light of the Tinapa project and also because of the closure of Port Harcourt Airport. There is talk of building a new airport to meet the demand of visitors expected to Tinapa in the future.

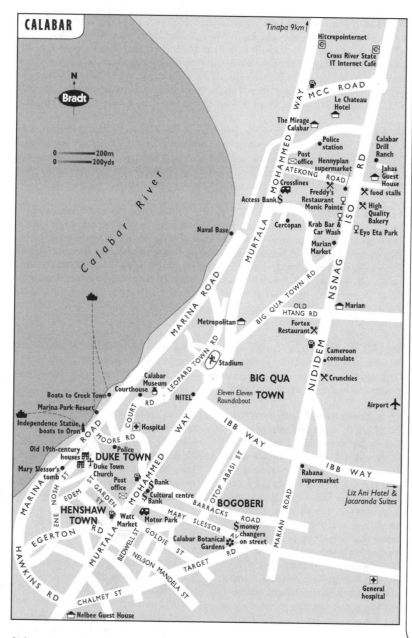

CALABAR

Tinapa 9km↑

Hitcrepointernet

Cross River State
IT Internet Café

MCC ROAD

Le Chateau
Hotel

The Mirage
Calabar

Police
station

Calabar
Drill
Ranch

Post
office
Hennyplan
supermarket

Jahas
Guest
House

ATEKONG ROAD

food stalls

Crosslines

Freddy's
Restaurant
Monic Pointe

High
Quality
Bakery

Access Bank

Cercopan

Krab Bar &
Car Wash

Eyo Eta Park

Marian
Market

Naval Base

BIG QUA TOWN RD

OLD
HTANG RD

Marian

Metropolitan

Fortex
Restaurant

Cameroon
consulate

LEOPARD TOWN RD

Stadium

BIG QUA

Crunchies

Calabar
Museum

TOWN

Boats to Creek Town

Courthouse

NITEL

Eleven Eleven
Roundabout

Airport

Marina Park Resort

Independence Statue,
boats to Oron

Hospital

Old 19th-century
houses

MOORE RD

DUKE TOWN

IBB WAY

IBB WAY

Mary Slessor's
tomb

Duke Town
Church

Post
office
Bank

Rabana
supermarket

Liz Ani Hotel &
Jacaranda Suites

Cultural centre
Bank

BOGOBERI

HENSHAW
TOWN

Watt
Market

Motor Park

MARY SLESSOR ROAD

money
changers
on street

EGERTON RD

Calabar Botanical
Gardens

HAWKINS RD

NELSON MANDELA ST

TARGET RD

CHALMEY ST

General
hospital

Nelbee Guest House

N

Bradt

0 ———— 200m
0 ———— 200yds

Calabar River

MOHAMMED WAY

MURTALA MOHAMMED ROAD

MARINA ROAD

NSNAG

NSIDEM

NSO RD

COURT RD

GARDEN ST

EDEM ST

ENE NOSH ST

MOHAMMED WAY

OTOP ABASI ST

BARRACKS

GOLDIE ST

BEDWELL ST

MURTALA RD

Southeastern Nigeria CALABAR

7

Airlines These airlines have flights between Calabar and Lagos at least once a day.

ADC Airlines ☎ 087 234477, airport desk;
www.adcairlines.com
Aero Contractors ☎ 080 5555 0556; www.acn.aero;
also has a daily flight between Calabar & the NAF
base in Port Harcourt.

Arik Air ☎ Lagos 01 496 6606; www.arikair.com;
also has daily flights between Calabar & Abuja.
Virgin Nigeria ☎ Lagos 01 460 0505;
www.virginnigeria.com

211

By road Minibuses and bush taxis arrive and depart from the **motor park** on Mary Slessor Avenue, for vehicles to Aba and Port Harcourt to the east and Ikom, Obudu and Ogoja to the north. It is advisable to arrive early, as we waited nearly two hours for a bush taxi to go-when-full from Calabar to Ikom, which is not that far away. Coming into Calabar vehicles may also drop off at Watt Market. The private bus company Crosslines (which specialises in three-across) has its own terminal just north of the Metropolitan Hotel, and has a service to Port Harcourt.

By boat Boats go to and from the wharf near the independence statue on Marina Road to Creek Town and to Oron (for onward boats to Cameroon see below). These are mostly motorised canoes that go-when-full, and the boat yard here is very similar to a typical motor park surrounded by stalls and food-is-ready joints. Both services cost little more than N100 and you can request a life jacket.

GETTING AROUND The original Old Calabar is split from the more modern areas by Murtala Mohammed Way, on which Watt Market is at the centre of things. To the west of this road are the old townships and busy wharfs along the river, where it is quite congested, so this area is best explored by *okada* or by foot, though it's fairly hilly. Getting around Calabar is straightforward enough, and shared taxis and minibuses run up and down Murtala Mohammed Way and Ndidem Nsang Iso Road, on the modern side of town, which are the two main arteries of the city, for little more than N30. The latter is also generally referred to as Marian Road, which it turns into further south.

WHERE TO STAY The choice of accommodation in Calabar is improving considerably and the Tinapa project is planning to build more hotels in the future. The infrastructure in Calabar is generally better than elsewhere in the country, so power and water are fairly consistent.

Metropolitan Hotel Murtala Muhammed Way; 087 230913; www.metropolitancalabar.com. Formerly Calabar's state hotel & built in the 1970s on the main road leading into town, this was sold to a private owner in 2005 who completely refurbished it in 2007. It's now the best & most expensive hotel in Calabar with 150 smart rooms in the main block or in chalets out the back near the swimming pool. Although there is a lot of concret, décor & furnishings are brand new & imported from overseas, there's a cocktail bar, very good but pricey restaurant serving buffet breakfasts & lunches & set continental dinners, or there's a separate Chinese restaurant. Facilities include gym, clinic, hair salon, internet access, car hire & foreign exchange. Rooms $$$$; suites $$$$$

The Mirage Calabar 230 State Housing Estate, MCC Rd; 0806 3537448; www.themirage calabar.com. Spacious, clean & tasteful rooms with large en-suite bathrooms, DSTV, wireless internet, room service, smart wooden furnishings, African paintings on the walls & a gym. Buffets in the restaurant cost around N2,000, plus there's an

additional Chinese restaurant with a limited menu but good food, & a karaoke bar & nightclub. Rooms $$; suites $$$$

Jacaranda Suites Plots C2–C6 G.D Henshaw Residential Layout, off Atimbo Rd; 087 239666; www.jacarandacalabar.com. Only a 3min drive from the airport, this offers very pleasant accommodation in 14 well-furnished rooms with DSTV & internet, set in attractive surroundings with a pool & outdoor thatched cocktail bar. There's a restaurant & bar serving continental dishes including pizzas, burgers, chips & salads, plus good fresh fish pepper soup. Rooms $$; suites $$$

Le Chateau Hotel Plot 56 MCC Rd; 087 238823; www.ths-lechateau.com. Set in a low white-washed building with cool arches, the 30 rooms have DSTV, clean bathrooms & motel-style parking outside the rooms. There's a small restaurant serving a few continental dishes, a bar, car hire services & laundry. $$

Liz Ani Hotel 12A Atimbo Rd; 0803 886 1130/543 9433. Basic but adequate & clean 11 rooms with AC, running water, a bar, & a laundry & simple plates of soup & starch on offer. $$

Marian Hotel Ltd 125 Old Ikang Rd; ☎ 087 220233/4. Affordable & comfortable 38 rooms & 4 suites in a newly painted block, with DSTV & secure parking in a compound. Nigerian & continental food is available for N1,200 a plate, & they can also organise car hire. $$

Jahas Guest House 107 Marian Rd; no phone. A dilapidated building, but the rooms inside are just about passable, with AC, local TV, leaky fridge & big bathrooms with buckets; it's in a quiet area close to the Drill Monkey Ranch. There are only 6 rooms that go from US$15. There's no food but they sell drinks. $

Nelbee Guest House 5 Dan Achibong St, off Calabar Rd; ☎ 087 232684. A good & friendly budget option close to the market, with parking in a compound, & a small restaurant serving up a dish of the day, & if you give them a bit of notice they will come up with something continental. It's Muslim-owned so there's no alcohol. Rooms are neat & clean with fridges, DSTV, running water in the showers, & are excellent value from only the equivalent of US$23. $

WHERE TO EAT AND DRINK The **Rabana Supermarket** (*56 Marian Rd*) sells some imported goods such as booze, tins and juice, plus useful items like razors and batteries. A similar store **Hennyplan** (*140 Ndidem Usang Iso Rd;* ☎ *0803 3925272*) has a more extensive range of imported products at slightly lower prices. **High Quality Bakery** (*102 Ndidem Usang Iso Rd*) serves a large range of breads, pies and cakes from N100. The best fish in town is available from chop stalls at the junction between Nididem Nsnag and Atekong roads to the north of town, where you can order a tasty fish with fried plantain for under N1,000. The fish is available to take away or you can ask for it to be served over at the **Monic Pointe** bush bar opposite, where beer and soft drinks are available. The best place to get *suya* is **Bogoberi**, where there are many stalls, each as good as the next, serving until the early hours.

Freddy's Restaurant 90 Atekong Dr; ☎ 087 232821; ⏰ 11.30–15.00 lunch Mon–Sat, 18.30–23.00 dinner daily. The best restaurant in town & an expat haunt, with a good atmosphere, nicely dressed tables, darts board, big, well-stocked bar, & DSTV. There's a long menu of Lebanese mezzes, steaks, *shawarmas*, kebabs, fish & prawns & a meal here for two with drinks will cost in the region of N5,000. $$$

Crunchies 39 Ndidem Usang Iso Rd; ⏰ 09.00–19.00. A good choice for fast food either to

eat in or takeaway, including fried chicken, *moi moi*, *jollof* rice, meat pies, kebabs, & you should be prepared to wait 15 mins, French fries. $

Fortex Restaurant Ioto Effiom St just off Ndidem Nsang Iso Rd. Good & cheap Nigerian food during the day in spotless surroundings with bright white plastic tables inside & on a small terrace. It serves a selection of garri, pounded yam, soups, fried rice & snails for as little as N500 a dish, but no alcohol. $

NIGHTLIFE Near the Marian Market on Ndidem Usang Iso Road is the **Eyo Eta Park** run by the Calabar Lions Club, where there are a couple of thumping outdoor bars selling beer and good *suya*. One of the best places for dancing with a truly Nigerian atmosphere is the **Krab Bar and Car Wash** (*98 Ndidem Usang Iso Rd*), a vast outdoor bar where you can conveniently get your car washed at the same time, and it's open until at least 02.00. This place is packed to the gills and you can get hot and spicy *suya* with your cold beer. After Krab has closed, it is possible to continue dancing at the **Pinnacle Nightclub** at the Mirage Hotel until 05.00 (*Wed, Fri and Sat; N1,000*). The atmosphere inside is smoky and hot but it can be a lot of fun. There is also a **karaoke bar** on site and the outside **Bom Bom Bar** serves good *shawarmas* but is often frequented by prostitutes and can be rather rowdy late at night.

PRACTICALITIES There are numerous internet cafés in town. **Hitecpro** (*140 Odukpani Rd*) offers wireless internet either on their computers or your own laptop. It has constant power and you can buy a cold drink and an imported chocolate bar to snack on while you browse the web. At the **Cross River State IT Village Internet Café** (*Woman's Development Centre, 37 Ekpo Archibong, Old Parliamentary Village Rd*) wireless facilities are also available and there's a coffee shop/restaurant serving starch and stew. At the **Metropolitan Hotel**, non-guests can surf for free providing they purchase something from the bar.

There are two **post offices** on Murtala Mohammed Way while the **NITEL** office is at 2 Club Road near the stadium, a few metres to the south of the Metropolitan Hotel. Most of the banks in Calabar **change money** but **Access Bank** at 45 Murtela Mohammed Way (✆ 087 238873-8) often offers the best rates. It's also possible to change currency with any of a number of Hausa money changers at **Bogoberi**, just off Mary Slessor Avenue.

The **Cameroon Consulate** is at 21 Ndidam Usang Iso Road (✆ 087 222782; ⊕ 09.00–15.30 Mon–Fri; pick up visas, 15.50–17.00). If you are travelling on in West Africa you need to write a letter to apply for the application form saying what you are doing and where you are going; the man at the gate will tell you what to write and will then hand the letter in, to be given to the consulate to read. Once the letter is approved, they give you two application forms, which you fill in and hand back with three passport photos; you'll need to buy a stamp for a few naira. The fee is currently N13,500 or CFA50,000 (approximately US$100). If you are in a vehicle you need to present photocopies of the vehicle's paperwork such as the carnet, etc. In theory visas should be processed in 48 hours, but it may be less if you go early and speak nicely to the officials. Be reasonably pushy (if the right person isn't there, politely ask them to go and find the right person).

WHAT TO SEE AND DO
The city
The Calabar Museum The **Calabar Museum** (⊕ 09.00–18.00 daily; entry N50) is housed in a beautifully restored old colonial building, built on top of a hill between Duke Town and Old Town, that was erected in 1884 for the British Council for the Bight of Benin and Biafra. Prefabricated and shipped from England, it is one of the finest examples of colonial architecture in the country, and is beyond doubt Nigeria's best museum.

From 1884 the building was the seat of the Oil Rivers and Niger Coast Protectorate, then from 1914 the Old Calabar Province, then in the 1950s it was used as a guesthouse. After the civil war it became the office of the new Southeastern State, and was fully renovated in 1986 to become the Calabar Museum. The building is painted a bright yellow and has wonderful wooden floors, shutters and original fittings. Unlike other Nigerian museums, which are often stuffed full of anything they can get hold of, here the items have been selected carefully for their relevance to the Calabar region, and there are some valuable items with weighty historical importance. It tells the story of old Calabar, colonial rule, the making of the Nigerian protectorate, palm oil production and export, and the road to independence. There are many knowledgeable staff and a surprising number of Nigerian visitors.

At the entrance is a craft and bookshop where you pay your entry fee. The library at the side of the museum is remarkable, and contains all the original paperwork, some of it in near-perfect condition, of the colonial office throughout the era that the British were here. These include the British parliamentary paper sent out yearly to Calabar on the roles of the civil service and police, and announcing any new or amended laws that were to be used to govern the colony; a set of *All England Law Reports* for 1951–70; and the *Nigerian Gazette* for 1926–55, which covered promotions, leave of absences, and new appointments in the colonial service. You can just pick these up and flick through them, when by rights they should be in the museum proper.

In the grounds of the museum is an old red British pillar box, and an old 1848 bell that was first used aboard ship and was rung to bring people together for instructions. Later it was erected at the site in Calabar where it was used to signify the start and finish of a working day in Old Calabar; many of the trading stations on the Calabar River had their own bells. The exhibits in the museum are excellently presented, but be warned that if the power fails the interior rooms are plunged into darkness.

The first thing you are likely to see is an early 20th-century motorbike (perhaps one of Nigeria's first *okadas*), which was generally used around Calabar by the missionaries. Downstairs there's a very good hall on the production of palm oil that was the 'red gold' of southern Nigeria for the first half of the 20th century; the most successful period was during World War II, when palm oil was used as industrial oil for military machines. On display are pots used to carry the palm oil, which were inspected on the beach for quality before being sealed and taken to the waiting ships. Young boys collected the palm husks from 10m palms and they were boiled until the oil floated to the surface and could be scooped off.

There's a selection of money on display that's been used in the region over the centuries, including cowrie shells, 17th-century manilas of copper and brass, flat iron bars used in the early 19th century (when you reputedly needed 36 of them to buy a slave), and a very rare Republic of Biafra one pound note. Other displays cover the slave trade, the arrival of the Portuguese, the British penetration of Nigeria, and trade on the Calabar River. There are some original documents and memoirs of the trade ship captains, some 19th-century furniture (including an 1885 organ), some pictures of the Queen's 1956 visit to Calabar when she visited Mary Slessor's grave, and a hall dedicated to the culture of the local Efik people.

From the upstairs rooms are fabulous views of the old town and the river, and it's not difficult to imagine the colonial officers surveying the river full of boats carrying palm oil on to waiting ships. In the grounds is a bush bar, which serves *suya*, fried plantain, pepper soup, and roasted fish and chicken, and you can sit in the huts and watch football on TV surrounded by nice gardens and trimmed hedges.

Marina Road and around From the museum you can stroll to the river down Court Road, past the old brick courthouse, the hospital and the Governor's Lodge, a very elegant white building with a green roof surrounded by manicured gardens. Towards the bottom of Court Road look out for a restored colonial house that is now the headquarters for the Crosslines bus company, and next door, rather amusingly, is the Basic Detective School.

Marina Park Resort is another new development on the riverfront opposite Moore Road (*N100*), where there are a number of tables and chairs scattered around the tree-lined lawns facing the river – an ideal spot for a picnic. There is also a clutch of bush bars, children's fairground rides, and a 200-seater amphitheatre for local performances.

On Marina Road next to the river are more old warehouses with shuttered windows, and an **independence memorial** with a lion on top. This is an atmospheric place to walk and everyone is busy on the wharfs hauling fish in or waiting for boats to cross the river; there are few bars to sit at, distinguished by the Star and Maltina flags. From Marina Road you can climb the hill again at Edem Street, to the 1904 **Duke Town Church** established by Presbyterian missionaries, where you'll see its still-working clock on the steeple, and its bell across the street. On Boco Street, the next road back down the hill at No 19, is a dilapidated old 19th-century pre-fabricated British building; look out for the brass wind chime and weathercock on the top. Around the corner of Enendem Street is another similar building, again hopelessly falling down, which was once the home of Chief Ekpo Bassey, who ordered the building from England.

Mary Slessor's tomb and cottage At the top of Enendem Street is the **Mary Slessor Memorial Tomb**, in a nicely tended graveyard with tall palm trees overlooking the river, though you may find the gate locked. Mary Slessor was one of Nigeria's most influential missionaries in the 19th century. Her tombstone notes her Scottish roots and describes her as the heroine who ended the killing of twins and their mothers in the Calabar region, a practice which once used to go on among the highly superstitious Efik people. **Mary Slessor's cottage** is in Ekenge across the river from Calabar, and it's a fine, double-storied house with an outside staircase and wooden doors and windows, and a roof made from corrugated iron sheets, that has been reasonably well preserved. Apart from the outside of the house, there's nothing to see, but you can get there by catching a boat from the wharf on Marina Road.

Watt Market Back in town, **Watt Market** is a huge outdoor market which opens daily and sells everything from home wares and beauty products to electrical goods, car parts, meat and cloth. This is also the place to have your hair braided or have a manicure. The smaller **Marion Market** is also worth a visit and has an excellent fruit and vegetable market every Thursday.

The Botanic Garden The old Calabar **Botanic Garden** (*corner of Target Rd and Mary Slessor Ave;* ⊕ *11.00–23.30 daily; free entry*) was established in Nigeria by the Royal Botanic Gardens, Kew, in 1893. The Cross River State Forestry Department converted the garden into a zoo in the 1970s for a brief spell, but then the grounds were derelict for about 20 years. In 2004 the Iroko Foundation, a UK-based NGO, together with Cercopan (see below), began to rehabilitate the gardens, and again the design for the layout came from Kew Gardens in London. (You can find more details on the website *www.irokofoundation.org.*) When completely finished, the new garden will incorporate a nature trail, medicinal plant nursery, primate rehabilitation facilities and an environmental education centre, and will educate Nigerians about the endangered African rainforests of Cross River State. For now you can wander around the lawn and buy drinks, fish, *suya* and goat's head pepper soup and eat them either at the café or at any of the benches that are dotted around.

Tinapa Calabar's newest development is Tinapa (*www.tinapa.com*), which has been built on a 68ha block on the riverbank several kilometres to the north of town and one kilometre away from the port. This is a huge and ambitious project, which will eventually cover a vast indoor area exceeding 80,000m^2, and was the brain child of former Cross River State Governor Donald Duke. Its estimated final cost is US$320 million. There is an incredible list of what is planned for the site, a joint venture between the state, the government and private investment: a huge duty-free shopping centre, both retail and wholesale (it is expected that many of the traders will be from China) with a food court and parking for 3,000 cars (this has been largely completed); and an 'entertainment strip' with five restaurants, a casino, a cinema complex, a ten-pin bowling alley, an arts and crafts village, a nightclub, a 300-room hotel, a wave park, tennis and volleyball courts and two film studios, which it is hoped will attract Nollywood filmmakers. A monorail is also planned between the complex and the airport.

This is just phase 1; phases 2 and 3 include a whole array of things like clay pigeon shooting, quad bike tracks and an exotic bird aviary! At the time of writing, the initial construction of the shopping centre had been completed, but the rest is a building site. Like the new shopping centres in Lagos, the anchor tenants are likely to be South African brands, and Shoprite, the large supermarket chain, is to be one of the the first to open a store.

Around Calabar

Calabar Drill Monkey Ranch The Drill Monkey Ranch (✆ *087 234310, 0903 5921262;* e *drill@hyperia.com;* ⊕ *09.00–17.00 daily; no entry fee but a donation is greatly appreciated*) is a rehabilitation centre and captive-breeding programme to establish a viable captive population in natural-sized groups and re-introduce drill monkeys to the wild. To get to the ranch turn off Ndidem Usang Iso Road at the Atekong Drive junction and follow the road behind the Jahas Guest House around to the left. Not all *okada* drivers know where it is and may automatically take you to Cercopan (below). It is run by Pandrillus, an NGO directed by Peter Jenkins and Liza Gadsby, and is the most successful primate captive-breeding programme in the world. The couple got to Nigeria in the 1980s during their own tour of West Africa by Land Rover, and after several years of research started Pandrillus in 1991. Their first drill

DRILL MONKEYS

Drill monkeys, *Mandrillus leucophaeus*, are short-tailed rainforest monkeys that survive only in Cross River State, Nigeria, in southwestern Cameroon, and on Bioko Island, Equatorial Guinea, and they are one of Africa's most endangered primates. Drills should not be confused with the more common mandrill, *Mandrillus sphinx*, found from southern Cameroon down to Gabon and the Congo Basin. Male mandrills have bright red and blue faces, while the male drill has a smooth black face, but otherwise they look fairly similar. Groups are led by an alpha male who is similar in size and shape to a large male baboon, and can reach over 40kg.

Drills are impressive creatures, especially the males with their bright fuchsia and purple skin, beautiful grey fur and 7cm fangs, and defined white frame around their faces that is displayed when the males reach adulthood; similar to a dominant male gorilla becoming a silverback. Unlike most monkeys, drills are semi-terrestrial and spend much of their time on the ground searching for roots, insects and leaves, and they climb trees in search of fruit and to sleep at night. They are semi-nomadic, travelling long distances in the forest, perhaps following fruiting seasons of certain trees. They communicate with each other using facial and vocal expressions, and like most primates they live in highly social groups of 15–30 animals.

On mainland Africa, the natural range of drill monkeys is only about 40,000km^2, about the same size as Switzerland, an area that is frequently at the mercy of loggers, hunters, farmers and encroaching development. Hunting for bushmeat is the biggest threat to their survival, and as most of this trade is commercial (not just to feed a hunter's family but to provide bushmeat for cash at local markets) then hunters kill as many animals as they can. It's not known for sure how many drills remain in the wild, but the population is certainly fewer than 10,000 and possibly as low as only 3,000. On Bioko Island in Equatorial Guinea, numbers are put at only 500. In zoos in Europe and the USA, drills number only about 60 and they have bred poorly. In the wild, female drills give birth to only one infant a year at most. It's against the law to hunt drills in both Nigeria and Cameroon, but laws are difficult to enforce, even in the protected areas of national parks. In reality, drills in these areas do not receive effective protection from being poached out of existence forever.

was a female named Calabar who was found in a shoebox in a bush bar with a mangled finger that had been chewed by a rat, and who is now the mother of seven and grandmother of five, and is presently enjoying her retirement at the Calabar ranch.

The project has a total population of 262, which represents 70% of all the world's captive drills. The first drill was born at the ranch in 1994, and since then over 200 drills have been born to mothers that arrived as orphans. Most of the drills that turn up at the centre are donated by local people, or by park rangers who liberate them from hunters after their mothers have been shot. Two were recovered from Asia, where they had been taken by international smugglers. In 1996 the first drill group was taken by helicopter to their new home at Afi Mountain Drill Ranch on the edge of Afi Mountain Wildlife Sanctuary in the Cross River region, north of Calabar, and released into a solar-powered electric enclosure of naturally forested drill habitat (a visit to Afi is covered on page 223). There are five such enclosures at Afi for five separate groups of drills, and one family lives at the Calabar ranch.

The Calabar and Afi ranches also provide a home to orphaned chimpanzees and have a total of 28 individuals. The 24 biggest and oldest (aged 5–24 years) live in their own spacious natural forest enclosure at Afi, while the younger ones are cared for in Calabar until they are self-sufficient enough to make the move to Afi. Chimpanzees are again highly threatened in Nigeria, and the project offers needy Nigerian chimps a chance to live with their own kind, but they are not allowed to breed. Unlike the drills, which are bred simply to save the species, chimpanzees, once partially habituated to humans, are more difficult to return completely to the wild and breeding chimps in captivity would fill limited space needed for wild-orphaned chimps. Two of the young chimps currently at the Calabar Drill Ranch were found in a box at Calabar Motor Park.

The Pandrillus project has done much to educate local people at Afi and Calabar and has taught them that it is not socially and environmentally acceptable to kill endangered primates; it has worked with various levels of government to enforce existing laws which protect wildlife. The project is solely funded by donations, large and small. It has no regular income and non-Nigerian staff such as Liza and Peter work for free, gainfully employing 42 Nigerian staff on a salary. Long-term financial support for the project is seriously needed. Future projects include establishing another 20ha enclosure at the Afi Drill Ranch for chimpanzees and to prepare the first drill group for complete release back into the wild. The Pandrillus Foundation in Oregon in the USA helps raise funds to support the projects in Africa. Contact them if you would like to make a donation (e *pandrillus@earthlink.net*). The ranch accepts volunteers on placements, but applicants should have proven skills that can help the project.

At the Calabar ranch there is always someone around to show you the drills and chimpanzees, and you will undeniably have an informative and educational visit. If you want to stay at Afi Mountain Drill Ranch, you will also need to arrange this here.

Cercopan Primate Sanctuary Calabar's other excellent primate sanctuary, Cercopan, is at 4 Ishie Lane off Murtala Muhammed Way, behind Access Bank (e *info@cercopan.org; www.cercopan.org;* ⊕ *09.00–17.00 daily; no entry fee but a donation is very much appreciated*). Founded in 1995 as a non-profit NGO involved in primate protection, rainforest conservation, education and research, it offers sanctuary to orphaned monkeys that have been victims of habitat loss and the ever-increasing bushmeat trade. Whereas the Drill Ranch is home to drills and chimpanzees, Cercopan is home to guenons and mangabeys – both indigenous to the tropical forests of West Africa.

The project currently has six species – Sclater's guenon, only found in Nigeria between the Cross and Niger rivers and highly endangered; Preuss's guenon, only found around the Obudu Plateau in Nigeria, Mount Cameroon and on the island of Bioko; red-eared guenon; putty-nose guenon; mona guenon; and red-capped mangabeys. Most are orphans whose mothers were shot for bushmeat or sold as pets, and were either donated or were confiscated by park rangers, though some of the animals were born here. Leo, a mona guenon, was the first monkey of the project, and at the time of writing was a respectable 15 years old.

The project now cares for 122 monkeys, of which about three-quarters are at the Calabar site. You can visit the centre and someone will show you around and introduce you to the monkeys. The rest of the monkeys – 18 mangabeys and 7 mona guenons – live in a large forested electric fenced enclosure at Rhoko Forest (see page 233) on the edge of the Cross River National Park.

The centre gets around 30,000 visitors a year, and Jerry Akparawa, the senior education officer, runs an excellent education project which also goes out to over 70 schools around Calabar, and has set up a conservation club that meets at Cercopan once a month. There's a similar project at the schools and churches around the Rhoko Forest. Jerry talks to the children about the plight of monkeys, and produces an activity booklet for kids explaining why monkeys should be with their families, and in simple terms why 'monkeys are finishing' – using language that Nigerian children can understand easily –'Monkeys will finish if the number of monkeys killed is more than the number of monkeys born.'

The centre employs 35 Nigerians including management staff, who are assisted by volunteers mainly from North America and Europe. Volunteers needed include vets, biologists, researchers, builders and mechanics, so if you are at all interested in a placement, please contact them. Cercopan also relies on donations and overseas grants to survive, so again if you have any interest in conserving Nigeria's natural heritage, this is a worthwhile project to support. Future projects include the reintroduction of mona guenons to the wild, and expanding tourist accommodation at Rhoko Camp, including building a tree house.

Creek Town A short relaxing trip up the river from Calabar is the small settlement of Creek Town. To get there **boats** go from the wharf near the independence statue on Marina Road at approximately 12.00 and return at 14.00, and depart again at 16.00 (but don't return). Note that there is no accommodation at Creek Town. It's a pleasant one-hour ride and you'll get to see the fishermen and villagers going about their business among the thick mangroves and dense palms on the banks of the Calabar River. There's nothing really to see once at Creek Town, though look out for the church, a fine colonial building that is thought to be older than the Duke Town church in Old Calabar. You can also wander through the small market and chat to the locals, and maybe indulge in a gourdful of palm wine.

Oron Oron is a small town across the creek from Calabar and makes for an interesting excursion, and it's also the departure point for boats to Cameroon. **Boats** to and from Calabar go-when-full from the wharf, cost about N100 and take a little over 20 minutes. Pay for your ticket in the boat shed and one of the touts will show you to the right boat. Once in Oron, you can get boats to Tiko, Limbé and Doula in Cameroon, and these can be found a few hundred metres to the left of where the boats from Calabar dock (a short hop on an *okada* through the back streets). Again they are small motor boats that carry 20 people and go-when-full, at roughly 07.00 and 12.00 daily, and they cost N3,000. Unlike the ferries, these boats carry two engines as a back-up, though they are often perilously overloaded and in poor condition, so you may want to consider taking a drop boat (and have the boat to yourselves), though this will cost considerably more and you'll have to negotiate hard over a price. More recently a larger vessel has also been used with outside bench seating and an inside area with bus-type seating. Ask around for the 'Oil Corsair' boat.

There's an immigration shed near where the boats depart, where the boatman will take you to have your passport stamped out of Nigeria, and the police here will undoubtedly search your luggage, and on arrival in Cameroon (where you need a visa) you go through the same procedures.

If you need to stay overnight in Oron, find the perfectly acceptable **Bakibum Beach Hotel** (*1 Oron Rd; no phone; $*), which is easily spotted as it's the tallest building in town very close to the wharf, and is quite a surprise with new windows, new doors, new AC units, stone floors, satellite TV and hot water, and fabulous views of the river and all the activity in the streets below. It's on six storeys, but has only 19 rooms, and is excellent value. The chef will cook Nigerian food or chicken and chips on request, but give him plenty of notice.

The **Oron Museum** (⊕ *09.00–17.00 daily*; *entry N50*) is a worthy distraction while you're waiting for a boat, just a few metres to the right of the Calabar boats. The most important exhibit here is the Ekpo wood carvings, mostly heads, which were used to contact ancestors and pray for assistance. Ekpo is the local traditional religion and refers to souls and ghosts that haven't yet reached their resting place in the underworld. The museum opened in 1959 to preserve over 600 of these statues of deities, as the traditional religion had fallen away in the face of Christianity, but the museum was shelled during the Biafran War in 1967, and many of the statues were destroyed or lost, though around 100 remain here today.

There are also some elaborate Ekpo masquerade costumes and masks made of wood and straw. Some of the masks are quite ugly and strange; some are skin masks, presumably made from animal hide, though they were once made from human skin and look spookily lifelike. There's an exhibit on the Ibibio puppet plays, which before the advent of Christianity used to be used as entertainment, but also to spread moral tales, and the plays featured subjects such as abortion, adultery, theft or greed (the male puppets on display have enormous genitals).

There are ceremonial calabashes for drinking palm wine at special events such as weddings or funerals, and it was believed that if a witch or thief drank from a ceremonial pot they would die. In the grounds of the museum is a bunker from the Biafran War with a rather frightening-looking, life-size model of a soldier, and beyond here is a lovely patch of gardens right next to the riverbank called the **Prince Chris Abasieyu Garden**. It's a very tranquil spot with tables and chairs and an outdoor pool table popular with courting couples. From here you can watch the fishermen on the river and the jungle of palms on the other side, and sip a malt drink, or occasionally palm wine, bought at the museum kitchen.

Kwa Falls The impressive Kwa Waterfalls are located at the southern edge of the Oban Division of Cross River National Park, about 40km north from Calabar at Aningeje, towards the town of Oban on a newly tarred road. You can drive right to the top of the falls, which are in a deep valley with beautiful forest surroundings, and walk down the 150 or so steps to the river below and swim. When there's lots of water there is quite a torrent of white water flowing down the rocks.

A signpost at the turn-off to the falls says 'Kwa Falls Police Station and Plantation'. From here, follow this road for two to three kilometres up a gravel track, go over a concrete bridge, and then turn right at a small junction and go to the end of this road down a dip and past a couple of buildings until you get to a white building on its own. If you are self-sufficient, you can negotiate with the local people to camp here, and they can arrange to get beers and soft drinks from one of the local villages, or possibly even palm wine.

CROSS RIVER NATIONAL PARK

The Cross River National Park is the largest area of undisturbed rainforest in the country, and has been described as the Amazon of Nigeria; it seemingly goes on forever, over into Cameroon. The park is spectacularly beautiful, with green, rainforest-cloaked mountains and enormous trees. It is split into two parts, the Oban Division and the Okwangwo Division (that also includes parts of the Obudu Plateau), which are approximately 40km apart on either side of the Cross River to the north of Calabar.

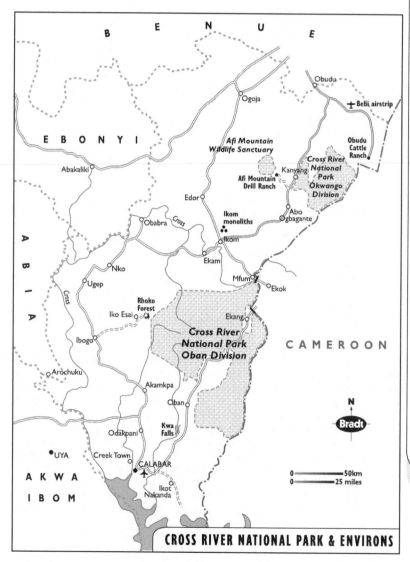

CROSS RIVER NATIONAL PARK & ENVIRONS

In the late 1980s news reached the outside world that gorilla populations still survived in the mountainous region on the Nigeria–Cameroon border, an area in which it was thought that gorillas were long extinct. Nigeria's gorillas are the most northerly and westerly in Africa. There are two distinct populations of gorillas in Cross River National Park. These populations were probably in contact in the past but are almost certainly isolated from each other today. One occurs at the northern end of the park in the forests of the former Boshi Extension Forest Reserve, originally established as a gorilla sanctuary in 1958. The other is found in the southwestern part of the former Okwangwo Forest Reserve, immediately adjacent to Cameroon's Takamanda Forest Reserve. There are some indications that the Boshi gorillas migrate seasonally across the Nigerian border into Takamanda Forest Reserve.

The Nigeria–Cameroon gorillas are recognised as a subspecies of the western lowland gorilla, and are dubbed the Cross River gorilla. It has been difficult to get accurate numbers, but it's generally believed there are fewer than 300 gorillas in this region; they are critically endangered, facing an extremely high risk of extinction in the wild in the immediate future. The chances of seeing these gorillas are minimal and they are not habituated to humans; if they were their lives would be under even more of a threat from hunters. One researcher we spoke to had spent two months in Cross River National Park, and although he had heard them and saw their night nests, he never saw the gorillas themselves.

The park covers approximately 4,000km² of the Cross River State and the terrain is tough, with hilly escarpments and steep valleys, and with peaks that generally rise higher than the surrounding deep forest, some of which reach nearly 1,000m. These rainforests are some of the oldest and richest in the whole of Africa, and many reports written by biologists, going as far back as the 1920s, emphasise the extreme biological richness of the area, their relatively intact status and the increasing threat from uncontrolled farming, logging and hunting.

The Oban division has an estimated 1,558 plant species, while the Okwangwo division has 1,545 species, 77 of which are endemic to Nigeria. The unique nature of Cross River State tropical forest is due in part to its high annual rainfall of over 4,000mm, and its relatively short dry season. Consequently, this forest, together with that immediately adjacent in southwest Cameroon, is classified as the only true evergreen rainforest in Africa. Over 60% of Nigeria's endangered plant and animal species are found only within these forests. These include 132 tree species listed by the World Conservation Monitoring Centre as globally threatened. As many as 200 species have been recorded from a single 0.05ha plot, a diversity matched only in exceptionally rich sites in South America. These trees also attract butterflies, and these forests are richer in butterflies than any other part of Africa.

The Okwangwo Division, home to about 80% of all wild primate species in Nigeria, is where Cross River gorillas share the same habitat with other primates, including chimpanzees and drills. Other rare species include possibly leopard, small antelope, a variety of monkeys, as well as buffalo and forest elephants. The gorilla, which had been declared extinct in Nigeria 40 years earlier, was rediscovered in 1987, and the huge amount of international publicity that this generated helped to persuade the government to gazette Cross River National Park in 1988.

Nevertheless, as in Nigeria's other parks, mismanagement and neglect have taken their toll, and, although the forests of the park are largely intact, they have been subjected to recent small-scale logging in some areas, and hunting continues to be practised throughout, endangering many species, notably the drill, chimpanzee, some of the monkeys such as Preuss's and Sclater's guenons, and the forest elephant.

The Cross River Forest is best appreciated from the Kwa Falls, the Cercopan Rhoko Camp or the Afi Drill Ranch (see below), which occupy good positions on the edge of Cross River National Park. Alternatively contact the Nigerian Field Association, who have in recent years organised group hikes in the forest (*www.nigerianfield.org*).

RHOKO FOREST

This is the forest monkey sanctuary of Calabar's Cercopan (see page 218). It's a lovely forested spot and since 2003 has been home to 18 mangabeys and 7 mona guenons, who live in a spacious electric fenced enclosure as part of a long-term reintroduction and research programme. The enclosure is inside a 400ha area of protected forest in the Akamkpa Local Government Area near the village of Iko Esai, on the edge of Cross River National Park to the north of Calabar, where there is also an education centre and signposted nature trail.

Cercopan works closely with the local community of Iko Esai on developing alternative sustainable livelihoods to hunting, and in developing revenues for the community through tourism. The relationship has developed so strongly, that Bobby Baxter, a trustee for Cercopan, has been made a local chief. Basic entrance (which includes a community tourism levy), is N1,500. This includes a guided tour around Rhoko, the monkey enclosure and a 1.5km nature trail. On a day visit you can also take a picnic, relax at camp, go to a nearby river for a refreshing swim, and explore the canopy via a tree platform in the rainforest, which is excellent for bird watching. You can also stay overnight, which is similar to the set-up at Afi (see below) and costs N1,500 per person. There are three raffia-roofed sleeping huts, one sleeping four, and two sleeping two people, a kitchen hut with a wood fire, an open shower and long-drop toilets. Cooking and eating utensils, mosquito nets, sheets, towels and drinking water are provided, and solar panels provide electricity, but you'll need to bring all your food. For both Rhoko and Afi, take things that are easy to cook – instant noodles, tins of baked beans, sweet corn, tuna, packet soup, bread, tea bags, powdered milk and the like. You'll need to get these items from one of the supermarkets in Calabar as they are not available locally. For those staying overnight, extra activities include guided forest night walks when you may spot some of the nocturnal animals such as bush babies.

GETTING THERE AND AWAY Iko Esai is a 3½-hour drive north of Calabar, and 18km east of the main Ikom road, from where the Rhoko Camp is accessible by *okada* or 4x4. To arrange a visit, and possibly a transfer if any of the staff are going up there, you first need to go to Cercopan in Calabar where they will radio through to the camp. To get there by public transport, take a vehicle towards Ikom and get off at the Ibogo junction (opposite the Biase Local Government Offices). From here you can hire an *okada* to Rhoko. Staff in Calabar can give you detailed directions.

AFI MOUNTAIN DRILL RANCH

The Afi Mountain Wildlife Sanctuary was created in 2000 by the Cross River State Government and the dense forests, jutting pinnacles and sheer rock faces are one of the most scenic areas in the state. The region is a natural home to chimpanzees, drill monkeys and gorillas, and many other forest animals, including bush pig, several species of monkey, parrots, eagles, pangolin, civet cats and mongooses. The Afi Drill Ranch is located on the edge of Afi Mountain Wildlife Sanctuary, from where there are tremendous views of the Afi massif towering above. The ranch provides local people with jobs at the ranch and supports local farmers by buying food for the ranch's animals. (For a complete background on Pandrillus, who operate the Afi and Calabar ranches, see page 223.)

In 1996 the first drill group was taken by helicopter to their new home at Afi, a solar-powered electric enclosure of naturally forested drill habitat. Today, there are five such enclosures at Afi and one for chimpanzees, and there are around 25ha of enclosed forest. In 2001 ex-President Obasanjo visited the ranch, went for a walk to see the animals, and planted a tree. The path from the camp to the enclosures is now dubbed Obasanjo Way.

This is a stunning and remote spot, and the views from the camp of the giant tangled trees and brooding mountains are outstanding. The mist-filled air is full of bats and soaring raptors in the early mornings and evenings, and butterflies and twittering insects during the day. There are easy hikes and walks to the swimming holes and waterfalls on the Bano Stream; one of the staff will go with you into sections of the Afi Mountain Wildlife Sanctuary. You can visit the demonstration tree nursery of native fruit and tree seedlings, and guides will take you for a walk into one of the drill enclosures. At the chimpanzee enclosure you can watch the animals through the fence playing, eating or grooming each other, or simply lying back on the grass contemplating their surroundings. There are also other wild monkeys, which are lighter than the chimps and drills and can therefore move through the enclosures at treetop level.

Cross River State (another Donald Duke initiative) has built a canopy walkway within an easy walk from the ranch. It spans 400 metres, and nine bridges connect ten platforms built in the trees, the highest of which is 23 metres above the forest floor. It's a lovely and unintrusive way to see the birds, butterflies and monkeys in the tree tops.

The camp consists of a kitchen with dining table, fire, fridge, and the manager's desk and radio; six comfortable fully screened raised sleeping cabins with wooden verandas with great views of the forest canopy; and a long-drop toilet and open-air bush shower. You need to bring all your own food and although water is available for cooking from a borehole, bring your own drinking water. A torch is essential. Warm beers and soft drinks can be ordered from the local village, but you will need to pre-arrange delivery as the staff only go in and out of the ranch by truck once daily.

The nearest petrol station and markets are in either Ikom or Obudu. If you want a cabin, it's essential that you arrange a visit through the Calabar Drill ranch in person, or by phone or email, so they can radio through to Afi to tell them when you are coming. Camping isn't a problem, and if you are fully equipped you can just pitch up. Cabins are N3,500 per person per night, camping is N1,500, plus N500 per vehicle, and every visitor is required to pay an additional N150 per night, which goes into a fund for environmental projects. The forest at Afi is full of insects, and closed shoes, socks and long trousers are essential despite the heat, though take swimming gear, as during most times of the year you can swim at the waterfalls at Bano Stream.

GETTING THERE AND AWAY If coming from Calabar and the south, follow the road from Ikom to Obudu. Some 56km north of Ikom there is a dirt track on the left (10km after Abo Ogbagante). If you get to Kanyang you've gone too far. Drive 6km west to the village of Katabang, crossing the Afi River, then turn right at the T-

On two occasions in Nigeria we were offered primates to buy. The first was in Katsina in the north when a man approached us and asked if we wanted to buy a patas monkey (he pointed up to the creature chained to a balcony on his house). The second and more shocking time was while talking to a director of one of Nigeria's (appalling) zoos; he candidly told me that he was on very good terms with the local hunters, could give them a specific order, and could get me (or anyone else for that matter) a chimpanzee for US$5,000. He added 'They are more expensive than other monkeys because they are quite rare you know', and 'We do not cheat the hunters over their prices, so they don't stop coming here'. This was the same zoo that was responsible for illegally sending two captive gorillas to a Malaysian zoo in 2002.

Primates are critically endangered in Nigeria, and some, such as the Sclater's guenon, which are endemic to Nigeria, are so rare that no-one knows how many individuals remain in the Cross River forests. You are more likely to see primates dead than alive in Nigeria, as black magic ingredients on a *juju* doctor's stall. Indeed, in the forests of southeastern Nigeria monkeys are still eaten. The chimpanzee incident shocked me to the core, and for this reason I would like to highlight and encourage support for both the Pandrillus and Cercopan projects detailed above. They are both excellent community-based charities working towards primate conservation and education and their work is imperative; without them many primate species will disappear from Nigeria's forests forever.

junction in Katabang and continue north for 6.5km to the marked turn into Drill Ranch. If coming from the north go south from Obudu on the Ikom road 60km (55km from the Obudu Cattle Ranch turn-off). The dirt track is on the right, 4km south of the village of Kanyang. There is a small police post at the turn-off and an 'anti-logging' gate managed by the State Forestry Commission to prevent logging vehicles going into the forest. Large vehicles, overland trucks for example, need to contact the Calabar ranch to arrange for this to be open on arrival. The road into the ranch is windy and steep in parts, and you may need a 4x4 vehicle with high clearance in the wet season.

By public transport get a bush taxi between Ikom and Obudu and ask to be dropped off at Kanyang. This is past the turn-off to Katabang if you are coming from the south, but you will have more of a chance of getting *okada*s here than in the Abo Ogbagante further back. Ask in the village for *okada*s and it shouldn't take long for them to miraculously appear. The journey from the main road through the forest to the ranch is thrilling by bike and takes roughly an hour. There is another road between Ikom and Obudu via Ogoja; make sure you are on the right road and in the right bush taxi.

OBUDU CATTLE RANCH

The Obudu Cattle Ranch is somewhat of an institution from colonial days. It's not far from the Cameroon border and is situated on a beautiful plateau 1,576m high on the Oshie Ridge at the base of the Sonkwala Mountains. The ranch has a long history and was originally a cattle ranch established in 1951 by Scottish farmers. The mountain range was first explored in 1949 by a Mr McCaughley, who camped on top of the mountain for a month, when he presumably decided that it would be the ideal spot for raising a few cattle. He returned a couple of years later with a Mr

Jones and a Dr Crawford, who between them established a ranch on the rolling green plateau.

The heyday of the ranch was in the 1950s and 1960s, when it was a retreat for colonials and the wealthy, but since then it has been a shadow of its former self and became an extremely dilapidated place, where you couldn't even get anything to eat or drink. Then in 2002 it became Cross River State Governor Donald Duke's pet project, as he remembered it fondly when visiting as a child. Funded by the State Government, he has instigated some remarkable refurbishments, pulled in South African hotel chain Protea for a couple of years to train the management, and it's now back up there as one of Nigeria's leading places to visit.

Accessed by a dramatic switch-back road that climbs up the mountain, the malaria-free plateau is fabulously situated on a land area of about 10,000ha, with a semi-temperate climate; it rarely reaches over 20°C (you'll need warm clothes) and it makes a refreshing change from the rest of the sweaty south. The best time to visit is between October and March just before the rainy season. It's tremendously scenic and the resort has beautiful and captivating scenery of rolling grassland, deep wooded valleys and waterfalls. The region is frequently referred to as 'land of the clouds'.

GETTING THERE AND AWAY The highlight of the Obudu Plateau is getting there. At the bottom of the hill is a wooden gate, which has a wooden bull's head above it and an office where you are required to sign in. Newly built facilities here include a waterpark with diving boards and slides, which is located at the bottom of the plateau as temperatures are much warmer for swimming here than at the top. Then a wonderfully scenic and exhilarating road climbs the 11.25km from the bottom to the top of the plateau through 22 hairpin bends, the most dramatic being about half-way up (it is called the Devil's Elbow). The road is stunning, and at each turn the views of rolling hills and intensely green pastures get wider, and the mountain air fresher and cooler. And then there's the brand new cable car! Built in 2005 by an Austrian company, it's reputedly the longest of its kind in Africa. It follows the same course as the road, is nine kilometres long with 36 cars suspended every few metres; it takes 15 minutes to the top and at its highest point is 500m above the ground. It's a fantastic ride with sweeping views and it really does feel like you are hanging in the clouds.

To get to the ranch by public transport from Calabar you will need to take a minibus or shared taxi to Obudu Motor Park and then arrange a drop by taxi from there to the ranch 65km away. Aero Contractors (*Calabar;* ☎ *0805 555 0556; www.acn.aero*) have flights (35mins) from Calabar to the Bebi Airstrip roughly 40km from the ranch towards Obudu. These depart Calabar on Wednesday, Friday and Sunday at 13.05, and return from Bebi at 14.00. The ranch can arrange airport transfers to the bottom of the hill where you have the choice of being driven up or going on the cable car.

⌂ WHERE TO STAY AND EAT

⌂ **Obudu Ranch Resort** ☎ 0803 550 6257/472 9327, 087 239001/238994; http://crossriverstate. com/obudu.htm. For a couple of years until 2007, the South African hotel chain Protea was managing the resort in order to train local staff. Management has now gone back to Cross River State, so contact is not as reliable as it was under Protea – note the number of phone numbers above. Accommodation is in 80 double chalets, most of which have a log fire, & 30 suites in wooden cabins. All have DSTV, fridge, heater & phone. NEPA hasn't reached this far, so all the power comes from the gens, which are not put on during the day, but which stay on at night to fuel the room heaters. Up here in the clouds, this means that things are a little gloomy during the day & you can't watch TV, but it's a laudable way of saving fuel. The state government is currently working out an arrangement for a

Another Donald Duke success story is the Obudu Ranch International Mountain Challenge (www.obuduranchmountainrace.com), a running event held in November, which is now in its third year and was conceived by Duke to bring international attention to Obudu Plateau, and indeed Nigeria. It has certainly done that, and the 2006 race attracted 500 international runners and over US$250,000 worth of prize money. It follows the road from the bottom to the top of the plateau, with 22 switchbacks, and is 11.25km long, with an 810m ascent to a height of 1,600m above sea level. The race has now been endorsed by the Athletic Federation of Nigeria (AFN), the International Association of Athletic Federations (IAAF) and the World Mountain Running Association (WMRA).

Japanese company to supply electricity permanently to the plateau. The restaurant serves continental buffet meals at set times & breakfast is US$13, while lunch & dinner are US$18. The resort is fast becoming one of Nigeria's leading convention centres, so always check first if there's space, as it's a long way to come & find out it is full. Rooms $$$; suites $$$$

WHAT TO SEE AND DO Great hikes can be arranged from the resort from one to six hours; expect to pay roughly N300 per hour for a guide. These go to local waterfalls and various view points including the strangely named 'intestine' view point, which actually refers to what the switch-back road looks like from the top. There's a 60m-long newly built canopy walkway (*entry N200*) where there are two platforms, 15.5m and 20.5m above the ground, which offer great views into a pretty patch of forest that is home to a number of species of birds. There are also stables where horse riding can be arranged for about N1,000 per hour, and the ranch can also organise visits to the Afi Drill Ranch if you don't have your own vehicle.

Other facilities include floodlit tennis courts, squash court, mini-golf, brand new mountain bikes for hire, and a new nine-hole golf course. You can swim in a natural rock pool about a ten-minute walk away, and there's a gym.

The ranch itself now supplies most of its produce. Honey is sourced by the villagers from the forests around the plateau who sell it to the new honey factory, while the dairy produces meat, butter, cheese and fresh milk. There are two rather special bulls on the ranch. Three-year-old Donald weighs 680kg, while six-year-old Joshua weighs a staggering 1,080kg. Their names are derived from the fact that it was Governor Joshua Dariye of Plateau State who donated the two bulls to Donald Duke.

One of the most recent developments at the ranch has been the completion of the president's house equipped with heli-pad, barracks for security staff and presidential aides, and a state-of-the-art clinic (which will serve anyone who stays there). The intention in the future is for this to be used by the Nigerian government in a similar way as Camp David in the USA (to which the President of the USA goes for high-powered political retreats, to sign peace agreements and the like).

IKOM

Finally, there's nothing of note in Ikom, but if you are travelling by public transport in the southeast you may pass through the **motor park** here, which is big, square and less hectic than many of the other motor parks in Nigeria, with vehicles parked neatly in rows. You'll also need to be here to get transport to the **Cameroon border** 30km away, usually provided by Peugeot bush taxis with wooden signs on top saying 'border'. The town is on the small side, with a big aluminium plant, and it serves the local logging companies that are making their way into the Cross River forests; look out for the enormous logging depot just to the south of town if coming from Calabar. There's a decent hotel if you get stuck to the left of the main Calabar road as it comes into town, and it's unmissable as it's one of the town's few high-rise blocks. The **Heritage Hotel** (*no phone*; $) is fairly modern, with parking in a compound, satellite TV, and clean rooms with a bucket.

At Alok, 22km north of Ikom on the Ogoja road, are some **stone monoliths** on the roadside, which are curiously carved and set in circles with abstract human figures on them. It is thought that they could date back as far as AD200, but not much is known about them. They measure from about 30cm to almost two metres high, and are thought to be representations of ancestors. When someone died, the survivors of the dead person would carve a stone in memory of the departed. For some unknown reason the stones were set in a geometric pattern that eventually formed a circle. You don't have to come this far to see them, however, as there is one in the grounds of the Calabar Museum, and another at the Oron Museum. Finally, a reader has recommended Ikom bananas as being the tastiest in Nigeria.

8

Central Nigeria

Central Nigeria is loosely the broad band that separates the distinctive southern and northern regions of Nigeria, known locally as the middle belt. I have lumped these areas together not for any chronological order of visiting, but simply because they do not fit into the northern or southern regions, and you'll have to dip into this Central Nigeria chapter sporadically depending on which direction, and between what northern and southern points, you are travelling. Some of the cities dealt with here have a few distractions of their own and you will inevitably pass through them if driving along the freeways that connect the major cities to the north and south, or spend time in their thronging motor parks if travelling by public transport.

Some central areas warrant a visit in their own right, such as the highland city of Jos, while the likes of the country capital Abuja and transport hubs such as Makurdi and Bauchi need a little less attention, though again you will find yourself in these centres if travelling between the north and south. Lake Kainji National Park is geographically part of the north, but it's usually approached from the south via Ilorin or Abuja. In some places such as Jos you'll find a melting pot of fundamentalist Christianity and Islam, and this city, like Ilorin, is between the southwest and the north, in the buffer zone between the two religions.

ABUJA

The site of Abuja, the new federal capital of Nigeria since 1991, was chosen for its strategic position at the centre of the country, its good climate, and because it was at the time of choosing sparsely populated by people who didn't have any particular religious or ethnic allegiance. The original inhabitants were mainly Gwari people who farmed the central savanna region. The Gwari women are known for carrying their loads on their shoulders and not their heads, as the Gwari people believe the head is the most sacred part of the body, which is already saddled with the burden of thinking for the whole body and which therefore should not be over-burdened.

Abuja is a purpose-built capital surrounded by large granite hills, and much of it is still under construction. Very oddly for a new city, there's also much demolition going on and throughout the city you'll see big red crosses marked on buildings earmarked to be pulled down. As the city grew many buildings went up without formal planning permission, often on land allocated for parks or for drainage. The city is on federal land, and the government has been revoking the land titles, making occupiers re-register and demolishing structures that were built illegally. As it's fairly new, Abuja has the best infrastructure in Nigeria, with speedy expressways and traffic lights that actually work (when there is NEPA). But despite two new dams being built in the 1980s to supply the city, services such as water suffer the same fate as in the rest of the country, and Abuja is still NEPA dependent.

It's a moderately attractive place to live, with wide open spaces and parks, though given that construction started in the late 1970s, there's a fair amount of the

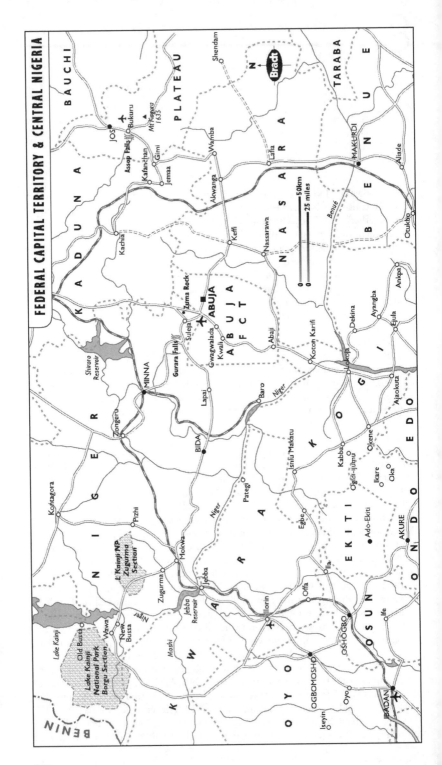

FEDERAL CAPITAL TERRITORY & CENTRAL NIGERIA

ugly concrete so fashionable in that era, and it's already starting to look very dated. Abuja is sometimes criticised, even by Nigerians, for being sterile and without much colour or culture, but nevertheless those who have made the move from Lagos say that the general standard of living is better in Abuja. There's hardly anything to see or do and it's not a city for walking, as everything is very spread out along wide freeways. Like Lagos it has some of the trappings of Westernisation, thanks to the embassies and conference centres, and you'll find a few luxury hotels, good food and some decent shops. Also like Lagos, you'll find prices are much higher in Abuja than in the rest of the country.

The annual four-day **Abuja Carnival** has been held every November since 2005, and features parades, exhibitions and a boat regatta on Jabi Lake. Cultural troupes from every state attend and the displays of dancing, horsemanship and musicians at the Eagle Square are very impressive. Although the event is well advertised there is unfortunately little information available about what is happening and when, though this may improve as the organisers get more practice.

BRIEF HISTORY By 1970 it was clear that Lagos, with its small islands, could no longer cope with the exploding population and inferior infrastructure needed for a country capital. General Murtala Mohammed set up a commission to decide on a central spot that was accessible from all parts of the country and that was ethnically neutral. Given that the civil war had just finished it was evident that Lagos, with its 75% Yoruba population, was not conducive to easing ethnic tensions. Abuja had neither a founder nor a settler, and even today it is populated by various ethnic migrants and no part is dominated by any particular group or religion, and there are no government reservation areas (GRAs) established by the British or townships for people from specific ethnic groups like in Nigeria's other cities, though areas are split by socio-economic divides.

Plans to build the capital were approved in 1976, and a 7,770km² Federal Capital Territory was created near the old town of Abuja (renamed Suleja), and with immediate effect the ownership and control of that land became vested in the federal government. Given that this was the era of the oil boom, the government also had money to spend. The land was designated from parts of the Kwara Plateau and Niger states and is 2½ times larger than Lagos State.

Abuja was an exiled king from Zaria who became king of the old settlement of Abuja (now Suleja) in 1825. His full name was Abubakar, but he was called Abu for short. Legend has it that because he was fair skinned, he was called Abu-ja (*ja* means red or fair in Hausa) or 'Abu-the-red-one'. The new name Suleja came from keeping the *ja* bit but adding the *Sule*, which was the shortened name of the emir at the time of the name swap.

Construction of the city began during the late 1970s, and from its outset it was reckoned that it would take 15–20 years to build, but towards the end of that decade the oil money began to dry up and, as a result of corruption among the building contractors and officials, construction slowed to a snail's pace and still continues today. It was decided that the land at the foot of Aso Rock would be the seat of government, and today this is where the main government buildings are located in the Three Arm Zone.

The first administrator of the Federal Capital Territory Authority (FCTA) was Mobboolaji Ajose Adeogun – who has an awful lot of streets in Nigeria named after him – who embarked on a massive recruitment of town planners, architects, engineers and other professionals to work on creating the new city. The FCTA started out with an office in Lagos in 1976 before moving operations closer to the new territory in Kaduna a year later, and then again to Suleja town, where the offices were set up in makeshift caravans as development began.

For the next three years until 1980 these mobile caravan units oversaw the construction of the first roads and land clearing, and the first housing development, which was erected to accommodate the officials and eventually the construction workers. Then a Federal Secretariat was built at the village of Garki to move officialdom officially in. This has since been dwarfed by the building of the New Federal Secretariat near the State House, which in parts is still under construction. Meanwhile whole villages that fell under the Abuja area were relocated from their original sites and transferred to land elsewhere in the FCT. These included Wuse, Maitama and Asokoro. The original villages were levelled by bulldozers and new districts with the same names were created in their wake. Garki village was allowed to survive on its original site as an experiment by one of the military regimes.

The development attracted a huge influx of people in a sort of 'gold rush' manner for the good job opportunities and better standard of living because of the modern, new and efficient services and infrastructure. First were the road builders and construction contractors, followed by the workmen and labourers, followed by the service providers – people had to sleep and eat after all. The development of housing and infrastructure could not keep pace with the torrent of new arrivals, unleashing an acute housing problem that still exists. Today, makeshift slums routinely appear, although the government frequently bulldoze these sites, despite them being people's homes. Most of the population cannot afford to live in Abuja itself and have to commute from satellite towns, which developed outside the original Abuja 'master plan' and have very little infrastructure.

From its inception Abuja has been a pet project of Nigeria's incumbent presidents, who often visited Abuja to survey the building sites, and who used its flashy new hotels as a retreat to escape from Lagos, and occasionally to receive foreign leaders. This tradition continued until the federal government officially moved here in 1991 during the presidency of General Babangida, when Aso Rock State House, the official residency of the head of state, was completed. In Lagos, Babangida signed the decree formally declaring Abuja as the new federal capital of the Federal Republic of Nigeria, before boarding the presidential plane and making the historic one-hour flight to Abuja in much pomp and circumstance. When he got there he was received at Abuja's concrete city gate, which straddles the highway from the airport, by all his ministers and top civil servants, before being whisked off to the new seat of government at the foot of Aso Rock. The subsequent migration of officialdom, business and governmental departments has been painfully slow, however, and many were reluctant to leave Lagos. Even today, many people who work in Abuja fly home to their families in Lagos at the weekends, but Abuja is more or less the proper working capital of Nigeria. In the 1991 census, the same time as the capital was officially moved, the population was put at 378,671. Today it's just under 1.5 million.

GETTING THERE AND AWAY
By air Nnamdi Azikiwe International Airport is the second-busiest airport in Nigeria after Lagos. The airport is about 40km west of the city centre along the Abuja–Lokoja highway. In 2006 the Abuja Gateway Consortium took over management of the airport and there are plans to upgrade it and build a new shopping centre, cargo warehouse, car parks and an airport hotel. For now the separate domestic and international terminals are far apart from each other, so it's worth noting that, like Lagos, some domestic airlines (Virgin Nigeria and Arik) operate from the international terminal. As in Lagos you can pitch up at the airport and book a flight to just about anywhere in the country on a first-come first-served basis, though here you can also go to the domestic airline desks at the Hilton and

Sheraton hotels and book a ticket as well as an airport transfer.

There are numerous flights to Lagos (one hour) throughout the day, as well as regular weekday flights to other major cities. Some European carriers fly directly into Abuja, too, such as British Airways and KLM. Check schedules on the websites. **ADC Airlines** flies between Abuja and Lagos, Sokoto and Yola; **Aero Contractors** flies between Abuja and Lagos and Owerri; **Arik Air** flies between Abuja and Lagos and Calabar; **Bellview** flies between Abuja and Lagos and Kano; **Chanchangi Airlines** flies between Abuja and Lagos and Owerri; **Overland Airways** flies between Abuja and Calabar, Ibadan and Ilorin; **Sosoliso Airlines** flies between Abuja and Enugu; and **Virgin Nigeria** flies between Abuja and Lagos, Sokoto and Kano.

To get from the airport to Abuja taxis line up in the car park outside the terminal building and the 40km is an expensive ride – roughly the equivalent of US$25 – but check in the airport what you should be paying. For budget travellers a shuttle bus service runs between the airport and Labour House in the Central District of the city for N800, supposedly every hour with the first bus from Abuja to the airport at 06.55 and the last from the airport to Abuja at 17.00 (✆ *09 273 1645 or 0806 552 1606*). Alternatively, ask around on the plane or at the airport if you can grab a lift with someone.

Airlines

✈ **Aero Contractors** Airport desk; ✆ 09 810 0197; www.acn.aero.com

✈ **Air France** Office at the Sheraton; ✆ 09 523 9965; www.airfrance.com.ng

✈ **Arik Air** Central Reservations; ✆ 01 279 9999; www.arikair.com

✈ **Bellview** Airport desk; ✆ 09 810 0089; www.flybellviewair.com

✈ **British Airways** Desk at the Hilton; ✆ 09 461 1002-6; www.britishairways.com

✈ **Chanchangi Airlines** Airport desk; ✆ 09 810 0143; desk at the Sheraton; ✆ 09 523 0225; the Hilton; ✆ 09 413 4301; www.chanchangi.com

✈ **IRS Airlines** Airport desk; ✆ 09 810 0447; www.irs-airlines.com

✈ **KLM and Kenya Airways** Office at the Sheraton; ✆ 09 523 0225; www.klm.com.ng

✈ **Overland Airways** Airport desk; ✆ 0803 535 1159; www.overland.aero

✈ **Sosoliso Airlines** Airport desk; ✆ 09 810 0122; www.sosolisoairline.com

✈ **Virgin Nigeria** Airport desk; ✆ 09 461 0505; www.virginnigeria.com

By road Jabi Motor Park, out past Berger Junction on Obafemi Awolowo Way (a continuation of Herbert Macaulay Way), is the city's main **motor park** for buses and taxis going just about everywhere, including Lokoja, Kaduna and Makurdi. There are two separate parts run by different organisations, and the touts out on the street can be annoying in their enthusiasm to get you into one of their cars. There are also 'luxury' buses to Lagos, Port Harcourt and Benin City, among other destinations, with companies such as ABC Transport (*www.abctransport.com*), Cross Country and Chisco, who all have terminals nearby on Obafemi Awolowo Way or along the street between Utako Market and the Jabi Motor Park. ABC operates three services to Jos a day for N890, for example. To get to Jabi you can pick up minibuses on Herbert Macaulay Way near Old Wuse Market in Wuse, but it's easier to take a drop taxi directly there.

ORIENTATION If you look at the map, the **Central District** of the city is like a spine that runs through from the foot of Aso Rock and the Three Arms Zone to the southern base of the ring road, which completely circles the city, though there is some development starting to happen on the outer side. The Central District has straight roads in a grid system and is the central business zone of the city,

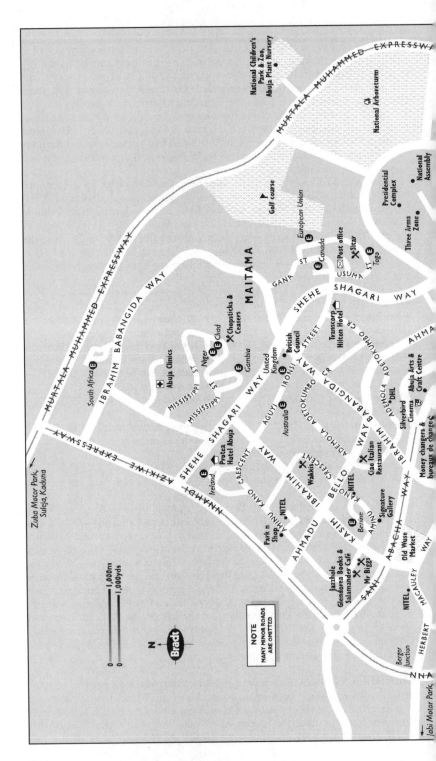

National Children's Park & Zoo, Abuja Plant Nursery

MURTALA MUHAMMED EXPRESSWAY

National Arboretum

MURTALA MUHAMMED EXPRESSWAY

IBRAHIM BABANGIDA WAY

Golf course

European Union

MAITAMA

South Africa

Abuja Clinics

Niger

Chad

Chopsticks & Ceasers

GANA ST

Canada

Post office

Sitar

Togo

USUMA ST

Gambia

SHEHE SHAGARI WAY

MISSISSIPPI ST

MISSISSIPPI ST

SHEHE SHAGARI WAY

United Kingdom

British Council

IRONSI STREET

ADETOKUMBO CR

Transcorp Hilton Hotel

Presidential Complex

National Assembly

Three Arms Zone

ADETOKUMBO WAY

AGUYI

Australia

ADEMOLA

DHL

AHMA

AZIKIWE EXPRESSWAY

Ireland

Protea Hotel Abuja

KANO CRESCENT

BELLO WAY

Ciao Italian Restaurant

Abuja Arts & Craft Centre

IBRAHIM BABANGIDA WAY

Silverbird Cinema

NNAMDI

Wakkis

IBRAHIM WAY

NITEL

Money changers & bureaux de change

Zuba Motor Park, Suleja, Kaduna

Park n Shop

AHINU KANO

NITEL

KASIM

Bernие

Signature Gallery

AMINU

NITEL

Old Wuse Market

A-BACHA WAY

Jazzhole

Glendorea Books & Salamander Café

Mr Biggs

SANI

ABACHA WAY

MACAULEY

NITEL

HERBERT

Berger Junction

NNA

Jabi Motor Park

N

Brädt

1,000m

1,000yds

0

0

NOTE
MANY MINOR ROADS
ARE OMITTED

ABUJA

Jos

Protea Hotel
Asokoro

IHEHE SHAGARI WAY

New Federal Secretariat

Crystal Palace

National Ecumenical Church

Women's Development Centre

Le Méridien Abuja

Abuja International Conference Centre

Fedex

UPS

ASOKORO

MURTALA MUHAMMED EXPRESSWAY

Post office

AKINTOLA BOULEVARD

Chelsea Hotel

Ceddi Plaza/Nu Metro

BALEWA AVENUE

MACAULEY

Afri Hotel

Police

WAY

Agura Hotel

BELLO WAY

Blakes Excellency Resort

CONSTITUTION

OLD DISTRICT

CENTRAL DISTRICT

HERBERT

Ship House

Post office

ROAD

Garki Supermarket

AHMADU BELLO

LADOKE SAMUEL

Mr Biggs

Browdi

CSS

Hotel

OLUEGUN OBASANJO WAY

INDEPENDENCE

Ghana

Royalton Hotel

ABIOLA

Sim Msira

Garden Kitchen

TAFAWA BALEWA WAY

Cool FM

US Embassy

Pridemark Luxury Suites & Tantalisers

Dannic Hotel

MOSHOOD

Area 1 Shopping Centre

GARKI

New Wuse Market

DIPLOMATIC DRIVE

Sudan

Post office

Police

NNAMDI AZIKIWE EXPRESSWAY

Protea Hotel Apo Apartments

Mali

Buses to Suleja

Africa Safari Hotel

United Nations

AVENUE

Old Federal Secretariat

Nigeria Tourism Development Corporation

OBASANJO WAY

Abuja National Hospital

OLUEGUN

INDEPENDENCE AVENUE

ZIKIWE

EXPRESSWAY AVENUE

Wonderland Children's Amusement Park

CONSTITUTION

National Stadium

Airport, Suleja

accommodating government and multinational corporation head offices and embassies.

The central district divides the city into southern and northern wings, with **Maitama** the location of more embassies and the Hilton Hotel, and **Wuse**, for Old Wuse Market and the Sheraton Hotel, to the north; and **Garki** and **Asokoro** to the south. Garki District is then subdivided into areas simply called Area 1, Area 2, and so on, while Wuse is separated into zones called Zone 1, Zone 2, and so on. Confusingly, then Garki and Wuse both have extensions – Garki II and Wuse II respectively – which are not the same as Area 2 and Zone 2. Street signs and signs showing house numbers have been introduced. These are colour-coded by district: Maitama is black on yellow, Wuse white on green, and Garki white on blue.

GETTING AROUND Abuja has very much been built with drivers in mind, and there are long distances to walk between places. City transport is nowhere near as frequent as in Lagos or other cities, though if you're prepared to wait around a bit for minibuses and shared taxis you should be able to navigate the city all right. Vehicles run up and down the main roads, and you just need to flag one down going in your general direction; expect to pay N30–50 for a short hop. City buses and taxis are green with a white horizontal stripe, but just about any vehicle serves as a taxi. Drop taxis are usually N200–300 within the city. A fleet of new dark green Peugeots and some London 'Hackney cab' taxis have appeared but they are very expensive, at around N1,000 for a drop.

Okadas were banned within the city limits in 2006, which has made travelling around Abuja much more expensive and less convenient. The reason for the ban, given at the time, was that they were too dangerous – which they were. But I suspect it also had something to do with the FCT government's vision of Abuja being seen as a shiny, modern city. *Okadas* still operate in the satellite towns (where the poorer people live) but are not allowed in the city centre where they may get in the way of the big men's cars. As a partial replacement for *okadas* large buses were introduced, which are mostly used to transport commuters between Abuja and the satellite towns.

WHERE TO STAY Because so many business people visit here from Lagos, there must be at least a couple of hundred hotels in Abuja and more opening all the time. As the hotels are newer than elsewhere in the country, they are of a reasonably good standard, though as in Lagos, despite the competition, room rates in Abuja are fairly hefty and there is little choice when it comes to budget accommodation. Many hotels offer discounts of 20–50% on Fridays and Saturdays, and sometimes Sunday nights, so it's always worth asking, though Abuja is very quiet at the weekends, and if you are here to get visas for somewhere else the embassies will be shut.

Abuja has some of the country's most upmarket hotels thanks to visiting presidents and the like, such as Le Méridien hotel, directly behind the Abuja International Conference Centre, and the Sheraton and the Hilton hotels to the north of the Central District. The South African chain, Protea Hotels, have also opened some properties. As they are international companies, it's perfectly feasible to book and pay for these hotels through their websites with no deposits. If paying by cash for them, budget approximately for another US$100 on top of the room rates. The cheaper hotels are to the south clustered around Garki.

Wuse and Maitama

Protea Hotel Abuja 412 Negreo Crescent, Maitama; ☏ 09 461 2741–3; www.proteahotels.com. Modern, purpose-built, comfortable & everything works, & on a par with Proteas across South Africa. This has 28 rooms, a business centre, wireless internet, restaurant, 24hr bar & room service, & the décor is muted browns & creams. The 4 double-storey executive lofts have a separate lounge & a jacuzzi. $$$$$

⌂ **Abuja Sheraton Hotel & Towers** Ladi Kwali Way, Wuse Zone 3; ☎ 09 461 2000; www.starwoodhotels.com. A huge hotel with 540 rooms & suites, several bars & restaurants (see *Where to eat and drink*), nightclub, tennis & squash courts, gym with sauna, swimming pool & business centre. The art gallery in the lobby has some good paintings & there are a number of useful shops & travel agencies, including a good bookshop. The Towers is the newly refurbished executive rooms on the 8th & 9th floors, with separate check-in, complimentary breakfast, flat-screen TV & coffee maker. Rates start from US$267 for a standard double in the main hotel. Don't forget the 15%. Rooms $$$$; suites $$$$$

⌂ **Transcorp Hilton Hotel** Shehu Shagari Way, Maitama; ☎ 09 413 1811; www1.hilton.com. Built in 1987, the enormous Hilton is the biggest hotel in West Africa, with 442 rooms & 228 suites on 10 floors, where you'll completely forget that you are in Nigeria. Queen Elizabeth II, Bill Clinton & George Bush have all stayed here. Facilities include everything you'd expect of a 5-star hotel, such as pool, tennis & squash courts, gym, sauna, beauty salon, nightclub, several bars & restaurants (dealt with under *Where to eat and drink*), business centre & internet café. The Hilton's banqueting hall, which can take about 1,200 people, was the venue for boxing matches during the 2003 All African Games. The rooms & suites are elegantly decorated with DSTV & minibars & all the trimmings. If you just want to use the pool & sporting facilities, non-guests are charged a fee of about US$15 per day. There's also a full-on shopping mall, with a bureau de change, travel agencies, airline desks, a handicraft village, a bakery & extensive duty-free shops selling booze & perfume. The Hilton has so many generators banked together it resembles an electricity sub-station. Non-resident room rates are presented in US$, but you will have to pay in naira at the hotel's exchange rate, & rates vary hugely, with no fewer than 18 types of rooms. A standard double starts from US$290. $$$$–$$$$$

Central District

⌂ **Chelsea Hotel** Plot 389, Cadastral Zone, Central District; ☎ 09 234 9080–4; www.chelseahotel abuja.com. A modern, professionally run & centrally located hotel with 75 rooms & suites in a bright white block set in a large car park & garden, with a pool, tennis courts, business centre, restaurant & bar. Rooms have got dreary dark red curtains & carpets but are comfortable with DSTV & a minibar. $$$

⌂ **Afri Hotel** 281 Herbert Macaulay Way, Central District; ☎ 09 234 2873/9724–7. This is a very modern, smart glass building with a car park out front behind a boom gate, & with 40, bright-white spotless rooms, with DSTV & a video channel that plays 'Nollywood' movies continually, & a well-stocked minibar. A full range of Nigerian dishes are available in the restaurant plus the odd continental special & the bar has so many bottles of drinks that it resembles a supermarket. This is very good value given how nice it is. $$

Garki and Asokoro

⌂ **Protea Hotel Apo Apartments** 2 Ahmadu Bello Way, Garki; ☎ 09 231 1234; www.proteahotels.com. Primarily aimed at long stayers (monthly & annually) but will take on short-stay guests if there's availability. There is a range of 34 self-contained modern apartments in a peaceful part of the city off the main southern ring road. Each has DSTV, fully equipped kitchen & modern furnishings. There's a small restaurant, room service, a lovely rooftop bar & a swimming pool. Foreign exchange & secretarial services are on offer. $$$$$

⌂ **Protea Hotel Asokoro** Bola Ige Close, Mohammadu Ribadu Street, Asokoro, Area 11; ☎ 09 314 6767; www.proteahotels.com. Newly opened in 2007, this features 83 rooms in a square white modern block with a pool, gym, wireless internet access, coffee shop, restaurant & 24hr bar. Like the other Proteas, décor is standard hotel furnishings with extras like DSTV. $$$$$

⌂ **Le Méridien Abuja** Tafawa Balewa Way, Area 11, Garki; ☎ 09 461 9000; www.starwoodhotels.com. Adjacent to the Abuja International Conference Centre, this hotel features international 5-star qualities with over 370 rooms & suites with luxury dark-wood furnishings, DSTV, balconies, wireless internet access, & spacious bathrooms with marble baths. There's a pool, gym, tennis & squash courts & 3 restaurants. This was actually one of the first hotels to be built in Abuja, but during Sani Abacha's reign in the mid-1990s he closed it down because he was paranoid that the rooms could be used to spy on nearby government buildings. In 2003, Le Méridien refurbished it & it reopened in 2004. Rooms $$$; suites $$$$

🏠 **Agura Hotel** Moshood Abiola Way, Garki Area 1; 📞 09 2341753/60. This was the first hotel to open in Abuja, in 1986, so furnishings are somewhat faded. According to the brochure 'the Agura is a haven of boundless delights where you will be teased with Tee-Vee & exquisite food & drinks'. Er, not quite, but nevertheless it's of a fairly good standard & the service is good, with 135 rooms, pool, gym, tennis & squash courts, a nice bar with Sky News & CNN on TV (and where a 'rumba' band plays most nights), bureau de change (guests only) & the modern Milky Way restaurant, with green-and-yellow plastic décor, where you can get a 3-course continental meal with a glass of wine. There are a couple of travel agencies & several domestic airline desks in the lobby & a bakery. $$$

🏠 **Crystal Palace Hotel** Plot 687, Port Harcourt Crescent, off Gimbiya St, Garki II; 📞 09 314 0033, 0803 937 6949. A very friendly hotel with well-equipped, clean rooms from a reasonable US$60. All rooms have AC, DSTV, hot water & free wireless internet. This place is very popular with NGOs & is in a lively area with bars right next door. The restaurant offers a N1,500 Nigerian buffet for lunch & dinner & breakfasts for around N400, including their special omelette toasted sandwich. $$

🏠 **Dannic Hotel** Plot 93, Oyo St, off Moshood Abiola Way, Garki Area 2; 📞 09 234 8183/5; www.abuja.dannichotels.com. The rooms here are tiny but spotless, with fridge & DSTV, & a key-card system (good job there's a 24hr gen). The reception staff are very friendly, but the real highlight here is the excellent restaurant serving all sorts of treats such as full English breakfasts, or prawn & avocado cocktails & excellent cream-based pasta dishes. Discounts of 50% are available from Fri to

Sun, but you have to stay a minimum of two nights. Rooms $; suites $$

🏠 **Royalton Hotel** Plot 1970, Gongola St, Garki Area 2; 📞 09 234 4914–17. This is a fairly neat tower up a quiet street with a modern lobby & has been recently refurbished. The 90 good-quality rooms have a fridge, DSTV & hot water. There's often a band in the Royal Bar & the Capital Restaurant has a daily changing menu of continental dishes such as beef goulash or chicken Maryland. $$

🏠 **Villa Hotel** Plot 1377, Borno St, Garki Area 10; 📞 09 234 2228–9/7650. The very nice 8 executive rooms here are above a branch of Tantalisers, & are geared towards the business traveller, but despite the lovely rooms this is not a terribly sociable spot, given that there is no restaurant or bar area, though you can order food to be delivered to your room & drink from the minibar. $$

🏠 **Africa Safari Hotel** Plot 11, Benue Cr, Garki Area 1; 📞 09 234 7881/1365. In a housing estate within walking distance of the Area 1 Shopping Complex, the rooms with fridge & DSTV are old-fashioned, but have new appliances, & there's a 24hr gen. You can get Nigerian dishes & simple Western items like egg & chips for around N800, & beers. Water is a problem here so keep your bucket full. $

🏠 **Browelf Hotel** Plot 16, Lagos Cr, off Ladoke Akintola Bd, Garki II; 📞 09 234 9596; 📧 browelfhotel@yahoo.com. Good budget option with clean doubles with TV & bucket. Pay a little more for extras such as a fridge & water heater. Room rates & deposit are both discounted at the weekend. There's a communal lounge & dark restaurant serving basics, or eat at the chop houses & bars on lively Lagos Crescent. $

🏠 **City Transit Inn** beside the ABC Transport terminal, 36 A E Ukukinam St, Utako; 📞 09 521 2342, 2338; www.abctransport.com. This is owned by ABC Transport & could be useful for an early start from the 'luxury' bus terminals or Jabi Motor Park. The basic but clean rooms have AC, DSTV & fridge. There's a simple restaurant & plenty of street food in the surrounding area. $

✕ **WHERE TO EAT AND DRINK** All the hotels have restaurants and most of them are fairly good. The area around Zone 4 Corner Shops and the adjoining Addis Ababa Crescent in Wuse district, close to the Sheraton, until recently had a reputation as the cuisine centre of Abuja, but after extensive demolition in the area only *suya* stalls and a branch of **Mr Biggs** remain. If you are on a budget and staying in Garki, head to the Area 1 Shopping Centre for cheap eating, where there are many chop and *suya* stalls – look out for *kilishi* (meat fried and dried in the sun with pepper and onions), and fruit stalls selling prepared slices of pineapple, coconut and mango. There's a branch of **Tantalisers** further up Moshood Abiola Way in Garki Area 10 on Borno Street, just round the corner from the **Sim Msira Garden Kitchen**, back on Moshood Abiola Way.

This is a lovely spot down some steps on a steep hill and it's a refreshing and unusual patch of manicured lawns and gardens, with shady palms and plastic chairs and tables scattered around the grass (and no rubbish). The outside thatched huts sell beers and soft drinks, *suya*, and food-is-ready, and it's open until 02.00 if the demand is there.

✗ **Abuja Sheraton Hotel & Towers** (see *Where to stay*); ◷ 12.00–15.00, 18.00–23.00. The Sheraton has a number of restaurants (none of them cheap) including the **Papillion Restaurant** with a nightly buffet of Nigerian food (better than at the Hilton) & theme nights such as Chinese or seafood, & **Luigi's** that has authentic Italian food & décor with a small but good menu of antipasti, pizza, steaks, veal & salmon dishes. There's also an espresso machine. The **Obudu Grill** is a standard steakhouse; there's a bakery in the lobby where you can get a trendy coffee & slice of cream cake. **$$$$**

✗ **Chopsticks** and **Caesar** 66 Mississippi St, Maitama; ☎ 09 413 1451; ◷ 12.30–16.00, 18.30–23.00 daily. Two adjoining restaurants in the embassy district & as the names suggest serving Chinese & Italian food. Both are pricey but the food is very authentic & Chopsticks is especially recommended by expats as having the best Chinese food in town, which is cooked from scratch in big woks. They also serve dishes from other parts of South East Asia & do takeaway & delivery. Caesars has an elegant dining room & specialises in veal & seafood, although there's plenty of pasta & sauces to choose from too. Both are popular with airline crews & they offer free pickups from the Hilton for groups of four or more. **$$$$**

✗ **Transcorp Hilton Hotel** (see *Where to stay*); ◷ 18.00–22.30 daily. There is a range of expensive restaurants in the Hilton, all which have recently been refurbished. The **Zuma Grill** has a nice patio for fine dining, with a Mediterranean à la carte menu, while the **Bukka Restaurant** has an extensive Nigerian & continental buffet. The **Oriental Restaurant** serves Chinese, Thai & Mongolian (make up your own) stir-frys; the **Fulani Pool Restaurant and Bar** (◷ 09.00–22.00 daily), with its thatched roof & African statues, has BBQs & a Tandoori oven, with themed BBQ nights & all-you-can-eat buffets. **$$$$**

✗ **Ciao Italian Restaurant** Plot 1173, Adetokunbo Ademola Crescent; ☎ 09 780 1435; ◷ 12.00–22.00 daily. This is probably the best Italian restaurant in Abuja, run by a friendly Italian woman so you can be guaranteed dishes are authentic. There's a full range of pasta, pizza & desserts, imported beer & Italian wine are available, & the real coffee is a joy to those who are fed up of Nescafé. **$$$**

✗ **Le Méridien** (see *Where to stay*). Here **Le Gwari Restaurant and Bar** is open 24hrs & serves continental dishes & a good range of imported booze, while **Le Splash Restaurant** (◷ 05.00–23.00 daily) is next to the pool & offers good local dishes & barbecues at the weekends with occasional bands. **$$$**

✗ **Sitar** 46 Usuma Crescent, Maitama; ☎ 0805 291 1815; ◷ 12.00–15.30 Mon–Sat, 18.30–22.30 daily. Run by the affable Mr Rahj & set in a smart house where uniformed staff serve good quality eat-in or takeaway Indian cuisine. There's a full range: biriyani, tikka masala, korma & plenty of vegetarian dishes. It's another spot that's popular with airline crews. **$$$**

✗ **Wakkis** Plot 171, opposite Kumasi Crescent, Aminu Kano Crescent, Wuse II; ☎ 09 780 2929/3000; ◷ 11.00–22.30 daily. This is an expat haunt with a great atmosphere, though the fabulous prawns & Indian curries are pricey. There's lots of imported booze & eating & drinking is very sociable, with everyone sitting at long bench tables. **$$$**

⌨ **Salamander Café** 72 Aminu Kano Crescent, Wuse II; ◷ 09.00–18.00 daily. Aims for the ambience of an upmarket European café, albeit with African-influenced décor, & is firmly targeted towards expats & rich Nigerians. Free wireless internet is advertised but was erratic on our visit. A breakfast costs N1–2,000, soup & a sandwich N2,000, an extravagant but real coffee N5–900, & a main course around N2,500. The 10% service charge is not included. **$$–$$$$**

✗ **Mr Biggs** 45 Lagos Crescent, Garki; 4 Addis Ababa Crescent, Wuse 4; 36 Amino Kano Crescent, Wuse Zone 2; ◷ 09.00–21.00 daily. There are several branches of this fast-food chain around the city for boxes off *jollof* rice, fried chicken, burgers, bean cakes, scotch eggs & sugary cakes. **$**

NIGHTLIFE If you want to hit a local bar, head to the south of Garki on Lagos Crescent, just off Ahmadu Bello Way, where there is a long line of bars and chop houses distinguished by the plastic tables and Star and Gulder beer crates stacked outside. This is a lively area in the evening, when there's some serious drinking to be done. It has survived the demolitions due to being in Garki village, which was exempt from Abuja's 'master plan'. There's also a branch of **Mr Biggs** at 45 Lagos Crescent and a couple of internet cafés that stay open late. Out of town past Asokoro on the road to Nyanya is Abacha Barracks (officially renamed Mogadishu Barracks), where you can sit, drink cold beer and eat spicy grilled fish in the busy 'mammy market'. In the centre of the market is a courtyard with open-air bars arranged around a circle of grills – just choose the fish you want – wandering musicians provide entertainment. To get there take a bus to Nyanya and ask to be dropped off at the barracks (just before the pedestrian bridge). Don't go there too late as soldiers come round at 22.00 to enforce closing time. Elsewhere in the city, the Sheraton and Hilton offer expensive bars for the less adventurous, where men must be aware that they will be hounded by prostitutes.

♀ **Abuja Sheraton Hotel & Towers** (see *Where to stay*). The **Lobby Bar** (⏰ 10.00–midnight daily) has a live band in the evening, & happy hour is 18.00–19.00. Here you will meet many other Abuja expats. The ☆ **Aquarium Nightclub** (⏰ 22.00–dawn Fri–Sat) thumps at the weekends, but expect to pay a huge cover charge if you're not staying at the Sheraton. The ♀ **Elephant Bar** (⏰ 17.00–03.00 daily; closed Sun) is an informal pub with nightly live music, & is located at the main entrance of the hotel.
♀ **Blake's Excellency Resort** Ahmadu Bello Way, to the northeast of Lagos Crescent. A popular bar with live music, where plastic tables are packed around a stage & on a rather wobbly balcony. It's usually full on Fri & Sat nights with a mostly local crowd & some expats. The house band, with their

energetic dancers, play highlife & Fela Kuti & Lagbaja covers, & other acts that appear during the evening play makossa or James Brown songs, & there's sometimes acrobats & comedians. In true Nigerian style, things don't get going until after 21.00. There's a N1,000 entry fee but this is negotiable if it's not busy.
♀ **Transcorp Hilton Hotel** (see *Where to stay*). The **Piano Lounge** in the lobby is open 24hrs & has live music in the evenings, as does the ♀ **Capital Bar** (⏰ 15.00–midnight daily), which is like an English pub & serves snacks such as chicken wings & burgers. Apparently, when Bill Clinton visited here in 2001, he had a good time listening to a James Brown impersonator! At the ☆ **Safari Nightclub** (⏰ midnight–dawn Fri–Sat) there is a cover charge of around US$20 for non-guests of the hotel.

PRACTICALITIES
Changing money You can try the bureaux de change at the Sheraton and Hilton, which, although they are supposed only to offer a service to guests, may not ask if you're staying there or not. The new Protea hotels also offer a foreign exchange service to their guests. Alternatively, head outside the gates of the Sheraton and turn left. Here are a number of Hausa money changers on the street who offer good rates of exchange, and they are not difficult to find as they will probably approach *oyibos* straight away. Some others have shops on Addis Ababa Crescent around Mr Biggs.

Cinemas Nu Metro Ceddi Plaza, 264 Tafawa Balewa Way, Central District; *www.ceddiplaza.com*. Nu Metro is a South African company which is opening up modern cinema complexes all over Africa. There are three screens showing Hollywood (not Nollywood) movies; be warned that sometimes the power goes off midway through a movie and there's a break until the gen kicks in. The Ceddi Plaza itself is a new shopping mall, largely empty at the time of writing, but Nu Metro also runs a book and music shop in the plaza, with reasonable prices for paperbacks.

Silverbird Cinema off Memorial Drive, close to the Sheraton (*www.silverbirdcinemas.com*). Although still under construction at the time of writing this 13-screen cinema complex should expand entertainment options in Abuja significantly if it's anything like the set-up they already have in Lagos.

Courier services The main branch of **DHL** is at 63 Ademola Adetokumbo Crescent, Wuse Zone 2; National Call Centre (℡ *01 270 0908*) though there are other branches around the city. **United Parcel Services (UPS)** is at 781 Emeka Anyakou Street, Garki (℡ *09 234 7979*); while **Fedex** is at 787 Malumfashi Close, Garki (℡ *09 234 9437*).

Cultural centres **British Council** Plot 2935, IBB Way (on the 'British Council Roundabout') (℡ *09 413 7870–7*; *www.britishcouncil.org/nigeria*). The Roof Top Cafe is a popular (but expensive) spot for coffee and excellent chicken *shawarma*.

Embassies and high commissions There are dozens of embassies and high commissions in Abuja. These are the most useful, in case you are travelling overland and need to pick up a few visas in Abuja for onward travel:

🅴 **Australia** Oakland Centre, 48 Aguiyi Ironsi Street, Maitama, ℡ 09 413 5226; www.nigeria.embassy.gov.au.

🅴 **Benin** Plot 342, Bamako St, Wuse Zone 1; ℡ 09 513 6105/6.

🅴 **Canada** 15 Bobo Street, Maitama; ℡ 09 413 9910.

🅴 **Chad** 10 Mississippi St, Maitama; ℡ 09 413 0751; ⏲ 08.00–16.30 Mon–Fri.

🅴 **European Union** Europe House, 63 Usuma St, Maitama; ℡ 09 413 3144. The EU represents a number of European member countries including Bulgaria, Finland, France, Germany, Greece, Italy, Portugal, Spain & Sweden.

🅴 **Gambia** Plot 25, Ontario Crescent, off Mississippi St, Maitama; ℡ 09 413 8545.

🅴 **Ghana** Plot 301, Olusegun Obasnajo Way, Garki Area 10; ℡ 09 234 5184.

🅴 **Ireland** Plot 415, Negro Crescent, Maitama; ℡ 09 413 1751.

🅴 **Mali** Plot 465, Nouakchott St, Wuse Zone 1; ℡ 09 523 0494.

🅴 **Niger** 7 Sangha St, off Mississippi St, Maitama; ℡ 09 413 6205.

🅴 **South Africa** 63 Usuma St, Maitama; ℡ 09 413 3862, 413 3574.

🅴 **Sudan** Plot 337, Mission Rd, Central District; ℡ 09 234 6265. Although at the time of writing it was not possible to cross Sudan overland because of the Darfur conflict, an overland company reported that in 2004 obtained at the Sudanese Embassy in Abuja cost in the region of US$50 & you needed 3 passport photos, a photocopy of the vehicle licence, *carnet de passage*, & a list of passenger names & passport details; on their visit it took 4 hours to issue all visas for the group. I have heard that they do not issue visas to US citizens, though an overland truck going through in early 2003 managed to successfully get one issued for a US passenger.

🅴 **Togo** Plot 664, Usuma St, Maitama; ℡ 09 413 9833.

🅴 **United Kingdom** Dangote House, Aguyi Ironsi St, Maitama; ℡ 09 413 2010/1; www.britishhighcommission.gov.uk.

🅴 **United States** Plot 1075, Diplomatic Drive, Central District; ℡ 09 461 4000; www.abuja.usembassy.gov.

Hospitals Like Lagos, it's a good idea to check with your embassy, or company if you're an expat, to find out which hospital they are currently recommending.

✚ **Abuja National Hospital** Yakubu Pam St; ℡ 09671 2526; www.nationalhospitalabuja.net. This 200-bed hospital opened in 1999.

✚ **Abuja Clinics** 22 Amazon St, Maitama; ℡ 09 413 7020–6; www.abujaclinics.com. Opened in 2004, this is the best of many private hospitals in Abuja, with good equipment & standards. Among many other specialities, they deal with tropical medicine & infectious diseases.

Information for visitors The head office of the **Nigeria Tourism Development Corporation** is at the Old Secretariat (*Garki Area 1;* ✆ *09 234 2764; www.nigeriatourism.net – although many of the pages on this website do not work*). The staff will be most surprised to see visitors but if you drop by they will try and rustle up some (old) brochures to give you.

The **National Parks Service** head office is on the Nnamdi Azikiwe Airport Expressway (✆ *09 234 5507/5568*). This office is roughly two kilometres out of town on the airport road, but there is no point in going there as it is the bureaucratic headquarters for the national parks service and they don't have any information to give out. Like the tourist offices, this is a largely dysfunctional organisation. Nigeria's most useful **tourist office** is in the arrivals hall of Abuja airport, which has a number of good books and a map of Abuja for sale, though the staff don't seem to know anything. Patchy information can also be found at *www.abujacity.com* and *www.abuja.net*.

Post and communications The main **post office** is on Moshood Abiola Way in Garki Area 10 (⊕ *08.00–16.00 Mon–Fri*). There are branch offices in the Area 1 Shopping Centre, on Mohammadu Buhari Way, both also in Garki and Maputo Street in Wuse Zone 3. There are a number of **internet** joints around, including flash internet cafés at the Sheraton and Hilton hotels, where you'll pay ridiculously expensive prices of about N250 for five minutes and N1,000 for 20 minutes. Cheaper places, where you'll pay a more standard N150 per hour, can be found around Wuse Market, and on Lagos Crescent, where there are a few 24-hour cyber cafés. **Cool Café**, in the Cool FM tower on Independence Avenue, is pleasant and reliable for internet during the day but gets busy in the evening. You can make (expensive) phone calls from any of the hotels, or from the public **NITEL** offices on M-Tel Street or Aminu Kano Crecent, both in Wuse Zone 2, at 251 Herbert Macaulay Way near the Old Wuse Market, or on Asa Street in Maitama near the Hilton. There are plenty of cell phone and landline **phone stalls** along the streets.

Sports Abuja has an 18-hole **golf course**, probably the best in Nigeria. The Ibrahim Badamasi Babangida (IBB) Golf and Country Club is in Maitama; non-members can play and there's a pleasant restaurant and bar in the club house. The course is a par 72 bisected by a number of streams, ponds and lakes with approximately 25 bridges and is set in some very attractive parkland. The Abuja **Hash House Harriers** usually meet at 15.00 on Saturdays in the car park of the Hilton.

Travel agents
Allstates Travel & Tours At the Hilton Hotel; ✆ 09 413 0405, 523 1811.
Air Transrapid Travel Agency At the Agura Hotel; ✆ 09 234 2671.

Habis Travel At the Sheraton Hotel; ✆ 09 523 0225/44.

SHOPPING **Old Wuse Market** is the largest market in Abuja, selling everything imaginable. It is on Sir Kasim Ibrahim Road, but you can get to it from off Herbert Macaulay Way if you walk through the newer buildings. When the city was built, it was designed to house 1,800 small shops, but the market attracted another estimated 13,000 illegal traders and stalls, and was so tightly packed that rescue vehicles such as fire engines couldn't get in (the main markets in Sokoto, Kaduna, Jos and Maidiguri have been destroyed by fire in recent years). In 2005 the government closed Wuse Market for four weeks, demolished the illegal structures and allowed just the originally intended number of 1,800 traders back on new

50-year leases. The market is now far less congested, but this was a controversial move and many people lost their livelihoods.

The **New Wuse Market** (main day Friday) is along Olusegun Obasanjo Way and is referred to as the 'poor' market. The government moved the old market here when they closed it, and although many of the formal traders went back the informal traders stayed on, working from underneath colourful umbrellas rather than from proper stalls; presumably prices are cheaper, hence the 'poor' title.

There are curio shops at the big hotels, and across Memorial Drive from the Sheraton is the **Abuja Arts & Crafts Centre**, a compound of traditional-style huts with people selling a variety of sculptures, textiles, clothes and paintings. Initial prices are high but if you're prepared to bargain they drop quickly.

Garki Supermarket Plot 465, Ahmadu Bello Way; ⏲ 09.00–18.00 daily. A Lebanese supermarket for expensive imported treats & useful items such as video tapes & camera batteries, next door to the Eddy Vic Hotel (the latter being truly awful & not recommended).

Jazz Hole and Glendora Books at the Salamander Café (see *Where to eat and drink*), 72 Aminu Kano Crescent, Wuse II; ⤫ 09 708 4518; *www.glendorabooks.net.* A branch of a wonderful Lagos chain (see page 134), this is a small shop within the Salamander Café, selling a limited but interesting range of books, but at much higher prices than the bookshop at Nu Metro. They also have a good selection of world music CDs.

Nike Art Village km 7.5, Abuja Airport Rd (behind a Texaco petrol station); ⤫ 080 231 31067; *www.nikeart.com.* This is another gallery of famous batik artist, Nike Okundaye (see page 154) though you'll need your own car or drop taxi to get out here as city transport doesn't go this far. There are art items on display & for sale similar to those in her other galleries in Lagos, Ogidi-Ijumu & Oshogbo, & Nike is currently building a 48-bed guesthouse here.

Park n Shop next to the Banex Plaza, Aminu Kano Crescent, Wuse Zone 2; ⏲ 10.00–18.00 Mon–Sat, 11.00–1800 Sun. Large supermarket popular with expats with a comprehensive range of imported goods from toothpaste to widescreen TVs, & sells wine & other alcohol.

Signature Gallery 65a Aminu Kano Crescent, Wuse Zone 2; ⤫ 09 523 3849; www.signatureafrica.com; ⏲ 10.00–1700 Mon–Fri, 10.00–16.00 Sat. This is the sister shop to the Lagos branch, with a wonderful collection of *objets d'art* from all over West Africa, & a few pieces from East & southern Africa, including oil & watercolour paintings, sculpture, exquisite furniture, antiques, fabrics, mirrors, vases & wood carvings.

WHAT TO SEE AND DO

The city There is very little to see or do in Abuja unless you are a fan of building sites and 1970s architecture. In fact, expats and Nigerians both generally find it a dull city, which explains why many fly back to Lagos at the weekend. When the city was being built, recreational facilities were not included in the grand scheme of things and as it's a new city there are no historic sights. There has been talk of building a National Museum in the city, but nothing has materialised yet, and when I trooped off to find the National Gallery of Art, which was marked on one map I had, I discovered it had not been built! Rather astonishingly, a new development is currently in the pipeline and is the brain child of a Nigerian businessman who has been living in the USA for a number of years: **Heritage City African Kingdoms and Empires** (*www.africanheritagecity.com*) is a proposed theme park with an African history theme and is to include fairground rides, amphitheatres, hotels, cinemas and other entertainment; 17,000 acres of land have been earmarked near Kusaki-Yanga, one of Abuja's satellite towns about 20 minutes' drive from the city centre. To date, just the website has been built!

Abuja's most interesting buildings are in the **Three Arms Zone** beneath the shadow of Aso Rock (*aso* means 'victory' or 'success'). The zone was fashioned after Capitol Hill in Washington DC, where Congress, the Supreme Court and the White House are within walking distance of each other. The Three Arms Zone derives its name from the three arms of the federal government structure, namely the executive, legislative and judicial arms. The zone is encircled by a ring road and includes the Presidential Villa (currently occupied by the State Security Service; the president lives in the fortress-like Aso Villa, hidden from public sight), the Federal House of Assembly, the Supreme Court of Nigeria and the **National Arboretum**. The latter is 100ha of land, natural forest and other vegetation that could be feasibly described as the president's back garden. At the beginning of Shehu Shagari Road is the **Tomb of the Unknown Soldier**, where in the past visiting foreign heads have laid wreaths. But mere plebeians are not permitted to get close to any of these buildings or even the tomb, as armed soldiers patrol the area, and the arboretum is fenced and closed off to visitors. Opposite the tomb is the **Eagle Square**, an open space with some tiered bench seating used for formal ceremonies, and on both sides of the square are the buildings of the **New Federal Secretariat**.

Two blocks further down are the **National Mosque** and **National Ecumenical Church**, facing each other from opposite sides of Independence Avenue and dominating the skyline of Abuja, underlining the determination of the government to ensure the right of every Nigerian to worship as they like. The mosque is a fine building with a golden dome and tall minarets. It was built in 1984, and inside is the main prayer hall, a library, conference hall and religious school. Non-Muslims (including women) can go inside outside of prayer time, and there's an office beside the entrance where you fill out a form and pay a *dash* to get permission. On Friday afternoons there is a street market outside the mosque. The church was completed in 2006 after it had spent 16 years as just a concrete shell due to lack of funds. It's a bright white building with a copper roof and stained glass windows and a rather ugly concrete tower.

Also in the Central District on Better Life Street is the **Women's Development Centre**, where in the entrance of the main auditorium is a hall of fame of portraits and sculptures of leading Nigerian women, overlooking some friendly women selling a few crafts and books, including the bright orange beads worn by brides on their wedding day. First Lady, Laura Bush visited here in early 2006 when the US president was on a tour of West Africa, and she addressed the organisation and attended a round table on women's empowerment.

Other buildings of note include the new **Abuja International Conference Centre** on Herbert Macaulay Way in Garki, a vast glass building set in well-attended grounds with a row of flags outside and with several meeting rooms and a main hall that can seat 2,000 people. It hosted the Commonwealth Heads of Government Meeting (CHOGM) in 2003, and one of the more recent important events held there was the 2006 signing of the Abuja Peace Agreement by 31 African Union countries, who called upon the international community to pressurise the Sudanese government to accept UN troops to help defuse the situation in Darfur. **Ship House**, on Olusegun Obasanjo Way in the Central District and built in the shape of a ship, is the headquarters of the Ministry of Defence.

The National Stadium On the outskirts of the city, on the airport road, is the **National Stadium**, which was built at a staggering cost of US$330 million for the eighth All Africa Games that were held in Abuja in October 2003. All facilities within the stadium were designed and engineered in compliance with the requirements of international sport associations, the Fédération Internationale de Football Association (FIFA) and the International Association of Athletics Federations (IAAF). It can seat 60,000 under cover, has an eight-lane running track, indoor sports hall, gym, Olympic-sized swimming pool, a 3,000-seater velodrome, a full-size football pitch and practice pitches, tennis courts and hockey fields. Look out for the enormous and deserted games village on the road from the airport that has nearly 700 flats where the athletes and coaches stayed during the games. Some 15,000 attended from 51 countries. The boxing and table tennis events were held in the ballrooms of Abuja's Hilton and Sheraton hotels.

The stadium was also scheduled to host the 2002 Miss World beauty pageant, as the winner the year before had been a Nigerian. Unfortunately, the stadium was not fully completed by then and because of violent clashes over the competition in some of the northern cities (see page 39), the pageant was forced to relocate to London.

Abuja is bidding to become the first African city to host the Commonwealth Games in 2014 (*www.abuja2014.org*), which in terms of numbers of athletes and spectators involved is actually smaller than the All Africa Games, so Abuja clearly has the capacity to host them. The only other city it is competing against is Glasgow in Scotland. Former Nigerian military leader from the 1960s, General Yakubu Gowon, is heading up the games bid team, and so far the Abuja bid has received strong support from African Commonwealth member countries (which indeed make up the bulk of the Commonwealth) as well as Australia. There are plans to upgrade the airport, build a mass rail transit system, and 'beautify', as Nigerians like to call it, the city. The stadium is also the home ground for the national football team, the Super Eagles, and it's also used for large religious events.

Other than that there's the **Wonderland Children's Amusement Park** near the stadium, (⊕ *13.00–22.00 Tue–Fri and 09.00–22.00 Sat–Sun; entry N300, and the rides inside N150–300*), which has pretty tame amusement rides for small children.

National Children's Park and Zoo This is the newest and nicest zoo in Nigeria, located at the foot of Aso Rock in Asokoro (⊕ *10.00–18.00 Mon–Fri, 10.00–18.30 Sat–Sun; entry N200 adults, N50 children*). To get there you'll have to take an *okada* or a drop taxi, and you may need to ask them to come back in an hour or two as there's little public transport in the car park once you get out here. It's off the ring road, the Murtala Muhammed Expressway, to the east of the city. This was only built in 2002 with the help of the National Zoological Gardens of South Africa, so the design reflects a better attitude to caged animals than in Nigeria's other archaic concrete nightmare zoos built decades ago. It's a pretty tract of countryside that has been kept clean and rubbish free (there are rubbish bins everywhere!). The modern animal enclosures, with informative display boards, are spacious and thoughtfully designed with the welfare of the animals taken into consideration. It's essentially a children's activity park with many playgrounds, climbing frames, paths leading to rocks to climb, a football pitch, and other treats, but there's no reason why grown-up children cannot enjoy a wander around the pleasant gardens, and it's nice to see all the Nigerian school kids ooing and ahhing at the animals that they clearly have never seen before.

Animals include wildebeest, various antelope, buffalo, giraffe, ostrich, zebra, lion and cheetah (presumably from other parts of Africa), a few monkeys and some domestic animals such as chickens, ducks, camels and donkeys. There's a very pretty lake right beneath Aso Rock where the **Lake Café** serves water and soft drinks. This is a good spot to admire the rock, which is the largest of the rocks in the immediate vicinity of Abuja city; look out for birds and (supposedly) crocodiles around the edges of the lake. It may be possible to arrange a walk up the rock from the zoo.

A few metres before the gate of the park is the **Abuja Plant Nursery**, a botanical garden with many species of flowering and fruit trees and many other plants originally created to supply trees to landscape the new city.

Zuma Rock, Suleja and Gurara Falls The **Zuma Rock** is proclaimed as the gateway to Abuja, as the Federal Capital Territory (FCT) begins at the foot of the rook, where Niger State ends. It's also reputed to be the geographical centre of Nigeria. Located just outside the town of Suleja, on the Abuja–Kaduna Expressway, 55km from Abuja, it's a huge rounded rock, 1km long and 300m high, with sheer cliffs on all sides and vertical lines carved on it by centuries of rainfall running down from the summit. Before the founding of the new federal capital, Suleja used to be called Abuja, and when the capital was being built many construction workers stayed in Suleja and commuted daily by taxi and lorry. The road from Abuja goes directly to the base of the rock before curving off to the left towards Kaduna. Big green buses to Suleja go from the Federal Secretariat in Abuja for N80. From Suleja you can take a drop or *okada* closer to the rock. Zuma Rock is impressive, but not necessarily worth a special trip out to Suleja and it only takes a minute to look at. Rather, look out for it on a drive or bus journey between Abuja and Kaduna.

Before the creation of the Federal Capital Territory, the region was known for its pottery. Near Suleja, **Bwari Pottery** is a training centre where one of the students was Ladi Kwali, a local woman who became internationally famous and now graces the N20 note. For a long time the centre was sadly derelict but several former students have now set up their own businesses, and have a showroom and kilns; they offer tours of the workshops and there's a picnic area. It's a popular excursion for expats and embassy staff. To get there take a bus from Abuja's Berger Junction to Bwari and drop at the T-junction, from where you can take an *okada* past the Law School to the pottery.

Another impressive attraction is the **Gurara Falls**, which are 32km from Suleja on the Minna Road. There's a sign saying 'Nigeria's Top Tourist Attraction'! They are at their best in the wet season when a torrent of foamy water spans a width of up to 200m and drops 30m. This reduces to a mere trickle in the dry season, though you can take a shower in them and swim in the Gurara River. There's a car park and picnic spot, some well worn paths at the top and bottom of the falls, and local boys may try and wrangle a small fee out of you. You'll need to organise a drop from Suleja to get to the Gurara Falls or take a bush taxi to Minna from either Suleja or Abuja and ask them to drop you at the junction for the falls, from where you can try to flag down an *okada* or walk the 10–15 minutes to the car park.

LOKOJA

Roughly 140km south of Abuja on the A2, Lokoja is the capital of Kogi State, and is principally known as the location of the confluence of the Benue and Niger rivers. You can see the spot from the Confluence Hotel, where there's a nice view of the brown sludgy rivers drifting slowly alongside one another between separate sand banks until there are no more sand banks and the river is one. During the dry season Fulani herdsmen bring their cattle to the banks of the Niger–Benue confluence around Lokoja and you can spot solitary fishermen in tiny canoes. Now a busy, and not especially clean, market town, one of the first things you'll notice in Lokoja, apart from the piles of rubbish, are the very odd abstract statues on the roundabouts. One of them I can only describe as a giant concrete triangle supporting a fish.

Lokoja was the first town in the hinterland to be settled by Europeans in what is now Nigeria in the British quest to control trade on the Niger. The African Association in London sent the likes of Mungo Park, Clapperton and the Lander brothers to trace the course of the Niger in the early 19th century, and they were followed by another multi-purpose expedition that set out by steamship in 1841 from the coast until it reached the confluence of the two rivers. Their quest was to open up the hinterland for trade, evangelism and Western civilisation, and it was on this journey that Bishop Samuel Crowther first preached the gospel along the banks of the Niger. At the confluence area the local chiefs ceded a plot of land 8 × 5km to the British expedition to build a model farm, from which Lokoja grew into a town under the leadership of Scottish explorer, Doctor William Baikie.

In the course of sailing up and down the Niger, Baikie discovered that white men could survive the scourge of malaria by using quinine, and he lived at Lokoja for over 30 years where he was dubbed 'King of Lokoja'. He nurtured trade links with the Hausa to the north and learnt their language, wrote a Hausa dictionary, and translated with the missionaries parts of the Bible into Hausa. The settlement of British traders continued to thrive and in 1879, under the leadership of British administrator George Goldie, all the British companies working along the Niger were amalgamated into the Royal Niger Company with headquarters in Lokoja, which had its own constabulary and gunboats on the river protecting the company's interests. The company negotiated trade treaties with Sokoto, Gwandu and Nupe in the north.

Meanwhile, the French were making progress in a southerly direction down the Niger from the French colonies in the northwest, and the company employed a Captain Frederick Lugard to form a military force to protect the northern states from possible invasion by the French. These military operations against a rival European colonial power soon proved too expensive for a private company and in 1897 the British government ended the charter. By 1900 the British had taken control of the north, and Lugard became High Commissioner of the Protectorate of Northern Nigeria. His capital was Lokoja from 1900 to 1902, before it was moved to Kaduna. Lokoja remained an important centre on the river as a collection point for goods that were transported down the Niger to the port at Warri for export. These days trucks do that along the A2, and there is surprisingly little river traffic on West Africa's greatest river.

GETTING THERE AND AWAY If you are coming from Abuja note that the road to Lokoja is another blackspot for accidents, and there are loads of wrecks on the side of the road. At the time of writing the road was being upgraded to a dual carriageway, which should reduce the number of deaths due to reckless overtaking manoeuvres. Lokoja's **motor park** is in the centre of town on Murtala Muhammed Way, which is the town's main street that more or less runs parallel to the River Niger, where shared taxis run up and down for N30. At the motor park you can pick up buses on short hops to neighbouring towns and long-distance vehicles to Abuja, Kaduna, Kano, Zaria and Ilorin.

For the south you need to get buses to Agauba or Ankpa and then change. If you prefer to travel by bush taxi note that the smaller Governor Ibro Motor Park is by the pedestrian bridge in the New Market area north of town, close to the Abuja junction. Until recently the only way to get to the south on the other side of the Niger was by car ferry, but there's now a new road going directly south of Lokoja to Ajaokuta, roughly 30km, where there is an enormous steel-processing plant and a new and very impressive 3km-long bridge over the Niger.

WHERE TO STAY

Confluence Beach Hotel literally on the beach overlooking the confluence of the two rivers & roughly 2km to the south of town on Ganaja Rd; ☎ 058 221726, 221751/2; e confluencebeachhotel @yahoo.com. The principal state-owned hotel under the same management as the Federal Palace Hotel in Lagos is a huge & popular conference venue with a vast car park. Facilities include a small bar, a basic restaurant serving Nigerian staples, a swimming pool (empty), tennis, volley ball

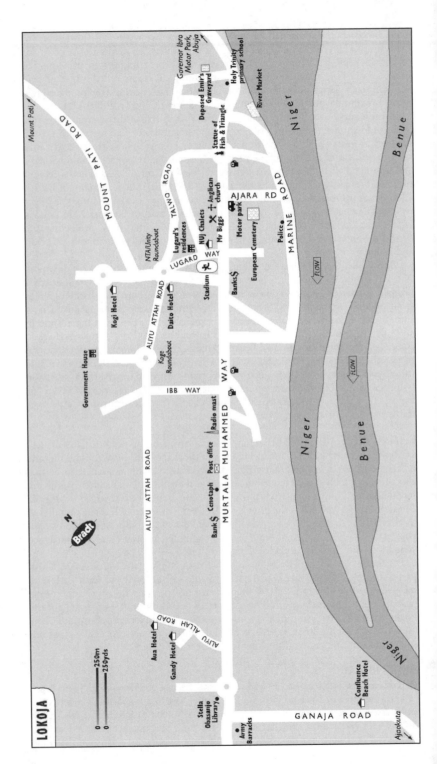

LOKOJA

0 ____ 250m
0 ____ 250yds

Mount Pati

MOUNT PATI ROAD

Governor Ibro Motor Park, Abuja

Holy Trinity primary school

Deposed Emir's Graveyard

River Market

Niger

Benue

Statue of Fish & Triangle

TAIWO ROAD

NTA/Unity Roundabout

Lugard's residences

NUJ Chalets

AJARA RD

Anglican church

Mr Biggs

Motor park

LUGARD WAY

European Cemetery

Police

MARINE ROAD

Kogi Hotel

Daito Hotel

Stadium

Banks $

FLOW

ALIYU ATTAH ROAD

Koge Roundabout

Government House

IBB WAY

MURTALA MUHAMMED WAY

Niger

Benue

FLOW

Radio mast

Post office

ALIYU ATTAH ROAD

Bank $ Cenotaph

Aua Hotel

Gandy Hotel

ALIYU ALLAH ROAD

Stella Obasanjo Library

Confluence Beach Hotel

Niger

Army Barracks

GANAJA ROAD

Ajaokuta

& basketball courts (overgrown), & a children's playground (rusting); it must have been grand in its day. Nevertheless, it's still the best spot in town, with a peaceful view of the two rivers gliding into one another, & the 156 rooms, spread around in low blocks, are comfortable & have AC, fridge & DSTV. Rates start from a not unreasonable US$45 & deposits are roughly half of the room rates. Rooms $$; suites $$$

⌂ **Diato Hotel** close to the NTA Roundabout on Aliyu Attah Rd; ✆ 0803 523 1853/0808 585 6288. Shiny & new with everything working. Rooms are compact but well equipped with AC, TV & hot water. $$

⌂ **Ava Hotel** Aliyu Attah Rd; ✆ 0803 587 3885. It's not brilliant, with a noisy gen & an outside bar in the car park where large groups of men come & watch football on TV, & not much to eat except a chipped plate of soup and *amala*, though there's a *suya* stand at the gate. But the cheap rooms are passable, with clean sheets & slow-moving fans, & it's always busy. $

⌂ **Gandy Hotel** Inikipi St; ✆ 0803 586 7026. Freshly painted with fairly modern furnishings, the rooms have either a fan or AC but are small & dark, but nevertheless cost only US$10. $

⌂ **Kogi Hotel** I Janet Ekundauyo Street in the GRA; ✆ 0802 902 6987/0806 570 5920. A good & friendly option in a quiet area. The 30 rooms, all with AC & fan, are either in the main block or in stand-alone stone buildings, but these are not very private. In the pleasing grounds there are palm trees, lots of parking, shady gardens with outside tables, & the restaurant & bar serves the odd continental dish & breakfast of tea-bread-and-eggs. Rates are inclusive of the 15%, & if you pay in advance by cash there's no need to pay a deposit. $

⌂ **NUJ Chalets** Lugard Way, not far from the museum; ✆ 0803 745 0708. The cheapest stay in Lokoja, with very basic & tiny rooms with fan & spotless bathrooms for just US$7. $

✗ **WHERE TO EAT** There's a branch of **Mr Biggs** on Murtala Muhammed Way close to the stadium, or you can eat at one of the many local chop houses. There are good bars and chop houses in the grounds of the museum that offer local starch-and-soup meals for N250 a plate.

WHAT TO SEE AND DO Queen Elizabeth II came to Lokoja to survey the relics of colonial history on her visit to Nigeria in 1956. She'd have a great deal of difficulty finding them now, as nothing has been maintained or looked after and as usual everything is seriously dilapidated, but if you persevere there are a couple of fairly interesting things to see. Near the motor park is the **European Cemetery**, which has some fine, well-established trees and early graves of missionaries, colonial officers and servicemen; some of the tombstones date back to 1867. Just to the north, beyond the roundabout with the funny statue on, is another cemetery, the **Deposed Emir's Graveyard**, with some graves of emirs from Kano, Zaria and Bida, exiled to Lokoja by Lugard during the British occupation of these cities in the early 1900s. Today both are used as ad hoc rubbish dumps.

Across from the Emir's Graveyard is the **Holy Trinity Primary School**, a broken building with a tin roof and outside gallery for classrooms, which was the first school in Nigeria, founded by Bishop Samuel Crowther in 1885. The newer block of classrooms on the site is still functional as a school. Also in the compound is the **Iron of Liberty**, the spot where slaves were freed in 1900; there are two upward iron poles, through which slaves passed through to freedom, and the spot where the Royal Niger Company's flag was lowered on 1 January 1900 and the British flag hoisted by Lugard – marked with a 2.5m concrete pillar.

Back at the roundabout, take one of the roads towards the River Niger to Marine Road and the (rubbish-strewn) embankment, from which there is a nice view of the busy, informal **river market**, full of people and colour. Tuesday is the big day here, when many women in gaily patterned dresses bring firewood from across the river to sell to the townsfolk of Lokoja. There are big wooden barges packed with people who are poled across to the other side of the river, and it's best to go and look at the activity in the late afternoon when all the market traders make

FREDERICK JOHN DEALTRY LUGARD (1858–1945)

- Born in 1858 in Madras (now Chennai), India.
- Military education at the Royal Military College, Sandhurst.
- Joined the East Norfolk Regiment in 1878, and served in the Afghan War (1879–80), the Sudan Campaign (1884–85) and Burma (1886–87).
- In 1888, Lugard took command of an expedition organised by the British settlers in Nyasaland against Arab slave traders on Lake Nyasa.
- In 1889 he joined the British East Africa Company and was involved in the emancipation of slaves held by Arabs on Zanzibar.
- Went to Uganda where he secured British predominance, and was Military Administrator for Uganda 1890–92. During which time he mapped out much of the Ruwenzori Mountains and Uganda's lakes.
- Was dispatched by the Royal Niger Company to Borgu (now Nigeria and the Republic of Benin) in 1894, where he secured treaties with local kings and chiefs acknowledging the sovereignty of the British company, while distancing the other colonial powers that were in the region.
- From 1896–97 Lugard led an expedition on behalf of the British West Charterland Company to explore Lake Ngami (in present-day Botswana).
- Then recalled to Nigeria where he was commissioned to raise a native force, the West African Frontier Force, to protect British interests against French encroachment down the Niger River.
- In 1902 he married acclaimed journalist, Flora Louise Shaw, who worked as the Colonial Editor for *The Times*, who in 1898, whilst she was his mistress, joined together the word *niger*, meaning 'black', with the word 'area', to create the name Nigeria.
- After he relinquished command of the West African Frontier Force, Lugard was made High Commissioner of the Protectorate of Northern Nigeria, a position he held until 1906.
- By the time Lugard resigned as commissioner, all of Nigeria was being peacefully administered under indirect rule under collaboration with local leaders supervised by British officers.
- Lugard was appointed Governor of Hong Kong, a position he held until March of 1912.
- Returned to Nigeria as governor and completed the amalgamation of protectorates into one single British colony, which he led until 1919.
- Returned to England and wrote *The Dual Mandate in British Tropical Africa* (1922), which detailed his theory of indirect rule and his belief that British imperial power was responsible for the development of Africa.
- Lugard never resumed service abroad but remained an active figure until his death in 1945, and was member of the Permanent Mandates Commission of the League of Nations from 1922 to 1936. He was knighted in 1902 and became a peer in 1928.

their watery way home. The Niger is still and khaki green and very picturesque, and there are a few fishing canoes and some boat-building going on along the shore. It's possible to hire a boat to take you down to the confluence or to some of the nearby Fulani villages for a few hundred naira. The locals firmly believe that tourists should travel in motor boats, so it may take some persuasion to hire one of the (much more pleasant) hand-pulled canoes instead.

To the north of Murtala Muhammed Way, follow the streets towards the Kogi Hotel, where in the grounds is the **first prison** in Nigeria, built by Lugard in 1903 and used until 1945. There's not much to see: it's just a small squat building now used as the hotel laundry, with a few remains of a watchtower and some walls. Notice the door to the laundry is the original gate, with its heavy iron bars. On Lugard Way are **Lord Lugard's Residence and Office**, two houses next to each other, one of which Lugard lived in and the other of which was the house of his senior staff. Both were built in 1901 on stilts because of the reptiles and floods, with wooden shutters and tin roofs to keep the interiors cool; they were prefabricated buildings sent from England. On each there are steps at the front leading up to the main front door, whilst at the back is a ramp to the service entrance.

You can go inside both of them. In Lugard's house on the left is the Kogi State Tourism Board, where you might be able to pick up a guide to show you around town for a small *dash*. The house on the right is a museum, though there is very little on display here, except a few faded photos of Lokoja, but someone there will tell you a little history if you make a donation. In the grounds are some old buoys that used to indicate the depth of the river, and an 1865 anchor. The museum has collected many of Lugard's things, including many old photographs and original treaties he signed with the Africans. Unfortunately they've chosen to display a gallery of photographs of Nigerian leaders from early colonial times to the end of the First Republic instead of these items.

To the northwest of the Kogi Hotel is **Government House**. It's a modern

OGIDI-IJUMU

Ogidi-Ijumu is a small village in a valley surrounded by beautiful hills in Kogi State, 10km to the southwest of the town of Kabba, which is 86km west of Lokoja. Surrounded by large domed rocky outcrops, it has a collection of small red-roofed houses, a small Catholic church and a mosque, and is home to about 3,000 people. It is the home village of Nike Okundaye, the famous Nigerian woman artist of the popular Oshogbo art movement who now lives in Lagos where she also manages her art gallery (see page 154). At Ogidi-Ijume, Nike has opened a traditional weaving centre and provided vertical looms to up to 50 women. They currently produce richly detailed patterns of hand-spun cotton and silk *aso-oke* cloth, and adire cloth which is hand painted with cassava paste by chicken feathers and then dyed with indigo. Nike learnt her skills from her great-grandmother in this village as a child.

Today cotton is still grown on local farms and indigo collected from trees in the region. Nike says that the centre has empowered the women of the village: 'What I have done in Ogidi-Ijumu is to give the women a strong economic tool so that their feelings and voices can be respected.' You can buy the cloth here or at her other galleries in Lagos, Abuja and Oshogbo.

Nike can organise accommodation in the village at her guesthouse, which is a smart, modern, whitewashed building with comfortable rooms with mosquito netting and ceiling fans and spacious lawns outside where meals are taken on long tables ($$). For groups Nike can also arrange transport from Abuja, which is about a four-hour drive away. There are various possible activities: guests can see the women demonstrating their artistic skills in the centre; local guides can take guests on walks into the nearby hills for great views of the village; a day trip can be arranged to Lokoja; and in the evenings the women put on a great show of singing and dancing. The women at the centre are delighted to meet visitors and many wear the wonderful indigo and white gowns Nike is so famous for. Contact Nike in Lagos to arrange a visit.

8

structure, but the front gate is the original, and was again built in 1901. Back on Murtala Muhammed Way, beyond the post office, is the **Cenotaph Monument**, a square concrete memorial behind a fence erected to commemorate the soldiers who died in both World Wars, with the names of the dead carved into it, and a few rusty cannons.

Above the town is **Mount Pati** (a Nupe word meaning hill) with great views of the town and confluence. You can hire an *okada* (pick a new-looking one, it's a steep road) to take you there for a couple of hundred naira or drive up if you have a car. It's roughly 1,500m high, with a 2km radius at the summit, on which are a number of radio masts. Reputedly Lugard used to go up here to watch the river with his telescope, and local residents claim that until about 20 years ago hyenas used to come down from Mount Pati to prey on domestic animals in Lokoja. On the road up, don't be surprised if you encounter naked *okada* drivers. Seemingly they make use of the mountain streams running off the hill to wash their bikes, their clothes and themselves!

MAKURDI

Makurdi, 323km to the southeast of Abuja, is the capital of Benue State, and is neatly bisected into north and south by the Benue River, which supports a boat-building industry that is supplied by the city's numerous sawmills. The combined road and rail bridge that spans the Benue here was built in 1932, opening up transport links between northeastern Nigeria and the southeast, and ultimately the sea. The newer, multi-laned expressway bridge is close to it.

The city is one of the most important homelands for the Tiv ethnic group, and has some Islamic influence, with several Muslim organisations and mosques. The Tiv people are traditionally farmers and the region grows cassava, yams, groundnuts, grain and rice; for this reason, on car number plates Benue State is dubbed 'Food Basket to the Nation'.

In the run-up to independence the Tiv people resented being governed by the Northern Region and the capital of Kaduna, and formed the United Middle Belt Congress (UMBC) to campaign for regional self-government separate from the north. Although the leader of the congress, Joseph Tarka, was based in Jos, he was a Tiv. The movement peaked in 1960–61, with a series of riots and demonstrations demanding a separate region, during which hundreds of Tiv activists in Makurdi were arrested and imprisoned. After the military coup staged by General Gowon in 1966, when Nigeria was split into 12 states, the creation of the Benue/Plateau State was generally regarded as a victory for the Tiv people. It was administered from Jos until 1976, when Benue State was restructured as its own, with Makurdi as the capital. There's nothing to see or do, but Makurdi is a transport hub for travel between the southeast and Abuja to the north, and the extreme west of Nigeria, and the chances are you may spend the night here.

Between Abuja and Makurdi you will pass through Lafia, a Hausa city and the capital of Nassarawa State, with an economy relying on the local coal mining industry. It was founded in the 1700s by the Hausas and developed into an important market town before being seized by the son of the Sultan of Sokoto in the early 1900s and becoming part of the Fulani Empire. Nassarawa State is dubbed the 'Home of Solid Minerals' and is one of Nigeria's newest states, created by General Abacha in 1996.

GETTING THERE AND AWAY Where you get dropped off in Makurdi by public transport rather depends on what direction you've come from. From the southeast you're likely to be dropped off on Gboko Road, the main road between the university and the town, from where you'll have to get an *okada* to the accommodation options another kilometre or so further on, again on or around Gboko Road in the Old GRA. Just before the university you'll find clutches of vehicles going south to Enugu and Katsina Ala (change here for Obudu and anywhere else south of Obudu).

If coming from the north, you'll get dropped off at the Lafia Motor Park in the north of the city, on the main road that crosses the river on the new bridge. The motor park is roughly 500m north of the bridge, and it's not very obvious. It's opposite the Amajechris petrol station, concealed behind a row of trucks and grimy engine oil and tyre stalls. From this motor park, vehicles go to Jos, Abuja, and Suleja, to the north.

WHERE TO STAY AND EAT

🏠 **Benue Hotel** 5/7 Ahmadu Bello Way; ✆ 044 532228/532178/533719. This is within walking distance to the north of the Gboko Rd roundabout; take Kashim Ibrahim Rd & then turn right on to Ahmadu Bello Way. The faded state hotel, with 87 rooms, has seen better days, but it's still probably the best option in town, with a car park & 24hr gen, restaurant & bar for excellent breakfasts that you make up from a list of breakfast items for about US$1 each. According to the tariff it costs slightly more for a non-resident, but you are unlikely to be charged the extra. Rooms $; suites $$

🏠 **Father Moustache Hotel** 5 Kashim Ibrahim Rd; ✆ 044 531072/532073. Around the corner from the Benue is the delightfully named Father Moustache Hotel. It's a small house with a few cheap rooms (from US$18) in large grounds, where there is a popular outside bar & *suya* stand. $

🏠 **Niima Hotel** 24 Gboko Rd, also near the roundabout; ✆ 044 533731, is a Muslim spot, so there's no booze, although there is cheap but dire food that you can order to be sent to your room. Rooms are adequate, with satellite TV, big beds, & a bucket.

On the roundabout itself is a branch of **Mr Biggs**, which maybe the better option for food if staying here. $

JOS

The region around Jos has its origins as far back as AD500, attested to by the discovery of the Nok terracotta on the Jos Plateau that's now on display in the Jos Museum. But Jos itself is a relatively new town, built by the British in the early 1900s as a tin-mining centre and developed rapidly following the completion of the railroad from Port Harcourt in 1914. Capital of Plateau State, Jos is located 288km northeast of Abuja on the Jos Plateau, which is about 1,250m above sea level on the Delimi River. Although not part of the north, if you have travelled from anywhere in the south, this is the first place you'll notice the distinctive northern scenery of scrub plains and rocky plateaus, and sandy fields littered with mud-brick homesteads; it's all very different to the green and lush scenery in southern Nigeria.

There are two theories about how Jos got its name. The first is that the original village at the foot of a hill where the present Jos Museum is located was called Gwosh and the early settlers mispronounced it; the second is that the early Christian missionaries gave it its name as an acronym for 'Jesus our Saviour'. Around 1903, agents of the Niger Company discovered that local people were smelting tin and traced its origin to the traditional tin furnaces on what is now Jos Plateau, though Captain Clapperton reported that he had seen tin for sale in Kano Market in the 1820s.

The exploitation of the tin ores began in earnest by the British from 1904, supported by an armed escort from the West African Frontier Force. Until the railway arrived, first the Zaria–Bukuru railway in 1914 and then the main railroad in 1927, the tin was carried by labour gangs of some 4,000 men to Loko, a port on the River Benue some 200km away, *en route* to the sea ports for export to Europe. The same gangs on their return journey brought back imported commodities to Jos. Barclays Bank and the Bank of British West Africa had opened their doors in the rapidly growing town by 1917, and encouraged more British, Indian and Lebanese settlers to a town that had a fast-growing reputation as a place where you could grow rich overnight. Output grew to 10,000 tons a year during World War I thanks to the demand for tin, but production had all but died out in the 1930s because of a fall in prices. By the end of the 1950s, with investment chasing the smell of oil, production slowed even further, and the tin mines eventually closed.

With average monthly temperatures ranging between 21°C and 25°C, Jos is considerably cooler and more comfortable than other cities in Nigeria. During colonial days, British officers were encouraged to spend some of their leave in Jos for the good of their health, and this requirement used to be written into the civil service code. The climate is also good for the growing of produce not found elsewhere in Nigeria, such as watermelons, lettuce and spinach.

Today Jos has a population of at least a couple of million, and curiously it's also home to lots of bread factories and many subsidiaries of NASCO, a food-manufacturing company; you'll see the enormous NASCO biscuit factory on Murtala Muhammed Way. Also look out for the hill to the south of town covered in aerials and satellite dishes, and the enormous blue storage tanks of Swan Water, bottled water that is produced in the region. Like other Nigerian cities, Jos has its collection of weird-looking roundabout statues. There used to be one of a 5m-tall woman with a child hanging on to her back and an enormous pot on her head in black concrete, of almost cartoon-like appearance, on the Terminus Roundabout near the market. However, it has been knocked down, apparently because the new Plateau governor believed that it was offensive to people of his tribe as it implied they're all poor.

One of the first impressions you'll get of Jos is the colourfully dressed Fulani people, many in bright fluorescent colours and lots of layers. In the cooler months you'll also see people bundled up in woolly cardigans and children wearing imported snow suits. There's a big Muslim presence, and you'll perhaps notice the numerous little parks scattered around the roads near the museum and on the road to the Hill Station Hotel. Some of these have benches and thatched seating areas, and are used for Muslim contemplation.

UNREST IN JOS As the crossroads between Nigeria's Christian south and Muslim north, Jos has witnessed violent clashes in recent years. Tension between the two communities erupted in riots in 2001 and the violence has continued intermittently since then. Thousands of people have been killed and tens of thousands more have now fled the state, and around the city are burnt-out mosques and churches. The violence has had ripple effects elsewhere in the country, and in Kano Christians were targeted in an uprising in 2004 that was supposedly in retaliation for the killings of Hausa in Jos. In 2004, the former governor of Plateau State, Joshua Dariye, was suspended for failing to control the crisis. Shortly afterwards he was arrested in the UK on money laundering charges but fled bail. Following the end of his term of office in 2007 he lost his immunity and has now been arrested on corruption charges in Nigeria. In recent years, there's often been a strong link in the northern cities with 'ethnic' or 'religious' trouble covering the tracks of crooked state governors, Kano and Zamfara states as well as Plateau State being other prime examples.

Additionally, both Muslims and Christians blamed each other for a fire which destroyed Jos Market in 2002, which still hasn't been rebuilt. Thankfully it started

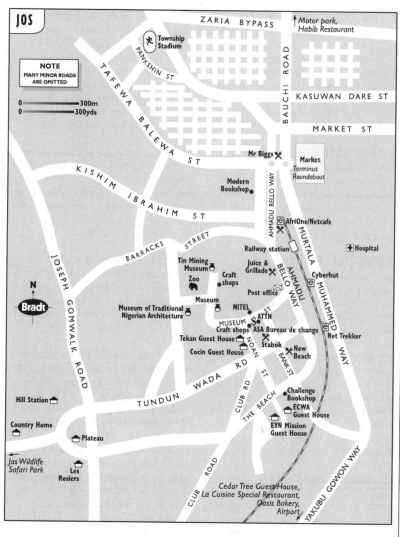

NOTE
MANY MINOR ROADS
ARE OMITTED

0 ——————— 300m
0 ——————— 300yds

ZARIA BYPASS

↑ Motor park,
Habib Restaurant

Township
Stadium

PANKSHIN ST

BAUCHI ROAD

KASUWAN DARE ST

MARKET ST

TAFEWA BALEWA ST

Mr Biggs

Market
Terminus
Roundabout

KISHIM IBRAHIM ST

Modern
Bookshop

AHMADU BELLO WAY

AfriOne/Netcafe

BARRACKS STREET

Railway station

Hospital

MURTALA

Tin Mining
Museum

Craft
shops

Zoo

Juice &
Grillade

Cyberhut

JOSEPH GOMWALK ROAD

Museum

Post office

AHMADU BELLO WAY

MUHAMMED WAY

Museum of Traditional
Nigerian Architecture

NITEL

ST

ATTN

MUSEUM

Craft shops

ASA

Bureau de change

Net Trekker

Tekan Guest House

NOAN RD

Stabok

New
Beach

Cocin Guest House

BANK ST

TUNDUN WADA RD

CLUB RD

THE BEACH

Challenge
Bookshop

Hill Station

ECWA
Guest House

Country Home

EYN Mission
Guest House

Plateau

Jos Wildlife
Safari Park

Les
Rosiers

CLUB ROAD

Cedar Tree Guest House,
La Cuisine Special Restaurant,
Oasis Bakery,
Airport

YAKUBU GOWON WAY

N

Bradt

at 04.00 so no-one was hurt, though the 4,300 densely packed stalls reputedly burnt for many hours and it must have been quite an inferno. Today it remains in its burnt-out state, with rather sad-looking charred Milo and Indomie advertising hoardings, and the stalls have shifted to the sides of the roads instead, making this area very congested. Because of this, some of the traders started moving back into the burnt-out shell, and there were further violent clashes in January 2007, when security forces attempted to evict them. In retaliation Muslim traders burnt down a police station.

GETTING THERE AND AWAY The **airport** is 29km to the south of the city, and the only option of getting to and from there is by drop taxi, which will cost in the region of N2,500. **Arik Air** (↘ *01 279 9999 central reservations; www.arikair.com*) have previously operated a service between Lagos and Jos, but check first if flights are operating. The main **motor park** is Bauchi Motor Park to the north, 3km from the city centre on the Bauchi Road, for vehicles going to Makurdi, Abuja, Bauchi, Zaria and Kaduna, though you may find yourself being dropped off at a number of smaller motor parks in the centre around Terminus Roundabout and Tafewa Balewa Street. 'Luxury' buses go overnight to Lagos and Port Harcourt from here and from the streets around the Township Stadium, but you'll have to ask around. Be wary in the old town around the stadium as it's pretty rough and ready. Jos is located at the terminus of a spur (first built in 1915) of the railway from Port Harcourt to Maiduguri. The **railway station** is centrally located on Bauchi Road, just south of the market. It's still open and staffed, despite there being no trains for years.

GETTING AROUND Once in the city centre, most of the attractions are within walking distance of each other and it's easy enough to wander around. The hotels and some restaurants are further outside from the centre, but there are plenty of *okada*s, and minibuses and shared taxis run up and down the long main road that runs north to south through the city. In the north it's called Bauchi Road, then turns into Murtala Muhammed Way in the middle of the city, before being renamed Yakubu Gowon Way to the south.

WHERE TO STAY There are a couple of mid-range hotels, and budget accommodation can be found at the various missions around Jos. However you'll need to be subdued to stay in these as they are venues used for Bible-study classes and church services, and you may look somewhat out of place. Nevertheless, if you are well behaved – no smoking or drinking and in bed by the curfew – they will let you stay and they cost next to nothing.

Cedar Tree Guest House 17 Yakubu Gowon Way, close to the Nigerian Television Authority building, some 5km from the centre of town beneath the hill with the Swan Water tanks on; 0806 090 9996. Formerly a Lebanese restaurant, this has been converted to a small but pleasant guesthouse. The rooms all have TV, AC, fridge & tea & coffee facilities & differ only in size of the room, bed & TV. $$

Country Home Hotel NEPA Close; 073 462479, 0803 700 7102/9454. This is a well-maintained hotel, with lots of new, bright-green paint. Good breakfasts of fresh rolls & juice are available, as are non-Nigerian dishes for dinner. The 59 rooms have giant beds with new, crisp white sheets, hot water, new satellite TV, AC units & fridges, & are exceptionally comfortable. $$

Hill Station Hotel 10 Tudun Wada Rd; 0807 297 7077. Built in 1938, & way past its prime but with faded charm, this is a bit of an institution in Jos, from the times when British colonial officers were instructed to spend their leave here for the good of their health. There's a functional swimming pool with a *suya* spot, established terraced gardens with jacaranda trees & good views over Jos & the hills beyond, & a few shops at the entrance selling curios, pottery & religious books. There's good uniformed service in the restaurant & bar with set

menus of soup, a continental dish & a piece of fruit. In total, there are about 10 different kinds of rooms & chalets ('shaletts') on the tariff. While there are higher rates on the tariff for non-residents, you are unlikely to be charged them. $$

Les Rosiers opposite Plateau Hotel, 1 Rest House Rd; 0803 357 5233; www.lesrosiers. sampasite.com. A friendly French–Nigerian couple run this small B&B in the grounds of their colonial house. Two outbuildings have been converted into beautifully decorated chalets with TV, fridge, hot water & tea & coffee facilities. Electricity is provided by batteries when there's no NEPA, so there's no gen to disturb the peace & quiet. The 1-bedroom chalet is US$50 & the 2-bedroom one US$80; both include a continental breakfast. Extra mattresses can be provided for US$16, which also includes breakfast. $$

Plateau Hotel Rest House Rd; 073 455741. Located in a hilly & leafy suburb in pleasant grounds with plenty of parking, but it's deadly quiet & there's no water in the swimming pool. There's a comfortable lounge, a shop selling books & men's shirts, & the restaurant has a changing daily menu, which includes continental dishes such as beef goulash or chicken casserole. As with all the other old state hotels, everything is seriously dilapidated, & the rooms are stuffed with ancient furniture, but they all have satellite TV & clean bathrooms. The generator is unreliable & only used in the evenings. The standard rooms have problems with water so the helpful staff may put you in one of the more expensive rooms for the same rate. $$

COCIN Guest House 5 Noad St; 073 452286. It's spartan but clean, & rooms have been freshly painted, with bed & desk, bucket & separate toilet, cool stone floors, & mossie netting in the windows. There's a restaurant that serves a dish of the day in big pots, & a sitting room with a TV. It's cheap but only admits single people or married couples, & there's a curfew of 22.00. $

ECWA (Evangelical Church of West Africa) Guest House on a road behind the Challenge Bookshop; 073 454482. This is another church mission with accommodation. There are several blocks in peaceful gardens where you can also camp, centred around a large hall used for evangelist church services, where there is a canteen serving a basic dish, & a TV. You may also get similar basic

accommodation at the **Eyn Mission Guest House** across the road (073 452056). As you can imagine, there are lots of Bibles for sale along this street. $

Tekan Guest House 6 Noad St; 073 453036. A friendly mission that has a few rooms & which is conveniently located near the museum complex. The rooms (no couples allowed) are only twins & singles of monastic proportions, but they are clean, with a simple bed & a bucket in the bathrooms, & for US$6 for a single & US$9 for a twin they're dirt cheap. There's also a 22-bed dorm here, & for US$4 you get a sheet & a blanket & use of a communal bathroom. Simple meals are also available but meal times must be strictly adhered to. TEKAN is an acronym derived from a Hausa phrase, '*Terayyar Ekklesiyoyin Kristi a Nijeria*', which translates as Fellowship of Churches of Christ in Nigeria (COCIN), which explains the name of the mission next door (above). $

✗ WHERE TO EAT AND DRINK There's a branch of **Mr Biggs** next to Terminus Roundabout near the market. **Oasis Bakery** has opened a branch at Secretariat Junction on Yakubu Gowon Way.

✗ La Cuisine Special Restaurant a few metres north of the Cedar Tree Guest House on the other side of Yakubu Gowon Way; 10.00–22.00 daily. Easily the best place to eat in Jos, with set tables with starched napkins & wine glasses. The fully continental menu includes lots of treats such as prawns, good steaks with sauces & sweet & sour chicken; vegetarians will love the vegetarian lasagne or fried noodles with vegetables & nuts. There's a full bar with some wines (don't forget the 15%). The atmosphere is spoilt a bit by blaring TVs though. $$$–$$$$

✗ Elysur 12.00–15.00 & 19.00–22.00 daily. An excellent Chinese & Lebanese restaurant just inside the entrance gate of the Hill Station Hotel, with an expansive menu, attentive service, lots of tables in AC, & the food is fairly authentic. $$$

✗ Habib Restaurant 82 Bauchi Road by the Zololo junction; 10.00–22.00 daily. Good Nigerian food (N300–600). About a dozen tables & a flashy modern front. $$

✗ Juice and Grillade 5 Ahmadu Bello Way. Serves

Nigerian fast food (mostly fried or grilled chicken) for around N600 on the ground floor & traditional soups & starches upstairs, & there's also an outdoor eating area. The food is good but not always very fresh. $$

Net Café/AfriOne 24 Ahmadu Bello Way; 10.00–21.00 daily. This has tinted windows so you may easily miss it. It's a lovely café with tasteful décor & fresh flowers on the counter, serving fresh bread, cappuccino, pastries & ice cream plus internet access & spotless toilets. A good option for an early dinner too, with a long menu of pizzas, burgers, pastas & sandwiches. $$

✗ Stabok Bank St. A plain restaurant set back from the street in a compound, with standard Nigerian food & some continental dishes such as chicken & chips, omelette & spag bol, though most things on the menu are seldom available. There are also beers & a few tots of spirits in the bar. $$

✗ New Beach Restaurant 5 Bank St; closed Sun. Nigerian food-is-ready in a busy & spotlessly clean spot with a lively bar next door. $

PRACTICALITIES If you need to **change money**, ASA Bureau de Change is on Museum Street opposite **NITEL**, which is very handily open 08.30–18.00 daily, and changes GBP, US$ and eastern and western CFAs (Communauté Financière

8

de l'Afrique francs) used in the West Africa Francophone countries. You'll also find Hausa money changers at the entrance of the Hill Station Hotel. There's an occasionally staffed **tourist office** at the Plateau Hotel (⊕ *08.00–16.00 Mon–Sat*); although nothing is given out, there is a useful list of hotels in Jos available.

Reliable **internet access** can be found at the Cyberhut at 3 Murtala Muhammed Way, which has a satellite connection, a dozen or so terminals and is packed with students (⊕ *09.00–20.30 daily except Sun; N110 per hour*). Net Trekker is another internet joint at 38 Murtala Muhammed Way on the same side of the road. Internet access at Net Café/AfriOne (see above) is expensive but fast at N300 per hour. The **post office** is on Ahmadu Bello Way, at the junction with Museum Street.

SHOPPING The **Modern Bookshop** (*16 Rwang Pam St*) sells maps of Jos, Kaduna and Kano that are difficult to find elsewhere and is surrounded by other stationery and computer shops. The **Challenge Bookshop** is near the mission guesthouses and has a small handicraft section.

The **Alternative Trade Network of Nigeria** (ATNN) shop at 1 Museum Street (✆ *073 450178; www.catgen.com/atnn/EN;* ⊕ *08.00–17.00 Mon–Fri, 10.00–18.00 Sat*) opposite NITEL, was in the midst of reconstruction when we visited but may have reopened by the time this book is published. It's run by a very well-meaning organisation that is the only Nigerian member of the International Fair Trade Association. ATNN supports small producers of craft items from all over the world, from disadvantaged or impoverished communities and developing economies, and mobilises and empowers them to continue their craft, as well as providing markets for what they produce. The fair trade principles include helping producers receive fair and appropriate value for their skills and labour, encouraging adequate working conditions and the positive use of working materials and traditional skills, and teaching local people the benefits of making a fair and equal business from their skills. Thus the fair trade movement supports grass-roots producers of mainly crafts and supports them by finding a market – for example, many craft items you find in Oxfam shops in the UK have originated from fair trade initiatives from all over the world.

The small nucleus of staff in the shop are very keen to chat – one of them even told me his mother lives in Chalfont St Peter in the UK, the home of Bradt! The ATNN has a membership of 120 co-operatives and individuals all over Nigeria that make handicrafts that are sold in the shop. These include silver jewellery, baskets, pots, leather, paintings and well-made cotton indigo dresses. There are other craft stalls selling leather, carved calabashes and clothes; the latter you can get made up, on Museum Street and around the corner on Noad Avenue, and at more places in the museum complex.

WHAT TO SEE AND DO
Jos Museum Complex The Museum Complex is best approached from Museum Road. It's a pleasant walk down the hill through lovely gardens full of gum and mango trees, and there are paths up to some rocky outcrops for local views. There are a number of attractions, and the UNESCO-sponsored School for Museum Technicians and the University of Jos Teaching Hospital are also located here.

The **main museum** (⊕ *08.00–17.30 daily; entry N50*) is to the right as you reach the bottom of the hill, and is spread out on the light and airy downstairs floor and in the garden behind, so you can see just about everything if there is no NEPA. Established in 1952, exhibits include currencies, such as feathers, tobacco, manilas, kuntu cloth, and of course cowries, all of which have been used as money in West Africa over the centuries; in the 17th century a cupful of cowries equalled a wife or a slave.

The museum also houses five pieces of the Nok terracotta sculptures (500BC) dug up in the Jos Plateau in 1943; they are all broken, but one head is more or less intact, and there's a 13th-century brass bust from Ife that's in very good condition. Another interesting item among the masquerade costumes and masks is an 18th-century brass royal throne with an elaborate python coiled around its feet. There's a selection of durbar horse attire, and the usual weapons and musical instruments.

Outside, and leaning against a wall, is the original Kano city door, once erected at one of Kano's gates before the British knocked it down on their arrival in 1903. There's also a similar section of the original 1845 Bauchi town gate. At the back of the museum is a very peaceful garden full of birds and trees, and a delightful, bright green rectangular pool with tilapia fish in it, surrounded by hundreds of old pots for a variety of different uses.

The small **Tin Mining Museum** (⏱ *08.00–17.30 daily*; *entry N20*) is at the end of the lane that runs past the main museum, and as you can imagine is dedicated to the (not terribly) interesting industry of tin mining. Outside the building are some early railway engines and carriages on display. Near here is a fine line of craft and **curio stalls** where you can watch and have a friendly chat with the artists at work, including a wood-turner, a painter and an indigo dyer. Also at the museum complex and opposite the main museum is a dreary **zoo** (*entry N50; N200 for cameras*), which you can easily give a miss as it's depressing, despite housing a collection of highly endangered species. But they are trapped in cages that are old and way too small; this is especially true of the chimpanzees and monkeys, which are thrown unsuitable food and sweets by ignorant Nigerians.

Further down the hill, the **Museum of Traditional Nigerian Architecture** (*free entry, but dash for a guide if you want one*) holds a collection of full-size replicas representing different styles of Nigerian architecture, including Katsina Palace, Zaria Mosque, Illorin Mosque and the Kano Wall. The replicas are much more impressive than the real things, which have been largely destroyed or neglected, or have over time been altered. It contains various architectural designs of major Nigerian ethnic groups, and there are huts with carved wooden door posts. No-one could tell me when this site was opened, but evidently it was before 1982, as there is a monument at the entrance to the Polish professor who designed the museum, commemorating his death in 1982.

The huts are built of mud and straw 'plugs' – round-shaped bricks – and the walls are then finished off with a smooth layer of the same mixture. This building material is fine for the drier climate in the north where the original buildings were once located, but in Jos's high climate the buildings get routinely battered by the rain, though very encouragingly they do get regularly repaired. You can walk along the top of the Kano Wall and go inside the Zaria Mosque. Further replicas from other parts of the country were planned but construction has been on hold for several years.

Also at the entrance is the Bight of Benin restaurant (⏱ *until 16.00 daily, bar until 18.00*) in a replica of an old chief's house, with an ornamental snake above the door and a red tin roof. Inside is a bar and a courtyard with plenty of tree trunks to sit on, and the eaves are made from bamboo. It's dusty and tatty, but you can still get a steaming plate of stew here during the day, and a cold drink.

Jos Wildlife Park The Jos Wildlife Park, also sometimes referred to as the Jesse Aruku Wildlife Park after a former manager, is situated to the west of the city and is signposted off Yakubu Gowon Way, but it can also be reached via back roads off the Zaria Bypass in the north of Jos. This is eight square kilometres of grassy hills and streams, though most of the animals at the safari park are housed in a collection of cages near the entrance (⏱ *10.00–18.00 daily*; *entry N50, N20 for a vehicle, N150 for a camera, N300 for a video camera*). If you don't have transport an *okada* will take you here for around N100 from town and it's an interesting ride though the backstreets of the edge of the city, where Fulani cattle ranchers graze their cows on the patches of scrub. The Plateau State Tourism office is located near the entrance gate, but was staffed by sullen students on work experience on our visit.

Also at the entrance is the Wildlife Museum, which is full of badly stuffed animals and birds, and some snakes in jars. There's a buffalo head and two sets of buffalo feet, a shrunken elephant head with a droopy trunk and a sign saying 'of great potential because size attracts visitors' (?), and mangy lion and leopard heads – the taxidermy is so bad they look like corpses. Cages are set in a shady garden of mango, eucalyptus, jacaranda and pine trees, but despite the pretty location, the animals (and especially the lions) at the wildlife park are kept in cages that are too small so it's a depressing place to visit, though on a more positive note the two remaining elephants are free-ranging in a large space of land. Other animals on display include a variety of birds such as barn owls and parrots, and two enormous Marshall eagles, a big python in a pit, various monkeys, giant tortoises and a pygmy hippo. The café here is stuffed full of ornate velour lounge furniture and has some outside tables on a terrace above the lion cage with views over the surrounding countryside.

AROUND JOS If you have your own transport you can explore other areas on the Jos Plateau. The Shere Hills are good for hiking and are among the highest ranges of mountains in Nigeria; they're home to the **Riyom Rock Formation**, a dramatic valley of balancing rocks 25km from Jos along the Jos–Abuja road. If you are travelling by public transport you can see them from the road from a vehicle from Makurdi or Abuja. For anyone familiar with southern Africa, they are similar to the balancing rocks of Zimbabwe, where weather erosion has shaped the rock pinnacles in such a way that the once-solid structures are now a series of smooth boulders sitting on top of each other.

On the same road and 64km south of Jos are the **Assop Falls**, a serene set of tumbling waterfalls where it is possible to swim in the pool at the bottom. If you are prepared to continue by infrequent bush taxi, you can break your journey between Jos and either Abuja or Makurdi here, but set out early as there is no accommodation outside of these centres. From the main road there is a Coca-Cola sign saying 'Assop Falls Tourist Resort' and there may be someone around to collect the N200 entry fee. Birdlife International has recorded 165 species of birds here, and it's a popular spot for filming Nollywood movies.

The owners of Les Rosiers B&B (see *Where to stay* on page 256) can arrange guided hiking tours of the plateau, costing N500 per person for a half day plus N1,200 for a guide. They'll make up a picnic for you for N900 per person.

WEST OF ABUJA

BIDA AND MINNA The two principal cities due west of Abuja are Bida and Minna. **Bida** is a Hausa–Fulani town dating back to around the 10th century, and has traditionally always been Muslim, with several ancient mosques built by the Hausa kings. When the British visited Bida in the 1870s they reported that the walls surrounding the city were 24km in circumference, but despite this considerable defence, the British still laid siege to Bida in 1897. Parts of the wall are still here, but they are mostly eroded.

Bida is about a four-hour drive, or roughly 230km, west of Abuja on a reasonably good road, and the only reason for being here is to perhaps change vehicles in the motor park or fill up with fuel on the way through. The main motor park, known as the Ilorin Garage, is on Ilorin Road in the heart of town. The limited accommodation in Bida is truly awful – move on.

To the north, **Minna** is 150km from Abuja and is the capital of Niger State with a population of a little over 300,000. It grew as an exporter of ground nuts after the Lagos–Kano railway arrived in 1915, but has earlier roots as a caravan stop for the Saharan trade route, probably in the 15–16th centuries. It's again Muslim dominated with prolific mosques, and today is home to the Federal University of Technology. Famous author Ben Okri and former military ruler General Ibrahim Babangida (who still has a mansion here) were born in Minna. The city has one major street with a string of roundabouts on it and the main motor park is Abdulsalam Abubakar Garage, which is out of town on the road to the barracks. There's a branch of Mr Biggs on this road too. There are two adequate hotels; Doko International Hotel (*Suleja Rd;* ☎ *066 223810, 0803 8134832;* $$) and the state-run Shiroro Hotel (*on the bypass;* ☎ *0807 6835866;* $$).

NEW BUSSA New Bussa is an unremarkable and very sleepy town that's more like a big village, but it's exceptionally friendly and has one feature that's totally unique to Nigeria – constant, uninterrupted electricity! Thanks to the nearby Lake Kainji hydro-electrical dam, that supplies much of Nigeria's patchy electricity, New Bussa (as the nearest place to the dam and as the home to many NEPA employees) receives an unbroken supply of electricity.

Getting there and away To get to New Bussa you need to turn off the main A1 108km north of Ilorin at Mokwa, and it's a further 100km to New Bussa along this road. There are direct bush taxis from Ilorin (N800); otherwise, you may find yourself changing vehicles at the junction in Mokwa. Alternatively you can cut across country from Abuja via Suleja and Bida to Mokwa. New Bussa's **motor park** is located in the centre of the town – look for the Peugeots and other clapped-out cars parked under a small shelter. From here you can get buses the short distance to Wawa, 10km to the west and the nearest point to Lake Kainji National Park.

Practicalities The **NITEL** office and the **post office** are together, a few metres to the north of the motor park; as usual look out for the unmistakable NITEL tower. The Lake Kainji National Park office is 2km from New Bussa on the approach road (☎ *031 670315/670424; note these landlines have been long dead*), though it's just as easy to go straight to the Kob Amusement Centre in Wawa, where you'll get more than adequate information about visiting the park (see below). The road from Mokwa goes over the dam wall just before New Bussa and an *okada* to the dam should cost around N150. It may be possible to take a ferry from the dam to Bin Yauri at the northern end of the lake, but this depends on the water level. Ask the local fishermen if it is operating.

Where to stay and eat

✗ **Kainji Motel** about 2km to the north of town on Niger Crescent at the end of Murtala Muhammed Way, in the GRA; ☎ 031 670032, 0803 861 0604. This is owned by NEPA & is where many employees stay. It offers comfortable & clean accommodation with 24hr power in peaceful & quiet gardens, with a car park behind a security boom gate. There's a restaurant for basic meals & the staff will knock on your door in the morning & bring tea-bread-and-eggs. Rates are just US$13 for a clean, bright room with DSTV, fridge, & a big vat of water in the bathroom. In theory there's a deposit of twice the room rate but this is not usually collected. The helpful staff will sneak into town to fetch (illegal) beer for you. The hotel is federal land but the state government have intimidated hotel management into keeping it dry. Across the road is a huge football field, & if you ask nicely you can watch the kids from the nearby NEPA school in their smart blue uniforms play football. They are delightfully polite & you'll get lots of 'good afternoon madam/sir'. $

✕ **Hydro Hotel** 26 Wawa Rd; ☎ 062 234089. Very neat & tidy, with everything working, though it's conservative, with a mosque & ornate Arabic décor with bronze pillars & gilt mirrors. There's also a simple restaurant; ask in advance if staff can rustle up something like an egg or chicken & chips or salad if you want something other than soup & starch. There are 40 or so rooms & you pay more for a bathtub or bigger room & bed. Closer to town, & also on Wawa Rd, beside the Ahmadiyya Muslim Hospital, is a supermarket selling imported goods such as chocolate, breakfast cereals & batteries. $

LAKE KAINJI NATIONAL PARK

The park is closely linked with the famous Lake Kainji hydro-electric complex, which supplies a greater part of Nigeria with electricity, and the Borgu Game Reserve, which was established in 1975 on completion of the Kainji Dam, the largest dam in Nigeria. The 136km-long artificial lake behind the dam covers Old Bussa, where Mungo Park, the British explorer, was said to have been killed in 1805 when the local people mistook him and his party for Fulani jihadists. The Zugurma Forest section was added in 1991, when both Zugurma and Borgu were renamed the Lake Kainji National Park, covering in total 5,382m^2.

WHERE TO STAY AND EAT

🏠 **Oli Camp** within the park. There are 32 old & worn out chalets; you have to notify the staff there if you are going to turn up by way of unreliable radio contact from the Roan Gate. The rooms are air-conditioned but the generator is only used at night. At Oli Camp there is a basic restaurant & bar serving beer, but as there are few visitors you'll have to try & arrange your visit in advance to ensure the camp staff are prepared for your arrival; expect to be reasonably self-sufficient. If you are camping then there is no problem, you'll be charged N2,000 for a tent space. Rooms $; suites $$

🏠 **Kob Amusement Centre** This is an alternative to staying in the accommodation in New Bussa, 10km away. There is a lounge & restaurant/canteen with fat velour sofas, where beer is available (the national park is on federal land), though you will have to order meals in advance so they have time to locate ingredients. There's basic accommodation in a range of flatlets in a 2-storey building, each with 2 bedrooms & a shared living room, a reasonable bathroom with bucket, a fridge & local TV, though none of the rooms have entertained visitors for a very long time, so expect to stay in a room that has been unused for years. Unlike New Bussa, NEPA is a far from guaranteed commodity here, despite the Centre's proximity to the Lake Kainji Dam. $

THE BORGU SECTION The park vegetation in the 4,000m^2 Borgu Section, to the northwest of the tiny settlement of Wawa and stretching to the Benin border, is characterised by tall grassy savanna, patches of woodland and riverine vegetation. According to the National Parks Service, it has 241 species of birds, 63 mammals, 28 reptiles and amphibians, and 259 species of plants, but this is highly debatable and their statistics are likely to be very outdated.

As in the other Nigerian national parks, an animal census hasn't been carried out for decades and most of the big game has probably been poached, though there are possibly still some buffalo, roan antelope, kob, western hartebeest, warthog, aardvark and olive baboon, and perhaps even lion, which the game rangers report hearing and spotting their footprints. There's also a fair number of hippo in the Oli River, though in the dry season the amount of water is fairly patchy, but there are enough pools of water to sustain some hippo pods. The hippo have been known to get out of the park and destroy local crops in villages around the edge of the park boundary, which puts them at risk of being shot. There used to be elephants here, and in the 1970s the population was put at around 1,000, but today these appear to have left the park and crossed the border into the Republic of Benin as a result of hunting pressure. Birdlife is abundant, especially at the Oli River near the camp inside the park, but animals are less often seen here than in Yankari National Park. There's very basic but underused accommodation within the park (see above).

THE ZUGURMA SECTION The Zugurma section is nowhere near the Borgu section and lies some distance away on the road from Mokwa to New Bussa, approximately 25km on the left-hand side of the road if coming from Mokwa. As it is relatively new, there are few roads or trails within this section and, given the state of the parks in Nigeria today, it's unlikely that any development will happen in the park soon. However, it's a pretty patch of green forest, and if you're driving do stop at the well-signposted gate to see if there is anyone around, and ask if you can go inside. There could still be monkeys present, including baboon, red patus monkeys, and black and white colobus monkeys. Accommodation was built here a few years ago at the Ibbi Tourist Camp, but today it's all shut up simply due to lack of visitors. If there is any future demand, the National Parks Service may staff and reopen it, but for now you'll have to be completely self-sufficient for camping and negotiate with the local people to gain entrance.

KOB AMUSEMENT CENTRE The Kob Amusement Centre is in the village of Wawa, 10km west of New Bussa, and some 24km south of the main gate to the Lake Kainji National Park. This used to be where trips into the park were arranged, but that is now done at Roan Gate on the other side of Wawa. You can tour the wildlife museum; the staff will be completely bowled over and hugely delighted that any interested visitors have turned up. In the museum is a range of lion and antelope skins, various bones and skulls, including those of elephants, which are now extinct in the park; in fact, if you go by the animal skins decorating the walls of the museum, in Kainji there once resided leopards, cheetahs, genets and civet cats, but whether these still exist within the park is impossible to determine and highly unlikely.

There is a whole heap of dried-out python skins, hedgehog and porcupine husks, and emaciated bird and monkey heads. One of the more interesting features of the dusty museum is the collection of poacher's weapons collected by the rangers, which includes very rudimentary handmade rifles that use some sort of homemade gunpowder and that shoot poison darts and arrows.

Hanging on the wall above the weapons is a collection of charms, some containing *juju* powders, taken from the poachers when captured. The museum guide tells you that given that poachers will lose themselves in the forests for a number of days in pursuit of their prey, some of these charms are used to ward off sickness, to help with navigation when lost, to empower them with strength to run away from a dangerous animal, and, in the event that they can't find an animal, to give them the vision or luck to find their prey. It's an odd collection of bits of feather, leather, and strange and unexplainable *juju* animal charms.

Getting there and away The Kob Amusement Centre is in the small town of Wawa, 10km west of New Bussa. If you have made it to New Bussa by public transport, then it is a short N50 hop in a shared taxi or N200 by *okada* on to Wawa. When you arrive in Wawa you will almost immediately hit a T-junction – the main body of the town and the road into Lake Kainji National Park is to the right, while to the left you'll see the entrance of the Kob Amusement Centre a few metres along this road. Taxis and buses drop off and pick up at this junction. Lake Kainji National Park is open from December to June, when the grass has died down and the animals have moved closer to the water.

Although you can get as far as the Kob Amusement Centre by public transport,

ANTI-POACHING AT KAINJI

Lake Kainji National Park, despite being nearly devoid of visitors and game, has today got to be one of the most protected national parks in Nigeria. There are continuing problems with poachers, and most of the big game has been poached out of the park since the 1970s, particularly antelope hunted for bushmeat, and especially waterbuck, of which large herds have been depleted. However, thanks to the conservation-aware game rangers at Kainji, poachers get prosecuted if caught and the punishments are fairly severe.

On our visit we were most impressed with the calibre and the enthusiasm of the park rangers. When we asked rather flippantly, 'Have you caught any poachers recently?' we were surprised when one ranger replied casually that he had, only three days previously, when he caught a man with a dead kob. 'We took his shirt off and beat him,' he replied.

When caught the poachers are under the jurisdiction of the national park rangers, with the assistance of the local police, as Lake Kainji National Park is federal land, and poachers are not accused, tried or sentenced under the local state laws, but under federal laws. We were also told that there was a 5km buffer zone around the park where the same sentences apply, and a culprit caught in this area was not necessarily entitled to a lawyer or trial in a local court. Poachers receive a variety of fines depending on the 'crime', from illegal entry and introducing domestic animals such as dogs or cows on to national park property, to carrying weapons within the park boundaries. If caught with a slain animal a poacher can receive a term in jail.

you need your own vehicle to enter the park, or take a chance on a lift from one of the park rangers. The Roan Gate entrance is a further 23km from Wawa, signposted off the road heading north out of town; this is where entrance fees are paid. Oli Camp within the park is 45km from the entrance, and in total 68km from Wawa. The road into Oli is rough but negotiable in a normal saloon car.

All prices below are non-resident rates; residents pay half but you should come with evidence of residency in Nigeria, if you don't look Nigerian. Entry fees are N400 for adults, N100 for children, camera N2,000, video N4,000, binoculars N200, car N400, truck N1,000. Daily game drives are advertised for N500 (N250 for children); a fairly new bus was parked at Wawa when I visited, waiting for visitors. Once at Oli Camp you can hire a guide to accompany you in your own vehicle on a game drive for N600 per day. You can hire a vehicle for N10,000 for a truck, bus or pickup; N6,000 for a Peugeot station wagon or N20,000 for a Land Cruiser. Boats can be hired for trips on the lake for N6,000; you have to buy this ticket at Roan Gate but the very bored guide and boat driver are waiting at the lock back at Kainji Dam.

9

East and Northeast Nigeria

The east and northeast of Nigeria are home to three of Nigeria's national parks. To the southeast of the region is the largely unexplored Gashaka-Gumpti National Park, which supports a range of habitats, from densely forested valleys to Nigeria's highest mountain, and possibly some good populations of animals that have survived without the attention or accessibility of man. Nearer Abuja is the more accessible Yankari National Park and the fabulous Wikki Warm Spring, probably Nigeria's most famous highlight, though this park has not been unscathed and for many years game was decimated by poachers. It's recently changed to new management, and already animal numbers are improving.

The isolated northeast of Nigeria is probably the country's least-visited region, and few *batauris* have ever even made it to the extreme east on the Cameroon border or the extreme north on the border with Niger or Lake Chad. Again, Lake Chad National Park has only ever been visited by a handful of people. Maiduguri is the major city of the northeast, which you can easily reach from Kano or Gombe to the south. But away from the main roads, unless you want to spend days travelling in and waiting for the infrequent bush taxis that ply this remote region, the only option is to explore it in your own self-sufficient vehicle and be prepared to bush camp.

To the north and northwest of Maiduguri is the Chad Basin that once contained Africa's superlake. Much of the region now is part of the Sahel, the southern reaches of the Sahara Desert and an arid flat area of palms, sun-baked earth, and ancient people that have adapted to the heat and the harsh living conditions. By contrast, in the large Adamawa State that spreads southwards from Maiduguri along the Mandara Mountains on the Cameroon border to Taraba State, you will find the most haunting and spectacular mountain scenery, where traditions among the local people haven't changed for thousands of years. Some of these regions are so remote that there are tales bandied around of tribes locked in the mountains who still don't wear clothes (or perhaps these are just stories to appease watchers of Nollywood movies and the Nigerian six o'clock news).

BAUCHI

Bauchi is the capital of Bauchi State and is located on the northeastern edge of the Jos Plateau at just over 900m, and is 132km (or about one-and-a-half hours' drive) from Jos to the east. Despite its elevation it's a very dusty and searingly hot city. Bauchi is primarily an industrial city and home to an enormous truck and tractor assembly plant and large asbestos and cement factories. It's also the closest city to one of Nigeria's leading tourist attractions, the Yankari National Park, which is about 50km to the southeast, so you are likely to spend the night in Bauchi before entering the park.

Bauchi was established in 1809 as an emirate and slaving centre by Yakubu

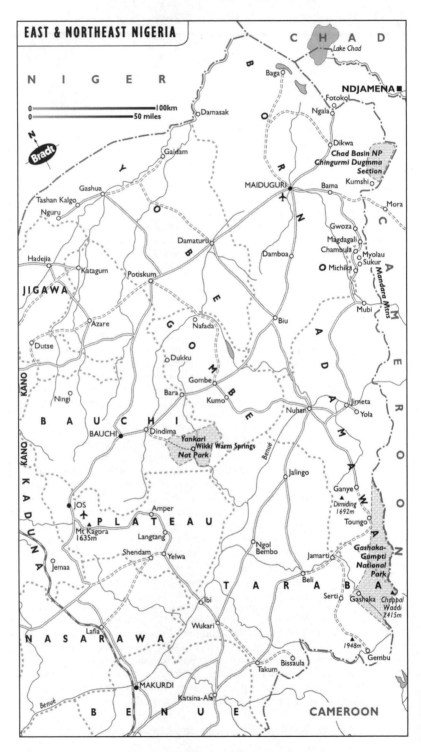

EAST & NORTHEAST NIGERIA

C H A D

Lake Chad

N I G E R

0 ————————— 100km
0 ————————— 50 miles

Baga

NDJAMENA ■

Fotokol

Ngala

Damasak

Gaidam

Dikwa

Chad Basin NP
Chingurmi Dugmma
Section

Kumshi

Gashua

MAIDUGURI

Bama

Mora

Tashan Kalgo

Nguru

Damaturu

Gwoza

Damboa

Magdagali

Chambula

Myolau

Sukur

Hadejia

Katagum

Potiskum

Michika

Mandara Mtns

JIGAWA

Biu

Mubi

Azare

Nafada

Dutse

Dukku

Gombe

Ningi

Bara

Kumo

Nuhan

Jimeta

Yola

BAUCHI

Dindima

Yankari
Wikki Warm Springs
Nat Park

Benue

BAUCHI

Jalingo

Ganye

Dimiding
1692m

Toungo

JOS

Amper

Mt Kagora
1635m

Langtang

PLATEAU

Shendam

Yelwa

Ngol
Bembo

Jamarti

Gashaka-
Gumpti
National
Park

Jemaa

Beli

Serti

Gashaka

Chappal
Waddi
2415m

Ibi

T   A   R   A

Lafia

Wukari

1948m

Gembu

N A S A R A W A

Bissaula

Takum

MAKURDI

Katsina-Ala

Benue

B   E   N   U   E

CAMEROON

Germa, a commander appointed by Fulani chief and Islamic leader Usman dan Fodio during the jihad of the 19th century. The word *bauchi* means slave or pagan in the Hausa language. Many immigrants were attracted to the region for its good arable land and it soon blossomed with mosques, markets, wards and quarters.

In 1902 the British occupied Bauchi, incorporating the emirate into northern Nigeria. Bauchi was to play a historic role during the de-colonisation of Nigeria thanks to it being the home of Abubakar Tafawa Balewa, a Bauchi teacher, who formed a social club in the town during the 1940s as a forum for discussing current affairs that went on to become the Northern People's Congress (NPC) – the political party that dominated the politics of the north in the run-up to independence. In 1960, Balewa became Nigeria's first prime minister, and he remained in office until his assassination in 1966. Balewa is buried in Bauchi in a tomb which is arguably the only interesting thing to see in the city.

GETTING THERE AND AWAY The **motor park** is 1km north of the central market in Ran Road just off Murtala Muhammed Way, and there are direct vehicles to Abuja, Kaduna, Jalingo, Gombe, Makurdi and Jos. Bauchi is a stop on the railway from Port Harcourt to Maiduguri, and the train station is to the east of the city on the road to Gombe. You need an early start from Bauchi if heading towards Yankari (see below) on public transport.

WHERE TO STAY

Protea Hotel Bauchi VIP Suites opposite Government House on Yakubun Bauchi Rd; ☎ 077 541760; www.proteahotels.co.za. This is another South Africa-run Protea so you can book through the website or the South African office; ☎ +27 (0)21 430 5300. Bauchi's newest & best hotel has 12 very smart suites in a modern cream block, in a secure compound with a small swimming pool & comfortable restaurant & bar serving continental fare. Each unit is double storey with a bedroom & bathroom upstairs & a spacious lounge & fully equipped kitchenette downstairs. There's DSTV, flat screen TVs & DVD players on both floors, & wireless connectivity throughout the complex. Décor is in warm hues of creams & browns, service & standards are on an international level, & this is easily the best hotel in the northeast of the country, with a price tag to match. $$$$$

Zaranda Hotel approximately 3km to the east of the centre of town on the Jos Rd; ☎ 077 543814–20, 0802 362 2255/6. A peeling, white, 10-storey building with an impressive row of flags outside, with 184 rooms, giant gens for 24hr power, & a water truck to keep the water tanks filled. If you are coming from Jos by public transport ask to be dropped off outside. In the vast car park are a couple of craft stalls selling carved calabashes &

cloth. There are two very nice restaurants with flowers on the table, serving buffet meals or set Nigerian & continental menus & snacks such as toasted sandwiches or burgers, & there's also a well-stocked cocktail bar. Bauchi is a Sharia state so the swimming pool is empty. In the lobby is the booking & information office for the Yankari National Park (🕐 08.00–20.00 daily). The helpful staff here will tell you how to get to Yankari (see below) & give details of entry fees, but there's not much point coming here, as there is never any need to book the park. $$

Obunna Royal Hotel Murtala Muhammed Way; ☎ 077 541941, 540011/21. A good option & a 5min walk around the corner from the motor park or a quick hop by *okada*. From the motor park, head towards the enormous football stadium on Murtala Muhammed Way & you'll see the hotel about 200m before the stadium. It's very friendly & comfortable & the 60 rooms on 3 storeys have enormous beds, spotless bathrooms where hot & cold water comes out of the taps, & some have balconies. There's good food in the restaurant, such as chicken & coleslaw & yam chips and, unusually, some vegetables such as carrots & beans. A big bar has an outside courtyard. $$

WHERE TO EAT
The street outside the Obunna Royal Hotel has most of Bauchi's very few bars, as well as stalls selling *suya* and egg-and-bread. Mr Biggs and Oasis Bakery have both recently opened branches on Jos Road, close to the stadium.

WHAT TO SEE AND DO The **tomb of Nigeria's first prime minister**, Abubakar Tafawa Balewa, who was assassinated in Lagos in 1966, is 300m north of the central market roundabout on Ran Road (⊕ *08.00–17.30 daily; free entry but dash for the guide, which you can pick up at the office to the left of the gate*). Opened in 1975, it's a square concrete block some 10m high and you can walk up a pitch-black concrete ramp and then down some stairs to the square outside the compound in the middle of it. The dark and light symbolise colonial repression and independence, respectively. It's decorated with lots of different-coloured tiles that represent the different ethnic groups in Nigeria, and the square concrete stepping stones and the spaces in between on the floor symbolise the troubles of the Nigerian government, the coups, crises and civil disorder since Balewa was assassinated (the tomb was built in 1975). In the middle is a simple grave with a mound of stones, and the open top symbolises Balewa's open mindedness to all the people of Nigeria.

Outside is a tall structure that was intended as a platform for a statue of Balewa, but his family never permitted a statue to be erected as Balewa was a Muslim and the Islamic faith prevents life representation in any form. In a room at the back of the complex is a display cabinet exhibiting a ceremonial sword presented to Balewa on a visit to Argentina, his watches, his radio, and a mini Sony TV presented to him by Queen Elizabeth II, and a small vial of oil, that is reputedly the first drop of oil to be extracted from the Niger Delta in the late 1950s and which was presented to Balewa in 1957 by Shell. Upstairs is a small library of his personal books, and if there is NEPA you can ask to watch a video of his speech at independence in 1960 – he was known as the Golden Voice of Africa for his good speaking voice. He was obviously good at other things too, as when he died Balewa left behind four wives and 19 children.

Other than the tomb, in the early evening it can be quite pleasant to walk around the area near the (recently reconstructed) Emir's Palace. On most evenings you'll see horses being exercised and local youths playing football on the dusty pitch outside the prison.

YANKARI NATIONAL PARK

Yankari National Park and its Wikki Warm Spring is probably Nigeria's best-known tourist attraction. It was upgraded to its present status as a national park by the government in 1991 and covers an area of 2,244km². Most of the park is made up of rolling hills of woodland savanna and is dominated by two rivers, the Gaji and the seasonal Yashi, that flow through the middle of the reserve, providing the main source of water for the wildlife.

The park was established in 1950 after the then Minister of Animal and Forest Resources went to Sudan and visited the White Nile Game Reserve, saw herds of elephant, antelope and buffalo, and decided that game reserves should be created in Nigeria. On his return he gazetted Yankari, which was a region already rich in game. Between 1955 and 1962, local hunters and farmers were moved out of the area, jeep tracks were ploughed through the forest to allow visitors to go on game drives, and a base camp was built close to Wikki Warm Spring. But in the 1970s and 1980s, wildlife populations declined dramatically due to a rinderpest epidemic and extensive and well-organised poaching by nomadic herdsmen. Marauding cattle were also sometimes killed by the lions leading to retaliation by herdsmen.

Several species of large mammal have become locally extinct since the area was first created as a game reserve, including African hunting dog, cheetah, giraffe, western kob, red-fronted gazelle and bohor reedbuck. But there are still approximately 500–600 elephant, perhaps 1,000–1,500 buffalo, roan antelope, patas monkeys, western hartebeest, various duikers, and approximately 50 lion. The

African rock python, the Nile crocodile and the Nile monitor lizard are fairly common and there's a pod of hippo in the Gaji River; baboons, warthog and waterbuck are regularly seen even in the camp. Yankari is good for birdwatching, and more than 350 species of bird have been recorded in the park – of these, 130 are residents, including saddlebill stork, grey-headed kingfisher, pied and giant kingfisher, hammercock, ibis, black magpie and cattle egret.

GETTING THERE AND AWAY The gate to Yankari is about 120km to the southeast of Bauchi and the clearly signposted turn-off is 69km from Bauchi on the Gombe road, at the village of Dindima. From here follow the road for 52km to the village of Mainamaji and the gate, and then Wikki Camp is another 43km through the park from the gate. The final stretch of road through the park has recently been re-tarred and is suitable for a normal car. All the other subsidiary roads are nothing short of sand tracks that are only suitable in a 4x4.

You can get here by public transport but you will have to set off from Bauchi early in the day. From Bauchi there are direct vehicles to Mainamaji, though expect to wait for some time until one fills up. Once at the village's motor park the Yankari gate is 200m further on, and in the motor park you can negotiate a drop by taxi to take you to Wikki for around N2,800, or cheaper still take an *okada* the 43km, which should cost in the region of N800. Once at Wikki there is no transport, so your only option is to arrange with the driver to come and pick you up at a pre-arranged time (there is no cell phone reception in the park) or hope that you can get a lift back to the gate with someone else, but remember Yankari only receives a handful of visitors at a time.

When you fill in the register and pay the fees at the gate, it's a good idea to see if there is anyone else staying in the park whom you could approach to ask for a lift out. Entrance fees to Yankari again include the ridiculous fees for cameras, which are often more than the fee per person to get in. They are: park entry fee for a resident, N200 (expats will need to show copies of their residency permits to get this rate); for a non-resident, N300 (N200 for a child); car, N500; camera, N1,000; and video camera, N2,000. Access to Wikki Warm Spring is another N200 for residents and N300 for non-residents, which is paid at reception when you pay for accommodation and is a one-off fee for your whole time there.

WHERE TO STAY AND EAT Wikki Camp (+882 16 5065 0578; e ynkwikki@ yahoo.com; www.yankarigamereserve.com; $$). For many years, Wikki Camp was hopelessly dilapidated and very run down; of the 110 chalets only about 40 or so were functioning and (barely) habitable. However, if you stay at Wikki Camp over the next couple of years, you will find yourself in what has effectively become a building site. All the accommodation at Wikki Camp is currently being upgraded: 30 of the original units are being refurbished, and new luxury rooms, villas and even a house for the president are being built. The road into the camp has already been tarred and new safari viewing vehicles have arrived.

The former governor of Bauchi State, Alhaji Mu'azu, like Donald Duke in Cross River State, is an advocate for tourism in Nigeria, and after vigorous campaigning Bauchi State took over the management of Yankari from the government's National Parks Services in 2006. The state has a master plan not only to improve the accommodation and facilities at the camp but eventually to fence the park to protect it from poaching. There are some rather fanciful, Disney-like images on the website about what the new 'resort' may look like when it's finished, but no one can deny that Yankari was in desperate need of refurbishment. Hopefully, animal (and visitor) numbers will increase now that it has been paid some attention.

For now though you can still stay in some of the old chalets. Rates start from the equivalent of US$30 for a small and sparse double rondavel that is very old and damp (be very wary of touching the old AC units or even light sockets which sprout wires like old man's whiskers), to US$45 for a large suite with running water. You can also camp. If you do, you can get water from the big water tanks in the grounds, and there's a loo in the activity centre, but this is not really advised as the baboons that habituate the camp are fairly aggressive.

The old, original restaurant is quite cosy, with football on the TV and friendly service, and the food is good though choice is limited to set menus. For N850 you can get a Nigerian main course followed by a piece of fruit, or for N900 you get a continental main course and dessert. The activity centre has a bar and DSTV where most of the staff watch movies all day, and two shops selling biscuits, chocolate, swimming costumes, rubber rings, batteries and camera film among other bits and pieces. Outside is a nice terrace with a good view over the savanna and a few odd plastic chairs, which is not a bad place to sit with a cold beer as a sundowner, but you are unlikely to see any animals except for the birds and baboons that occupy the giant mahogany trees and baobabs around the camp.

WHAT TO SEE AND DO

Game viewing Safaris used to take place on Yankari's famous big green truck, which was an enormous and ancient beast of a thing that was in the park for decades, and had to be pushed down a hill to get it started. It has now been scrapped, and replaced by a new fleet of safari vehicles. You can hire one of these with a driver for N5,000–7,000 per day, or use your own vehicle, but you'll need to be in a 4x4. Alternatively, jump on the daily guided game drives. The morning game drive goes at 07.30 and the afternoon one at 15.30. Both last two hours and cost N200 for residents and N300 for non-residents, which is paid at the office just in front of reception. The dry season of November to March is the best period to visit the reserve as the dense vegetation has thinned and game gathers at the rivers. The tsetse flies are a problem in Yankari and administer a wicked bite.

Just to give you an idea of the sort of game-watching experience you can expect in Yankari, while we were in the park we saw three baboons in the camp, one male waterbuck walked past our chalet during the night, we think we heard a lion, and on the game drive we saw one ground hornbill, one python in the river, and very, very luckily, a herd of about 40 elephant. More recently, readers have reported seeing a pride of one male and three female lions not from the camp.

Wildlife Museum The closest you are likely to get to most animals in Yankari is the Wildlife Museum at the reception block (⌚ *08.00–12.00 and 15.30–17.00 daily*). Exhibits include bits of old stone and iron picked up in the park and the various remains of what used to be Yankari's inhabitants, such as lion, leopard and cheetah pelts, a few stuffed antelope, an elephant rib bone, an elephant pelvis, an elephant head, elephant feet, an elephant ear, an elephant eyebrow, and an elephant nipple! Oh, and a pair of hippo ears. There's also a whole bunch of animal droppings on display. Judging by all the animal remains, Yankari was obviously once fairly packed with game, but poaching has sadly taken its toll, and in the museum is also a collection of weapons taken off poachers and the head of a dead ground hornbill that poachers have been known to wear as a disguise when they approach animals.

Archaeological sites The **Dukke Wells** were dug out about a century ago and used as reservoirs to store water by the early settlers. There are 130 shallow wells at the site between 2.5m and 3.5m deep and around 50cm across, which are interconnected below ground and hued out of red sandstone rock. These are roughly midway along the main access road into the park so you can stop and take a brief look. To get to the **Marshall Caves** you'll need your own 4x4 and a guide from the camp. These are all about the same age and are man-made shelters that people used to live in up until the 1950s to 1960s when people were moved out of the region to create the park. They are roughly 1.5–4m in diameter and there are some 60 of them in the area around Borkono Gorge. They were named after a Mr P. J. Marshall, an ex-game ranger who found them in the 1980s. Bats inhabit some of the caves.

There are several old iron smelting sites in the park, crumbling conical clay furnaces that were once used to make farm implements and weapons, and several abandoned village sites from when the people that lived in the region were relocated when the park was gazetted in the 1950s.

Wikki Warm Spring The real reason to come to Yankari and one of Nigeria's highlights is to visit the beautiful Wikki Warm Spring, a natural clear and pure swimming pool gushing out from under a cliff of red sandstone rock. Behind the camp restaurant a steep path takes you down to the spring in a lovely forested valley of dense greenery.

Wikki has a constant temperature of 31°C and over 4,500,000 litres of water a day empty into the spring and are then carried to the Gaji River. The water is at least 2m deep, and the bathing area extends for about 200m to a large sandy beach, where you can take a soothing wallow in the warm shallows, which are about 9–10m wide. It's a lovely bright blue swathe of crystal-clear water with a sandy and mossy bottom surrounded by a thick forest of sausage and tamarind trees. Despite the ugly concrete platform built on the access side, it's an impossibly pretty spot and well worth the effort of getting to Yankari, even if you don't see many animals. You'll have to guard your possessions from the baboons and if you are fortunate you may see elephant from the springs themselves.

GOMBE If you are heading east from Bauchi then the next city is Gombe, the capital of Gombe State – it is 187km due east of Bauchi past the turn-off to Yankari National Park. It was founded as an emirate in 1804 during the jihad of Usman dan Fodio. There's not much here and it's a sprawling city spread out in a wide valley with, unusually, a lot of road-building going on, but you are likely to swap vehicles here if you are heading to Maiduguri in the northeast or to Yola in the southeast. The motor park is close to a big central roundabout, and it's easy enough to swap vehicles without leaving the motor park, though if you get stuck late in the day try the **Gombe State Hotel** (*GRA Road, Gombe;* ☎ *072 620230*).

YOLA AND JIMETA Spacious and flat, this is a twin town situated south of the Benue River in the Benue Valley. Jimeta, 5km north of Yola, is the newer settlement and administrative centre; Yola is the commercial hub and older Fulani town. Yola was founded in the mid-19th century from a war camp during the course of the jihad movement, when an emirate was established and trade links with the wealthier of the northern cities were established by way of the Benue and Niger rivers. By 1885 the valley had become a scene of European interest, with the British, German and French imperialists all trying to stake their claim. Eventually the British took the town by force in 1901, while the southern part of the emirate fell to the Germans (now in Cameroon). The British built the new town of Jimeta as the river port, to send hides, cotton and groundnuts down the Benue to Warri for export.

Today the two towns are regarded as one community. There's nothing to see there, but they are situated in some of the most scenic countryside in Nigeria, along the mountains of the Cameroon border. It can get very hot here in the dry season when temperatures reach over 40°C.

The motor park is in Jimeta on Galadima Aminu Way, where you will also find the **Yola International Hotel** on Kashim Ibrahim Way. This was the local state hotel that was opened in 1990, but standards became so dire one guest called it the 'hotel from hell'. It closed in 2006, supposedly for refurbishment. Hopefully it will reopen soon as there are good views of the sludgy Benue River from the terrace. For now, simple accommodation and food can be found at the **Friendship Guest House** (*near the Police Roundabout, off Kahim Ibrahim Way, Jimeta;* \ *080 2450 2555;* $$), the **Meridian Hotel** (*opposite the police barracks, 6 Galadima Aminu Way, Jimeta;* \ *080 5495 0251;* $$), or at the **Chemian Heritage Hotel** (*8A Mohammed Mustafa Way, Jimeta;* \ *080 3242 1749;* $).

GASHAKA-GUMPTI NATIONAL PARK

Located in the southeastern corner of Nigeria to the north of the Mambila Plateau and across Taraba and Adamawa states, Gashaka-Gumpti is an extension of the mountains of Cameroon, and at 6,600m^2 is one of the largest and least-explored territories in the whole of Africa. The largest park in Nigeria, it became a game reserve in 1972 and a national park in 1991 and is a vast expanse of wilderness. It comprises two sectors, each rich in its own unique flora and fauna species. The Gumpti sector is located on its northern fringe while the Gashaka is on the southern fringe.

Until recently, very little was known about what was in the park and it received only a handful of visitors each year. But this is now set to change thanks to the Gashaka Primate Project (*www.ucl.ac.uk/gashaka/home*), which was established as an NGO in 2000, and now has set up residence in the park. In conjunction with University College London, and largely sponsored by the UK's Chester Zoo, the project is run by a team of international volunteers and local field assistants. This is another excellent worthwhile NGO dedicated to conservation in Nigeria as well as undertaking research activities to study how chimpanzees and other primates interact with the environment.

The park has a diverse range of habitats from guinea savanna, riverine forest and tropical rainforest, to steep mountains, deep jungle-filled gorges, and montane cloudforest, as well as montane meadows high up. The terrain supports hot springs, waterfalls and many networks of rivers and streams including the Taraba, a major tributary of the River Benue. Much of the park is mountainous, with steep hills rising 500–900m from their bases, and spectacular scenery. It is home to Nigeria's tallest mountain at 2,415m, Chappal Waddi, which simply means 'mountain of death'.

The many different habitats of Gashaka-Gumpti support a great diversity of plant and animal species. Both savanna and forest animals are present, including buffalos, hartebeests, yellow-backed duikers, giant forest hogs, warthogs, lions, leopards, hyenas, African hunting dogs, hippopotamus, chimpanzees, olive baboons, and colobus, patas and mona monkeys. The park is home to the largest populations of primates in Nigeria, since the local people (Muslim Fulanis) do not traditionally hunt these animals. Some 366 bird species have been recorded here, including 13 species found only in this mountain chain along the Cameroon border, and the park is also a spawning ground for some fish species such as Nile perch, electric fish and tilapia.

In the past the park was under threat of conversion to other forms of land use. Increased population pressure had led to encroachment of the park by farmers who cut the dense forest to farm; and, in the dry season, thousands of cattle were illegally put into the park to graze, causing serious destruction. Poaching pressure was also high, and commercial bushmeat hunting was increasing on both sides of the border, and carnivores like lions and hyena were killed by cattle owners.

However, the Gashaka Primate Project has breathed new life into the park. To date the management has installed a radio mast so staff can communicate with each other across the park, employed a team of armed rangers, and demarcated several hundred kilometres of park border by cutting a five-metre-wide corridor through the bush and beaconing it with oil drums filled with stones. This was necessary as cattle grazers had previously used the fact that they didn't know where the border was as an excuse to bring their herds into the park. Already, with the presence of rangers and researchers, poachers have been deterred.

If you plan to head there, contact them in advance, explore the excellent website, and remember this is another of Nigeria's worthwhile wildlife projects, which is always looking for volunteers. If you are prepared to spend time in the park and are confident about off-road driving (a GPS is essential here), this is the best place in Nigeria to look for its elusive wildlife, and the park is especially recommended for overlanders travelling through West Africa.

GETTING THERE AND AWAY If you are in your own vehicle, bring plenty of fuel. Serti on the main road between Bali and Gembu is the usual access point to the southern Gashaka section of the park, which is 15km from the park gate at the village of Bodel. The entry fee is N1,000 (which includes cameras!). In the dry season (December to May) it is possible to drive to Gashaka Village within the park, some 30km from the gate, where the Gashaka Primate Project has a field centre, though a 4x4 is essential and this route involves crossing three rivers. It can only be done by foot in the wet season (April to November), when these rivers can become so swollen they can become impassable, although at times canoes maybe available. Visitors without their own vehicle may be able to find transport on a local commercial truck or in one of the project's vehicles, and once there it might be possible to hire a 4x4 and driver. Contact them in advance.

WHERE TO STAY AND EAT There's hutted accommodation in Serti, or you can camp at the park's newly refurbished Tourist Transit Camp, which you should report to anyway before entering the park. Rooms cost US$10–20. Food-is-ready can be found at Serti's motor park. At Gashaka and at their other field station 10km further in the park at Kwano, the project provides simple self-catering accommodation: huts with beds, outdoor kitchens under thatch, bucket baths and long drop loos. If you don't bring your own food, they can provide simple meals (rice, yams, beans and tea) and clean water. Bed and board costs US$10 per day. Gashaka has 2–3 hours of electricity in the evenings, while Kwano has 24-hour electricity. If you're self-sufficient you can basically camp anywhere in the park; however there are several designated campsites though they have no facilities.

WHAT TO SEE AND DO The project has tagged more than 50km of **hiking trails**, and there are a few rough jeep tracks, but it's essential to take a guide as it's very easy to get hopelessly lost. Ranger escorts and porters can be arranged at the village of Serti, or at Gashaka and Kwano within the confines of the park. They have been trained by the Gashaka Primate Project, cost N500 a day, and many are ex-hunters who have an intimate knowledge of the park and know where the animals are to be found. Day hikes from Gashaka include walks to the bat forest, which is home to a large population of fruit bats and some primates, and to a hippo pool on the Kam River.

Kwano is located in a dense tract of beautiful rainforest and is the best place in the park to view primates. It may be possible to accompany a researcher to study a group of increasingly habituated chimpanzees here. Self-sufficient overlanders can take a ranger escort and go on longer multi-day trips to isolated spots of wilderness on the Cameroon border and up into the mountains.

Visitors planning to climb **Chappal Waddi** should collect a ranger escort from Serti and then drive to Njawai on the northeastern corner of the Mambilla Plateau, about a six-hour drive. Porters can be hired at Njawai, where you can leave the vehicle, and a two-day trek is then needed to reach the top of the mountain. This approach is fairly gentle with no steep ascents, and it's broken by a night at the small, friendly village of Jauro Hammasaleh. Expect to trek about 6–7 hours each day. The mountain summit itself is bisected with the international border with Cameroon. Die-hard trekkers can approach the mountain from Gashaka and walk through the park to the top of the mountain. This round trip takes 8–10 days.

MAIDUGURI

Maiduguri, the densely populated capital of Borno State, is in the extreme northeast of Nigeria on the edge of the Sahel, and is a blindingly hot and sandy city. It's surrounded by savanna scrubland and the encroaching sand belt of the Sahara, and camels, date palms and the indigenous Kanuri people, with their striking elaborate hair and colourful scarves, are a common sight. You may find yourself here if continuing into northern Cameroon, as Maiduguri is the closest Nigerian city to Cameroon, and there are two border posts within 140km to the east (see *Getting there* in Chapter 2 for more details). It's also only a 1½-hour drive southwest of Lake Chad and is the nearest city to the country of Chad. Ndjamena, the capital of Chad, is roughly 250km from Maiduguri and can be reached in a day via a short transit through Cameroon.

Maiduguri was founded as a British military post in 1907 and, like Kaduna and Jos, was a creation of Lord Lugard's empire building. Maiduguri grew quickly and within 20 years of its establishment was home to 15,000 people, many of whom were from other parts of Nigeria. Although it is predominantly Muslim, the Sabon Gari concept never really took off here, and unlike in other northern cities people live together without being warded off in their own sections of town. The population was boosted again after World War II when many returning servicemen settled here with their families; today the population is just under two million. Mosques are prolific throughout the city (each hotel has its own mosque) and hundreds of thousands of men pray several times a day. Remember to be sensitive around the mosque areas, which are often open prayer compounds on the side of the road. In 2006 Maiduguri witnessed riots over the Prophet Mohammed cartoons published by a Danish newspaper, which left at least 16 people dead and over 40 churches destroyed.

From February to June this city is intolerably hot, with temperatures reaching well over 40°C, and the annual rainfall is a scanty 600mm. Go sightseeing early, though there isn't much to see. The state government started an initiative telling people it was their duty to plant trees to provide shade, and there are some hardy neem trees lining the streets. Again this city is spattered with odd-looking roundabouts; the welcome roundabout is a green and white concrete circle and the west end roundabout has a curious giant fish on it. Borno State is a strict Sharia state, and you will not find alcohol anywhere in Maiduguri. Some bars and hotels serving alcohol were burnt down in 2001 in riots over the lunar eclipse; Muslims claimed that immoral activities caused the phenomenon! Unlike in some of the other Sharia states, however, some of the hotel swimming pools have water in and foreigners may be permitted to swim.

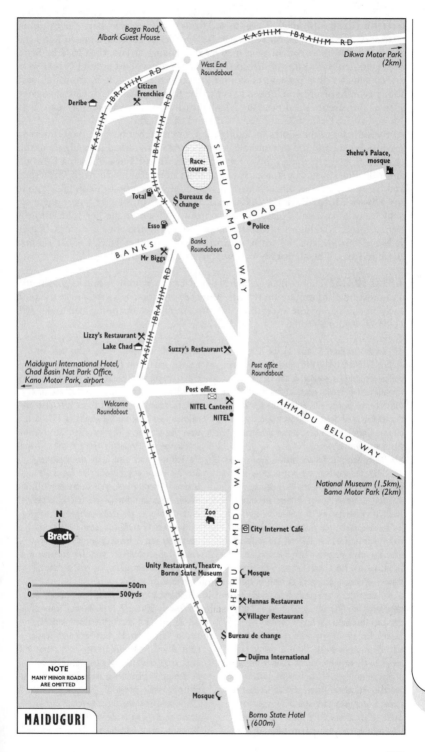

Baga Road,
Albark Guest House

KASHIM IBRAHIM RD

West End
Roundabout

Dikwa Motor Park
(2km)

Citizen
Frenchies

Deribe

Shehu's Palace,
mosque

Race-
course

SHEHU LAMIDO ROAD

Total
Bureaux de
change

Police

Esso

Banks
Roundabout

BANKS RD

Mr Biggs

Lizzy's Restaurant
Lake Chad

Suzzy's Restaurant

Maiduguri International Hotel,
Chad Basin Nat Park Office,
Kano Motor Park, airport

Post office
Roundabout

Post office

AHMADU BELLO WAY

Welcome
Roundabout

NITEL Canteen
NITEL

National Museum (1.5km),
Bama Motor Park (2km)

N

Bradt

Zoo

City Internet Café

SHEHU LAMIDO WAY

0   500m
0   500yds

Unity Restaurant, Theatre,
Borno State Museum

Mosque

Hannas Restaurant

Villager Restaurant

Bureau de change

KASHIM IBRAHIM RD

Dujima International

NOTE
MANY MINOR ROADS
ARE OMITTED

SHEHU LAMIDO ROAD

Mosque

MAIDUGURI

Borno State Hotel
(600m)

GETTING THERE AND AWAY To get to and from here from anywhere else by public transport you need to set off very early. It's over seven hours in a bus to Kano and around six hours to Bauchi (you may have to change at Potiskum in Yobe State, depending on the whims of drivers), and both journeys cost around N1,000. On arrival vehicles drop passengers around the main road coming in from the west, though for departure you'll need to get to the **Kano Motor Park** (*Tashar Kano* in Hausa) on Airport Road near the Maiduguri International Hotel for vehicles to Kano, Bauchi, Gashua, Gombe and Baga on Lake Chad.

For vehicles to the south, including the Cameroon border near the Cameroon town of Mora, and the distant Yola, capital of Adamawa State (though along this road bush taxis are scarce), head for the **Bama Motor Park** on Bama Road off Ahmadu Bello Way. For transport to the most northerly border with Cameroon and the road that goes through a small section of Cameroon to reach Chad, go to the **Dikwa Motor Park** on Dikwa Road to the east of the city, where there are vehicles to Dikwa and Ngala, where you can swap on to another vehicle to the border itself. Maiduguri is the terminus for the terminally ill eastern branch railway from Jos, and the **train station** is 250m to the northeast of Sir Kashim Ibrahim Road. The **airport** is 6km west of town but is closed.

WHERE TO STAY There isn't a great deal of choice of accommodation in Maiduguri, and most hotel rooms are pretty dire. But they are popular so try and get a room early in the day before everything fills up. You'll pay no more than N4–5,000 (US$30–40) for a room.

⌂ **Borno State Hotel** 1 Talba Rd, Old GRA; ✆ 076 371008/233919. Overpriced for what you get but nevertheless popular, & has seen some refurbishment in recent years. Accommodation is in different-sized chalets with new mossie netting on the windows, new doors & windows, & a fresh lick of paint. There's also a basic restaurant serving starch staples & soup. $$

⌂ **Deribe Hotel**, Sir Kashim Ibrahim Rd; ✆ 0802 372 5999. This was once the best place to stay in town but now the 100 rooms have peeling wallpaper & broken fittings. If there are enough guests the generator will be turned on; otherwise it's hot & dark. On the plus side, the restaurant serves Nigerian food but the chef can rustle up something more Western if asked in advance, & the swimming pool has a quiet terrace with seats & shade — it's not a bad place to come in the heat of the afternoon, & non-guests & non-Muslims can swim for a fee. $$

⌂ **Lake Chad Hotel**, Sir Kashim Ibrahim Rd; ✆ 076 232400. Has 60–70 very worn rooms decorated with 1970s plastic bucket chairs & couches with plastic covers on them, but it's clean & the service is good, even if few of the facilities work. The very amicable chef in the kitchen will do his best to please, & may even cook something vegetarian; dishes go for around N600. There's a very good stand here for international magazines &

newspapers. Sometimes the swimming pool has water; a small fee is charged for non-guests. $$

⌂ **Maiduguri International Hotel** Stadium Rd, at least 3km out of town just past the Kano Motor Park; ✆ 0802 637 7910. This vast state hotel was officially opened by General Abacha in 1997 & is something of a white elephant despite its modern appearance. It's also largely empty & only a few of the 300 rooms are used, hence the cheap rates. Bats live in the empty rooms! The rooms are fabulous & modern with great bathrooms, DSTV, & modern furnishings, but the gen is only turned on in the evening so you could find yourself slogging up the stairs to an AC-less room. The lobby is ridiculously vast & there's a bright blue pool outside but no shade or chairs. The expensive & deserted restaurant serves not very authentic continental dishes. $$

⌂ **Dujima International Hotel** Shehu Lamido Way, Old GRA; ✆ 0802 637 7910. Recently repainted, this has tatty but comfortable rooms with AC, satellite TV & fridge, big bathrooms with running water, & some with working showers, & there's lots of parking, though this is a busy place, so get there early to guarantee a room. The restaurant is pretty unreliable though. $–$$

⌂ **Albarka Guest Inn** after the Texaco filling station on Baga Rd to the north of town, about 10mins by *okada* from the post office roundabout (no phone). This is a brand-new & comfortable guesthouse with just a few cramped but pleasant standard rooms with TV, AC & hot water. There's a tiny restaurant serving a limited selection of soup & starch for around N600 a plate & a bar serving alcoholic drinks – the only place I am aware of in Maiduguri that does. §

✗ WHERE TO EAT

Not much happens in Maiduguri after dark; things tend to close quite early, not least because there are no bars. Restaurants shut by about 21.00 at the latest and the later you go the less choice of food-is-ready there will be. It's a good idea to have a main meal during the day here. If you are not eating at the hotels, there are few non-Nigerian options. If you're in Maiduguri around the start of the rainy season and feeling adventurous you can try the fried grasshoppers sold from stalls around the post office roundabout.

Citizens Frenchies Restaurant around the corner from the Deribe Hotel, stuffed full of tables and with ancient chandeliers hanging from the ceilings, serves chicken, fried and *jollof* rice, and spaghetti but the food is not always ready and if you don't drop by in advance there may not be any food at all (*no phone*). **Jil's Restaurant** on Leventis Road, further south after the Total petrol station, is open all day for food-is-ready. It's busy with lots of customers coming in for takeaways. Outside is a news stall with a good selection of foreign magazines and newspapers.

At the banks roundabout is a branch of the predictable **Mr Biggs**, the fast-food chain selling the standard scotch eggs, chicken and *jollof* rice, pies and cakes. One of the most popular places to eat in town is **Lizzy's Restaurant** (⊕ *09.00–21.00 daily except Sun*) next door to the Lake Chad Hotel, an unmissable bright red and yellow building with a huge gen outside, which is completely decked out in red and white Coca-Cola posters, flags, tables and fridges. It's always packed to the gills with guests and there's a huge menu offering *semovita*, rice, pounded yam, *garri* and a variety of soups and fabulous salads with additional hard-boiled eggs and baked beans. **Suzzy's** restaurant is a similar set-up on Shehu Lamido Way, just to the north of the post office roundabout. There's another branch of Lizzy's called **Unity Restaurant** just off Shehu Lamido Way, at the entrance to the museum and theatre.

Opposite the zoo, also on Shehu Lamido Way, are a couple of grimy chop houses next door to each other, **Hannas** and **Villager**, which serve basic chop and rice and sometimes spaghetti, and a few doors to the south is a *suya* spot and curio shop selling leather bags and carvings. Finally, at the post office roundabout, next door to the NITEL office in a smashed-up building, is the **NITEL canteen**, which is decidedly grubby and full of flies but serves good food-is-ready, enormous salads with lots of vegetables, eggs and a dollop of mayonnaise, and cheap tea and coffee, doughnuts and pies during the day, so fill up here at lunchtime.

PRACTICALITIES

Getting around is easy enough by *achaba* (motorbike), or shared taxis and minibuses up and down the main roads, and will cost little more than N30. Walking would be a good option if it wasn't so hot. The City Internet Café on Shehu Lamido Way opposite the zoo (⊕ *09.00–21.00 daily*) has reliable **internet** access (thanks to its big gen) for N150 per hour. There is a whole bunch of banks around banks roundabout, but to change money try the bureau de change further back, opposite the Esso petrol station in a row of wooden shops with a clear signpost above it. It's open from 08.00–18.00 but closed on Fridays and Sundays and will change US$ and CFAs. There's another bureau de change on Shehu Lamido Way near the Dujima Hotel, but again it's closed on Fridays. The **post office** and the **NITEL** office are on the corner of post office roundabout and there are landline and GSM **phone stalls** on the streets around them.

WHAT TO SEE AND DO **Kyani Park** on Shehu Lamido Way (☉ *09.00–17.00 daily; entry N20*) is a 42-acre dilapidated and neglected zoo. It is fairly spacious, though, and thanks to the neem trees it attracts a number of bats and wild birds. It's a popular place for many locals to spend a few hours, including the street children. But despite some of the enclosures being fairly large, they only have the odd antelope in them, spread out as individuals rather than living together in a natural social group. And the first things you will see are the chimps locked up in tiny cages, and two elephants in a ridiculous pit full of their own shit. All the animals are a long way from their natural homes and look so dreadfully hot. Don't go there.

There are two museums in Maiduguri: the **Borno State Museum** (*entry N50*) is just off Shehu Lamido Way next to an open-air and rarely used theatre to the south of the zoo, and the **National Museum** (*entry N10*) is on Bama Road, to the north of Ahmadu Bello Way (*both* ☉ *09.00–16.00 Mon–Thu, 09.00–12.00 Fri*). They house the usual collection of musical instruments, weapons, masquerade outfits and pots, but nothing of any special value, except for a replica of the Dufuna Canoe in the National Museum, reputedly the oldest boat ever found in Africa, which dates from perhaps 6000BC, unearthed near Damaturu in Yobe State. Nigeria's Commission for Museums and Monuments still has the original locked up somewhere. The National Museum also has a replica of a traditional hut housing a Muslim culture exhibit, including a display of circumcision instruments, which the guide will explain the use of in great detail. The only other mildly interesting sight is the **Shehu of Borno's Palace** at the end of Banks Road, a colonial building with a clock on top, and a huge mosque next to it, though you can't go inside. You might want to call in to the **Chad Basin National Parks office** next to the Maiduguri International Hotel (✆ *076 342184*) if you are heading to that region, but though staff are friendly they can't really tell you very much about the facilities of the park, though they can usefully give you directions to the different sections (dealt with under Chad Basin National Park, below).

AROUND MAIDUGURI

BAGA AND LAKE CHAD

In the extreme northeast of Nigeria lies Lake Chad, a small body of water which it shares with Niger, Chad and Cameroon. Lake Chad was once one of Africa's largest freshwater lakes, but it has dramatically decreased in size owing to climate change and human demand for water. According to one study working with NASA's Earth Observing System, the lake is now one-twentieth of the size it was 35 years ago. In the 1960s it had an area of more than 26,000km^2, but by 2000 this had fallen to less than 1,500km^2 – a puddle by comparison. The rapid shrinkage has been due to reduced rainfall combined with greatly increased amounts of irrigation water being drawn from the lake and the rivers which feed it. Droughts are quite common within the Chad basin, and by the end of each dry season evaporation occurs, and because it is very shallow, only 7m at its deepest, it always shows seasonal fluctuations in size.

Although the shrinking of Lake Chad is widely regarded as an environmental tragedy, it has provided benefits in some ways, especially in northern Nigeria. The water loss has uncovered more farmland, which is periodically moistened as the lake expands during the rainy season, and when the water contracts again at the onset of the dry season, valuable agricultural land is exposed, along with fish manure, which makes it even more fertile. And most importantly it's got soil moisture, which can sustain agricultural crops another three months into the dry season. Although other parts of Africa's Sahel are parched and prone to famine at times, the Lake Chad Basin remains agriculturally productive for an expanding population, and there haven't been any major famines there at all.

The most common species of vegetation currently found in the Lake Chad region are acacia, baobab tree, desert date, palm, African myrrh and Indian jujube. The most common species of aquatic plants are papyrus, ambatch, water lilies and reeds. Before the turn of the 20th century, those visiting the medieval Kingdom of Kanem reported an abundance of wildlife throughout the Lake Chad region. However, within the past hundred years there has been a dramatic decrease in the number of wildlife still living in the region. The main causes of this decrease are habitat loss, hunting and competition from livestock. Reptiles and amphibians have fared somewhat better, and monitor lizards, crocodiles, rock pythons and spitting cobras are all still fairly common in the Lake Chad region.

The migration of birds to Lake Chad each year is phenomenal. There are hundreds of species of bird that migrate to or live in the Lake Chad region. Some of the most abundant terrestrial birds of the region are the ostrich, secretary bird, Nubian bustard and ground hornbill. There are also many different types of water and shore birds such as the garganey, marabou stork, shoveler, fulvous tree duck, Egyptian goose, pink-backed pelican, glossy ibis and African spoonbill. The lake is also known for its excellent fishing resources – there are over 40 species of fish that are caught and sold by local fishermen. Accompanying all of these relatively commonplace animals are some ancient species, which are native to Lake Chad. Both the lungfish and sailfin are and have been unique to this region for hundreds if not thousands of years.

You can visit Lake Chad from Baga (see below) but don't expect an endless vista of water. Today it's made up of watery channels that cover and create seasonal islands and it's similar in ecological character to the Okavango Delta in Botswana. There's not much to see in the way of lake scenery, but a trip to one of Lake Chad's channels is a great way to see and meet the people of the lake, who are just as interesting as the lake itself, and it's a huge adventure just getting there. The best time to go is between December and February when the water is at its highest. Be warned, it can get very hot here and summer temperatures reach 45°C.

Getting there and away Expect to pay in the region of N500 for a bush taxi and a little less for a minibus from Maiduguri to Baga. Note there is no accommodation in Baga, and although there was once a hotel called the Baga State Hotel, it's presently being used as military accommodation, so you'll have to visit here on a day trip from Maiduguri. It takes just over two hours and is a little less than 200km. The taxi ride takes you into the Sahel proper, a vast wasteland of sand and scrub where you may see camels and more of the Kanuri people, with their olive skins, plaited hair and layers of patterned clothes. You may also see open trucks or land cruisers carrying sacks of maize, and perched on top you'll see hundreds of fantastically dressed men in flowing robes and brilliantly coloured turbans, wrapped so tightly around their faces because of the sand and wind that only their eyes are showing.

The Sahel villages are made up of huts with pointed conical thatched roofs, with chickens and toddlers scratching around in the sand outside. The scenery is stark but eerily beautiful – this is one of the remotest corners of Nigeria. Baga itself is a sprawling town, much larger than the small settlements you pass through on the way here. Once at Baga motor park (which also serves as an enormous open-air mosque, where you will see many hundreds of men praying at the allotted times), negotiate with an *achaba* driver to take you to Lake Chad. Very few speak any English, though some understand French, and you may have to enlist the help of a local trader to explain that 'you want to see Lake Chad'. In any event your arrival in Baga will draw quite a crowd, but don't be intimidated as everyone will be delighted to see you and will be completely curious about how and why *batauris* have made it this far. We went to a place called Fish Dam, but there are several other tributaries of Lake Chad within 10km of Baga. If you have your own 4WD, just get someone to point you in the general direction and you can simply go exploring in the sand. A good tip is to follow the other well-worn tracks to the north of Baga, as they will inevitably lead to the edge of the lake.

You are doubtless going to have your own experience here depending on what you arrange when you get to Baga, but our experience went like this. We managed to negotiate a couple of *achabas* for N500 each for the round trip and waiting time – gutsy, fiery Suzukis, bikes much more suitable for the sandy terrain here than the normal Jinchengs, the Chinese bikes seen in the cities. The drivers took us through the backstreets of Baga, where everyone we passed stopped and stared, and then out into the desert on a track of deep sand for about 6–7km. It was an exciting ride.

When we got to Fish Dam, a busy little port area with a few shacks, our drivers deposited us at the immigration post where we duly sat down for a chat under a thatched shade, produced our passports for inspection, and asked very nicely if we could 'see Lake Chad'. I am presuming there are more of these at the other tributaries around Baga. They let us continue to the edge of the water, where we spent an hour or so observing what was going on, chatting to the people, and admiring the rippling channel surrounded by reeds. Here was a remarkably simple port on an ancient lake, of traditional lake people: men hauled sacks on and off wooden canoes, robed and turbaned traders sat on their haunches and discussed deals in numerous languages, fishermen hauled in their nets on the little beach, gaily dressed women sorted fish into baskets on their heads, numerous trucks and vehicles rumbled up with various boxes and sacks and were unloaded and loaded up again by the muscular porters, sacks of grain and maize arrived by canoe from other shores of the lake, regal-looking men in the most elaborate robes sat beneath thatched shelters and counted out wads of naira, deals were done, payments were made, and the atmosphere was that of such rich tradition, they might as well have been counting in cowries. It was a magical experience.

CHAD BASIN NATIONAL PARK At 2,258km², Chad Basin National Park is dotted across Borno and Yobe states in three independent sectors. The Chingurmi-Duguma sector is in Borno State on the Cameroon border south of Lake Chad. The Bade-Nguru Wetlands and the Bulatura Oasis are both located in Yobe State, some 400–500km to the northwest of the Chingurmi-Duguma sector. The park is generally described as the conventional basin of the famous but rapidly shrinking Lake Chad, though none of the sections are near to the shores of present-day Lake Chad itself. Prince Philip visited the Lake Chad Basin when he was president of WWF in 1989 and parts of the park were visited by Charles and Diana in 1990, but since then the park has received only a handful of visitors and can only be visited if you are in a self-sufficient 4x4 vehicle.

You may want to stop at the Chad Basin National Park office in Maiduguri (see above) to get some information, but the staff know very little about the areas of the park themselves, and don't even know what the park entrance fees are or if accommodation is available! It's not. Like Nigeria's other national parks, accommodation was built some time ago, but at Dagona and Gulumba base camps, at Bade-Nguru and Chingurmi-Duguma respectively, accommodation has simply fallen into disuse, there's no-one around to collect any park entrance fees and your only option is to bush camp. To gain access to any of the regions below you'll simply have to drive off road into the bush and hope for the best. Alternatively you could perhaps hire a guide from the office in Maiduguri.

Chingurmi-Duguma, the largest of the three areas, covering 1,228km² of

Borno State, was first proclaimed a forest reserve in 1975, and is dominated by savanna dotted with acacia woodland, elephant grass and swampy areas, and it effectively joins the Waze National Park on the other side of the border in Cameroon and shares a similar eco-system. Wildlife is seriously limited and although there used to be giraffes here, they are long gone, though there may still be a few ostriches and hardy spotted hyenas, and antelopes including the western hartebeest and red-fronted gazelle, and many birds such as marabou storks, secretary birds and bateleur and tawny eagles. There is a possibility of there still being elephant in the region that migrate over the border from Cameroon from time to time.

Both the Bade-Nguru Wetlands and the Bulatura Oasis are found within an area known as the Hadejia-Nguru Wetlands, one of West Africa's most important stopover points for birds migrating from Europe; it has been proclaimed a Ramsar site (an important wetland habitat for birds under the 1971 Convention of Wetlands, and today supported by Birdlife International). During the dry season, many thousands of European birds seeking sanctuary in Africa during the harsh European winter come to these serene wetlands next to a vast desert terrain – a sudden belt of greenery on the edge of the Sahel. The birds' watering ground also serves a large human population of thousands who depend on the annually flooded wetlands for their agriculture, grazing and fishing. Floods in the wet season play a critical role in recharging groundwater, on which Nguru town and the string of settlements along the channel and lake are dependent.

Bade-Nguru covers 938km^2 and the wetlands are centred around a more permanent ox-bow lake, fed by the Jama'are River that rises in the Jos Plateau, and by the Hadejia that rises in the hills around Kano. Over winter a total of 377 species of birds have been recorded here, and birds that have nested in Europe and Asia begin to migrate to Africa from August and some stay as late as the following May. Roughly a quarter of a million birds make the Sahel zone of Nigeria their wintering range and families include ducks, geese, herons, storks, cattle egrets, ibises, pelicans, long-tailed cormorants, spotted redshanks, wood sandpipers, spur-winged plovers and ruffs (waders) in their thousands.

The **Bulatura Oasis** is an area to the north of Bade-Nguru on the border with Niger, and it's a highly scenic chain of sand dunes some 10–30m high and 300–400m wide in the Sahel. The area is 92km^2 in size, made up of sand and swampy palm-filled valleys, hence its name. The water in the area attracts some antelope, and sometimes Fulani cattle herders and camels, but the tracks these make through the sand soon disappear after winds. This is the only spot where flamingoes have been recorded in Nigeria. The drive up here along sand tracks leading north of the Nguru–Gashua road will take you past nomadic Fulani settlements, easily some of the remotest in Nigeria.

Getting there and away To visit these areas, you will need to have your own vehicle and be completely self-sufficient. The Bulatura Oasis and the Bade-Nguru Wetlands are best visited from Nguru, where there is a small information centre. Very basic accommodation can be found at the **Nguru Guest Inn** in large double rooms with fans and a bucket for N600. The Bade-Nguru Wetlands are located 15km from Nguru in the direction of Gashua. The route goes through a village midway along the Nguru–Gashua road called Tashan Kalgo, where there is a sign for the wetlands (though for its old name of Dagona Waterfowl Sanctuary), which is roughly 5km further on down this turning. It is advisable to ask in the village for permission to visit the sanctuary and request a guide to take you there. Someone will find the right person for you and you may also be able to negotiate to rent a canoe from the local fishermen. To get to the Bulatura Oasis a guide is essential.

Chingurmi-Duguma is accessible only during the dry season and is located approximately 140km, or a two-hour drive, to the southeast of Maiduguri, near the village of Kumshe.

SUKUR To the southeast of Maiduguri, a worthwhile if difficult excursion is to travel to the ancient village of Sukur (*www.sukur.info*) right on the border with Cameroon in the Mandara Mountains. It's one of Nigeria's two UNESCO World Heritage Sites, proclaimed in 1999 for its cultural landscape (the other one is the Osun Groves; see page 180). It's a beautiful settlement of perhaps 3,000 people, high up in the mountains with tremendous views of the valleys below dotted with villages and herdsmen, and of terraced hillsides. The word Sukur means 'vengeance' in Margi and Kilba, and *ta sukur* means 'feuding' in the Bura language, so presumably the Sukur people settled in their mountain stronghold after a local spat centuries ago.

Sukur's existence was kept from the British until 1927, and not much has changed here for a very long time – people still go about their daily rural lives in much the same way as their ancestors did. It's a small chieftaincy consisting of kin groups of various origins, with one chiefly lineage headed by the *hidi* or chief. The settlement is divided into 'Sukur Sama' and 'Sukur Kasa', referring to upper Sukur and to lower Sukur, and the Palace of the *xidi*, a large stone enclosure with its various gates, dry stone walls and niches, is in the top part on a hill dominating the village below. It has a little compound of huts where the chief lives with his wife, a stable for his horse and a bull-fattening pen. You are more than welcome to visit the chief and he will happily make a welcome speech and tell visitors a little of the history of the Sukur people, which the guide will translate into English. You may want to present him with a gift; one reader took kola nuts and biscuits which he was very happy with.

Since the settlement has gained worldwide interest, in recent years it's been visited by a number of curious researchers, anthropologists and archaeologists, so these days the people are a little more used to the sight of *batauris*, and they have even set up a small museum and five simple stone chalets for visitors with a generator ($). Buckets of water and a small kerosene stove are available. This is a delightful experience and you will feel most welcome. Since its inclusion on the World Heritage list a festival is held here each year on 2 February.

Getting there and away The proper procedure is for foreigners to get written permission to visit Sukur from Nigeria's National Commission for Museums and Monuments, so try and organise this in advance at one of the museums in Maiduguri, or Jos, Kano and Kaduna. If you are not in your own vehicle, from Maiduguri you need to set off early and be equipped with ready-prepared food to last a day or two, and if everything works smoothly you should reach Sukur by mid-afternoon.

First get a bush taxi from Maiduguri's Bama Motor Park to Bama, than swap on to another one to Madagali, 82km to the south on the A13. You may be able to get a direct vehicle from Maiduguri to Madagali that is probably heading for Mubi further south. From Madagali, it's a short ride by *achaba* to the small settlement of Mildo, where there's a sign: 'Sukur World Heritage Site'. Here it is customary to go to the local museum office, which is next to the district chief's house, where you should ask permission to visit Sukur and they will organise a guide to take you there. If the office is closed ask around for the museum guide's house.

Sukur is way up in the mountains to the southeast of Madagali and your only option is to walk. It takes about three hours and is fairly steep, so you need to be reasonably fit for the round trip. The track is clearly marked out, and once here it's another 5km to the village of Mydlau; the final part of the walk is on an ancient set of 500 stone steps that climb the mountain from behind the school at Mydlau. If you are driving, ask at the school if you can park your vehicle there. The walk up is tremendous and small children line the steps chanting and blowing horns. Once at the top the views are fabulous and the steep terraced valleys fall away in every direction. It is possible to return by a different route to Mefir Suku, the village on the plain further down the hill, which every Tuesday holds a market visited by the people of Sukur.

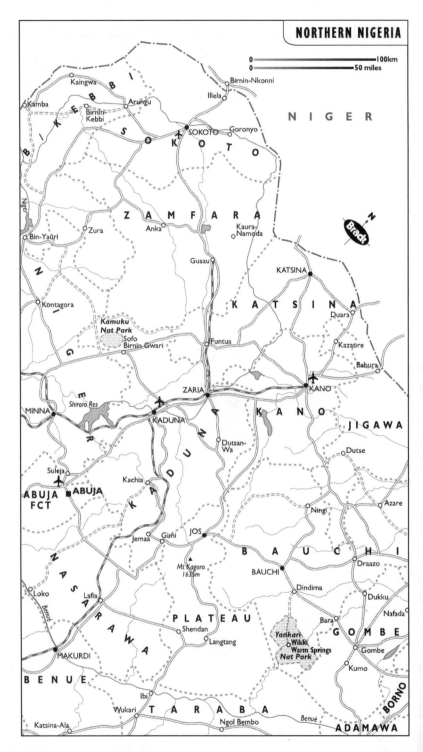

10

Northern Nigeria

Parts of the north, such as Lake Kainji National Park, Maiduguri and Lake Chad, have been covered in earlier chapters, simply because of their accessibility from the south, but it is the northern ancient emirates of Kano, Katsina and Zaria that hold perhaps Nigeria's most evocative atmospheres. These are cities steeped in Islam, with prolific mosques, ancient city walls, and old Hausa architecture. In Kano, today a city of almost ten million people, there's a market where trade in the impossibly congested lanes has been going on for a millennium, and less than a hundred years ago it was still the West African hub for camel caravans arriving from North Africa and Arabia across the Sahara. Sokoto is still ruled by a sultan, and each of the cities have grand emir's palaces in which trumpeters still herald the presence of the emir.

Away from the cities and in the far north, the stark and arid savanna of the Sahel region is an area dotted with mango and gum trees that is still frequented by camels and nomadic Fulani herdsmen with their sheep and goats, as it has been for thousands of years. You'll see farmers using hand hoes or ox-driven ploughs, ancient villages of low mud houses with no windows to keep them cool, beehive huts used as grain containers topped with straw roofs balanced on rocks and logs, curling smoke from charcoal burners, and women and children collected around wells with clay water pots on their heads. Here it is sandy and dusty and blindingly hot, and when it rains there are violent electrical storms and the region is littered with burning trees. Although barren, the region surprisingly produces a variety of fruit and vegetables not seen so readily in the south, and in all the cities you will see pineapples, watermelons, bananas, mangos and oranges for sale on the side of the road, and in restaurants you'll find salads with lettuce and tomatoes on the menu.

The north is dominated by Islam, and most of the states operate to a certain degree under Sharia law. The very essence of the religion gives the north a very different personality from that in the south, where millions of Muslim men pray several times a day, and hundreds of thousands of little girls go to school cloaked head to foot. The implications of Sharia are not as intrusive to the traveller in this region as you might expect, and because of the presence of many Christians in the cities, who mostly live in the Sabon Gari districts (Hausa for 'foreigner's town'), as a non-Muslim visit or you will encounter no problems. This is not the case on a local level, however, and the north has famously been known over recent years as the region for violent religious spats between the two religions, and tension among the communities is high. The Sahel roads are littered with police checkpoints where policemen in faded uniforms stand on the hot road all day collecting *dash*, and it's not uncommon to see lorry-loads of robed men carrying AK47s. When visiting the north, always keep your ear to the ground for possible disturbances.

Kaduna is a relatively modern city on the Kaduna River. It is the capital of Kaduna State, and is usually regarded as the first city of the north, but as a new city it doesn't hold the same appeal or charm as the older emirates. The city was founded by the British in 1913 and was the capital of Nigeria's former Northern Region from 1917 to 1967. After the British government took control of the colony in 1900 from the Royal Niger Company, Lord Lugard first settled in Lokoja, which he made his capital, but he found it too far south in the territory to have effective control and moved to a more favourable site, where the Lagos–Kano railway crossed the Kaduna River, known then as Mile 570. It was of strategic importance and in easy reach of the emirates, and as a new town it also had the advantage of being free from the clamours of local chiefs and traditional leaders. In the early days Kaduna was only inhabited by government agencies and officials and was dubbed then simply Government Town before being renamed Kaduna after the river. (*Kadduna* means crocodile in Hausa and there was once an abundance of them in the river.)

The transfer of 366 British officers and around 5,000 African troops to Kaduna in 1913 marked the birth of the town, although for some years facilities were basic and the town was referred to by the early officers as 'a hole in the bush' or 'Lugard's folly'. But clerks, labourers, railway workers, staff of colonial companies and a good deal of immigrant Nupe, Yoruba, Hausa, Igbo, Edo and Fulani followed in their wake, building urban Kaduna into a multicultural city. As the capital of the Northern Region, Kaduna was a nerve centre for politics, and Lugard's policy of indirect rule during the colonial period. He repeatedly requested that it was to be the national capital as he thought there was too many Africans in Lagos, but Britain refused to finance the transfer.

Later, Kaduna was also at the centre of the de-colonisation period from 1951 to 1960, as it was also the home of Ahmadu Bello, the leader of the Nigerian People's Congress party (NPC), who became premier of the Northern Region at independence. The British town planners built an expansive and well-laid-out Government Reservation Area (GRA), which today is still home to Kaduna's elite. They also carefully planned the separation of the northern Nigerian residents, who were forced to live in Tudan Wada, and the immigrants, who lived in the Sabon Gari. Some claims have been made that this caused the mistrust that has since led to more recent religious and ethnic clashes between the two communities. In 1967, with the creation of 12 states, Kaduna ceased to be the capital of the whole of Northern Nigeria and became instead the capital of North Central State. In 1976, when the country was divided into even more states, it became the capital of Kaduna State.

Today Kaduna is northern Nigeria's political centre and there are a number of training colleges for teachers, police and the military, and two universities. It's a busy commercial and industrial centre and has a pipeline that connects the city's oil refinery and petrochemical plant to the oil fields in the Niger Delta, a Kronenbourg brewery and a large Peugeot assembly plant. There are Christians who have lived in Kaduna their entire lives, migrating here from the south decades ago to work in the factories, but since Kaduna State adopted Sharia law in 2000 the tension between Muslims and Christians has been almost palpable. Kaduna has witnessed violent riots and religious clashes, most notably in 2000 when 400 people were killed, and again in 2002 when 200 people were killed over the Miss World controversy (see page 39). The city remains segregated today, with Muslims living mainly in the north of the city and Christians in the south.

GETTING THERE AND AWAY The **airport** is some way out of the city, roughly 40km to the north, and the only option is to take a drop taxi for around N1,500. Chanchangi Airlines has an office in the city at 8 Ahmadu Bello Way (062 249949); there's another desk at the Hamdala Hotel (062 235440–9), and a desk at the airport (062 234595; www.chanchangi.com). There is one flight a day from Kaduna to Lagos Monday to Friday at 07.30, and at 08.00 on Saturdays and Sundays. From Lagos to Kaduna there are flights Monday to Friday at 10.00 and 13.30 on Saturdays and Sundays, and the flight takes one hour. Staff in the city office (09.00–18.00 daily) can organise a taxi to the airport, but this is more expensive than organising it yourself.

The **motor parks** are a few kilometres out of the city in several directions. From the Television Garage in the south of the city, vehicles arrive and depart for all places south, including Abuja and Suleja, and Zaria and Kano to the north. To get to the garage from the centre of town, look out for minibuses calling 'before bridge, garage'.

'Luxury' buses also go from here overnight to Onitsha, Aba and Port Harcourt. A bus to Abuja is around N600, and one to Zaria costs just over N200, and there are also direct minibuses to Zaria, only one hour away from the city centre on the corner of Ahmadu Bello Way and Ibrahim Taiwo Road. The biggest and busiest motor park is Kawo Motor Park at the top of Ali Akilu Road to the north of the city, which has minibuses and shared taxis going in all directions. To get there, catch a minibus that calls out 'Kawo' or 'Mando'. Kaduna was built on the railway, and, the **train station** is just south of the Kaduna River on Constitution Road. The train between Kano and Lagos passes through Kaduna (see page 304).

GETTING AROUND The city is fairly spread out but is bisected neatly by one major straight road that runs south to north, but rather confusingly it changes its name frequently. In the south, from the Junction–Constitution road roundabout, which has a huge concrete football on it, it's called Junction Road, before changing names to Ahmadu Bello Way through the guts of the city, and then Ali Akilu Road in the north of the city. **Minibuses** and **shared taxis** run up and down the main drag for N30, and to get to any of the motor parks is a N30 ride on a minibus, all of which are probably too far on an *achaba*. Public transport is rather organised in Kaduna, with formal bus stops that have names in Hausa (indicated in italics in the text below). Shared taxis run on the routes that minibuses don't, such as Independence Way. You will find drop taxis at the major hotels and at the motor parks.

PRACTICALITIES For **changing money** there is a whole bunch of bureaux de change in kiosks in the car park at the Hamdala Hotel, as well as money changers outside, and more on the street across Mohammed Buhari Way outside the Habil Restaurant. **Post offices** are located opposite the train station to the south of the city, and on Yakubu Gowon Road to the northeast of the market. The **NITEL** office is on Golf Course Road, and there's a branch of **DHL** at 16 Ahmadu Bello Way. The most reliable **internet** café with several terminals is Webcafé, 11 Ali Akilu Road, just round the corner from the French Café – for both of these it is worth the effort of catching a bus the 1km or so to the north of the city. Webcafé (09.00–21.00 daily; N100 per hour) is next to an ISP, so email access is consistently good.

WHERE TO STAY

Command Guest House 10 Mohammed Buhari Way (formerly Waff Rd); 062 242918/21. Easily Kaduna's nicest hotel with over 200 modern rooms

in a 3-storey block surrounded by established gardens & with tennis & squash courts. The garden bar is a great place to enjoy a sundowner even if you're not staying here. The rooms, while being exceptionally good by Nigerian standards, with DSTV, constant power & hot water, & sparkling bathrooms, are very plain, with bare white walls, but they are very comfortable. You can arrange car hire here, there's a functional business centre, & a good restaurant serving a range of Western food with changing daily menus. There are a couple of other hotels a few doors along but they are pretty dire & overpriced. Rooms $$; suites $$$

🏠 **Hamdala Hotel** 26 Mohammed Buhari Way; ☎ 062 245440/7. This huge complex was built in 1961 & opened by Ahmadu Bello, so as you can imagine it is very dated, but it's busy, so has a lived-in feel with good service & a 24hr gen. The excellent bookshop in the lobby stocks *Newsweek*, *Time* & the like, European glossies, & somewhat of a surprise for a Sharia state, *Penthouse* & *Playboy*. The restaurant in the hotel itself is not bad, though a little shabby, but it is always busy & there's a comfy bar serving alcohol. At the hotel entrance is also the Unicorn Chinese Restaurant (⏰ 11.30–15.00, 18.30–22.30 daily; $$) with a basic menu of mostly chop suey. At the back of the complex is a huge laned pool with diving boards, & in the car park are curio shops & bureaux de change. There is a confusing array of over 200 different-sized rooms here, so it's just a case of looking at them until you find something that suits. Apart from the rooms in the main hotel block & in its extension block, at the back are some chalets, & another 'motel' block (which doesn't look anything like a motel). $–$$

🏠 **Catholic Social Centre** Independence Way; ☎ 062 240167. A secure compound with parking & cheap & comfortable accommodation in rooms in 2 blocks; pay more for TV. There's a restaurant for basic food & soft drinks & nice gardens with benches. The curfew is midnight & they strictly don't open the gate for anyone after that. $

🏠 **Durncan Hotel** 6 Katsina Rd; ☎ 062 217486, 0802 794 1218. Efficient, friendly & popular, though there's no booze or parking & meals are cheap but very ordinary, & you're not going to get much more than a plate of rice or *semovita*. It's also right next door to a mosque, so expect to be woken early by the call to prayer. There are about 20 small & old-fashioned rooms with buckets on 2 storeys. Rooms with a fan go for US$14, pay a bit more for AC. $

🏠 **Gloria Moria Hotel** 222 Ahmadu Bello Way/Zaria Rd; ☎ 062 240720. This is the best of the budget options, with a nice tiled lobby & it's all newly refurbished with new blinds, wrought-iron furniture in the restaurant, & there's a fridge in reception selling juice & cold drinks. There's no car park, though, & only parking space for about 4 cars on the street with a security guard. The small rooms have DSTV & working bathrooms. $.

🏠 **Mussafir Hotel** 15 Constitution Rd; ☎ 062 240470. Small but clean & comfortable rooms with a TV & bucket, some with balconies overlooking the horrendous traffic on Constitution Rd & the football stadium opposite, & food & beer is brought to your room. There's a small parking bay out front that is locked at night. Adequate doubles all have AC & the gen stays on all night & go for a cheap US$20. $

🏠 **Traveller's Inn** 19 Argungu Rd; ☎ 062 217912. Also a good budget option & cheap, but it's unashamedly run-down & on a noisy street & there's no parking. The rooms, however, are very clean, with AC, two enormous beds & a bucket in the bathroom. Tea-bread-and-eggs for breakfast & plates of fried rice for dinner are brought to the room. $

✕ **WHERE TO EAT AND DRINK** There's little point in eating in your hotel, which mostly only offer plates of plain starch in any case, and Kaduna has a fair amount of excellent alternative places selling non-Nigerian food thanks to there being a large expat community here. For fast food there's a branch of **Mr Biggs** ($) with an internet café behind on the corner of Yakubu Gowon Road and Ahmadu Bello Way near the post office. Around the Hamdala Hotel on Mohammed Buhari Way is **Habil Fast Food** ($) opposite the main entrance of the hotel, for boxes of rice, chips and fried chicken (although often little is actually available) in a spotless AC environment, and there's also a swimming pool behind it that you can use for a small fee. It's clean with a shaded bar area, but is very busy and women may feel exposed swimming here as it's mostly frequented by young men. Further along is **Ali Baba** ($), a small Lebanese spot serving good pizzas and *shawarma* for as little as N350.

Kaduna
National Museum
Kano–Abuja Expressway,
Airport,
Abuja Junction Motor Park,
Kawo Motor Park,
NAF Club, Arewa House
School
French Café
Sou's Palace
Webcafé
Food Palace
Government College
COLLEGE ROAD
DOKA CRES
NORTH RD
AKILU
ROAD
CORONATION
WAZIRI RD
ALKALI ROAD
Lugard Hall
SULEIMAN CR
YAKUHU AVENUE
COLLEGE ROAD
BANK ROAD
DOKA CRESCENT
ALI
B'YARO RD
MADAMA RD
AHMADU
DENDO RD
ALIMI RD
RACE COURSE RD
Murtala Square
(Racecourse)
KASHIM IBRAHIM RD
Hospital
NEPAU
Roundabout
SOKOTO RD
Command
Guest
House
Habil Fast Food,
swimming pool
Kaduna
Rugby
Club
Ahmed's,
Kaduna
Club
TAFAWA WAY
Ali Baba
Changchangi Airlines
Ostrich Bakery
MOHAMMED
Saman
Pharmacy
Hamdala
BUHAR
INDEPENDENCE
BELLO
DHL office
BIDA RD
LAFIA WAY
ROAD
BALEWA WAY
Baker's Delight,
Byblos Restaurant
Arewa
Leventis
Roundabout
Mr Biggs
YAKUBU
WAY
GOWON
WAY
Golf course
BROADCASTING RD
Post office
Stadium
State
Secretariat
Regal
Cinema
High
Court
NITEL
GOLF COURSE ROAD
Central
Market
IBRAHIM
BIDA RD
TAIWO ROAD
INDEPENDENCE
Direct buses
to Zaria
Police
Prison
BORIN ROAD
KANO RD
OGBOMOSHO ROAD
SABON GARI
Traveller's Inn
Safari Bar
Durncan
WAY
Katsina
Roundabout
FORCE RD
Gloria Moria
Catholic Social Centre
N
ABUJA RD
Bradt
JUNCTION ROAD
Stadium
Roundabout
CONSTITUTION ROAD
Gamji
Park
Mussafir
0   1,000m
0   1,000yds
Ahamadu Bello
Stadium
Kaduna
Railway
station,
Television
Garage
KADUNA

For very cheap chop, look out for the men selling grilled chicken on the side of the road; it's freshly cooked and quite delicious – there's a particularly dense crop along Mohammed Buhari Way, around the Command Guest House. For a fun local eating experience try the **unnamed restaurant** ($) just off Ahmadu Bello Way on Gwandu road, to the north of Katsina roundabout. It's recognisable from the bright yellow-and-red Maggi adverts painted on the outside and, in the evening, from the crowds of *okada* and bus drivers going in for their dinner. Huge plates of fresh food-is-ready are only around N150.

If you're in Kaduna on a Friday or Saturday night then the ☆ Nigerian Air Force Club (**NAF Club**) on Rabah Road is worth a visit. You can take a bus north from the centre to bus stop *Minista*, then an *achaba*. The club has a large outside bar and live music, usually starting around 21.00 and continuing until dawn. Food is available from the bar or you can eat at one of the chop stalls nearby.

✗ **Byblos Restaurant** off Ahmadu Bello Way; ☎ 062 241901, 0803 311 9480; ⏲ 12.00–15.00, 19.00–23.00 daily. It's pricey, but this is one of the nicest restaurants in Kaduna with a full bar of imported spirits, liqueurs & some wines, nice décor, subdued lights & background music. There are unusual items on the menu such as Chateaubriand, Champignon de Paris (mushrooms baked in wine with melted cheese), lots of delicious steaks & sauces, Lebanese mezzes & pizzas on Wed & Fri nights. $$$

✗ **Sou's Place** Waziri Ibrahim Crescent in Abakpa GRA; ☎ 062 295474, 0803 619 1292, 349 6198. Difficult to find but well worth the effort for their excellent pizzas cooked in a proper pizza oven & in a lovely, peaceful setting. Take a bus north from the centre & drop at the Total petrol station on Ali Akilu Rd, follow the road (Doka Crescent) at the southern side of the petrol station & take the first left. The restaurant is behind the first house on the right. It usually opens around 19.00 but if you're early the friendly staff will usually open up for you. $$$

✗ **Arewa Chinese Restaurant** 28 Ahmadu Bello Way, next door to the defunct Nigerian Airways office; ☎ 062 240088, 0803 506 2023; ⏲ 12.00–15.00, 19.00–22.00 daily. This is located in a pagoda-like building, with the restaurant on the upper floor, in a big car park with sparkly lights outside. It offers very authentic Chinese food, a good atmosphere, & a cosy bar serving beer & spirits. The extensive menu has mostly meat dishes, so vegetarians may need to ask for something special, & nearly all the dishes except for seafood cost the same for small, medium or large portions, & there's an all-you-can-eat buffet at Sun lunch. $$–$$$

🍴 **French Café** 2 Ali Akilu Rd; ⏲ 11.00–23.00 daily. A very lovely, if expensive, restaurant & bakery run by Lebanese expats. The bakery out front sells delectable chocolate éclairs & Black Forest gateaux, & the AC café to the back has a huge menu of sandwiches with fillings such as salmon, smoked turkey, shaved beef & Italian mozzarella, real salads with shrimps & avocado, pastas, burgers, steaks & chicken. On Sun afternoons (13.00–16.00) there's a buffet for N2,000. There's a huge range of imported spirits & French wine; finally, the toilets are fabulous. $$–$$$

✗ **Food Palace Restaurant** 1 Alkali Rd, next door to the International Trust Bank; ☎ 0803 349 4052, 0805 919 1523; ⏲ 12.00–21.00 daily. New, with immaculate plastic chairs & one room with mats to eat sitting on the floor, which is the traditional rural Hausa way of eating. Traditional food is on offer such as excellent pepper soup & *garri*, & unusual local items such as *waina*, ground rice soaked in yoghurt & then steamed. They also serve local drinks; *kunu* is made from millet, with plenty of ginger, & *zobo* is made from the flowers of a hibiscus-like plant. $$

✗ **Ahmeds/Kaduna Club** near the Hamdala Hotel on Mohammed Buhari Way; ⏲ 09.00–midnight daily. This offers plenty of cold beers, fish/steak/chicken & chips, & snacks such as pies & spring rolls all accompanied by CNN on the TV. There is a members-only lounge next door & a couple of tennis courts outside. This was closed for refurbishment at the time of writing but should have reopened by the time you read this. $–$$

✗ **Kaduna Rugby Club** near Habil Fast Food, Mohammed Buhari Way; ⏲ 11.00–23.00 Fri–Sun, 15.00–23.00 Mon–Thu. A restaurant popular with the expat crowd serving both European & Nigerian food, including chicken or fish & chips & mixed grills, which are reasonably priced. $–$$

♀ **Safari Bar** Argungu Rd, Sabon Gari. When I looked in, this was packed to the gills with men (and some Muslims I think) getting labouredly drunk. But it's a lively spot & women will feel quite comfortable here as it appears to be run by women who flap around the sottish men & help them out the door if necessary. Tables are arranged around an outside courtyard; it's decorated with beer flags, & hawkers do the rounds selling popcorn. $

SHOPPING

Bakers Delight More or less opposite the Arewa Chinese Restaurant on Ahmadu Bello Way; ⊕ 10.00–22.00 daily. A supermarket with some Lebanese & other imported tins & packets & a bakery counter.

Dalema Supermarket tucked away on Isa Kaita Rd in Malali GRA; ⊕ 09.00–18.00 daily. This has a good deli counter & a wide selection of imported goods at expensive prices. To get there take a bus north to *Minista* and then ask the *achaba* riders at the junction.

Ostrich Bakery 22 Ahmadu Bello Way; ⊕ 07.00–22.00 daily. Sells cold drinks, tubs of ice cream, fresh bread, cakes & pies & stays open late. There are branches of these in most of the northern cities, which are confusingly sometimes called Oasis Bakery. $

Saman Pharmacy 3 Mohammed Buhari Way, a block to the east of the Command Guest House; ⊕ 08.00–22.00 daily. They have a huge range of imported medical items & lots of recognisable brand names in a tiny building. The pharmacist in the office next door will give advice on minor complaints.

WHAT TO SEE AND DO

Kaduna National Museum Kaduna has limited sights, but you are very likely to pass through here, as it's an important transport hub to other points in the north, and there are a couple of worthwhile distractions. **Kaduna National Museum** is opposite the Emir of Zaria's house on Ali Akilu Road about 300m north of the French Café (⊕ 09.00–17.00 daily; entry N100). To get there by bus ask them to drop you at *Gidan Sarki* (Emir's house in Hausa) as locals don't know the museum. It's not one of the better Nigerian museums and there are only two dusty rooms with a few replicas of Benin brass plaques, and carved ivory from the old Benin Palace. Again the pieces of Nok terracotta are disappointingly also replicas. The collection is mostly bits and pieces from southern Nigeria, though there is a small display of Islamic tablets and Koran writing, some especially evil-looking Epa cult masks and an elaborate knitted and raffia masquerade costume, and the usual collection of calabashes and pots.

Hausa Village The best reason for coming here is the reproduction of a mud-walled **Hausa Village** with about ten buildings covered in corrugated tin roofs, and some open courtyards and gardens under the shade of flowering jacaranda and flame trees. It's outside and at the back of the museum and not obvious, so get someone to show you the gate. This is a popular spot for many Kaduna families, and you can wander around the huts; the people inside will be happy to talk to you. In one is a women's hairdresser; leave your shoes at the door, go in and chat to the women and young girls sitting on mats or traditional Hausa ten-legged stools as they have their hair done. Once braids are unleashed some of their hair is very long and bushy until it is tamed again by straighteners, perms or plaiting.

In the other huts are weavers and painters, and at the far end is a long hut with a brass maker, blacksmith and silver craftsman. Here you can buy brass rings fashioned out of bullets! Try and be here on Thursday–Sunday when at 17.00 there is a display of drumming and dancing followed by a Hausa drama that lasts about an hour. Everything is in Hausa but you can enlist a guide to sit next to you to try and explain what is going on. Ask one of the museum staff or a trader in the huts. The chances are you still won't have any idea what's going on as the tales are of mythical escapades, but it's very musical and atmospheric, with the graceful dancers with hennaed feet and hands, deep decorative scars on their faces and vibrant drumming, and as far as I am aware it's the only performance of its kind in Nigeria. Each performance attracts about a hundred people who sit on basic wooden benches or on the mud floor. There's a small entry fee to pay at the gate.

Arewa House Further north, off Ali Akilu Way at 1 Rabah Road, is **Arewa House** (*bus stop Minista;* ⊕ *08.00–16.00 Mon–Fri*; *entry N50*), the former residence of Ahmadu Bello, the first Premier of Northern Nigeria until the first military coup. Its museum features many of his personal effects, plus his office records and government publications, and various other artefacts, as well as displays from each northern state.

In the city centre Back in the city centre off Ibrahim Taiwo Road, the **Central Market** sells the usual assortment of manufactured plastic goods and clothes, though the fruit and vegetable section on the railway tracks at the back is particularly colourful, and again it comes as a surprise to find so much variety of produce in such a barren region. In the northeast corner of the market, the **Regal Cinema** shows Bollywood movies every night at 20.15. Imported from India they are not subtitled, but Hausas generally enjoy the singing and dancing, and these old colonial cinemas feature in many of the northern cities.

    Gamji Park (officially Hassan Usman Park), in a peaceful location by the river to the southeast of town, is a popular spot with families at the weekend and it's a relaxing place to sit with a cold drink or ice cream. You can take an *achaba* from the stadium roundabout to Gamji Gate and from there walk past the street food stalls. There's a swimming pool here, which is not quite as nice as the one at Habil Fast Food but it is more family-orientated. There are also a few mangy ostriches and some cramped crocodiles in run-down enclosures, and **Lord Lugard's Foot Bridge**, which he originally built in Zungeru in what is now Niger State in 1904, which was rebuilt in the park in 1954.

    The only other attraction in Kaduna is **Lugard Hall** on Independence Way, built by Lord Lugard and used by the colonial government as their headquarters when they administered northern Nigeria. Today it is the State House of Assembly and an impressive example of colonial architecture, painted green and white in dramatic well-tended grounds, but you can only peek through the gate.

Kamuka National Park Kamuka National Park lies some 125km west of Kaduna on the A125 near the town of Birnin Gwari, and the park gate is 23km to the south of here off the Lagos–Kaduna road near the village of Dagara. Kamuka covers 1,121m^2 of savanna woodland marshes and was gazetted as a national park in 1999 from an older forest reserve and named after a local ethnic group. However, the park has only ever received a handful of visitors and it's poorly protected. It reputedly has some elephants, roan antelopes, western hartebeest, a number of species of duikers, warthogs, baboons and jackals, and a variety of birds including guinea fowl and ground hornbill. The park is supposedly open from December to June; if you manage to gain access and find anyone to pay, the entry fee is supposed to be N300. There's no accommodation and you'll need to be in a self-sufficient vehicle and be prepared for camping, and remember that none of the tracks within the park have been maintained.

ZARIA

The ancient walled city of Zaria to the north of Kaduna retains much of its old character and has a fine mosque and Emir's Palace. It is an exceptionally friendly place and one of the most pleasant of the northern cities. First known as Zazzau, it was founded in about 1000 and became one of the 15th-century Hausa states (see box on page 316). It was once an important city on the trans-Saharan trade route, where camel caravans from the north exchanged salt for slaves, cloth, leather and kola nuts. With them came Arabian influences, and the court of Zazzau increasingly became interested in the teachings of Islamic scholars. Like their contemporaries in Kano and Katsina, the Sarkis (kings) of Zazzau converted to Islam in the 15th century.

The jihad of the early 19th century (see page 35) was successful in Zaria, and an emirate was established in 1808 under the control of the wider Sokoto Caliphate. A century later it was incorporated into the British Protectorate and cotton, groundnuts, leather and tobacco from the region were sent by rail to Lagos for export.

The old walled city still exists, inhabited by mainly Hausa-Fulani – the main market is on the original site where the camel caravans used to stop from the Sahara, and where there are still many Islamic schools. The population is just over one million, of which about three-quarters are Muslim. Western education has gained much ground here, with the establishment of the Ahmadu Bello University (ABU) (*www.abu.edu.ng*), the first university in northern Nigeria, located on the northern approach to town, which has one of the largest teaching hospitals in the country. The university has witnessed some violent clashes in recent years between the more radical students and the security forces. The Nigerian Aviation College, with its own airfield, is also on this road.

GETTING THERE Zaria's **motor park** is under and around the bridge of the Kaduna–Kano Expressway on Sokoto Road to the north of the city between the river and university, with rows of vehicles parked up on either side of the road going to Kaduna, Kano, Gusau, Sokoto, Katsina and Jos. A bush taxi from Kaduna, only 83km or one hour to the south, costs around N180. The **train station** is near the Union Bank, just to the north of Queen Elizabeth II Road, and the train between Lagos and Kano stops here (see page 340).

GETTING AROUND From south to north, the old walled city overflows into Tudun Wada, the newer part of the city built after the British came. There is then a big overgrown gap of around 500m of undeveloped land where maize is grown and rubbish thrown, around the swampy Kubani River, to the GRA to the north of the river. Sokoto Road then continues north past the golf course for another kilometre or so to the Sabon Gari and the motor park, before heading out for another couple of kilometres to the university campus. From the motor park it's easy enough to jump on an *achaba* or any of the constant stream of shared taxis and minibuses that run up and down the Sokoto–Kaduna road, the main artery of the city (which in parts is also confusingly known as Hospital Road), for little more than N30.

WHERE TO STAY

🏠 **Zaria Hotel** Sokoto Rd; ☎ 069 333092. The city's principal hotel, set in nice grounds with an empty swimming pool, but you can get alcohol here as it's run by the Arewa Hotels chain. The bookshop here sells mostly law & medical books for the university students. Bizarrely for a Muslim city, there is a functioning nightclub here on Wed, Fri & Sat nights, an additional big comfy bar, & a very neat restaurant with a menu of Nigerian food & one continental dish such as fish & chips, & attentive service. The 52 rooms have satellite TV with CNN. Rooms $$; suites $$$

🏠 **Kongo Conference Hotel** Old Jos Rd, on the right-hand side roughly 1.5km from the junction of Kaduna Rd close to ABU's Kongo Campus; ☎ 0805 915 7048. A large, dated hotel & another 1970s concrete eyesore in a big 3-storey block. The restaurant here is the oddest, most kitsch inter-galactic building I have ever seen, with a few tables dotted around, miles away from each other. Architecture buffs should come here just to look at the place. The old-fashioned 80 rooms, however, have reasonable bathrooms with running water, satellite TV, & there's an all-night gen. But the rooms are very musty & stuffy & perhaps are not used that often – the one we were in spat all sorts of rubbish out of the AC unit when it was switched on. $$

🏠 **Teejay Palace Hotel** 6 Western Way Close, GRA; 📞 0803 607 2070, 0804 237 6619. Here are 50 comfortable & cool rooms arranged around tiled courtyards, with satellite TV, an all-night generator, established gardens, a mosque & no booze. It's well signposted off the Sokoto Rd in the peaceful GRA. The restaurant serves the usual Nigerian dishes but also has curries & vegetarian dishes. Attached to the hotel is the Teejay Amusement Park, with swimming pool, gym & internet. All the facilities are complementary for hotel guests; non-guests can use the pool for a small fee. $$

🏠 **Zazzau Royal Chalets** across the railway line from the Beauty Guest House; 📞 0802 650 4749. This is a quiet compound of colonial bungalows, each with its own garage, a large sitting room & bedroom, satellite TV, AC. The helpful staff will bring hot water on request. The restaurant will prepare Nigerian food if you order in advance. $$

🏠 **Aifaas Motel** by MTD junction, 9 Sokoto Rd; 📞 0802 358 4341, 0806 729 5661, 0803 968 3560. A lovely hotel decorated with roses & pot plants, with old-fashioned décor, but it is spotlessly clean & comfortable, & the rooms have hot water & satellite TV, & the suites have tea & coffee in the rooms. In the restaurant you may get the likes of chicken with soy sauce or spag bol, & good breakfasts. No alcohol is served. Outside is a kiosk in an old shipping container serving doughnuts, burgers, samosas, pre-cooked toasted sandwiches, terrible pizza (no choice of topping, just small, medium or big), *moin moin* & meat pies, & there's a shady outside seating area in a little garden. $

🏠 **Beauty Guest House** Sokoto Rd, 📞 069 334038. Very rough & ready but popular, with an unkempt, tatty dining room serving Nigerian staples & a horrendously noisy gen. It has recently had a coat of paint, sheets on the beds are clean & rooms have fans; there is running water in the shower, & an ancient one-station TV. Central location. All rooms are a flat N2,500 (US$20). $

🏠 **New Zaria Motel** off Queen Elizabeth II Rd, in the GRA opposite the Sharia Court; 📞 0806 323 0945. This is a government-owned motel in shady, tree-filled grounds – it is unashamedly shabby but it's friendly with a great atmosphere. It's non-Muslim (as attested to by the Gideon Bibles in the rooms), & this is the place where people come for illicit drinking – there are some raucous parties going on in the rooms & car park (despite its proximity to the Sharia Court across the road). There's a small restaurant, or they will deliver the usual Nigeria food to your room, & there's excellent *suya* available in the car park. Most rooms don't have hot water but the staff will heat a bucket for you. The generator is kept on all night. $

✖ **WHERE TO EAT AND DRINK** You may get the odd continental dish in the hotels, but Zaria is a good place to try out northern Nigerian food in the many chop houses. Additionally there's a branch of **Mr Biggs** close to the river and an **Ostrich Bakery** opposite the motor park. If you want a beer go to one of several **bars** in the 'PZ' area on IBB Road opposite Union Bank and backing onto the railway line, with paths through the bushes for surreptitious access. The **Easy Life Spot** has a particularly nice garden and a pool table. Another recommended bar is outside the **Soho Guest Inn** on New Kano Road close to the motor park. There's a large area for sitting outside and the barman has a huge collection of LPs, making the music selection very different from the usual Nigerian and American R&B and rap.

✖ **Shagalinku Restaurant** Kongo Rd; 🕐 10.00–21.00 daily. Well-known locally for excellent Nigerian food & elaborately decorated with several carpeted private rooms where you can do as the locals do & sit on the floor while eating. It has a small shop with some imported goods on the ground floor. $–$$

✖ **Al-Nasiha Restaurant** 4 Sokoto Rd; 🕐 10.00–18.00 daily. This has cheap food-is-ready during the day on 2 levels, with white-coated waiters & a full range of good Nigerian food. Nearby is the Al-Nasara, another branch of the same restaurant. $

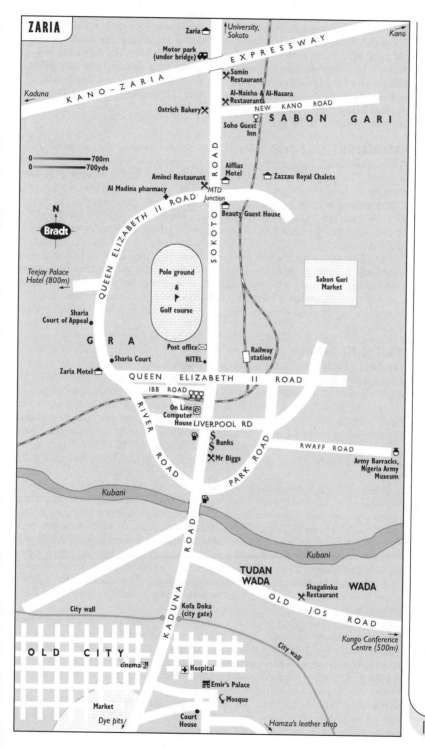

ZARIA

Zaria
University, Sokoto
Kano
Motor park (under bridge)
Kano-Zaria Expressway
Kaduna
Samin Restaurant
Al-Naisha & Al-Nasara Restaurants
Ostrich Bakery
New Kano Road
SABON GARI
Soho Guest Inn
0 ——— 700m
0 ——— 700yds
Aiffias Motel
Aminci Restaurant
Al Madina pharmacy
MTD Junction
Zazzau Royal Chalets
N
Bradt
Beauty Guest House
Teejay Palace Hotel (800m)
Sokoto Road
Queen Elizabeth II Road
Polo ground & Golf course
Sabon Gari Market
Sharia Court of Appeal
G R A
Sharia Court
Post office
NITEL
Railway station
Zaria Motel
QUEEN ELIZABETH II ROAD
IBB ROAD
On Line Computer House
LIVERPOOL RD
River Road
Banks
Mr Biggs
Park Road
RWAFF ROAD
Army Barracks, Nigeria Army Museum
Kubani
Kubani
TUDAN WADA
WADA
Shagalinku Restaurant
Old Jos Road
Kaduna Road
City wall
Kofa Doka (city gate)
Kongo Conference Centre (500m)
Old City
cinema
City wall
Hospital
Emir's Palace
Mosque
Market
Dye pits
Court House
Hamza's leather shop

✗ Aminci Restaurant opposite the Aifaas Motel at MTD junction; ⊕ 08.00–21.00 daily. Chicken or goat's head pepper soup with choice of starch from N250 – it boasts bright white tiles & refreshing fans, & is not a bad place for tea-eggs-and-bread in the morning. $

✗ Samin Restaurant close to the motor park on Sokoto Rd; ⊕ 08.00–22.00. This is a very popular chop house serving a variety of traditional northern food including some unusual & delicious dishes such as *fate* (a kind of thick soup with couscous, fish & vegetables), *waina* (fluffy yoghurt & rice cakes) & *fura da nono* (fresh yoghurt mixed with millet & ginger) all for N150 a plate. $

PRACTICALITIES The **NITEL** building is on Sokoto Road, to the east of the Zaria Motel (just look for the tower), and it's open unusually late (until 21.00, closed Sunday). The **post office**, also on Sokoto Road, is close by. For **internet**, On Line Computer House, on Sokoto Road near the level crossing is a well-set-up internet café; browsing is N150 an hour and if you have your own laptop you can plug it in. There are also many good internet cafés out in Samaru (N30 bus from the centre), opposite the main gate of the university, which are popular with students and lecturers.

Money changers hang out in the car park of the Zaria Hotel, should you need to **change money**. At 28 Queen Elizabeth II Road is the **Al Madina Pharmacy and Clinic**, which is very clean and well stocked with imported medical items. Another recommended pharmacy is **Farmeks** in Samaru Market near the university, with a good range of genuine products, a doctor and a laboratory for malaria tests.

WHAT TO SEE AND DO

The Emir's Palace The **Emir's Palace** is a fairly new construction, built in 1995, with a façade that is a wonderful, brilliantly coloured mosaic wall surrounding an imposing gate. The grandstand for watching the durbar is perched on the top of the wall to the left of the gate, and to the right is the smaller old gate of brown mud bricks from the original palace that's around 100 years old. The vast durbar ground, full of swallows, is in front, which is also used as the overflow for Friday prayers from the mosque to the southeast of the palace. The emir is leader of the Zazzau Emirate (see box) and the present emir, Dr Shehu Idris, has ruled since 1975.

If the emir is at home, you can usually arrange with one of the palace guards to see inside the palace and even meet him. Someone hanging around outside the palace will assist and the palace secretary may even approach you. Everyone is very friendly and accommodating. The guards have obviously been with the emir throughout his reign and are incredibly elderly men dressed in marvellously elaborate bright red robes and turbans, with a black piece of cloth as a sign stitched on their backs saying Zazzau. Reputedly, there are some 350 palace guards in total, and 100 stay with him in his apartments at all times. The old name for a palace guard is Dogarin, and they once used to collect taxes from the townsfolk of Zaria on behalf of the emir.

To the left of the palace is a busy primary school where the teachers and pupils will happily show you around, and a *batauri* will be received with much excited enthusiasm by the children. Again, as in many places in Nigeria, some of these kids may never have seen a white face before. In the streets around the school, look out for the old, double-storeyed mud buildings that are good examples of the old Hausa mud-brick architecture, with carvings around the door posts and windows that could feasibly be centuries old. They are practically falling down, but you can still see the geometric patterns and frescos in yellow, green, blue and red, shuttered windows, tin roofs, and high, small windows.

The central mosque The **central mosque**, a few metres to the southeast of the palace, is an unremarkable modern building with concrete monolith minarets surrounded by trees, built on the site of the old mosque. Parts of the old mosque, such as the original internal vaulted ceiling, can still be seen inside, and a reproduction of the old mosque can be seen in the Museum of Traditional Nigerian Architecture in Jos (see page 259). At Friday prayers the mosque holds around 3,000 people, with another 2,000 in the square outside, and it is quite a spectacular event to watch.

You could go to watch Friday prayers, but be very discreet and stay well in the background – women, of course, are not welcome and even the local women melt away during prayer time. It's a spectacular event when many thousands of beautifully dressed men in their brightly coloured and multi-layered robes, with extravagant turbans and headdresses, simultaneously pray. They stand and bow in lines towards Mecca, and despite the thousands of people the silence is deathly at the most intense time of prayer – it's an extraordinary spectacle. All the northern emirs traditionally wear white robes and a lacy white or black turban that is tied under the chin and that covers the chin up to the mouth. At Friday prayers you may see the emir, who is heralded by trumpeters playing long thin trumpets, as he walks to and from the palace and the mosque, when a cannon goes off. He walks with his entourage to the mosque, shaking hands as he goes with all the men who greet him.

As a woman, I unfortunately did not witness any of the Friday prayers in northern Nigeria, so here is an account from a male traveller who watched Friday prayers in Zaria: 'As I passed through the old city's gate on the back of my *achaba*, the road was just chock-a-block with worshippers, young, old, and extremely old, walking up to the mosque – so much so that I had to get off the motorbike and walk the last couple of hundred metres. The buzz was all-encompassing, but the actual prayers only went on for a relatively short time, and the silence was deafening. The 'after-prayer session' was even more interesting, as the emir of Zaria wandered back to his palace. His path was preceded by trumpeters, bodyguards and by many assorted hangers-on. I stood at the gateway to his palace with hundreds of others waiting to get a look at him, just like some teeny-bopper waiting to get a glimpse of one of the Backstreet Boys as they run from the back of the concert hall into a waiting limousine. He was brilliantly robed in about 20m of the whitest cloth, with red slippers and Ray Ban sunglasses. I thought he gave me a slight wave and nod of acknowledgement, but he may well have been swatting one of the 50 million flies that were present. Following along behind him was a large variety of majestically robed gentlemen looking very important, shaking hands with those offered and doing the old after-Friday prayer business deals and perhaps even collecting debts. I enjoyed it immensely and didn't feel too overwhelmed.'

Hamza's Leather Shop Another worthwhile place to visit in Zaria is **Hamza's Leather Shop** on Kaura Road (you will have to enlist the help of a guide to find this – ask outside the Emir's Palace and you should find someone). It's a shop and tannery for goat, lizard, snake and crocodile leather and there's a variety of good-quality bags, briefcases and duffel bags on offer, though you may balk at the material being used, and to purchase some of these items could present a problem when taking them home. Crocodile hides come from the Maiduguri River, and there are also monitor lizard briefcases, cobra wallets and iguana cell-phone covers. Instead, go for the items made from soft goatskin. This is a treasure chest of quality leather items and the designs of the women's handbags in particular would give Louis Vuitton a run for his money. Hamza and his staff have been trading and working for over 40 years.

The older name for Zaria is Zazzau, and the inhabitants are called Zage-zage or Zazzagawa. Oral tradition has it that the name Zazzau is derived from a famous sword which was honoured by the Zazzagawa and which helped to give a kind of ethnic identity in the years before the recognition of any king. One of the earliest rulers of Zazzau was Bakwa Turunku (it's not certain whether Turunku was a king or queen), who had two daughters. The older daughter was called Amina, after whom the original 15km perimeter wall of Zazzau is named. Zaria, the younger daughter, gave her name to the modern emirate and its capital. Queen Amina ruled Zaria and was known as a great warrior, her territories stretching as far as Bauchi in the east and extending as far south as the River Niger, and she built a walled town wherever she conquered.

Tradition maintains that Queen Amina never married a full-time husband, but instead took a temporary husband for the night, usually one of her bodyguards, and had him killed the following morning so that he would never tell tales of his experiences with her. Queen Amina died near Bida in the present-day Niger State after she chased one lover who managed to get away. He had hidden in a river and Amina jumped in after him to catch him but drowned. There is a portrait of her inside the Emir's Palace. Zaria, Queen Amina's sister, did marry and succeeded Amina as queen, but later became bored with married life, and presumably with being queen, and ran away to the north.

The Queen Amina Walls, the dye pits and the old market The **Queen Amina Walls** of Zaria, which circumnavigate the old city, are between 14 and 16km long and are pierced by eight gates. The gates are concrete reconstructions, though startlingly and rather magically, the gates are still manned by palace guards carrying bows and arrows. The walls are thought to be about 1,000 years old, and are perhaps the best preserved among the cities of northern Nigeria, but the need for defensive walls has disappeared since the occupation by the British at the beginning of this century. Moreover, the rains of over 50 wet seasons have battered down the mud walls, and, like many other walls in the north, today it's a crumbling mound of brown earth with piles of plastic rubbish and goats on top.

Like the more famous ones in Kano, Zaria has its **dye pits**, but again you'll need a guide to take you there as they are off Zage Dantse Road, to the south of the main market. The family operating the pits has been here for over 200 years – today they are run by the one-eyed cloth-dyer O Yummar Idib, who has more dye pits in his nearby house. Art students from all over Nigeria still come to Zaria to discuss with him the ancient method of dyeing. It's a similar set-up to the one in Kano, but only a few dye pits are in operation, and they use red, green and yellow natural dyes as opposed to just the indigo blue used in Kano. Cloth is dyed to order and is used for ceremonial purposes for the emir and his staff.

The old **market** nearby is very clean and organised, very friendly and a pleasure to walk around. Despite the modern produce and manufactured clothes, looking at the herbs, spices, fresh produce, pulses, grains and various dried grasses, flowers, and roots, it's easy to imagine things have not changed much here for hundreds of years. About midway down Kaduna Road between the city gate and the market is an old colonial **cinema** that shows (un-subtitled) Bollywood movies to the Hausa community.

Outside the city Outside the old city, at the Chindit Army Barracks, is the small **Nigeria Army Museum**. To get there follow RWAFF Road to the end. You may have to request permission to visit through the guards at the gates and come back later to see if it has been granted. There are no set opening hours – it's more a case of waiting for someone to show you the museum. Inside is a collection of medals, weapons, army uniforms, maps, and many faded but interesting photographs of the colonial years and the major wars that Nigeria has been involved in during the last century, notably the civil or Biafran War and the Burma Campaign during World War II, where most of the Nigerian forces were sent. North of the river and not far from the railway station, the **Sabon Gari Market** is a good place to buy some local crafts, such as beads, raffia-work and decorated calabashes, but again you'll certainly need a guide to find anything in the maze of twisty passageways.

KANO

Kano is the oldest city in West Africa, and today is the capital of Kano State. It is a teeming and vibrant city with a variety of interesting things to see. Rather surprisingly, in the 2006 census, the population of Kano State was put at 9,383,682, which was just over 370,000 more than Lagos State, making Kano Nigeria's largest city. This has been highly disputed and Lagos is generally considered to be far bigger.

Nevertheless, Kano is a huge commercial city founded on the trade of the ancient Sahara routes, and it's in the centre of a major agricultural region where cotton, cattle, and about half of Nigeria's peanuts are raised. The traffic is especially chaotic here, and the pollution in the city is palpable, especially at the end of the dry season from April to May, when hot fumes scorch your throat. Kano has several districts, including the old city, which is walled and contains many clay houses, giving Kano a medieval atmosphere. The parts of the wall that can still be seen today were built in the 15th century, though as in other northern cities, most of it is seriously dilapidated and eroded.

Kano is popular for its traditional arts and crafts, including weaving and indigo cloth-dyeing, and it has long been known for its leatherwork; its tanned goatskins were sent to North Africa from about the 15th century, and were known in Europe as Morocco leather. The city is also recognised as a centre of learning, being the seat of Bayero University and the Kano State Institute for Higher Education, and the British Council Library and the Kano State Library are also located in the city. If you are in town at the end of Ramadan, then the traditional horse-riding celebrations are not to be missed. The emirs of Kano and Katsina both hold colourful durbars during the Muslim festival of Eid-el-Kabir and Id Al Malud. Performances include charges on horseback, knife-swallowers, camels, acrobats, snake charmers, drummers and horn blowers. The city has many good restaurants and accommodation options, and you'll welcome the coffee and cake shops and Western food.

Despite these attractions, however, be aware that Kano is a very conservative Islamic city and has also attracted fame as a hotbed for religious tension in recent years. There were serious riots in 2004, when many Christians lost their lives and churches were destroyed. The population is dominantly Muslim, with just 5–10% Christian who mostly live in the Sabon Gari part of the city, and Sharia law is very strict in Kano, and is becoming increasingly so. In the last couple of years Muslim women have been banned from riding on the back of *achabas*, alcohol has been banned, Muslim men and women must now use single sex public transport, and Muslim children must wear Islamic dress to school. In 2005 the state government recruited a force of 9,000 Muslim men as a sort of religious police to enforce these

10

Kevin O'Rourke

One striking feature of Nigeria's northern cities are the *almajiris*, crowds of young boys (some as young as four) found wandering with their begging bowls around the motor parks, markets and busy streets. *Almajiri* is a Hausa word but is derived from an Arabic word (*Al-Muhajirin*) meaning 'emigrant'. In the past these were boys who had been sent by their parents to study the Qur'an under a *mallam* (teacher); they would earn their keep and learn humility by begging for him. Failure to bring food and alms to their *mallam* usually earned them a beating.

Nowadays the *almajiris* tend to be younger sons of poor families, sent off to reduce the financial burden on their parents. They often get little or no Islamic education beyond being taught the few verses of the Qur'an they chant while begging and no Western education, ensuring that their opportunities for earning a living when they grow up are limited. Many sleep on the streets, even during the cold *harmattan* season, making them vulnerable to illness and abuse. The *almajiri* system has also been implicated in the various ethnic and religious crises in northern Nigeria since the return to democracy. Teenaged former *almajiris*, still living on the streets, are easily recruited by local politicians as hired thugs, who can be relied on to carry out intimidation, arson or even murder. In some cases their only payment has been one meal a day and access to a television to watch football matches.

laws – fining *achaba* drivers for carrying women who were not their wives, for example. But it was then believed that this force was responsible for demolishing more churches and persecuting Christians, and the national government stepped in and won a court order that branded it illegal and the force was disbanded in early 2007.

Additionally, anytime there is a problem elsewhere in the world – the Danish cartoon controversy in 2005, which caused a huge reaction in Nigeria, being a prime recent example – Muslims attack Christians. The result is that today many Christians are leaving Kano, and in the future it could become almost a secessionist Islamic state. In a more serious incident in March 2007 an armed group in Kano (including women and some children) shot and killed an imam while he was giving prayers at a mosque, which was followed by an attack on the central police station where 20 policemen and 25 of the gang were killed. It was thought that the imam had been criticised for not preaching a stricter Islamic line and was not telling his congregation to vote for the election candidate he was supposed to (the incident occurred just before the 2007 election). The attackers were dubbed by the press as a fundamentalist self-styled Nigerian 'Taliban'.

BRIEF HISTORY Kano was the largest of the seven Hausa states (see box on page 316) and Kano's written history dates back to 999, when the city was already several hundred years old. Legend has it that it was founded by a character called Bagauda, one of the six sons of Bawo, the founder of the Hausa states, who was sent here by his father to form a dynasty and monarchy based on the trans-Saharan trade routes when the region was of strategic importance to the trade route, and had wide contacts with North Africa. Many people from Arab North Africa, Mali and Songhai migrated here and were absorbed into the city – skilled traders and artisans mainly concerned with the gold trade and Islam – and city walls and ditches were built extending to the surrounding villages and settlements.

The walls and ditches were considerably extended during the reign of Mohammed Rumfa between 1463 and 1499. Islam was adopted probably between the 12th and 14th centuries from visiting sheiks from North Africa and Mali, and it was practised by almost all the city's occupants by the 16th century, when Kano was a centre for Islamic learning which attracted scholars from all over the Muslim world. Kano's traders went as far as the Mediterranean, Gonja (modern Ghana) and to what is now Gabon to the south. They exchanged Hausa leather, pottery, metal works and particularly cloth – Kano is still famous for its indigo dye pits and the bright blue cloth was once worn by the Tuaregs and other peoples of the Sahara – and groundnuts (sacks of groundnuts stored in pyramids were still a feature of Kano until the 1970s). In return they took back to Kano salt from Lake Chad, kola nuts from Yorubaland and Ghana, and weapons, silk, spices, perfume and Islamic books from across the Sahara.

Kano reached the height of its power in the 17th and 18th centuries, when city traders reputedly sent 300 camel-loads of cloth at a time to Timbuktu. The European explorer Captain Clapperton, who went to Kano in 1826, reported seeing a caravan arriving from the north with over 3,000 camels. Kano market was laden with commodities, and in *Travels and Discoveries in North and Central Africa* (1857) German traveller Heinrich Barth describes a list of imports to the city in 1850, which he called 'the great emporium of Negroland'. There were 'cotton prints from Manchester, silk and sugar from France, articles of Arab dress from Egypt and Tunis, embroidery from Tripoli, common paper, reading glasses, beads from Venice, copper, sword blades, needles and razors'. Kano was traditionally described as *Tumbi Giwa* – 'the capacious stomach of an elephant'.

Like the rest of northern Nigeria, the Kano region was taken during the Fulani jihad in 1809 and held by them under the Sokoto Caliphate until 1903. But it soon regained its leading commercial position before being taken by the British in 1903, when it became part of northern Nigeria. Lugard, the British governor-general, appointed a new emir, Mohammed Abbas, in place of Emir Aliyu, who was exiled and later died in Lokoja, and Kano became a laboratory for Lugard's experiment in indirect colonial rule. The railway arrived in 1911, and with this development and the road-building by the British, the trade routes across the Sahara began to die. The first international flight arrived in Kano in 1937 and it became Nigeria's second international airport after Lagos. Today Kano remains the most important commercial city in northern Nigeria, attested to by the frantic market that has stood on the same spot for perhaps a thousand years.

GETTING THERE AND AWAY

By air Aminu Kano (KAN) **Airport** (↘ *064 600310*) is 8km or 25 minutes' driving time north of the central Sabon Gari area of the city. Aside from scheduled services, it operates charter flights in season for the many hundreds of thousands of northern Nigerian Muslims making the pilgrimage to Mecca. The Nigerian Air Force is also based here. There is an international terminal and a domestic terminal and, as in Lagos and Abuja, Virgin Nigeria and Arik Air use the international one for all their flights. In both terminals, facilities are minimal with just a newsstand at check-in and a bar airside. Construction was started on a new domestic terminal a few years ago, but has since been abandoned. Buses from the airport leave for the city every ten minutes between 06.00 and 22.00, taxis are available and you can also hire a car and driver. There are direct flights to and from Kano and Amsterdam three times a week with KLM.

Arik air has a flight from Lagos to Kano (1½ hours) at 11.15 Mondays–Fridays, which returns to Lagos from Kano at 13.15, and one at 16.00 on Sundays, which returns to Lagos at 18.15. **Bellview** has one flight a day between Kano and Lagos at 10.10 on weekdays, and at 09.40 at weekends, which departs Lagos for Kano at 06.50 on weekdays and 07.30 at weekends. There's an Abuja to Kano flight (45

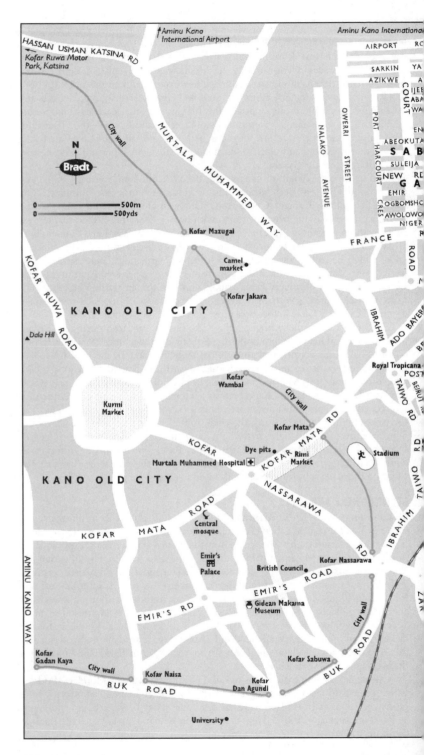

HASSAN USMAN KATSINA RD
Kofar Ruwa Motor
Park, Katsina

↑Aminu Kano
International Airport

Aminu Kano International

AIRPORT   RO

SARKIN   YA

AZIKWE   A

COURT   OJEE
ABA
WA

EN

ABEOKUTA
S A B
SULEIJA
NEW   RD
G A
EMIR
OGBOMSHO
AWOLOWO
NIGER

N

Bradt

City wall

KOFAR RUWA ROAD

0 ————— 500m
0 ————— 500yds

Kofar Mazugai

Camel
market

Kofar Jakara

KANO OLD CITY

▲Dala Hill

Kurmi
Market

MURTALA MUHAMMED WAY

NALAKO AVENUE

OWERRI STREET

PORT HARCOURT

COGBOMSHO CRES

FRANCE

IBRAHIM

ADO BAYERO

Royal Tropicana
POST

TAIWO RD

BEIRUT

Kofar
Wambai

City wall

Kofar Mata

KANO OLD CITY

KOFAR MATA RD

Dye pits

Rimi
Market

Kofar
Mata

Murtala Muhammed Hospital ✚

NASSARAWA

Stadium

IBRAHIM TAIWO RD

ROAD

Central
mosque

KOFAR MATA

RD

Emir's
Palace

British Council

ROAD

Kofar Nassarawa

AMINU KANO WAY

EMIR'S RD

EMIR'S ROAD

Gidean Makama
Museum

City wall

ZAR

Kofar
Gadan Kaya

City wall

BUK   ROAD

Kofar Naisa

Kofar
Dan Agundi

Kofar Sabuwa

BUK ROAD

BUK ROAD

University●

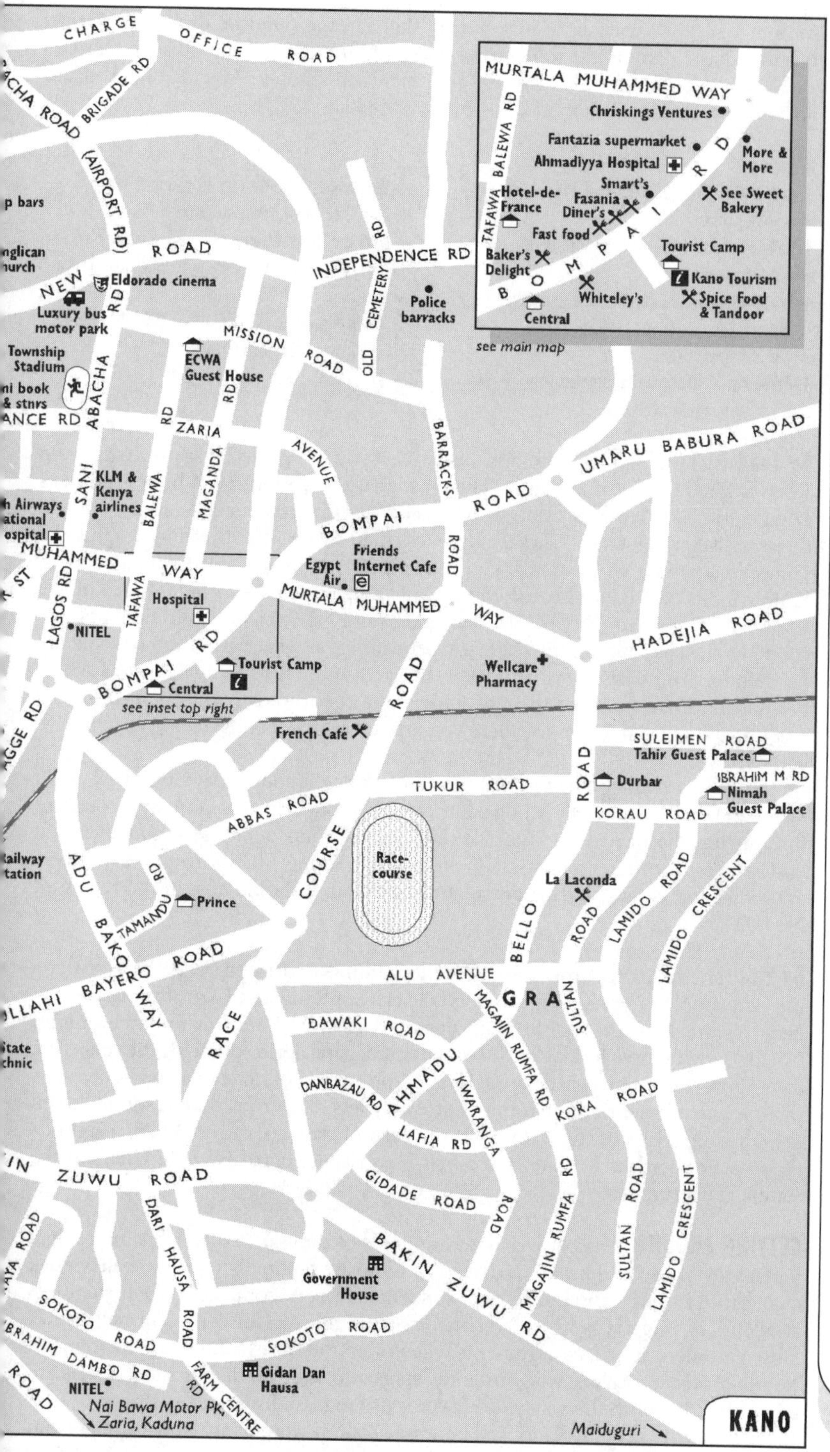

CHARGE
OFFICE ROAD
ACHA ROAD
BRIGADE RD
(AIRPORT RD)

p bars

nglican
hurch

NEW

ROAD

Eldorado cinema

Luxury bus
motor park

Township
Stadium

ni book
& stnrs
ANCE RD

ABACHA

RD

ZARIA

SANI

KLM &
Kenya
airlines

BALEWA

MAGANDA
RD

MISSION

ECWA
Guest House

ROAD

AVENUE

INDEPENDENCE RD

CEMETERY RD

OLD CEMETERY RD

Police
barracks

BARRACKS

ROAD

UMARU BABURA ROAD

h Airways
ational
ospital

MUHAMMED

WAY

TAFAWA

BALEWA

RD

BOMPAI

Egypt
Air

Friends
Internet Cafe

ROAD

MURTALA MUHAMMED

WAY

HADEJIA ROAD

LAGOS RD

ST

NITEL

Hospital

BOMPAI

Central

Tourist Camp

see inset top right

ROAD

Wellcare
Pharmacy

SULEIMEN ROAD
Tahir Guest Palace

AGGE RD

French Café

TUKUR ROAD

ABBAS ROAD

Durbar

KORAU ROAD

IBRAHIM M RD

Nimah
Guest Palace

Railway
tation

ADU

BAKO

ROAD

RD

TAMANDU

Prince

COURSE

Race-
course

RACE

BELLO

ROAD

La Laconda

SULTAN ROAD

LAMIDO ROAD

LAMIDO CRESCENT

LLAHI BAYERO WAY

ALU AVENUE

GRA

State
chnic

DAWAKI ROAD

DANBAZAU RD

MAGAJIN RUMFA RD

SULTAN

AHMADU KWARANGA

LAFIA RD

KORA ROAD

IN ZUWU ROAD

DARI HAUSA

RD

GIDADE ROAD

MAGAJIN RUMFA RD

KORA ROAD

SULTAN ROAD

LAMIDO CRESCENT

A ROAD

BAKIN ZUWU RD

Government
House

SOKOTO ROAD

SOKOTO ROAD

IBRAHIM DAMBO RD

FARM CENTRE RD

Gidan Dan
Hausa

ROAD

NITEL

Nai Bawa Motor Pk,
Zaria, Kaduna

Maiduguri

KANO

Inset (top right):

MURTALA MUHAMMED WAY

Chriskings Ventures

BALEWA RD

TAFAWA BALEWA RD

Fantazia supermarket

Ahmadiyya Hospital

More &
More

Hotel-de-
France

Smart's
Fasania
Diner's

Fast food

See Sweet
Bakery

Baker's
Delight

BOMPAI RD

Tourist Camp

Kano Tourism

Spice Food
& Tandoor

Central

Whiteley's

see main map

KANO

10

minutes) at 08.30 weekdays only, but no flight in the opposite direction. **Virgin Nigeria** has a daily flight to Abuja at 08.15 (45 minutes), which on Wednesdays and Fridays continues on to Sokoto (3½ hours with a stop in Abuja). The Abuja to Kano flight, Sunday–Friday, departs Abuja at 1830.

Airlines

✈ **Arik Air** 012 799999, head office; www.arikair.com.

✈ **Bellview** 064 231462, airport desk; www.flybellviewair.com.

✈ **British Airways** c/o Nasimatume Investments Ltd, FI Airport Rd; 064 637310, 637320; www.britishairways.com.

✈ **Egypt Air** 13 Murtala Muhammed Way; 064 630759; www.egyptair.com.eg.

✈ **IRS Airlines** 14C Murtala Muhammed Way; 064 637922; www.irs-airlines.com.

✈ **KLM and Kenya Airways** 17 Sani Abacha Way; 064 632632, 630061; www.klm.com.ng; www.kenya-airways.com.

✈ **Virgin Nigeria** at the airport, 064 947513/ 970/960; www.virginnigeria.com.

By road By bush taxi and minibus the furthest you can get to on any one trip from Kano is Maiduguri, 615km away. The journey takes around seven hours and costs around N2,000. Vehicles also go to Katsina (two hours) for around N500, and there are other vehicles to Zaria, a little less than two hours away and roughly the same price, where you can change for transport to Sokoto, and Kaduna and Jos. Kano's main Nai Bawa **Motor Park** is on Zaria Road about 5km south of the centre and it costs roughly N150 on an *achaba* and N50 in a bus from here into the centre of the city, though this will vary depending on what part of the city you are heading to. From Katsina, you are likely to arrive at the Kofar Ruwa Motor Park on the Katsina Road north of the city. There are other motor parks on all the main roads leading into the city, so where you arrive rather depends on where you have come from.

'Luxury' **overnight buses** to Lagos and Port Harcourt arrive on New Road in the Sabon Gari and it's a huge compound of big coaches and easy enough to find during the day to book a ticket. There are touts at the gate and they will lead you to a number of buses, including the Young Shall Grow and Bestway Transport companies, and an overnight bus to Lagos should cost in the region of N4,000.

By rail The **train station** is south of the Sabon Gari area on Fagge Road. After a gap of a couple of years, a weekly service between Kano and Lagos has supposedly been resumed. In theory, the train departs Lagos for Kano on Friday evenings, usually arriving on Monday or Tuesday, then departs again for Lagos the following day. There are often significant delays as 'the engine often spoils and sometimes there is a derailment', though this is probably less dangerous than it sounds given the crawling speed of the train. A seat in second class goes for N1,025; a second-class sleeper berth is N1,540; and a first-class sleeper berth N2,670. Check at the station if it's running.

GETTING AROUND Kano heaves with hundreds of thousands of *achabas*, more than perhaps even Lagos. The *achaba* drivers of Kano are reputedly reckless as they duck and weave through the traffic, and accidents are very common. When there are accidents in Nigeria between *achabas* or *okadas* and cars or buses, all hell breaks loose and there are fierce arguments when often the car is completely surrounded by other *achaba* drivers who instantly appear to join in the ruckus. If you are uncomfortable with the way your driver is driving, ask him to slow down.

New on the scene in Kano, and because Muslim women are now banned from riding *achabas* driven by strange men, are the lemon coloured three-wheeled *tuk-tuks* that can take three people across the back seat behind the driver and only carry men or only women at any given time. These are covered and some have side curtains for complete privacy for women. Minibuses and shared taxis ply the main roads from the motor parks into the city centre, though you may feel more comfortable in a drop taxi as the traffic is horrendously bad. Again some of these are for women only, but again only apply to Muslim women. Most of the *achaba*, drop and minibus drivers are northerners and speak little or no English, so expect some communication difficulties. If you want to tour Kano's sights, a half-day with a hire car and driver should be sufficient.

ORIENTATION The city has several districts, including the old city that is dominated by the sandstone Dala Hill and the heaving Kurmi Market, which is where most of the sights are, but it's also the most congested area of the city with narrow lanes and hundreds of thousands of people, so be wary of getting lost here. To the northeast of the old city is the Sabon Gari, generally known as the Christian quarter. If you follow Murtala Muhammed Way to the east of the city, you'll reach the GRA – which is much more spacious and peaceful than the old city, with wider streets and bigger houses – where some of the better hotels are located.

In the industrial centre, Bompai, in the middle of the city, the main focus is Bompai Road, where you will find the best and most useful shops and restaurants, as well as the Tourist Camp, which is where the helpful Kano State Tourism Board is located. You can hire a guide here but it's expensive, and Kano can easily be explored on your own if you have some experience of travelling in the bigger cities of Nigeria. If you don't, then a guide might be a good idea. They charge roughly N2,000 for half a day and organise a drop taxi to take you around the city for N500 per hour (let them do the negotiation for this as they'll get a cheaper price). The office is open daily 08.30–18.00, but if there is no-one around (the staff could be at the mosque) just ask and they will locate someone.

WHERE TO STAY A bill was passed through the Kano State government in 2004 banning all sales and consumption of alcohol within the state. However, no non-Muslims have been penalised as yet and alcohol is limitedly available in Kano at a few hotels and in the predominantly Christian quarters. Kano State charges a 1% tourism levy on room rates in addition to the usual 10% service charge and 5% VAT.

🏠 **Prince Hotel** Court Close, Tamandu Rd off Audu Bako Way; 📞 064 639402/633393; www.prince hotelng.com. Easily the best hotel in Kano, it's very modern & professionally run, with a bar, wireless internet, a swimming pool & 24hr power. The décor in the 51 rooms is all dark wood & blue rugs, & they generally look like international hotel rooms with working bathrooms & DSTV. It's popular with expats & international journalists, & pre-booking is advised, but in reality this is almost impossible as they require the full deposit for advance booking. Car hire is available & the Calypso Restaurant is here (see *Where to eat and drink*). Rooms $$; suites $$$

🏠 **Central Hotel** Bompai Rd; 📞 064 630000/9. Hopelessly run-down & a 1970s inter-galactic

eyesore, with very weird-looking lost-in-space architecture & a hideous concrete courtyard. However, the pool does have water in it & the receptionists advised that although local guests could not swim, foreigners were allowed to. At the bar tucked away at the back of the pool area you can buy cold beer & have an illicit drink on a plastic chair on the bare pool deck. Rates are high for the dreary & terribly old-fashioned rooms, with cracked windows, non-functional fittings & broken furniture. Only worth a mention because it has been privatised & will be refurbished soon. $$
🏠 **Durbar Hotel** 11B Ahmadu Bello Way; 📞 064 641657. Recently refurbished & the public areas are very grand with sparkling tiles, mirrors & fresh paint. Rooms are spacious & there's a restaurant

for simple meals & secure parking in the compound. This seems to be popular with visitors from southern Nigeria. $$

⌂ **ECWA Guest House** Mission Rd; ✆ 064 631410. A large leafy mission compound with spacious rooms, but you have to be on your best behaviour here (no smoking, drinking or visitors in your room), as this is a church guest house with a midnight curfew. Rooms in the old blocks start from a very reasonable US$10, while the spotless & well-equipped (AC, TV, fridge, hot water) rooms in the new building start from US$24. $$

⌂ **Hotel-de-France** 54 Tafawa Balewa Rd; ✆ 064 646416, 0803 286 8080. Here is a surprising oasis of flowering shrubs & trees & green lawns next to the Toyota plant & opposite the Mercedes plant, with very nice rooms refurbished in 1994 with spotless cool tiles, newish furniture, & modern bathrooms. The whitewashed & airy restaurant serves Nigerian food & good green salads, plus fish or steak & chips, but no alcohol. It's an historical 1920s building & was once French-owned. Charles de Gaulle stayed here on his way to Fort Lymeé to check on his troops. For a time in the1960s it was a cinema. $$

⌂ **Nimah Guest Palace** 8B Sulaiman Crescent; ✆ 064 642946/644557. This is popular with wealthy Muslim families, & it has its own mosque. Cordoned off at the back & behind tall walls is a swimming pool for non-Muslims. The rooms are luxurious, though the décor is very Arabic, with lots of gilt mirrors & marble. Nigerian meals are served in the rooms (but watch for those extra charges) & there's a separate breakfast restaurant upstairs, with booths & a TV (🕐 05.00–11.00). $$

⌂ **Royal Tropicana Hotel** 17–19 Niger St; ✆ 064 647496, 639352/3. Fairly modern hotel with a busy informal lobby with a few shops & a bakery, & a mosquito-ridden bar downstairs serving booze in what was once the hotel disco — an eerie mirrored dungeon that's pitch black if there is no NEPA. The

bar by the (functioning) swimming pool is much more pleasant. The rooms are very ordinary, but there are good views of the city from the top floors. Deposits are fairly hefty here, almost 50% of the room rates. $$

⌂ **Tahir Guest Palace** 4 Ibrahim Natsugune Rd, off Ahmadu Bello Way; ✆ 064 315281/317245/6; www.tahirguestpalace.freewebspace.com. This is very similar to the Nimah & the first thing you will notice here are the armed guards in the car park. Wealthy Nigerians & expats stay here, & former US Secretary of State Madeline Albright was a guest, though it's very reasonably priced. The Tahir has its own power source & water tower. It also boasts a huge breezy lobby, tiled hallways with nice fresh décor, wireless internet throughout, & in the 143 rooms your feet will sink into the thick carpets, & the modern pink bathroom suites have gold-coloured fittings. The restaurant serves a good range of food & the service is attentive, there's a small, inviting swimming pool between the giant satellite dishes, & outside awaits a line of newish cars with knowledgeable drivers if you require transport. $$

⌂ **Tourist Camp** 11A Bompai Rd; ✆ 064 642017. The rooms here are small, with minuscule bathrooms, but they have a fridge & local TV; there's usually water in the taps. The gen goes off here at night & it's unbearably hot, with no AC. The compound has a large lit car park with a security guard, & is an ideal spot for camping & for overlanders; they have received the odd truck & vehicle before in the past. There's also a 10-bed dorm with sheets & pillows & a communal bathroom block out at the back. Spice Food & Tandoor restaurant is located here, as is the Kano State Tourist Office & bureau de change, & you can also get laundry done. NB: On our last visit this was even more run down & the accommodation was closed for refurbishment. Reports welcome.

✕ **WHERE TO EAT AND DRINK** There are many restaurants for cheap eats in the $ category located on Bompai Road near the Tourist Camp, as well as *suya* stands and craft stalls on the street. **Baker's Delight** (*3 Bompai Road;* 🕐 *10.00–22.00 daily*) is a supermarket with some Lebanese and other imported tins and packets and a bakery counter. Next up is **Fast Food Bakery** (🕐 *07.30–22.30 daily*) with a big range of delicious snacks such as meat pies, pizzas, cakes, biscuits, spring rolls, proper French bread, tea, coffee and fresh juice, simple formica tables; oddly it's run by a Chinese man who also makes birthday cakes.

Next door is **Diner's Restaurant**, which has a limited selection of food-is-ready but in pleasant surroundings, with red and white checked tablecloths, fans and a TV, and it's dirt cheap. Then there is the **Fasania Chinese Restaurant** run by Chinese people who cook up reasonably priced authentic dishes, followed by **Smart's Indian Restaurant** for Indian sweets and pickles, falafel, *shawarmas* and burgers. Opposite is the Lebanese-run **Whiteley's** ice-cream shop for a variety of flavours.

More or less opposite the Tourist Camp is **Fantazia Supermarket** (⊕ *09.00–23.00 daily*), which has a huge but expensive range of imported goods, a deli counter with olives, feta cheese and good hams, British magazines, well-known products like Heinz Tomato Ketchup and HP Sauce, and a whole aisle of chocolate.

Continue along Bompai Road to the east of the Tourist Camp and on the same side of the road is **See Sweet and Bakery** (⊕ *09.00–midnight daily*). There are lots of treats on offer here, starting with biscuits and cream cakes, delicious sorbets and ice cream for about N150 a cup, a fresh juice bar, thick shakes, proper sandwiches and tasty *shawarmas* for around N400 (all the bread is baked freshly in the in-house bakery). Upstairs is an enormous and modern pool and table-football hall with a giant flat-screen TV for watching sports and music channels, and a bar serving non-alcoholic drinks, and an outside terrace with chairs. Next door is the **More & More** supermarket (⊕ *09.00–22.00 daily*), which is a new Lebanese place selling a very broad range of imported and expensive food and household items.

Elsewhere in the city, **Arabian Sweets** at 4 Beirut Road serves cheap pastries and burgers but in grimy surroundings, with dirty plastic tables out front. **Halal Meat Restaurant**, on Civic Centre Road opposite the end of Beirut Road, serves a variety of Lebanese and Nigerian food, including *jollof* rice, *suya*, *kafta* and *shawarma*, and is consistently busy. A plate of freshly grilled and delicious meat and chips or rice costs around N500 and a sandwich N150 (when they have bread). There's a branch of **Mr Biggs** on New Road in the Sabon Gari, just north of the Zamani Bookshop.

Also in the Sabon Gari is a whole bunch of illicit taverns and bars around Enugu Road; remember this is Hausa for 'foreigner's town', and as this is the city's non-Muslim quarter, beer and hard liquor are sold from numerous establishments with names such as the **Merry Guest Cool Spot** and the **Be Kind Cool Spot** – just look for the fluttering flags advertising beer. It's a lively and atmospheric place in the evening and you can watch with interest what goes on in the street, but be very wary in this area and stick to the busy and well-lit bars – if possible make sure the mamma in charge takes you under her wing and looks after you. There are also a few hotels in these streets, but most are fleapits frequented by prostitutes.

✕ **Calypso Restaurant** at the Prince Hotel (see *Where to stay* for location); ⊕ 07.00–11.00 for breakfast daily, 12.00–16.00 for lunch & 19.00–23.00 for dinner. The best restaurant in the city where you'll find fine dining & fine wines aimed at the international community of expats & press corps, with a full bar of imported alcohol & an extensive menu of Lebanese starters N400–800, pizzas from N1,000, & main meat dishes N1,500–2,000, all set among starched white table cloths & besuited waiters, so you'll need to dress up a bit. $$$$

✕ **La Locanda** 40 Sultan Rd, off Ahmadu Bello Way; ⊕ 12.00–15.00 Mon–Sat; 19.00–late daily. An OK Italian restaurant with reasonable pizzas, lasagnes &

pasta, & mixed grill, where a meal for two will cost in the region of N3,500. There's a bar with beers & some wines. It is set in a private house with shady palms & parking inside the gates, although later in the evening it becomes seedy, with male hardcore drinkers & prostitutes. $$$$

✕ **Spice Food and Tandoor** within the grounds of the Tourist Camp, Bompai Rd; ⊕ 12.00–15.30 Sat–Thu; 18.00–23.00 daily; last orders 22.00. An excellent Indian restaurant with a charming & chatty owner serving Chapmans & soft drinks, & a full menu of delicious food which is popular with Indians — always a good sign. Among the dishes on offer are mutton, chicken & beef jalfrezi, biriyani or korma, plus lots of vegetarian dishes using spinach &

cottage cheese, all from around N400 a dish, plus an assortment of nans & rotis or a whole tandoori chicken for N1,000. On our visit the owner was talking about opening a takeaway venture outside the complex on the main road. $$$

🖵 **French Café** Race Course Rd; ⏱ 11.00–23.00 daily. This is in a quiet location with a large

terrace & is not a bad place to have a beer & watch the sun go down. They serve the same excellent selection of Lebanese & continental food as their branch in Kaduna, such as delectable cakes, generous sandwiches, pastas, burgers, steaks & chicken. $$–$$$

LISTINGS

Books and maps Zamani Bookshop is at 84 Awolowo Road in Sabon Gari (⏱ 08.00–12.30, 14.00–17.30 Mon–Sat). Here you can pick up a map of Kano, and some local novels by well-known Nigerian writers. Because of Nigeria basing their school curriculum on that of the UK, you'll also find Chekhov and Shakespeare on the shelves. This is the best of a whole bunch of book and stationery shops on this road.

Changing money The government bureau de change at the Tourist Camp is the best place to change money, but you have to give them notice if you want to change a large sum. You'll also find money changers across the street from the Central Hotel.

Cinema There's another old colonial cinema near the luxury bus motor park on New Road, which shows regular Bollywood movies. These are popular across the north of the country but they are not subtitled.

Communications The main **NITEL** office is some way out of town on Zoo Road, but there's a more convenient one on Lagos Road. The post office is very central, on Post Office Road near the train station (⏱ 08.00–17.00 Mon–Fri, 09.00–13.00 Sat).

There are plenty of places to check the **internet** across the city. **Chrisking Ventures** next to Smart's Indian Restaurant on Bompai Road (⏱ 08.00–18.00 daily) charges N150 per hour, with plenty of fairly new terminals, and seems popular with families. **Friend's Internet Café**, 7c Murtala Muhammed Way, opposite the Golf Club (⏱ 08.30–23.00 daily), is a fabulous spot. This is a super-quality patisserie and one of the best places to eat in Kano, for coffees and soft drinks, the finest of cakes and pastries, and a huge variety of ice cream. There's even an oven outside, from which you can get fresh *zaatar* (cheese bread) first thing in the morning. The gen works all day and there are 18 hi-tech terminals on state-of-the-art office furniture for browsing the internet in glamorous style for N200 per hour; there's also a scanning and printing service.

Cultural centres

British Council 10 Emir's Palace Rd; 📞 064 646652/643489; www.britishcouncil.org/ nigeria-about-us-kano.htm (⏱ 10.00–20.00 Mon–Fri except during Ramadan when they close at 18.00; 11.00–16.00 Sat). The British Council has been in Kano since 1943 & is housed in a

historical building of similar architecture to the Gidan Dan Hausa (below). The library here is only open to members, but if you ask nicely you should be able to browse the British newspapers & magazines.

Hospitals

✚ **Ahmadiyya Musum Hospital** Bompai Rd; 📞 064 633376, opposite the See Sweet & Bakery. Has a laboratory for testing malaria.

✚ **International Hospital** Corner of Airport Rd & Murtala Muhammed Way; 📞 064 940032, 943595. Has 24hr emergency clinic & a dentist.

Pharmacies

✚ **Baker's Delight** 3 Bompai Rd (🕐 10.00–22.00 daily). This is a supermarket, but there is also an excellent & knowledgeable pharmacy here that imports drugs from Europe, including Cotexin (a malarial cure also found in East Africa).

✚ **Wellcare Pharmacy**, on Murtala Mohammed Way (🕐 10.00–18.00 daily) is a well-stocked supermarket & popular with Kano's expats.

WHAT TO SEE AND DO Most of Kano's worthwhile sights are in the old city, and you may want to consider hiring a guide to see some of them – though the guides at each of the places are good enough, and you don't really need an additional one to drive around with you in a taxi. If you find a good taxi driver, he will be sufficient to take you into the Kurmi Market, the Emir's Palace and perhaps the city walls unguided. Entry to the old city is through one of the city gates (not the originals but concrete replacements).

Dye pits Kano's dye pits are still in use and are some of the oldest in Africa. They are located along the road beyond Kofar Mata Gate, and the cloth market is behind a breeze-block wall on the other side of the street. They are privately owned and have been in the same family for over 500 years, and at the entrance the manager will meet you and give you a tour. Expect to pay *dash* all around, especially for photographs, so have plenty of small notes to hand. Here cloth is soaked in indigo dye in large vats, and the process starts with mixing various natural dyes with water in a calabash before mixing these ingredients with ash in the dye pits and leaving them to ferment for three days. Then the indigo sticks are added and it's again left for three days, before potassium is added, then another three days, before stirring, and another three days, when the ash and indigo sticks are removed.

After another two weeks of fermentation the dye is ready to use, and repeatedly used for one year, or longer for the deeper pits that are one to six metres in depth. The indigo provides the brilliant blue colour, the ash the brightness, and the potassium the colour-stay. The depth of colour depends on how long fabric is soaked for – if it is soaked for several hours the blue colour is so dark it becomes almost black. The dyers continually dip the cloth as the oxygen helps seal the colour. The residue that comes out of the pits, the ash, indigo sticks and potassium, is made into mud bricks that are burned until only the potassium is left, and this is then recycled back into the dye pits.

After the cloth is dry it's ironed by charcoal irons or pressed in the traditional way by pounding the cloth over a smooth tree trunk with a wooden mahogany pound. You can go inside the 'ironing shed' and watch the men pounding the cloth and expertly spitting water on the cloth. It takes about 20 minutes to pound one piece of cloth and the pounding gives it a lovely sheen; people pay extra for cloth that has been pounded on both sides, and Kano cloth is often used for ceremonial robes of the most important local leaders. Patterns are created by tying and stitching with raffia or cotton thread, or by using chicken feathers to paint on cloth. This acts as a resist to the dye, much as the wax method on batiks.

The indigo cloth is for sale in sheets of a couple of metres long and perhaps a metre wide; the machine-made cotton is roughly N1,500 a sheet, while the hand-woven cotton is N3,000 and these are some of the best souvenirs to take home from Nigeria. They have various abstract patterns on them with names such as 'zebra in the bush', 'widow's eye', 'star in the sky' or 'Emir's Palace'.

Grand Mosque and Emir's Palace Kano's Grand Mosque, further down Kofar Mata Road from the dye pits, is one of the largest in Nigeria, attracting up to 50,000 worshippers on a Friday, and is located at the back of the Emir's Palace near the servants' entrance. The building itself is not of any architectural value and is a fairly

Durbars are held in Katsina and Zaria, but the Kano durbar is considered the biggest and the best. It is usually held some time in November, but this depends on the dates of the Muslim calendar. It celebrates the culmination of the two great Muslim festivals, Eid-el-Fitir (commemorating the end of the holy month of Ramadan) and Eid-el-Kabir (commemorating the Prophet Ibrahim sacrificing a ram instead of his son).

Durbars are lively and colourful festivals and are known for their horsemen, who wear bright red turbans and copper armour, and their accompanying musicians, who wear feathered headdresses decorated with cowrie shells. They date back to the time when the northern emirate states used horses in warfare, and each town, district and nobility household was expected to contribute a regiment to the defence of the emirate. Once or twice a year, the emirate military chiefs invited the various regiments for a durbar (military parade) for the emir and his chiefs. Regiments would showcase their horsemanship, their preparedness for war, and their loyalty to the emirate. During the ceremony the participants are dressed in colourful gowns called *babanringa*, meaning big gowns in Hausa, and the horses are clad in tartan-like regalia.

Of all the modern-day durbar festivals, the Kano durbar is the most magnificent and spectacular, and begins with prayers outside town, followed by a colourful procession of gaily dressed riders on horses and camels accompanied by drumming, dancing and singing. They get to the public square in front of the Emir's Palace, where each village group, district, and noble house takes their assigned place. Last to arrive is the Emir and his splendid entourage and trumpeters, who take their place in front of the palace to receive the *jahi*, or homage, of their subjects. The festival begins with each column of seven to ten horsemen racing across the square at full gallop, swords glinting in the sun, who then stop abruptly to salute the emir with raised swords. At this moment the arena will be full of clouds of dust and cheering spectators. The last and most fierce riders are those of the emir's household and regimental guard, known as the Dogari. After the show, celebrations continue well into the night.

modern structure, and outside is a huge arena where many men pray outside that can't gain access to the mosque. If you are here on a Friday, it's well worth coming here to watch Friday prayers, when these thousands of men dressed in elaborately colourful robes kneel and fall deathly silent at the most intense section of the prayers, and when the *khatib* and *imam* talk to them over the loudspeaker. Unfortunately women will not be appreciated at the event, and non-Muslim men should stay discreetly in the background.

The Emir's Palace is next to the central mosque and you'll need to follow the wall around to the south of the vast complex to get to the front gate. Notice the emir's horses stabled around the walls. The present emir is Emir Alhaji Ado Bayero, who has reigned since 1963. Again, there is a vast arena at the front of the main gate where the annual durbar takes place (see box), and there's a royal grandstand on top of the wall to the right of the gate. Today, both here and at other Emir's Palaces in the north, the flag of Islam is raised if the emir is in, and is pulled down when he is out. It's a fairly grand building, though it's of little architectural interest, as although it's old and dates back to the 15th century, it has been renovated out of all recognition, and houses a number of administrative blocks, but you can peek through the main gate, Kofar Kudu, and see the series of courtyards and inner gates beyond, each manned by the traditional and elderly palace guards in their colourful and heavy robes. The entire complex of over 30 acres is enclosed by a wall 6–8 metres high, which was at one time surrounded by a moat.

The best time to come here is to watch the durbar, when many expats from Lagos come up, including embassy staff and international business people, and all the dignitaries from the emir's local councils and governments. Queen Elizabeth II watched the durbar on a visit to Nigeria in 1958, and obviously enjoyed the spectacle, as on a visit in 2003 she requested that it be held in her honour once again. Unfortunately the British security services considered that it would be too high a security risk, which disappointed many Nigerians.

Gidan Makama Museum Across the square from the Emir's Palace is the Gidan Makama (the Makama's House) Museum (*www.kanoonline.com/gidan_makama;* ☉ *09.00–17.00 daily; N200 entry for non-residents*), which was the first palace of the emir, before he moved across the road to the newer and larger premises. It's now a good museum with examples of local art, including photographs retracing Kano's history. The museum, with a small mosque next door, was built in the 15th century, and was completely restored in 1986, and is now a national monument. It's an old mud building today painted a dark chocolate brown, and there are 11 galleries, though you may have to tour by torchlight if the gen is not working. There's the old door on display from one of Kano's city gates, Kofa Dukauuyam, some very old photographs of jihad warriors and important members of the Sokoto Caliphate before the arrival of the British, an elephant-skin shield and other items from the jihad wars in the 18th century, and pictures of the old pyramids that were formed from sacks of groundnuts which used to be a feature around Kano up until the 1970s.

Outside is a craft shop and drinks stall, and in the grounds a reconstruction of a *madobi* (women's) hut, with a display of the items a woman may need in the preparation of a marriage. Look out for the similar houses that are about the same age as the museum in various states of repair in the nearby streets.

The city wall The old city had approximately 25km of city walls with 15 gates (*kofars*), which were first built about 900 years ago, but which were extended and enlarged in the 15th century. When the British arrived in Kano on 3 February 1903, through the Kofar Kabuga, the emir at the time escaped through the Kofar Waika, and even today out of superstition the emir does not pass through this gate.

South of the museum and between Kofar Saburwar and Kofar Dan Agundi is the 6km section of the city wall that has been rebuilt, thanks to funding from the German government, and it looks very impressive. It's several metres high with small turrets and a row of niches and is a smooth rich red colour. The method used is the traditional mud and straw 'plugs': rounded bricks made from a combination of mud, water and straw to bind them. Once the wall is built from the plugs, the outer surface is covered with a smooth layer of the same mixture. Unfortunately the rest of the walls are in a sorry state and are covered with rubbish, and you will have to look hard to imagine what the now small piles of brown earth with goats perched on top once looked like.

Kurmi Market The ancient Kurmi Market is in the centre of the old city and is hugely atmospheric; it is one of the most exotic and colourful places in the Sahel. The market has been trading on this very spot for perhaps a thousand years, and was first visited by European explorers in the 19th century. You might get totally overwhelmed and claustrophobic here (and most certainly sweaty) and will have patiently and politely to decline the continual entreaties from the traders. In any case you will get hopelessly lost and any sense of direction will be seriously challenged, so you will really have to go there with a guide. It's not for the faint-hearted, and the passages are very narrow and congested; the gap between some of the stalls is little more than a few centimetres.

You'll probably be taken to the craft section where carved calabashes, leather and beads are for sale, and nearby is the section for the horse attire worn at the durbars, including the richly embroidered Fulani horse blankets and decorations used at festivals. Possibly you'll be taken to the meat section which is so old the walls are falling down – it's covered in flies and the dismembered animal carcasses will send your senses reeling. At all times watch where you are stepping – if you look down you'll sometimes find yourself walking on rickety slats over running drains some metres below.

Dala Hill You'll see the flat-topped, red sandstone Dala Hill clearly on the horizon above the market, and it's more or less in the middle of the old city. Dala Hill first appeared on a map of the Arab geographer, Idrisi, in 1145 and is believed to be the original site of early Kano. From the top there are fine views of Kano spreading endlessly in every direction, but to get here you are going to have to find a knowledgeable taxi driver or take a guide from the tourist office, as it's a mind-boggling area of choking alleyways, and the 100 or so steps up to the top are obscured behind a mass of houses.

The views are spectacular, and you can see as far as the airport roughly 8km away to the north of the city, with the jets parked up on the apron, which is the only open space visible. In every other direction to the horizon the city is an unbroken vista of densely packed urban buildings: the old mud-brown low-rise houses of the old city immediately around Dala Hill, the congested alleyways and the vast **Kurmi Market** to the southeast. Beyond are Kano's modern tower blocks, and NITEL and TV aerials. This is one of the best opportunities apart from flying in over Lagos to witness what is the essence of Nigeria – its mass of humanity. Look out for the roof of the Central Mosque and the Emir's Palace. The best time to go up here is in the late afternoon when the sun is behind you, and the glow of the red houses and brown rusty roofs of the ancient city are at their most intense.

Gidan Dan Hausa Away from the old city, Kano's other attraction is the Gidan Dan Hausa (*gidan* means house in Hausa) on Dan Hausa Road (⊕ *08.00–16.00 Mon–Thu; 08.00–13.00 Fri; entry N100 plus a dash for the guide*). The Kano State History and Culture Bureau (❨ *064 632385*) is located here in a new building next door to the house itself.

The house, built in 1905, is an outstanding example of Hausa mud-walled architecture, and was used by the British until independence in 1960, and was Kano's first colonial residency. It was first built by the emir of Kano as a residence for a local chief; Hanns Vischer became the first British resident from 1908 and was the director of education for northern Nigeria. Vischer arrived in Nigeria in 1906 after travelling by caravan from Tripoli (see box) and first stayed at the Emir's Palace with Lord Lugard before moving to the house. His wife Isabella joined her husband in Kano from 1912, where they lived until World War I broke out in 1914. Vischer was known locally as Dan Hausa, the 'son of the Hausa' because he spoke the language so well.

The house was originally the house of a local chief who was responsible for managing the emir's farmland, and some of the rooms are over 150 years old. Vischer extended it in 1907 and by 1909 it was partly a school; the lessons were taken outside beneath the arms of some tamarind trees, and by 1914 blocks of classrooms had been built in the grounds. Other similar buildings in Kano include the British Council building near the Emir's Palace. If you are at all interested in the Vischer history, ask the director in the Culture Bureau (mostly a line of portrait photographs of past emirs and dignitaries), next to the house if you can look at the documents and photographs donated to the house by the Vischer Family Trust in the UK.

You enter the house through the waiting room as is Hausa tradition, and then go into the visitors' rooms, where there is a collection of pots, stone tools, and other bits and pieces from the Iron Age, plus some of Vischer's china pots from England. There are two pots roughly 1m high and 1m across that are thought to be

THE DEADLY ROAD

Hanns Vischer was a Swiss-born teacher who worked for the British colonial service in Kano at the turn of the 20th century. He is best remembered for being the pioneer of a revolutionary education system that gave due regard to the religion and background of the Hausa people in northern Nigeria, a system that was later copied throughout much of Britain's colonial empire, and for which he was subsequently knighted. He is somewhat less well known for an incredible journey he took in 1906. Vischer became intrigued about the 'deadly road', the centuries-old route across the Sahara that the camel caravans used to follow to transport goods and slaves between West and North Africa. It was referred to as the deadly road because of the amount of skeletons that littered the desert, from slaves and camels that perished on the march north.

In 1906 the 30-year-old Vischer undertook an audacious journey through the heart of the Sahara Desert from Tripoli in Libya to Lake Chad in northern Nigeria by camel, through what are today Libya, Niger and Nigeria. Accompanied by religious pilgrims and newly freed slaves, he travelled the route combatting torrid heat and tribal raiding parties, and where no water could be found for days. He completed the journey successfully with no loss of life in his party, many of whom were freed slaves who had attached themselves to the caravan for protection, going back to their homes in Nigeria. Vischer wrote a book of his journey in 1910, *Across the Sahara*, and he says of the Sahara, 'I had entered it frivolously, like a fool. . . I left it as one stunned, crushed by the deadly majesty I had seen too closely.'

Having completed the journey, and from his post in Kano, Vischer asked his boss in England if he could repeat the journey in reverse. He received this frosty reply: 'Dear Vischer, I prefer my staff to do the work they are paid for, rather than seek personal kudos or geographical advancement in foreign territory... If you are bent on the journey, you should resign and make room for a man who is satisfied with his job. Plain speaking but I like to run my own show. Yours Sincerely, W P Hewby.'

Nearly a century later the same route was followed by John Hare, a modern-day Swiss explorer and founder of the Wild Camel Protection Foundation (*www.wildcamels.com*). In 2001, Hare followed Vischer's wishes and did the journey in reverse, beating Vischer's time across the Sahara thanks to shorter oasis stops and a GPS. In 1906 Vischer travelled 1,581 miles over 5½ months, with 40 camels and 40 men, while Hare travelled 1,462 miles over 3½ months, with 25 camels and 12 men. In his party, Hare took a Chinese zoologist – the first Chinese man to cross the Sahara in recorded history. To read John Hare's full account of his journey, try and get a back copy of the December 2002 *National Geographic*, or check out the website www.nationalgeographic.com. His book of the journey is *Shadows across the Sahara* (2003, Constable & Robinson).

from 800–500BC – one was apparently used for mixing cement. There is also a copy of the Koran on display that was presented to Ahmadu Bello by the Egyptian president, Abdul Nasser, when Bello visited Egypt in 1963. The Vischers' dining room now houses a very grand horse's durbar costume, some musical instruments, and various celebration gowns and staffs used by previous emirs.

Upstairs is a display of local crafts, including an ancient pot with a slot in the top (that must have been the very first piggy bank in northern Nigeria!) and a skin from an unfortunate python that killed two goats in Kano in 1984. In the Vischers' bathrooms you can also view the original 1907 toilets, with (rather comically) newer loos erected alongside. They don't look that different. On the roof of the house you will see what was once Vischer's radio room, and the flat roof where his guests used to sleep outside. Rather delightfully, Vischer's gramophone in the master bedroom still works – ask the guide to play it for you. The scratchy tunes instantly cloak the house with a huge amount of atmosphere, especially as you get here at the end of the tour, and have already heard all the stories about Vischer and the house.

KATSINA

Capital of Katsina State, the city of Katsina is in the extreme north, only a few kilometres from the border with Niger and has an estimated population of just under half a million. The city was once surrounded by a 21km wall with seven gates, built in the 11th century, but little of it remains today. From the 14th century, Katsina was a centre for Islamic teachings and like Kano and the other northern cities, a caravan hub for the Hausa States. At the end of the 16th century Katsina replaced Timbuktu as the main centre for Islamic study in West Africa, and back then the city was made up of sections inhabited by various immigrants, traders or professions, and there were quarters for the people of Mali and Borno, students and Islamic scholars.

In the 17th and 18th centuries, Katsina was one of the seven Hausa kingdoms, before being conquered by the Fulani jihad in 1804, when emirs were put in place under the Sokoto Caliphate. When the British took northern Nigeria a century later, the emirate system was upheld by the British as part of Lugard's system of indirect rule. The Katsina College was established in the early years of the colonial era in 1922. The college provided education to the elite of northern Nigeria and was modelled on the British public school system, which subsequently provided educated administrators for the colonial bureaucracy.

Many northern political key players attended Katsina College, including Abubakar Tafawa Balewa, the first prime minister of Nigeria, and Ahmadu Bello, the first premier of the Northern Region, as well as many prominent ministers and emirs. In 1938 the college was moved from Katsina to Kaduna, when Kaduna was capital of northern Nigeria, and where it is now known as Barewa College. There's little to see or do in Katsina, but, like the other northern cities, it is steeped in ancient atmosphere, and unlike Kano, which is an older city but has some trappings of the Western world, life in Katsina, with its markets, frenetic street life and old mud buildings, hasn't changed much for hundreds of years. Domestic animals roam the alleyways, robed and turbaned men do deals on the street, cloaked women carry vegetables on their heads, and children in Islamic uniforms chant passages from the Koran and write on wooden scripture boards in the many outdoor schools.

GETTING THERE AND AWAY A highway links Katsina to Kano and to Maradi over the border in Niger (for details on crossing the border see 'Getting there' in Chapter 2). From Kano to Katsina it costs roughly N500 for the 173km or two-hour trip. There is no direct road or transport link between Katsina and Sokoto to the west, but it's possible to swap vehicles in Funtua – give yourself all day for this journey as it's a big distance. You can also swap vehicles in Funtua for Zaria or alternatively go via Kano. It's also possible to head into Niger, 45km north of Katsina, and follow the highway from Maradi through to Birnin-Nkonni, and cross back into Nigeria, where it's 85km to Sokoto. Local people use this route and there is public transport, as there is trade between Nigeria's Hausa people and the markets of Maradi, but foreigners will require a multi-entry visa for Nigeria and a visa for Niger, so although it involves a shorter distance, it's not terribly practical. The roads up here from Kano and Zaria have been recently repaired but are already crumbling again. There are fabulous views of mud villages and the arid landscapes as you head into the Sahel proper. On arrival, vehicles will drop you somewhere along IBB Way, the road that runs the entire length of Katsina in a north–south direction. On departure you'll either need to get to the **motor park** on the Kano Road or pick up a vehicle on IBB Way.

The **Limited Bureau de Change** is on the corner of IBB Way and the road that goes towards the Gobarau Minaret, and the **post office** and the **NITEL** building are centrally located on IBB Way opposite the Unity Bank.

🏠 WHERE TO STAY

🏠 **Liyafa Palace Hotel** ↘ 065 431165, 0807 642 2116; on IBB Way roughly 3km outside of town towards Kano; there's a sign but look hard as all the paint has worn off. If you're coming from Kano you can ask to be dropped at Liyafa Junction. This is easily one of the nicest hotels in the north of Nigeria, with 108 rooms in 3 spacious blocks of chalets, real hotel furniture, all-night AC, great bathrooms with hot water, & DSTV. It was opened by General Ibrahim Babangida in 1991 & has been fairly well looked after since. Facilities include a tennis court & mosque, but the swimming pool is sometimes empty & there is only a selection of Fanta available in the bar. In the very good restaurant you can get snacks such as burgers & omelettes, & there's a choice of daily specials of main dishes. Ignore the tariff that says foreigners must pay in US$ – the reception staff wouldn't know what to do with a dollar bill if they saw one. Given the standards, rates are not bad & include the 15%. $$

🏠 **Katsina Motel** | Mohammed Bashir Rd, in the GRA; ↘ 065 430017, 0802 649 5234. To get here, from the first roundabout on the Kano Rd as it enters the town & turns into IBB Way, turn right (if coming from Kano) until you reach Yar'adua Rd after about 2km. Then turn left & take the first right, then the first right & you should be on Mohammed Bashir Rd. You'll have to arrive early to get a room as it's deservedly popular, & the only choice for those on a budget. There is a standard restaurant serving a variety of bland food, but they are good at dealing with late arrivals & if you speak to the chef in advance he can come up with something vegetarian or vaguely non-Nigerian. The recently refurbished chalets are set in established gardens, with a few gazebos to sit in the shade, & there's a mosque. A double costs just over US$30. Next to the motel is the Katsina Club, which looks derelict but has well-maintained tennis courts. You may be allowed to play if you ask nicely. $$

🍴 **WHERE TO EAT** At night along the length of IBB Way are night-time chop stalls selling prepared fruit such as pineapple, and very good hot-and-spicy *suya* cooked over charcoal under paraffin lamps. A branch of **Oasis Bakery** has opened on Nagogo Road, opposite the hideous pyramid-shaped Diamond Bank.

🍴 **Katsina City Restaurant** 115 IBB Way, in the centre of town; ⏰ 08.00–18.00 daily. This serves big & filling Nigerian meals & the likes of spaghetti with tomato sauce, & exceptionally good salads with eggs & tinned baked beans. It's always packed, with loads of tables decorated with fake roses, fans & blaring TVs, & the service is instant. $

WHAT TO SEE AND DO The centre of activity spreads around IBB Way, Katsina's main thoroughfare between the concrete Kofar Kaura, one of the city gates built on the site of an older mud brick one, and the domed **central mosque**. Just beyond the mosque and to the left is Kangiwa Square that serves as the overflow for the mosque during Friday prayers, and where the **Emir's Palace** flanks the eastern side. It's relatively traffic free and is a pleasant place to wander around. On top of one of the green, yellow and white palace walls covered in faded bill posters is the emir's grandstand, to watch the occasional durbars that take place in the square, and a modern breeze-block clocktower and a flagpole indicating if the emir is in or out. The façade of the palace is fairly modern, but inside the compound are myriad older, squat mud buildings, and if you want to look around you can approach one of the palace guards. Around the square are some colonial buildings with flat roofs built of grey and white blocks of stone, one of which is the police station and another the Sharia Court.

THE FORMATION OF THE SEVEN HAUSA KINGDOMS

Duara, a town that is today a tiny dot on the map some 82km west of Katsina and 145km north of Kano, in Katsina State on the Niger border, is an important place in Hausa history, as it is generally believed to be the founding town of the seven Hausa states, one of the most powerful of West Africa's dynasties. It was first created in the 10th century by a woman called Daurama, who was the queen of her kingdom Daura. Meanwhile, a character called Bayajidda, who was a son of the king of Baghdad, left his homeland after a spat with his father and came to West Africa. He first settled in Borno, but after falling out with his father-in-law he fled Borno and abandoned his pregnant wife, and arrived in Daura where he sought water for his horse.

The Kusugu Well in the town was occupied by a notorious and terrifying snake called Sarki (the word later became a word for king), which was terrorising people and only allowed them to fetch water once a week, on a Friday. Bayajidda asked the way to the well where he laid his calabash down, and the snake seized it. He then pulled the snake to the surface and cut off its head with his sword. He returned to his lodgings with his calabash of water and the snake's head and the next morning, which was a Friday, the townspeople were amazed to find the snake's body next to the well. Queen Daurama proclaimed that she would give half of her town to the man that killed the snake. Bayajidda presented the head of the snake to the queen but he replied that he would rather marry her than have half the town, which she promptly agreed to. They had a son called Bawo, who later became king of Daura himself and had six sons: Gazaure succeeded Bawo as the king of Daura, Kumayo was sent to Katsina where he overthrew the Durbawa dynasty, Bagauda was sent to Kano where he overthrew the Tsunburbuwa people, while Duma, Gunguma and Zamnakogi went to Gobir, Zazzau and Rano respectively, and established their own dynasties.

Together with Bayajidda's son by the other woman in Borno, who ruled Biram in Hadejia, this completed the list of seven Hausa states, all descended from Bayajidda. By linking these seven kingdoms through trade, and with trade routes to North Africa across the Sahara that also brought Islam, they grew into powerful states and melting pots of new ideas and knowledge, great international markets, and seats of scholarly learning. For centuries, the Hausa dynasty ruled what was to become northern Nigeria, until the Fulani jihad in 1804, led by Usman dan Fodio, who overthrew one after the other of the Hausa kingdoms and appointed an emir in each. Today, the water from the Kusugu Well in Duara is still drinkable and it is believed to cure many ailments.

The Gobarau Minaret The **Gobarau Minaret,** to the northwestern corner of Kangiwa Square, is a wonderful example of traditional architecture – to get there follow IBB Way to the end, round the corner to the left, walk 100–200m and take the first right-hand turn along Gobarau Street, and the minaret is easily seen about 100m on the right. It's best to visit around 08.00–10.00 as the guide is often elsewhere later in the day. The imposing minaret is built of mud and palm timbers, and is all that remains of a mosque constructed in the heyday of the dynasty of the seven Hausa states. It is thought to have been built between 1348 and 1398, though it has been refurbished a few times since then.

Today the remaining 15m tower is the tallest mud-built structure in Nigeria, and a national monument. There's a guide at the bottom, and for a small *dash* you can climb almost to the top; there are some fabulous views of the old rooftops of the city, and if you look to the north, you'll look into Niger. You can also see parts of the city wall, though you may have to ask the guide to point these out as the walls are little more than mounds of earth. To the west you can see Katsina's army barracks. The guide at the minaret lives in a compound at the bottom and you can wave to his wife and kids from the top. Also at the bottom of the tower is a large primary school.

If you make it as far north as Katsina, this is yet another region of Nigeria where older people may remember when white people were seen regularly in the north but children may never have seen them before. The chances are you will be completely mobbed by the school children, as was our experience, the little girls cloaked and their hands and feet covered in henna tattoos. They all wanted to touch our skin and hair, and hundreds of children followed us pied-piper style, mimicking everything we said until we had to make a polite escape by *achaba*.

The old market Katsina's **old market** spreads around the streets opposite the minaret and is worth a wander, but be warned about the abattoir and meat section almost directly opposite the minaret behind the first few rows of stalls, as the reeling smells here will somewhat stop you in your tracks. Elsewhere in the packed and sandy lanes are traditional blacksmiths at work at smithies over charcoal burners, Fulani women selling milk and yoghurt from calabashes, piles of grains, cereals and pulses on perilously overloaded stalls, and livestock herded into pens for easy inspection, including long-haired, chocolate-brown goats, and the odd camel.

GUSAU

Gusau is the capital of Zamfara State, and is located on the Sokoto River, which is an important source of water during the dry season. Once a leper colony, the city is Hausa-Fulani and strictly Muslim. Like Kano State, Sharia law is followed to the letter here and even public minibuses and shared taxis are designated for women only, and women are not allowed to ride *achaba*s. Disaster struck here in October 2006, when a dam collapsed, which killed over 40 people and hundreds of livestock and destroyed some 500 homes.

You are only likely to find yourself here *en route* to Sokoto, and if it gets too late to continue the 219km to Sokoto you may need to stop in Gusau as there is nowhere else after here. The **Du-Ludeo Hotel** (*no phone; $*), on Bypass Road to the south of town on the Zaria road, is adequate. It's a new brown and yellow building with a restaurant in a compound with secure parking, and comfortable doubles with fan and working bathrooms, and they will be able to rustle up something in the restaurant. The gen is only on for a few hours in the evening though. There are also several other hotels around the bypass.

Sokoto, the capital of Sokoto State, is situated near to the confluence of the Rima and Sokoto rivers in the extreme northwest of Nigeria, and with an average annual temperature of 38.3°C it is one of the hottest cities in the world. Sokoto is in the dry Sahel, surrounded by sandy savanna and isolated hills, where camels are used throughout the area, and there's a camel market in Sokoto. The region's lifeline is the floodplains of the Sokoto-Rima River system, which are covered with rich alluvial soil (deposited by running water) for the growing of crops. In dry and drought seasons, power and water are a particular problem this far north, and generator use is restricted.

Sokoto is a sprawling city of 3.7 million people (according to the 2006 census) and is an important centre of Nigerian Islam – there are dozens of mosques all over the city, and new ones being built all the time. It's not a particularly attractive city, and I think I saw more rubbish here than in the other northern cities, though it is surprisingly green, and the roads are lined with neem trees. Despite having a long history, it lacks the Sahel atmosphere of Katsina and the friendly charm of Zaria.

BRIEF HISTORY Originally the capital of the Hausa kingdom of Gobir, established around the 10th century, Sokoto was one of the seven walled Hausa kingdoms, and in the 13th century Islam arrived from the north by way of the trans-Saharan caravan routes. In the early 19th century, Fulani chief and Islamic leader Usman dan Fodio chose Sokoto as the capital of his caliphate and as a base for the spread of Islam and the expansion of the Fulani Empire. 'Caliph', or 'Khalifa' in Arabic, is a leader of Islam and literally means 'successor of Mohammed', the Islamic prophet.

From Sokoto, Usman and his followers administered the holy war known as the Fulani jihad, which lasted from 1804 to 1830 (see page 35). The jihad took control of most of northern Nigeria and adjacent parts of Cameroon and Niger and succeeded in spreading the Islamic faith throughout West Africa. They were attracted to Sokoto for its strategic position and its steep escarpments protecting it from any surprise cavalry attacks. From humble beginnings as a war camp, Sokoto grew in leaps and bounds into a haven for supporters and followers of the jihad, with most of the early inhabitants being jihad warriors and their families. The erection of city walls in 1809 led to increased security in the town, but with an ever-increasing population there came a need to fortify these with another outer city wall 20 years later.

Dan Fodio died in 1817 and his tomb in Sokoto is still an important place of pilgrimage for many Nigerian Muslims. He was succeeded by his son, Muhammadu Bello, who was made the first sultan of Sokoto, and who built up the city in the 1820s as the capital of all the new emirates. He was the spiritual leader to whom all the other emirs of the Fulani Empire answered, and the presence of many mosques, Koran schools and religious scholars made Sokoto the centre for Islam in West Africa.

This political system still exists today and the sultan of Sokoto is effectively the spiritual leader of Muslim Nigeria. The caliphate continued to be successful through a series of sultans, when the emirs in all parts of the caliphate were expected to shuttle to and from Sokoto to pay homage, to take counsel on state matters or to partake in Islamic learning, until the arrival of the British in 1903. Frederick Lugard conquered the caliphate relatively easily with weapons that included rocket launchers and newly invented machine guns against a Sokoto cavalry equipped with bows and arrows and the odd barrelled pistol. All of the emirates of the Sokoto Caliphate were absorbed into the colonial Protectorate of

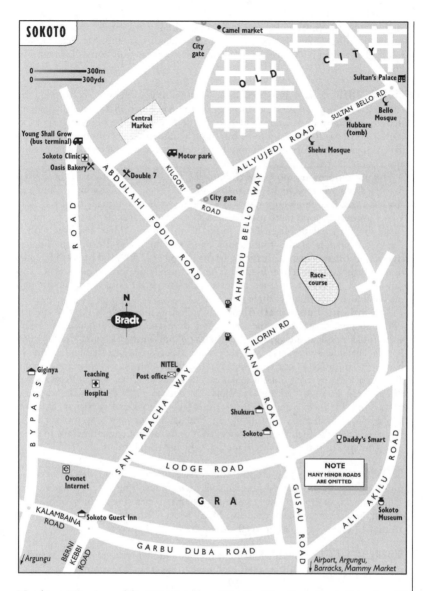

SOKOTO

- Camel market
- City gate
- OLD CITY
- Sultan's Palace
- Sultan Bello Rd
- Bello Mosque
- Hubbare (tomb)
- Shehu Mosque
- Central Market
- Young Shall Grow (bus terminal)
- Sokoto Clinic
- Oasis Bakery
- Double 7
- Motor park
- Kilgori
- Abdulahi Fodio Road
- Allyujedi Road
- City gate Road
- Ahmadu Bello Way
- Race-course
- N
- Bradt
- Ilorin Rd
- Giginya
- Teaching Hospital
- NITEL
- Post office
- Sani Abacha Way
- Kano Road
- Shukura
- Sokoto
- Daddy's Smart
- Bypass
- Ovonet Internet
- Lodge Road
- GRA
- Gusau Road
- Ali Akilu Road
- Sokoto Museum
- Kalambaina Road
- Sokoto Guest Inn
- Berni Kebbi Road
- Garbu Duba Road
- Argungu
- Airport, Argungu, Barracks, Mammy Market

0 ——— 300m
0 ——— 300yds

NOTE
MANY MINOR ROADS
ARE OMITTED

Northern Nigeria, and by 1914 into one Nigeria. Thanks to Lugard's policy of indirect rule, the sultan of Sokoto and the northern emirs were quickly appeased by the British, who allowed indirect rule through the sultanate and network of emirs, with colonial officers overseeing their governments.

After independence, the assassination of the sultan of Sokoto in 1966 was a major cause of the outbreak of the Nigerian civil war (see page 16). More recently, the Sultan of Sokoto since 1996, Muhammadu Maccido, died in a plane crash in October 2006 along with 104 other people. The crash took place as the plane took off from Abuja's runway, and the flight was heading for Sokoto. His son and one of his grandsons also perished, as did the son of the former Nigerian president Shehu Shagari. Crowds of mourners from all over northern Nigeria kept vigil outside the Sultan's Palace for weeks, and Muslims came from other West African countries including Niger, Chad and Sudan to pay their respects. He was replaced as Sultan by Mohamed Sa'ad Abubakar, a great grandson of Usman Dan Fodio.

GETTING THERE Sokoto is located at the junction of two highways connecting the city to Zaria along the A218, and to Jega on the A1, a road that eventually goes all the way to Lagos. Give yourself plenty of time to get here by public transport, as these are not roads you want to be travelling along after dark. Although improved in recent years they run through remote regions, are badly pot-holed, and domestic animals on the road may cause accidents.

Sokoto's enormous **motor park** is to the north of town, next to the central market, from where vehicles go to Jos, Abuja, Gusau, Zaria, Kaduna, Kano and Argungu (see box below), though you would be advised to initially head for Zaria as any journey beyond there may be after dark. There's also plenty of transport to Illela, the border with Niger 85km to the north, costing N350. The Young Shall Grow terminal is at the roundabout on Abdulahi Fodio Road, and 'luxury' **overnight buses** depart daily for Lagos for roughly N3,500, and to Port Harcourt in the southeast for just over N4,000. This is probably the longest bus journey you can take in Nigeria, a distance of some 1,200km or 20 hours by road (though inadvisable as they travel at night).

The **Sultan Abubakar III Airport** is 9.5km to the south of the city and the only transport to and from the airport is a drop taxi for around N1,500. ADC airlines has a desk at the airport (✆ *060 230606*) and in the Shukura Hotel (✆ *060 239206; www.adcairlines.com*), and they have a Lagos–Sokoto flight (2 hours 40 minutes) via Abuja (1 hour 40 minutes) at 08.55 on Wednesday, Friday and Sunday. The flight returns from Sokoto to Abuja and Lagos at 12.05. **Virgin Nigeria** has flights from Lagos to Sokoto via Abuja that depart at 12.10 on Wednesday and Friday and 11.10 on Sunday. Flights from Sokoto to Lagos depart at 13.00 on Wednesday and Sunday and 12.00 on Friday. Always check as times change frequently and the flights will be cancelled if there are not enough people to make it worthwhile or if the visibility is too poor during the Harmattan.

GETTING AROUND Getting around Sokoto is easy enough and shared taxis and minibuses ply Kano Road. Motorbike taxis here are just little 50cc scooters and are called *kabuskis* or *express*. They can struggle to go up even the slightest of hills but at least they are incapable of excessive speed. Most of the riders appear to be either around 12 years old or closer to 60 – there are few in between.

WHERE TO STAY Inexplicably Sokoto has a huge number of hotel rooms for such a remote city and most of the hotels each have in excess of 100 rooms.

🏠 **Giginya Hotel** By-Pass Rd; ✆ 060 231263/ 231466. The best hotel in Sokoto, & completely refurbished in 2003, so everything here is reasonably fresh & functioning, with 200 newly painted rooms with new hotel furniture imported from Italy, thick carpets, balconies, DSTV & fridge. There's an all-night generator, spacious tiled lobby with coffee bar & lounge area, an empty swimming pool, & a restaurant, though it's a bit hit & miss with continental food – chicken chasseur is no different from chicken pepper soup. Rooms $$; suites $$$

🏠 **Shukura Hotel** Kano Rd; ✆ 060 230006. Popular, with good service & had a bit of a refit in 2006. The restaurant has only 4 tables so presumably most people eat in their rooms. Other than food-is-ready, there may be also chips, omelettes & spaghetti on offer. There is a good source of water here, as attested to by the local women & children collecting water from the taps in the car park. There are 230 rooms, & a standard room has a double bed, so you don't need to pay more for the bigger rooms. $$

Sokoto Guest Inn Kalambaina Rd; 📞 060 233205/232672/232955. Here are good-value 122 rooms in big chalets painted hospital green in pleasant grounds full of cats, offering dingy but spotlessly clean & cheap accommodation with bucket & fan. There's TV with a good selection of satellite channels but there's no AC when the gen's on. $

Sokoto Hotel Kano Rd; 📞 060 232126. A vast concrete block of 244 rooms with broken windows & big car park, & very tired-looking & dirty, though it's often surprisingly full, despite there being much better places to stay for the money. Rooms with fan start at US$8; double this for AC. $

✗ WHERE TO EAT AND DRINK

Apart from the *suya* stands in the old city that serve all the bits of a sheep, eating out in Sokoto is really limited to the hotels and the **Double 7** (*9 Abdullahi Fodio Rd;* 📞 *060 234709*) run by one of only three Lebanese families in Sokoto and lit up like a Christmas tree at night, with strings of coloured flashing lights leading from the building to the road. Downstairs is a supermarket (🕐 *07.00–23.00 daily*) selling imported goods, with a snack bar outside for *schawarmas* and burgers, and a counter in the back selling fresh bread, good meat pizza slices, cakes and cold drinks. Upstairs is the formal Lebanese restaurant (🕐 *08.00–23.00 daily*) with a huge menu of mixed grills, pizzas, falafels, *schawarmas*, steaks and chicken dishes. The dishes are not necessarily authentic, but they make a change from Nigerian food and they're not too expensive.

The **Oasis Bakery** is beside the Sokoto Clinic, and in a green corrugated shed in the clinic car park is the excellent and very busy **Clinic Restaurant**, which offers salads and couscous as well as the usual food-is-ready. Options for entertainment in the evening are very limited and Sokoto is 'dry'. However, if you are feeling adventurous and are desperate for a beer, the army barracks close to the airport have a '**mammy market**' with bars but the atmosphere is very unpleasant due to fighting among soldiers and prostitution. A much nicer option, and where the local young middle class gathers, is **Daddy's Smart**, an (alcohol-free) bar and sports club near the Lodge Road/Kano Road roundabout. You can sit with a mineral and watch people enjoying themselves playing volleyball, badminton and basketball.

PRACTICALITIES

The **NITEL** office is on Sani Abacha Way and there's no sign, but you'll see the tower, and it's next door to the green and white **post office**, where there's an EMS Speedpost service. **Ovonet Internet**, opposite Usman Danfodio University Teaching Hospital on Custom Barrack Road, is good and fast at only N100 per hour.

WHAT TO SEE AND DO

The Sokoto Museum

The **Sokoto Museum** is on Ali Akilu Road to the east of Kano Road (🕐 *09.30–16.00 Mon–Fri; entry N500, plus dash for the guide*) and is also dubbed locally as the History and Culture Bureau. It houses an excellent collection of local exhibits telling the story of Usman dan Fodio's jihad, and the guide is very good and (unusually) able to answer questions about the exhibits. Many of Usman dan Fodio's personal items are on display, such as original Islamic scriptures, maps, weapons, and copies of the Koran.

One exhibit is devoted to the colonial era, and includes a wooden throne given to the sultan of Sokoto by Queen Elizabeth II during her visit to Nigeria in the 1950s. Rather crudely and insensitively of the British at the time, the throne has a carving of a naked boy on it, and reputedly the sultan had the boy's head removed before he would sit on it. The issue wasn't about the nakedness as such, but it is forbidden under Islam to represent a person in art. Another exhibit of note are the original carved city doors that once were erected in the old gates.

The annual Argungu (pronounced 'ar-goon-goo') Fishing Festival is a major week-long event, and one of the leading festivals in West Africa. It takes place near the town of Argungu, 99km southwest of Sokoto. It originated in 1934 when Sultan Dan Mu'azu of Sokoto made a visit to the region, and a grand fishing festival was organised in his honour on the Argungu River. Hundreds of men and boys dived into the water and the biggest fish caught was presented to the sultan. Since then, it's become a celebrated yearly event held during February or March, and it marks the end of the growing season and the harvest. Events include art and craft exhibitions, cultural dances and music, local drama, traditional boxing and wrestling, archery competitions, bicycle races, donkey and camel races, and a motor rally. On the river itself are canoe and swimming races, deep-diving competitions, bare-hand fishing and wild-duck hunting. The festival's grand finale is the fishing show, when thousands of men and boys enter the water, armed with large fishnet scoops. They are joined by canoes filled with drummers, plus men rattling huge seed-filled gourds to drive the fish to shallow waters. During the allotted time, they fight for the fish in the river and a wealth of fish is harvested, including giant Nile perch reaching weights of over 60kg. A 1.6km stretch of the Argungu River is protected throughout the year, so that the fish will be plentiful for this 45-minute fishing frenzy. It's all finished off with singing and dancing well into the night. In 2004 the winning fish weighed in at 82kg; in 2005 it was 75kg. It takes at least four men to hoist these weights on the scales. Unfortunately, since 2006, there has been no fishing as the waters have been too low. When the festival does take place, the nearest accommodation is in Sokoto and there's regular public transport to and from Argungu.

The central market and the old city The well-organised Sokoto **central market**, next to the motor park, unfortunately burnt down in 2006, but it has since been rebuilt, with a highly organised network of neat stalls. It doesn't quite have the same atmosphere as the old Kano and Katsina markets, but it's pleasant enough to wander around under the shade of the neem trees. Look out for the reams of brightly coloured cloth, the male tailors bent over ancient black Singer sewing machines, and the abundant arrangements of fruit and vegetables.

By contrast, the **old city** around Sultan Bello Road is very run down and congested, and could feasibly be described as a slum, with its intense rubbish problem and rank drains. Little remains of the city's walls, which are concealed beneath haphazard housing, and the only remaining gates, the Kofar Alivu Jedi on Aliyu Jedi Road, and the Kofar Kade on Old Market Road, are concrete replicas.

The Sultan's Palace, two great mosques and a camel market The **Sultan's Palace** is a huge modern complex built from 1970s concrete, and is not as impressive as some of the other Emir's Palaces of the north. It is nothing more than a simple compound of office buildings with a line of fat-cat councillors' Mercedes and some horses tethered in the car park, though you may see one of the elderly palace guards in their heavy red and white robes. The main gate is beyond a green and white roundabout on Sultan Bello Road.

Two of Sokoto's greatest **mosques** can still be seen near the Sultan's Palace – the Sultan Bello and Shehu mosques – and while their golden domes and minarets are impressive to look at on the outside, non-Muslims or women are not allowed inside. Just before the Shehu Mosque, a dirt alleyway leads off to the **Hubbare**, a squat one-storey mud building that was once the home of Usman dan Fodio, and where he is buried along with most of his family and his imam; the spot still attracts pilgrims who come to pay homage, but again non-Muslims are not very welcome here, though it may be possible for men to visit. Women are allowed into the compound but not into the tomb itself.

There is a **camel market** in this area though, which could have perhaps been trading in camels for a thousand years or more. I was reliably informed that these days the starting price for an adult camel is N80,000 and for a youngster N10,000, which of course is negotiable. On one ancient tourism leaflet, I found a listing for sights in Sokoto that said: 'There is a camel market that is well attended by both Nigerians and camels.'

Appendix 1

English is the official language of Nigeria and is widely spoken and understood just about everywhere except for some of the more rural areas and distant northern towns. In all the cities that have universities, English is used for education, so all younger people speak it. Generally you'll find that English is often spoken rather formally – 'good afternoon madam', 'you are welcome sir', etc. You may struggle to understand some of the quirky pidgin-English sayings and phrases, though you just might find yourself peppering your own speech with some of them. 'O' is the classic example, which is added on to all sorts of words – I would imagine that former expats of Nigeria would continue to say *Sorry-o* for the rest of their lives.

PIDGIN ENGLISH Pidgin or 'broken' English is a mixture of English and indigenous Nigerian words often used in casual conversation, and has been spoken and understood by almost all Nigerians for more than a century. It's spoken with a lot of spirit and gesticulation. Many English words are used differently in pidgin English and it can be confusing, and the many misspellings and mispronunciations are so popular that they have entered colloquial use. Some of my favourites include: *chop* – meal; *small chop* – snack; *sistah* or *brudda* – anyone from the same village; *take leg* or *with feet* – walk; *on it* – switch on; *off it* – switch off; *tossed* – out of order; *move for front small* – go forward a little; *hello* – I can't hear you; *easy yourself* – go to the toilet; and the very best: *raincoat* – condom (see also *Glossary of Nigerian phrases* on pages 328).

These days pidgin English is a language in itself, and is used in plays and novels and on the radio in Nigeria. Indeed, the United Nations has translated the Declaration of Human Rights into Nigerian pidgin English (*www.unhchr.ch/udhr/lang/pcm.htm*). So, 'everyone has the right to life, liberty and security of person' translates as 'everi one naim get right to live, get right to do as e like and right to see say im life safe for where e dey'.

There is also a mine of proverbs in pidgin English. 'Man wey fool na him loss' ('It is the fool that loses'); 'Lion de sick no be say goat fit go salute am for house' ('Just because the lion is sick does not mean the goat can go to the lion's house to greet him'); 'Monkey no fine but im mamma like am so' ('The monkey may not look handsome, but his mother likes him as he is'); and 'Cow wey no get tail na god dey drive him fly' ('God drives away the flies from the cow without a tail').

NIGERIAN LANGUAGES AND DIALECTS Of the 400 or so Nigerian languages and dialects (in some areas such as the Niger Delta someone in the next village will speak a different language), the most common are Yoruba, spoken in the southwest, Igbo, spoken in the southeast, and Hausa, spoken in the north. In the north, only educated people speak English, and it can be a problem for visitors to find an *okada* driver, chop seller or stall keeper who speaks English, though they will usually find someone around who can. Although you will get by with English, it is, as always, considered polite to learn a few local greetings, and all Nigerians will be delighted if you make the effort to say a few words in their own tongue. Once in Nigeria, look out for a small pamphlet *Teach Yourself Yoruba, Hausa & Igbo*, by

J. O. Odetunde (try the bookshops in Lagos, see page 328). This is a humorous little book containing all sorts of useful phrases such as 'On the way to school I saw a snake' and 'Where can I barb my hair?' More recent editions also come with a cassette.

BASIC WORDS AND PHRASES
Essentials

	Yoruba	Hausa	Igbo
Good morning	Ekuojumo	Ina kwana	Igbolachi
Good afternoon	Ekaasan	Ina wuni	Ezigbo ehihie
Good evening	Ekuirole (Ekaale (after 19.00)	Ina wuni	Mgbede oma
Good night	Odaaro	Said a safe	Kachifo
How are you?	Se daadaa ni?	Kana Lafiya?	Kedu ka idi?
I'm fine	Adupe	Lafiya lau	Odi mma
My friend	Ore mi	Aboki na	Enyim
Thank you	Rse/Aagbabire	Na gode	Dalu
Please	E joo	Faranta zuciya	Biko
You're welcome	E kaabo	Sannu da zuwa	Nno
What's your name?	Kini oruko re?	Yaya sunanka?	Kedu afa gi?
My name is…	…ni oruka mi	Suna sa…	Aham bu…
Where is the toilet?	Nibo ni ile igbe yin wa?	Ina bayin ku?	Ebeka ulo nsi unudi?
I don't understand	Ko ye mi	Ban fahimta ba	A ghota ghim
I want to see a doctor	Mo fe ri dokita	Ina son ganin likita	Achoro m ihu dokinta
White person	Oyibo	Bature	Ncha

Questions

	Yoruba	Hausa	Igbo
How?	Bawo?	Yaya?	Kedu?
Where?	Nibo?	Ina?	Ebee?
Why?	Torikinni kilode	Don me?	Maka gini?
When?	Nigbawo?	Yaushe?	Ole mgbe?

Shopping

	Yoruba	Hausa	Igbo
How is the market? (a greeting to any trader)	Bawo loja?	Ya ya kasuwa?	Kedu maka ahai?
What are you selling?	Kinni o n ta	Me ka ke sayarwa	Gini ka l na-ere
I want to buy bread	Mo fera buredi	Zan sayi biredi	Achorom igote ach icha
How much is it?	Elo ni?	Nawa ne?	Ego ole ka obu?
How much do you want to pay?	Elo lo fe san?	Nawa ne kake so ikwu?	Ego ole ka ichoro ikwu?
How much is it last? (literally 'what is your final price'?)	Elo ni jale?	Nawa ne gaskiya?	Gini bu ezigbo onu ya?
Bring 30 naira last	Mu ogbon naira wa jale	Kawo naira talatin gaskiya	Weta iri naira ato

Travelling

	Yoruba	Hausa	Igbo
Is it far?	Se o jinna ni?	Akwai nisa?	O tere aka?
Please, show me the way	Ejoo efi ona han mi	Yana jan saniya	O n'adokpu ehi
I want to go to Lagos	Mo fe lo si Lagos	Ina so in je Lagos	A choro I ga Lagos
Please, where can I get a vehicle going to Lagos?	Ejoo, ni bo ni moti leeri oko Lagos?	Dan allah ina zan samu mota zuwa Lagos?	Biko, ebe ka mga-enweta ugbo ala na-aga Lagos?
Where is the way to the motor park?	Nibo ni oju ona de ibudo iwoko?	Ina hanyar zuwa tashar mota?	Ebe ka esi aga na odu ugbo ala?
Take me to the motor park	Gbe mi de ibudo iwoko	Ka kai ni tashar mota	Buru m ga na odu ugbo ala
What is your fare?	Elo le fe gba?	Nawa za ka, karba zuwa tasha?	Ego ole ka ina ana?
Driver, you're going too fast	Direba ere re ti poj	Mai tuki, gudun ka ya yi yawa!	Okwougboala, ina-agbasi ike nnukwu
How many hours' journey?	Irin wakati melo ni?	Tafi yar awa nawa ne?	Obu njem awa ole?

Eating

	Yoruba	Hausa	Igbo
I want to eat	Mo fe jeun	Ina so in ci	Achoro m iri
Do you have…?	Se o ni…?	Kana da…?	Inwere…?
Which type of food do you have?	Iru onje wo lo wa?	Wane irin abinci ne kuke dashi?	Kedu udi nri inwere?
Give me a spoon	Fun mi ni sibi	Ba ni cokali	Nye m obere ngaji
The food is ready	Onje ti setan	Abinci ya yi	Nri adigo
vegetable	efa	ganye	ugu
fruit	eso	ya yan itatuwa	mkpuru osisi
meat	eran	nama	nwere
fish	eja	kifi	azu
egg	eyin	kwai	akwa
yam	isu	doya	ji
plantain	ogede	ayaba	ogede
pepper	ata	yaji	ose
rice	iresi	shinkafa	osikapa
potato	anomo	dankali	nduku
tomato	tomati	tumatur	tomanto
water	omi	ruwa	mmiri
OK, give me rice	Fun mi ni iresi	To, ku ba ni Shinkafa	O dimma, niye m osikapa

Time

	Yoruba	Hausa	Igbo
What says the time?	Kinni asiko so?	Karfe nawa ne?	O gini na-aku?
Yesterday	Ana	Jiya	Unyahu
Today	Oni	Yau	Tata
Tomorrow	Ola	Gobe	Echi
Morning	Aaro	Safe	Ututu
Afternoon	Osan	Rana	Ehihie
Evening	Irole	Dare	Mgbede

Days of the week

	Yoruba	Hausa	Igbo
Monday	Ojo aje	Luttinin	Monde
Tuesday	Ojo isegun	Talata	Tuzde
Wednesday	Ojo ru	Laraba	Wenesday
Thursday	Ojo bo	Alhamis	Tosde
Friday	Ojo eti	Jumma'a	Fraide
Saturday	Ojo abameta	Asabar	Satude
Sunday	Ojo aiku	Lahadi	Uka

Numbers

	Yoruba	Hausa	Igbo
1	okan/meni	daya	otu
2	eij/meji	biyu	abou
3	eta/meta	uku	ato
4	erin/merin	hudu	ano
5	arun/marun	biyar	ise
6	efa/mefa	shida	isii
7	eeje/meje	bakwai	asaa
8	ejo/mejo	takwas	asato
9	esan/mesan	tara	iteghete/itolu
10	ewe/mewa	goma	in
11	mokanla	goma sha daya	iri na otu
12, etc	mejila, etc	goma sha biyu, etc	iri na abuo, etc
20	oogun	ashirin	iri abuo
30	ogbon	talatin	iriato
40	ogoji	arbain	iri ano
50	edegbeta	dari biyar	puku ise
60	ogota	sittin	iri isii
70	adorin	sabain	iri asaa
80	ogorin	tamanin	iri asato
90	adorun	casain	iri iteghete
100	ogorun	dari	out puku
1000	egberunkan	dubu	out nnari

Note: There are regional dialects within the languages for numbers

Appendix 2

419	Any type of fraud, though it originally means financial fraud after the number of the section of the Nigerian penal code that addresses fraud schemes
Area Boys	Lagos hoodlums who steal from people using intimidation
batauri	White person (Hausa); you'll hear this in the northern cities
black shirt	Policeman
chop	A meal
chop house	A restaurant or café
dash	Bribe, tip; used as both a noun and a verb as in 'what will you *dash* me?'
drop	Can mean to get off a bus or taxi, but if you want a taxi to yourself (with no other passengers), you want a drop taxi. You're more likely to use the phrase 'no drop' as it is assumed that all *batauris* or *oyibos* want their own vehicle.
easy yourself	Go to the toilet
emir	Northern Muslim leader
expat	Foreign expatriate worker; there are more than 20,000 expats in Nigeria working in sectors such as oil or telecommunications, and as embassy staff
food-is-ready	Where you'll see this sign, it means that there is some kind of food ready. Stalls cook up pots of pounded yam, *eba* etc, with some kind of soup from the morning and keep them going all day. You will have limited choice towards the end of the day, when the food-is-ready starts to run out.
go-slow	Traffic jam
GRA	Government reserved area; mostly created by the British in colonial years as the residential district for British officers, but in more recent years it has been the area where governors, councillors and civil servants live. The GRA is invariably the poshest or nicest part of a city, with the biggest houses.
moto	Any kind of vehicle, but usually used to refer to a car or bush taxi
NEPA	Nigerian Electric Power Agency; or Never Expect Power Again (Nigerian slang)
NITEL	Nigerian Telecommunications (telephone company)
oba	Traditional Yoruba king and leader, also referred to as an *alafin*
off	The verb to switch something off, as in 'off the light'
off seat	Out of the office
okada	Motorbike taxi named after a defunct airline; called *achaba* in the north
on	The verb to switch something on, as in 'on the AC'
on seat	In the office

oyibo	White person (Yoruba slang); you will hear this everywhere
pijott	Peugeot car commonly used as a bush taxi that usually has three rows of seats and can carry nine passengers plus the driver
pure water	Half-litre plastic bags of (not always good) drinking water sold everywhere
Sabon Gari	Hausa 'for foreigners' town'; often meaning the Yoruba or Igbo, or sometimes the Christian, quarter of a northern city
small chop	Snack
sorry-o	Expression of sympathy
suya	Barbecued meat, often served on sticks
take leg	Walk
wahalla	Trouble; 'no wahalla' means no trouble or no worries
welcome	Hello
with feet	Walk

Appendix 3

BOOKS

History and background These are the most useful books, but they are all out of print today.

General

Bradley K *The Living Commonwealth* Hutchinson & Co Ltd, 1961

Hallett R *Africa to 1875* Heinmann Educational Books Ltd, 1974

Oliver R and Atmore A *Africa Since 1800* Cambridge University Press, 1972

The Biafran War

Draper M *Airlift and Airwar in Biafra and Nigeria 1967–1970* Howell Press Inc, 2000. The author was involved in an airlift to Biafra during 1968 and, later, an attempt to ferry other aircraft there. This technical book about the military aircraft used by the Nigerians and the Biafrans fuses first-hand accounts with original documentation.

Sherman J *War Stories: A Memoir of Nigeria and Biafra* Mesa Verde Press, 2002. This is a memoir of the Biafran War as seen though the eyes of John Sherman, an American who served with a Red Cross food distribution and medical team during the civil war. It brings the reader uncomfortably close to the horrors of war, especially in the team's attempt to prevent hundreds of children dying from extreme malnutrition.

20th-century and contemporary history There are a number of prolific Nigerian writers who in the last few decades have used their medium as a tool to challenge the state. Nobel Prize winner **Wole Soyinka** is one of Nigeria's most outspoken writers, who for decades has protested against Nigerian authoritarianism in plays, novels, newspaper articles and poetry. His activism landed him in jail in the late 1960s, and in 1994 he was thrown out of the country by Abacha, who he still refers to as the 'diminutive, demented dictator'.

One of his Soyinka's important critical books on Nigeria is *The Open Sore of a Continent: A Personal Narrative of the Nigerian Crisis* (Oxford University Press, 1997), written during the Abacha term of the mid-1990s, when Soyinka said that Nigerians were 'primed for a campaign of comprehensive civil disobedience'. In the book he covers the two decades of military rule and the strife between the ethnic groups, condemns the country's leadership, which he calls illegitimate, and muses over questions of nationalism and international intervention. Soyinka's latest book, *You Must Set Forth at Dawn: a Memoir* (Random House, 2006), covers his political activity in the last few decades, and includes an account of his 1967 attempt to avert the Nigerian civil war by travelling to Biafra and speaking to the leader of the seceding state. For this he was imprisoned without trial for 27 months, most of it spent in solitary confinement.

Another author who wrote dozens of novels is **Ken Saro-Wiwa**, Nigeria's foremost environmentalist and literary writer, best known for *A Month and a Day: A Detention Diary* (Penguin Books, 1996), which he wrote and smuggled out of jail during his detention by

Abacha before being executed on trumped-up charges in 1995. Wiwa led his Ogoni people in the Niger Delta to challenge the environmental degradation of their environment by Shell through gas flaring, oil spillage and soil degeneration, and the various military regimes that exploited the oil wealth. Wiwa called this 'environmental racism'. The book promotes the idealism that all ethnic nationalities must be allowed to shape their destiny and control their resources.

Ike Okonta and **Oronto Douglas** discuss the same subject in *Where Vultures Feast: Shell, Human Rights, and Oil in the Niger Delta* (Lub Books, 2003), which describes the efforts of the people in the Niger Delta to battle the devastation of their homeland by Shell. The company has colluded with a series of corrupt and repressive Nigerian governments.

A good contemporary book on Nigeria is *This House Has Fallen: Midnight in Nigeria* (Public Affairs Press, 2000) by **Maier K**, a journalist for the *Independent* who was stationed in Lagos for more than a decade. It's generally a historical account, but he also covers the civil disorder and poverty of recent years, and includes first-hand discussions with Nigerians, from taxi drivers and religious leaders, to business and military men. It's an excellent assessment of Nigeria's chaotic state, and he gives dire warnings that Nigeria is a time bomb ready to go off.

FICTION AND BIOGRAPHY

Ben Okri Nigeria has produced some outstanding novelists whose work has graced the shelves of bookshops the world over. Nigerian-born Ben Okri has published many books, including *The Famished Road*, which won the Booker Prize in 1991, *Songs of Enchantment*, *Astonishing the Gods*, *Infinite Riches* and *Dangerous Love*. He has also published two books of poems, the most recent being *Mental Fight*, and a collection of non-fiction, *A Way of Being Free*. His first book, *Stars of the New Curfew* (Vintage, 1999), is a collection of African short stories about greed and violence. They are vivid tales about the gritty desperation of his characters, hanging on to life by hook or by crook in the slums of Lagos and provincial towns.

The Famished Road (Vintage, 1992) tells the story of Azaro, a spirit-child who in the Yoruba tradition of Nigeria exists between life and death, and who maintains ties to the supernatural world. Survival in his chaotic African village is difficult and Azaro and his family must contend with hunger, disease and violence, as well as the boy's spirit-companions, who are constantly trying to trick him back into their world. *Infinite Riches* and *Songs of Enchantment* follow on from *The Famished Road* with other adventures of Azaro.

Chinua Achebe Another famous Nigerian author is Chinua Achebe, who wrote *Things Fall Apart* (first published in 1958; reprinted in 2006 by Penguin), a gripping study of the problem of European colonialism in Africa. The introduction states that the story is about 'a clan which once thought like one, spoke like one, shared a common awareness and acted like one. The white man came and his coming broke this unity. In the process many heads rolled: new words, new usages and new applications gained entrance into men's heads and hearts and the old society gradually gave way.' The story is about an African tribe that lived in an African village called Umuofia at the turn of the 20th century, led by a character called Okonkowo. The white missionaries arrived and started to convert Africans to Christianity. Okonkowo's self-dignity and power were taken away and his life and beliefs began to fall apart.

Although a work of fiction, the novel very specifically mirrors the way in which the Igbo in the southeast first encountered the European missionaries and colonialists at the beginning of the 20th century, and how this changed the essence of their society. Achebe took the phrase 'things fall apart' from a poem penned by the Irish poet W. B. Yeats entitled 'The Second Coming' – 'Things fall apart; the centre cannot hold. Mere anarchy is loosed upon the world.'

Chris Abani A praised new Nigerian novelist is Chris Abani, whose debut novel, *Graceland* (Picador, 2005), is the story of an innocent child growing into a hardened young man in Nigeria during the late 1970s and early 1980s. The main character is Elvis Oke, who impersonates the American rock-and-roll singer he is named after. The story alternates between Elvis's early years in the 1970s, when his mother dies of cancer and leaves him with a drunk and disapproving father, and his life as a teenager in a Lagos ghetto, a place one character in the book calls 'a pus-ridden eyesore on de face of de nation's capital'. Abani followed this first novel with the equally powerful *Becoming Abigail* (Akashic Books, 2006), which is a harrowing coming-of-age story about a sexually abused Nigerian teenage girl who is sent to London, where her family forces her into prostitution.

Helon Habila *Waiting for an Angel*, by Helon Habila (most recently published by Penguin, 2004), was winner of the Caine Prize for African Writing 2001, and voted fifth-best debut novel by the UK's *Observer* newspaper in 2002. In the novel Lomba is a young journalist living under Sani Abacha's military rule in Lagos in the 1990s. He is trying to write a novel in his shabby apartment on Morgan Street (dubbed Poverty Street) and covering arts for a city newspaper, the *Dial*. His life changes drastically after his room-mate is brutally attacked by soldiers, his first love is forced to marry a wealthy old man, journalists are arrested all over the city and the *Dial* offices are set on fire. Lomba decides to take part in a pro-democracy demonstration but is arrested and imprisoned for three years with no access to lawyers or friends. Powerful and vivid, the story moves backwards in a series of closely connected incidents that show Lomba's life before his incarceration. Habila paints an extraordinary picture of life on Poverty Street, which he calls 'one of the many decrepit, disease-ridden quarters that dotted the city of Lagos like ringworm on a beggar's body', bringing their sounds, sights and smells to life.

Habila's second novel, *Measuring Time* (WW Norton, 2007), follows the story of the relationship between twin teenage boys who want to escape their Nigerian village. The loud, boisterous twin gets involved in the wars of West Africa during the 1980s and 1990s and even comes into contact with Liberia's notorious warlord Charles Taylor. One twin becomes a soldier; the other, quiet and weak with sickle-cell disease, is forced to stay at home with his father, who both boys hate as they believe that he made their mother's life so miserable she died at an early age. It's a moving story about the strong and weak side of the human personality balancing each other out.

Chimamanda Ngozi Adichie Chimamanda Ngozi Adichie is an extraordinary 30-year-old Nigerian writer. Her first novel, *Purple Hibiscus* (Harper Perennial, 2005), offers an intensely personal account of growing up in Nigeria in the early 1990s. Shortlisted for the Orange Prize and winner of the Commonwealth's Writer's Prize, it is set in the context of social extremes, political upheaval and religious intolerance. Yet its real strength is in the minutiae of Nigerian family life through the eyes of a 15-year-old girl slowly moving towards maturity. *Half of a Yellow Sun* (Fourth Estate, 2006) did win the 2007 Orange Prize and is a profoundly gripping story about Nigeria during the Biafran War. It's primarily told through the eyes and lives of Ugwu, a 13-year-old peasant houseboy, and twin sisters Olanna and Kainene, who are from a wealthy and well-connected family. Adichie's skilful depictions of food rationing, soap-making and running from air raids enable the reader to imagine the horrors of war and death and it describes how war wilfully destroys communities, relationships and harmonies.

Ken Wiwa After his father's death in 1995, Ken Saro-Wiwa's son, Ken Wiwa, wrote an extraordinary book called *In the Shadow of a Saint* (Spectrum Books Ltd, 2002) about what happened to his father, and about his own personal journey of accepting his loss and of being the son of a martyr. In it he describes the remarkable meetings he had after his father's death with one of Nelson Mandela's daughters, the son of another South African activist who was killed, Steven Biko, and Aung San Suu Kyi, the daughter of another martyr and the founder of Burma. It also describes in detail how he campaigned for his father's release from prison with the world's leaders, who didn't take Abacha's threats of execution seriously and who were as surprised as anyone when Ken Saro-Wiwa was murdered.

Music For anyone interested in Nigerian music, I recommend Michael Veal's *Fela: The Life & Times of an African Musical Icon* (Temple University Press, 2000). Fela Kuti was Nigeria's greatest musician and the inventor of Afro-beat, a fusion of African music and jazz. He studied music in London and went on to discover James Brown and black politics in the USA in the 1960s. When he returned to Nigeria Kuti created songs and music with a strong protest element that attacked such targets as corrupt politicians and businessmen. Fela's complete rejection of governmental authority, his promiscuity and his flagrant use of marijuana were other challenges to the establishment, and the government unleashed a series of attacks on Fela, his family and property. Fela died of AIDS in 1997. The book surveys Fela's life at home and worldwide, detailing his imprisonments and physical abuse, and his performances and song writing.

Here are a few lines from one of his songs that serve as a fitting end to a book about Nigeria:

Why black people suffer today
Why black people don't have money today
Why black people haven't travelled to the moon today
THIS is the reason why:
We were in our homeland, without troubles
We were minding our own business
Some people came from a faraway land
They fought us and took our land
They took our people as slaves and destroyed our towns
Our troubles started at that time
Our riches they took away to their land
In return they gave us their colony
They took our culture away from us
They gave us their culture which we don't understand
Black people, we don't know ourselves
We don't know our ancestral heritage
We fight each other every day
We are never together at all –
THAT is why black people suffer today

Health and Safety

Wilson-Howarth, Dr J., *Bugs, Bites, and Bowels*, Cadogan, 2002.
Warrell, D. and Anderson, S. (eds) *Expedition Medicine*. Handbook of the Royal Geographical Society covering tropical medicine.
Lankester, Dr T., *The Traveller's Good Health Guide*, Sheldon Press, 2006. Health advice for long-stay travellers including expats and employees of NGOs.
Pelton, R. Y. *The World's Most Dangerous Places*, Harper Collins, 2003. Nigeria is listed.
Dawood, R., *Travellers' Health: How to Stay Healthy Abroad*, Oxford University Press, 2002. Health matters in the developing world.
Wilson-Howarth, Dr J. and Ellis, Dr M., *Your Child Abroad: A Travel Health Guide*, Bradt Travel Guides, 2005.

WEBSITES

General information There are dozens of websites produced in Nigeria that cover news, sport or discussion, but most are badly designed, many of the links or pages don't work, and they produce dozens of pop-ups. However, there are some good news sites that are updated regularly. Many of the individual states also have their own websites, but most list the different governing departments or have profiles of the state governor so are not terribly useful:

www.motherlandnigeria.com Fairly good country information and general features, but much of it has not been updated for a number of years

www.nigeria.com Probably the most comprehensive site for general information, and has a good selection of features and news covering politics, sport and environmental issues

www.nigeria.gov.ng The formal government website listing government departments, with a few patchy and outdated pages on tourism

www.nigeria-arts.net A good resource if you are interested in Nigerian literature, music and visual arts

www.nigeriabusinessinfo.com Tourism blurb and some economic information

www.nigerianoil-gas.com Industry news and links to all the major corporations in Nigeria

www.nigeriasports.com The latest sports news from Nigeria; also covers Nigerian sports people based overseas

www.nigerpost.com Pulls in news from other sites from across Africa

www.voiceofnigeria.org Website for Nigeria's popular radio station covering news, sport and politics.

Health and Safety

Blood Care Foundation (UK) *www.bloodcare.org.uk*. A charity 'dedicated to the provision of screened blood and resuscitation fluids in countries where they are not readily available'.

British Travel Health Association (UK) *www.btha.org*. Official site for the organisation of travel health professionals.

Foreign and Commonwealth Office (UK) *www.fco.gov.uk*. Up-to-date general travel advice with a full list of UK embassies and consulates.

Medic Alert (UK) *www.medicalert.co.uk*. Site for the foundation that issues internationally recognised bracelets and necklaces for those with an existing medical condition or allergy. The bracelet/necklace holds key medical information in the event of you passing out and not being able to tell your doctor what your condition is.

World Health Organization *www.who.int*. Advice on malarial risks and vaccination requirements, with a link to the WHO Blue Book, which lists diseases around the world.

WIN £100 CASH!
READER QUESTIONNAIRE

Send in your completed questionnaire for the chance to win £100 cash in our regular draw

All respondents may order a Bradt guide at half the UK retail price – please complete the order form overleaf.
(Entries may be posted or faxed to us, or scanned and emailed.)

We are interested in getting feedback from our readers to help us plan future Bradt guides. Please answer ALL the questions below and return the form to us in order to qualify for an entry in our regular draw.

Have you used any other Bradt guides? If so, which titles? . . . .
. . . .
What other publishers' travel guides do you use regularly? . . . .
. . . .
Where did you buy this guidebook? . . . .
What was the main purpose of your trip to Nigeria (or for what other reason did you read our guide)? eg: holiday/business/charity etc.. . . . .
. . . .
What other destinations would you like to see covered by a Bradt guide?
. . . .
Would you like to receive our catalogue/newsletters?
YES / NO (If yes, please complete details on reverse)
If yes – by post or email? . . . .
Age (circle relevant category) 16–25   26–45   46–60   60+
Male/Female (delete as appropriate)
Home country . . . .
Please send us any comments about our guide to Nigeria or other Bradt Travel Guides. . . . .
. . . .
. . . .
. . . .

Bradt Travel Guides
23 High Street, Chalfont St Peter, Bucks SL9 9QE, UK
☏ +44 (0)1753 893444 f +44 (0)1753 892333
e info@bradtguides.com
www.bradtguides.com

CLAIM YOUR HALF-PRICE BRADT GUIDE!

Order Form

To order your half-price copy of a Bradt guide, and to enter our prize draw to win £100 (see overleaf), please fill in the order form below, complete the questionnaire overleaf, and send it to Bradt Travel Guides by post, fax or email.

Please send me one copy of the following guide at half the UK retail price

Title	Retail price	Half price
. . . .	. . . .	. . . .

Please send the following additional guides at full UK retail price

No	Title	Retail price	Total
. . .	. . . .	. . . .	. . . .
. . .	. . . .	. . . .	. . . .
. . .	. . . .	. . . .	. . . .

Sub total . . . .
Post & packing . . . .
(£2 per book UK; £4 per book Europe; £6 per book rest of world)
Total . . . .

Name . . . .

Address . . . .

Tel . . . .   Email . . . .

☐ I enclose a cheque for £ . . . . made payable to Bradt Travel Guides Ltd

☐ I would like to pay by credit card. Number: . . . .

Expiry date: . . . / . . .   3-digit security code (on reverse of card) . . . . .

Issue no (debit cards only) . . . . .

☐ Please add my name to your catalogue mailing list.

☐ I would be happy for you to use my name and comments in Bradt marketing material.

Send your order on this form, with the completed questionnaire, to:

Bradt Travel Guides NIG2
23 High Street, Chalfont St Peter, Bucks SL9 9QE
☎ +44 (0)1753 893444   f +44 (0)1753 892333
e info@bradtguides.com   www.bradtguides.com

Bradt Travel Guides

www.bradtguides.com

Africa

Africa Overland	£15.99
Algeria	£15.99
Benin	£14.99
Botswana: Okavango, Chobe, Northern Kalahari	£15.99
Burkina Faso	£14.99
Cameroon	£15.99
Canary Islands	£13.95
Cape Verde Islands	£13.99
Congo	£15.99
Eritrea	£15.99
Ethiopia	£15.99
Gabon, São Tomé, Príncipe	£13.95
Gambia, The	£13.99
Ghana	£15.99
Johannesburg	£6.99
Kenya	£14.95
Madagascar	£15.99
Malawi	£13.99
Mali	£13.95
Mauritius, Rodrigues & Réunion	£13.99
Mozambique	£13.99
Namibia	£15.99
Niger	£14.99
Nigeria	£17.99
Rwanda	£14.99
São Tomé & Príncipe	£14.99
Seychelles	£14.99
Sudan	£13.95
Tanzania, Northern	£13.99
Tanzania	£16.99
Uganda	£15.99
Zambia	£17.99
Zanzibar	£12.99

Britain and Europe

Albania	£15.99
Armenia, Nagorno Karabagh	£14.99
Azores	£13.99
Baltic Capitals: Tallinn, Riga, Vilnius, Kaliningrad	£12.99
Belarus	£14.99
Belgrade	£6.99
Bosnia & Herzegovina	£13.99
Bratislava	£6.99
Budapest	£8.99
Bulgaria	£13.99
Cork	£6.99
Croatia	£13.99

Cyprus see North Cyprus	
Czech Republic	£13.99
Dresden	£7.99
Dubrovnik	£6.99
Estonia	£13.99
Faroe Islands	£15.99
Georgia	£14.99
Helsinki	£7.99
Hungary	£14.99
Iceland	£14.99
Kiev	£7.95
Kosovo	£14.99
Lapland	£13.99
Latvia	£13.99
Lille	£6.99
Lithuania	£14.99
Ljubljana	£7.99
Luxembourg	£13.99
Macedonia	£14.99
Montenegro	£14.99
North Cyprus	£12.99
Paris, Lille & Brussels	£11.95
Riga	£6.95
River Thames, In the Footsteps of the Famous	£10.95
Serbia	£14.99
Slovakia	£14.99
Slovenia	£13.99
Spitsbergen	£15.99
Switzerland: Rail, Road, Lake	£13.99
Tallinn	£6.99
Transylvania	£14.99
Ukraine	£14.99
Vilnius	£6.99
Zagreb	£6.99

Middle East, Asia and Australasia

Borneo	£17.99
China: Yunnan Province	£13.99
Great Wall of China	£13.99
Iran	£14.99
Iraq: Then & Now	£15.99
Kazakhstan	£15.99
Kyrgyzstan	£15.99
Maldives	£13.99
Mongolia	£16.99
North Korea	£14.99
Oman	£13.99
Shangri La	£14.99
Sri Lanka	£13.99
Syria	£14.99
Tibet	£13.99

Turkmenistan	£14.99
Yemen	£14.99

The Americas and the Caribbean

Amazon, The	£14.99
Argentina	£15.99
Bolivia	£14.99
Cayman Islands	£14.99
Chile	£16.95
Chile & Argentina: The Bradt Trekking Guide	£12.95
Colombia	£16.99
Costa Rica	£13.99
Dominica	£14.99
Falkland Islands	£13.95
Guyana	£14.99
Panama	£13.95
Peru & Bolivia: Backpacking & Trekking	£12.95
St Helena	£14.99
USA by Rail	£14.99

Wildlife

100 Animals to See Before They Die	£16.99
Antarctica: Guide to the Wildlife	£14.95
Arctic: Guide to the Wildlife	£15.99
Central & Eastern European Wildlife	£15.99
Chinese Wildlife	£16.99
East African Wildlife	£19.99
Galápagos Wildlife	£15.99
Madagascar Wildlife	£15.99
Peruvian Wildlife	£15.99
Southern African Wildlife	£18.95
Sri Lankan Wildlife	£15.99

Eccentric Guides

Eccentric Australia	£12.99
Eccentric Britain	£13.99
Eccentric California	£13.99
Eccentric Cambridge	£6.99
Eccentric Edinburgh	£5.95
Eccentric France	£12.95
Eccentric London	£13.99
Eccentric Oxford	£5.95

Others

Your Child Abroad: A Travel Health Guide	£10.95
Something Different for the Weekend	£9.99

Index

Page numbers in bold indicate major entries; those in italics indicate maps

Aba **199–200**
  Museum of Colonial History 200
Abacha, Sani **20**, 22
Abeokuta **163–6**, *165*
  Olumu Rock 165–6
  Ikota Market 166
  where to stay and eat 164–5
Abuja **229–46**, *234–5*
  airlines 233
  getting around 236
  getting there and away 232–3
  history 231–2
  National Children's Park and Zoo 244
  National Stadium 244–5
  nightlife 240
  orientation 233–6
  practicalities 240–2
  shopping 242–3
  where to eat and drink 238–9
  where to stay 236–8
  Zuma Rock, Suleja and Gurara Falls 246
accommodation **72–7**
  glossary of accommodation terms 74–7
  long-term 73
Achebe, Chinua 21, **331**
Ade, Sunny 43
administrative regions 29
Afi Drill Ranch 50, 218, **223–4**
airlines (domestic) 64
airlines (international) 55
Argungu Fishing Festival 42, **322**
art **40**, 82
Asaba 193–5
Assop Falls 260
ATMs 63

Badagry 9, 125, **159**
  slave relics 159–61
  where to stay and eat 125
Baga and Lake Chad 278–80
Bauchi 265–8
  Balewa's tomb 268
  where to stay and eat 267

Benin City 8, 41, **186–91**, *187*
  bronze casters 41, **190–1**
  National Museum 190
  where to stay and eat 189–90
Benin, Kingdom of 9, **186–8**
Biafran War **16–18**, **197–9**
Bida 260–1
bilharzia 94
Bonny Island 207
bush taxis 68–70
business hours 82
Brass Island **208**

Calabar **209–21**, *211*
  Botanic Garden 216
  Calabar Drill Monkey Ranch **217–18**, 224
  Calabar Museum 214–15
  Cercopan **218–19**, 223
  Creek Town 219
  getting around 212
  getting there and away 210–12
  Mary Slessor's tomb and cottage 216
  nightlife 213
  practicalities 213–14
  Tinapa 216–17
  where to eat and drink 213
  where to stay 212–13
camping 73
Central Nigeria **229–64**, *230*
Chad Basin National Park 278, **280–2**
charities *see* Cercopan and Pandrillus
chimpanzees **50**, 218, 224, 272
cholera 90, **95**
Christianity 33, 161, **34–5**, 38
climate **5**, 51, 96
crime and corruption 103–5
Cross River National Park 220, **221–5**, *221*
Crowther, Bishop Samuel 14, 247, 249
culture 39–44
cultural etiquette 83–5

dashing *see* tipping
   Davies-Okundaye, Nike **154–5,** 176,
      178, 243, 251
diarrhoea 100
disabled travellers 106
distance chart 66
dress **42,** 58
drill monkeys 50, **217–18,** 224
drinks 80–1
Duke, Donald **210,** 226–7
durbar 296, 299, **310–11**

East and northeast Nigeria **265–84,**
   266
eating **73–81**
economy 26–31
electric devices 87
embassies and high commissions
   foreign 138
   Nigerian 54–5
endangered species 48–50
Enugu 195–7
   where to stay and eat 196–7
ethnicity **30–1,** 32, 33
Eyo Masquerade 148

family life 39–40
festivals 41–2
foreign exchange **62–3,** 136–7
fraud 102–3
Fulani 30–1
further reading 94, **320–34**

Gashaka–Gumpti National Park 272–4
gay travellers 83
geography 3–5
getting around **64–72**
   by air 64–5
   car rental and driving 65–7
   by rail 67
   minibuses and bush taxis 68–70
   okadas and city transport 70–2
getting there and away **55–7**
   by air 55
   by sea 55
   overland 55–7
glossary of Nigerian phrases 328–9
Gombe 271
gorillas **50, 222**
government *see* history and government
   Gowon, Yakubu **16–9,** 245
greetings 83–4
Gusau 317

Hausa 30
Hausa States, Seven 30–1, **316**
health **89–101**

preparation 89–94
healthcare in Nigeria 94–101
heat and humidity 96–7
hepatitis 97
high commissions *see* embassies
   history and government 5–26
HIV/AIDS and sexually transmitted
   diseases 97

Ibadan **166–73,** *168*
   getting there and away 167–9
   Mapo Hill 172–3
   practicalities 169
   The Alhaji Jimoh Bamidele Crafts
      Centre 172
   Transwonder Amusement Park 172
   University of Ibadan 171–2
   where to eat and drink 170–1
   where to stay 169–70
Ife **173–5**
   Ife Museum 174–5
   Oba's Palace 174
   Obafemi Awolowo University 175
   Opa Oranmiyan 175
   where to stay and eat 173–4
Igbo 16–18, **31,** 197–9
Ikom 56, **227–8**
Ilorin 185
immunisations 90
information **61,** 242
infrastructure 28–31
insects and bugs 97–9
insurance **90,** 106
internet and email 88
Islam 7, 33, **35–9**

jihad 7, **35–7**
Jimeta 271–2
Jos **253–60,** *255*
   getting there and away 255–6
   Jos Museum Complex 258–9
   Jos Wildlife Park 259–6
   practicalities 257–8
   shopping 258
   where to eat and drink 257
   where to stay 256–7

Kaduna **286–92,** *289*
   getting there and away 287
   Kaduna National Museum 291–2
   practicalities 287
   where to eat and drink 288–9
   where to stay 287–8
Kamuka National Park 292
Kano **299–314,** *302–3*
   city wall 311
   Dala Hill 312

dye pits 309
getting there and away 301–4
Gidan Dan Hausa 312–14
Gidan Makama Museum 311
Grand Mosque and Emir's Palace 309–11
history 300–1
Kurmi Market 311–12
listings 308–9
orientation 305
where to eat and drink 306–8
where to stay 305–6
Katsina **314-7**
Gobarau Minaret 317
where to stay and eat 315
Kuti, Fela **43–4**, 132, **333**
Kwa Falls 220–1

Lafia 252
Lagbaja **44**, 133
Lagos **109–61**, *118, 128–9, 144–5*
changing money 136–7
embassies and high commissions 138
getting around 117–21
getting there and away 113–17
history 110–13
Ikoyi 152–3
Lagos Island 142–52
Lekki Peninsula 154–6
National Museum 143–7
National Theatre and Gallery 158
nightlife 131–3
Oba's Palace 152
practicalities 136–42
safety 139–40
shopping 133–6
sports 140–1
Tarkwa Bay 156–8
Victoria Island 153–4
visas 141–2
where to eat and drink 125–31
where to stay 121–5
Lake Chad *see* Baga
Lake Kainji National Park **262–4**
Borgu Section 262–3
Kob Amusement Centre 263
where to stay and eat 262
Zugurma Section 263
language **32–3, 324–7**
Lawal, Amina 38
location 3
Lokoja 12, **246–52**, *248*
colonial relics 249–52
getting there and away 247
where to stay and eat 247–8
Mount Pati 252
long term accommodation 73

Lugard, Captain Frederick 12–13, 247, **250**
luggage 57–8
luxury buses 70

Macaulay, Herbert **14**, 35, 112
Maiduguri **274–8**, *275*
getting there and away 276
practicalities 276–7
where to stay and eat 277
Makurdi **252–3**
malaria 90–2
maps **61**, 138–9
marine dangers 101–2
media and communications 85–8
medical facilities 94
medical kit 94
meningitis 99
minibuses and bush taxis 68–70
Minna 260–1
Miss World 39
money 62–4
motor parks 68
music **43–4**, 131–3

natural history 45–50
national parks 45–8, *46*
New Bussa 261–2
newspapers and magazines 88
Niger Delta 10–11, 26, 200–1, **207–9**
Niger River 10–11, **3–4**, 246–7
Nigerian Tourism Development Council **61**, 242
Nok 6, 41
Nollywood movies **77**, 88, 158
Northern Nigeria **285–323**, *284*

Obasanjo, Olusegun 19, **22–5**, 224
Obudu Cattle Ranch 225–7
Ogbomosho 185
Ogidi-Ijumu 251
oil 18, **27–8**
okadas and city transport 70–2
Okomu National Park 191–2
Old Oyo National Park 184
Onitsha 193–5
Oron 219–20
Oshogbo **175–82**, *177*
art galleries 178
Osun Festival 182
Osun Sacred Groves and Forest 180–2
where to stay and eat 176–8
overland borders 55–7
overland from Europe 55
Oyo **182–4**
drum shops 183–4
where to stay and eat 183

palm oil 11, 215
passports 53
people 31–2
petty theft 105
poaching 47, 264, 268, 272
political risks *see also* religious clashes
   105–6
population 31–2
Port Harcourt **200–7**, *202*
   getting there and away 203
   Port Harcourt Tourist Beach 207
   practicalities 206
   where to eat and drink 205–6
   where to stay 204–5
Portuguese 8, 186
post 87
prices *see* money
   public holidays 2, **62**
public toilets 85

rabies 99
radio 87–8
railways 67
red tape 53–4
religion 33–9
religious clashes *see also* political risks
   38–9
restaurants *see* food
   Rhoko Forest 218, **233**
Riyom Rock Formation 260
road accidents **101**, 65, 140
roadblocks 28, **71**

safety **101–6**, 139–40
Saro-Wiwa, Ken **21**, 24, 330–1
Sharia law **27–9**, *36*, 285, 299
Shere Hills 261
shopping and bargaining 81–2
slave trade **8–11**, 34, 110–11
small change 63–4
Sokoto **318–23**, *319*
   getting there and away 320
   history 318–20
   Old City 322–3
   Sokoto Museum 321
   where to stay and eat 320–1
Sokoto Caliphate 7, 8, 10, **35–7**, 318–9

Southeastern Nigeria **193–228**, *194*
Southwestern Nigeria **163–92**, *162*
Soyinka, Wole 16, 17, 330
sport 44–5
states 29
   street food 79
Sukur 282–3

telephone 86–7
television 77, 87–8
tetanus 100
Tinapa 216–17
tipping (dashing) 84–5
tour operators 53
traditional dress 42–3
traditional religions **33–4**, 180
travel clinics 92–3
tuberculosis 100–1
Twins Seven Seven 179
typhoid 101

Umuahia 197–9
   National War Museum 197–9

visas **53–4**, 141–2
Vischer, Hanns 312–4

Warri 209
websites 333–4
Wenger, Susanne 175, 178–82
what to take 57–60
where to stay *see* accommodation
wildlife 47–50
women travellers 83

Yankari National Park **268–71**
   getting there and away 269
   where to stay and eat 269–70
   Wikki Warm Spring 271
Yar'Adua, Umaru 24–6
Yola 271

Zaria **292–9**, *295*
   Central Mosque 297
   Emir's Palace 296
   getting there and away 293
   where to stay and eat 293–6